pres ce que maistre Gautier
mappe ot traitie des aventu-
res du saint Graal soffisa-
ment si com il li sambloit. Si fu au-

MS 229, f. 272v *(slightly enlarged)*

Catalogue

of Medieval and Renaissance Manuscripts
in the Beinecke Rare Book
and Manuscript Library
Yale University

Volume I: MSS 1-250

medieval & renaissance texts & studies

VOLUME 34

Catalogue

of Medieval and Renaissance Manuscripts
in the Beinecke Rare Book
and Manuscript Library
Yale University

Volume I: MSS 1-250

BY

Barbara A. Shailor

medieval & Renaissance texts & studies
Binghamton, New York
1984

© Copyright 1984

Center for Medieval & Early Renaissance Studies
State University of New York at Binghamton
Binghamton, New York

Library of Congress Cataloging in Publication Data

Beinecke Rare Book and Manuscript Library.
   Catalogue of medieval and renaissance manuscripts in the Beinecke Rare Book and Manuscript Library, Yale University.

   (Medieval & renaissance texts & studies ; v. 34)
   Contents: v. 1. MSS 1-250.
   Includes indexes.

   1. Beinecke Rare Book and Manuscript Library—Catalogs. 2. Manuscripts—Connecticut—New Haven—Catalogs.   3. Manuscripts, Latin (Medieval and modern)—Catalogs.   4. Manuscripts, Greek (Medieval and modern)—Catalogs.   5. Middle Ages—Manuscripts—Catalogs.   6. Renaissance—Manuscripts—Catalogs.   I. Shailor, Barbara A., 1948-   II. Title. III. Series.

Z6621.B4213   1984   011'.31   84-667
ISBN 0-86698-065-2

Printed in the United States of America

For

Cora E. Lutz

Board of Advisors

Walter Cahn

Consuelo W. Dutschke

Jane Greenfield

Walter N. Nichipor

Richard H. Rouse

Contents

Abbreviations	ix
Introduction	xv
MSS 1–250	3
Indices	365
Plates	423

Abbreviations

Achten-Knaus	G. Achten and H. Knaus, *Deutsche und niederländische Gebetbuchhandschriften der Hessischen Landes- und Hochschulbibliothek Darmstadt* (Darmstadt, 1959).
Aristoteles Latinus	G. Lacombe, *et al.*, *Aristoteles Latinus*. Pars prior (Rome, 1939); Pars posterior (Cambridge, 1955).
BHG³	*Bibliographica hagiographica graeca*, ediderunt Socii Bollandiani, 3rd ed. (Brussels, 1957).
BHL	*Bibliotheca hagiographica latina*, ediderunt Socii Bollandiani.
B. L.	British Library.
B. N.	Bibliothèque Nationale.
Branner	R. J. Branner, *Manuscript Painting in Paris during the Reign of Saint Louis: A Study of Styles* (Berkeley, 1977).
Briquet	C. M. Briquet, *Les Filigranes: Dictionnaire historique des marques du papier ... 1282 jusqu'à 1600*, facs. of the 1907 edition with supplementary material, ed. A. Stevenson (Amsterdam, 1968).
CAG	*Commentaria in Aristotelem Graeca*, 23 vols. + 3 supp. vols. (Berlin, 1882-1909).
Canart	P. Canart, "Scribes grecs de la Renaissance," *Scriptorium* 17 (1963) pp. 56-82.
CC	Corpus christianorum.
CC Cont. Med.	Corpus christianorum: Continuatio medievalis.
CLA	E. A. Lowe, *Codices latini antiquiores* (Oxford, 1934-71).
Colophons	*Colophons de manuscrits occidentaux des origines au XVIe siècle* (Fribourg, 1965-79).
Copinger	W. A. Copinger, *Supplement to Hain's Repertorium bibliographicum* (Berlin, 1926).

Cosenza	M. E. Cosenza, *Biographical and Bibliographical Dictionary of the Italian Humanists and of the World of Classical Scholarship in Italy, 1300-1800* (Boston, 1962-67).
CPL	*Clavis patrum latinorum*, ed. E. Dekkers, *Sacris erudiri* 3 (2nd ed., 1961).
CSEL	Corpus scriptorum ecclesiasticorum latinorum.
CTC	F. E. Cranz and P. O. Kristeller, eds., *Catalogus translationum et commentariorum: Mediaeval and Renaissance Latin Translations and Commentaries* (Washington, D.C., 1960-).
Delaissé, Marrow and de Wit, *Waddesdon Manor*	L. M. J. Delaissé, J. Marrow and J. de Wit, *Illuminated Manuscripts. The James A. De Rothschild Collection at Waddesdon Manor* (Fribourg, 1977, for the National Trust by the Office du Livre).
De Meyier	K. A. de Meyier, "Scribes grecs de la Renaissance. Additions et corrections aux répertoires de Vogel-Gardthausen, de Patrinelis et de Canart," *Scriptorium* 18 (1964) pp. 258-66.
De Ricci	S. de Ricci, *Census of Medieval and Renaissance Manuscripts in the United States and Canada* (New York, 1935).
DNB	*Dictionary of National Biography*.
EETS	Early English Text Society.
Emden, BRUC	A. B. Emden, *A Biographical Register of the University of Cambridge to A. D. 1500* (Cambridge, 1963).
Emden, BRUO	A. B. Emden, *A Biographical Register of the University of Oxford to A. D. 1500* (Oxford, 1957-59).
Exhibition Catalogue	W. Cahn and J. Marrow, eds., "Medieval and Renaissance Manuscripts at Yale: A Selection," Yale University Library *Gazette* 52 (1978) pp. 174-284.
Faye and Bond	C. U. Faye, *Supplement to the Census of Medieval and Renaissance Manuscripts in the United States and Canada*. Continued and edited by W. H. Bond (New York, 1962).
Gazette	Yale University Library *Gazette*.
GKW	*Gesamtkatalog der Wiegendrucke* (1925-).
Graux and Martin	C. Graux and A. Martin, *Rapport sur une mission en Espagne et en Portugal. Notices sommaires...* in Nouvelles archives des missions scientifiques et littéraires 2 (1892) pp. 1-322.
Hain	L. F. T. Hain, *Repertorium bibliographicum, in quo libri omnes*

Abbreviations

	ab arte typographica inventa usque ad annum M. D. (Stuttgart, 1826-38).
Harlfinger	D. and J. Harlfinger, *Wasserzeichen aus griechischen Handschriften* (Berlin, v. 1: 1974; 2: 1980).
HBS	Henry Bradshaw Society.
HE	C. Wordsworth, ed., *Horae Eboracenses*, Surtees Society, 132 (1920).
Heawood	E. Heawood, *Watermarks: Mainly of the 17th and 18th Centuries* (Monumenta Chartae Papyraceae I) (Hilversum, 1950).
IMEV	C. Brown and R. H. Robbins, *Index of Middle English Verse* (New York, 1943). *Supplement* by R. H. Robbins and J. L. Cutter (Lexington, 1965).
Karpozilos	A. Karpozilos, "The Yale University Manuscripts of Andreas Darmarius," *Hellenika* 26 (1973) pp. 67-71.
Ker, MLGB	N. R. Ker, *Medieval Libraries of Great Britain* (London, 2nd ed. 1964).
Ker, MMBL	N. R. Ker, *Medieval Manuscripts in British Libraries* (Oxford, 1969-).
Leroquais, LH	V. Leroquais, *Les Livres d'heures manuscrits de la Bibliothèque Nationale* (Paris, 1927-43).
Lieftinck, *Maatschappij*	*Codices 168-300 Societatis cui nomen Maatschappij der Nederlandsche Letterkunde* descripsit G. I. Lieftinck. Bibliotheca Universitatis Leidensis. Codices Manuscripti, v. 1 (Leiden, 1948).
Lyell Cat.	A. de la Mare, *Catalogue of the Collection of Medieval Manuscripts Bequeathed to the Bodleian Library Oxford by James P. R. Lyell* (Oxford, 1971).
Meertens	M. Meertens, *De Godsvrucht in de Nederlanden naar Handschriften van Gebedenboeken der XVe Eeuw*. Leuvense Studieen en Tekstuitgaven 1-3, 6 (1930-34).
Missale Romanum	R. Lippe, ed., *Missale Romanum Mediolani 1474* in Henry Bradshaw Society, 17, 23 (1899, 1907).
MSS datés	*Catalogue des manuscrits en écriture latine portant des indications de date, de lieu ou de copiste* (Paris, 1959-74).
OCT	Oxford Classical Texts.
Olivier	J. M. Olivier, "Les manuscrits grecs de l'Archivo-Biblioteca del Cabildo metropolitano (La Seo) de Saragosse," *Scriptorium* 30 (1976) pp. 52-57.

Omont	H. Omont, *Facsimilés de manuscrits grecs des XVe et XVIe siècles* (Paris, 1887).
Pächt and Alexander	O. Pächt and J. J. G. Alexander, *Illuminated Manuscripts in the Bodleian Library* (Oxford, 1966–73).
Parkes, *Keble College*	M. B. Parkes, *The Medieval Manuscripts of Keble College Oxford* (London, 1979).
Patrinelis	C. G. Patrinelis, " "Ελληνες κωδικογράφοι," 'Επετήρις τοῦ Μεσαιωνικοῦ 'Αρχείου vols. 8–9 (1958–59) (Athens, 1961) pp. 63–125.
Perdrizet	P. Perdrizet, *Le Calendrier Parisien à la fin du Moyen Age.* Publications de la Faculté des Lettres de l'Université de Strasbourg 63 (Paris, 1933).
PG	*Patrologia cursus completus, series graeca*, accurante J. P. Migne.
Phillipps Studies	A. N. L. Munby, *Phillipps Studies* (Cambridge, 1951–60).
Piccard	G. Piccard, *Wasserzeichenkartei Piccard im Hauptstraatsarchiv Stuttgart* (Stuttgart, 1961–).
PL	*Patrologia cursus completus, series latina*, accurante J. P. Migne.
PMLA	*Publications of the Modern Language Association of America.*
PO	*Patrologia orientalis* (Paris, 1907–).
RH	U. Chevalier, *Repertorium hymnologicum* (Louvain, 1892–1921).
Sarum Missal	J. W. Legg, *The Sarum Missal, edited from three early manuscripts* (Oxford, 1916).
Schneyer	J. B. Schneyer, *Repertorium der lateinischen Sermones des Mittelalters für die Zeit von 1150–1350.* Beiträge zur Geschichte der Philosophie und Theologie des Mittelalters 43 (Münster, 1969–).
Sinclair	K. V. Sinclair, *Descriptive Catalogue of Medieval and Renaissance Western Manuscripts in Australia* (Sydney, 1969).
Sonet	J. Sonet, *Répertoire d'incipit de prières en ancien français.* Société de Publications Romanes et Françaises 54 (Geneva, 1956).
SR	*Statutes of the Realm*; with references to 1810–28 ed., v. 1.
Stegmüller	F. Stegmüller, *Repertorium Biblicum Medii Aevi* (Madrid, 1950–).
Stegmüller, *Sent.*	F. Stegmüller, *Repertorium commentariorum in Sententias Petri Lombardi* (Würzburg, 1947).
Tenneroni	A. Tenneroni, *Inizii di antiche poesie italiane religiose e morale* (Florence, 1909).

Abbreviations

Teubner	Bibliotheca scriptorum graecorum et romanorum teubneriana.
Thomson, *Latin Bookhands*	S. H. Thomson, *Latin Bookhands of the Later Middle Ages 1100-1500* (Cambridge, 1969).
Thorndike and Kibre	L. Thorndike and P. Kibre, *A Catalogue of Incipits of Medieval Scientific Writings in Latin* (2nd ed., 1963).
Ullman	B. L. Ullman, "Petrarch Manuscripts in the United States," *Italia medioevale e umanistica* 5 (1962).
Vogel and Gardthausen	M. Vogel and V. Gardthausen, *Die griechischen Schreiber des Mittelalters und der Renaissance*. Beihefte zum Zentralblatt für Bibliothekswesen 33 (Leipzig, 1909).
Walther, *Initia*	H. Walther, *Initia carminum ac versuum medii aevi posterioris latinorum*, Carmina medii aevi posterioris latina, i (Göttingen, 1959).
Walther, *Sprichwörter*	H. Walther, *Lateinische Sprichwörter und Sentenzen des Mittelalters*, Carmina medii aevi posterioris latina, ii (Göttingen, 1963-67).
Weale, *South Kensington*	W. H. J. Weale, *Bookbindings and Rubbings of Bindings in the National Art Library, South Kensington Museum* (London, 1894, 1896).
Wilmart	A. Wilmart, *Auteurs spirituels et textes dévots du moyen âge latin* (Paris, 1932).
Ziskind Catalogue	B. M. W. Knox, "The Ziskind Collection of Greek Manuscripts," Yale University Library *Gazette* 32 (1957) pp. 38-56.

Introduction

THE COLLECTION OF MEDIEVAL AND RENAISSANCE MANUSCRIPTS preserved in the Beinecke Rare Book and Manuscript Library of Yale University is one of the major holdings in the United States. It is the purpose of this introduction to discuss briefly the history of the collection and to present the format of the entries and the layout of the catalogue.

Although Yale University has been acquiring early manuscripts since 1714 when Elihu Yale presented a handsome copy of the "Speculum Humanae Salvationis", the collection in the Beinecke Library is a relatively new one. Many manuscripts were purchased in the 1960's and early 1970's after the opening of the Beinecke Library; many others came to Yale between 1942-83 from distinguished private collections. A few individuals who contributed greatly to the recent growth of the Yale holdings merit special attention (see also H. W. Liebert, "Reflections on Medieval and Renaissance Manuscripts at Yale," *Gazette* 53 [1978] pp. 116-19).

In 1942 James T. Babb assumed the position of Acting University Librarian and then Librarian. An avid book collector himself, Babb shared his interests with a number of people who would eventually donate or bequeath their early manuscripts to Yale. It was perhaps his personal friendship with David Wagstaff that induced Wagstaff to present his remarkable library of sporting texts, a library composed of works on hunting, fishing and falconry. It was also under Babb's auspices that the Yale Library Associates purchased the first significant group of illuminated manuscripts in 1954 ("Eight Medieval Manuscripts," *Gazette* 29 [1955] pp. 99-114). The group includes the lavishly illustrated Arthurian Romances (MSS 227 and 229) as well as a French translation of Caesar's *Gallic Wars* produced for Jacques Donche, counselor of Charles the Bold of Burgundy (MS 226). Babb's enthusiasm for illuminated manuscripts received the support of several collectors, most notably Louis M. and Hannah D. Rabinowitz, Henry Fletcher, and Thomas E. Marston. Additionally, Edwin J. Beinecke's profound interest in the Yale libraries and the opening of the Beinecke Rare Book and Manuscript Library in 1963 were largely the result of Babb's leadership as University Librarian.

The scope of the holdings in the Beinecke Rare Book and Manuscript Library is extensive, encompassing two distinct bodies of material: the general collection (presently 640 items and still expanding) and the Marston manuscripts, a collection formed by Thomas E. Marston (234 items) and obtained by Yale in 1962. The manuscripts in both collections are written in many languages one might expect, such as Latin, Greek, French, German, Italian, Spanish, and English, as well as in a few surprising ones, for example, Icelandic and Nahuatl. They date from the 4th to the early 18th century. Although there are other groups of medieval and Renaissance manuscripts housed in the Yale University Library system we shall concentrate in the first three volumes of this catalogue on the two main holdings in the Beinecke Library: Vol. I MSS 1–250; Vol. II MSS 251–500; Vol. III Marston MSS. We shall eventually catalogue the fine manuscripts in the James Marshall and Marie-Louise Osborn Collection, also in the Beinecke Library. A catalogue of the Paul and Mary Mellon alchemical manuscripts has been recently published by L. C. Witten and R. Pachella (*Alchemy and the Occult*: Vol. III Manuscripts 1225–1671 [New Haven, 1977] with numerous reproductions).

There is no single focus or principle of organization for the general collection of medieval and Renaissance manuscripts. The nucleus of the collection, as listed in De Ricci and Faye and Bond, was transferred to the Beinecke Rare Book and Manuscript Library in 1963 from the Rare Book Room in the Sterling Memorial Library. A few items subsequently entered the Beinecke Library from other Yale collections; they were added to the general collection as they were transferred. Other manuscripts, although they received Beinecke shelf numbers, are not deposited in the library and are therefore not included in this catalogue. We have noted wherever appropriate the present location of manuscripts not described. Each new codex or fragment is now placed in the manuscript vault and assigned a number; if several manuscripts arrive at the same time and from the same donor or source, they are usually numbered consecutively. Hence, the materials are arranged, for the most part, in chronological sequence according to the date of acquisition.

The general collection is a fascinating mixture of manuscripts of various dates and from far-ranging geographical locations. It increased in size gradually until the 1940's, when there occurred the surge of growth noted above. In addition to the sporting texts donated by David Wagstaff and the illuminated manuscripts obtained by the Yale Library Associates in 1954, Yale purchased an impressive number of Greek manuscripts in 1957 through the Jacob Ziskind Charitable Trust (MSS 234–74, 288–304). The trust was established by the bequest of Jacob Ziskind, a Fall River (Massachusetts) textile industrialist and philanthropist. The earliest codex from the Ziskind Collection has been attributed to the beginning of the 10th century while the later manuscripts contain inscriptions that clearly date them, wholly or in part, to the early 18th century. The works in these Greek manuscripts represent the various fields and areas of interest generally associated with Greek scholarship. There are treatises on astrology, cosmography, and geography, in

Introduction XVII

addition to classical, biblical and patristic texts. Many of the codices were formerly in the Guilford and Phillipps collections. Frederick North, fifth Earl of Guilford (1766-1827) was an eccentric philhellene who assembled a library on the Greek island of Corfu. A few of his manuscripts are preserved in the British Library; a significant group, however, was purchased by Sir Thomas Phillipps. The remainder of the Ziskind manuscripts had been located for several centuries in the library of the Santa Iglesia del Pilar in Saragossa, Spain (C. Graux and A. Martin, *Manuscrits grecs d'Espagne et de Portugal* [Paris, 1892]; J. M. Olivier, "Les manuscrits grecs de l'Archivo-Biblioteca del Cabildo metropolitano [La Seo] de Saragosse," *Scriptorium* 30 [1976] pp. 52-57). Among these are texts copied by the well-known Renaissance scribes Andreas Darmarius and Camillus Venetus.

In 1971 the Beinecke Rare Book and Manuscript Library was fortunate to receive a considerable bequest from Henry C. Taylor whose library consisted of many illustrated volumes on geography and navigation (J. S. Kebabian, *The Henry C. Taylor Collection* [New Haven, 1971]). Taylor began collecting with a single book written by Captain John Smith entitled *Sea Grammar, With the Plaine Exposition of Smith's Accidence for Young Sea-men*. Following the list of works suggested by Smith for the well found ship, Taylor first acquired all of those treatises recommended and then enlarged his holdings with suitable early manuscripts and printed books. The medieval and Renaissance manuscripts from his collection are currently catalogued as Beinecke MSS 556-69, 574.

Not all of the early material in the Beinecke Library consists of complete codices; there are numerous fragments that have, for the most part, received little attention. Hans P. Kraus presented two interesting groups of fragments (MSS 481 and 482) to Yale in 1966. Each is composed of 144 separate folios or portions of folios that trace the development of writing from the 8th through the 15th centuries; both contain some unusual items, including specimens of Beneventan and Visigothic scripts. Smaller groups of fragments were donated by Henrietta C. Bartlett in 1954 (MS 483), by the Yale Library Associates (MS 484), and by James Osborn in 1973 (MS 525).

The general collection of medieval and Renaissance manuscripts has grown very rapidly over the last twenty years. When Faye and Bond published in 1962 the *Supplement* to De Ricci's *Census*, they listed 291 items in the University Library (pp. 25-50). Since 1963 the Beinecke Library has acquired almost 350 additional manuscripts, most of them of extraordinary importance to scholars. This growth would not have been possible without the generosity of the Beinecke family; no fewer than 115 items were selected by Edwin J. Beinecke personally or were purchased with the gifts and endowment funds contributed by members of the family. Among these 115 we should note some of the more remarkable acquisitions: the mystical and devotional miscellany often referred to as the "Rothschild Canticles" (MS 404), the elaborate "Heures de Savoie" (MS 390), the richly decorated "Albergati Bible" (MS 407), a fifteenth-century commonplace book named the

"Book of Brome" after Brome Hall in Suffolk (MS 365), and an early volume dated ca. 875 containing the capitularies of Charlemagne, his son Louis the Pious, and Charles the Bald (MS 413).

The collection of manuscripts we shall describe in the third volume is that assembled by Thomas E. Marston and acquired by the Yale University Library in 1962 (see Faye and Bond, pp. 64–96). While still a graduate student at Yale, Marston began to hunt for the early texts of classical authors he was enthusiastically studying. Somewhat later, he developed a more far-reaching principle for adding to his personal library: his aim was to acquire a collection of manuscripts and early printed books similar to that possessed by a humanist of the Italian Renaissance. Therefore, in addition to the works of Juvenal, Persius, and Martial, he searched for those of Bruni, Traversari, Guarino of Verona, and their circle of friends. Some of his manuscripts are modest in appearance and were clearly intended to be working texts; others are elaborately illuminated by famous artists. Marston has also donated many important manuscripts to the general collection of the Beinecke Library and continues to serve as Adviser on Medieval and Renaissance Manuscripts.

IN 1969 CORA LUTZ BEGAN THE ARDUOUS TASK of trying to organize both the general and Marston collections. She assigned numbers to those items acquired since Faye and Bond's *Supplement* to De Ricci's *Census* and compiled descriptive entries for all of the manuscripts. Her impressive work has served as the in-house reference tool and has been the foundation for all subsequent investigations. Cora Lutz accomplished a great deal before her retirement in 1975, particularly with respect to the identification of texts. Our task during the past seven years has been to build upon her work, to supplement it, and to put the information into an appropriate format that will make it accessible to scholars, whether they be art historians, paleographers or textual critics. We are fortunate that the National Endowment for the Humanities has granted funds to carry on our research and to begin publication of a comprehensive catalogue.

The matter of a suitable format for cataloguing medieval and Renaissance manuscripts is a difficult one since there are few firmly established guide-lines. For the Beinecke catalogue we have adopted an entry similar to that used by the late N. R. Ker in his multi-volume *Medieval Manuscripts in British Libraries* (Oxford, 1969-) and to that used in the forthcoming catalogues of the Huntington and Newberry Libraries. R. H. Rouse has been most helpful in designing and implementing the format. Our entries attempt to fulfill three essential functions of a good catalogue description: first, to note accurately the textual contents and physical make-up of the fragment or codex; second, to relate briefly the material in the Beinecke Library to manuscripts preserved elsewhere; third, to serve as a point of departure for further inquiry by scholars and collectors.

It is inevitable, however, that in a work of this nature there will be errors; a

Introduction XIX

cataloguer of medieval and Renaissance manuscripts cannot be versed in every field or discipline. We hope that our readers will find something of value here concerning the collections housed in the Beinecke Library and will excuse those errors that have crept in through either ignorance or oversight. Additions and corrections will be most welcome and may find their way into a future volume.

Some methodological considerations and explanations of format are presented in the following sections.

I. *Heading*

The heading for each entry consists of the call number, in bold type, in the first line to the left; the probable country of origin and date or approximate date to the right. The suprascript notations *in.*, 1, *med.*, 2, *ex.*, refer to the beginning, first half, middle, second half, end of the century; 2/4 denotes the second quarter of a century whereas s. XIV/XV denotes the period around the turn of a century. Multiple dates appear for composite codices. The second line provides a short title, to the left, and a reference to a plate at the end of the volume, on the right.

II. *Contents*

We endeavor to record all texts in the sequence in which they occur in the manuscript and to give a leaf citation for the beginning and conclusion of each article. Arabic numerals designate the particular texts (articles). Roman numerals appear if the manuscript is composed of physically discrete sections; in many instances separate items produced by various scribes at different times and in different geographical locations were lumped together and bound by a later owner. Text identifications and bibliographical citations, when available, follow immediately the incipits and explicits for an article.

Rubrics are in italics; transcriptions of incipits and explicits retain the original orthography of the text. Parallel oblique lines (//) indicate that the text begins or ends imperfectly. Square brackets ([ ]) denote editorial intervention or problems of interpretation (e.g. [?]). The use of [*sic*] is restricted to readings that may appear peculiar to the reader but which do, in fact, appear in the text. Asterisks are used when a word or phrase is illegible due to damage by water, rodents, etc.

III. *Physical Description*

The physical specifications of the codex (with multiple descriptions for composite items) are divided into several small paragraphs arranged in this order, though it has sometimes been advisable to adopt slightly altered formats.

a. Material on which a manuscript is written. Adjectives that describe the quality of the parchment or references to watermarks listed in Briquet or elsewhere may follow in parentheses. Number of leaves and foliation is given, with flyleaves designated by small Roman numerals before and after the number of leaves of the text (e.g., iv + 22 + iii). It is presumed that flyleaves are contemporary with the binding unless otherwise stated. Dimensions of the folio, with dimensions of the written space in parentheses, record the height and width respectively. After the number of columns and lines is the description of the physical arrangement of the page: bounding lines (rulings that delineate the written space), the instruments or materials used for ruling (hard point, crayon, lead, ink), and prickings.

b. Collation; catchwords, leaf and/or quire signatures. If there are several designs or arrangements of catchwords and signatures, we attempt to list them and where they occur.

c. Scribes, scripts. This section is often less precise than we would wish because of the difficulty of determining a suitable nomenclature for later gothic scripts. We hope that the Plates at the end of the text will complement and clarify some of our designations for script. Information on scribe(s), if available, occurs under the section devoted to Provenance.

d. Decoration. The main kinds of decoration are described hierarchically, beginning with the most elaborate and proceeding to the simplest. If this portion of the description is exceedingly long, as is true in the case of lavishly illuminated manuscripts, we divide the discussion into several distinct paragraphs. Attributions by art historians and bibliographical citations concerning the illuminator or school of illumination are noted whenever possible.

e. Imperfections. We record significant damage or repair to the bookblock that is not mentioned elsewhere in the entry. When the manuscript is in good physical condition, the paragraph is omitted.

f. Binding. Extensive comments on binding have been compiled by J. Greenfield, Director of the Yale Conservation Studio. Plate 1 illustrates selected binding terms found in the descriptions. Pastedowns composed of manuscript fragments are also discussed here; often, however, their poor state of preservation hinders us from describing them in great detail or from identifying precisely the text(s).

IV. *Provenance*

This portion of our catalogue entry addresses the questions: Where and when was the manuscript produced? Who were its former owners, both individuals and institutions? When did Yale University or the Beinecke Rare Book and Manuscript Library acquire the item? Evidence of prior ownership is presented even if its importance is unclear. Opening words of the *secundo folio* are appended to the end of the paragraph for most Western manuscripts produced before 1500.

V. *Bibliography*

Bibliographical citations occur in the following order: 1. De Ricci and/or Faye and Bond; 2. *Exhibition Catalogue* prepared by Cahn and Marrow; 3. hand-list of

Introduction XXI

Ziskind Greek manuscripts compiled by Knox. Other references not cited in the text of the entry are listed in chronological order of publication.

VI. *Indices*

Multiple indices (1-7) provide access to information in the descriptions:

1. MSS arranged by country or region of origin and by century.

2. Dated MSS.

3. General index: persons, places, authors, etc. There are rather lengthy entries for Saints, Illuminations (listed by subjects illustrated), Bindings, and Watermarks.

4. Illuminators and Scribes.

5. Provenance: individuals and institutions associated with manuscripts.

6. Other MSS cited.

7. Incipits for both identified and unidentified texts.

VII. *Plates*

Financial considerations preclude photographic reproductions of each item or of each part of a composite codex; we do not illustrate some manuscripts for which facsimiles are already available (as in the fine *Exhibition Catalogue* of Cahn and Marrow) or materials that are poorly preserved. The Plates are grouped into four major sections:

1. Dated Western MSS: Latin, German, French, etc., manuscripts that can be dated with some certainty. We exclude account books, diplomas, documents, and the like.

2. Dated Greek MSS (no suitable examples in vol. 1).

3. Undated Western MSS arranged according to geographical location and approximate date of production.

4. Undated Greek MSS in chronological sequence.

I AM DEEPLY INDEBTED TO MANY SCHOLARS for their help and support in compiling this catalogue. I am especially grateful to researchers who shared their expertise when they came to New Haven to examine materials. Scholars who have contributed specific insights are acknowledged (thought not always, I am afraid) in the text; others who have offered advice on various subjects to both Cora Lutz and myself include L. Armstrong, J. Baker, B. Bischoff, V. Brown, M. Cole, A. C. de la Mare, C. Gilbert, K. D. Hartzell, T. Izbicki, G. Keiser, N. R. Ker, W. Kimnach, R. Lewis, J. Marrow, P. Meyvaert, P. Moraux, J.-C. Muller, F. Robinson, K. Scott, L. E. Voigts, N. G. Wilson, L. C. Witten, C. Wright.

I should like to thank as well my Board of Consultants: W. Cahn, C. W. Dutschke, J. Greenfield, W. N. Nichipor, R. H. Rouse. Their assistance continues to be invaluable.

Several individuals deserve special recognition. As my assistants, D. Creasy and J. Hamburger often suffered many of the tedious and less glamorous tasks of cataloguing; N. Warfield mastered the complexities of the computer so as to input the complete text together with indices and typesetting codes; N. Bowen helped to proofread and edit the final stages of the text; D. Cook labored to produce the photographic reproductions.

Without the cooperation of the Beinecke Rare Book and Manuscript Library, however, this project would not be possible. Throughout the years the librarians have created an atmosphere conducive to scholarly pursuits. P. Howell, H. Lobay, S. Parks, S. Rutter, C. Sammons, and M. G. Wynne have answered countless questions; S. Peterson, L. Dowler, R. Franklin, and R. Rogers have encouraged my work on the administrative level.

THIS WORK IS DEDICATED TO CORA LUTZ, who first introduced me to the medieval and Renaissance manuscripts in the Beinecke Library and who inspired me to undertake this catalogue.

B. A. S.

New Haven
October 1983

MSS 1–250

MS 1 Italy, s. XV/XVI
Livy, Ab urbe condita libri I-X Pl. 28

ff. 1r–335v Facturusne sim Opere precium si a primordio ... quod unum diem Aesculapio supplicatio habita est. Finis. f. 336 ruled, but blank

R. Conway and C. F. Walters, eds., OCT (1914–1919) 2 vol.; revised edition of Books I–V, R. M. Ogilvie, ed. (1974).

Parchment, ff. iv (paper) + 336 + v (paper), 358 x 252 (227 x 160) mm. Written in 31 long lines; double vertical bounding lines; ruled in lead.
I–XVI^{10}, XVII^{8}, XVIII–XXXIII^{10}, XXXIV^{8}. Catchwords perpendicular to text, between vertical guide-lines.
Written by a single scribe in round humanistic script.
On f. 1r: the initial F historiated with a view of Rome, full-page illuminated border in gold and colors into which are introduced the Trivulzio arms of Milan (paly of 6, or and vert) and a set of unidentified arms (gules, a cross saltire sable). Initials of books, 8-line, of painted gold on background of blue, green and red, and partial floral border.
Initial on f. 2r damaged by crease.
Binding: s. xviii. Brown leather, gold-tooled, edges marbled and gilt, rebacked, with T. LIVII DECAS PRIMA on spine.

Written in Milan in the late 15th or early 16th century; arms of the Trivulzio family of Milan on f. 1r. According to A. C. de la Mare it is presumably part of the same set of Livy as Vienna, Öst. Nationalbibl. Cod. 13, Livy, *Dec.* III, made for Marshal Gian Giacomo Trivulzio (1436–1518), which is copied by the same scribe (see Hermann, *Beschreibendes Verzeichnis* VI, 1, no. 69 and Taff. XLVII, XLI 3) and has decoration very close in style. The scribe copied several famous Milanese manuscripts of the late 15th century, such as Milan, Trivulziana 2163 and 2167, the elaborately illuminated abecedario and grammarbook of Massimiliano Sforza (b. 1493), son of Duke Lodovico il Moro; also Geneva MS lang. étr. 210, the dedication copy of Luca Pacioli, *De divina proportione*, presented to Lodovico il Moro, 1498, with diagrams attributed to Leonardo da Vinci.

Brought from Palermo by Dr. Anthony Askew (1722-1772); at his sale (London, 1785, no. 482), bought by Sir William Burrell (1732-1796). Note in the hand of M. Wodhull (f. ii recto): "This appears to be the very Book which I saw Sir W. Burrell purchase in Dr. Askew's manuscript Auction No. 482 for thirty two Guineas; in Sir W. Burrell's Auction May 1796 it is said to have gone for about five, No. 657. The note in 'Bib. Askev. manuscripta' is: 'ex Panormo in Sicilia hunc cod. adduxit secum Cl. Askevius,' & '300 Annor. MSS longe pulcherrimus'. " Bought by the same Michael Wodhull, Esq. (1740-1816), of Thenford, Northamptonshire at White's sale (London, 26 March 1798), with his signature and notes; his sale (London, 1886, no. 1570) to Quaritch for William Loring Andrews (bookstamp and bookplate inside front cover). Presented to Yale by William Loring Andrews in 1894 (A. van Name, comp., *Catalogue of the William Loring Andrews Collection of Early Books in the Library of Yale University* [New Haven, 1913] pp. 3-4, no. 2).

secundo folio: cum bonis

Bibliography: De Ricci, v. 1, p. 161, no. 1.
  Catalogue of an Exhibition of Illuminated and Painted Manuscripts Together with a Few Early Printed Books with Illuminations ... (New York, The Grolier Club, 1892) p. 5, no. 7.

MS 2
Jacopo Zeno, Vita Caroli Zeni

Italy, ca. 1458

1. ff. 1r-6r *In libros vitae morum rerumque gestarum. Caroli zeni veneti. Ad pium secundum pontificem maximum. Iacobi feltrensis et bellunensis antistitis. Praefatio. Gloriosa sanctitatis tuae. Ad Sublime pontificatus maximi culmen ... gratiae tuae non expertem tuae Beatitudinis pietate et amore foveri.*

   Dedicatory preface to Pope Pius II.

2. ff. 6r-191r *Vitae morum rerumque gestarum caroli zeni. Ad pium secundum pontificem maximum. Liber primus. Qui venetae urbis originem incrementaque tradidere rerum scriptores ... Pro laudantium officio gloria ut quidem par est. Haudquaquam fraudatam esse cognouimus. Finis.* ff. 191v-192v ruled, but blank

   This manuscript is of special importance because it contains the complete work. Beinecke MS 2 is Codex A in the modern edition of G. Zonta, *Vita Caroli Zeni auctore Iacobo Zeno* in *Rerum Italicarum Scriptores*, Nuova ed., 19, Parte 6, fasc. 1-2 (Bologna, 1940-41). In the edition of Muratori (*Rerum Italicarum Scriptores* 19 [Milan, 1731] pp. 202-372), made from a manuscript in Padua (Episcopal Seminary MS 46), the last seventeen lines are missing.

   Parchment, ff. ii (parchment) + 192 + i (paper), 271 x 177 (177 x 106) mm. written in 28 long lines, double vertical and horizontal bounding lines, all full across. Ruled in hard point on hair side; remains of prickings along upper, lower and outer edges.

I-XIX^{10}, XX^2. Quires signed with letters of the alphabet on verso of final folio and recto of following folio; letters placed between inner vertical bounding lines.

Written in humanistic script by Franciscus de Tianis of Pistoia (see below).

On f. 1r, a foliage border which includes hares, stork, vase, and arms of the Piccolomini family (argent, a cross azur with 5 crescents or; surmounted by keys in saltire argent and a papal tiara; supported by a pair of angels). Eleven elaborate initials, 11- to 7-line, in gold, red, blue, and green entwined with foliage. The style of decoration is decidedly Roman (see G. M. Canova, "Un saggio di gusto Rinascimentale: I libri miniati di Iacopo Zeno," *Arte Veneta* 32 [1978] pp. 46-55).

Binding: s. xviii. Brownish-red goatskin, gold-tooled; pale green and gold, Dutch gilt paper boards.

Written in Italy by Franciscus de Tianis (who was also responsible for Paris, B.N. lat. 8910, 8911, and 4192) as the dedication copy to Pope Pius II, whose arms appear in the border of f. 1r; the manuscript is datable between the election of Pius II in August 1458 and the election of Jacopo Zeno as bishop of Padua on 26 March 1460. Unidentified shelf-marks include "Prato" and "R.66." According to a newspaper clipping from the Yale files [n.d., n.p.] the manuscript came from the Trivulzio Library in Milan and was auctioned by George A. Leavitt and Company (New York, 27 Nov. 1886, no. 7). Purchased by William Loring Andrews (bookstamp and bookplate inside front cover) who presented it to Yale in 1894 (A. van Name, comp., *Catalogue of the William Loring Andrews Collection of Early Books in the Library of Yale University* [New Haven, 1913] pp. 1-3, no. 1).

secundo folio: [ne]mine me uspiam

Bibliography: De Ricci, v. 1, p. 161, no. 2.
Exhibition Catalogue, pp. 229-30, no. 54, pl. 20 (f.1r).
Catalogue of an Exhibition of Illuminated and Painted Manuscripts Together with a Few Early Printed Books with Illuminations ... (New York, The Grolier Club, 1892) p. 4, no. 8.

MS 3
Fragments

MS 3 is a box of fragments, many of which were removed from bindings. Library records contain little information on these fragments; most are in a poor state of preservation. Since some have been reclassified as separate manuscripts or relocated in other collections, the numbering is not consecutive.

1. Gregory IX, *Decretales*   France, s. XIII^2
From Bk. 3, Tit. 21 (two fragments).

Parchment, each ca. 337 x 55 mm. (length of written space 185 mm.). Ruled in lead, 2 columns of 48 lines; between guide-lines for text, 4 mm.; writing below top line. Written in small cramped gothic textura, with at least 3 contemporary and later hands in the glosses. Initial, 2-line, in blue with red flourishes; guide-letters visible beneath. Text divisions, paragraph marks and headings in red. Removed from a binding; stains, creases and holes.

2. Breviary   France, s. XII^2

Contains parts of the offices for Christmas, Stephen and Silvester (four fragments).

Parchment, ranging in size from ca. 90 x 245 mm. to 132 x 245 mm. (width of written area 225 mm.). Ruled in hard point, 2 columns; writing above top line; between guide-lines for text, 9 mm. Written in 2 sizes of late Carolingian minuscule, with exaggerated ascenders on the smaller size. Initials 3- or 2-line, red or green, both with red dots attached. Headings and strokes on 1-line initials in red. Holes, stains, tears and traces of glue; removed from a binding.

3. Breviary   Germany, s. XIII^2

Contains part of the office for Simeon (one fragment).

Parchment, 178 x 139 (179 x 112) mm. Written in 10 long lines of text with staves, ruled in lead, double vertical bounding lines full across; between guide-lines for text, 15 mm. Written in early gothic bookhand. Initials of one staff plus one line in red; 1-line initials in blue or red; rubrics and 4-line staves in red; square musical notation. Probably a pastedown; portions missing at lower and outer edges, including some text and music; traces of glue at inner edge.

4. Missal   France, s. XII^1

Five fragments of a missale plenum. Portions of Dominica X post Pentecosten, Feria IV of that week, Dominica XI, and of votive masses for a priest to say on behalf of himself, and for the shedding of tears. Where they occur, the texts of the proper chants are notated in a compact, well executed, distinctive script of mixed Breton and French aspect. Some of the chants are cited by incipit. Unusually, the first of the votive masses is prefaced by a listing of chants which would be appropriate to it. The Alleluia for Dominica X is *Domine refugium*, and the proper collect for Vespers of that Sunday (not present in the fragment) was entered after the post communion.

Parchment, ranging from 215 x 98 to 161 x 42 mm. 2 columns (each 69 mm. wide), ruled in lead; between guide-lines 7 mm.; writing above top line. Written in 2 sizes of early gothic, with neumes above the smaller size. Initials 6- to 2-line, in blue and/or red, with red or blue flourishes; rubrics in red. Binding reinforcement from spine; rubbed, creased and stained, with traces of glue.

Written in France, probably in the diocese of Le Mans. The peculiarities of notations with mixed Breton and French forms are found in a similar mixture in various surviving manuscripts from Le Mans including a portion of the Office of St. Julian of Le Mans contained in Oxford, Bod. Lib. MS 596, ff. 211v–213r (W. H. Frere, *Bibliotheca Musico-Liturgica* [London, 1901–32] no. 126, and plate 6 [212v]). See also M. Huglo in *Acta musicologica* 25 (1963) 75f. The most distinctive neume is the porrectus whose left portion resembles an incomplete standard mathematical symbol for infinity. (We thank K. D. Hartzell for his assistance with these fragments.)

5. Theological text, in Lat. France, s. XIII^1

Possibly a sermon (two fragments).

Parchment, ca. 245 x 117 and 40 x ca. 100 mm. Written in 2 columns (each 203 x 65 mm.) of 25 lines, ruled in lead [?]; between guide-lines for text, 9 mm. Written in early gothic bookhand. One-line initials with red strokes. Torn, stained, and with remains of paste; much text obliterated. Removed from a binding.

7. Thomas Aquinas, *In libros Ethicorum Aristotelis* Italy, s. XIV^{in}

Sancti Thomae Aquinatis ... Opera omnia..., V. J. Bourke, ed. (New York, 1949) v. 21, pp. 140–45; parts of Bk. 4, lectiones 12 and 13. Opening words of the text of Aristotle underlined, followed immediately (without paraphrases) by the full text of Aquinas' comments (one leaf).

Parchment, 291 x 197 (228 x 168) mm. Written in 2 columns of 48 lines, ruled in lead; between guide-lines for text, 5 mm.; written below top line. In small round gothic with many abbreviations. Space left for a 2-line initial. Stained and creased, with much text lost due to rubbing and two holes; once a pastedown.

8. Lectionary or Choir Breviary Germany, s. XIV^2–XV^1

Readings (up to 3), including one from Luke 9.1 (one leaf).

Parchment, 396 x 292 (300 x 204) mm. Written in 2 columns of 27 lines; ruled in brown ink, double horizontal and single vertical bounding lines, full across; between guide-lines for text, 11 mm. Written in well formed gothic textura with few abbreviations. Calligraphic initials, 5- to 2-line, in red or blue with blue and/or red penwork and flourishes. Rubrics and strokes on 1-line initials in red. Part of a dismembered manuscript.

10. Unidentified text, on Civil Law [?] Germany, s. XV

Includes rubrics *De ludo* (two fragments).

Paper (thick, with broad laid lines; watermarks similar to Piccard Ochsenkopf I. 113), 193 x 153 mm. Written in 2 columns frame-ruled in ink (each column 71 mm. wide). Written in small gothic cursive with many abbreviations. Initials, 2-line, in red or blue; rubrics and paragraph marks in red; in margin, Arabic numerals to mark sections of text, each bracketed by red dots. Once the cover of a pamphlet in the Yale University Library ("Curieuse Staats-Frage Wer in dem grossen Monarchischer Königreich Spanien der rechtmässige Successor seyn soll im Fall der jetztregierende König Carolus II" [Cologne: Peter Marteau, 1699]); removed ca. 1929.

11. Legal contract, in Lat.   Italy, 1474

Agreement between nuns of a convent of Sta. Lucia and one Raynaldus, concerning a house.

Parchment scroll, measuring 470 x 255 mm. Written in humanistic notarial script, on one side only. Worn.

12. Simone da Cremona [?], *Sermones*   Germany, s. XV^2

Sermons for the Temporale, including the beginning of one for the third Sunday after the octave of Epiphany (two leaves). (Text: Nolite esse prudentes apud vos [Rom. 12.16] ... Augustinus sermone .4. ad suos fratres heremitas sic inquit Beatus qui prudens est et felix...) Attribution from a sales slip; as yet unverified.

Paper (watermarks: unidentified bull's head), 300 x 212 (211 x 138) mm. Written in 2 columns of ca. 45 lines; frame-ruled in lead, prickings at corners of columns. Consecutive folios from 2 different quires; catchword in inner lower margin of first, quire signed (as the fourth) on second. Written in a large gothic cursive with many abbreviations; marginal notes by original and later hands. Initial, 4-line, red and green; headings, underlining, and initial strokes, in red.

Dealer's slip in library files (dated 1926) states that the leaves were taken from a manuscript prepared in the Carthusian monastery at Buxheim, and signed by Caspar Misnensis, 1434; see *Colophons* v. 2, no. 4840-42. Early provenance listed in De Ricci: sale of Graf Hugo von Waldbott-Bassenheim (Munich, 20 Sept. 1883, no. 2756); Charles F. Gunther sale (New York, 11 Nov. 1926, no. 268) to Ellner. Sold leaf by leaf by the Foliophiles, New York (1926, T. F. 1); folios now in Tampa, Fla. Public Library, no. 1 (De Ricci v. 1, p. 508) and Geneva College Library, Beaver Falls, Pa., no. 1 (De Ricci v. 2, p. 1984).

13. Unidentified text, in Lat.   Italy [?], s. XV^{med}

Possibly sermons (one leaf).

Parchment, 325 x 205 mm. Written in 2 columns of 45 lines (each column 232 x 70 mm.), no rulings visible. Written in highly abbreviated gothic cursive. Initial, 3-line, in blue with elaborate red flourishes, followed by a line of gothic textura, then text. Probably a pastedown; most of text illegible due to tears, stains, creases and mold. Signature in outer margin: "Samuel Johnson, 1884 [?]".

16. Legal document, in Fr.   France, s. XVI

Involving Nicolas Hubert, maestre Claude Hesines, Jehan Cousin and his sheep; probably incomplete at end.

One strip of parchment, 68 x 320 mm. French notarial script. Apparently used as a binding reinforcement.

17. Theological notes, in Lat. Italy [?], s. XV/XVI

Notes on the definitions of *consilium, fortitudo*, and *pietas* (one fragment).

Paper (no watermarks), 90 x 80 mm. Written in 22 long lines, no ruling. Written in tiny gothic cursive. Creases and stains.

27. Philosophical text, in Lat. Germany, s. XIII[1]

Major theme of this section of the work is *voluptas* (one fragment). Portion of text reads: Cum autem indefinitum est problema uno modo contingit destruere ut si dixerit uoluptatem bonum esse uel non bonum....

Parchment, 127 x 40 mm. (width of written space 70 mm.). Written in long lines, ruled in lead, double vertical bounding lines; between guide-lines for text, 4 mm. Written in small early gothic bookhand, with later marginal notations. One 1-line red initial. Binding reinforcement, with remains of glue.

28. Hours France, s. XV^{med}

Contains part of the Penitential Psalms (one bifolium). Portions of Pss. 6.7-11; 31.1-4; 50.6-16.

Parchment, 177 x 125 (101 x 62) mm. Written in 15 long lines; ruled in pale red ink, single horizontal and vertical bounding lines, full across; between guide-lines for text, 7 mm. The text shows that one bifolium was between these two leaves. Written in a well formed liturgical gothic bookhand. Initials 2- and 1-line in gold, against irregular blue and red grounds with white filigree, infilled red or blue with white or gray filigree; trailing black hairlines at corners. Line-fillers red or blue with white and gray filigree and gold dots or designs. Well preserved. Removed from Nicolaus de Hanapis' *Biblia pauperum* (Venice, 1480), which was a gift of Laurence Gilman Noyes in 1950.

29. Psalter Franco-Flemish [?], s. XIII-XIV

Contains Psalms 106.40-107.11 (one leaf).

Parchment, 109 x 80 (74 x 54) mm. Written in 16 long lines, ruled in lead, single vertical bounding lines, full across; writing below top line; between guide-lines, 4 mm. Written in liturgical gothic bookhand. Original decoration: simple 2- and 1-line initials in red with blue penwork; 1-line initials in red or blue; helical line fillers in red and green. Over the 2-line initial with penwork was added, ca. 1300, a 3-line initial in gold edged with black, against an irregular blue and red ground, infilled red with white filigree; ground, red, blue and gold with white filigree and cusped terminals, extends the full length of the inner margin. Much worn and darkened.

30. *Corpus Iuris Civilis*   Italy, s. XIV[1]

Digesta 46.3.36–37, 44–47 and 46.6.5–47.5; P. Krueger and T. Mommsen, eds., *Corpus Iuris Civilis*, v. 1 (Berlin, 1892) pp. 749, 750 and 759–60 (fragment of a conjugate leaf).

Parchment, total size 200 x 290 mm. (width of written space 107 mm. without glosses, 180 mm. with glosses). Written in 2 columns, ruled in lead, double outer, single inner vertical bounding lines, with 4 mm. between guide-lines for text; ruling in all margins for commentary. Written in round gothic; tie marks are used to link text to commentary. Initials 3- to 2-line, blue, in margins; 1-line red initials in text; paragraph marks in red and blue; rubrics. Stains and holes; verso partly illegible due to rubbing. Probably removed from a binding.

31. Gradual   Germany, s. XIV/XV

Services from the first Sunday in Lent through part of the following Tuesday. In the margin, in red, XXIX and XXX (one bifolium, continuous text).

Parchment, 275 x 198 (223 x 137) mm. Written in 10 lines of text with music; no ruling visible; 1 line plus 1 staff equals 22 mm. Written in liturgical gothic bookhand. Initials 1-line or 1-line plus 1 staff, in red, one with a face inside; line fillers and rubrics in red. Black square notes on 4-line red staves. Fragment of an unidentified 15th-century manuscript pasted on the first folio recto; remains of a parchment place-marker. Stained and rubbed. Probably used as flyleaves.

33. Commentary on an unidentified Lat. legal text, in Fr.   France, s. XIV[2]

Two fragments of parchment, 211 x 177 and 211 x 145 mm. (width of written space 142 mm.). Written in 2 columns; ruled in lead, single vertical bounding lines; between guide-lines for text, 5 mm. Written in rounded gothic bookhand; a few contemporary marginal notes. Lord's Prayer in English (s. xvi/xvii) between columns. Pen trials by one "Thomas". Crude 16th-century drawings of flowers in margins. Removed from the binding of Yale's copy of Aristotle, *Ethica*, ed. P. Vettori (Paris, 1560).

34. Grammar Handbook   England, s. XV[2/4]

Portions of a grammar handbook, including parts of a nominalium and rhetorical works (23 pieces).

Paper (watermarks similar in design to Piccard Fabeltiere 1342–48), each fragment 158 x 100 mm. Long lines ruled in ink or (in lexicon) 2 columns, unruled. Written in Anglicana bookhand. Signature of an early owner on what appears to have been the paper flyleaf of the codex: "Johannes carter est verus possessor huius libri." Boards from a binding.

MS 3

37. Petrus Comestor, *Historia scholastica*   France, s. XIII[1]

Portions of *Historia numeri: De recessu israel a monte synai* to *De xii. exploratoribus*, accompanied by many marginal glosses (2 fragments).

Parchment, each fragment 137 x 159 mm.; the 2 fragments fit together, with a written space 200 x 103 mm. Written in 2 columns of 52 lines; ruled in lead, double outer and triple center vertical bounding lines, double horizontal bounding lines, all full across; additional ruling in outer margin for glosses; between guide-lines for text, 5 mm. Remains of prickings in outer margin. Written in early gothic bookhand, with very neat contemporary marginal notes. Initials 3- to 2-line in red or blue with blue or red penwork; 1-line initials in text red or blue; paragraph marks, headings and chapter numbers in red. Probably used as flyleaves.

38. Giovanni Boccaccio, *Filocolo*   Italy, s. XIV/XV

Contains 5.2.5 to 5.4.5 and 5.11.1 to 5.14.1 (3 fragments, the third without text). The text is quite close to the printed text of A. E. Quaglio, ed., *Tutte le opere di Giovanni Boccaccio* (Verona, 1967) v. 1, pp. 551-53 and 569-71.

Parchment; the 2 fragments with text are 335 x 210 (233 x 154) mm. each. Written in 2 columns of 51 lines, ruled in lead; between guide-lines for text, 5 mm. In a beautiful fere-humanistic script. Initials 4-line, in blue or red, with fine elaborate penwork in red and a color which has completely faded out, extending full length of text column. Written in Tuscany (Florentine decoration?). Holes and stains; octagonal white paper tag with blue edging, holding "No. 333" (crossed out and replaced with "111"). Probably used as pastedowns. We thank D. Dutschke for information on the text and localization of these fragments.

39. Sermon, in Lat.   England or Germany, s. XIII[2]-XIV[1]

Portions of an unidentified sermon and a sermon for *Dominica decima* (one bifolium).

Parchment, 165 x 270 mm. (width of written space 116 mm.). Written in 2 columns, ruled in lead; between guide-lines for text, 3 mm. Written in small gothic textura. One 4-line initial in red; remnants of a long red flourish; rubrics. Used as a book binding; reinforced with a printed text of s. XVI or later which covers the entire back of the parchment. Removed from a rare book in the Yale University Library.

40. Legal document, in Lat.   Italy, s. XVI

Subject unidentified, as much of the upper portion of the document is missing. Signed at bottom by "Guillermus de fonte, clericus".

One piece of heavy parchment, 284 x 190 mm., and a very small fragment. Written in cursive with heavy bâtarde influence. Used as a cover; upper right corner as well as right edge of text missing, with charred edge. Stains, holes, and remains of glue.

41. Legal document, in Lat. Italy, s. XVI

Florence is mentioned, also the date 157* [trimmed]. Subject unidentified, as much of the text is missing.

Parchment, 194 x 302 mm. No ruling. Written in an untidy running hand. Used as a binding; creased and rubbed, with large holes.

42. Unidentified liturgical work, in Lat. Germany [?], s. XIII-XIV

Includes rubrics for responses, versicles, and a *sermo* (2 fragments).

Parchment, each fragment a portion of a conjugate leaf, each 30 x 168 mm. (width of written space 70 mm.). Written in long lines, ruled in lead; writing begins below top line; between guide-lines for text, 5 mm. Written in small gothic textura. Initials (3- to 1-line), headings, underlining, and strokes on 1-line initials in red. Probably used as a binding reinforcement.

44. Hours France, s. XV^{med}

Contains Psalm 5. 6-13, perhaps from the Office of the Dead (one leaf).

Parchment, 163 x 115 (104 x 73) mm. Written in 17 long lines, ruled in pale red ink, single horizontal and vertical bounding lines, full across; between guide-lines for text, 6 mm. Written in liturgical gothic bookhand. Initials, 1-line, gold against an irregular pink and blue ground with white filigree; line-fillers pink and blue with white filigree and gold. According to an unidentified printed note (from a bookseller?), the manuscript was found in Lyons, and its identification verified by La Bibliothèque Sainte Geneviève of Paris. Bought in New York by Mrs. Arthur Greenfield; her gift to Yale in 1973.

45. Prayers, in Armenian Armenia, 1454

Three prayers, including the Lord's Prayer; part of a set for use as a talisman (3 strips).

Paper (soft but heavy, no watermarks), each piece ca. 364 x 68 mm. Written in long lines on one side only, no ruling, varying number of lines. In a small neat script by the priest Melkiseth in 1454. Headpiece with palmette ornament, in yellow, red and blue. All pieces damaged by water. Gift of Harold S. Burr in 1963.

46. Ecclesiastical document, in Lat. France, s. XVI

Precise subject unidentified; mentions Brother Robertus Guelloti, papal bulls and the date 148* [trimmed] (2 fragments).

Parchment, each piece ca. 135 x 102 mm. Written in long lines on one side only; ruled in hard point; between guide-lines for text, 7 mm. In an informal bâtarde. Used as pastedowns; a few holes, remains of glue, portions of text obliterated by rubbing.

47. Unidentified scholastic text, in Lat. England, s. XIV[ex]

Two fragments of parchment, each 206 x 72 mm., which fit together to form a single leaf measuring ca. 210 x 140 (161 x 115) mm. Written in 2 columns of ca. 38 lines; frame-ruled in brown ink; prickings at corners of the written space. Written in Anglicana bookhand with many abbreviations. Creased; perhaps a binding reinforcement.

50. Sermons, in Lat. and It. Italy, s. XV

Short sermons on death, 2 full [?] and 2 partial (one leaf).

Paper (unidentified watermark in upper corner, partly trimmed), 150 x 113 (119 x 93) mm. Written in 23 long lines, not ruled. In a neat italic. Probably used as a flyleaf.

52. Unidentified work, in Lat. England, s. XIV[1]

Possibly a sermon (one fragment).

Parchment, 170 x 110 mm. Written in 2 columns of 36 lines (1 column 140 x 46 mm.); ruled in lead; between guide-lines for text, 4 mm. Written in small gothic textura (on recto); a less formal style of gothic, with marginal notations of s. XVI (verso). Used as a pastedown. Gift of James Tanis in 1965.

53. Legal documents, in Fr. France, s. XVI

Subjects unidentified. One document mentions the date 1525.

Two leaves of parchment, each ca. 555 x 441 mm. Written in 66 or 79 long lines; one side only, no rulings. Written in 2 different hands, both informal bâtarde. Stains and remnants of paste; used as pastedowns and binding reinforcements.

MS 4 (olim Z109.7) Italy, s. XV[ex]
St. Antoninus, Confessionale

ff. 1r–120v *Incipit confessionale fratri*[s erased] *Antonini de florentia Ad omnes. Defecerunt scrutantes scrutinio ait ... Si percussit aliquem praedicatorum vel iniecit manus temerarias.//* [ends abruptly at quire twelve; catchwords: vel violentis]

The text does not correspond closely to any of those listed in GKW, v. 2, nos. 2080–2140.

Paper (watermarks: unidentified bull's head), ff. ii (fragments of 14th-century liturgical manuscript used as pastedown and flyleaf i, with modern paper for ii) + 120 + i (fragments from same 14th-century manuscript used as back flyleaf and pastedown), 154 x 103 (95 x 69) mm. Written in 23 long lines; horizontal lines ruled in ink, vertical in lead, full across; prickings along upper and lower edges.

I–XII¹⁰. Catchwords, surrounded by four symmetrically arranged flourishes, in center of lower margin.

Text written by one person in humanistic script; numerous marginal and interlinear notes in a slightly later hand.

Many ornamental capitals of various sizes, 9- to 3-line, in red and blue with purple penwork, mark each section of text; some with pale shades of yellow, peach, and purple as background. Rubrics (except toward end); red, blue, and yellow paragraph marks.

Binding: s. xv^{ex}. Original sewing on three tawed, slit straps, kermes pink, laced through tunnels in the thickness of wooden boards into rectangular channels on their outer face. Twisted, tawed cores of plain, wound endbands laid in grooves. All supports pegged and gypsum [?] used to fill in around them. Spine lined with brown calf, wanting except under endband tie-downs. Covered in brown calf, blind-tooled with a rope interlace panel border. Corner turn-in tongues. Two catches on lower board, stubs of straps on upper. Boards worm-eaten and detached and most of the cover wanting. Minor repairs to endleaves and headband made ca. 1976.

Written in Italy at the end of the 15th century; early provenance unknown. Gift of James Hosmer Penniman, 1921.

secundo folio: soluas tu

Bibliography: De Ricci, v. 1, p. 162, no. 4.

MS 5 (olim Z109.20)   Germany, s. XV²
St. Birgitta, Regula Sancti Salvatoris, etc.

1. ff. 1r–10r   *Incipit Regula Sancti Saluatoris confirmata pro Constitutionibus De humilitate Castitate et paupertate. primum*. Principium itaque huius religionis et salutis est vera humilitas ... Et cogitent in cordibus suis quod terra sunt et in terram reuertentur.

    S. Eklund, ed., *Opera minora Sanctae Birgittae,* (Lund, 1975) v. 1, p. 11, MS U^e and pp. 146–72.

2. ff. 10r–11r   *Vrbanus Quintus Vt nichil a nouicijs omnino exigatur*. Urbanus Episcopus seruus seruorum dei Ad perpetuam rei memoriam ... datum Rome Apud sanctum Petrum ii° nonas aprilis pontificatus nostri Anno vii°. f. 11v blank

    Eklund, *op. cit.*

3. ff. 12r–16r   *Incipit Regula sancti Augustini episcopi.* Ante omnia fratres karissimi diligatur deus. deinde proximus ... orans ut sibi debitum dimittatur et in temptationem non inducatur *Explicit Regula sancti Augustini.*

    Pseudo-Augustine, *Disciplina monasterii*; PL 32. 1449–52.

4. ff. 16r–28v *Incipiunt Additiones domini Prioris Petri super Regula sancti Saluatoris de humilitate capitulum primum.* Humilitas vera est timere deum omni hora ... veniat in contemptum. dum habitus canonice religionis despicitur indignis. *Deo gracias.*

The order of the text in this manuscript differs somewhat from that published by T. Nyberg, ed., *Dokumente und Untersuchungen zur inneren Geschichte der drei Birgittenklöster Bayerns 1420–1570* in *Quellen und Erörterungen zur bayerischen Geschichte*, N.F. 26, part 2 (Munich, 1974) pp. 49–110.

5. f. ii [One leaf of another manuscript laid in:] *Reuelacio Sancte Birgitte.* Cantus sit modestus grauis et simplex non fractis uocibus non cum discantu sed omni humilitate et deuotione plenus. *Uenerabilis pater Beatus Bernhardus Clareuallis abbas praecepit ... ita dicens.* Psalmodiam non nimium protrahamus sed rotunde et viua voce... [a short text on singing psalms, seemingly incomplete, follows; this is followed by a note, partially erased, dated "Anno domini mccclxiii die sancti vitalis"].

Parchment, ff. 28 + i (1 leaf of 15th century parchment manuscript laid in), 236 x 160 (177 x 118) mm. Written in 30–39 long lines, frame-ruled in ink; some prickings visible at top and bottom; outer edges have been trimmed.

I–II^{10} (small parchment fragment containing marginal notes on f. 17v that were partially lost through trimming is bound between folios 17 and 18), III^8. Catchwords along lower right edge of verso.

Written by a single scribe in bâtarde (no loops).

Primary plain initials, 11- to 1-line, in red; rubrics throughout.

Binding: s. xv. Original sewing on four slit, tawed straps laced into beech boards as are the tawed cores of plain, wound endbands. Covered in cream-colored skin, cut or worn away so that the endbands are visible on the spine. Traces of five bosses on each board and of a strap-and-pin fastening, the strap attached to the lower board with a brass plate. Pin and strap wanting. Front pastedown: fragment of 15th-century manuscript, on paper; back pastedown: fragment of another 15th-century manuscript glued in upside down. Watercolor sketch of St. Birgitta (115 x 67 mm.) pasted on front cover, probably s. xvi.

Written in Germany in the second half of the 15th century (see art. 5); early provenance unknown. Belonged to comte Paul Riant, 1836–1888 ("2470", in red, inside front cover; bookstamp inside back cover; L. de Germon and L. Polain, *Catalogue de la bibliothèque de feu M. le comte Riant* [Paris, 1896] v. 1, p. 359, no. 2470). Presented to Yale by Mrs. Henry Farnam, 1896 ("Yale University Library 1896" written on front pastedown; A. B. Benson, "The Scandinavian Collection," *Gazette* 8 [1933] pp. 49–53).

secundo folio: Ad conseruandam

Bibliography: De Ricci, v. 1, p. 162, no. 5.

MS 6 (olim Z109.28) Italy, s. XIV^{ex}
St. Bernardine of Siena, Tractatus de restitutionibus

ff. 1r–77r *Incipit tractatus de restitutionibus. editus a venerabili patre fratre Bernardino de senis. Prohemium.* Restitues hereditatem meam mihi. Inter cetera quae ad christianam religionem ... [text:] *Prima principalis pars. Quis restituere tenetur. Sermo 33.* Primo est considerare necesse est. Quis restituere obligatur ... Putredini dixi pater meus es. mater mea. et soror mea vermibus. f. 77v ruled, but blank

The text is a part of the *De christiana religione* of St. Bernardine, often copied as a separate work. See *S. Bernardini Senensis ordinis fratrum minorum opera omnia...* (Florence, 1950) v. 1, pp. 400–532. The Beinecke codex is listed as no. 90, p. xxxix, in this edition; the sermons in MS 6 are numbered 33 through 40.

Parchment, ff. ii (paper) + 77 + iii (paper), 135 x 97 (98 x 65) mm. Written in 28–30 long lines, with the single bounding lines usually ruled in lead, the guidelines for the text in ink; prickings for bounding lines at outer edge.

I-VI^{10}, VIII^{10} (-8, 9, 10). Horizontal catchwords in lower right hand portion of verso, with two dots and a flourish at beginning and end of word(s).

Written by a single scribe in fere-humanistic script.

Initials, headings and paragraph marks in red.

Binding: s. xix/xx. Vellum case.

Written in Italy at the end of the 14th century; early provenance unknown. Bought with the income of the Edward Wells Southworth Fund in 1910.

secundo folio: quis inuenta

Bibliography: De Ricci, v. 1, p. 162, no. 6.

MS 7 (olim Z109.30) Germany, s. XV
Breviary (diurnal)

1. f. 1r Scarcely visible text under the remains of a damaged woodcut of the Pietà; f. 1v Portions of an office for Stephen protomartyr.

2. ff. 2r–7v Graded calendar in red and black with additions in a contemporary [?] hand supplying readings, other saints, and obits; among the saints are Richard King (7 Feb., added), Walburga (25 Feb.), Cunigundis (3 March), Castulus (26 March), Rupert (27 March), Trudpert (26 April), Translation of Walburga (1 May), Boniface (5 June, in red), Erentrude (30 June), Ulric (4 July), Willibald (7 July), Kilian (8 July, in red), Henry emperor (13 July), Octave of Kilian (15 July), Oswald (5 Aug.), Sebald (19 Aug.), Translation of Erentrude (4 Sept.), Translation of Cunigundis (9 Sept.), Translation of Rupert and Chuniald (24 Sept.), Translation of Virgilius (26 Sept.), Burchard (14 Oct.), "dedicacio maioris [?] ecclesie" (24 Oct., added), Willibrord (7 Nov.),

Virgilius (27 Nov.), Odilia (13 Dec.). The added obits are "obiit Elizabet Ebyn mater mea Anno et cetera [14?]16" and 4 others, illegible, on 2, 3 and 17 September, and 5 November.

3. f. 8r   Diagram for determining calendar; f. 8v   Portions of an office for Stephen protomartyr and notes on indulgence *in ecclesia magd[eburgensis?]* and on the feast of the relics *dominica die post corpus christi* or *sequenti die post mauricii*; prayer to the Virgin; f. 9r–v   Prayers to the Trinity.

4. ff. 10r–14v   Partial table of contents in a later hand; temporale for the day offices for the week following Pentecost.

5. ff. 15r–20r   Day offices for the dedication of a church, Trinity Sunday and the feast of Corpus Christi.

6. ff. 20v–66v   Day offices of the sanctorale from Urban (25 May) through Virgilius (27 Nov.), including offices for Ulric, Kilian, Henry emperor, Reginswindis, Oswald, Cunigundis, Rupert, Chuniald and Gislar, Willibald, Burchard and Willibrord.

7. ff. 66v–69v   Antiphons and responses *de hystoriis*; prayer to the Virgin added in a different hand.

8. ff. 70r–78v   Capitula, prayers and antiphons for the Sundays from the 1st through the 24th Sunday after Trinity; f. 79r–v additional capitula and antiphons.

9. ff. 80r–94r   Antiphons and responses for the common of saints.

10. ff. 94v–115v   Readings for the common of saints; f. 115v added prayers to Mary Magdalen; f. 116r–v added confessional prayer.

11. ff. 117r–128v   Hymns for the sanctorale (Holy Spirit through Catharine), for the dedication of a church and for Compline, Matins and Lauds.

12. ff. 129r–145r   Psalms, antiphons and hymns, many by cue only, arranged for the week, day offices only.

13. ff. 145r–147v   Prayers before and after mass.

14. ff. 147v–154r   Penitential psalms and litany, including among the 27 martyrs Kilian (17) and Oswald (25), among the 22 confessors Henry (14), Otto (15), Ulric (16), Willibald (17), Burchard (19), Rupert (21) and Virgilius (22), and among the 25 virgins Cunigundis (12) and Walburga (23).

15. ff. 154r–165v   Office of the Dead with two unidentified sets of responses to the lessons at matins: 1. Credo quod; 2. Qui lazarum; 3. Domine quando; 4. Heu michi; 5. Cum veneris; 6. Peccantem me; 7. Domine secundum; 8. Libera me ... de viis; 9. Libera me ... de morte. The second set, under the rubric *pro parentibus lecciones*: 1. Redemptor meus; 2. Manus tue; 3. Memento [? badly rubbed] quod sicut lutum; 4. Absolue domine; 5. Ne tradas; 6. Rogamus te; 7. Deus eterne; 8. Domino confitebor; 9. Libera me ... de morte.

16. ff. 166r-173v   Ferial capitula, an office for the Virgin (9 lessons at matins), offices for the Holy Cross, Kilian, Translation of Nicolas, Benedict, Erentrude, Translation of Martin, Dominic, Presentation of the Virgin, Willibald.

17. ff. 173v-181r   Added material in several hands: offices for Willibald, Anna and Sebald; hymns at Lauds; a lesson for the Office of the Dead.

18. ff. 181v-182v   Table on the Golden Number and on lucky or unlucky sections of the zodiac; capitula; last leaf torn out.

Parchment (sturdy, of uneven quality), ff. i (modern paper) + 182 + i (modern paper), 105 x 75 (ca. 82 x 60) mm. Written in ca. 26 long lines; frame-ruled or with single vertical bounding lines only, in ink. Remains of prickings in lower margin.

An accurate collation is impossible due to tight binding. Some catchwords along lower edge.

Written primarily by a single scribe in a small running script. Additions by several contemporary and later writers.

Plain initials, 4- to 1-line, in red. Rubrics throughout.

Portions of text, badly worn or trimmed, have been lost.

Binding: s. xv-xvi. Resewn on two tapes. Wooden boards. Covered in dark brown calf, blind-tooled in a diamond pattern with indistinguishable ornaments within the diamonds and at their intersections. Traces of five round bosses, larger on lower board, metal corner pieces and a catch plate on the upper board. Rebacked, with leather formed in the shape of endbands in the turn-ins at head and tail of the spine and with a strap and pin (a modern nail?) fastening added.

Written probably in Southern Germany, in or near Magdeburg (see art. 8), during the 15th century; early provenance unknown. Presented to Yale in 1898 by Albert H. Buck, M. D.

Bibliography: De Ricci, v. 1, p. 163, no. 7.

MS 8 Germany, s. XV^2
Psalter, etc.

1. f. 1r   Invitatories and the hymn Nocte surgentes for Sundays.

2. ff. 1v-120v, 185r-196v, 121r-172v   Liturgical psalter with invitatories, antiphons, versicles and hymns.

3. ff. 172v-184v, 197r-199v   Hymns for Matins for the temporale (Advent through Corpus Christi), the sanctorale (John the Baptist, Peter and Paul, Mary Magdalen, Lawrence, Augustine, Michael archangel, All Saints), the dedication of a church and the common of saints (apostle, one martyr, many martyrs, one confessor, one virgin, one virgin not martyr, many virgins).

MS 9

Paper (watermarks similar to Briquet Lettre P 8598), ff. 199 + i (contemporary paper). The codex was bound incorrectly; ff. 185-196 should follow f. 120. 152 x 107 (104 x 70) mm. Written in 15 long lines; single vertical bounding lines, double horizontal lines, full across. Ruled in ink; prickings visible in lower and outer margins.

I-XIV^{12}, XV^{16}, XVI^{12} (+ 1 leaf at end), XVII^2. Catchwords located along bottom of folio near binding.

Written by a single scribe in bold gothic textura.

Initials, 3- to 1-line, at beginning of each verse, in red; rubrics throughout.

Most leaves are stained and repaired.

Covers and spine missing.

Written probably in Western Germany in the second half of the 15th century; early provenance unknown. Purchased by Yale with the Ann S. Farnam Fund in 1909.

secundo folio: sic inpij

Bibliography: De Ricci, v. 1, p. 163, no. 8.

MS 9 (olim Z109.32)   Germany, s. XVI^{in}
Hours, Premonstratensian use   Pl. 16

1. ff. 1r-3v Prayers as follow: *De mane dum primo surgis lege istam orationem.* In christi surgo nomine ... resuscita me in nouissimo die ad laudem et gloriam nominis tui. Amen. Pater noster et cetera. Credo in deum patrem. Credo in spiritum sanctum. Aue maria et cetera. *Trine orationes ad patrem Oratio.* Pater de celis deus miserere uobis. Domine sancte pater omnipotens eterne deus qui coequalem...; Domine ihesu christe fili dei uiui...; Domine sancte spiritus qui coequalis ... et ignem sanctissimi ac suauissimi amoris tui. Qui uiuis et regnas deus. Per omnia secula seculorum. Amen. [HE 124-25]

2. ff. 3v-48v Hours of the Virgin, Premonstratensian use.

3. ff. 49r-71v Penitential Psalms, beginning defectively in Ps. 6.9, and Litany. Among the 24 martyrs, Gereon (19); among the 23 confessors, Servatius (9), Severinus (10), Godehard (15), Willehad (16), Anskar (17), and Rembert (18); among the 18 virgins, Walburgis (12), Aldegundis (14) and Ursula (18).

4. ff. 72r-127v Office of the Dead, Premonstratensian use.

5. ff. 127v-132r Prayer. *De paives* [sic] *vincencius devant dit bet. So we dat leset eyn iar lanck alle daghe myt innicheit vor ene sele. de wert vorloset.* Criste mortalium spes vna. qui tue misertus tantum es facture ... propter nos induere dignatus est formam visibilem ihesus christus filius tuus dominus tuus dominus noster ... Per omnia secula seculorum. Amen.

6. ff. 132r-136v Suffrages to the Body of Christ to be said *ad matutinas, ad salue regina, ad quindecim gradus, ad psalterium sancti spiritus, ad psalterium corporis christi, In vigilia dedicationis ad psalterium..., antequam psalterium..., finito psalmo....*

7. ff. 136v-139r *Sequuntur Antiphone de domina nostra.* Nigra sum sed formosa ... [Canticum Canticorum, 1. 4]; (f. 137r) Uox turturis audita est; (f. 137r) Salue regina [RH 18147]; Alma redemptoris mater ... [RH 861]; (f. 138r) Aue beatissima ciuitas diuinitatis eterne felix gaudium ... [RH 1701]; (f. 139r) Botrus cypri dilectus meus michi ... [cf. RH 2506].

8. ff. 139r-153v Offices *In vigilia pasche Ad capitulum, De corpore christi, Ad sepulchrum psalmi* (cues of Pss. 5, 6, 114, 115, 129, 141 in full, 142), *Commendacio animarum* (Pss. 115, 116, 117 followed by versicles), *In vigilia natalis domini Ad capitulum*, Gospel readings (John 1. 1-14 and John 17. 1-26), prayer *Pro sepultis in cimiterio.*

9. ff. 153v-156r Short Hours of the Cross.

10. ff. 156v-159r Hours of the Compassion, short form.

11. ff. 159r-160r Prayer to the Five Wounds of Christ, *Lyell Cat.*, pp. 61-62. f. 160v ruled, but blank

12. ff. 161r-187r Saturday office for the Virgin (9 lessons at Matins).

13. ff. 187r-192r Suffrages. 2 each *de Sancta cruce, de venerabili sacramento, de domina nostra, de apostolis, de sancto Augustino,* and *de omnibus sanctis.* f. 192v ruled, but blank

14. ff. 193r-198v Office for the first, seventh, or thirtieth day anniversary of a burial or for its commemoration, beginning *Vita in ligno moritur, infernus ex morsu despoliatur, Domine miserere anime famule tue....*

15. ff. 198v-201r *Oratio sancti Augustini quam qui homo qualibet die ...* Domine iesu christe qui in hunc mundum propter nos peccatores ... ut peruenire valeat ad societatem ciuium supernorum ... per omnia secula seculorum. Amen.

Lyell Cat., p. 379, no. 160.

16. ff. 201v-209v *Commendacio animarum.* Subuenite sancti dei..., *Oratio.* Tibi domine commendamus animam famule tue..., *Oracio.* Misericordiam tuam domine sancte pater, Ps. 113 (cue only) with antiphon, *Oracio.* Omnipotens sempiterne deus qui humano corpori..., *Oracio.* Suscipe domine creaturam tuam..., Ps. 114 (cue only) with antiphon, *Oremus.* Diri uulneris nouitate percussi..., *Oracio.* Deus cui soli competit medicinam dare..., *Oracio.* Suscipe domine animam serui tui quam..., *Oracio.* Deus cuius misericordie non est numerus..., *Oratio.* Tibi domine commendamus animam famule tue..., *Oracio.* Deus origo pietatis pater misericordie..., [no rubric] Gratias ago tibi domine ihesu christe pro sexaginta et quadringentis..., *Oracio.* Domine ihesu christe qui portando crucem pro me....

17. ff. 209v-217v Suffrages to the angels, John the Baptist, the apostles and

evangelists, martyrs, confessors, virgins, Pro pace; Ps. 138; Aue sanctissima maria mater dei regina celi ... [indulgence conceded by Sixtus IV]; Aue maria ancilla sancte trinitatis ... [indulgence revealed to Bernard].

18. ff. 217v-246r Suffrages to Michael Archangel, one's Guardian Angel, all angels, John the Baptist, all patriarchs and prophets, Bartholomew, one apostle, all apostles, Gregory, one martyr, all martyrs, the 15 helpers, Jerome, one confessor, all confessors, Anna with indulgence conceded by Alexander VI (*quas confirmauit rome in festo pasche Anno domini M. CCCC XCIIII.*), Mary Magdalen, Catharine of Alexandria (2 suffrages), one virgin, all virgins and widows, all saints, for Holy Mother Church.

19. ff. 246r-248v Miserere mi domine animabus que singulares apud te non habent intercessores...; Saluete vos omnes fideles anime quarum corpora hic et ubique requiescunt...; Sal[u]ete vos omnes fideles anime que iacetis...; Respice quesumus omnipotens deus super animas ... [prayers for the dead with indulgences conceded by Pius II and John IV]; Auete omnes christifideles anime ... [prayer for the dead with indulgence conceded by John XII].

20. ff. 248v-251r Second nocturn of an office for the dead *secundum Paderbornense ordinarium* added by a later hand. ff. 251v-254v ruled, but blank

Parchment, ff. v (i, iii, iv = contemporary parchment; modern paper leaf added [ii]; v, with miniature, added separately) + 254, 137 x 95 (83 x 52) mm. Written in 15 long lines per page, ruled in black ink; double horizontal, single vertical bounding lines, all full across.

I^4 (original flyleaves; -1, + modern paper inserted between i and iii and glued to iv), II^8 (+ 1 leaf added at beginning), III-VII^8, VIII^8 (-1, 2), IX-X^8, XI^8 (-2), XII-XVI^8, XVII^8 (folio between ff. 120 and 121 not numbered), XVIII-XIX^8, XX^6, XXI^8, XXII^6, XXIII-XXXIII^8, XXXIV^8 (-6).

Written by a single copyist in two sizes of liturgical gothic script.

One miniature, f. v verso: Saul on the Road to Damascus, an addition (s. xvi^{in}) of fair quality, in an arched frame, brown and gold; a scatter border of flowers and insects on a beige ground, brown edging. Large initials, one (f. 4r) 8-line (45 x 45 mm.) on burnished gold with tooling, the others either on burnished gold with tooling (ff. 1r, 38r, 72v, 127v) or on pink and blue grounds (ff. 154r, 161r, 193v), set in full scatter borders of acanthus twigs (either gold with pink and brown or red, blue, and/or pink), flowers and, in some cases, birds, over compartmentalized (blue/gold, pink/beige, blue/dark blue, beige/brown), beige and parchment (with and without a background of black pen flecks) grounds; some borders without bounding lines. On f. 1r, an unidentified coat of arms in each corner of the border. Upper left and lower right, sable, in chief 2 wreaths vert with dots gules and or, in base a rose per pale gules and argent, barbed vert, seeded or. Upper right, or, a bear [?] rampant argent, langued gules. Lower left, ermine, a fess gules with 4 plates, cottised sable. Small initials, 3-line, gold, either filled with pink with gold filigree on a blue ground decorated with acanthus and black flecks, or filled with blue on a pink ground decorated with black filigree; some with additional flowers or pink and blue acanthus; all associated with short border strips, as above. Numerous 3- and 4-line initials, blue, filled with red curling acanthus drawn in pen, surrounded by red or crimson penwork. 2- and 1-line initials in red or blue. Rubrics throughout.

Pieces of the illuminated borders have been cut from ff. 4, 38, 127, 154, and 193. Ink has run or been rubbed in several places, including ff. v verso and 1r.

Binding: s. xvi. Sewn on three double vegetable fiber cords laced into wooden boards. The book is so tightly bound that it is impossible to determine whether or not the sewing is original. No endband grooves. Edges gilt. Covered in dark brown calf with a panel stamp of the Virgin and Child on a crescent, within a flambent aureole in the center of each board, hearts pierced with an arrow and a dagger [?] in a diamond, stars in circles above and below the central stamp, all within a vine scroll border. Traces of one fastening, two later fastenings added. Rebacked, very possibly by the binder who rebacked MS 7 as there is a similar, unusual, endcap treatment.

Written in Northwestern Germany, probably near Cologne, as indicated from the saints in the Litany (art. 3), and the style of the borders (derivative from Ghent-Bruges School models of ca. 1500). The codex may have belonged to a woman, given the presence (although not exclusive) of feminine forms. Arms of early owners (coat of arms in each corner, all unidentified; later additions?) in border of f. 1r. Given 11 June 1598 by Bernardus Kniperus of Lübeck, to Leonardus Rubenus, abbot of the Benedictine monastery of Abdingkhoff, near Paderborn (inscription on flyleaf, recopied on a leaf inserted later after the flyleaf). Old shelf-mark N. 35 of the monastery (f. v recto). In 1807 belonged to Ant. Jos. Rosenmeyer (inscriptions on ff. iii recto and v recto); later belonged to A. Gelsenthal (inscription on f. iv recto). Given to Yale by Addison van Name in 1922.

Bibliography: De Ricci, v. 1, p. 163, no. 9.

MS 10 (olim 4.4.17 and Z109.34)   England, s. XV^{med}
Hours, use unidentified   Pl. 20

1. ff. 1r–54v   Office of the Dead, beginning and ending imperfectly; use undetermined. The responses to the lessons at Matins are 1. Credo quod, 2. Qui lazarum, 3. Domine dum ueneris, 4. Subuenite sancti dei, 5. Heu michi domine, 6. Ne recorderis, 7. Peccantem me, 8. Domine secundum, 9. Memento mei domine; the 9th lesson begins Vir fortissimus iudas.

2. ff. 55r–86v   Penitential Psalms and Litany. Among the 27 martyrs Thomas (2; cancelled), Austremonius (7), Marcellus (11), Quentin (12), Edmund (13), Olanus (14), Alban (15), Irenaeus (17), Julianus (20), Fortunatus (24); among

MS 11

the 30 confessors, Silvester (1), Hilary (2), Gregory (4), Germanus (5), Taurinus (6), Eucherius (11), Eligius (12), Florus (14), Augustine (15), Dunstan (16), Cuthbert (17), Edmund (18), Philibert (22), Columban (23), Aegidius (24), Odo (25), Majolus (26), Odilo (27), Hugo (28), Geraldus (29), Leonard (30); among the 23 virgins, Cyrilla (11), Ethelreda (13), Milburga (14), Radegundis (15), Walburgis (16), Florencia (17), Consortia (18), Daria (19), Columba (20).

3. f. 87v   Prayer in a later hand. Paucitas dierum meorum timetur breui dimitte me domine ... Libera me domine de morte eterna in die illa tremenda// f. 88 ruled on both sides, but blank except for short passage from John 1.6 and pen trials.

Parchment (coarse), ff. iii (paper) + ii (contemporary parchment, with large pieces torn from outer margins) + 88 + i (paper), 185 x 120 (110 x 67) mm. Written in 12 long lines per page; single bounding lines; ruled in pale brown ink.
I^8 (-1, 2, 3, 4), II^8 (-5), III-VII^8, VIII^8 (-4), IX-XI^8, XII^2, XIII^2 (+ 1 leaf, glued to f. 86v). Catchwords below written space, near bounding line.

Written in liturgical gothic script of two sizes, by one person. Prayer on f. 87v is added in a very similar script, but by a less firm hand.

A pencilled note on f. 55r refers to a miniature cut out between ff. 54 and 55. 2-line initials in blue, with red penwork often extending along left border. 1-line initials in blue or red. Rubrication to mark headings within sections in crimson or orange ink.

Binding: s. xviii. Brown calf, blind-tooled. Rebacked; back cover detached.

Written in England, as is clear from script and decoration, but perhaps from a French exemplar, given the number of Central and Southern French saints in the litany; the liturgical use of the Office of the Dead remains unidentified. The name of Thomas of Canterbury and "dompnum apostolicum" in the litany (ff. 71v and 76v) have been cancelled. Note on the second flyleaf reads: "Enoch Huntington's the Gift of Mr. William Cone a Book which he took out of the Ruins of a House at Morrisania in New York in the Campaign of the Year 1776. February 10th. 1777. Middletown in the State of Connecticut in America." Along the inner edge of the same leaf, in a different hand, "Presented to the Library of Yale College" [date unknown]. On f. 11r a name in pencil: Hinnit [?]; on f. 27r, in pencil, possibly in the same hand, Mary Demery [?].

Bibliography: De Ricci, v. 1, p. 163, no. 10.

MS 11   England, 1704
Statuta collegii reginalis, etc. (partly in English)

All bibliographical citations for this manuscript refer to *Documents Relating to the University and Colleges of Cambridge* (London, 1852) 3 vol.

1. f. ii *Statuta Collegij Reginalis. Index Statutorum Collegij Reginalis.* Cap. 1 Praefatio Reginae Fundatricis Pag. 1 ... 37. De Interpretatione Statutorum. 62. Finis Index Statutorum. [v. 3, pp. 72-73]

2. pp. 1-63 *Statuta Colegii Reginalis. Praefatio Reginae Fundatricis.* Elizabeth Dei gratia Angliae Franciae et Domina Hiberniae dilectis ... contraria et repugnantia sub poena incurrendi manifestum perjurium ipso facto. [v. 3, pp. 17-55]

3. pp. 63-89 *Interpretationes Statutorum.* A. D. 1529 per Praesidentem et majorem partem sociorum huius ... alii Collegii fundationis pro omnibus benefactoribus locum obtinent. Finis. [v. 3, p. 56 ff.; the manuscript differs considerably from the printed text]

4. p. 90 *Index Interpretationum Statutorum Collegii Reginalis.* De tempore Aestatis et Hyemis. Pag. 63 ... De ordine et senioritate Sociorum et Bibliotistarum. 89. Finis Interpretationum in hoc libro.

5. pp. 1-3 Epistle from Queen Elizabeth I dated 1570. [v. 1, pp. 454-55]

6. pp. 4-59 *Leges siue Statuta Academiae Cantabrigiensis.* Deum timeto, Regem honorato, Virtutem colito, disciplinis bonis operam dato ... Unum in communi Arario repositum alterum apud Cancellarium et duo Procuratores habeant. Cancellarius: Gulielmus Cecilius. Procancellarius: Dr. May, Mr. A. Cath, Procuratores: Thomas Aldridg, Reuben Sherwood. Finis. [v. 1, pp. 455-95]

7. pp. 60-66 *Statuta de Oratore eligendo et ejus officio ex Libro Procuratorum.* Quoniam plerumque periclitata est Respublica nostra ... ends with a list of orators for the years 1522-1696. [v. 1, pp. 431-34; the final portion of this section differs from the printed text]

8. pp. 66-77 Quare's to which the Vicechancellour and head of the university are desired to send an answer [followed by Answers; in English].

9. pp. 71-122 Miscellaneous collection of "Interpretationes, decreta et statuta" (some in English) ranging in date from 1571-1673 (not in chronological order).

10. pp. 123-124 *Index Interpretationum Decretorum et Statutorum Academiae Cantabrigiensis.* Pag. 60 Statuta de Oratore eligendo et ejus officio ... [continued on f. i verso at the beginning of the volume where it ends:] 120 Instructions to the Vicechancellour and Heads for Government, by Charles I.

Paper (no watermarks), ff. ii (contemporary paper) + 90 + 124 (pagination by original scribe), 183 x 117 (170 x 95) mm. Written in ca. 30 long lines; frame-ruled in ink; two vertical bounding lines along left side of writing area to form narrow column for chapter numbers and notations.

The codex is too brittle to be collated; no signatures or catchwords.

Written by a certain Langwith according to a note on f. i recto (see below); a fine calligraphic italic hand.

Binding: s. xviii. Written upside down in a brown calf, blind-tooled, ready-made blank book. Split along spine.

Written apparently by the copyist Langwith (probably Benjamin, 1684?-1743, who received his degree from Cambridge in 1704) on 5 October 1704, for John Hayes; inscription on f. i recto: "Langwith writ over these Statutes for me (out of Mr. Bedford's Book). I gave him a guinea for his pains. October 5 1704." Signature of John Hayes (publisher of *Statuta quaedam academiae cantabrigiensis* ... [Cambridge, 1684]), inside front cover; followed by note; "Of two statutes, the restraining doth bind/ If neither restrain, the latter doth bind." Bookplate of James Bindley (1739-1818); autograph note inside front cover: "This Volume contains the Statutes of Queen's College Cambridge and also those of the University itself J.B." Bindley sale (Evans, 1819, 3, no. 925) to Richard Heber (1773-1833); his sale (London, 1836, 9, no. 20) to Rodd. Sold by Thorpe (Cat. 1863, no. 148) to Sir Thomas Phillipps (no. 9314 on f. i recto); his sale (London, 1895, no. 124) to Ridler. Sale by Sotheby's (27 Feb. 1899, no. 390) to Dobell (Cat. 24, 1923, no. 80); sold by him in 1924 to James Hosmer Penniman of Philadelphia who presented it to the Penniman Memorial Library of Education of Yale University in the same year.

Bibliography: De Ricci, v. 1, p. 163, no. 11.

MS 12 Italy, s. XV[1]
Prayers, Hymns, etc., to the Virgin Mary (Lat. and It.)

1. f. 1r-v   Canti go [*sic*] zoiosi e dolce melodie/ tutti cridiamo alla humile maria/ ... [Tenneroni, p. 74].

2. f. 2r   Benedecta verzenella madre de dio/ chel mi conuene ... [Tenneroni, p. 70].

3. ff. 2r-3v   Regina del cor mio/ a ti cum mente pia/ ... [Tenneroni, p. 227].

4. ff. 4r-7r   *Laude deuotissime della gloriosissima Verzene* ... O aula e masone della uniuerssale propiciatione. Casone della generale reconciliatione....

5. ff. 7r-8r   [Prayers to the Virgin with responses:] *Corona sacratissime uirginis matris marie. In primis ad matutinum dicitur. Verssus.* Domine labia mea aperies. *Responsio.* Et os meum annutiabit laudem tuam ... *Postea.* Aue maria....

6. f. 8r   Seven Temporal Joys of the Virgin [HE 63-64].

7. f. 8r-v   Seven Joys (unspecified). Gaude ergo de cetero et exulta mecum quia gloria mea excellit....

8. ff. 8v-9r   Seven Spiritual Joys of the Virgin [HE 64-65] followed by Oratio [HE 66] ending: et ad gaudia tue eterne beatitudinis feliciter ueniamus. Qui uiuis et cetera// ff. 9v-15v blank

Paper (watermarks obscured by binding and trimming), ff. 16 (contemporary foliation, 3 bis; modern foliation, used in contents above, begins on second leaf [i, 1-15]), 225 x 172 (161 x 118) mm. Written in 33 long lines or lines of verse; single (sometimes double) bounding lines. Ruled in hard point; prickings visible at outer corners of written space for ff. 9-16.

Composed of a single gathering of sixteen leaves.

Written by one scribe in round gothic bookhand.

Four poorly executed initials in gold and colors on ff. 1r, 2r (two), and 4r; the last accompanied by green and gold dots. Red initial strokes; rubrics throughout.

Binding: single quire tacketed to a piece of folded vellum.

Written in Italy in the first half of the 15th century; early inscription on front cover "Questa sie de madona felippa da thano [for Tanno near Sondrio?]." Purchased by Yale in 1911 with the income of the Edward Wells Southworth Fund.

secundo folio: Benedecta

Bibliography: De Ricci, v. 1, p. 164, no. 12.

MS 13 (olim Z109.85) Italy, s. XIV^2
Hugo de Folieto, Moralitates de avibus, etc.

1. ff. 1r-13r [Prologue:] *Incipit libellus cuiusdam ad rainerum conuersum cognomine. corde benignum. de quadam auium significacione mistica et morali. Et primo de simplicitate.* Cum scribere illiterato debeam non miretur diligens lectorum si ad ... Qui enim sapientem verbis instruit. quasi pleno vasculo latices infundit. [text:] *De simplicitate columbe. Capitulum primum. Si dormiatis inter medios cleros, penne columbe de argentate et posteriora dorsi ejus in pallore auri.* In scriptura sacra frater tres columbas legendo reperi ... id est mutacio eorum non sinit homines crescere [?] in virtute. *Expliciunt moralitates de auibus. deo gracias.*

2. ff. 13r-14r *Incipit tabula de moralitatibus auium.* Primum capitulum istius operis est de simplicitate ... vel de hominibus lucem veritatis odientibus. *Explicit tabula de moralitatibus auium.*

3. f. 14v *Incipiunt moralitates de piscibus. Capitulum primum.* Est belua in mari que dicitur grece aspis chelone ... ut putaretur infernum esse. dicente ipso iona propheta. *Exaudiuit me de ventre inferi. Expliciunt moralitates de piscibus. deo gracias.*

4. f. 14v *Incipit tabula de piscibus.* Primum capitulum est de belua ... et de natura eiusdem. moralitas de illis qui sunt modice fidei.

5. ff. 14v-16r *Incipiunt moralitates de lapidibus.* Sunt lapides igniferi in quodam monte orientis quos greci vocant cheroboles ... nobis concedat qui sine fine vivit et regnat. *Expliciunt moralitates de lapidibus. deo gracias.*

6. f. 16v *Incipit tabula de lapidibus.* Primum capitulum de lapidibus est de

cherobolibus ... moralitas de beata maria virgine. *Explicit tabula de moralitatibus lapidum. deo gracias.*

This work is often attributed to Hugh of St. Victor in manuscripts; it is printed with his works in PL 177. 13-164, without tables, and the order of the individual sections varies considerably from that in this manuscript (see R. Goy, *Die Überlieferung der Werke Hugos von St. Viktor* [Stuttgart, 1976] pp. 491-92).

Parchment, ff. ii (paper) + 16 + ii (paper), 237 x 180 (176 x 115) mm. Written in 2 columns, 46 lines, ruled in lead; single bounding lines, full across; prickings at top, bottom, and in inner margin, for bounding lines only.

I-II[8]. Catchwords for first gathering (enclosed in red rectangle), located in center of lower margin on verso.

Written by a single scribe in gothic bookhand; many abbreviations.

Painted initial at beginning of prologue in blue, brown, pale yellow, green, and orange; smaller initials in red or blue with penwork designs. Paragraph marks in red and blue; rubrics throughout.

Binding: s. xx. Quarter paper case.

Written in Italy in the second half of the 14th century; early provenance unknown. Given to Yale in 1913 by the Yale Club of Boston.

secundo folio: praemium

Bibliography: De Ricci, v. 1, p. 164, no. 13.

MS 14 (olim Z109.140)   Italy [?], s. XV[1]
Plutarch and Xenophon, Lat. tr. Leonardo Bruni

1. ff. 1r-3r blank; ff. 3v-4v [O]cioso mihi nuper ac lectitare aliquid cupienti oblatus est libellus ... Ciceronis honor ut uehementer exoptem a multis de hoc ipso scribentibus superari. Vale.

   Dedicatory epistle of Leonardo Bruni to Niccolò Niccoli; H. Baron, *Leonardo Bruni Aretino humanistisch-philosophische Schriften* (Leipzig, 1928) pp. 113-14; V. R. Giustiniani, "Sulle traduzioni latine delle 'Vite' di Plutarco nel Quattrocento," *Rinascimento* 2[a] ser., v. 1 (1961) p. 38, no. 22, b.

2. ff. 5r-46v [T]ulliorum familia que et Ciceronis postea cognomentum recepit ex municipio Arpinati ... Ita omnes Ciceronis inimici misere tandem ignominioseque perierunt. Explicit Feliciter.

   Plutarch, *Vita Ciceronis*; Giustiniani, *op. cit.*, p. 38, no. 22, b.

3. ff. 47r-67r [D]emostenis Pater demostenes ut Theopompus historicus tradit imprimis ... quod sepe predicenti demosteni credere noluerat. Feliciter Explicit

   Plutarch, *Vita Demosthenis*; Giustiniani, *op. cit.*, p. 38, no. 22, a.

4. ff. 67v-69r [X]enophontis philosophi quendam libellum quem ego ingenii exercendi gratia e greco sermone ... in his primiciis studiorum nostrorum nullo modo ausi sumus attingere.

Dedicatory epistle to Niccolò Niccoli; Baron, *op. cit.*, pp. 100-01.

5. ff. 69r-87r [C]um ad hieronem tirannum simonides poeta aliquando uenisset ... Que omnia si tu feceris cunctarum que in humana sunt uita pulcerrimam ac beatissimam rem possidebis felix enim cum sis nemo tibi invidebit. Explicit. ff. 87v-90v blank, except for "O fortuna mea quam numquam" on f. 90v

Xenophon, *Hiero*.

In this manuscript the treatises are not identified, nor is the translator, but the dedicatory epistles to Niccolò Niccoli serve to indicate both author and translator.

Parchment, ff. ii (parchment) + 90 + ii (parchment), 202 x 128 (127 x 79) mm. Written in 21 long lines, ruled in brown crayon; single bounding lines, full across; prickings along upper, lower, and outer edges for bounding lines only.
I^4, II-IX^{10}, X^6. Horizontal catchwords on lower right-hand edge of verso, between bounding line and gutter.
Written in humanistic script by a single scribe.
No headings or ornamentation; the manuscript was apparently never finished.
Binding: s. xix. Straight-grained black goatskin, gold-tooled.

Written in Italy [?] in the first half of the 15th century; early provenance unknown. Library files indicate that the manuscript was no. 42 in a Rodd catalogue; we have not been able to verify this. Abate Luigi Celotti sale (Evans, London, 14 March 1825, no. 235) to Payne and Foss for Sir Thomas Phillipps (stamps on ff. i and ii with double entry: 963 and 2738); his sale (London, 1899, no. 383) to Lovering; V. G. Simkhovitch collection; sale by Anderson's (New York, 14 Dec. 1903, no. 398) to N. T. Bacon. Presented in 1926 by Leonard Bacon and Susan Bacon Keith in memory of their father Nathaniel Terry Bacon.

secundo folio: ab initio

Bibliography: De Ricci, v. 1, p. 164, no. 14.

MS 15 (olim Z109.150) England, s. XV$^{1/4}$
Prosper Aquitanus; Johannes Shepey

1. f. 1r [Preface:] Iste Prosper fuit equitaneus vir eruditissimus omniumque arcium dogmate ... vel quid si maxime vitent siderium celi cupiunt qui scandere regnum.

2. ff. 1r-30r Dum sacris mentem placet exercere loquelis/ Celestique ... [text:]

Innocencia dei vera est que nec sibi nec alteri nocet ... sed mens. quoque nobis. Vna sit atque duos spiritus vnus alat. Amen. Explicit prosper de verbis sancti doctoris Augustini quod [?] I. C. Da gloriam deo. f. 30v blank

Prosper Aquitanus, *Epigrammata ex sententiis Sancti Augustini*; PL 51. 497-532. The manuscript follows the text in PL up to f. 27v, but concludes with additional unidentified material as printed by Christopher Plantin (Antwerp, 1560) p. 114.

3. ff. 31r-107v   Johannes Shepey, *Sermones* (no title). The sermons are listed here according to numbers assigned by Schneyer (v. 3, pp. 765-68): 1, ff. 31r-33r; 2, ff. 33r-34v; 3, ff. 34v-36v; 4, ff. 36v-38v; 5, ff. 38v-40r; unlisted sermon on Psalm 97 for Christmas, ff. 40r-44v (*De Nativitate domini. Cantate domino canticam* ... Verba ista scripta sunt in psalmo et sunt verba spiritus sancti inuitantis nos ad sacrosanctam ecclesiam ... dei perfecta sunt opera. Rogemus et cetera.); 6, ff. 44v-46v; 7, ff. 46v-49r; 8, ff. 49v-51v; 9, ff. 52r-56r; 10, ff. 56r-59v; 11, ff. 59v-61r; 12, ff. 61r-63r; 13, ff. 63r-65v; 14, ff. 65v-67v; 15; ff. 67v-69v; 16, ff. 69v-71v; 17, missing; 18, ff. 71v-74r; 19, ff. 74r-75v; 20, ff. 75v-78r; 21, ff. 78r-80r; 22, ff. 80v-83r; 23, missing; unlisted sermon for Psalm Sunday, ff. 83r-87v (*Dominica in ramis palmarum. Ecce Rex tuus venit tibi mansuetus* ... [Mat. 21.5]. Verba ista scripta sunt in euuangelio hodierno in quibus verbis tria possunt notari scilicet christi dignitas cum dicit ... viuet in eternum ad hanc vitam nos perducat. Amen.); unlisted sermon for Easter, ff. 87v-99r (*In die pasche*. Mortuus erat et reuixit legimus in quadam historia scilicet hester 1 quod rex assuerus ... in corde crucem et passionem christi rogemus ergo deum vt det nos clauem crucis per quem possimus venire ad requiem ... Amen.; on f. 90r in the middle of the sermon there is a brief English quotation of a stanza from Augustine's *Candet nudatum pectus*; see IMEV, 4088); 24, ff. 99r-100v; 25, ff. 100v-103r; 26, ff. 103r-104v; 27, ff. 104v-105v; 28, ff. 105v-107r; 29, f. 107r-v (ends imperfectly on verso).

Parchment, ff. ii (paper) + 107 + ii (paper), 176 x 122 (122 x 80) mm. Written in 24-29 long lines; frame-ruled in lead, ink, or hard point; prickings at corner of written space.

I^{12}, II^{16}, III-V^{12}, VI^{12} (+ 1 leaf after 10, f. 75), VII-VIII^{12}, IX^{6}. Catchwords, enclosed in rectangle, only appear on verso of ff. 6-12.

Written in various styles of Anglicana, with some portions in gothic bookhand, by four scribes. Scribe 1: ff. 1r-10r; Scribe 2: ff. 10v-30r; Scribe 3: ff. 31r-107v; Scribe 4: f. 75r to the top of 76r (perhaps to supply text missing from the exemplar).

Blue initials with elaborate red, blue, and black penwork borders that almost totally encompass the written space on ff. 1r and 31r (trimmed along upper and outer edges); similar initials in blue with red penwork designs extending entire length of folio introduce each new section of text.

Binding: s. xix. Brown sheepskin, blind- and gold-tooled. Rebacked.

Written in England in the first quarter of the 15th century; belonged ca. 1640 to Thomas Fairfax (signature on f. 1r); sale of the Fairfax library from Leeds Castle (London, 1831; has not been identified in the catalogue). Sold by Thorpe (Cat. 1836, no. 163) to Sir Thomas Phillipps (no. 9520 inside front cover); his sale (London, 1898, no. 481) to Sotheran. Given in 1926 by Leonard Bacon and Susan Bacon Keith in memory of their father Nathaniel Terry Bacon.

secundo folio: Uera eternitas

Bibliography: De Ricci, v. 1, p. 165, no. 15.

MS 16 (olim Z109.175) Flanders, s. XV^2
Hours, use of Rome

1. f. 1r–12v   Calendar, rather empty, in French; among the saints, Juliana (16 Feb.), Honorina (27 Feb.), Leodegar (27 March, *sic*), Magloire (9 April, *sic*), Germanus of Alexandria (29 April), Quiriacus (4 May), Germanus of Paris (28 May), Medard (8 June), Gertrude (20 June, *sic*), Eligius (25 June, in red), Germanus of Auxerre (31 July), Audomar (16 August, *sic*), Aegidius (1 Sept., in red), Donatianus of Algiers (6 Sept.), Lambert (17 Sept.), Maclovius (14 Nov., *sic*), Eligius (1 Dec., in red).

2. ff. 13r–16v   *Deuote oroison a nostre dame*. O intemerata ... [masculine forms; Wilmart 488–90].

3. ff. 17r–22v   *A la vierge marie oroison*. Obsecro te ... [masculine forms; Leroquais, LH 2.346–47].

4. ff 22v–25r   *Oroison a nostre dame*. Stabat mater dolorosa ... [RH 19416].

5. ff. 25r–26v   Five Joys of the Virgin [HE 63–64].

6. ff. 27r–106v   Hours of the Virgin, use of Rome.

7. ff. 107r–147v   Offices, in short form, for each day of the week beginning with Sunday: Trinity, Dead, Holy Spirit, All Saints, Eucharist, Cross, Virgin.

8. ff. 147v–154v   Mass of the Virgin.

9. ff. 155r–183r   Penitential Psalms and Litany; among the 14 confessors, Romanus (2) and Albinus (6); among the 19 virgins, Geneviève (11 and 16), Juliana (12), Gertrude (15), Ursula (18).

10. ff. 183r–194v   Suffrages (headings in French) to Peter and Paul, the Cross, John the Baptist, John the Evangelist, Peter and Paul (different text than above), James, Nicolas, Lawrence, Antony abbot, Sebastian, Barbara, Catharine, Margaret, and Apollonia.

11. ff. 195r–237v   Office of the Dead, use of Rome.

12. ff. 238r–241v   *Octo versus sancti bernardi*. Omnipotens splendor eterne lucis per

signum sancte crucis. Illumina oculos meos ... et in tua misericordia pia et in gracia tua semper gaudere. Amen [RH 27912].

Parchment, ff. 241 + ii (paper), 133 x 99 (82 x 55) mm. Calendar written in 17 long lines per page, text in twelve, ruled in pale purple ink; single bounding lines at sides and bottom, double at top of written space, all full across; some prickings at top and bottom of leaves.

I^{12}, II^8, III^6, IV-XXIX^8, XXX^6 (+ 1 leaf added, f. 238). Catchwords along lower edge, near gutter.

Written in formal bâtarde script; ff. 238r-241v in a different hand than the preceding folios, but probably almost contemporary.

Thirteen undistinguished historiated initials (6-, 4-, and 3-line), ca. 1460-70, blue or pink with white highlights on brown grounds with gold highlights, enclosing, on f. 44v (Lauds) the Visitation [the initial for Matins, f. 27r, contains a butterfly, inserted by the same artist who did the borders]; f. 62v (Prime) the Nativity; f. 69v (Terce) the Annunciation to the Shepherds; f. 76v (Sext) the Adoration of the Magi; f. 82v (None) the Presentation in the Temple; f. 89r (Vespers) the Massacre of the Innocents; f. 100v (Compline) the Flight into Egypt; f. 112v (Hours of the Dead, for Monday) Angels carrying souls to heaven; f. 118v (Hours of the Holy Spirit, for Tuesday) Pentecost; f. 123r (Hours of All Saints, for Wednesday) Saints; f. 131v (Hours of the Sacrament, for Thursday) Adoration of the Host; f. 136v (Hours of the Cross, for Friday) the Crucifixion; f. 142v (Hours of the Virgin, for Saturday) Pietà. The subjects of the historiated initials as well as the collation indicate that no miniatures were originally planned.

Six other initials (ff. 13r, 17r, 27r, 107r, 155r, and 195r) enclose carefully studied flowers. Scatter and compartmentalized borders of average quality (ff. 13r, 62v, 76v, 82v, 89r, 100v, 107r, 112v, 118v, 131v, 142r, 155r, and 185r) added later, ca. 1480-1500, for the most part to pages with historiated or flower initials, similar to borders in manuscripts of the "Ghent Associates"; the majority with acanthus branches, flowers, and birds, or flowers alone scattered on backgrounds of pink, bright blue, slate blue, gold and/or black, or flowers set within a lattice of twigs, the diamonds so formed alternately pink and blue (f. 123r) or green, pink and blue (f. 238r). (Cf. the "Hours of Mary of Burgundy and Maximilian of Austria," Berlin, Kupferstichkabinett, MS. 78. B. 12, ca. 1475.) Three borders (ff. 27v, 69v, and 136v) with thistles, brown and blue or brown and green, touched with gold, arranged in a wallpaper-like pattern over grounds of slate-blue or red cross-hatched with lines in a darker shade of the same color. (Cf., for a similar type of border, Madrid, Bib. Nac. Vit. 25-5, ca. 1477-80, and Berlin Kupferstichkabinett MS. 78. B. 13, ca. 1480. We thank A. H. van Buren for bringing these comparisons to our attention.) In the border on f. 107r, a grotesque with the torso of a man and the hind legs of a large cat; on f. 185r the same, holding a bow. 2-line initials in gold on pink and blue with white highlights, except on ff. 238r-241v, gold on blue and brown with white highlights. 1-line initials in blue with red penwork, or gold with black penwork, or black with a red stroke; a few spaces for such initials have not been filled. In the text, headings and marks for antiphons in red; in the calendar, headings for months, dates, and important feasts also in red. Line-fillers: two oblique lines, blue or gold, with dots attached.

Binding: s. xviii. Brown calf. Paste-decorated edges. Rebacked. Spine stamped with gold leaves and the words "GETEY BOEK".

Written in Flanders, ca. 1460-70, as indicated by the style of the initials and script. Borders added later, in Flanders, ca. 1480-1500. Owned ca. 1840 by Henrietta Flirtmann [?]; signature and date on f. 1r. Baggett Collection. Sale by Anderson (New York, 5 June 1901, no. 133) to N. T. Bacon. Given in 1926 by Leonard Bacon and Susan Bacon Keith in memory of their father, Nathaniel Terry Bacon.

Bibliography: De Ricci, v. 1, p. 165, no. 16.

MS 17 (olim Z109.227) France, s. XV^2
Hours, use of Paris

1. ff. 1r-11v   Full calendar in French, with major entries in gold, the others alternating red and blue, of the type printed by Perdrizet; the leaf with the month of November is missing.

2. ff. 12r-15v   Sequences of the Gospels. //nomine eius. Qui non ex sanguinibus neque ex voluntate ... qui uiderunt eum resurrexisse a mortuis non crediderant//

3. ff. 16r-18v   Obsecro te, beginning abruptly: [speran]//cium. Uirgo ante partum, uirgo in partu et uirgo post partum ... et uictoriam contra aduersitates huius// [masculine forms; Leroquais, LH 2.346-47].

4. ff. 19r-22v   O intemerata, a long form. //enim dei ipse christus filius uerus omnipotens deus ... cum sanctis et electis suis uitam et gloriam sempiternam. Amen [Wilmart 494-95].

5. ff. 23r-62v   Hours of the Virgin, use of Paris. //et in psalmis iubilemus ei. Dominus tecum. Quoniam ... R. Dei genetrix. *Oratio*. Deus qui de beate marie//

6. ff. 63r-77v   Penitential Psalms and Litany. //delictum meum cognitum tibi feci ... ut indulgenciam quam semper optauerunt pijs supplicationibus ... Amen. Pater noster. Aue maria. Among the martyrs, Eustachius; among the confessors, Remigius and Taurinus; among the virgins, Geneviève, Avia.

7. ff. 77v-83v   Short Hours of the Cross; rubric on f. 77v, text begins abruptly on f. 78r: //christe et benediximus tibi ... per omnia secula seculorum amen.

8. ff. 84r-89v   Short Hours of the Holy Spirit. Domine labia mea aperies ... Omnipotens sempiterne deus da nobis illam sancti//

9. ff. 90r-130v Office of the Dead, use of Paris. //vocem orationis mee. Quia inclinauit ... semper optauerunt pijs supplicationibus consequantur. Qui uiuis et regnas deus per omnia secula seculorum. amen.

10. ff. 131r-134v Fifteen Joys of the Virgin, in French. Doulce dame de misericorde ... pries lui quil enlumine mon cuer. Aue maria. E tres doulce dame pour ycelle grant ioye que// [Leroquais, LH 2.310-11].

11. ff. 135r-137v Seven Requests, in French. //conseil et ayde en lonneur de celuy ... Sire si comme ce fu uoir regardes moy en pitie. Pater noster [Leroquais, LH 2.309-10].

12. ff. 137v-138r Saincte uraye croix aouree. Qui du corps dieu ... [Sonet 1876].

13. ff. 138r-140v Suffrages addressed to the Holy Trinity, Michael, John the Baptist, Dionysius, Catharine, and Margaret, ending imperfectly.

Parchment, ff. iii (paper) + ii (contemporary parchment) + 140 + ii (paper), 196 x 142 (93 x 63) mm. Written in 17 long lines per page in the calendar, 15 in the text, ruled in pale red ink; single bounding lines, full across; prickings visible at outer edges.

The volume was misbound, with many folios out of order; it was corrected by N. R. Ker in 1971. The collation is now as follows: I^{12} (-11), II^8 (-1, 6, 7), III^8 (-3, 8), IV^8 (-1), V^8 (-4), VI^8 (-3, 5, 7, 8), VII^6 (-4), VIII^6 (-1, 5), IX^8 (-1, 3), X^8 (-2), XI^6 (-1), XII^8; XIII^8 (-3, 6), XIV^8, XV^8 (-1), XVI^8 (-2, 4), XVII^8, XVIII^8 (-1), XIX^6; collation of ff. 124-140 uncertain; leaves missing after ff. 124 and 134. Catchwords in the lower margin of last folio of quire, verso, slightly right of center.

Written in gothic script of two sizes, verging on bâtarde, by one person.

Two miniatures (ff. 84r and 131r) of poor quality remain. The location of the other miniatures can no longer be determined due to rebinding. On f. 84r Pentecost, in an arched frame; miniature and text in a 3/4 bar border, gold with flowers, attached to an historiated initial (Dove) and a full acanthus border (blue and beige acanthus, flowers, birds, and gold dots) with four scenes inserted in corners, clockwise from lower right: Christ on the road to Emmaus, Christ appearing to Mary Magdalen, Noli me tangere, and the Ascension; the entirety within a blue bounding line. On f. 131r the Virgin and Child enthroned, with two angels in a thick brown arched frame; miniatures and text in a 3/4 border, a twig with branches lopped off, in blue with white highlights, attached to an historiated initial (Joseph) and a full acanthus border, as above, with a green bounding line. 6-line historiated initial in the same style on f. 139v, with St. Dionysius and his companions, Rusticus and Eleutherius. On all other pages, outer margin, traced border as above, with green bounding line, except ff. 23-29 (quire III), in red. 2-line initials, blue or pink with white highlights on gold ground, filled with flowers, fruit, or ivy. 1-line initials and line-endings, gold on pink and blue grounds, with white highlights. KL monograms in Calendar, as 2-line initials; names of months, dates, and important feasts in gold; other feasts alternately in red and blue.

Water damage on ff. 2 and 3; portion of border on f. 35 cut out; last folio damaged by moisture and acid.

Binding: 1976. Dark brown calf over wooden boards, blind-tooled. Bound in Yale Library Conservation Studio. Previous French binding, s. xix, boxed with the codex.

Written in Northern France in the second half of the 15th century as indicated by Saints in the Litany, perhaps in Rouen judging by the style of the miniatures. Belonged in 1590 to Alexandre Ramon of Nemours (note on f. iv verso). Belonged to Caroline M. Street (signature and date 1845 on f. 141r). Bookplate of Augustus Russell Street; gift of Mrs. Augustus Russell Street in 1869.

Bibliography: De Ricci, v. 1, p. 165, no. 17.

MS 18 (olim Z109.232) France, s. XIV^{ex} and 1578
Missal Pl. 9

I. 1. ff. 1r–40v Temporale, principal masses of the liturgical year, winter season, with musical notation; rubrics for: In die Natiuitatis domini, In die epyphanie, In purificatione sancti marie uirginis, Dominica in ramis palmarum, In die pasche, In annuntiatione beate marie, In die Ascensionis domini, Missa de sancto spiritu, De sancta trinitate. Two staves for music at the bottom of f. 40v have not been filled.

II. 2. ff. 41r–47r Common prefaces, with musical notation throughout. f. 47v blank

III. 3. ff. 48r–56v Te igitur...; Canon of the Mass, parts with musical notation.

4. ff. 57r–60v Mass of the Virgin Mary, noted (rubric partly erased).

5. ff. 60v–67v Mass of the Dead, noted.

6. ff. 67v–72v Votive masses (collect, secret and post communion only): Pro defunctis in aniuersario, Pro episcopo uel sacerdote, Plurimorum episcoporum et sacerdotum, Vnius defuncti [two masses, for a man and for a woman, both with plural forms suprascript], Pro patre et matre, Pro sepulti [*sic*] in cymiterio, Pro congregatione, Pro benefactoribus, [Pro familiaribus].

IV. 7. ff. 73r–92r Temporale, principal masses of the liturgical year, summer season, without musical notation; rubrics for: Missa de sacramento, De Assumptione beate marie, De natiuitate beate marie, In inuentione sancte crucis, In exaltatione sancte crucis, In festo omnium sanctorum, De sancto macuto episcopo et confessore, In dedicatione ecclesie.

8. ff. 92r–94r   Gloria and Credo for principal and Marian feasts, with musical notation.

9. ff. 94r–97v   *1578. Missa de sancta christi lachrima.*

10. ff. 97v–100v   *Missa nostre domine pietatis.*

11. ff. 100v–101v   *Oratio ante missam dicenda a sacerdote.* O dulcissime atque amantissime domine iesu christe quem nunc deuote desidero suscipere ... amor corda purificans et intellectum illuminans. Amen.

12. ff. 101v–102v   *Oratio post sacram communionem.* Aue sanctissima caro summa vita dulcedo ... misericordia inenarrabili dignetur indulgere. Amen.

13. flyleaf, after f. 102   Passages from Matthew (recto) and Wisdom (verso) in a modern cursive hand.

Parchment, ff. ii (contemporary parchment) + 102 + i (modern parchment), 240 x 167 (172 x 110) mm. The manuscript is composed of four parts.

I and III (ff. 1r–40v, 48r–72v): written in 16 long lines (the Canon in 14 lines); single horizontal and vertical bounding lines full across. Ruled in pale brown ink. Catchwords to right of inner bounding line. Written in liturgical gothic of two sizes, by one scribe. On f. 48r, a 5-line historiated initial (65 x 58 mm.), white-decorated red and blue on a gold ground, enclosing a priest serving Communion; from the corners sprout blue vines with white, gold, and red trilobe leaves, extending around 3 sides of the page. On f. 1r, an 8-line illuminated initial of white-decorated blue and red (63 x 65 mm.), filled with blue and red trilobe leaves, on a gold ground; the base of the letter is extended around the inner and lower margins as a gold, blue, red, and white bounding line; from the lower two corners of this line and the upper left corner of the initial sprout vines, as for the historiated initial. 3- and 2-line initials in orange-tinted red or blue; rubrics throughout. Square notes in brown on 4-line orange-tinted red staves (the red ink has bled so that the whole written space has an orange glow).

II and IV (ff. 41r–47v, 73r–102v) were intended to be integrated into the earlier portion: written in 7 long lines in II, where text is accompanied by musical notation throughout, and 18 long lines in IV, where no musical notation occurs. Ruled in pale brown ink with single bounding lines, full across. Catchwords right of center in lower margin. Written in liturgical gothic of the late 16th century, in two sizes by a single scribe; the letters slant slightly toward the left. 4- to 1-line initials in red and blue. Rubrics are sometimes set off on the right side of the page by a narrow vertical border in brown. Musical notation: square notes on 4-line staves, all in brown.

I–V^8, VI^8 (-1), VII^9 (structure uncertain), VIII–X^8, XI^{10} (-3, 7), XII^8, XIII^6.

Binding: 1981. Quarter cloth case, retaining brown mottled paper covered boards, s. xix. Traces of earlier bindings.

Written in Northern France at the end of the 14th century (Parts I, III) and in

1578 (Parts II, IV; see art. 9); the prominence of St. Maclovius (Macutus) in art. 7 suggests that Parts II and IV were produced in Brittany or Normandy. Bought in Paris by Caroline M. Street in 1847 (signature and date on f. ii recto). Bookplate of Augustus Russell Street (inside front cover). Given to Yale by Mrs. Augustus Russell Street in 1868.

secundo folio: populum

Bibliography: De Ricci, v. 1, p. 165, no. 18.

MS 19 (olim Z109.250) France, s. XIV^2
Hours (fragment)

ff. 1r–19v Penitential Psalms, text begins imperfectly: 6. 6–11 (Quoniam non est in morte...), 31, 37, 50, 101, 129, 142. Folio 19v ends with the rubric: *Ci apries commencent les xv saumes*.

Parchment, ff. i (contemporary parchment) + 19, 152 x 113 (73 x 53) mm. Written in 11 long lines; single vertical bounding lines, double horizontal bounding lines, full across. Ruled in ink; prickings in upper and lower margins.
I^6 (-1), II^4 (missing one folio; structure uncertain), III^2, IV^{10}.
Written by a single scribe in liturgical gothic script.
Carefully executed initials, 3-line, on blue or pink rectangles outlined in black, mark the beginning of each psalm; partial cusped borders, also in blue and pink, attached to each. Initials infilled with intertwining vines, often on gold ground, sometimes with small animals; modest use of gold dots inside rectangular grounds and borders. 1-line initials of blue with red penwork with blue dots and of gold with blue penwork and red dots. Line-fillers in combinations of red, blue and gold (various linear and flower designs).
Binding: s. xix. Bound in a piece of blind-tooled brown calf, once part of a 17th–18th century binding. Front pastedown and flyleaf from a Bible concordance, version 3 (France, s. XIII/XIV; see R. H. and M. A. Rouse, "The Verbal Concordance to the Scriptures," *Archivum Fratrum Praedicatorum* 44 [1974] pp. 5–30). Back pastedown from 15th-century antiphonal, with musical notation, containing a portion of the office for Nicolas (6 Dec.).

Written in France toward the end of the 14th century, probably as part of a Book of Hours. Signature and date at the top of f. 10r in faded ink: "Godefroid 1705." Given in 1926 by Leonard Bacon and Susan Bacon Keith in memory of their father, Nathaniel Terry Bacon.

Bibliography: De Ricci, v. 1, p. 165, no. 19.

MS 20

MS 20 (olim Z109.04)   Germany, 1452
Albertus Magnus, Commentarii in Librum IV   Pl. 5
   Sententiarum Petri Lombardi

ff. 1r–317r   *Sapientia edificauit sibi domum. excedit columpnas septem* [Prov. 9.1]. In isto verbo praepostero ordine narrantur ... De pedibus sedentis super solium. Istud accipitur *de ysaya* [7.1] et licet aliter exponitur a beato dyonisio tam in celesti ... breuis totius libri sentenciarum epilogus. In quo et finitur ... Amen. *Et sic est finis Scripti sentenciarum quarti Doctoris Alberti magni Completus Anno domini millesimo Quadringentesimo Quinquagesimo Secundo tercia die Augusti De quo laus detur qui in celis dominetur Per me laurencium de mechlinia.*

Stegmüller, *Sent.*, v. 1, p. 26.

Paper (watermarks similar to Briquet Ancre 381, Balance 2427, Tête de boeuf 15102), ff. ii (parchment, stubs only) + 317 + ii (parchment, stubs only), 283 x 212 (218 x 155) mm. Written in 2 columns, 50–60 lines; frame-ruled in hard point; some prickings at top and bottom of folio.

I–XVI^{12}, XVII^{16}, XVIII^{12}, XIX^{12} (6 and 7 glued together; the glued sides are blank), XX–XXIV^{12}, XXV^{14}, XXVI^{16} (-13, 14, 15, 16).

Gothic cursive script of three hands. Scribe 1: ff. 1r–156v; Scribe 2: ff. 157r–274r; Scribe 3, Laurence of Mechlin, wrote ff. 274r–317r and dated the codex 1452 (see colophon above). The first and third copyists placed catchwords along lower edge near binding and signed leaves in lower right corner of recto for first half of quire (e.g., bi, bii, etc.). Scribe 2 used catchwords underlined in red, located under written space in the margin. Some folios are also signed in Arabic notation, in red, on recto of first leaves of gathering.

Plain initials in red and rubrics throughout.

Binding: s. xv. Original sewing on five slit, tawed straps laced into wooden boards. Endband cores laid in grooves. Covered with white, tawed skin, blind-tooled with a St. Andrew's cross within panel borders. The covering leather is sewn around the endbands, from spine to edges, with a back-stitch. Traces of round bosses, probably brass, and of two strap and pin fastenings, the pins on the upper board.

Written by two unidentified scribes and by Laurence of Mechlin (*Colophons*, v. 4, p. 25, no. 12308) in Germany in 1452. Was 0.55 in the library of the Carthusians of St. Barbara at Cologne (C. Löffler, *Kölnische Bibliotheksgeschichte in Umriss* [Cologne, 1923] p. 71, no. 182; R. B. Marks, *The Medieval Manuscript Library of the Charterhouse of St. Barbara in Cologne* in *Analecta Cartusiana* 21–22 [Salzburg, 1974] v. 1, p. 89, fig. 82; v. 2, pp. 382–83). Evidently it was copied as part of the effort to rebuild the library after it burned in 1451. Belonged to Leander van Ess, Darmstadt (no. 189, on spine); his sale to Sir Thomas Phillipps (no. 573; stamp inside front cover, tag on spine). Phillipps sale (London, 1910, no. 9) to Dobell. Given to Yale in 1929 by Mrs. J. L. Leipziger.

secundo folio: et insuper

Bibliography: De Ricci, v. 1, p. 166, no. 20.
H. S. Garrison, "D. Alberti Magni Commentarii in Librum IV Sententiarum," *Gazette* 5 (1930) p. 14.

MS 21 (olim Z109.08) England, s. XIII^2
Aristotle, Physica (fragment)

ff. 1r-2v //quies medium est quare si aliquis motus statu occupetur neque unus est neque continuus repitur [corrected to *recipitur*] ... erunt alie quidem uio//[lente]

Physica, Book V (in Latin translation); *Aristoteles Latinus*, Pars prior, p. 248, no. 27. Early printed text by M. Herbipolensis [Martin Landsberg], *Summi philosophorum principis Aristotelis libri octo de phisico* ... (Leipzig, 1512) I iii verso-I vi recto.

Parchment, ff. 2 (central bifolium of a quire), 245 x 197 (160 x 92) mm. Written in 29 long lines; double vertical bounding lines full length of page, with two pairs of additional rulings (to form columns for marginal notes) in inner and outer margins; ruled in lead.

The text was written by a single scribe in gothic textura; the interlinear and marginal notes and commentary at bottom of the folio are in several less formal hands.

Paragraph marks in red or blue; running titles in same colors.

The bifolium was apparently removed from a binding for it bears evidence of trimming, folding, rubbing, and pasting.

Written in England in the second half of 13th century; provenance unknown, for there are no Beinecke library records concerning this manuscript.

Bibliography: De Ricci, v. 1, p. 166, no. 21.

MS 22 (olim Z109.020) England, s. XIV^{med}
Nicolaus de Lyra, Postilla super Psalterium (fragment)

ff. 1r-3v Commentary on Psalms 4-8 //cantus huius psalmus magis erat aptus decantari ... quam eius mouente et sic ista laus puerorum uidentur pref//

Parchment, ff. 3, 360 x 228 (304 x 213) mm. Written in two columns of 62 lines; single bounding lines, full across, with two additional rulings in upper margin. Ruled in ink; prickings (horizontal slits) in outer margin.

The three consecutive folios were written by a single scribe in gothic textura.

Three 4-line initials, in blue, with red penwork designs, including foliage in center of initials; passages from the Bible underlined in red; paragraph marks in red and blue.

The leaves are worn and have been trimmed (some text lost). They appear to have been removed from a binding.

Written in England in the middle of the 14th century; provenance unknown, for there are no library records concerning this manuscript.

Bibliography: De Ricci, v. 1, p. 166, no. 22.

MS 23 Yale Law School

MS 24 (olim Z109.031)   Germany, s. XV^2
St. Birgitta, Revelationes, etc.

1. f. 1r [Table of Contents for *Revelationes*, Book 1:] //mirabilia continetur. *Capitulum liii*. Verba angeli ad sponsam de spiritu cogitacionum ... predicanda per dei amicos personis ignorantibus. *Capittulum lx. Expliciunt rubrice primi libri celestis reuelacionum dei beate Birgitte diuinitus reuelate.*

2. ff. 1r-398v *Sequitur prologus in libris celestibus reuelacionum dei Beate Birgitte diuinitus reuelatus.* Stupor et mirabilia audita sunt in terra nostra mirabile si quidem erat ... cum maxima deuocione et reuerencia inter manus predictarum personarum emisit spiritum. *Explicit liber ultimus celestis reuelacionum dei beate Birgitte principisse Nerecie de regno Suecie diuinitus reuelatus. Deo gracias.*

Beinecke MS 24 appears in the critical edition (MS H) published in *Samlinger utgivna av Svenska fornskriftsällskapet* (Lat. ser.); see C.-G. Undhagen, ed., *Sancta Birgitta Revelationes Book I* (Uppsala, 1978) pp. 178-79, 199. Undhagen believes that the Yale codex was copied from MS Oa (Katrineholm, Ericsberg Slottsbibliothek, Library of Ericsberg Castle).

For a detailed analysis of articles 3-7, see Undhagen, *op. cit.*, p. 179, n. 7.

3. ff. 399r-400r *Incipit vita beate Birgitte in teutonico sub breuitate conpilata.* Sancta Birgitta ist geboren von den konigklichem stamme von gotlant ... degelich nach irem dode an manchem enden in mancherhande wonder wercken von czeichen.

C. Selmer, "Die spätmittelhochdeutschen Bestandteile der lateinischen Birgitta-Handschrift der Universitätsbibliothek zu Yale und ihre Dialecktbestimmung," PMLA 51 (1936) pp. 38-40.

4. f. 400r-v *Oratio de sancta Birgitta*. O amantissima christi sponsa summo principi in celestibus ualde....

5. ff. 400v-401r *Oratio de beata Birgitta in teutonico*. Ggegruset sistu werde heilge muder sancta Birgitta eyn behegelich brut....

Selmer, *op. cit.*, pp. 40-41.

6. f. 401r   Three short prayers *de beata Birgitta*.

7. f. 401v   Incomplete prayer *De sancta Birgitta,* with seven parts: *De ortu et origine eius ... De ipsius commendacione.*

Paper (watermarks similar to Briquet Lettre P 8619 and 8625), ff. iii (paper) + 401 + iv (paper), 276 x 208 (222 x 145) mm. Written in two columns of 39-42 lines; frame-ruled in ink or lead, with some double inner vertical guide-lines and an occasional additional ruling in lower margin.
I^8, II-XL^{10} (+ 3 leaves at end; structure uncertain). Remains of catchwords along lower edge of folio in gutter; most trimmed.
Written in a well formed running hand by a single scribe who has been identified as Freiherr von Greifenclav (see Provenance). Divisions for indexing carefully noted in margins.
Large penwork initials of mediocre quality, in red and blue; foliage designs in center of letters and penwork borders, in red, are sometimes accompanied by vulgar green dots. Many simple initials, 7- to 1-line, in red or blue; running titles in red. Rubricated throughout.
Binding: s. xix^2. Mottled, brown calf case, gold-tooled with monogram of comte Paul Riant on spine. Detached from bookblock.

Written in Germany in the second half of the 15th century by a scribe identified as Freiherr von Greifenclav, abbot of the monastery of Maria Forst (near Cologne). See Selmer, *op. cit.,* pp. 56-57. Belonged (ca. 1860) to the Bischöfliche Seminar-Bibliothek at Hamburg (stamp on f. lr); in 1882 it was sold by C. H. Beck of Nördlingen (Cat. 155, no. 52) to comte Paul Riant (booklabel; L. de Germon and L. Polain, *Catalogue de la bibliothèque de feu M. le comte Riant* [Paris, 1896] v. 1, p. 360, no. 2472). His Scandinavian library was presented to Yale University by Mrs. Henry Farnam, in 1896 (A. B. Benson, "The Scandinavian Collection," *Gazette* 8 [1933] pp. 49-53).

secundo folio: vane glorie

Bibliography: De Ricci, v. 1, p. 166, no. 24.
U. Montag, *Das Werk der heiligen Birgitta von Schweden in oberdeutscher Überlieferung* (Munich, 1968) p. 40.

MS 25 (olim Z109.041)   England, s. XV/XVI
Giovanni Gigli, Quaestiones de observantia quadragesimali

ff. 1r-34v   *Iohannis de giglis iuris utriusque doctoris apostolici subdiaconi et collectoris ... questiones de obseruancia quadragesimali.* [text:] Quod iam diu promiseram vt scilicet de iis de quibus nuper non parua questio fuit super ... Et hec de iis ad presens sufficiant que dicta sunt sine preiudicio veritatis et recte fidei. *Finito libro Laudes redde deo.*

For the author see Emden, BRUO, v. 1, pp. 764-65. The text, which is unpublished, also occurs in London, B. L. Harley 336.

Paper (watermarks similar to Heawood 2473, 2475), ff. ii (same paper as text) + 34, 300 x 211 (198 x 152) mm. Written in 24-28 long lines; frame-ruled in ink or hard point.
I^8, II^{12} (+1 leaf added at beginning, f. 9), III^{12} (+1 leaf at end).
Written by a single scribe in English secretary script.
Large crude initials, in red, at beginning of each section of text, accompanied by simple penwork designs in brown ink; paragraph marks in red.
Binding: s. xvi-xvii. Original sewing on four double, tawed cords. No endbands. Cords laced through slanted round holes in oak boards. Covered in dark brown calf with traces of two sets of strap-and-pin fastenings, not contemporaneous, going from upper to lower board and vice versa. An outer covering of 19th-century leather and marbled paper has been added. Sewing breaking. Covers lined with a parchment fragment of a Missal (England, s. XIII); (front pastedown:) portions of the Gospel and the Secret for the Annunciation (25 March); (back pastedown:) portions from the Masses for the Nativity of John the Baptist (24 June), for John and Paul Martyrs (26 June), and for the Vigil of Apostles Peter and Paul (28 June).

Written in England at the end of the 15th or beginning of the 16th century. Signature on f. ii verso: "liber doctoris dyngley", probably Roger Dingley, All Souls College, D. D. 1526. Belonged to John Wildgoose (signature of late 18th or early 19th century on f. ii recto). Purchased by the Yale University Library in 1896.

secundo folio: canetur

Bibliography: De Ricci, v. 1, p. 167, no. 25.

MS 26 (olim Z109.071m) France, s. XIII^2
Petrus Comestor, Historia scholastica, etc. Pl. 10

1. ff. 1r-247r *Incipit scolastica historia. Prefatio.* Imperatorie maiestatis est in palatio tres habere mansiones. Auditorium uel consistorium in quo iura decernit ... quinte ferie sollempnitas et processio translata est ad dominicam.

    Stegmüller, v. 4, nos. 6543-64; Beinecke MS 26 is listed in v. 4, p. 289.

2. ff. 247r-279r *Incipit explanatio actuum apostolorum.* Anno nonodecimo imperij tyberij cesaris adhuc procuratore iudee pilato ... gladio enim perimebantur nobiles et in loco magis honorabili scilicet in catacumbis. *Explicit ecclesiastica hystoria.* f. 279v blank

Stegmüller, v. 4, nos. 6865 and 6785; attributed to Petrus Pictaviensis.

Parchment, ff. iv (paper) + 279 + ii (paper), 264 x 176 (189 x 119) mm. Written in two columns of 38 lines; double vertical bounding lines and three lines between two columns; triple horizontal bounding lines with additional ruling in upper margin for running titles, full across. Ruled in ink or lead; prickings at top of folio.
I-XXXIV^8, XXXV^8 (-8).
Written in small neat gothic textura by two scribes. Scribe 1: ff. 1r–214v; Scribe 2: ff. 214v (bottom of first column) –279r. Writing is above top line.

Numerous calligraphic initials in red or blue with simple penwork designs of the same colors; some letters have green added as well. Running titles in red.

Portions of the text are faded and difficult to read.

Binding: s. xviii. Red goat-skin, gold-tooled. Two paper flyleaves inserted at beginning contain extracts from the library catalogue of the duc de la Vallière and from the *Nouveau dictionnaire historique*.

Written in Southwestern France [or perhaps Spain?] in the second half of the 13th century; early provenance unknown. Belonged to the duc de la Vallière (G. de Bure, *Catalogue des livres de la bibliothèque de feu M. le duc de la Vallière*, v. 1 [Paris, 1783] p. 29 no. 109 and Additions, p. 6); his sale to Jean-Baptiste L'Ecuy (not located in his sale catalogue, Paris, 8 Dec. 1834). Collection of M. F. Tomkinson (bookplate); his sale to Maggs (London, 4 July 1922, no. 1298; clipping inside front cover). Goldschmidt's Cat. 13 [n.d.], no. 48. Presented to Yale in 1928 by Frank Altschul.

secundo folio: ita nox

Bibliography: De Ricci, v. 1, p. 167, no. 26.

MS 27 (olim Z109.073) England, s. XV^{in}
Speculum humanae salvationis, etc. Pls. 19, 32

1. ff. 1r–2r *Tabula super speculum humane saluacionis. Aubacia quedam in prologo*. Absalon suspenditur. 25....

2. ff. 2r–6v Incipit prohemium cuiusdam noue copulacionis [*sic*] cuius nomen et titulus est speculum humane saluacionis. Expediens uidetur et utile quod primo ... In xlv^{to} capitulo agitur de septem gaudiis eiusdem gloriose uirginis. Et sic terminantur capitula huius libelli et uoluminis. *Expliciunt capitula super speculum humane saluacionis.*

3. ff. 7r–90v Incipit speculum humane saluacionis. In quo patet casus hominis ... Quod nobis omnibus prestare dignetur, dominus noster ihesu christe,/ Qui cum patre et spiritu sancto est imperpetuum benedictus. Amen.

J. Lutz and P. Perdrizet, eds., *Speculum humanae salvationis*, 2 vol. (Mülhausen and Leipzig, 1907).

4. ff. 91r–104v   *Hic incipiunt meditaciones de passione domini, et primo ponitur meditacio, de cena domini. Secundo, de passione generali et cetera infra patet per ordinem.* [A]dueniente et minime te tempore miseracionum et misericordiarum domini ... Benedictus dominus deus israel, quia uisitauit et fecit redempcionem plebi sue. Explicit, et cetera. [f. 104v, a prayer now only faintly visible under ultraviolet light, beginning: Christus factus est pro nobis ...]

M. J. Stallings, *Pseudo-Bonaventura's Meditationes de passione Christi* (Washington, D. C., 1965) pp. 87–130 (line 22); Beinecke MS 27 seems to belong to the *h* family.

Parchment (thick, furry), ff. 104 (original pagination in red on ff. 7r–90v), 280 x 190 (203 x 129) mm. Written in 33–34 lines of verse on ff. 2v–90v, 36 long lines on ff. 91r–104v and 2 columns of 33–34 lines on ff. 1r–2r; ruled in ink, single vertical and horizontal bounding lines, full across (on ff. 7r–90v a 16-line space in the upper right corner of each folio, recto and verso, is left unruled for illustration). Prickings in outer, upper and lower margins; an additional pricking in the center of the outer margin marks the lower edge of space reserved for illustrations. I–IV^8, V^8 (–1 following f. 32; –8 following f. 38), VI^8 (–1 following f. 38; –3, 4, and 5 following f. 41), VII^8, VIII^8 (–1 following f. 48; –8 following f. 54), IX^8, X^8 (–1 following f. 62, –3 following f. 63), XI–XIV^8, XV^8 (–5, 6, 7 and 8 following f. 104). Catchwords below written space, to right (most trimmed); signatures throughout (e. g., di, dii, diii). A new series of signatures (same form) begins on f. 92r (beginning of quire XIV).

Written by two scribes in similar gothic textura bookhands. Scribe 1 (ff. 1r–90v) in brown ink. Scribe 2 (ff. 91r–104v) in a darker ink and more compressed script. A few marginal comments and corrections of s. xv–xvi.

The manuscript originally contained 192 miniatures, of which 29 have been entirely and 1 (f. 53r) partially removed. The remaining miniatures, comparable to New York, Pierpont Morgan Library MS 766 (County of York, s. XIV^{ex}) and Oxford, Bod. Lib. Bodley MS 758 (Norfolk, 1405; see Pächt and Alexander, v. 3, no. 794), are drawn in light brown ink and tinted in brown and yellow washes with touches of red. The miniatures on ff. 7r–38v have been redrawn in black ink by a second hand, related in style to Oxford, Bod. Lib. Don. d. 85 (s. XV^{in}; Pächt and Alexander, v. 3, no. 803. Compare especially f. 38v, Sampson and the Philistines, with fig. 803a). A dirty tan ground has been added to miniatures on ff. 67v and 68r.

The subjects of the miniatures are as follow: (Chapter 1) f. 7r Good and Evil angels/ Lucifer thrown into hell-mouth, f. 7v Creation of Eve, f. 8r Marriage of Adam and Eve, f. 8v Temptation of Eve; (Chapter 2) f. 9r Fall, f. 9v Expulsion, f. 10r Adam delving and Eve spinning, f. 10v Noah's Ark; (Chapter 3) f. 11r Annunciation to Joachim, f. 11v Vision of Astyages, f. 12r Closed Garden and the

Sealed Fountain, f. 12v Balaam's prophecy of the star; (Chapter 4) f. 13r Birth of the Virgin, f. 13v Tree of Jesse, f. 14r Closed Door, f. 14v Temple of Solomon; (Chapter 5) f. 15r Presentation of the Virgin, f. 15v Golden Table, f. 16r Sacrifice of Jephthah's daughter, f. 16v Queen of Persia in the hanging garden; (Chapter 6) f. 17r Marriage of Mary and Joseph, f. 17v Marriage of Sarah and Tobias, f. 18r Tower of Baris, f. 18v Tower of David; (Chapter 7) f. 19r Annunciation, f. 19v Burning Bush, f. 20r Gideon's fleece, f. 20v Rebeccah gives drink to Eliezar; (Chapter 8) f. 21r Nativity, f. 21v Dream of Pharaoh's butler, f. 22r Aaron's rod, f. 22v Octavian and the Tiburtine Sibyl; (Chapter 9) f. 23r Adoration of the Magi, f. 23v Magi see the star, f. 24r Three mighty men bring water to David from the well of Bethlehem, f. 24v Throne of Solomon; (Chapter 10) f. 25r Presentation of Christ in the Temple, f. 25v Ark of the Covenant, f. 26r Seven-armed candelabra, f. 26v Presentation of Samuel; (Chapter 11) f. 27r Flight into Egypt, f. 27v Egyptian's image of the Virgin and child, f. 28r Child Moses casts down Pharaoh's crown, f. 28v Dream of Nebuchadnezzar; (Chapter 12) f. 29r Baptism of Christ, f. 29v Brazen vessel, f. 30r Naaman washes in the Jordan, f. 30v Ark borne over Jordan; (Chapter 13) f. 31r Three temptations of Christ, f. 31v Daniel destroys Bel and the Dragon, f. 32r David slays Goliath, f. 32v David kills the lion and the bear; (Chapter 14) [two miniatures missing: Penitence of Mary Magdalen and the Penitence of Manasses], f. 33r Return of the prodigal son, f. 33v David and Nathan; (Chapter 15) f. 34r Entry into Jerusalem, f. 34v Jeremiah weeping over Jerusalem, f. 35r Triumph of David, f. 35v Heliodorus repulsed from the Temple; (Chapter 16) f. 36r Last Supper, f. 36v Fall of manna, f. 37r Passover—Jews with the Paschal lamb, f. 37v Abraham and Melchizedek; (Chapter 17) f. 38r "Ego sum," Men sent to arrest Jesus fall backwards, f. 38v Samson kills 1000 Philistines with the jawbone of an ass [four miniatures missing: Shamgar kills 600 men with an ox-goad, David kills 800 men, Betrayal of Christ, Joab kills Amasa]; (Chapter 18) f. 39r David plays before Saul, who tries to kill him, f. 39v Sacrifices of Cain and Abel/ Cain kills Abel [eight miniatures missing: Mocking of Christ, Jews spit on Hur, Noah mocked by Ham, Blinding of Samson, Flagellation, Achior bound to a tree, Lamech beaten by his two wives, Job beaten by his wife]; (Chapter 21) f. 40r Christ crowned with thorns, f. 40v Zerubbabel points to Appemen and Concubine of Darius [two miniatures missing: Shimei casts stones at David, and Hanun, King of Ammon, insults David's ambassadors]; (Chapter 22) f. 41r Bearing of the Cross, f. 41v Isaac carries the wood for his sacrifice, f. 42r Wicked husbandmen kill the heir, f. 42v Spies with the grapes of Eshcol; (Chapter 23) f. 43r Christ nailed to the Cross, f. 43v Tubalcain smites the anvil and Jubal invents music, f. 44r Isaiah sawn in two, f. 44v King of Moab sacrifices his first-born son; (Chapter 24) f. 45r Christ crucified, with Mary, her heart pierced by a sword, John, and the two thieves, f. 45v Nebuchadnezzar's dream of the tree, f. 46r Death of Codrus, King of Athens, f. 46v Eleazar Maccabaeus kills the elephant [two miniatures missing: Christ on the Cross mocked by the Jews, and Michal derides David]; (Chapter 25) f. 48r

Death of Absalom, f. 48v Evilmerodach cuts the body of his father Nebuchadnezzar into 300 pieces; (Chapter 26) [two miniatures missing: Deposition, Jacob mourns Joseph]; f. 49r Adam and Eve mourn Abel, f. 49v Naomi mourns her husband and sons; (Chapter 27) f. 50r Entombment, f. 50v David laments Abner, f. 51r Joseph in the Pit, f. 51v Jonah cast into the Sea; (Chapter 28) f. 52r A four-level depiction of Hell — Hell of the descendants of Abraham, of Purgatory, of the non-baptized children, and of the damned and demons, f. 52v Three children delivered from the fiery furnace, f. 53r [partially cut out] Daniel in the lions' den fed by Habakkuk [f. 54v, one miniature cut out: The ostrich delivers its young]; (Chapter 29) f. 54r Christ tramples on Satan, f. 54v Benaiah slays the lion in the pit [two miniatures missing: Samson and the lion, Ehud kills Eglon]; (Chapter 30) f. 55r Virgin overcomes the Devil/ Arma Christi, f. 55v Judith kills Holofernes, f. 56r Jael kills Sisera, f. 56v Tomyris kills Cyrus; (Chapter 31) [two miniatures missing: Harrowing of Hell, Moses leads Israel out of Egypt]; f. 58r Abraham delivered from the fire of the Chaldees, f. 58v Lot escapes from Sodom; (Chapter 32) f. 59r Resurrection, f. 59v Samson carries off the gates of Gaza, f. 60r Jonah cast up by the fish, f. 60v Cornerstone; (Chapter 33) f. 61r Ascension, f. 61v Jacob's ladder, f. 62r Lost sheep brought back, f. 62v Translation of Elijah; (Chapter 34) [two miniatures missing: Pentecost, the tower of Babel]; f. 63r Moses receives the Ten Commandments, f. 63v Elisha supplies the widow with oil [two miniatures missing: Virgin visits the holy places and Return of Tobias]; f. 64r Finding of the lost piece of silver, f. 64v Michal married to Phaltiel; (Chapter 36) f. 65r Assumption of the Virgin, f. 65v Ark brought home, f. 66r Woman clothed with the Sun, f. 66v Solomon sets Bathsheba on his right hand; (Chapter 37) f. 67r Virgin, baring her breasts, intercedes for mankind, f. 67v Abigail appeases David, f. 68r Woman of Tekoa appeases David, f. 68v Wise women cast out head of Sheba to David; (Chapter 38) f. 69r Virgin as the defender of mankind, f. 69v Thearbis, princess of Sabba, defends her city against Moses, f. 70r Abimelech killed by the woman of Thebes, f. 70v Michal helps David escape; (Chapter 39) f. 71r Christ displays his wounds to God the Father, f. 71v Antipater shows his wounds to Julius Caesar, f. 72r Virgin shows her breast to Christ [Christ is seated on the conventional globe, to which have been added (s. xvi?) several numbers], f. 72v Esther intercedes for her people; (Chapter 40) f. 73r Last Judgment, f. 73v Parable of the talents, f. 74r Parable of the ten Virgins, f. 74v Writing on the wall; (Chapter 41) f. 75r Torments of Hell, f. 75v David punishing the men of Rabbath, f. 76r Gideon punishing the men of Succoth, f. 76v Pharaoh and his army drowning in the Red Sea; (Chapter 42) f. 77r Mary and the saints in heaven, f. 77v Solomon and the Queen of Sheba, f. 78r Feast of Ahasuerus, f. 78v Job feasting with his children; (Chapter 43) f. 79r (*Miraculum de passione Christi*) Christ bearing the Cross appears to the Hermit in his tower, f. 79v (Vespers) Last Supper, f. 80r (Compline) Agony in the garden [the artist has added in the margin a lamp dangling from the upper bounding line], f. 80v (Matins) Betrayal of Christ, f. 81r (Prime) Christ before Pilate, f. 81v (Terce) Flagellation, f. 82r

(Sext) Condemnation of Christ and Pilate washing his hands, f. 82v (None) The Crucifixion; (Chapter 44) f. 83r (*Miraculum de dolore Christi et sue gloriose matris*) A monk, his hands and feet pierced by nails and his heart by a sword, f. 83v Presentation in the Temple, f. 84r Flight into Egypt, f. 84v Christ in the Temple, found by Mary and Joseph, f. 85r Mary observes the Betrayal of Christ, f. 85v Crucifixion, with Mary's heart pierced by a sword, f. 86r Lamentation, f. 86v Mary surrounded by objects recalling events from the life of Christ; (Chapter 45) f. 87r (*Miraculum de septem gaudiis beate marie*) Mary appears to the sick priest, f. 87v Annunciation, f. 88r Visitation, f. 88v Nativity, f. 89r Adoration, f. 89v Presentation, f. 90r Christ among the Doctors, f.90v Coronation of the Virgin.

2-line calligraphic initials, blue, at the beginning of each chapter and *"figura"* or type (*I*-initials, 6-10 lines; at the bottom of the page, e.g., f. 29v, the *I* breaks and runs beneath the lowest line of text), with elaborate, angular penwork and flourishes, in red (some, e. g., ff. 17r and 21r, with faces). On ff. 91r-104v, 2-line blue initials, plain; spaces for some initials, including a 6-line initial on f. 91r, left blank. 1-line red or blue initials, some of the blue with red penwork. Capital *A*'s in each *Amen* alternate red and blue. Guide-letters for initials throughout. Paragraph marks, blue. Tituli, inscriptions in miniatures, chapter numbers, and pagination in red throughout. Guide-numbers for pagination still visible, especially on ff. 58v-60r.

The parchment is worn and dirty, with many torn and slashed folios. Apart from the folios which are missing entirely, the upper portions (with miniatures) on ff. 47, 53 and 57 have been removed.

Binding: s. xv. Dutch or German? Sewn on six double, tawed cords laced into beech boards and pegged in three holes. Endband cores laid in grooves and pegged. There is an inner cover of pink, tawed skin. Over this is a chemise of thin, white tawed skin stitched to a heavy outer, tawed pigskin cover which extends about 25 mm. at the head, 70 mm. at the fore-edge, and was whip-stitched at the edges. The tail edge has been cut down. Two straps are attached to the upper cover and tacked to the extending skin at the fore-edge with a narrow, tawed thong. There are two square marks where pins were attached to the lower cover. The original sewing cords have broken and have been replaced, a part of the book resewn, and part of the chemise pocket cut away. The ends of the fastening straps and the endbands are wanting. The binding was described by Dorothy Minor in *The History of Bookbinding, 525-1950 A. D.*, an exhibition held at the Baltimore Museum of Art, 1957, p. 55. no. 128.

Written in England at the beginning of the 15th century, as indicated by the style of the miniatures. The *Meditationes de passione Christi* were added to the volume in the 15th century by a different, but contemporary, scribe on blank folios in the last quire of the *Speculum* (ff. 91-92) and on two new quires (XIV-XV). Presented to Yale in 1714 by Elihu Yale (note on front cover: "Yale College Library, 1715"); believed to be the first illuminated medieval manuscript in any

American collegiate library. Signature of John Bentley (f. 57r, s. xvii or xviii?). Several annotations by Ezra Stiles, Professor of Divinity and President of Yale University from 1778 to 1795 (ff. 25r, 40r, and 90r; on f. 90v, "Januarii 26th 1793. Perlegi hunc Librum Ezra Stiles.").

secundo folio: [table, f. 2:] Octauianus cesar
[text, f. 3:] Et hec oblacio

Bibliography: De Ricci, v. 1, p. 167, no. 27.
Exhibition Catalogue, pp. 211-12, no. 37.
W. H. McCarthy, "An Exhibition of Bookbindings," *Gazette* 7 (1932) p. 15 and illustration of binding.
Illuminated Books of the Middle Ages and Renaissance (Baltimore: Walters Art Gallery, 1949) pp. viii and 51, no. 139.
A. L. Kellog, "Susannah and the Merchant's Tale," *Speculum* 25 (1960) pp. 275-76 and fig. 3 (of f. 11r).
T. E. Marston, "The *Speculum humanae salvationis*," *Gazette* 42 (1968) pp. 124-30.
C. E. Lutz, "The 'Gentle Puritan' and the 'Angelic Doctor'," *Gazette* 52 (1978) pp. 122-26.

MS 28 (olim Z109.073)   Germany, 1513
Prayers (in Ger.)   Pl. 7

1. ff. 1r-2v   Prayers to the Holy Trinity. *Ein löblichs vnd andechtigs gepett zu der heiligenn vnd vngetaylten trinitet* ... O du heylige trinitet. O du ware aynikait du helige götliche maiestat...; (f. 1v) *Ain anderß gepet zu der heiligen vnd vngetailten trinitat*. O herr mein got künig ob allen künigen vnd...; (f. 2r) *Ain anderß gepet zu der heiligenn vnd vngetailten trinitet*. O heyliger got. O starcker got. O vntötlicher got erparm dich...; (f. 2v) *Ain anderß gepet* ... O heilige trinitet warer ewiger got du hochstes güt ob allem güt. Ich dein arme creatur....

For a similar sequence of prayers see San Marino, Huntington Library HM 195 (art. 9).

2. ff. 3r-9v   Prayers to Christ. *Ein gepet von der zükunfft vnseres liben herren ihesu cristi*. O herr Ihesu criste ewiger parmherziger got Schöpfer aller welt Ich dein armer...; (f. 3r) *Von der kindthait cristi ain gut gepett*. O herr almechtiger got ihesu criste, piß genedig nur ellend [text trimmed]...; (f. 3v) *Von dem leben cristi vnd von dem liechtmess tag ain gut andechtig gepet*. Herr Ihesu criste Ich gedenck als du geopffert pist worden in den tempel...; (f. 4r) *Von dem palmtag ain andechtigs gepet*. O Guettiger herr ihesu criste Ich gedenck das du an dem palmtag loblich pist...; (f. 4v) *Von dem abentessen vnsers lieben herren ihesu cristi ain gepet*. O ewiger parmherziger got herr ihesu criste dein heilgs abentessen betracht ich...; (f. 4v) *Von der angst an dem ölperg ain güts gepet*. Herr ihesu criste mein got nach deinem heyligen abentessen pistu außgangen...; (f. 5r) *Von der gefängknuß zu*

Metten zeit. O himlischer künig mein got vnd herr ihesu criste. Durch vnseren willen...; (f. 5v) *Zü preym vnd Terz zeit ain andechtigs gepet, etc.* Eya du parmherziger got ihesu criste dein grosse vnschuld gedenck ich...; (f. 5v) *Von der gayßlung ain gut gepet*. O aller liebster herr ihesu criste Ich betracht dein großpitters leiden das du gelitten hast...; (f. 6r) *Von der krönung ain gepet mit andacht, etc.* O du mein aller liebster herr ihesu criste du zier der engel du spiegel der götlichem...; (f. 6v) *Zü der Sext zeit ain gepet*. O du höchster got. O liebhaber menschlichs geschlechts nach der...; (f. 7r) *Zü der Nonn zeit ein gut gepet*. O ewige weißhait. O gruntlose väterliche lieb herr ihesu criste dein grosse...; (f. 7v) *Zü vesper zeit ain andechtig gepet*. O du schein des ewigen liechts. Wie pistu nun so gar erloschen...; (f. 8r) *Von der auffart vnsers herrenn Ihesu cristi ain gepet*. O bewaltiger schöpfer himels vnd der erdenn Herr ihesu criste Nach deiner...; (f. 8v) *An dem heiligen pfingstag ain gepet, etc.* O du mein aller höchster schaz vnd trost meiner armenn seel herr...; (f. 9r) *Von dem Iüngsten gericht ain gepet*. O ewige götliche parmherzigkait. O ernstliche gerechtigkait herr ihesu criste Nun gedenck ich....

3. ff. 9v-14r   Prayers for Indulgences. *Der heilig vater vnd pabst benedictus der xii hat* ... O du aller liebster herr ihesu criste Ich pit dich durch die übertreffenlichen lieb...; (f. 10v) *Von dem nachuolgenden gepet hat man fünfftaüsent* ... O du aller liebster herr ihesu criste Schöpfer vnd erlediger der welt...; (f. 11v) *Hye nachuolgt ein gepet des heiligen pischolffs sandt Augustins ... das gepet*. O Got herr ihesu criste der du vmb erlösung willen der welt hast wollen...; (f. 12r) *Hye nachuolgen die gepet S. gregory* [rubric begins again on f. 12v:] *Hye nachuogen andechtige gepet sandt gregory da von hat man vill vnd grossenn ablas* ... O herr ihesu criste Ich pet dich an. am creuz hangenden vnd ein durue kron [each section followed by a pater noster and ave maria] ... [cf. San Marino, Huntington Library HM 195, art. 19].

4. ff. 14r-20r   Prayers to Christ. *Ain schöns andechtigs gepet von dem pitteren leiden vnsers herren ihesu cristi*. O herre ihesu criste des waren lebendigen gottes sun in der ewigkait...; (f. 15v) *Ain andechtigs gepet zu vnserem lieben herren ihesu cristo. dem menschen nütz an seel vnd an leib*. O herr almechtiger got parmherziger himlischer vater. laß erscheinen In mein herz...; (f. 16v) *Ain anders andechtigs vnd gützs gepet zu vnserm lieben herren ihesu cristo*. Herr ihesu criste almechtiger ewiger got tail mir mit dein heiligs...; (f. 17r) *Ain anders gepet* ... O herr ihesu criste du ewiger parmherziger got aller welt schöpfer vnd des menschlichen ... [cf. San Marino, Huntington Library HM 195, art. 8]; (f. 18r) *Ain anders andechtigs gepet* ... O almechtiger ewiger got vnd herre mein beschaffer erlöser vnd helffer...; (f. 19r) *Ain danckpers guts vnd andechtigs gepet zü got dem himilischenn vater mit andacht zesprechenn*. O himlischer vater in der ewigkait du parmherziger got. Ich lob dich mit ganzer...; (f. 19v) *Ain gepet zu dem Sun gottes* ... O herr ihesu criste des lebendigen waren gottes Sun....

5. ff. 20r-24v   Miscellaneous prayers, mostly to Christ. *Ain gepet zu got dem heiligen geist*. O heiliger geist vnd ewiger got. vaterliche ewige lieb tröster aller...; (f. 20v) *Das nachuolgende gepett Sol man sprechen vor einem Crucifix vnsers herrenn ihesu*

cristi. O herr vnd got Ich kom für dich als ain armer pettlär...; (f. 21v) *Ain gepet von der angst vnsers lieben herren ihesu cristi am ölperg.* O aller liebster herr ihesu criste. Ich betracht vnd gedenck mitleidenlich von...; (f. 22v) *Ain anders gepet ... am ölperg.* O herr ihesu criste warer go [end hidden by tape] vnd mensch du pist der aingeporen...; (f. 23v) *Ain andechtigs gepet fur die sündt vnd zü begeren güt tugend wider die sündt.* O almechtiger ewiger got. Ich vnwirdiger sunder pit vnd beger von dir...; (f. 24v) *Ain gepet von dem heiligen Creuz ihesu cristi.* Ich pit dich du heiligs creuz dar an vnser hail gewurckt ist wordenn....

6. ff. 24v-34r Prayers attributed to specific individuals. *Die fünff gepet hugonis.* Aller suessister herr ihesu criste. Durch die wirdigkait deines leichnams...; (f. 25r) *Die drew gepet des heiligen vaters Sandt fransiscen.* Got vater von himel. Ich pit dich in dem namenn ihesu cristi nazareni ... [cf. Beinecke MS 134, f. 45v]; (f. 26r) ... *Dise gepet hat gemacht der heilig vater vnd pabst Vrban der funff* ... [series of prayers, each with a Collect; for Matins:] Ich gebenedey vnd wolsprich dir o aller guettigister ihesu Wann vmb vnser armen ... [Prime:] Ich lob dich o allerdurchleuchtigister ihesu Wann du mit falscher ... [Terce:] Ich lob vnd ere dich o aller höchste weisshait Wann du vmb des veloren ... [Sext:] Ich grossmach dich o aller suessister ihesu Wann die hämmerschleg haben ... [None:] Ich sag dir großmechtig danck o aller suessister vnd erwirdigister herr ihesu criste ... [Vespers:] O aller verwundtister herre ihesu criste Ich sag dir vnaußsprechenlich danck Wann du ... [Compline:] Ich armer sunder hochwirdig dich mit den stercksten krefften meines liebs ... *Item es ist zewissen das am yedlicher mensch er sey gaistlich oder weltlich mag die vorgeschriben gepet Sandt Brigitten petten pey tag oder pey nach mit einander oder nacheinander wann er die weil mag haben etc.*

7. ff. 34v-36v Prayers revealed by Christ. *Es war ain andachtiger priester der die muter gottes gar lieb halt* ... Gegrust seist du suesser herre ihesu criste Ain wort des vaters Ain Sun der Iunckfrawen...; (f. 35v) *Ain gepet sich tailhafftig zu machen des heiligen sacraments* ... O herr almechtiger ewiger got Wir pitten dich durch deinen eingepornen Sun...; (f. 35v) *Ain andechtigs gepet wider den gächen todt vnd fur die pestilenz.* Allmechtiger ewiger parmherziger got Ain anfangk vnd endt aller ding...; (f. 36r) *Der sogen ist zesprechen zu morgens vnd gegen der nacht vnd in aller widerwertigkait vnd truebsalen.* Dye almechtigkait gottes vaters die weißhait gottes Suns die sennftmuetigkait gottes heiligen geists....

8. ff. 36v-47r Prayers for the rosary. *In dem namen vnsers lieben herren ihesu cristi vaher sich hye an der heilig vnd sälig rosenkranz der lobsamen Iunckfrawen marie ... sprich als hernachgeschriben stast.* Gruest seist maria genadenvol der herr mir dir du bist gesegent...; (f. 42r) *Hye nachuolgt ain schöne rubrick von dem ablas vnnd nutzperkait des rosenkranz* ... [parts of rubric obscured by gray ink] O aller erwirdigiste kunigin der parmherzigkait, Ich grueß den erwigen temel...; (f. 44v) *Hye nachuolgt ain ander schöner vnd besuder andechtiger rosenkranz ... Gegruest seist maria etc. vnd nach yedlichem artikel sprich Amen vnd nit [sic] nach dem Aue maria. Ihesus Christus* den du hast empfangen von dem heiligen geist in aller raynigkait....

9. ff. 47r-69v   Prayers to the Virgin. *Ain schönes gepet zu der raynen Iunckfrawen maria fur die pestilenz.* O maria du pist das wolgeriert vaßlem des heiligen geists...; (f. 48r) *Ain gepet von herzenlichen mitleiden vnser lieben frawen der himelkunigen.* O eya du allerwirdigiste muter des aingepornen Sun gots...; (f. 49r) *Ain andechtigs gepet von den siben klagen vnd schmerzen der muter gottes* ... O maria ein Iunckfraw ob allen Iunckfrawen ein muter ihesu cristi...; (f. 50r) *Hye nachuolgen die Syben tagzeit vnser liebenfrawen marie etc.* Maria muter rayne mayd, Zu mötten zeit ward dir herzlichs laid ... [includes sections for Prime through Compline and *zu der Aue maria zeit*]; (f. 51r) *Ain andechtigs gepet von vnser lieben frawen marie.* O liebe vnd aller liebste maria edle suesse kunigin Ich vnwirdiger aller creatur naig mich...; (f. 54v) *Ain andechtigs vnd guts gepett zu vnser lieben frawen vmb ein säligs endidises mussäligen lebens.* O du lobsamiste vnd raynngiste junckfraw vnd muter gotts maria. O du reicher schaz der gotlichen genaden. O du...; (f. 56r) *Ain schönes gepet zu vnser lieben frawen das solten mensche mit aufferhebtem herzen sprechen.* O werde Iunckfraw maria O du himelische kunigin du zier der engel erparm dich...; (f. 57v) *Das gepet hyenachuolgent ist genomt das guldin. Aue maria etc.* Pys gruesset maria ein dierren der heiligen drinältigkait ein muter...; (f. 58r) *Ain löblichs gebet zu vnser liebenn frawen in dem sygleicht wret edlem gestain.* Maria du gewaltige kunigin der himel. Du heilige kaiserin der engel ... [cf. San Marino, Huntington Library HM 195, art. 11]; (f. 59r) *Pabst Sextus der vierd des namens hat geben von dem nachgeschriben gepet xj tausent iar antlas als offt man es spricht.* Pis gegruest allerheiligiste maria, muter gots kunigin der himel porten des paradeis...; (f. 59v) *Von dem nachuolgenden gepet hat man funff iar antlas.* O maria ain laitter der himel, Ain saul der welt...; (f. 59v) *Hye nachuolgen andechtige gepet von vnser lieben frawen An yren vnd yres liebsten Suns* ... O Maria du edle junckfraw, Du liechter morgen stern, vnd wirdigiste muter...; (f. 60r) *Ain gepet zu vnser frawen von yrer heiligen gepurt.* O kunigin der himel junckfraw maria trosterin aller betruebten Widerpring...; (f. 60v) *Ain gepet zu maria von der verkundung vnsers herren ihesu cristi.* O du ynnigkliche Iunckfraw ob allen Iunckfrawen, O du wirdigister tempel...; (f. 61v) *Ain andechtigs gepet zu maria von der haymsuechung Sand Elizabeth.* O du trösterin aller betruebten Herzen. O du spiegel...; (f. 62r) *Ain gepet zu maria von der heiligen gepurt vnsers herrenn ihesu cristi.* Gegruesset seist du himlische kindel petterin, Du du vns geporren hast...; (f. 63r) *Ain andechtigs gepet zu maria von der beschneidung vnsers herren ihesu cristi.* O du suesse muter gottes vnd vnuermailigte junckfraw maria, Ich pit dich...; (f. 63r) *Ain gut vnd andechtig gepet zu maria an dem öbersten oder heiligen drey kunig tag.* O maria ein kayserin des himels vnd der erden, Ich pit dich durch die vnmassig freudt...; (f. 63v) *Ain gepet von maria von dem liechtmess tag.* O aller raynigiste wirdigiste junckfraw maria, O du sälige muter ob allenn muttern...; (f. 64v) *Ain gepet zu maria von der vrstend vnsers herren ihesu cristi.* Gegruesset seist du aller lobsamiste muter gots rayne Iunckfraw maria in der aynigkait...; (f. 65r) *Ain andechtig vnd gut gepet zu maria von der Auffart cristi ihesu.* O du wirdigiste aller creatur zartte Iunckfraw maria, Ich betracht die vnmässig vnd vnbegreifflich...; (f. 65r) *Ain*

andechtigs vnd guts gepet zu maria an dem heiligenn pfingsttag das gepet. O maria du suesse Iunckfraw, du heiliger tempel der heiligen trinältigkait...; (f. 65v) *Ain gepet von vnser frawen schidung auß disem jamer.* O du vnvermälgite Iunckfraw vnd wirdigiste muter vnsers herren ihesu cristi maria, O du thron götlicher maiestat...; (f. 67r) *Man list wie der heilg [sic] erzpischoff Sandt Thoman von Kandelperg Sprach mit grosser freudt vnd andacht die siben freudt marie ... Hye nachuolgen die yrdischen freudt marie etc.* Frew dich o kunigin der himel widerpringer [trimmed] aller creatur, Iunckfraw vnd muter gots maria, Aber sprich ich frew dich ... [ends f. 68r:] dir verlihen hat. Amen. *Ave maria.* [Seven Joys of the Virgin; Leroquais LH 2.343-44] *Anfang, Bedenck, mitel vnd endt. Bedenck auch pauls wigg. 1513.* (f. 68v) *Man list das vnser liebe fraw erschain dem heiligen erzpischoff vnd martrer sandt Thoman von Kandelperg, vnd offerbart im selbs yr Siben himlisch freudt ...* Frew dich junckfraw maria ein muter vnsers herren ihesu cristi, Wann du vor allen engelen vnd heiligen erhöcht...; (f. 69v) *Ain gepet auff all vor geschriben freud.* O junkfraw gepererin gots maria lieb, freudt, kurzweil, trost vnd hoffnung meiner seel....

10. ff. 70r-76v Various prayers. *Vnser frawen Klag vnter dem heiligen creuz.* Marie klag die was so gross, da sy yr liebs kind sach...; (f. 72v) *Babst Julius der ander gibt achzig tausent jar ablas ...* O aller erwirdigiste kunigin der parmherzigkait, Ich grues dem Iunckfreulichs herz...; (f. 73r) *Zu der muter gots ain guts petlin.* O muter gots du engel zier, mit ganzer krafft schrey ich zu dir...; (f. 73r) *Von dem nachuolgenden gepet hat pabst Syxtus xj tausent iar ablas.* Gegruest seyst aller heiligiste maria, muter gots, kunigin der himel, ain porten des paradeiß...; (f. 73v) *Hye nach wirdt vermeckt in welicher maynung man got dienen sol vnd gutte werck vnd gepet volpringen. Merck eben.* Es ist aygentlichen zu wissen das man got mit dar vmb sol dienen, das er vns behuet...; (f. 74r) *Nach zeuolgen diser leer sol ain yedlicher cristen mensch warnämen vnd mit fleiss merckenn.* Das der gross lerer Scotus vnd auch ander lerer mit jm sprechen vnd vermaynt ... [sections: *Von der lieb gots; von dem glauben; von der hoffnung; von der forcht gots*]; (f. 76v) *Ain schöne rubrick von der veronica.* Item der heilig vater vnd pabst Siluester verleicht allen den die yr sund warlich....

11. ff. 77r-85v Fifteen prayers of St. Birgitta. *Die nach geschriben funfzehen gepet seind der heiligen frawen sand Brigitten ...* O herr ihesu criste ewige suessikait.... ff. 84v-85v blank

12. ff. 86r-93r Prayers to be said before Communion. *Hye nachuolgen etliche schöne gepet so der mensch enpfahen wil das hochwirdig sacrament gots leichnam.* O ewige weishait herr ihesu criste meiner durssigten seel speis...; (f. 86v) *Ain anders gepet vor der enpfahung gots leichnams.* Ihesu criste du genadenreicher schaz meiner seel gemahel laß heut erfult werden...; (f. 86v) *Ain anders gepet vor der enpfahung gots leichnams.* Eya du ewigs wort geflossen auß dem herzen deines hymlischen vaters ... [cf. San Marino, Huntington Library HM 195, art. 12]; (f. 87r) *Ain anders gepet vor der enpfahung gots leichnam.* Ich pit dich herr ewiger got, du wollest mich

heut genedigklich erhörren...; (f. 87v) *Ain anders gepet vor der enpfahung gots leichnams.* Ewiger got herr ihesu criste, schöpfer himels vnd der erden, Ich glaub von ganzen herzen...; (f. 88r) *Ain anders gepet vor der enpfahung gots leichnam.* In mein herz senck dein lieb du vrsprung aller genaden ... [cf. San Marino, Huntington Library HM 195, art. 12]; (f. 88r) *Ain anders gepet vor der enpfahung gots leichnams zu got dem vater.* Herr got heiliger himlischer vater, der du deinen aingepornen Sun vnsers herren...; (f. 88v) *Ain anders gepet vor der enpfahung gots leichnam.* Herr ihesu criste der du vmb vnsers hails willen deinen lieb in den pitteren todt geantwürt...; (f. 88v) *Ain anders gepet vor der enpfahung gots leichnams zu got dem heiligen geist.* Got heiliger geist, der du wo du wilt dein götliche genad wurckest...; (f. 89r) *Ain gepet zu der heiligen drinältigkait vor der enpfahung.* O heilige trinältigkait du ainiger got, Bross erschrockenlich vnd volparmherzigkait...; (f. 89r) *Ain gepet zu der Iunckfrawen maria vor der enpfahung.* Helige junckfraw maria, die du deinen aingepornen Sun...; (f. 89v) *Ain anders gepet zu der Iunckfrawen maria, vor der enpfahung gots leichnams.* O du aller rainieste vnd wirdigiste muter meines herren ihesu cristi heilige maria, du ewige Iunckfraw die du den selben schöpfer...; (f. 90r) *Ain gepet zu allen engelen vor der enpfahung gots.* O yr heiligen engelischenn geist die der almechtig got vor dem hellischen vall enthalten...; (f. 90r) *Ain gepet zu allen patriarchen vnd propheten vor der entpfahung.* O yr heiligen patriarchen vnd propheten die den tag des herren begert, vnd in zukunfft...; (f. 90v) *Ain gepet zu allen zwelffpoten vnd ewangelisten vor der enpfahung.* O yr heiligen zwelffpotenn vnd ewangelisten Die der almechtig got als er mit euch...; (f. 90v) *Ain gepet zu allenn martreren vor der enpfahung gots leichnams.* O yr heiligen martrer die da vmb die lieb vnsers herren ihesu cristi, ewer plut vergossen ... [cf. San Marino, Huntington Library HM 1176, art. 13]; (f. 91r) *Ain gepet zu allen heiligen peichtige* [trimmed] *vor der enpfahung gots leichnams.* O yr heiligen peichtiger, die der almechtig got vmb bekennung seines heiligenn namens...; (f. 91r) *Ain gepet zu den heiligen Iunckfrawen vor der enpfahung.* O yr heiligen Iunckfrawenn die yr nun in keuschait vmbfangen...; (f. 91v) *Ain gepet zu allen heiligen vor der enpfahung gotz leichnams.* O yr all lieb heiligen Die der almechtig got von ewigkait gehailigt...; (f. 91v) *Ain gepet vor der enpfahung zu cristo ihesu.* O du parmherziger tröstlicher trost aller betruebten menschen, Ich kom heut zu dir....

13. ff. 93v–98r Prayers to be said after Communion. *Hye nachuolgen etliche schöne gepet, nach der enpfahung des hochwirdigen Sacraments gotzs leichnams ...* Herzenliche danckparkait ewigs lob, ere vnd alle säligkait...; (f. 94r) *Ain anders ... gepet nach der enpfahung gots leichnams.* O du ware speis der engel, O du wares himelprot der ellenden menschen...; (f. 94r) *Ain anders gepet nach der enpfahung gots leichnams.* Herr ihesu criste Ich glaub das ich dich waren got vnd menschen enpfangen hab...; (f. 95v) *Ain anders gepet nach der enpfahung gots leichnams.* Ich danck dir milter vater genädiger herr vnd parmherziger got das du mich vnwirdigen...; (f. 95v) *Ain anders gepet nach der enpfahung gots leichnams zu der muter gots. Das gepet.* O du erwidige kaiserin du heligen gepererin gots, heilige maria, die du den

Sun des himlischen vaters geporren hast...; (f. 96r) *Ain anders gepet nach der enpfahung gots leichnams zu got dem vater.* O himlischer vater ewiger got, wer pin ich, oder wer hat mir dein genad erworben...; (f. 96v) *Ain anders gepet nach der enpfahung.* O du suess himelprot herr ihesu criste ain Sun gottes himlischen vaters in der ewigkait geporen...; (f. 97r) *Ain anders ... gepet nach der enpfahung gots leichnams.* Mein seel lobt auch got den heiligen geist durch des wurckung der heilig frouleich ... [cf. San Marino, Huntington Library HM 195, art. 12]; (f. 97v) *Ain anders gepet nach der enpfahung gots leichnams.* O heiliger got, O starcker got, O vntödlicher got, O du heilige drinältigkait....

14. ff. 98v–106r Prayers to various saints and angels. *Ein gepet in der gemain das mag einer petten zu ainem yedlichen zwelfpotten ihesu cristi. Das gepet.* O du genadenreicher vnd heiliger herr sand .N. ein junger ihesu cristi, Vnd besunder...; (f. 99r) *Ain gemains gepet das mag ain mensch sprechenn zu ainem yedlichen ewangelisten.* O du heiliger vnd wirdiger sand .N. ain warer ewangelist der gotlichen warhait...; (f. 99r) *Ain gemaines gepet das mag ain mensch sprechen zu ainem yelichenn heiligenn der ain martrer ist gewesenn.* O du hochwirdiger vnd strenger ritter gots heiliger sandt .N. du starcker vnd großmechtiger martrer...; (f. 100r) *Ain gepet in der gemain zu vill martrer als sandt Achacj vnd der gleichen.* O yr vnvberwindtlichenn lobsamen vnd heiligen martrer sandt .N. vnd .N. Wann yr vmb lieb vnd ere vnsers herren ihesu cristi...; (f. 100v) *Ain gemains gepet zu ainem peichtiger der ein pischoff ist gewesen etc.* O du hochwirdiger vater sand .N. ain schein vnd zier der newen stat iherusalem...; (f. 100v) *Ain gepet in der gemain von vill peichtigeren.* O yr durchleuchtigistenn peichtiger ihesu cristi von got wirdig vnd außer welt abgeschaiden...; (f. 101r) *Ain gepet in der gemain zu einem peichtiger der nit pischoff ist gewesen als sant Benedict Sandt leonhart egidius vnd der gleichenn.* O du säliger vnd lieber peichtiger ihesu cristi heiliger sand .N. Ich vnwirdiger sunder pit dich...; (f. 101v) *Ain gepet in der gemain das mag ain mensch sprechen zu ainer yedlichen junckfrawenn die ein martrerin ist gewesen als sandt katherein barbara vnd ander.* Gegruest seist du allerheiligiste v̈berwinderin deiner pittrikait vnd leiden sand .N. Ich pit dich...; (f. 102r) *Ain gepet von vil junckfrawen in der gemain als Sand vrsula, vnd der gleichenn.* O yr aller säligisten vnd aller raynisten junckfrawenn in raynigkait des herzens leibs...; (f. 102r) *Ain gepet in der gemain das mag ein mensch sprechen zu ainer yedlichen junckfrawen die mit ain martrerin ist gewesen als sandt Scolastica, vnd der gleichenn.* O du rainiste vnd heiligiste junckfraw sand .N. du gesegnete praut...; (f. 103r) *Ain gepet in der gamain von den frawen die mit junckfrawen oder martrerin sein gewesen, als sandt Anna, Elizabeth vnd der gleichen.* O du wirdige aller genaden heilige sandt .N. red ain guts wortt fur mich vor dem ewigen got...; (f. 103v) *Ain gepet zu deinem heiligen engel.* O heiliger engel gots dem ich auß götlicher fursichtigkait beuolhen...; (f. 104r) *Ain gepet zu deinem aygen zwelfpoten.* O du hochwirdiger zwelfpot vnsers herren ihesu cristi heiliger sand .N. du hast treulich...; (f. 104v) *Ain andechtigs gepet zu allen heiligen gottes.* O du wirdige hochgelobte vnd rainigiste gepererin gottes heilig junckfraw maria,

vnd du mein allerliebster vnd heiligister engel...; (f. 105r) *Ain anders gepet zu allen heiligen gottes*. O yr allheiligen der nam vnd gedachtnuss ist geschriben...; (f. 105v) *Ain gepet zu allen heligen engelen gottes mit andacht*. O yr hochwirdigen vnd heiligen himelfursten heiligen engelen, erwelt diener des almechtigen kunigs....

15. ff. 106r–117v   Prayers to various saints. *Hye nachuolgen andechtige gepet, in Sunderhait zu ainem yedlichen heiligen zwelffpot, vnd am ersten zu dem heiligen sant Andre.* O du hochgelobter vnnd hochwirdiger himelfurst vnd heiliger zwelffpot sand peter, O du gutter getrewer herter...; (f. 107v) *Ain gepet zu dem heiligen zwelffpoten Sand Pauls*. Frew dich vnd frolock du außerwelts vas der heiligen kirchen gottes heiliger apostel sand pauls...; (f. 108r) *Ain gepet zu dem heyligen Sand Johannes ewangelisten*. Johannes du himlischer adler, Du besunder freundt gottes ... [cf. San Marino, Huntington Library HM 195, art. 13]; (f. 108v) *Ain gepet zu dem heiligen zwelffpoten Sand Andre*. O du heiliger Sand Andre, zwelffpot vnsers herren ihesu cristi, durch das lieb du gelitten hast...; (f. 108v) *Ain gepet zu sand Iacob dem zwelffpotten genant der großer*. O heiliger zwelffpot sant Iacob den wir glauben nach menschlicher gestalt...; (f. 109r) *Von sand philip vnd Iacob apostelen ein gepet*. O yr lieben heiligen apostelen cristi sand philip vnd iacob die yr durch vberwundunig der marter...; (f. 109v) *Ain gepet zu dem heiligen Sand Thoman apostelen*. Heiliger sand Thoman du apostel vnd sand pott des herren der du verdient hast...; (f. 109v) *Ain gepet von sand matheo dem zwelffpoten vnnd ewangelistenn*. O du säliger apostel vnd ewangelist Sand matheus, Durch die vnendtlichen parmherzigkait...; (f. 110r) *Ain gutt vnd andechtig gepet zu Sandt Bartolme dem zwelffpottenn*. O heliger sandt Bartolmee, Du apostel vnsers herren ihesu cristi der du in dem land India...; (f. 110v) *Ain gepet von Sand Symon vnd Iudas den heiligen zwelffpottenn*. O yr lieben himelfurstenn Symon vnd Iudas apostelen vnsers herren ihesu cristi, Die yr die ganzen gegent...; (f. 111r) *Ain gepet zu den vierzenhen notthellfferen Sprichs mit andacht*. O yr vnvberwintlichen ritter gottes vnd löblichen Sighafften heiligen Sand Sixt, sand Erasm, Sand blasi...; (f. 111v) *Ain gepet zu dem heiligen martrer vnd ritter sand Sebastian*. O du wirdiger vnd strenger ritter gottes heiliger sand sebastian, du großmechtiger martrer...; (f. 112r) *Ain gepet zu dem heiligen martrer vnd kunig sand quirein haubtherren zu Tegernsee*. Ich pit dich heiliger hochwirdiger martrer vnd kunig sand quirein der du durch die lieb gots...; (f. 112v) *Ain gepet zu dem heiligen martrer vnd ritter sand Jorgen*. O strenger ritter vnd heiliger notthelffer sand Jorg der du krefftigklich...; (f. 113r) *Ain gepet zu dem heiligen martrer sand laurenz*. O säliger vnd großmechtiger martrer sand laurenz Ich armer sunder...; (f. 113v) *Ain gepet von dem heiligen martrer Sand Cristoff*. Heiliger martrer sand cristoff Ich pit dich durch den heiligen namen ihesu cristi...; (f. 114r) *Ain andechtigs gepet zu dem heiligen pischoff vnd peichtiger sand Wolfgang*. O du säliger vnd wirdiger pischoff ihesu cristi heiliger sand Wolffgang, vnter der regel sand Benedicten gehailigt...; (f. 114v) *Ain gepet zu der heiligen Iunckfraw sand katherina*. Pis gegruesset sälige Iunckfraw vnd martrerin

sand katherina, ein tochter des vngelaubigen kunigs...; (f. 115r) *Ain gepet zu der heiligen Iunckfraw sand margaretha.* O du heilige Iunckfraw vnd martrerin sand margaretha, durch dem heiligs leben pist du in diser welt...; (f. 115v) *Ain gepet zu der heyligen frawen Sand Anna der muter vnser liebenn frawen.* O du wirdige muter der hymlischen kaiserin vnd aller raynisten vnd hochgelobten Iunckfrawen marie...; (f. 116v) *Ain gepet zu der heiligen sandt maria magdalena ein ware puesserin.* Erfrew dich du heilige magdalena, ein hailsame hoffnung vnd durch scheynender spiegel...; (f. 117r) *Ain gepet zu der heiligen frawen vnnd kunigin sand Elizabethenn.* O du edle fraw sand Elizabeth erlang mir von got...; (f. 117v) ... glori vnd freudt Amen. *Bruder Paulus vorzeiten genant Melchior Wigg auß dem rieß geporen, Vnd das puechlin geschriben zu Tegernsee Anno domini 1513.*

16. ff. 118r–129v Prayers for the sick. *Hye pin ich bezaichen wie man fur ein krancken menschen pitten soll. Vnd die seel got beuelhenn die denn von hynnen schaiden will.* Gelaubige vnd cristenliche seel far hyn far hyn von diser welt, In dem namen des vaters...; (f. 118v) *Die gepet soll man sprechen ob dem krancken menschen Ain anderß gepet fur den krancken menschen.* O parmherziger got, O guettiger got, der du mit deiner grossen parmherzigkait...; (f. 119v) *Mer ain gepet fur den.* O herzen lieber N mein dem almechtigen got beuilch ich...; (f. 120v) *Ain anders gepet fur den krancken menschenn.* Herr ihesu criste hailer der welt, wir beuelhen dir dises menschen seel...; (f. 121r) *Ain anders gepet fur den krancken menschenn.* Herr ewiger got wir pitten dein parmherzigkait mit andacht...; (f. 122r) *Ain anders gepet fur den krancken menschen zu der heiligen trinitet.* O aller höchste gothait, vngemeßne guet, aller guttigiste vnd aller löblichiste...; (f. 122v) *Ain anders gepet zu vnserem herren ihesu cristo fur den krancken.* Herr ihesu criste vmb den grossen schmerzen den du an dem creuz hast vmb vns gelitten...; (f. 122v) *Ain gepet zu vnser lieben frawen fur den krancken menschen.* O heilige vnuermälgte vnd gesegnete in ewigzeit Iunckfraw maria helfferin vnd trösterin...; (f. 123r) *Das nachuolgend gepet zway oder dreymal ob dem krancken mensch* [trimmed]. Der frid vnsers herren ihesu cristi, Das zaichen des heiligen creuz, die raynigkait...; (f. 123v) *Ain gepet zu dem aigen engel fur den krancken menschen.* O allerheiligister engel gottes herr dem diser mensch von got is beuolhen...; (f. 123v) *Hye nach pin ich setzen drey Pater noster die gesprochen hat eines pabsts Capellan fur den pabst da er lag an seinen zugen vnd wolt von hynnen schaiden vnd seiner seel ward dar mit gehollffen als er darnach dem Capellan das was verfunden Sprich am erstenn.* Kyrieleyson, Kyrieleyson, Kyrieleyson, Herr almechtiger got erparm vber vns...; (f. 125v) *Das nach geschriben gepet ist die vor geschriben gepet alle beschliessen.* O allmechtiger got herr ihesu criste Der du vns mit deinem heiligen plut erlösen pist...; (f. 126v) *Fur die krancken menschen soll man die heyligen anrueffen vnd ob in peten die letaney wie hernach stät.* Kyrieleyson ... [includes Abel among the righteous men; Abraham among the patriarchs; among the 12 martyrs, Vitus (4), Quirinus (7), Chrysogonus (8), Achatius (10); among the 8 monks, Wolfgang (2) and Corbinian (3); among the 13 virgins, Thecla (6), Scholastica (7), Ursula (10)]; (f. 128v) *Es ist zewissen das der menschen*

sicherlichen stirbt, der dise nachgeschriben frag erkent vnd spricht ia darauff [?] *frag den krancken. Ereyest du dich das du stirbst in dem heiligen cristenlichenn glauben....*

17. ff. 130r-140v Various prayers. *Ain gepet fur all glaubig seelen zu der heiligenn drinältigkait.* O heylige drinältigkait du aynigs wesen, ewiger got, Erparm dich vber all glaubig seelen ... [cf. San Marino, Huntington Library HM 195, art. 15]; (f. 130r) *Ain anders gepet fur all glaubige seelen.* Seit gruest all ellend glaubig seelen habt rue ... [cf. San Marino, Huntington Library HM 195, art. 15]; (f. 130r) *Ain anders gepet fur all glaubig seelen.* O heyliger got, O starcker got, O vntodlicher got herr ihesu criste, Erparm dich vber all glaubig seelen...; (f. 130v) *Ain anders gepet fur all glaubig selen.* O du reicher prunn der parmherzigkait, tail mit dein väterlich lieb...; (f. 131r) *Ain anders gepet fur all glaubig selen.* Ewiger vnd almechtiger got Erparm dich vber all edlendt glaubig selen...; (f. 131r) *Ain anders gepet fur all glaubig selen.* Die ewigen rue gib herr allenn glaubigen selen, vnd das ewig liecht leucht...; (f. 132r) *Merck ein schöne leer.* O mensch wiltu leben in sicherhait, So hab vmb dein sund...; (f. 132v) *Ain gepet zu deinem aigen engel mit andacht zesprechen.* O heiliger engel gots, Dem ich auß götlicher fursichtigkait...; (f. 133r) *Ain andechtigs vnnd guts gepet zu deinem aigen xij potten wie ob* [trimmed; this rubric followed immediately, on f. 133v, by another rubric:] *Ain andechtigs gepet zu Sand katherina dar von auch vil antlaß ist geben* ... Lobent den herren all heiden, lobent in alle volcker...; (f. 134r) *Hye nachuolgen die Acht verß des heiligen Bernhardj im von dem pösen geist auß dem psalter* ... Almechtiger schein des ewigen liechts durch das zaichen des heiligen creuzes ... [cf. RH 27912, in Latin]; (f. 136v) *Von sant Cristoff ain andechtigs schöns gebet zu sprechenn.* O heiliger herr sandt Cristoff der eren [?] du bist ain wirdiger martrer gottes, Ich pit dich...; (f. 137r) *Ain anders andechtigs gebett zu dem heiligenn sant Cristoffel.* O heiliger vnd lieber herr sant cristoffel Ich pit dich, meer [?] mir mein freid offt...; (f. 137v) *Ain andechtigs guts vnd hailsams gebet zu dem heiligen sant Erasm* ... Heiliger vnd erwirdiger pischoff sant erasm edler gottes martrer...; (f. 139r) *Hye nachuolgt Ain taglig vnd notturfftige peicht mit herzen vnd gemuet zu got morgens so der mensch auff steett* ... O herre got dir bekenn ich vnd gib mich schuldig, das ich wider ... sunden huetten. Amenn. Das ganz puechelin Mein hantschri [trimmed]. f. 140v blank, except for later notes

Bound in with the manuscript are 3 printed works, each paginated separately; all with full-page engravings and full engraved borders: *Das Leben der allerheyligsten vnnd vbergebenedeyten Jungkfrawen vnd Mutter Gottes Maria* (Augspurg: Christoff Mang, 1609); *Von den Siben Engelfurstenbetrachtungen vnd Gebett. Item. Von dreyerley Ambtern deß Heiligen Schutz Engels* (Augspurg: Chrisostomo Dahertzhofer, 1612); *Sunder Spiegel, Das ist* (Augspurg: Chrisostomo Dahertzhofer, 1612).

Paper, ff. ii (paper) + 140 (watermarks at top of folio, trimmed) + 85 (printed text) + i (paper), 131 x 90 (125 x 72) mm. Written in 23-26 long lines; frame-ruled in pale red ink.

I⁸ (-4, 5?), II-IV⁸. Rest of manuscript bound too tightly for accurate collation. No catchwords or signatures.

Written by Melchior Wigg (alias Bruder Paulus; see under Provenance) in a small even gothic cursive script, with loops. The scribe's signature on f. 117v is executed in large gothic textura, in blue ink, with red.

A few initial *I*'s extend the length of the written space in blue with red or red alone; crude. 7- to 5-line initials in blue, with red penwork. On f. 77r, an elaborately split uncial *d* in blue. 4-, 3-, and 1-line initials in red or blue, sometimes with black or red penwork. Capitals stroked with red. Rubrics and red paragraph marks throughout.

Some water stains and wax spills, none affecting the text. Reinforced in gutter by adding paper strips. Many pages trimmed, with loss of text.

Binding: s. xix-xx. Rebinding using original [?] wooden boards covered in dark brown goatskin, roughly gold tooled. All edges gilt. Strap-and-pin fastenings.

Written in 1513 at the Benedictine monastery of Tegernsee, by Melchior Wigg (alias Bruder Paulus), according to notes of ff. 68r and 117v (see arts. 9 and 13; also prayers to St. Quirinus, patron of Tegernsee [on f. 112r], and to St. Wolfgang, "vnter der regel sand Benedicten gehailigt", f. 114r). Tegernsee was dissolved in 1803. Given by H. Holbrook Curtis (signature, second flyleaf) to Dr. Franklin Carter, who gave it to Yale in 1910.

Bibliography: De Ricci, v. 1, p. 167, no. 28.

MS 29 Spain, s. XVII
Aristotle, Ethica, Sp. tr. Pedro Simon Abril, etc.

1. f. vii recto [Title page:] Los diez libros de las Ethicas de Aristotelis Traducidos originalmente de lengua griega Por Pedro Simon Abril.

2. ff. 1r-10v [Dedicatory epistle to King Philip II, 1527-98:] A la S. C. R. M. de el Rey Dn. Phelipe nuestro señor Pedro Simon Abril, profesor de letras humanas, y philosophia ... que con tanta razon tiene entre los doctos de tantos años a esta parte ganada y adquirida.

3. ff. 10v-30v [Prologue to the translation followed by summary of Book I:] Prologo de el interprete al letor en el qual se le declara el modo ... las riquezas por la felicidad que se cree ó espera hallar en las riquezas.

4. ff. 30v-545r [Translation of Aristotle, *Ethica*:] Qualquier ante, y qualquier doctrina, y asi mismo toda accion, y eleccion parece que a algun ... [end is mutilated:] comenzandolo a tratar*** a manera. ** in [?] de los X. libros morales. f. 545v blank

Paper (thin; unidentified watermarks concealed in gutter), ff. vii (paper) + 546 (foliation should begin on vii, which is part of the first quire) + iv (paper),

201 x 145 mm. The physical format of the codex varies considerably, with 14–26 long lines per page; bounding lines (when present) in hard point.

The codex is too tightly bound to be collated.

Written by a single scribe in elegant italic script.

Many folios at end are stained and repaired; some text lost.

Binding: s. xix. Brown mottled calf, gold- and blind-tooled, by B. Miyar (note on f. i recto).

Written in Spain in the 17th century; early provenance unknown. Belonged to Diego del Monte, Madrid (inscription with date 1852 on f. i verso). Acquired by Yale in 1888.

Bibliography: De Ricci, v. 1, p. 167, no. 29.

MS 30 (olim Z111.69k) Italy, s. XVI/XVII
Jeronymo Osorio, Della nobiltà civile, It. tr. Bernardo Gandino, etc.

1. ff. 1r–2v [Preface with signature of translator:] Non è alcun dubbio (signor illustrissimo) che era la uarità [*sic*] delle cose create dal sommo Fattore ... supplicandola ni tanto à seruirsi di me, si come di fedel, humile, et obligatissimo seruitore ... Seruitor humilissimo. Bernardo Gandino. D. f. 3r–v blank (table of contents on verso in a later hand)

2. ff. 4r–44v *Della nobilta ciuile de M. Girolamo Osorio Portoghese libro primo tradotta in lingua italiana da Bernardo Triuigiano.* [Books I–II] Poiche, o Ludouico Principe illustrissimo, la benignità tua mi ha inuitato à seguir ... della famiglia ha hauuto l'origine dal fonte della uirtù. f. 45r–v blank

3. ff. 46r–81v *Trattato delle uirtù et operationi ciuili della Nobiltà produttrici.* Se da gli antichi la uirtù cotanto pregiata si degni et nobili effetti ... li nobili amatori del publico bene, uiuendone in pace, et tranquillità, si conseruerà lungamente felice.

Paper (watermarks: unidentified angel similar to Briquet Ange 662, but with BFF as countermark), ff. 82 (foliation begins on 2), 215 x 162 (176 x 111) mm. Written in 22–25 long lines; frame-ruled in hard point, often with double outer vertical bounding lines.

I^{78}, II^5 (1 is front pastedown; structure of 2–5 uncertain). Catchwords for each folio at bottom of written space.

Written in a calligraphic italic script by Bernardo Gandino of Treviso, with frequent corrections.

Binding: s. xix–xx. Paper case with decorated paper sides. Bookblock detached.

Written in Italy, presumably by Bernardo Gandino of Treviso, at the end of the sixteenth or beginning of the seventeenth century; early provenance unknown.

Belonged to James Luce Kingsley (1778-1852; signatures on front and back covers). Acquired by Yale in 1853.

Bibliography: De Ricci, v. 1, p. 168, no. 30.

MS 31 (olim Z111.81) Denmark [?], s. XVI^{ex}
Christian III and Frederick II of Denmark, Laws (in Low Ger.)

1. ff. 1r-88r "Receß" of Christian III of Denmark, dated 1558, with a Register of the 70 articles. ff. 1v and 88v-89v blank

   Cf. *Stormectigste Hønborne Førstis oc Herris Her Christians den Eredie Danmarckis ... Recess* (Copenhagen: Laurentz Benedicht, 1567), in Danish.

2. ff. 90r-147r "Dat Dänische See-Recht" of Frederick II of Denmark dated 1561, with a Register of the 73 articles. ff. 90v and 147v-153v blank

   Cf. *Den Danske Søraet Som Stormectigste Hønborne Første oc Herre Her Frederick den Anden ...* (Copenhagen: Andrea Gutterwiß, 1577), in Danish.

3. ff. 154r-176r Laws of Frederick II of Denmark (*Krieges Schepes Artickell*), dated 1565, with 69 articles. ff. 154v and 176v-177v blank

4. ff. 178r-207r "Handtuestung" of Frederick II of Denmark dated 1559, with a Register of the 48 articles. f. 178v blank; ff. 207v-209v blank

   Cf. *Konning Frederich den Andens Handfaestning ...* (Copenhagen: Andrea Gutterwiß, 1577), in Danish.

5. ff. 210r-233v "Hoffrecht" of Frederick II of Denmark with a Register of the 47 articles, dated 9 May 1562. f. 210v blank

   Cf. *Baards Retthen Huorledis holdis skal paa kronens Slotte oc Gaarde offner alt Danmarckis ...* (Copenhagen: Andrea Gutterwiß, 1577), in Danish.

Paper (sturdy; watermarks buried in the gutter), ff. iii (paper) + i (contemporary paper) + 233 + iii (paper), 200 x 150 (ca. 135 x 95) mm. Written in 15-16 long lines, ruled in hard point, single vertical bounding lines only.
I-XXVIII^8. First 4 folios of quire signed in lower margin, recto (e.g., Bij, Biij, etc.).
Written by one scribe in cursive script.
Headings in large gothic textura, with flourishes.
Binding: s. xix^2. Tan and brown mottled calf, gold-tooled; on the spine, "DESZ BRODMECHTIGESTEN [*sic*] HOCHGEBARNEN FÖRSTENVIMD," and the crowned monogram of comte Paul Riant. By the same binder who did MS 24.

Written in Northern Germany or Denmark in the late 16th century, after 1565; perhaps copied by Pawel Hansen whose signature appears on ff. 154r, 178r. (The copy seems to have been made all at one time, not in separate sections as the laws were decreed.) Early provenance unknown. Sold by Weigel (Leipzig, 1881; note on original front flyleaf) to comte Paul Riant (bookplate, and monogram on spine; L. de German and L. Polain, *Catalogue de la Bibliothèque de feu M. le comte Riant* [Paris, 1896] v. 1, p. 362, no. 2487), whose Scandinavian library was given to Yale in 1896 by Mrs. Henry Farnam.

Bibliography: De Ricci, v. 1, p. 168, no. 31.

MS 32 (olim Z111.155) Netherlands, s. XV
Hours, use of Utrecht (in Netherlandish)

The contents of the surviving folios were worked out by N. R. Ker. Because the folios are so badly out of order, the contents are given by sections rather than by the present sequence of folios.

1. ff. 32-39   Penitential Psalms (incomplete at beginning) and Litany (breaks off before invocation of saints). Responses present (for lessons 1, 7, 8 and 9) correspond to Utrecht use.

2. ff. 24-26, 30-31, 27-29, 5-12, 16-23, 1, 40-41   Office of the Dead, Utrecht use, beginning at the third nocturn of Matins; prayers at the end to the Virgin and St. John the Evangelist. ff. 42r-43v ruled, but blank

3. ff. 2r-4v   Prayers in Netherlandish. //ende vereinghe mi mit di ... *Ene ghebet vanden sacrament*. Ic groet di inder afgronde diinre ewigher godliker minnen...; (f. 4r) *Een heilich man leert*. Als wy onsen heren sullen ontfaen so sellen wi gaen...; (f. 4v) *Dit seltu lesen alstu onsen heren ontfanghen hebste mit innich*//

4. ff. 13r-15v   Prayers in Netherlandish. //tende boven allen lichten want sonder di gheen lichtenis...; (f. 14r) *Ene ghebet vanden sacrament*. Danc segghen wi di almachtighe vader want du mi arme sondersche ... [Meertens, v. 6, p. 243]; (f. 14v) *Een goet ghebet*. Heer godstadighe in ons dattu heuest gewrocht in mi...; (f. 15r) *Een ghebet*. O heer ihesu christe die alle tut voer ons gheoffert wordste ... [Meertens, v. 6, p. 282]; (f. 15v) Here ihesu christe die mit wille des vaters ende des heilighen gheests ... die mi toe gheuoecht siin te bidden//

Parchment, ff. 43, 135 x 102 (72 x 52) mm. Written in 18 long lines; ruled in pale brown ink; double horizontal and single vertical bounding lines, full across; prickings in outer margins.

The manuscript is misbound. The collation of the surviving folios should probably be: I^8 (ff. 32-39), II^8 (ff. 24-26, 30-31, 27-29), III^8 (ff. 5-12), IV^8 (ff. 16-23), V^8 (ff. 1, 40-43; -2, 7, 8; 7 and 8 probably blank), VI^8 (ff. 2-4, 13-15; -4 and 5). The original position of VI is uncertain, but it probably came towards the end of the manuscript.

Written in liturgical gothic bookhand by a single scribe.

3-, 2-, and 1-line initials with very fine penwork: gold with dark blue penwork or blue with red penwork. 1-line initials within the text black with one or two red strokes. Line fillers: blue cables. Rubrics in orange-tinted red.

Water damage on ff. 8v, 38v and 39v has obliterated some initials; the text is still legible.

Binding: Date? Bookblock tacked to a vellum folder. The light rectangular patch on the front cover, lower left, was probably left by the removal of a shelf tag.

Written in Utrecht [?] in the 15th century. Signatures and notes on f. 42r (s. xix) with the name Anna Bogardus and "Bedelaer [?]"; another hand has added a note with reference to "Haerlem." Gift of John B. Galbraith in 1922.

Bibiliography: De Ricci, v. 1, p. 168, no. 32.

MS 33 (olim Z111.015)   France, s. XIV
Roman de la Rose

ff. 1r–114v   *Cest est le rommant de la rose.* Maintes gens dient que en songes/ Na se fables non et menconges/ ... Ainsi ai la la [*sic*] rose vermeille/ Atant fu iour et ie mesueille. Explicit.

F. Lecoy, *Le Roman de la Rose*, 3 vols. (Paris, 1966–70). Seventeen leaves containing lines 8242–10751 are now missing between ff. 39 and 40; in addition, the text has been abridged to 16272 lines.

Parchment, ff. iii (parchment) + 114 + ii (parchment), 315 x 223 (234 x 173) mm. Written in 2 columns, 36 lines of verse per column; double left, single right bounding lines for each column, full across; single horizontal bounding lines full across. Ruled in ink; remains of prickings in all margins except inner.
I–IV^8, V^8 (-8; also missing two quires of 8 after f. 39), VI–VIII^8, IX^6, X^9 (structure uncertain), XI^{10}, XII^8, XIII^{10}, XIV^8. Catchwords near lower edge, in gutter.

Written by a single scribe in neat gothic textura.

Plain initials, 2-line, alternating red and blue, throughout the text; headings in red. First letter of most verses stroked with yellow.

Slits in parchment on ff. 42–44, some affecting text.

Binding: s. xix, before 1881. A very fine Grolieresque binding in brick red goatskin, gold-tooled, by Rivière.

Written in France in the 14th century; early provenance unknown. Belonged to B. M. Pickering for whom it was rebound by Rivière. Bequeathed to Yale in 1883 by Joseph J. Cooke (1813–1881).

secundo folio: Semblot bien

Bibliography: De Ricci, v. 1, p. 168, no. 33.

P. Meyer, "De quelques manuscrits français conservés dans les bibliothèques des États-Unis," *Romania* 34 (1905) p. 88.

E. Langlois, *Les manuscrits du Roman de la Rose* (Lille, 1910) p. 196.

R. L. Hawkins, "The Manuscripts of the *Roman de la Rose* in the Libraries of Harvard and Yale Universities," *Romanic Review* 19 (1928) pp. 17-20, with plate of f. 94v.

MS 34 (olim Z111.0134m)   Spain, 1487, 1686
Carta Ejecutoria, etc. (in Sp.)

I. 1. ff. 3v-13r   Carta ejecutoria, or letter of nobility, granted to Don Alfonso Rodríguez (Tinagero Rodríguez de la Escalera) by the authority of King Ferdinand and Queen Isabel of Castile. Issued in Salamanca, 1487. Seal missing. ff. 13v-18v blank

II. 2. ff. 19r-74v   Numerous documents (all dated 1686) concerning a lawsuit involving Don Diego Tinagero Rodríguez de la Escalera of Seville, a descendant of Alfonso Rodríguez.

The codex is composed of two distinct sections bound together in the 18th [?] century, but with additional folios inserted: ff. iv (paper; watermarks similar in type to Heawood 743, with letters BL in central circle, heart in lower circle, and the number 4 below) + ii (parchment bifolium, s. xvii, with illumination) + 11 (Part I: parchment; ff. 3-13) + ii (parchment bifolium) + iii (paper; watermark similar in design to Heawood 743, with three circles in central circle and blank lower circle) + 56 (Part II: paper, several watermarks similar in design to Heawood 743 and 259-262; ff. 19-74) + iii (paper with same watermarks as first four flyleaves). The manuscript is too tightly bound to collate precisely.

Part I: 292 x 209 (218 x 150) mm. Written in 52 long lines; single bounding lines; ruled in hard point or lead. Round gothic script by a single scribe. Crude decorative border on f. 3v and REY (in gold, outlined in black) may be later additions.

Part II: 307 x 204 mm. This section has no uniform format. Written in various cursive hands. Many of the documents included appear to have once been folded. Some loss of text due to trimming.

Folios 1v and 2r have crudely illuminated full-page miniatures, s. xvii. Folio 1v: members of the Rodríguez family offering prayers to the Madonna and Child. Folio 2r: arms of the Tinagero Rodríguez de la Escalera family (per pale, vert, a tower argent, being climbed by a lion or holding a sword or in its teeth, on a ladder or, as a Moor [?] proper falls headlong from the top; or, 4 staves [?] palewise in fess, points to the base gules, hilted in brown [?]; border azur, with 8 crosses potent argent).

Binding: s. xviii? Thin wooden boards covered with dark brown leather, flesh side out. Vermilion and green ribbon fastenings.

Part I was written in Salamanca in 1487; Part II in Seville in 1686. Nineteenth-century ownership inscription of Juan Antonio Bula [?] on f. 77r. Presented to Yale University by Joseph M. Andreini in 1932.

secundo folio: pagar

Bibliography: De Ricci, v. 1, pp. 168-69, no. 34.

MS 34A Peru, 1740
Legal document (in Sp.)

The document establishes the rights of Don Bernardo Antonnio Ramirez Tinagero to property in the district of Ríobamba; dated 20 April 1740, Ciudad de los Reyes del Peru (Lima).

Paper (watermarks similar to Heawood 294-295 [with the number 4 added beneath circles] and to 740), ff. 8, 311 x 215 mm. The manuscript has no uniform format; it consists of a single gathering written in a fine italic hand. It was previously laid in Beinecke MS 34. The tops of ff. 1r and 8v bear stamps for the years 1739-1740.

Provenance and Bibliography: see MS 34.

MS 35 (olim Z111. + 0134n) Spain, 1550
Carta Ejecutoria (in Sp.)

1. f. 1r [Title, in same hand as text:] Executoria de fidalguia de Lope gonçalez de Ualdes y Pedro gonçalez de Ualdes hermanos uezinos del lugar de uillar del aguila.

2. ff. 1v-52v Carta ejecutoria, or letter of nobility, issued in the names of Lope Gonçalez de Valdes and Pedro Gonçalez de Valdes, by the authority of Charles V, Emperor of the Holy Roman Empire, dated 12 September 1550 in Granada. Seal missing.

3. ff. 52v-53v Official recording of the document in Villar del Aguila (Huete), dated 21 October 1550 (signed by scribe inside back cover: Don Antonio Larrillo).

Parchment, ff. 54 (contemporary foliation begins on 2), 325 x 226 (230 x 156) mm. Written in 36 long lines; double vertical and double upper horizontal bounding lines, full across. Ruled in ink; prickings in margins for bounding lines only. Consists of a single gathering.

Written in round gothic by one scribe who added decorative designs in upper and lower margins. Addition on ff. 52v–53v by Don Antonio Larrillo is in a similar hand.

The ornamentation of the codex is poorly executed. Folio 1v: miniatures representing the crowning of the Virgin (upper left) and the arms of the Gonçalez de Valdes family at bottom of folio (quarterly per cross potence gules throughout, first and fourth argent, 3 bars azur between 10 roundels chequy or and gules; second azur, a sword palewise argent, hilted in base or, between 4 fleur-de-lis or; third or, a tower triple-towered argent with a lion dormant brown [sic], langued gules, in chief a crescent argent); f. 2r: miniature of Justice, with scales (lower half of page). Both folios have elaborate decorative borders in gold and colors that are badly rubbed. Folios 4v and 52r have historiated initials with portraits of a seated king (Rey Don Iohan?). Twenty-five small painted initials, 7- to 5-line; gold letters with black pen designs on white-decorated blue and dark red backgrounds.

Binding: Bookblock laid in a contemporary vellum wrapper with an envelope flap.

Written in Granada and Villar del Aguila in 1550; early provenance unknown. Pencil notation inside front cover: "22/1.450". Gift of the Yale Library Associates in 1931.

Bibliography: De Ricci, v. 1, p. 169, no. 35.

MS 36 (olim Z111.0147)   Italy, s. XVII
Cesare Speciano, Propositioni christiane   Pl. 32
   et civili subalternate a Dio

1. f. 1r   [Title page:] Propositioni christiane et ciuili subalternate à Dio ... Questo libro si commincio à Roma d'Ottobre l'anno 1585.

2. ff. 2r–3v   Monitione, followed by Preface to the reader in which the author states that he completed the work while he was serving as Papal nuntius of Pope Clement VIII in Prague in 1597.

3. ff. 4r–271r   Chi hà luoco principale appresso un Prencipe sauio è buon mezzo dà conseruarselo ... perche ne riuscirà male al sicuro e darà occasione di disgusti in abondanza.

N. Mosconi, "Per la storia della riforma Cattolica," *Convivium* 3 (1931) pp. 347–63.

Paper (unidentified watermarks: paschal lamb, with countermark PP plus clover; bird on mountain enclosed in a circle), ff. 273 + iv (paper; iv = pastedown), 282 x 200 (216 x 155) mm. Written in ca. 23 long lines; no visible system of bounding lines or prickings.

The binding is too tight to permit collation. Catchwords appear on most folios, below written space, on both recto and verso.

Written by a single scribe in a neat italic hand.

Binding: s. xvii. A fine binding of vermilion goatskin, gold-tooled, with unidentified arms of a cardinal (vair) stamped in gilt on both covers. Edges gilt and gauffered. Unobtrusive repairs at head and tail of spine and joints.

Written in Italy in the seventeenth century, possibly for the unidentified cardinal for whom it was bound. Ownership evidence includes the following, but the precise sequence of owners is unclear: inscriptions on ff. 1r and 271r "G. Stork a Milano 1802 In. No. 12203"; mutilated tag of bookdealers inside front cover "Milano. Pietro e Giusseppe Vallardi"; circular stamp in f. 1r "HL Musée Napoléan épreuve d'essai"; signature on f. 271r: "Ex libris Albertus Comes Potocki"; this appears to be the same Potocki family from whose collection a Psalter (now Bib. Narodowa 8003) was acquired by the National Library in Warsaw in 1933 (see Z. Ameisenowa, *Francuskie rękopisy illuminowane z Wilanowa w Bibljotece Narodowej* [Cracow, 1933] p. 4) and who owned Paris, B. N. n. a. l. 540. Bequeathed to Yale University in 1883 by Joseph J. Cooke.

Bibliography: De Ricci, v. 1, p. 169, no. 36.

MS 37 (olim Z111.0155)   Italy, s. XV, XVII
Vita di San Petronio, etc. (in It. and Lat.)

I. ff. 1r-18v [Vita de S. Petronio] Questa sie la legenda del nostro padre mesiere sam petronio ... corpo de ihesu christo lo quale sostene pena per mij peccadurj insu//

   The text is defective throughout.

II. ff. 19r-53v [Tommaso Nacci Caffarini:] *Incipit quidam Tractatus de stigmatibus extractus de secunda parte libelli. Qui intitulatur Libellus de supplemento legende beate Katerine de senis* ... Quoniam in secunda parte legende uirginis beate katerine de senis et signanter in sexto capitulo fit mencio de stigmatibus ... Propter sacra vulnera et cetera vt supra in laudibus.

   The text is accompanied by marginal notes, some trimmed.

III. ff. 54r-89r [Federico Borromeo, *Vita S. Caroli Borromei:*] *Antonio Caraffae Cardinali Amplissimo*. Historiam esse ueritatis testem, nuntiam uetustatis, et magistram uitae optime nosti ... [text:] *Caroli Cardinalis Borromei uita*. Quae est naturae humanae peruersitas ut quae imitari nos posse diffidimus falsa putemus ... qui uiuunt quos sanctissimis suis donis in dies magis dita et pro tua benignitate ditabit. f. 89v blank

IV. ff. 90r-146v   *Aeneae Siluij Piccolominei Foederici Rom. Regis Secretarij et oratoris*

De morte eugenij Quarti creationeque et coronatione Niccolai V oratio ... Cupere te Princeps serenissime que nostra in legatione sunt gesta referre tibi ... reddes et ad suscipiendam coronam Imperij iter habebis apertum. Finis. ff. 147r–148v blank

V. ff. 149r–166r [Thomas Obicinus; title on f. 149r:] Motiuo Celeste diretto in questo segnato tempo [f. 149v blank; text begins on 150r:] Vedendo il negotio tanto graue per il quale mi sono partito ... la uolontà de Prelati e Prencipi simile che l'opera del signore si farà. Amen.

The codex is composed of five separate manuscripts bound together (one flyleaf of paper contemporary with binding at front and back).

Part I: Paper (sturdy; watermarks: unidentified mountain with cross, in gutter), ff. 18 (contemporary foliation lxxxii–c; the order of the folios is lxxxii–iii, lxxxv–vi, lxxxviii–viiii, lxxxxii–iii, lxxxiii, lxxxvii, lxxxxviii, lxxxx, lxxxxviiii–c, lxxxxv–vi, lxxxxiiii, lxxxxvii; modern foliation 1–18), 259 x 195 (185 x 147) mm. Written in two columns of 28 lines; frame-ruled in hard point. Round humanistic by a single scribe. Simple penwork initials in red or blue, some with penwork designs of the other color. Waterstained and mended throughout.

Part II: Paper (sturdy; watermarks: unidentified unicorn, in gutter), ff. 35 (old foliation, in same hand as marginal notes: 1–35; modern foliation: 19–53), 272 x 201 (206 x 140) mm. Written in ca. 39 lines; frame-ruled in lead. Small neat round textura in a single hand; catchwords in center of lower margin. Uninspired and badly rubbed historiated initial (Christ [?] displaying stigmata) on gold background with three gold dots, f. 19r; small decorative initials in red with black penwork designs, or blue with red. Paragraph marks in red or blue. Folios have been trimmed with some loss of marginalia.

Part III: Paper (watermarks similar to Briquet Fleur de Lis 7107), ff. 37 (old foliation: 199–233; modern foliation: 54–89), 280 x 200 (205 x 140) mm. Written in 20 long lines (no visible guide-lines or prickings) by one scribe in a calligraphic italic hand. Catchwords under written space on each page, on verso. Waterstained throughout.

Part IV: Paper (watermarks: unidentified eagle on a mountain, enclosed by a circle), ff. 58 (contemporary foliation: 37–94; modern foliation: 90–147), 274 x 197 (195 x 112) mm. Ca. 17 long lines; single vertical bounding lines ruled in hard point; italic hand by a single scribe. Catchwords under written space on verso of each folio.

Part V: Paper (unidentified watermarks obscured by text), ff. 20 (modern foliation: 148–67), 259 x 199 (226 x 155) mm. 28 lines per page written in a small italic hand by one scribe; single vertical bounding lines produced apparently by folding the leaves. Catchwords under written space on verso of each folio.

The manuscript has been damaged and repaired too extensively to permit an accurate collation.

Binding: s. xviii–xix. Vellum and paste paper case.

All five parts were written in Italy; I and II in the 15th century and III-V in the 17th century. The codex as it is now composed belonged to Abate Matteo Canonici; his sale in 1835 to the Rev. Walter Sneyd (1809-1882; see Sir T. Phillipps, *Catalogus manuscriptorum in bibliothecis Angliae*, p. 15, no. 20). Sneyd sale (London, 16 Dec. 1903, no. 164) to Quaritch. Unconfirmed library note indicates that the manuscript went to Germany. Purchased by Yale in 1907 with the Ann S. Farnum Fund.

Bibliography: De Ricci, v. 1, p. 169, no. 37.

MS 38 France, s. XIV/XV
Boethius, Fr. tr. Renaut de Louhans Pl. 11

ff. 1r-55v [Author's Prologue consisting of eighteen 8-line stanzas; his name is spelled by the first letter of each stanza:] Fortune mere de tristesce/ de douleur et de affliction/ ... [text begins on f. 2r:] *Ci parle boece au commencement du primier liure*. Je souloye jadis penser/ dicter ensaigner et escripre/ ... [epilogue ends:] Il en sera tout elerement/ Fait cy apres Rebrichement.

As Renaut de Louhans states in the prologue, his work incorporates material from a commentary on Boethius made by another member of the Dominican order (Nicholas Trevet) as well as his own digressions. See F. Nagel, *Die altfranzösische Übersetzung der Consolatio philosophiae des Boëthius von Renaut von Louhans* (Halle, 1890); R. H. Lucas, "Medieval French Translations of the Latin Classics to 1500," *Speculum* 45 (1970) p. 232; R. A. Dwyer, *Boethian Fictions: Narratives in the Medieval French Versions of the De Consolatione Philosophiae* (Cambridge, Mass., 1976) p. 130, no. 9. Critical edition in preparation by J. K. Atkinson (see *Speculum* 56 [1981] p. 227).

Parchment, ff. i (paper) + 55 + i (paper), 282 x 205 (225 x 145) mm. Written in 2 columns of 33 lines; three single vertical bounding lines, one at the left edge of each column and one along outer edge of folio; single horizontal bounding lines; all full across. Ruled in lead; prickings in upper, lower and outer margins, for bounding lines only.

I-V^{10}, VI^{2}, VII^{6} (-4, 5, 6). Catchwords in lower margins within decorative rectangle, on verso; some quire-marks (e.g., bi, bii, etc.) in lower right corner, on recto.

Written in bâtarde by a single scribe.

Two intricate penwork initials, 5-line, on ff. 1r and 2r in red and blue; less detailed penwork initials, 3-line, in same colors throughout text; first letter of each verse stroked in red.

Binding: s. xvii-xviii. Brown spattered calf, with peculiarly striped turn-ins. Title, in gold, on spine: BOECE EN VER FRANC.

Written in France at the end of the 14th or beginning of the 15th century; early provenance unknown. Purchased by Stanley W. Childs in 1932 from Goldschmidt's (cat. 26, appendix, no. 203A) for the Albert H. Childs Memorial Collection.

secundo folio: Par enuie qui

Bibliography: De Ricci, v. 1, p. 170, no. 38; Faye and Bond, p. 25, no. 38.

MS 39 (olim Z113.21) Denmark, s. XV
Sjaelland, Denmark: Logbok

We thank W. F. Hansen and F. Blaisdell for assisting with the following Danish transcriptions.

1. ff. 1r–227r *Hær børies een fortale aa danske ther man kaller prolgus* [sic] *aa latine. Capitulum primum.* Meth logh scal land bygges Æn vilde hwer man orues at sit eget oc lade man nyde jæffnet tha ... [text begins, f. 4r:] *i. Om Arff.* Fader oc mother ær søn oc datter næst ... hører koning enæ som guld eller sylff oc ængen æmbetzm** [erasure]

   The text differs considerably from that in the edition of the *Laws of Siaelantz* published in Copenhagen, 1495 [?], "in ... Hoos gotfrid aff geme," ff. 2r–96r.

2. ff. 227r–232r [Heading:] Thette ær then rætt som sat var a malstæffnæ i Ringstæde ... [text:] Kircke om vigd vorter maa æy annen sinnæ vighes vtæn løøs vorter ... hwndertæ vinter oc syntyng vinter oc sy [ink blotch] maanede oc tolff daghe.

   Ibid., ff. 96r–99v; text similar, but not identical.

3. ff. 232r–240r [Heading:] Thette ær then log ther koning Eric ... [text, f. 232v:] Thet hauer oc koning jæt riget at ængen man scal fanges vtæn han ... alle som i hans raat æren Oc serdeles høwetzmen.

   Ibid., ff. 99v–106v; text similar, but not identical.

4. ff. 240r–244v [Heading:] Hwilke oc sonne rætt haue skule e huan the legge eller ære [followed by "tafflen"]. [Text, f. 240v:] Hwilken man annen slar i hiell. Oc vorter han gerpen juz færske ... tha næffnæ hwer therræ thre mæn aff garden// [ends imperfectly in section 21]

5. ff. 245r–265v //I guts naffn amen aar æffter guts byrd ... scal hawe wij latet vort sechret hænghe//

   Unidentified legal work, apparently imperfect at beginning and end.

Paper (light-weight; watermarks in gutter similar to Briquet Main 11417 and Lettre P 8636), ff. 265, 191 x 136 (135 x 85) mm. Written in 19–22 long lines; frame-ruled in lead.

I^{10}, II^{12} (-12), III^{14}, IV-XVIII^{12}, XIX^{12} (-1), XX^{12} (-12), XXI-XXII^{14}.
Written in a running script with some looped ascenders, by one scribe.

Crude 2-line initials, in orange. Paragraph marks and slashes between sentences, also in orange.

Waterstains and signs of wear on most folios, some affecting the legibility of the text.

Binding: s. xvi-xvii rebinding? Sewn on three vegetable fiber, double cords, the previous sewing caught up. No endbands. The cords are laced and pegged into oak boards. Between the cords the spine is lined with vellum strips which extend into the inside of the boards. Covered in reddish-brown calf, blind-tooled with a vine scroll St. Andrew's cross set in a panel border of the same on the lower board; concentric panels, two with vine scrolls on the upper. There is a brass catch on the upper board, the stub of a vellum strap attached to the lower one. The leather is wanting in the spine area.

Written in Denmark in the 15th century; early provenance unknown. Inscription in a cursive hand (s. xviii?) inside front cover: "Then Rätte Sialanske Logh Bog, in sex libros diuisos, quos Ordinationes Ecclesiasticae excipiunt." Sold by Cohn of Berlin in 1884 (entry from catalogue pasted inside front cover) to comte Paul Riant (bookplate; L. de Germon and L. Polain, *Catalogue de la bibliothèque de feu M. le comte Riant* [Paris, 1896] v. 1, p. 360, no. 2474) whose Scandinavian library was given to Yale in 1896 by Mrs. Henry Farnam.

secundo folio: oc værieløse

Bibliography: De Ricci, v. 1, p. 170, no. 39.

MS 40
Attainder of Lord Cromwell

England, s. XVII

ff. 2r-10r *Anno xxxii H: 8 In⁰. The Attainder of the Lord Cromwell. Soit faict come il est desire* ... In their most humblewise shewing to your most Royal Majestie the Lords ... this said Article of Attainder or any other Article Provision or thing heretofore had or made to the contrary Notwithstanding. ff. 1r-v and 10v-12v blank

For this Act of Attainder (of which Beinecke MS 40 is a later copy) see *Rotuli Parliamentorum* ... (London, n.d.) 32. h. 8; calendared in detail but not verbatim in *Letters and Papers, Foreign and Domestic, of the Reign of Henry VIII, 1509-47*, XV, 498 (60).

Paper (watermarks similar to Heawood 348), ff. 12, 330 x 212 (277 x 151) mm. Written in ca. 25 lines; frame-ruled in ink; prickings at corners of written space, plus one along each vertical bounding line in outer margin.

The manuscript is composed of a single gathering, unbound.
Written in a neat cursive script by one scribe.

Written in England in the 17th century; provenance unknown; no Beinecke library files concerning it.

Bibliography: De Ricci, v. 1, p. 170, no. 40.

MS 41 Germany, s. XV^{in}
Breviary, pars aestivalis, use of Carmelites

1. f. 1r   blank except for ownership notes (see below); f. 1v   antiphons and capitula.

2. ff. 2r–7v   Graded calendar in red and black with numerous later additions; among the feasts are those of Basil (8 Jan., duplex, added), Honoratus (16 Jan., 9 lessons, added), Faustinus and Jovita (15 Feb., 9 lessons, added), Cyril (6 March, duplex, in red), Joseph (19 March, duplex, added), Angelus "ordinis carmelitarum" (5 May, duplex, added), Albert of Trapani "confessoris ordinis nostri" (7 Aug., duplex, in red), Conception of the Virgin (8 Dec., totum duplex, added). Many other saints from the Roman Martyrology have been added incorrectly: wrong date, wrong attribute or wrong gender (e.g. Crescentiana and Juliana virgins on 12 August).

3. ff. 8r–62r   Temporale from Easter through the Saturday after the first Sunday in November. ff. 62v–63v ruled, but blank

4. ff. 64r–74v   Gospel readings for the 24 Sundays after Trinity.

5. ff. 75r–78v   Offices of the anniversary of the dedication of a church, and of its octave.

6. ff.79r–194v   Matins of the Sanctorale from Ambrose (4 April) through Linus (26 November).

7. ff. 194v–198v   Suffrages added by a later hand throughout the liturgical year to the Virgin, Anna, all angels, all saints and for peace; benedictions for Matins.

8. ff. 199r–224r   Common of saints.

9. ff. 224v–228v   Commemoration of the Virgin, for Matins only, with 2 sets of 9 lessons.

10. ff. 229r–258r   Lauds through Compline of the Sanctorale from Ambrose (4 April) through Linus (26 November) with some later additions in the margins.

11. ff. 258r–259r   Added by several different hands: antiphons to the Virgin; an antiphon *De sancto angelo carmelitarum*; an office to John the Evangelist before the Latin Gate; antiphons to Gereon and for the octave of Martin.

12. ff. 259v–260r   Added in a later hand, a list of feasts, January to November,

with a note of local veneration (usually Ravenna, Florence and Rome); many of these feasts were also added to the calendar. Of particular interest are the entries for 6 March, "Cirilli presbiteri et confessoris ordinis nostri in monte Carmeli", and for 16 May, "Simonis [Stock] ordinis nostri confessoris burdegale". f. 260v, versicles and responses from the common of saints.

Paper (with parchment conjugate leaves at beginning and end of quires; calendar on parchment), ff. ii (parchment) + 260 + ii (parchment), 143 x 100 (90 x 63) mm. Written in ca. 36 long lines; single vertical bounding lines ruled in ink; horizontal guide-lines for written space in lead. Prickings in upper and lower margins.

The binding is too tight to permit precise collation, but most gatherings seem to be composed of 12 leaves. Remains of catchwords along lower edge near gutter.

Written primarily by a single scribe (see below) in an informal, but careful, gothic script. Numerous additions by contemporary and later writers.

Plain initials and KL monograms, 6- to 1-line, in red. Rubrics throughout. Paragraph marks, underlining, and initial strokes in red. The verso of the final folio bears the partially erased image of a large decorative initial, in green, over which the later text was written (see art. 12).

Binding: s. xix. Head and fore-edge gilt, with tawed, pink markers on the fore-edge. Bound by William Matthews, a leading American binder (second half of the 19th century) in a dark brown goatskin Jansenist binding (plain outside with gold-tooled doublures).

Written probably in Mainz at the beginning of the 15th century by the scribe Gerhardus de Castris for Carmelite use, as shown by the saints in the calendar: the feasts of Basil, Albert, the Conception and daily commemoration of Anna (cf. art. 7) were incorporated into Carmelite liturgy in 1411; all appear here as subsequent additions. The feast of Cyril, here in the main hand, was introduced in 1399. Ownership note (s. xv) on f. 1: "Ad Carmelitas Conventus Moguntinensis fratrum beatissime marie virginis Breviarium Estivale de tempore et de sanctis Manu Venerabilis patris Gerhardi de Castris quondam ibidem prioris scripti [*sic*] et cetera". On f. 2 (s. xvii) "Carmeli Moguntino, N. n. 8". On f. 1r (s. xvii?) "Ling[?] N. 148". Of s. xix, the signature of Leander van Ess with the number 65 (f. 1r); the book has been rebound and there is no evidence to suggest that it was sold with the van Ess collection to Sir Thomas Phillipps. Bequeathed to Yale by John W. Sterling (1844-1918; no. 80 in the inventory of his estate).

secundo folio: [calendar, f. 3:] KL Marcius
　　　　　　　 [text, f. 9:] [in exi]tu hij

Bibliography: De Ricci, v. 1, p. 170, no. 41.

MS 42 Italy, s. XV^2
Gradual

1. ff. 1r–3r   Rubrics for the mass, under the heading *Incipit ordo Graduale secundum consuetudinem romane curie.*

2. ff. 3r–97v   Graduale from Andrew to Clement, including full offices for Agatha (f. 18r), Zenobius (f. 39r), John the Baptist (f. 42v), Felicitas (f. 52v) and Lawrence (ff. 63v and 72v).

3. ff. 97v–215r   Commune sanctorum.

4. f. 215r–v   Office for Ansanus.

5. ff. 215v–219v   Dedication of a Church.

6. ff. 219v–224v   Office of the Dead. Ends imperfectly: Requiem eternam dona eis domine et lux perpetua luceat// Catchword: eis.

7. first flyleaf at back: Index in a later hand, titled "Repertorium rerum omnium quae in hoc libro continentur dispositum a Fratre Elia Pinelli." Arranged alphabetically under the headings Introitus, Graduales, Alleluia, Tractus, Offertoria, and Communiones.

Parchment, ff. i (cardboard) + i (slightly later parchment) + 226 (foliated by original scribe with red Roman numerals, beginning with *i* on f. 1 verso and including 98 *bis*; modern foliation in pencil, used above, includes 59 *bis*) + i (slightly later parchment) + i (cardboard), 645 x 438 (425 x 270) mm. Written in long lines, 6 staves with 6 lines of text; ruled in lead, double vertical bounding lines full across.

I–V^{10}, VI^{10} (–3, after f. 52, cut out; traces of off-set color from a full border remain on f. 52v), VII–XXII^{10}, XXIII^6. Catchwords to right of the inner bounding lines, perpendicular to text, surrounded by flourishes with yellow wash or three dots.

Written by one scribe in large round gothic bookhand. Index added later by Frater Elia Pinelli, in humanistic script.

Three historiated initials; that on f. 3r (Sts. Peter and Andrew), the Calling of Sts. Peter and Andrew, is of high quality and close in style to work of Francesco di Lorenzo Roselli; purple, with white floral highlights; ornate purple, blue and green fruit and floral border, inner margin, with candelabra, hair-spray and gold dots. The two other historiated initials are of inferior quality: f. 78v (Holy Cross) Cross with Arma Christi and f. 22r (Mass of the Dead) two roundels: skull and cross-bones against a landscape and skeleton with scythe against a black ground. Very fine penwork 3- and 2-line initials comparable to, but more ornate than initials by Guinifortus de Vicomercato (cf. Indiana University, Lilly Library MS Ricketts 240, in *Two Thousand Years of Calligraphy*, exhib. cat. [Baltimore, 1965] pp. 54 and 59, no. 38; Oxford, Bod. Lib. Canon. Pat. Lat. 177, in Pächt and Alexander, v. 2, no. 253; and Vatican, Lat. Ottob. 183); done in red or blue (one on f. 57r in gold), decorated with white bands and jewels, with blue and red penwork, large illusionistic jewel studs and simple fruit and floral borders, painted in purple, blue, green, and yellow or in pen, red, blue with some black and yellow; initial on f. 189r with two seraphim. Some 2-line initials incorporate ivy or fruit swags. 1-line initials, red or blue, divided, with blue or red penwork, jewel studs, circles and lozenges, in green, yellow and tan. Square musical notation on 4-line red staves. Rubrics throughout.

Binding: s. xvii-xviii. Original sewing on 6 double cords, each covered with brown leather and probably nailed to inside of boards. Red and gold wound endbands. Heavy wooden boards are covered with thick leather [cowskin?] and the spine is covered separately with leather nailed to the edge of each board. There are four brass corner pieces and a large central boss on each board, bosses protruding from the three outer edges, and a strap-and-pin fastening, the pin on the lower board.

Written in Italy in the second half of the 15th century; the offset on f. 53v of an elaborately decorated border for the opening leaf of the office of St. Felicitas suggests that the codex was originally produced for an institution associated with this saint. Given in 1679 to a church of Sta. Lucia by R. P. Jo. Ant. Disdotti of Bergamo; inscription on verso of second front flyleaf, reads: "D. O. M. R. P. Jo. Ant. Disdotti Bergomensis Ecclesiae Chori Sacristi atque Conuenti huius Procurator, nec non et assiduus Benefactor, Qui dum operabatur pro sacris paramentis reficiendis, et ex nouis ornando Sacristiam, In vigilia S. Andreae Apostoli Anni Domini MDCLXXIX ad Chori decus istum Librum transmisit, et omnia in honorem eiusdem Dei, atque Beatae Virginis Mariae, ac Sanctae Luciae Virginis et Martyris huius Ecclesiae Titularis quo eius solemni die primo Liber apertus fuit ad cantandum." On verso of end flyleaf, crude arms done in pen and ink (s. xviii?) of the Convent at Prato and Santa Maria Novella of Florence. Obtained in Florence in 1903 by Addison van Name. Gift of Victor O. Freeburg in 1953.

Bibliography: De Ricci, v. 1, p. 170, no. 42.

MS 43 (olim ZZ109.55)   Italy, s. XV^2
Psalter, etc.

1. ff. 1r-2v   Invitatories: Venite exultemus, Preoccupemus faciem, Quoniam deus magnus, In manu tua domine, Venite adoremus, Dominum qui fecit nos, Adoremus dominum, followed by the hymns Primo dierum omnium and Nocte surgentes.

2. ff. 3r-176r   Liturgical Psalter (Pss. 1-108) with hymns, canticles, and antiphons. Capitals *A* and *B* in outer margins every two Psalms, perhaps to denote change in reader.

3. ff. 176r–195v   Hymns for Matins and Lauds, ends imperfectly: (f. 176v) *In aduentu domino Ad nocturnum hymnus*. Verbum supernum prodiens a patre olim exiens ... [RH 21391]; (f. 177r) *Ad laudes hymnus*. Uox clara ecce intonat obscura queque increpat ... [RH 22199]; (f. 177v) *In natiuitate domini Ad nocturnum hymnus*. Christe redemptor omnium ex patre patris unice ... [RH 2960]; (f. 178r) *Ad laudes hymus*. A solis ortus cardine adusque terre limitem christum canamus principem natum maria uirgine Beatus auctor ... [RH 26]; (f. 178v) *In epyphanya domini*. Hostis herodes impie christum uenire quid times ... [RH 8073]; (f. 179v) *Dominica in XL^a Ad nocturnum hymnus*. Ex more docti mistico seruemus hoc ieiunium deno dierum circulo ducto quatuor notissimo. Lex et...; (f. 180v) *Ad laudes hymnus*. Iam christe sol iustitie mentis deiscant tenebre uirtutum ... [RH 9205]; (f. 181r) *Dominica de passione Ad nocturnum hymus*. Pange lingua gloriosi prelium certaminis et ... [RH 14481]; (f. 181v) *Ad laudes hymus*. Lustris sex qui iam peractis tempus implens corporis ... [RH 10765]; (f. 182v) *Dominica prima post pascha Ad nocturnum hymnus*. Rex eterne domine rerum creator omnium qui eras ante secula ... [cf. RH 17392]; (f. 183v) *Ad laudes hymnus*. Aurora lucis rutilat celum laudibus intonat mundus exultans ... [RH 1644]; (f. 183v) *In natiuitate apostolorum a pascha usque ad pentecosten. Ad nocturnum hymnus*. Tristes erant apostoli de nece sui domini quem pena mortis ... [RH 20589]; (f. 184v) *In ascensione domini ad nocturnum hymnus*. Eterne rex altissime redemptor et fidelium quo mors soluta ... [RH 654]; (f. 185v) *Ad laudes hymnus*. Ihesu nostra redemptio amor et desiderium deus creator ... [RH 9582]; (f. 186r) *In festo pentecostes. Ad nocturnum hymnus*. Iam christus astra ascenderat regressus unde uenerat ... [RH 9215]; (f. 186v) *Ad laudes hymnus*. Beata nobis gaudia anni reduxit orbita cum ... [RH 2339]; (f. 187v) *In festo Sanctissime trinitatis. Ad nocturnum hymnus*. O lux beata trinitas tres unum trium ... [RH 13155]; (f. 188r) *Ad laudes hymnus*. Festi laudes hodierni ritu ductas annuo ciues gaudio ... [RH 6151]; (f. 188v) *In festo corporis christi. Ad nocturnum hymnus*. Sacris sollemnijs iuncta sint gaudia et ... [RH 17713]; (f. 189v) *Ad laudes hymnus*. Uerbum supernum prodiens nec patris linquens dexteram ad opus ... [RH 21398]; (f. 190r) *In conuersione sancti pauli. Ad nocturnum hymnus*. Doctor egregie paule mores instrue et mente polum nos transferre ... [RH 4791]; (f. 190r) *Ad laudes hymnus. In cathedra sancti petri [ad nocturnum* crossed out] *hymnus*. Iam bone pastor petre clemens accipe uota ... [RH 9196]; (f. 190v) *Ad nocturnum hymnus*. Quodcumque uinclis [*sic*] super terram strinxerit erit in astris religatum ... [leaf missing after f. 190; RH 16918]; (f. 191v) *In festo omnium Sanctorum. Ad nocturnum hymnus*. Christe redemptor omnium conserua tuos famulos beate semper uirginis ... [RH 2959]; (f. 192r) *Ad laudes hymnus*. Ihesu saluator seculi redemptis ope subueni et pia dei genitrix ... [RH 9677]; (f. 192v) *In natiuitate apostolorum Ad nocturnum hymnus*. Eterna christi munera apostolorum gloriam laudes canentes ... [RH 590]; (f. 193r) *Ad laudes hymnus*. Exultet celum laudibus resultet terra gaudijs apostolorum gloriam sacra canunt ... [RH 5832]; (f. 193v) *In natiuitate unius martyris ad nocturnum hymnus*. Deus tuorum militum sors et corona premium

laudes canentes martyris absolue martyres et bestiarum dentibus ... [cf. RH 25455]; (f. 194r) *Ad laudes hymnus*. Rex gloriose matyrum [*sic*] corona confitentium qui respuentes terrena ... [cf. RH 32927]; (f. 194v) *In natiuitate confessorum ad nocturnum hymnus*. Iste confessor domini sacratus festa plebs cuius celebrat per orbem ... [RH 9136]; (f. 195r) *Pro confessoribus pontifex. Ad laudes hymnus*. Ihesu redemptor omnium perpes corona presulum in hac die ... [RH 9628]; (f. 195v) *Pro confessor non pontifex. Ad laudes hymnus*. Ihesu corona celsior et ueritas sublimior qui confitenti seruulo reddis ... Anni recurso tempore, dies illuxit lumine//

Parchment, ff. i (contemporary parchment) + 195, 575 x 385 (385 x 250) mm. Written in 15 long lines; single horizontal bounding lines; double rulings for each line of text; ruled in ink or crayon.
I-XIX^{10}, XX^{10} (-1, 7 through 9). Catchwords in center of lower margin.
Written in a large round gothic bookhand; space between double rulings ca. 13 mm.
One crude historiated initial, 6-line (Ps. 1): David seated on ground with both hands raised in prayer, against a blue ground, the letter-form tan, orange, and red with white filigree; large blue, green, pink, and red acanthus leaves at the corners, against a gold ground, edged with two thick black bands, penwork, gold dots, and hair-spray. In bottom margin a "YHS" monogram, against a blue ground, inside sunburst and green, pink, and blue wreath, supported by large bud from which sprout two large acanthus leaves, red berries, gold dots and hair-spray, as above. 6- or 5-line initials (ff. 37v, Ps. 26; 60r, Ps. 38; 79v, Ps. 52; 98v, Ps. 68; 126r, Ps. 80; 148r, Ps. 97; 176r, Hymns for Matins and Lauds) red and/or blue, with large green or red dots, elaborate purple calligraphic decoration, portions filled with green and tan. 2-line initials, red or blue, with calligraphic ornament and flourishes, as above. 1-line initials, blue or red, with guide-letters throughout. On f. 160v a large pen drawing of a hand pointing to text.
Binding: s. xvi-xvii. Sewn on five tawed skin straps. Plain, wound endbands on cores laced into tunnels in the edges of heavy wooden boards. Covered with three separate pieces of dark brown leather [cowskin?] with leather straps extending across the spine and nailed to the boards over the sewing straps. Each board has four corner pieces, a central boss and a strip of metal, probably iron, nailed around the four edges. Strap-and-pin fastening, the pin on the lower board, stubs of pink, tawed straps attached to the upper one. Fragments from several parchment manuscripts and early printed texts used as binding reinforcements.

Written perhaps in Northern Italy in the second half of the 15th century; early provenance unknown. The number "383" is written inside front cover. There is no record of its acquisition by Yale.

secundo folio: [expi]atos sordibus

Bibliography: De Ricci, v. 1, p. 171, no. 43.

MS 44 Yale Art Gallery

MS 45   England, s. XVII
Basilici tyranni umbra, etc.

1. f. 1r-v   On f. 1r, pen trials and signatures (see provenance); f. 1v seems to contain a portion of art. 2 omitted by the scribe.

2. ff. 2r-39v   Basilici tyranni umbra. Argumentum. Anno a virginis partu 492 Zeno genere Isauritus [precise reading marred by later correction] homo luxuriae atque immanitate infamis orientis regebat imperium....

   Latin tragedy with a list of characters drawn partly from Byzantine history, including *Umbra Basilici tyranni* (d. 497), Zeno *Imperator*, Longinus *eius frater*, Gazeus *Rhetor*, Euphemianus, Castor *tribunus militum*, and various *pupilli* and *ephebi*.

Articles 3-28 are primarily poems in Horatian meters on early Jesuits, e. g., St. Francis Xavier (1506-52), Brother Rudolph Acquaviva (1550-83), St. Ignatius of Loyola (1491-1556), St. Aloysius Gonzaga (1568-91), and Edmund Campion (d. 1581).

3. ff. 40r-42v   Ingreditur Iaponia amictu lugubri, altera manu fractam crucem, altera pugionem tenens. [text:] Siste focum te causa manet nunc altera iudex/ non duxit sortes vrna citata meas/....

   Signed at the conclusion by R. P. G.

4. ff. 42r-44v   Satis est Domine Satis est. [text:] Liquerat astrorum fulgentia culmina sedes/ Atque iter in terras sollicitabat Amor/....

5. ff. 44v-46r   Aloisius amore divino accensus velut Narcissus in Lilium convertitur. [text:] Quid Nymphe resonae filia verulae/ Quae gaudes vitreis garrula fontibus/....

6. ff. 46r-47v   Idem ffratri Rudolpho suadet ne rebus caducis fidat. [text:] Non semper viridem Cirrha superbiam/ Lactat, nec croceis halat odoribus/....

7. ff. 47v-49r   Ignatius more militari arma sua consecrat Deiparae. [text:] Exurge apricis Calliope rosis/ Regina collis musa biuertitis/....

8. f. 49v   In chastitatitis [*sic*] lilium proseucticon. [text:] Amoenus ipse amoenos/ fert flosculos Hymettus/....

9. ff. 50r-51v   Mortalia quaeque esse caduca. Ode. [text:] Heu! heu rapaci gloria labitur/ Correpta gressu: nec datur insuper/....

10. ff. 51v-53r   Valerianus a Sponsa conversus ex divino amore opprimitur. Elegeia. [text:] Ah! quanta aethereos pertentant gaudia cives/ cum tanto humanus langueat igne sinus/....

11. f. 53r [Untitled poem added at bottom of folio:] Arma belluosa pubes/ Bellici propago Martis/....

12. ff. 53v-54v Xauerius Mercurio melior In virgine regnat. [text:] Formosa virgo Zodiaci decus/ Amor leonis seu Marathonia/....

13. ff. 54v-55v Xauerio Templum extruitur. [text:] Huc adsit omnis Pyramidum situs/ Eductus astris, Mulciberi gravis/....

14. ff. 55v-58r Hercules Antaeum siue Xauerius Trauancorem expugnat. [text:] Iam lux emoriens tacitam caligine noctem/ Induerat terris serpitque per ossa cubant/....

15. ff. 58r-60r Mercurius Alcidae comes siue Xauerius fortis simul et Eloquens. [text:] Est vbi sidereas stant regia tecta sub auras/ Sylua alta et densis medio surgentibus antrum/....

16. f. 60r-v Extruitur ara Xauerio. [text:] Adesto celsis Aemoniae iugis/ Vates loquaci saxa trahens chelis/....

17. ff. 60v-62r Gemitus Xauerij cum in naui aegrotantes videret. [text:] Vos o Taenario quondam Ludibria regi/ Nunc picturato gloria nata polo/....

18. f. 62v Enigma et Logogryphium. [text:] Cum Deus egelido natus vagiret in antro/ Ilevi [?] ego nec fraenos adduxi fletibus illa/....

19. ff. 63r-64r Felix China quae Xauerium morientem excepit. [text:] Gorgones nuper iacui cum fessus in antro/ Lenis Hyanteae qua fluit error aquae/....

20. ff. 64v-65v Miratur rex Molucensij Xauerium nullius rei creatae amore flagragre. [text:] Quae tale Mauri prodigium Iubos/ Tellus ectegit [?] quos Pycij patens/....

21. f. 65v [Unidentified poem (?) added in three compact columns at bottom of leaf:] Huc ad regem pastorum/ Pastores currite/ Huc ad regem Amorum/ Amantes pergite/....

22. ff. 66r-67r Xauerius vt Phoenix ex contemplatione Diuina flammas concipit. [text:] Ardua qua surgit Nabathaeo vertice rupes/ Ac patet intonso proxima flamma Deo/....

23. ff. 67v-68v Xauerius ex Philosophiae cursu Palmam magisterij consequitur. [text:] Cernis vt frontem pugilis decoram/ Impedit Daphne radians metallo/....

24. f. 69r-v In pedes Xauerij. [text:] Quid miri Aesonidem Phryxei uelleris igne/ Accensum ignotas Phasidos isse vias/....

25. f. 70r-v Tropaeum subaudiae Principi Thomae. Dythirambus. [text:] Vnde Lesbois animata neruis/ Pegasi rupes salit? Hippocrenes/....

26. ff. 71r-72r Anglia. Haeresi oppressa Sociorum adventu recreatur. Ode. [text:] Sic aestuanti glissit anhelitu/ Vindicta diuum sic penitus graui/....

27. ff. 72v-74v Thamesis. In Edmundi Campiani nece amnem sistit. [text:] Tem-

pore quo faedo regia Britannia bello [several corrections in this first line render the readings uncertain]/ Heroumque parens natorum vndauit alumno/....

28. ff. 75r–76r Ignatius perluctantem Xauerium conuertit. [text:] Xauerius. Fastidiosas terrere vlterius moras/ Desiste verbis: haec pruinosam decent/....

Dialogue between St. Ignatius of Loyola and St. Francis Xavier, signed at the conclusion by I. M.

29. ff. 76v–78v Imperator deflet suum casum. [text:] Quisquis fugacis lubricum mundi decus/ Et blandientis dona fortunae stupet/....

30. ff. 78v–81r Imperator desperabundus. [text:] Quis me profundit dirus habitator stygis/ Furore verset? Quae furia miserum feris/....

31. f. 81r De violae natura. [text:] Scilicet vt rosa quam ros educat, irriget imber/ Sol firmat, lactat Cynthia, flora fouet/....

32. f. 81r–v Descriptio hyemis aduentantis. [text:] Tristis hyems tumidis acuens Stridoribus iras/ Imbriferos coniungit equos. Boreasque Notusque/....

33. ff. 81v–82v Laus vitae Pastoritiae. [text:] Frondosis si nosse iuuat quam dulcia Campis/ Otia Pastor agit quae solus gaudia captet/....

34. ff. 82v–86r Naenia. [text:] Ite procul laetae laeto cum carmine Musae/ Naenia sola placet lugubris; Ite procul/....

35. ff. 86v–90v Descriptio Imaginis B. Virginis. [text:] Pernassus [sic] gemino quam lambit vertice nubes/ Aethaeriumque caput sublimibus inserit astris/....

Paper (unidentified armorial watermarks), ff. 90, 172 x 108 (ca. 160 x 85) mm. Folios 15–62 ruled for 26 long lines or lines of verse, but ruling is often ignored; ruled in hard point, prickings at inner side of written space and at outer edge. Folios 1–14 and 63–90 written in ca. 25 long lines, single bounding lines ruled in hard point.

I^6, II–III^8, IV^8 (–3, cut out after f. 24), V–XI^8, XII^6 (–6, after f. 90). Catchwords for each folio on ff. 76v–82r.

Written by several cursive hands, some clearly later additions. A few headings in square capitals.

Binding: s. xviii. Vellum case, blind-tooled. Bookblock almost detached. Front pastedown may be part of art. 2 of text, but is too badly mutilated to be certain.

Written in England (cf. arts. 25 and 26) in the 17th century, by or for Jesuit(s). Various inscriptions in 18th-century cursive inside the front cover and on f. 1r: "R** D. P. Compton," "Gulielmus Elisius hunc librum tenet," "Johano Colfordo," "Stephanus Faulknerus," and "Johannes Hortonus [?]". Purchased from Goldschmidt's (cat. 26, appendix, no. 231) by Sterling W. Childs for the Albert H. Childs Memorial Collection in 1932.

Bibliography: De Ricci, v. 1, p. 71, no. 45.

MSS 46-54 France, s. XV-XVIII
Legal documents of the Barony d'Ursay

MSS 46-54 contain both original documents and later transcripts relating to the Barony of Ursay. They were classified and calendared for Catherine Amable de La Haye Montboult by her "feudiste" Charles-Felix Lheureux (see "Avertissement" of v. 10, MS 54). The first volume of the collection was not included in the purchase of these papers. Given below is a transcription of the title page of each volume.

MS 46 (Vol. 2) Aveus fois-hommages de la baronie d'ursay au comté de Passavent depuis 1436 jusqu'en 17 ... [the last 2 numbers are not given] Tome 2, Cotté B. 188 ff., followed by an alphabetical table.

MS 47 (Vol. 3) Avertissement. Ce volume contient des baux a cens des aveus, fois-hommages declarations contracts d'aquets d'echanges d'arentement partages sentences et autres titres au soutient de la mouvance de la baronnie d'Ursay depuis 1419 jusqu'en 1584. Tome 3, Cotté C. 482 ff., followed by an alphabetical table.

MS 48 (Vol. 4) Avertissement. Ce volume contient des aveus fois-hommages declarations contracts d'aquets, d'echanges, d'arrentement partages sentences et autres titres au soutient de la mouvance de la Baronnie d'Ursay depuis 1585 jusqu'en 1621. Tome 4, Cotté D. 615 ff., followed by an alphabetical table.

MS 49 (Vol. 5) Avertissement. Ce volume contient des baux a cens des aveus des declarations, fois-hommages, contracts d'aquets, d'echanges, partages arentements sentences et autres titres au soutient de la mouvance de la baronnie d'Ursay depuis 1622 jusqu'en 1653. Tome 5, Cotté E. 593 ff., followed by an alphabetical table.

MS 50 (Vol. 6) Avertissement. Ce volume contient des baux a cens des aveus, des fois-hommages des declarations des contracts d'aquets, d'echanges, d'arentement partages, sentences et autres titres au soutient de la mouvance de la Baronnie d'Ursay depuis 1654 jusqu'en 1694. Tome 6, Cotte F. 717 ff., followed by an alphabetical table.

MS 51 (Vol. 7) Ce volume contient des baux a cens, des aveus, fois-hommages, des declarations, des contracts d'aqueter d'echanges sentences et autres titres au soutient de la mouvance de la Baronnie d'Ursay depuis 1695 jusqu'en 17 ... [the last two numbers are not given] Tome 7, Cotté G. 244 ff., followed by an alphabetical table.

MS 52 (Vol. 8) Assises de la Baronnie d'Ursay 1771. Tome 8. 202 ff., followed by an alphabetical table.

MS 53 (Vol. 9) Liasse d'anciens censifs, ecrous et memoires de la baronnie d'Ursay depuis 1567 jusqu'en 1700. 228 ff.

MS 54 (Vol. 10) Avertissement. Le present censif de la Baronnie d'Ursay Fait en l'an 1773 a la Requete de Haute et Puissante Dame Catherine Amable de la haye montbault ... par Le Sieur Charles Felix Lheureux feudiste.... 315 ff., followed by an alphabetical table.

Parchment and paper (watermarks vary with each document). Covers of volumes 2-9 are 340 x 215 mm., and of vol. 10, 400 x 260 mm. Many of the individual documents are much smaller than the size of the cover; those larger are folded to fit inside. Documents may be single leaves or quires. Script ranges from 15th-century cursive with bâtarde influence to 18th-century cursive; text sometimes difficult to read because edges are hidden in gutter.
 Binding: s. xviii. Vellum mended with canvas, inscribed with brief title. The cover of MS 46 is a fragment of a Ritual, with notes on 4 red lines.

Written in France, in or near the barony of Ursay, at various times from the 15th to the 18th centuries; collected in the 18th century. Early provenance unknown. Purchased by Yale in 1922 through the Richard S. Fellowes Fund.

Bibliography: De Ricci, v. 1, p. 171, nos. 46-54.

MS 55 Yugoslavia, s. XV-XVI
Documents (Sebenico)

Documents and accounts (ca. 1400-1530) pertaining to the church of St. Gregory in Sebenicó (Dalmatia). Folios 63v-64r contain a copy of a will, in Latin, of Gregory of Sebenico. Other items, including an inventory of the church of St. Gregory (dated 8 Sept. 1403) are in Italian.

Paper (sturdy; watermarks: unidentified mountain) ff. 139, 410 x 155 mm. Arranged in a tabular format and written in many different cursive hands. Some entries have been crossed out.
 Too fragile to be collated. Numerous folios are stained and partly illegible; final leaves mutilated; loss of text throughout.
 Binding: Date? Sewn with coarse thread on seven double, wound thongs. Tacketed to a brown goatskin wrapper with seven sets of four tawed, pinkish-brown thongs, wound around each other on the outside of the spine. Sewing holes about 10 mm. apart outline the edges of the spine, sides, fore-edge and envelope flaps. Mold has eaten into cover and book, and the wrapper has shrunk so that it is now much smaller than the bookblock. Home-made notarial binding? Covers are lined with fragments of a noted antiphonal (s. XII); part of one sheet containing responds and antiphons for Epiphany and its octave is legible. Ca. 17 lines of text. Diastematic notation on a dry point staff with one red line. C and f are used as clefs, but from the condition of the sheet it is not possible to tell which clef should be associated with the red line. The neume style (of French aspect)

is similar to that in Rome, Bibliotheca Apostolica Vaticana, MS Urbin. lat. 393, of unknown provenance, which H. M. Bannister groups with North and Central Italian manuscripts (*Monumenti Vaticani di paleografia musicale latina* [Leipzig, 1913] I, no. 477; II, pl. 92a). We thank K. D. Hartzell for his assistance with these fragments.

Written in Yugoslavia during the 15th and 16th centuries presumably at the Church of Saint Gregory in Sebenico. Given to Yale in 1935 by Gustave R. Sattig.

Bibliography: De Ricci, v. 2, p. 2252, no. 55.

MS 56
Antiphonal (fragment)

Italy, s. XVI

The fragment contains the responsories and antiphons for the octave of Epiphany (one bifolium with continuous text).

Parchment, ff. 2 (paginated in red: cxlvii–cl), 550 x 336 (377 x 265) mm. Written in 9 lines of text with musical notation. Ruled in lead, double vertical bounding lines; no prickings, but there are marks, in lead, for guide-lines.
Written in round gothic script.
Four red staves with black square notes; crude initials in red.

Written in Italy in the 16th century; early provenance unknown. Gift of James Hillhouse in 1932.

Bibliography: De Ricci, v. 1, p. 225, no. 56.

MS 57
Vergil, Aeneis

Italy, s. XIV^{ex}, XV^2

ff. 1r–112v [1.46]   //Ast ego que diuum incedo Regina iouisque/ Et soror et coniunx una cum gemte [*sic*] tot annos/ ... [final folio mutilated] **tuisti infandum accendere bellum/ **et luctu miscere hymeneos// [12.805]

The following lines are lacking; most were presumably on leaves that became detached and have fallen out: 1. 1–45, 467–756; 2. 1–33, 567–88, 644, 682–742; 4. 10–72, 197–257, 570–695; 5. 166–351; 6. 587–901; 7. 1–744, 809–17; 8. 1–238, 431–96, 689–730; 9. 1–11; 12. 160–415, 676–739, 806–952.

Prefaced to each book are ten or eleven lines in verse (Walther, *Initia* 8699). R. A. B. Mynors, ed., OCT (1969) pp. 104–418. The text of Vergil is accompanied on ff. 1r–5v by marginal and interlinear glosses, the greater portion of which are derived from or an adaptation of Servius. The commentary does, however, include notes (some in Greek) independent of Servius. (We thank M. L. Lord for her assistance with the commentary.)

Composed of three parts: the first (ff. 1-6) was apparently added to replace lost leaves, the second and third (ff. 7-112) were written somewhat earlier and are contemporary with each other. There are marginal and interlinear notes in several hands throughout, especially at the beginning of the volume on ff. 1r-5r, as well as catchwords added later.

Part I: Paper (sturdy; unidentified watermarks obscured by text), ff. 6, 282 x 192 (187 x 83) mm. Written in 35 lines of verse; double vertical and horizontal bounding lines, full across. Ruled in hard point; remains of prickings for upper horizontal bounding lines in outer margins. One gathering of six folios written in italic by a single scribe.

Part II: Paper (sturdy; several unidentified watermarks including two circles with a cross), ff. 51 (7-57), 283 x 193 (212 x 112) mm. Written in 31 lines of verse; single or double upper (and sometimes lower) horizontal bounding lines, full across. Ruled in lead; prickings at corners of written space. Catchwords below written space are accompanied by decorative flourishes. Written in fere-humanistic script by one scribe. Spaces left for initials. A large gap in the text occurs between Parts II and III (6.587 to 7.744).

Part III: Paper (sturdy; watermarks: unidentified crossed swords), ff. 55 (58-112), 283 x 193 (204 x 102) mm. Written in 32 lines of verse; single or double upper (sometimes lower) horizontal bounding lines, full across. Ruled in lead; some prickings in gutter for guide-lines. Remains of signatures (Roman numerals) along lower edge of recto. Written by a single scribe in a script similar to that in Part II. Spaces left for initials.

The binding is so brittle (with many pages unattached) that it is not possible to collate Parts II and III.

Binding: s. xvi-xvii? Sewn on three slit leather straps. There is no indication of an earlier sewing, but the book was extensively mended before it was sewn. Tawed cores of plain wound endbands laid in grooves. Beech boards with rectangular channels on the outside in which the straps are nailed. The spine is lined with brown leather and the book covered in dark brown sheepskin faintly blind-tooled with a central diamond made up of arches with small ornaments scattered in and around it. Tongue turn-ins. There are two catches on the lower board and traces of red and cream silk ribbons nailed to the upper one with star-headed nails. The title is painted in red on the spine.

Written in Italy, Parts II and III at the end of the 14th century and Part I in the second half of the 15th; the three sections were apparently bound together during the 16th or 17th century. Evidence concerning early provenance includes the signatures Pietro Paulo Santino on f. 1r and Gian Maria Ferduno [?] inside back cover. Presented to Yale in 1934 by Carl B. Spitzer.

Bibliography: De Ricci, v. 2, p. 2252, no. 57; Faye and Bond, p. 25, no. 57.

MS 58

MS 58 Italy, 1461
Sozomenus Pistoriensis Pl. 6

ff. 1r–77r *Persius* Flaccus Satiricus poeta uulterris nascitur omni mundi ... mentes nostras cui sit honor et gloria in secula seculorum. Amen. *Ego bartholomeus de baldinottis scripsi anno mcccclxi.* f. 77v blank

This commentary on Persius by Sozomenus Pistoriensis is found anonymously in the Beinecke manuscript and in London, B. L. Harley 3989, the latter written by the author ca. 1427. See CTC, v. 3, pp. 253–55.

Paper (unidentified watermarks, trimmed) and parchment (f. 1), ff. 77, 166 x 121 (115 x 85) mm. Written in 27 long lines; frame-ruled in lead or hard point; remains of prickings along outer edges.
I–VII^{10} (+ 1 leaf at beginning, f. 1), VIII^6. Catchwords perpendicular to text along inner bounding lines.
Written in a neat humanistic script in 1461 by Bartholomaeus Baldinotti.
Small initials, in red, mark the beginning of prologue and each satire.
Binding: s. xix. Vellum case.

Written in Italy in 1461 by Bartholomaeus Baldinotti (*Colophons*, v. 1, p. 213, no. 1711); early provenance unknown. Presented to Yale in 1936 by Thomas E. Marston (bookplate).

secundo folio: Nec fonte

Bibliography: De Ricci, v. 2, p. 2252, no. 58.

MS 59 Italy, 1534 [?]
Catalogus librorum (Aldine Press)

ff. 1r–4v Catalogus liborum [*sic*] qui in officina Aldi Manutii plaerique omnes intra annum Domini MDXXXIII Venetiis ... Erotemata Constantini Lascaris graecè et latine cum tabula Cebetis ... M. Antonii Flaminii/ si [?] bene memini explanatio in Psalmos. Italicisque sic se habet suprascriptus Catalogus.

The catalogue consists of four sections: Libri graeci, Alii libri graeci, Libri latini, Italici libri; it was unknown to A. A. Renouard, *Annales de l'imprimèrie des Alde* (Paris, 1834) pp. 329–45.

Paper (sturdy, brown; watermarks: unidentified coat of arms in gutter), ff. iv stubs + 4 + ix stubs, 323 x 102 mm. No written space delineated.
A single quire written in italic by one scribe.
All folios are stained, damaged, and/or repaired.
Binding: 1850. Bound by George Bretherton in quarter red-brown leather with blue-black cloth sides.

Written in Italy in 1534 [?]; the date 1541 in one entry appears to be a later addition; early provenance unknown. The manuscript was in England as early as 1850 when it was bound by Bretherton (label inside front cover). Acquired by Sir Thomas Phillipps ca. 1860 (no. 15644; signature on f. 4v and tag on spine); his sale (London, 1899, no. 13) to J. E. Hodgkin; his sale (London, 12 May 1914, no. 26) to Tregaskis. Sold in 1934 by C. A. Stonehill's to Thomas E. Marston, who presented it to Yale in 1935.

Bibliography: De Ricci, v. 2, p. 2252, no. 59.

MS 60
Registrum brevium; Novae narrationes

England, s. XIV[1]

1. ff. i-x (unfoliated)   List of chapters for Registrum brevium (follows approximately the order given in W. S. Holdsworth, *A History of English Law*, v. 2 [London, 1923] pp. 617-32). Concludes with: Sequuntur capitula breuium de ingressu.

2. ff. 1r-138r   Registrum brevium. The first chapter Breue de recto patens (in margin) begins with a writ of King Edward (Edwardus dei gracia ... balliuis suis Ebor' salutem...); ends with a paragraph labelled De annua pensione. ff. 138v-144v blank, except for miscellaneous scribblings and mathematical calculations

    The text starts in a manner similar to Register R in *Early Registers of Writs* edited by E. de Haas and G. D. G. Hall in Seldon Society, v. 87 (London, 1970) pp. 108-18, but differs considerably after section 43.

3. ff. 145r-204v   Novae narrationes. The manuscript follows primarily Text C (with numerous variations) edited by E. Shanks, Seldon Society, v. 80 (London, 1963) pp. 144-305; it breaks off in C. 286: et exil en le maner et les tenemenz auantditz s. abatu vn sale pris de xl, vn chambre pris de v,// ff. 205r-209v random notes, signatures, etc.

4. f. 210r   Part of an article of indenture (13 lines; 18th-century hand), in English, concerning William Jenninges of Birmingham. f. 210v mathematical calculations

Parchment, ff. ii (contemporary parchment) + 214 (no foliation for table; medieval foliation for text, 1-204: leaf between 134 and 135 unnumbered, -101; the same person who foliated the text added the appropriate folio numbers to the table in the margins) + vi (contemporary parchment; modern foliation, 205-10), 120 x 80 (81 x 49) mm. Written in 27 long lines; single inner, double outer vertical bounding lines, with additional ruling in outer margins; double horizontal bounding lines (sometimes full across). Ruled in lead or ink; remains of prickings in lower and outer margins.

I^{12} (unfoliated table; -11, 12, no loss of text), II-XI^{12}, XII^{12} (-5, f. 126), XIII-XVIII^{12}. Catchwords along lower edge, near gutter.

Written in small, cramped Anglicana bookhand by one scribe.

Twelve illuminated initials (crudely drawn and much rubbed), in dark red, blue, gold, green, and orange, with simple borders extending the length of the folio (cf. Pächt and Alexander, v. 3, no. 545). Paragraph marks in blue or gold throughout.

Lower half of ff. 33, 78 torn; large portions of text stained and illegible.

Binding: s. xv-xvi. Original sewing on four double, tawed cords laced into flush wooden boards. The covering extends over the endbands and is sewn around them. Traces of a secondary embroidery. Spine lined with tawed skin extending to outside of boards. Covered with tawed, cream-colored skin. A brass catch on the lower cover and traces of a clasp attachment on the first few leaves. Lower board detached, upper board and most of the spine covering wanting, probably for some time.

Written in England in the first half of the 14th century; the codex bears evidence of extensive use. Owners of the 18th [?] century: Thomas Cowper (signatures: ff. ix verso, x recto, 140v); Ambrose Davenporte (note on f. 141r: "Ambrose Davenporte is a good boye"); John Knighte (note on f. 205v; perhaps of the 17th century?). Belonged to Mrs. Doctor James of New Hartford, New York (newspaper clipping [n.d.] inside cover). Signatures of "Theo. H. Bradish, Utica, N.Y. 1856" on f. 209v and on clipping; "James P. Bradish, Philadelphia, 1857" on f. 209v; "George G. Kennedy, Roxbury Mass., Sept. 16 1857" on f. 206v. Purchased from Malcolm Kennedy with the anonymous gift of a Yale undergraduate in 1932.

secundo folio: Rex et

Bibliography: De Ricci, v. 2, p. 2253, no. 60.

MS 61
Boethius, De consolatione philosophiae

Italy, 1430
Pl. 5

ff. 1r-36r   Carmina qui quondam studio Florente peregi/ Flebilis heu mestos cogor inire modos/ ... cum cuncta agamus ante oculos iudici cuncta cernentis. Explicit liber boetij de consolatione philosophica vi kal. ianuarij 1430. [another explicit in a modern (?) hand follows] f. 36v blank

L. Bieler, ed., CC ser. lat. 94 (1957) pp. 1-105.

Parchment, ff. 36, 246 x 176 (190 x 132) mm. Written in 36-37 long lines or lines of verse; vertical bounding lines in hard point, horizontal guide-lines in ink; prickings along lower edge.

I-IV^8, V^4. Remains of signatures, in red, on recto of first leaves (ai, aii, etc.);

catchwords appear in center of lower margin, with a small flourish on each side and below.

Written in round gothic bookhand by one scribe.

Historiated initial with partial border contains the portrait of Boethius (f. 14r); four illuminated initials of similar design and colors (dark red, red-orange, green, blue, gold) on ff. 6r, 12v, 22r, 29v (beginning of Books II-V). Small initials and paragraph marks in red throughout.

Binding: Date? Original sewing on two thick, slit leather straps, the endbands sewn on leather cores. Flush beech boards with straps laced through tunnels in the edge to channels slanted up to the outer face. The ends of the straps therefore protrude well above the face. Straps nailed and endband cores laid in V-shaped grooves and nailed. The spine and about one quarter of the boards covered by brown calf with a nailed parchment strip at the edge, fragments only remaining. No adhesive on the spine. Channels for straps cut in the upper board. Holes for pins in the lower, but no marks of pin plates. This binding could be contemporary or 19th-20th century. It is interesting to note that the manuscript was bought because of the binding and not because of the text.

Written probably in Northern Italy in 1430; early provenance unknown. Purchased from Gabriel Wells in 1935 with funds from the Yale Library Associates.

secundo folio: Rimari

Bibliography: De Ricci, v. 2. p. 2253, no. 61.

MS 62 England, 1391[?]
Coram Rege Roll (fragment)

Nearly contemporary copy of an extract from a Coram Rege Roll, involving Iohannes de Burgh, his wife Sibilla, and Nicholas de Burgh; concerns property dispute in West Bagborough (Somerset). Title reads: "In banco Regis de termino Michaelis anno regis Ricardi quartodecimo. Rotulum lviii."

Single parchment membrane measuring 435 x 244 mm. Written in Anglicana bookhand. Badly mutilated with loss of text; stains along left margin suggest it formerly served as a flyleaf.

Written in England at the end of the 14th century; provenance unknown for there are no library records concerning it.

Bibliography: De Ricci, v. 2, p. 2253, no. 62.

MS 63 Italy, s. XV²
Excerpts from Greek & Latin authors (all in Lat.)

Excerpts are listed according to the headings given in the manuscript; the divisions and titles indicated by Roman numerals suggest a rationale for the arrangement.

I. Orations

1. ff. 1r-7r   Excerpta ex oratione eschinis contra tesiphontem [Lat. tr., Leonardo Bruni]

2. ff. 7r-11v   Ex oratione demosthenis contra eschinem

3. f. 12r-v   Ex philippica Demosthenis

4. f. 12v   Demosthenes ad alexandrum

II. Lives

5. f. 13r   In Vita Tiberij et Gaij graccorum

6. f. 13r   In Vita thimoleonis

7. f. 13v   In Vita Sertorij

8. ff. 13v-18v   Ex Vita Pauli emilij

9. f. 19r   Ex Vita Eumenis

10. f. 19r-v   Ex Vita Sertorij

11. ff. 20r-23v   Ex Vita Marci antonij [Lat. tr., Leonardo Bruni] f. 24r-v blank

III. Exempla

12. f. 25r   Ex prefatione Fr. philelphi in aphotegmata plutarci

13. ff. 25r-42r   Ex prefatione Plutarci ad Traianum [followed by a series of *exempla externa* which include Dionysius, Archelaus, Alexander, Ptolomeus, et al.]

14. ff. 42r-50v   Sequntur domestica. 1. Romana [includes Fabius, Scipio, Cato the Elder, et al.]

IV. Excerpts from Valerius Maximus

15. ff. 51r-54v   Excerpta ex Valerio maximo [selections from Book 1, arranged under the headings: de religione, de neglecta religione, de ominibus, de prodigiis, de somniis, de miraculis]

16. ff. 54v-60v   Liber secundus [selections: de institutis antiquis; de disciplina militari; de iure triumphandi; de censura; de maiestate]

17. ff. 60v-67r   Incipit tertius [selections: de indole; de fortitudine, de patientia, de humili loco natis qui clari euaserunt, qui a parentibus claris degenerauerunt, qui ueste aut cultu ultra patrium morem usi sunt, de fiducia sui, de constantia]

18. ff. 67r–72v   Incipit IIII [selections: de moderatione, qui ex inimicis iuncti sint amicitia uel necessitudine, de abstinentia et continentia, de paupertate, de uerecundia, de amore coniugali, de amicitia et dilectione, de liberalitate]

19. ff. 72v–78v   Liber quintus [selections: de humanitate et clementia, de gratis, de ingratis, de pietate erga parentes fratres et patriam, de parentum in liberos amore et indulgentia, de seueritate parentum in liberos]

20. ff. 78v–85r   Liber sextus [selections: de pudicitia, libere dicta aut facta, de seueritate, grauiter dicta aut facta, de iustitia, de fide publica, de fide uxorum in uiros, de fide seruorum in dominos, de mutatione morum ac fortune]

21. ff. 85r–90v   Liber septimus [selections: de felicitate, sapienter dicta aut facta, uafre (?) dicta aut facta, de stratagematibus, de repulsis, de necessitate]

22. ff. 91r–93r   Liber octauus [selections: infames rei, de testibus malis, de studio et industria, de ocio, quanta uis sit eloquentie, de senectute, de cupiditate glorie]

23. ff. 93r–95v   Liber nonus [selections: de luxuria, de crudelitate, de ira et odio, de auaritia, de superbia et insolentia, de perfidia, de errore, de ultione, dicta improba aut facta, de moribus non uulgaribus, de cupiditate uite, de similitudine forme] f. 96r–v blank

See D. M. Schullian, "A Revised List of Manuscripts of Valerius Maximus," *Miscellanea Augusto Campana* in *Medioevo e Umanesimo*, v. 45 (Padua, 1981) p. 712.

V. Excerpts from Xenophon [Lat. tr., Francesco Filelfo]

24. ff. 97r–102v   Ex libello Xenofontis de Vita Cyrri Regis Persarum

VI. Lives

25. ff. 103r–108v   Ex Vita M. Catonis uticensis per aretinum e greco traducta

26. ff. 109r–112v   Ex Vita Catonis Censorini

27. ff. 113r–115r   Ex Vita Aristidis

28. ff. 115v–116r   Ex Vita Phocionis

29. ff. 116v–117r   Ex Vita Pompei

30. ff. 117v–119r   Ex Vita Ciceronis

31. ff. 119v–120v   Ex Vita Ligurgi

32. f. 121r–v   Ex Vita Nume Pompilij. ff. 122–124 blank

VII. Seneca's Tragedies

33. ff. 125r–127r   Excerpta ex prima tragedia senece que inscribitur hercules furens

34. ff. 127r–130r   Sequitur athreus et Thiestes

35. f. 130v   Thebays

36. ff. 131r–134r   Ipolitus

MS 63

37. ff. 134r–135r   Edippus sequitur
38. ff. 135v–136v   Trohas
39. ff. 136v–137v   Sequitur medee
40. ff. 137v–139r   Incipit Agamemnon
41. ff. 139r–140v   Sequitur Octauia
42. ff. 140v–142r   Sequitur hercules oethei

VIII. Miscellaneous

43. ff. 142v–146v   Ex Seuerino siue Boetio de consolatione philosophye
44. f. 147r–v   Ex Libello Guarrini de Assentatoribus
45. ff. 147v–148v   Ex Aristotelis economica
46. ff. 149r–150v   Ex libello Basilij
47. ff. 151r–152r   Ex Epistola Beati Bernardi
48. f. 152r–v   Epistola Phallaris demotelli

IX. Roman Comedy

49. ff. 153r–158r   [Terence] f. 158v blank
50. ff. 159r–167v   Ex Plauto. ff. 168–171 blank

Paper (sturdy; unidentified watermarks buried in gutter include hat, ladder, crossed arrows, cross bow), ff. i (paper) + 171 + i (paper), 255 x 183 (158 x 112) mm. Written in ca. 29 long lines or lines of verse; paper has been neatly folded to make the vertical bounding lines for written space.

I^{10}, II^{14}, III^{16}, IV–XI^{14}, XII^{10}, XIII^{10} (-10). Remains of signatures in lower right corner, recto; catchwords in lower margin near gutter, verso.

Written by two scribes: Scribe 1 (ff. 1r–152v) wrote in a careful humanistic script for text and modified capitals for headings; Scribe 2 (ff. 153r–167v) retained the overall format but used a less elegant style of writing.

Binding: s. xviii. Plain sheepskin case.

Written in Italy in the second half of the 15th century with great care, as is indicated by the ample margins (perhaps for later annotations?) and by the arrangement of excerpts; early provenance unknown. No. 33 in an unidentified sale. Presented to Yale in 1931 by Thomas E. Marston.

secundo folio: Pacem dum

Bibliography: De Ricci, v. 2, p. 2253, no. 63.

MS 64
Martial, etc.

Italy, s. XV²
Pl. 26

1. ff. 1r-193v   *Marci Valerii Martialis. Xenia. Incipiunt.* Te toga cordilis et penula desit oliuis/ Aut inopem metuat sordida blata famem/ ... *Ientacula.* Surgite iam uendit pueris ientacula pistor/ Cristateque sonant undique lucis aues.

The codex was misbound; the order of the epigrams is as follows (based on the Teubner edition of W. Heraeus and J. Borovskij, 1976): f. 1r-v: Xenia [Liber 13] 1-10 (continued on f. 6r); ff. 2r-3v: 12. 84-98; ff. 4r-5v: 13. 29-64; f. 6r-v: 13. 11-28; ff. 7r-87v: 1. 41-6. 88 (missing 1. 47); ff. 88r-186v: 7. 2-12. 83; ff. 187r-188v: 13. 65-100; ff. 189r-193r: 14. 149-222.
Excerpts from the critical commentary of Domizio Calderini (Professor of Rhetoric at Rome in 1470) surround the text on ff. 1r-24v and 165r-193r. See CTC, v. 4, pp. 261-65 (the first edition of this commentary was published in Rome in 1474).

2. ff. 193r-194v   [Unidentified prose text outlining the development of civilization:] In noua terra credibile est fuisse omnia semina rerum nulla mixta [corrected to *mista*] et si qua sunt aut industria ... Antoninus non solum pius sed***commodus Gordianus Iunior//

Parchment, ff. i (paper) + 194 + i (paper), 162 x 100 (114 x 62) mm. Written in 27 lines of verse; double vertical bounding lines, with an additional line in outer margin; ruled in hard point or lead.
I^6, II-IX^{10}, X^{10} (-2, 9), XI-XX^{10}.
Written by one scribe in a neat italic for the text and a less formal hand for the commentary and for the unidentified text on ff. 193r-194v.
Gold initials, 5-line, on blue, dark red and green grounds, with white and gold highlights, mark the beginning of each book. Small, plain initials, alternating red and blue, for each epigram. Commentary and titles, in various shades of red.
Final folios creased and rubbed; some loss of marginal text due to trimming and wear.
Binding: s. xviii-xix. Vellum case, blind-tooled.

Written in Italy in the second half of the 15th century for or by an individual interested in the scholarly commentary of Domizio Calderini; early provenance unknown. Presented to Yale in 1936 by Thomas E. Marston.

secundo folio: Nolueram

Bibliography: De Ricci, v. 2, p. 2253, no. 64.

MS 65 Italy, s. XV²
Martial

ff. 1r–238v *In amphitheatrum Caesaris*. [B]arbara pyramidum sileat miracula memphis/ Assiduus iactet nec babillona labor/ ... Dic mihi simpliciter comedis et citharedis/ Fibula quid prestas carius ut futuant.//

Ends abruptly at Bk. 14. 214; also missing Bk. 14. 79–93.2; W. Heraeus and J. Borovskij, eds., Teubner (1976) pp. 1–343.

Paper (sturdy; watermarks: several unidentified in gutter, including the letter R), ff. iii (paper) + 238 + iii (paper), 217 x 143 (131 x 80) mm. Written in ca. 22 lines of verse; double vertical bounding lines; ruled in hard point.
I–II⁸, III–XXII¹⁰, XXIII¹⁴, XXIV¹⁰ (-1, 10).
Written in informal humanistic scripts by multiple scribes. Each made notes in the margins for the rubricator (at least two distinct hands that alternate through the manuscript; some rubrics are illegible). Various types of catchwords; on f. 96v one is encompassed by a bird with a long beak.
Plain initials in red; rubrics stop on f. 220r.
Binding: s. xix. Bound by Zaehnsdorf (established ca. 1842) in half green goatskin with green cloth sides.

Written in Italy in the second half of the 15th century, apparently in some haste. Lines were frequently omitted (then added in the margins) and poor planning resulted in a big blank space on f. 186r–v; some rubrication bled from one folio to the next. Belonged to Thomas Hodgkin of Newcastle-on-Tyne (1831–1913; bookplate). Presented to Yale by Thomas E. Marston in 1936.

secundo folio: Denique supplicium

Bibliography: De Ricci, v. 2, p. 2253, no. 65.

MS 66 Italy, s. XV²
Leonicenus Omnibonus, De arte metrica, etc.

1. ff. 1r–13v *Omniboni Vicentini Viri Eruditissimi Artis Metricae Tractatus Incit* [sic]. Pes in metro dicitur quod pedis fungitur officio [sic] metra enim per pedes quodammodo incedunt ... Mezenti ducis exuuias. Breuis in hoc Nemorosa Zacynthos. τέλος

   L. Omnibonus, *De arte metrica* (Padua, ca. 1476).

2. ff. 14r–24r [B]*arbarismus Est Vna Pars Orationis Vitiosa in Communi* sermone in poemate. Metaplasmus itemque barbarismus in loquela nostra ... ledeamque helenam troianas uexit ad urbes.

   Donatus, *De Barbarismo et soloecismo* (Ars maior, Part 3); H. Keil, ed., *Grammatici latini* (Hildesheim, 1961) v. 4, pp. 392–402.

3. ff. 24r-35v [S]olet aliquotiens in scripturis ordo uerborum causa decoris aliter quam uulgaris uia dicendi ... παραβολή est rerum genere dissimilium [?] comparatio ut regnum celorum grano sinapis et sicut moises exaltauit [ink blotch]//

Lorenzo Guglielmo Traversagni de Savone, O. F. M. (1425-1503), *Opusculum de re rhetorica* (see J. Ruysschaert, ed., *Bibliothecae Apostolicae Vaticanae codices manu scripti recensiti iussu ... Codices 11414-11709* ... [Vatican, 1959] MS 11441, art. 3).

4. ff. 36r-45v //*Lex et regula ad eleuandam et deprimendam unius cuiusque partis orationis syllabam qui sit ad similitudinem elementorum litterarum atque syllabarum ... Interiectio* uero nullam certam regulam retinet tamen in fine uel in medio acuitur ut papé euâx. τέλος περὶ τῶν προσωδίων. Δοξα.

Pseudo-Priscian, *De accentibus*; Keil, *op. cit.* (Leipzig, 1859) v. 3, pp. 519-28.

Paper (watermarks similar to Briquet Balance 2489), ff. ii (modern paper) + 45 + ii (modern paper), 215 x 120 (125 x 62) mm. Written in 28 long lines; double vertical and horizontal bounding lines, full across; ruled in hard point. I^{10}, $II-III^{12}$, IV^{11} (structure uncertain; one leaf with text missing between ff. 35 and 36). Catchwords arranged in a circle near gutter.

Written by a single scribe in italic for the text and marginal notes, and in modified capitals for headings.

Decorative initial and border outlined in red, but uncolored, appear on f. 1r. Frequent use of red ink in headings, marginalia and for long sections of the text.

Water and ink stains throughout; some loss of text.

Binding: s. xix. Brown calf, blind- and gold-tooled.

Written in Italy in the second half of the 15th century for a scholar interested in grammar and rhetoric; early provenance unknown. Sold by Thorpe (cat. 1836, no. 910; not verified) to Sir Thomas Phillipps (no. 9511, note on f. 1r; label on spine); his sale (London, 1935, no. 323) to C. A. Stonehill. Presented to Yale by Thomas E. Marston in 1936.

secundo folio: fieri uel

Bibliography: De Ricci, v. 2, p. 2253, no. 66.

MS 67
Juvenal; Persius

Italy, 1468, 1469
Pl. 6

1. ff. 1r-72v *Materiam et causas satirarum hac inspice prima./* [S]emper ego auditor tantum nunquam ne reponam/ Vexatus totiens rauci Theseide codri/ ... Pytagoras coeteris Animalibus abstinuit qui/ Tanquam homine et ventri indulserit omne ligumen. Telos. Finis. Laus Deo. *Iunius Iuuenalis Aquinas explicit per me donnum Franciscum cognomento Phylaretum scriptus die Iouis tertia Februarii Mccclxviiii presentibus discretis ac eruditis adolenscentibus Iuliano Pytio. Cristoforo Pyerio.*

Donno Berardino Aquilio. ac pientissimo Iohanni Baptista Pegaso patrono libri tempore quo Federicus Tertius Romanorum Imperator Secundo Italiam uenerat. f. 73r-v blank except for doodlings, etc.

Juvenal, *Satirae I-XVI* (with XVI preceding XV); W. V. Clausen, ed., OCT (1959) pp. 37-175. For the *argumenta* of Guarino of Verona (added at the beginning of satires) see S. Endlicher, *Catalogus codicum philologicorum latinorum Bibliothecae Palatinae Vindobonensis* (Vienna, 1836) p. 116 and Walther, *Initia* 10770.

2. ff. 74r-84v   *Nec fonte labra prolui caballino/ Nec in bicipiti sonniasse parnaso/* ... Iam decies redit in rugam depinge ubi sistam/ Inuentus crisippe tui finitor accerui. *Persius Flaccus Satyricus poeta uolateranus uolateris natus anni mundi v ccxxxvi Imperii Tiberii anno xxi mortuus autem anno aetatis sue xxix Imperii Neronis anno viiii. Telos. Ego Franciscus Seroddi Centinomius pulcriori autem cognomine et quo immodum glorior Phylaretus dictus hunc Libellum peregi ob imperium diui et pientissimi adolescentis Berardini Petri qui me gratis scribere iussit die lune xxviiii Mai mcccclxviii.*

Persius, Prologue followed by *Satirae I-VI*; Clausen, *op. cit.*, pp. 3-28.

3. ff. 85r-87v   Astrological notes on the moon in the twelve signs of the zodiac, beginning with a passage on *De luna arietis* (Cum luna fuerit in Ariete bonum est incipere iter...) and ending with *De luna piscis* (Cum luna fuerit in piscibus bonum est facere...).

Thorndike and Kibre, 315.

Paper (watermarks similar to Briquet Lettre R 8941 and Harlfinger Flèche 12), ff. i (contemporary paper) + 87, 235 x 165 (150 x 97) mm. Written in 27 lines of verse; double vertical bounding lines, single horizontal, most full across. Ruled in lead; irregular pattern of round prickings.

I-VII^{10}, VIII^4 (-3), IX^{10}, X^4. Catchwords perpendicular to text between inner bounding lines.

Written in humanistic script by three scribes. The principal scribe, Franciscus Seroddi Centinomius Phylaretus, wrote ff. 1r-72v and 79r-84v; he signed the manuscript on ff. 72v and 84v (see contents for colophons, the first of which is quoted in *Colophons*, v. 1, p. 108, no. 4395). Scribe 2 wrote ff. 74r-78v and Scribe 3 the notes on ff. 85r-87v. Marginal and interlinear glosses in several contemporary hands.

Argumenta of Guarino of Verona in red rustic capitals preceding each title; spaces for decorative initials never filled. Various schoolboy notes with drawings on flyleaf and pastedowns of both covers.

Binding: s. xvi? Vellum stays. Original sewing on three slit, tawed straps. Primary, plain and secondary, beaded endbands on twisted, tawed cores, laid in grooves and pegged or nailed. Spine lined with tawed skin, mostly lacking. Straps laced and pegged or nailed into beech boards covered in (originally) brick-red leather, blind-tooled with an inscription in a border around an inner panel of overlapping circles interspersed with dots. Four flower-shaped bosses on each board and two catches on the lower one. Two bosses and clasp straps wanting.

Written in 1468 and 1469 for Berardinus Petrus (unidentified, as are the other young men in the colophons who appear to be listed according to their nicknames). Signatures (16th century?) of one Franciscus on f. 13r and Frater Francischanus on f. i verso. Acquired from Maggs in 1932 by Thomas E. Marston (bookplate) who presented it to Yale in 1936.

secundo folio: Haec ego non

Bibliography: De Ricci, v. 1, p. 155, no. 2.

MS 68
Juvenal; Persius

Italy, s. XV^2

1. ff. 1r–75r Semper ego auditor tantum numquam ne reponam/ Vexatus totiens rauci theseide codri/ ... Vt qui fortis erit sit foelicissimus idem/ Vt laeti phaleris omnes et torquibus omnes. Iunii Iuuenalis aquinatis liber satyrarum quintus explicit. f. 75v blank

   Juvenal, *Satirae I–XVI*; W. V. Clausen, ed., OCT (1959) pp. 37–175.

2. ff. 76r–88v Nec fonte labra prolui caballino/ Nec in bicipiti somniasse parnaso/ ... Iam decies redit in rugam depinge ubi sistam/ Inuentus chrysippe tui finitor acerui. ff. 89r–90v blank except for some notes in Italian and cipher

   Persius, Prologue followed by *Satirae I–VI*; Clausen, *op. cit*, pp. 3–28.

Paper (watermarks similar to Briquet Tête de boeuf 14873), ff. iv (contemporary paper) + 90, 215 x 127 (150 x 80) mm. Written in 26 lines of verse; double vertical and single horizontal bounding lines.
I–IX^{10}. Catchwords perpendicular to text between inner bounding lines.
Written in humanistic script by a single scribe.
Six illuminated initials in blue or green, 6- to 5-line on gold rectangular grounds (ff. 1r, 20r, 32v, 45v, 59r, 76r); smaller initials, in blue, for the remaining satires.
Binding: s. xvi? Vellum stays and vellum reinforcement of own end leaves. Resewn on three slit straps bound in wooden boards covered in brown leather, blind-tooled, with two catches on the upper board. Too heavily restored to tell much about the binding.

Written in Italy in the second half of the 15th century; the arms of the original owner (f. 1r) have been mutilated. J. T. Adams sale (London, 7 Dec. 1931, no. 136) to Maggs; purchased by Thomas E. Marston (bookplate) who gave it to Yale in 1936.

MS 69

secundo folio: Exul ab

Bibliography: De Ricci, v. 1, p. 155, no. 3.

MS 69
Juvenal; Persius

Italy [?], s. XV^{med}

1. ff. 1r–81r Semper ego auditor tantum numquam ne reponam/ Vexatus tociens rauci theseide codri/ ... Pytagoras conctis animalibus abstinuit qui/ Tamquam homine et uentri indulsit non omne legumen. Explicit Satirarum Liber Decii Iunii Iuuenalis. Amen. [added in a later hand:] Aquini.

   Juvenal, *Satirae I–XVI* (with XVI preceding XV); W. V. Clausen, ed., OCT (1959) pp. 37–175.

2. ff. 81v–95v *Prima Satira*. [N]ec fonte labra prolui caballino/ Nec in bicipiti sompniasse parnaso/ ... Iam deties redit in rugam depinge ubi sistam/ Inuentus crisippe tui finitor acerui. Explicit Liber Persii Satirice. [added in another hand:] Satira Sexta.

   Persius, Prologue followed by *Satirae I–VI*; Clausen, *op. cit.*, pp. 3–28.

3. ff. 97r–98r Miscellaneous sententiae, all unidentified. One of the miscellaneous poems, said to have been by Petrarch, is no longer in the manuscript; it may have been on f. 96 which was already missing when Ullman included it in his index (Ullman, no. 55). ff. 98v–99r blank

4. f. 99v Excerpts from Seneca.

5. f. 100r [Poem attributed in the manuscript to Antonio Beccadelli; heading in codex:] *Panormita*. Dum mea me genetrix grauido gestaret in aluo [partly concealed by mending tape] ... femina uir neutrum flumina tella cruces [in a later hand:] mirabilis conclusio.

   A. Beccadelli, *Carmen de hermaphrodita* [Treviso, ca. 1475]; Hain 10502.

6. f. 100v Monaca: Me tibi teque mihi genus etas et decor equant ... Gaudeo quia uerbis sum superata tuis. f. 101r–v blank

   Short dialogue between a nun and a cleric; Walther, *Initia* 10852.

Paper (sturdy; watermarks: similar to Briquet Couronne 4639–40 and unidentified bird), ff. i (contemporary paper) + 100 (foliation begins on 2; f. 96 cut out), 212 x 143 (142 x 82) mm. Written in 24 lines of verse; single bounding lines; ruled in hard point.
I^{10}, II^{12} (-8; no loss of text), III^{16}, IV^{12}, V^{14}, VI^{10}, VII^{12}, VIII^{10}, IX^{6} (-1). Catchwords perpendicular to text along inner bounding line.
Written in humanistic script by a single scribe. Marginal and interlinear notes in several contemporary hands.

One original initial, in red, on f. 1r; all other initials appear to be later additions, some drawn in lead.

Most leaves mended in lower outer corner.

Binding: s. xix. Narrow brown calf spine with traces of gold tooling, small vellum corners and purple paper sides. Much rubbed and worn.

Written possibly in Italy in the mid-15th century; its origin is difficult to determine. The script is Italian in appearance, but the paper seems to be Northern European (watermarks similar in type to Briquet Couronne 4639: Düsseldorf 1438, and Couronne 4640: Colmar 1441). Obtained (ca. 1820) by Sir Thomas Phillipps (no. 292, note on f. 1r) from the Abbey of S. Ghislain in Belgium. His sale (1896, no. 785) to Leighton (Cat. 1, 1920, no. 252; 5, 1924, no. 56); J. T. Adams sale (London, 7 Dec. 1931, no. 137) to Maggs. Purchased from Maggs by Thomas E. Marston (bookplate) who presented it to Yale in 1936.

secundo folio: Exul ob

Bibliography: De Ricci, v. 1, p. 155, no. 4.

MS 70
Juvenal

Italy, 1475
Pl. 7

ff. 1r–81r *Semper ego auditor* tantum numquam ue reponam/ Vexatus totiens rauci teseide codri/ ... Vt qui fortis erit sit felicissimus idem/ Vt leti faleris omnes et torquibus omnes. *Finis. laus deo. Explicit liber satirici iuuenalis aquini.* Scripsit benedictus *1475* die secundo aprilis. f. 81v blank

Juvenal, *Satirae I-XVI*; W. V. Clausen, ed., OCT (1959) pp. 37–175.

Paper (watermarks similar to Briquet Lettre A 7918), ff. 81 + i (paper), 211 x 136 (151 x 80) mm. Written in 24 lines of verse; double bounding lines; ruled in hard point.

I^{10}, II^{12}, $III-VII^{10}$, VIII^{10} (-10). First catchword, enclosed in red flourishes, is located in middle of lower margin; others appear along bottom of page, some with red initial strokes.

Written in a poorly formed humanistic script by a certain Benedictus (see contents for colophon).

Initials, 5- to 3-line, in red, at beginning of each satire; initials stroked in red, for first letter of each verse.

Binding: s. xviii-xix. Vellum case, with "Satyre Iuvena Saphon Carmin M.S." on spine, in gold.

Written in Italy in 1475; early provenance unknown. Ex libris of Raimondo Ambrosini of Bologna (d. 1914), with notations "MS 474" and "7274" (codex not listed in G. Mazzatinti, ed., *Inventari dei manoscritti delle Biblioteche d'Italia*, 14 [Forlì, 1909]

pp. 9-58). Bought from Rosenthal's in 1932 by Thomas E. Marston (bookplate) who presented it to Yale in 1936.

secundo folio: cum populum

Bibliography: De Ricci, v. 2, p. 2254, no. 70.

MS 71 Italy, s. XV^2
Juvenal; Persius

1. ff. 1r-68v //Flos asye ante ipsum pretio maiore paratus/ Quam fuit et tulli census pugnacis et ancis/ ... Vt qui fortis erit sit felicissimus idem/ Vt leti faleris omnes et torquibus omnes.

   Juvenal, *Satirae V.56-XVI* (lines 29-94 of Satire XV are interpolated between lines 293 and 294 of XIV); W. V. Clausen, ed., OCT (1959) pp. 56-175.

2. ff. 68v-79v Nec fonte labra prolui cabalino/ Nec in bicipiti somniasse parnaso/ ... Continuo crassum ridet fulphennius ingens/ Et centum grecos curto centusse licetur.

   Persius, Prologue followed by *Satirae I-V.59*; and *V. 149-191*; Clausen, *op. cit.*, pp. 3-25.

Paper (watermarks similar to Briquet Echelle 5904, 5908 and Harlfinger Flèche 12), ff. ii (contemporary paper) + 79 + ii (nearly contemporary paper), 215 x 146 (140 x 95) mm. Written in 22 lines of verse; double vertical bounding lines ruled in lead; horizontal guide-lines in ink. Prickings at top and bottom of folio.
I-VII^{10}, VIII^8 (+ 1 leaf at end). Catchwords perpendicular to text between inner bounding lines.
Written by a single scribe in humanistic script. Marginal notes and corrections in several hands.
Plain decorative initials with vine work designs, outlined in ink but not painted, mark the beginning of satires. Initial of each verse stroked with red (much faded). Spaces left for headings.
Binding: s. xix-xx. Vellum non-adhesive binding.

Written in Italy in the second half of the 15th century; early provenance unknown. Presented to Yale in 1936 by Thomas E. Marston (bookplate).

secundo folio: Gurgite

Bibliography: De Ricci, v. 2, p. 2254, no. 71.

MS 72
Juvenal

Italy, s. XV^2

ff. 1r–69v   [S]emper ego auditor tantum numquam ne reponam/ Vexatus totiens rauci teseide codri/ ... [final five lines added in a later hand:] Pythagoras? c[u]nctis animalibus abstinuit qui/ Tamquam homine et uentri indulsit non omne legumen? Expliciunt.

Juvenal, *Satirae I–XVI* (with XVI preceding XV); W. V. Clausen, ed., OCT (1959) pp. 37–175.

Paper (watermarks similar to Harlfinger Huchet 18, 21, 22), ff. ii (paper) + 69 + ii (paper), 217 x 144 (150 x 85) mm. Written in 28 lines of verse; double vertical and horizontal lines, full across; ruled in hard point, on verso.
I^{12} (–1), II–V^{12}, VI^{10}. Catchwords in center of lower margin.
Written in italic script by one person; some marginal and interlinear glosses on first two satires.
Spaces left for initials and headings.
Binding: s. xix–xx. Vellum case.

Written in Italy in the second half of the 15th century. "Padoua 1678" on inside flap of front cover; inscription on f. 1r "del Conte Jacomo di Sterpeto [?]". Presented to Yale in 1936 by Thomas E. Marston (bookplate).

secundo folio: Cum leno

Bibliography: De Ricci, v. 2, p. 2254, no. 72.

MS 73
Juvenal, with commentary

Germany, s. XV^2

1. ff. 1r–61r   Semper ego auditor tantum nunquam ne reponam/ Vexatus tociens rauci theseide codri/ ... Vt qui fortis erit sit foelicissimus idem/ Vt laeti phaleris omnes et torquibus omnes.

   Juvenal, *Satirae I–XVI*; W. V. Clausen, ed., OCT (1959) pp. 37–175.

2. ff. 1r–61r   [Unidentified commentary on the sixteen satires of Juvenal, beginning at top of left hand column:] Theseus Egei athenarum Regis filius ex Ethra coniuge qui adolescens optante Medea ... torquibus: torques militares erant sumpto more a gallis ... followed by a few sentences explaining the distinctions between orator, rhetor, and declamator.

   This extensive commentary, written in the same hand as the text, draws upon some of the earlier scholia as well as works of later scholars; it is not listed in the CTC.

3. ff. 61v–62r   Miscellaneous passages on the nature of tragedy, satire, comedy,

plus a short life of Juvenal: Vita Iuuenalis aquinatis Satirici. Iunius Iuuenalis libertini locupletis incertum alumnus an filius ad mediam ... nobis non est longa disputacione confirmandum.

The *Vita* begins in the same manner as no. I printed by O. Jahn, ed. *D. Iunii Iuuenalis Saturarum libri V* (Berlin, 1851) p. 386.

Paper (watermarks similar to Briquet Tête de boeuf 14874), ff. iii (paper) + 62 (foliation in lower right corner, in pencil, runs from 70-131) + iii (paper), 315 x 211 (127 x 85) mm. Written in 32 lines of verse; double vertical bounding lines, with additional narrow column in inner margin and two columns in outer margin for extensive commentary; ruled in hard point, on verso.
I-IV^{12}, V^{14}. Signatures of later date on recto along lower margin.
Written by a single scribe in a well spaced informal bâtarde for the main text and in a very small cramped bâtarde for surrounding notes.
Crude illuminated initial, 9-line, on f. 1r; red initials, 3-line, at beginning of remaining satires. First letter of each verse stroked in red (ff. 13r-61r); some lines underlined in red.
Binding: s. xx. Cloth case, bound in Yale Conservation Studio post 1973.

Written in Germany in the second half of the 15th century; early provenance unknown. Gift of Thomas E. Marston (bookplate) in 1936.

secundo folio: Flaminieam

Bibliography: De Ricci, v. 2, p. 2254, no. 73.

MS 74 England, s. XVII^{med}
Juvenal, Satirae I-IV (in Eng.)

1. f. 1r [Dedicatory epistle to Sir Robert Wiseman:] To the Right Worshipfull Sr Robert Wiseman Knight all increase of happines. Right W^o: Notwithstanding the Greeke Proverb: δὴ κράμβη θάνατος ... and my rough-hude lines more welcome to all ingenuous, and honest-harted mens reading. Yours ever to be comannded. Jo: Billinge Jo: f. 1v blank

2. ff. 2r-35r Iunij Iuuenalis Aquinatis Sat. I. Argu: Here is describ'd the perfect ground./ Why he his Muse to Satyres bound./ [text:] Shall I alone for ever lend mine eare,/ And not repaie my wrongs, but still forbeare,/ ... Amongst the trades men to then did befall./ And with his dearest blood did pay for all. ff. 35v-44v blank, except for inscription (see below)

Juvenal, *Satirae I-IV*, in the English translation of Jo Billinge and Sir Thomas Hewitt; for a discussion of the text and its translators see G. M. Parássoglou, "A Seventeenth-Century Translation of Juvenal," *Gazette* 46 (1971) pp. 12-19. Jo Billinge explains in the dedicatory epistle "I have boldlie presumed to joyne the two first Satyres (which indeed belong unto your worthie kinsman, and my much respected friend Sir Thomas Huet) unto the third and fourth: partlie, because they'r all one mans worke, and so ought not to be parted or disjointed...."

The text of the translation is accompanied by Latin footnotes, some drawn from the *scholia uetustiora* (P. Wessner, ed., Teubner [1931]).

Paper (watermarks: trimmed and buried in gutter), iii (paper) + 44 + iii (paper), 154 x 96 mm. (the measurements of the written space vary according to the number of footnotes).
The binding is too tight to permit an accurate collation.
Written by a single scribe in a neat running hand.
Binding: s. xix. Blind-tooled calf.

Written in England probably in the middle of the 17th century, presumably by Jo Billinge who signed the dedicatory epistle; note (s. xvii-xviii?) written upside down on f. 44v: "Introibo ad altare dei as holy Martye [*sic*] sayd when He was a burning. by name Mill Master." Sold by Thorpe (cat. 1836, no. 738) to Sir Thomas Phillipps (no. 9178; inscription on f. i verso); Phillipps sale (London, 1896, no. 784) to Quaritch; sale by Sotheby's (London, 13 July 1921, no. 792) to Dobell. Purchased from C. A. Stonehill on 20 Sept. 1932 by Thomas E. Marston (bookplate); his gift to Yale in 1936.

Bibliography: De Ricci, v. 2, p. 2254, no. 74.

MS 75 England, s. XVII[1]
Lawyer's Commonplace Book of Precedents

1. ff. 1r-336v   The personal handbook of a legal scholar (perhaps from Gloucestershire?) arranged according to subject and with internal cross references; some theological and literary notes interspersed (e.g., ff. 202r-203v, 213v have brief excerpts from Sallust, Juvenal, Martial, Tertullian, Bacon, Horace, Cicero, Ovid, Lucan, Persius, and the Bible, some with translations into English). Includes sections devoted to: Constable and Marshall, Preachers and Preaching, Creeds, Barons, Constables and Marshalls, Barons, Seales, Seals of the King, Indictments ... London, Barons and Earles, Universities of Oxford and Cambridge, Corporations, Treason.

2. ff. 337r-347r   Abbeys: fo: 53:/ Abbey lands: fo: 52:/ Ability: fo: 195:/ ... Words: fo: 179:/ Writts originall: fo: 93:/ Writts of Right: fo: 93:

   Alphabetical index with many entries under the heading "First Book" and a few under "Second ["& third" suprascript]."

Paper (watermarks: unidentified arms with fleur-de-lis and various counter-

marks including IHS), ff. ii (original paper) + 348, 351 x 220 (ca. 330 x 161) mm. Written in ca. 82 lines; single horizontal bounding line at top of folio, and a single vertical bounding line on the left (and sometimes on the right) to delineate a column for marginal notes. Ruled in lead.
   The volume is too tightly bound to be collated.
   Written in a small cramped legal script by several writers.
   Binding: s. xviii. Brown leather, flesh side out or very worn.

Written in England in the first half of the 17th century, probably by several secretaries for the original owner; the addition of a column for "Second & third" book in the index suggests that MS 75 was the first volume in a series of three. Unidentified round paper tag with "151" on spine. Sold in 1830 by Jeffery of Pall Mall to Sir Thomas Phillipps (no. 4468; tag on spine); his sale (London, 1935, no. 131) to C. A. Stonehill from whom it was purchased by Thomas E. Marston (bookplate); his gift to Yale in 1936.

Bibliography: De Ricci, v. 2, p. 2255, no. 75.

MS 76   Italy, s. XV$^{3/4}$
Agogo Mago

ff. 1r-8v   *Lo libro medesynal* delli spariueri vuol chussi che quando lo spariuero se infirmo ... Sello spariuero auera nudhi dalli felle chaura cum olio et cum insenço. *Complito che lo libro de* agogo mago a grilliciano [?] Re de tute le passione vien a falchoni a hosthori et spariueri. ff. 9r-10v ruled, but blank

   Printed as the second part of Agogo Mago, *Libro de la natura de cavalli* ... (Venice, 1517) Gi-viii; A. Lupis, *Petrus de l'Astore* (Bari, 1979) p. 32, n.

   Parchment, ff. i (paper) + 10 + i (paper), 220 x 142 (155 x 100) mm. Written in 30 long lines; double vertical bounding lines. Ruled in hard point, hair side, for vertical lines; ink for horizontal; prickings along upper and lower edges.
   One gathering of ten leaves.
   Written by a single scribe in a neat humanistic bookhand.
   One gold initial (f. 1r), 7-line, filled and surrounded by white-vine ornament, on a dark blue, dark red, and dark green ground, with pale yellow dots; extends into inner and upper margins. In lower margin an unidentified coat of arms (or, on a chief azur a parrot vert beaked gules) in a laurel wreath; accompanied by gold balls, hair-sprays, and simple floral patterns. Four initials, 6- to 4-line, in blue with red penwork designs or red with purple; plain capitals alternating red and blue throughout.
   Binding: s. xix. Brown goatskin, gold-tooled.

Written in Italy (possibly Florence) in the third quarter of the 15th century according to A. C. de la Mare; unidentified arms on f. 1r (see above). Belonged to C. F. G. R. Schwerdt (bookplate; see catalogue *Hunting Hawking Shooting* [London, 1928] v. 2, p. 315, pl. 154 of f. 1r); his sale (Sotheby's, 12 March 1946, no. 2174). Purchased from Quaritch, 26 Oct. 1946, by the Yale Library Associates, with funds contributed by Mrs. Samuel Milbank.

secundo folio: [por]tato fioli tute

Bibliography: Faye and Bond, p. 26, no. 76.

MS 77
Albertus Magnus, De animalibus

Germany, s. XV^2

ff. 1r-388v Scienciam de animalibus secundum eam quam in principio premisimus diuisionem post scientiam de vegetabilibus ... Hec igitur de uermibus dicta sint a nobis ... et ego talium hominum parum curo reprehensiones. *Explicit edicio alberti magni quam scripsit diffuse et gloriose de naturis animalium. Deo gratias.*

A. Borgnet, ed., *B. Alberti Magni ... opera omnia,* v. 11-12 (1891).

Paper, with parchment bifolios at beginning and end of each gathering (watermarks: similar to Briquet Lettre P 8606 and 8625), ff. ii (paper) + 388, 285 x 209 (180 x 137) mm. Written in two columns, frame-ruled in crayon with double (occasionally single or triple) horizontal bounding lines full across; single inner and double outer vertical bounding lines; remains of prickings in upper, lower, and outer margins.

I-XIV^{12}, XV^{10}, XVI-XXXII^{12}, XXXXIII^{12} (-7 through 12). Catchwords along lower edge in gutter, on verso; some leaf signatures, on recto (e.g., d 1, d 2, etc.).

Written by a single scribe in a neat running script for the text and a more formal style for rubrics.

First initial on f. 1r, 10-line, painted blue, on red and green ground, yellow highlights. Many small plain initials in red and/or blue. Major headings lacking; minor rubrics and red initial strokes throughout.

Binding: s. xv-xvi. Sewn and wound on five slit, tawed straps laced into oak boards and pegged or nailed. Kermes pink, braided endbands attached to primary ones sewn on hempen [?] cores laced into boards. Covered in brown calf, blind-stamped in a diamond pattern filled in with roses, fleurs-de-lis, eagles, and lions [?]. Traces of five round bosses on each board and of three nails to attach a chain at the head of the lower board. Tongue turn-ins. Two clasps on the upper board and stubs of pink, tawed straps held to the lower with metal plates. Remains of a title on parchment on the upper board. Numerous place markers, some vermilion leather, some very small Turk's head knots of leather or tawed skin. Rebacked.

Written in Germany in the second half of the 15th century; early provenance unknown. Belonged to Sir Thomas Phillipps (no. 2234; inscription and stamp on f. 1r); his purchase from Longman. Collection of C. F. G. R. Schwerdt (bookplate; see catalogue *Hunting Hawking Shooting* [London, 1928] v. 2, p. 315); his sale (Sotheby's, 12 March 1946, no. 2176). Acquired from Goldschmidt's by David Wagstaff (bookplate); gift of Mr. and Mrs. David Wagstaff in 1949.

secundo folio: corporis animalis

Bibliography: Faye and Bond, p. 26, no. 77.

MS 78　　　　　　　　　　　　　　　　　　　　　　Spain, s. XVI, XVII
Antiphonal, etc.

I. 1. ff. 1r–33v　Common of Saints

　2. ff. 33v–37v　Dedication of a church.

　3. ff. 37v–38r　Commemoration of the Holy Cross.

　4. ff. 38v–43v　Antiphons for suffrages: Sancta Maria succurrere miseris iuua ... [lessons for Hours of the Virgin]; Petrus apostolus et paulus doctor gentium...; Salue sancte pater patrie lux forma minorum uirtutis ... [RH 40727, Saint Francis of Assisi]; Hic vir despiciens mundus et terrena triumphans ... [RH 37909]; Vos sancti dei incliti qui estis mente lucidi francisci [RH 22150, Sancti ordinis minorum]; Da pacem domine in diebus nostris quia non...; O Sacrum Conuiuium in quo christus ... [RH 13677]; Sub tuum presidium confugimus sancta dei genitrix...; Isti sunt due oliue et duo candelabra....

II. 5. ff. 44r–45r　Si queris miracula, mors, error, calamitas, demon, lepra fugiunt ... [RH 18886; Antony of Padua].

　6. ff. 45r–46r　Office for Peter of Alcantara, O.F.M. *S. Petri de Alcantara.* Domine Iesu christe, cui sanctus Petrus adeo fideliter in vita sua seruiuit....

　7. ff. 46v–47v　Office for Paschalis Baylon, O.F.M. Paschalis admirabilis insignis et prodigijs, qui magnus splendens meritus celestes ... [RH 14600].

　8. ff. 48r–50r　Hymn to the Virgin. Salue mater Saluatoris fons salutis vas honoris scala celi ... [RH 18044]. f. 50v blank

Paper (sturdy; staggered thumb holes at bottom of leaves), ff. i (contemporary paper, ruled for music) + 50, 505 x 375 (360 x 268) mm. Written in 5 long lines of text, accompanied by musical notation; single vertical bounding lines ruled in lead; double horizontal guide-lines, in pale brown ink, for each line of text; staves in red with black square notes.

The binding is too tight to allow an accurate collation.

Written by two scribes in a large round gothic bookhand. 1: ff. 1r–43v (s. XVI);

2: ff. 44r–50r (s. XVII). Scribe 2 attempts to replicate the work of Scribe 1, but uses 5-line staves rather than 4-line.

Decoration for ff. 1r–43v: initials, with foliage designs, in rectangular frame, often with ground uncolored; colors range from vibrant blue, yellow, and orange to olive green and dark purple. Initials for ff. 44r–50r, of similar design, with more subdued shades, and no frames.

Binding: s. xvi–xvii. Vellum stays, contemporary paper flyleaves and pastedowns. Original sewing on five supports attached to very thick, square wooden boards. Beaded and colored endbands. Red edges. Covered in brown calf [cow?] reinforced at spine with additional leather and straps nailed to the boards. Traces of a strap-and-pin fastening. Vellum label with notation "Antiphonar. Com. sanctorum" nailed to lower board. The badly warped upper board is reinforced with two strips of wood placed vertically on the upper surface.

Written in Spain during the 16th century presumably for Franciscan use (Part I) and supplemented (Part II) during 17th century; the second portion may have been added for use of the Reform Congregation of the Spanish Discalceates of which Peter of Alcantara was the founder (see art. 7). Presented to Yale in 1940 by Carl B. Spitzer.

Bibliography: Faye and Bond, p. 26, no. 78.

MS 79 Spain, s. XVI
Pedro López de Ayala, Aves de caça

1. f. i recto-verso. *Nostro Señor Dios.* Quando Crio el mundo e fízo el hombre todas las animalias ... podran sere Caminados y los aues Remediadas.

   Preface; J. Gutierrez de la Vega, ed., *Libros de cetrería* (Madrid, 1879) v. 1, pp. 143–46.

2. ff. ii recto – iii recto. *Tabla. Capitulo.* Primero de las aves que son llamadas de Rapinya ... Capitulo xxxxvij. de quales cosas ... el cacador e traer consígo para sus aues [followed by the heading for chapter 1, placed incorrectly at the end of the table] *Fin.* f. iii verso blank

   J. Gutierrez, *op. cit.*, pp. 146–49.

3. pp. 1–129 *De cada dia.* Vieron los hombres de como naturalmente vnas aues comen la las otras ... E ansi Aura tu Falcon Talante de Comer. ["H. M. D. L. V." added in a somewhat later hand] *Veni ad saluandum nos Domine deus noster.* pp. 130–32 ruled, but blank

   J. Gutierrez, *op. cit.*, pp. 151–344.

Paper, 3 leaves (presently unnumbered) + pp. 1–130 (pagination by a modern hand, in pencil) + 1 leaf, 215 x 159 (168 x 103) mm. Written in 30 long lines for preface, 27 for text; frame-ruled in lead.

I-IV^{16}, V^6 (-6). Signature for first leaves of gathering, on recto (a.i, a.ij, a.iij, etc.).

Written by a single scribe in a careful italic script.

Crude initial and heading (in gold and subdued water colors) on f. i recto and f. 1r; other small initials, 4- to 1-line, in similar colors throughout text. Headings in red; initials of each paragraph in blue or red.

Waterstained throughout.

Binding: s. xvii. Black goatskin, blind-tooled. Fragments of manuscripts (covered by paper pastedowns) serve as binding reinforcements.

Written in Spain in the 16th century; early provenance unknown. Belonged to Sir John Saunders Sebright; sale to Robinson's in 1939 from whom it was purchased by David Wagstaff (bookplate). Presented to Yale in 1944 by Mr. and Mrs. David Wagstaff.

Bibliography: Faye and Bond, p. 26, no. 79.

M. G. Wynne, "The Wagstaff Sporting Books and Manuscripts," *Gazette* 20 (1945) pp. 11-12.

MS 80 Italy, s. XIV^1
Remigius of Auxerre, etc.

1. f. 1r blank; f. 1v   Brief excerpts from Bede, *Super Canticum Canticorum* (Bk. 4; PL 91. 1142) and from Leo, *In sermone quodam.* Excedit quidem dilectissimj multumque supereminet humanj eloquij facultatem ... (A. Chavasse, ed., CC lat. ser. 138 [1973] p. 146).

2. f. 2r-v   Selections from Gregory, *Moralia in Iob* (from Prologue, Books 2, 20, 21; PL 75. 553 etc.).

3. ff. 3r-4r   Vt iuuet et prosit conatur pagina presens/ Dultius arrident seria picta iocis/ ... Nam prouisa minus ledere tela solent/ Iam metitur linum iam fiunt retia iam uir//

   Gualterus Anglicus, *Fabulae*; K. McKenzie and W. A. Oldfather, eds., *Ysopet-Avionnet: The Latin and French Texts* in University of Illinois Studies in Language and Literature 5 (1919). The order of the fables is 1-13, 15-18, 24-25.

4. ff. 4v-5v   Index of readings, in red and black, for items on ff. 31r-87v, beginning *Dominica prima de aduentu* and concluding *In festo beati francisci* (5 entries). f. 6r-v blank

Arts. 5-19 are composed of a series of sermons drawn from Remigius of Auxerre, *Expositio super Matthaeum* (PL 131. 865-932). See also H. Barré, *Les homéliaires carolingiens de l'école d'Auxerre* in *Studi e Testi* 225 (Vatican, 1962) pp. 125-29; Beinecke

MS 80 corresponds most closely to "r" (Vatican lat. 648). For each art. we have recorded the heading as it appears in the manuscript, followed by that portion of Matthew, with commentary, excerpted for the sermon.

5. f. 7r–v *Expositio remigij super Matthaeum. Initium sancti Euangelii secundum Matthaeum.* Initium est inchoatio uel alicuius rei principium quasi primum capud ... ad quam currebant omnes quasi ad fontem omnis doctrine.

    Preface; Stegmüller, v. 5, 7226.

6. ff. 7v–8r *In natiuitate beate marie. Liber generationis ihesu christi etc.*

    Matthew 1.1–3; Stegmüller, v. 5, 7226.

7. ff. 8r–9r *In uigilia natiuitatis domini. Cum esset desponsata mater ihesu maria ioseph.*

    Matthew 1.18–23; Stegmüller, v. 5, 7226, 1 (Sermo IV).

8. ff. 9r–10v *De epyphania. Cum natus esset ihesus in bethleem....*

    Matthew 2.1–12; Stegmüller, v. 5, 7226, 1 (Sermo VII).

9. ff. 10v–11r *In festo innocentium. Angelus domini apparuit in sompnis ioseph etc.*

    Matthew 2.13–18.

10. ff. 11r–12r *In uigilia epyphanie. Defuncto autem herode etc.*

    Matthew 2.19–23; Stegmüller, v. 5, 7226, 1 (Sermo VI).

11. ff. 12r–14v *Dominica prima xl^e. Ductus est ihesus in desertum a spiritu etc.*

    Matthew 4.1–10.

12. ff. 14v–15v *In festo sancti Andree. Ambulans ihesus iuxta mare Galilee etc.*

    Matthew 4.18.

13. ff. 15v–16v *Dominica .5. post pentecosten. Nisi habundauerit iustitia uestra etc.*

    Matthew 5.20–23.

14. ff. 16v–17v *Dominica .14. post pentecosten. Nemo potest duobus dominis seruire.*

    Matthew 6.24–33.

15. ff. 17v–19r *Dominica .3. post epyphaniam. Cum descendisset ihesus de monte etc.*

    Matthew 8.1–13; Stegmüller, v. 5, 7226, 1 (Sermo VIII).

16. ff. 19r–21r *Feria .5. post diem cinerum. Cum autem introisset ihesus capharnaum etc.*

    Matthew 8.5–13.

17. ff. 21r–22r *Dominica .4. post epyphaniam. Adscendente ihesu in nauiculam secuti sunt eum....*

    Matthew 8.23–27; Stegmüller, v. 5, 7726, 1 (Sermo IX).

18. ff. 22r–23r *Dominica .18. post pentecosten. Asscendens ihesus in naviculam transfretauit etc.*

    Matthew 9.1–8.

MS 80

19. ff. 23r-25r   Dominica .23. post pentecosten. Adhuc illo loquente ad eos ecce princeps unus etc.

Matthew 9.18-26.

20. ff. 25r-28r   Incipit liber beati Augustini de natiuitate et passione christi et de virgine maria. [O]mnis qui ad dominum hemanuel. Hoc est uerbum patris altissimi quo caro factum est et habitauit in nobis ... Benedictus tu a christo Benedictus a matre christi ipsius quem dilexisti ... in secula seculorum. Amen.

H. Thurn, *Die Handschriften der Universitätsbibliothek Würzburg* in Handschriften aus benediktinischen Provenienzen 2, 1 (Weisbaden, 1973) pp. 58-59, MS M, ch. f. 169, ff. 59r-62r. In other manuscripts this work is attributed to Bernard.

21. ff. 28r-30r   [S]ingna [sic] et mirabilia fecit apud me deus excelsus. Daniel. 3. Omnis speculatio sapientialis inquisitiam altissimarum intellectuali ... Nec fas dicere nec fas scire ... etc.

Rubric in upper margin: *In festo beati francissci Et in festo stigmatum.*

22. f. 30r   In natiuitate domini. [U]erbum caro factum est. Io. [John 1. 14]. Prima anime impressio in corpus est uita ita prima ... [27 lines; incomplete]. f. 30v blank

Unidentified sermon which appears again in art. 68.

Arts. 23-57 are composed primarily of selections from Luke accompanied by Bede's *Expositio super Lucam* (D. Hurst, ed., CC lat. ser. 120 [1960]) arranged as sermons. For each art. we have recorded the heading as it appears in the manuscript, followed by the reference to that portion of Luke, with commentary, excerpted for the sermon.

23. ff. 31r-32r   [Rubric missing; later note in upper margin:] *Euangelium secundum Lucam cuius expositio sit ignoro.* [text:] *Fuit in diebus herodis regis* ....

Luke 1.3-25.

24. f. 32r-v   In annuntiatione beate Marie uirginis. In mense autem sexto missus est angelus ....

Luke 1.26-38.

25. ff. 32v-33r   Feria .vi. quattuor temporum de Aduentu. Et discesscit ab illa angelus.

Luke 1.38-46.

26. f. 33r-v   In natiuitate sancti Iohannis baptiste.

Luke 1.57-68.

27. ff. 33v-34v   In prima missa natiuitatis domini.

Luke 2.1-14.

28. f. 34v   *In secunda missa natiuitatis domini.*
Luke 2.15-20.

29. ff. 34v-35r   *In circumcisione domini.*
Luke 2. 21.

30. f. 35r-v   *In purificatione beate Marie virginis.*
Luke 2.22-32.

31. ff. 35v-36r   *Dominica .I^a. oct. natiuitatis domini.*
Luke 2.33-40.

32. ff. 36r-37r   *Dominica .I^a. oct. epyphanie.*
Luke 2.42-52.

33. f. 37r-v   *Dominica .iiij. de Aduentu.*
Luke 3.1-6.

34. ff. 37v-38v   *Dominica prima de Aduentu.*
Luke 21.25-33.

35. ff. 38r-39r   *Dominica sexagessime.*
Luke 8.4-15.

36. ff. 39r-40r   *Dominica .iij. in quadragessima.*
Luke 11.14-28.

37. ff. 40r-42r   *Dominica quinquagessime.*
Luke 18.31-43.

38. ff. 42r-43r   *Feria secunda post pascam.*
Luke 34.13-35.

39. f. 43r-v   *Feria .iija. post pascam.*
Luke 34.36-47 (a portion of the text missing here is inserted on f. 55r-v).

40. ff. 43v-44r   *Dominica .ij^a. post pentecosten.*
Luke 14.16-24.

41. ff. 44r-45r   *Dominica .iiij. post pentecosten.*
Luke 5.1-11.

42. f. 45r-v   *Dominica .xvj. post pentecosten.*
Luke 14.1-11.

43. ff. 45v-46r   *Dominica .xv. post pentecosten.*
Luke 7.11-16.

MS 80

44. ff. 46r-47r   *Dominica .xij. post pentecosten.*
    Luke 10.23-37.

45. f. 47r-v   *Dominica .x. post pentecosten.*
    Luke 18.9-14.

46. ff. 47v-48v   *Dominica .ix. post pentecosten.*
    Luke 19.41-47.

47. ff. 48v-49r   *Dominica .iij. post pentecosten.*
    Luke 15.1-10.

48. f. 49r-v   *Dominica .viij. post pentecosten.*
    Luke 16.1-9.

49. ff. 49v-50r   *Dominica prima post pentecosten.*
    Luke 6.36-42.

50. f. 50r-v   *In festo Sancte Marie magdalene.*
    Luke 7.36-50

51. f. 50v   *Dominica .xiiij. post pentecosten.*
    Matthew 6.24.

52. ff. 50v-51r   *Dominica .iij. post epyphaniam.*
    Luke 5.12-14.

53. f. 51r-v   *Feria .vj. post pentecosten.*
    Luke 5.17-25.

54. ff. 51v-52v   *De dominica .iij. post epyphaniam.*
    Luke 7.1-10.

55. ff. 52v-53v   *Dominica .23. post pentecosten.*
    Luke 8.41-56.

56. ff. 53v-54v   *Dominica prima xl^e M^c.*
    Luke 4.1-13.

57. ff. 54v-55r   *Dominica .ij. xl^e.*
    Luke 9.28-36.

58. f. 55r-v   Brief section omitted from f. 43r-v (art. 39).

59. f. 55v   *De sepulcro David. Mouet fortassis aliquos qui tamen modo simplicia monumenta nouerunt ... sicut postea mendose dicere uoluerunt.*

60. f. 56r   [A]*udite obsecro uniuersi populi et uidete* ... [Lamentations 1.18]. *Hodie si uocem domini audierietis nolite obdurate corda uestra* ... [Psalms 94.8]. *In-*

uenitur per scripturam quod animalia quedam audientes uocem genitricis recognoscunt et statim secuntur ... Hunc dolorem et hanc tristiam ostendunt quatuor notarij et euangeliste christi ... etc.

61. ff. 56v-59v   In quo uerbo .5. per ordinem ostendit et predixit. Primo Locum sue passionis. 2º Modum proditionis ... et tanta lacrimarum eius effusione resoluta est unde omnia christi membra tergeret.

A collection of passages from Anselm, Augustine, Bede, and Ambrose on the Passion of Christ. One scribe wrote the main text on ff. 56v-59r, for which the incipit and explicit are given above; several others made extensive additions on f. 59r-v and in the margins of ff. 56v-58v.

62. ff. 60r-69v   *De passione christi.* Hec passus sum absque iniquitate manus mee cum haberem mundas ad deum preces ... [Iob 16.18-19]. Sicut narrat sanctus ylarius magnus doctor ecclesie ... Color uero monumenti et loculi rubicundo et albo dicitur esse permixtus.

63. ff. 69v-71r   *De passione christi.* Inter omnia digna memoria que annuatim recolit sancta dei ecclesia est precipue passio et mors christi ... milites romani ad custodiam sepulcri clausi et sigillo muniti. *M. 21. g. Altera autem die que est post pasceuen etc.*

64. ff. 71r-72r   *De resurrectione.* In sua resurrectione dominus et saluator noster suam potentiam suam sapientiam et suam bonitatem ostendit ... Decima et ultima [apparitio] fuit facta in monte oliueti hora nona ... *illis eleuatus est etc.* [Acts 1.9].

65. f. 72r-v   Series of passages from the Bible and various authors (added in a later hand).

66. ff. 73r-74v   Sermo pro beato francisco. Hic erat edoctus uiam dei et feruens spiritu loquebatur et docebat diligenter ... [Acts 18.25, followed by Exodus 38.8:] Legitur exo. xxxviij quod fecit moyses labrum eneum cum basi sua de speculis mulierum. [text:] Labrum hoc erat lauatorium in quo sacerdotes lauabant manus et pedes ... Ad cuius ibidem consortium eius meritis peruenire ualeamus. Amen.

67. ff. 74v-75r   [V]idi et ecce quadrige. 4^{or} ... [Zechariah 6.1]. Hanc uisionem reuelauit dominus zachiarie ... ut credetes [sic] uitam eternam habeamus.

Hugo de Sancto Caro; Stegmüller, v. 3, 3721.

68. f. 75r   Same sermon (complete?) as art. 8, but beginning Sicut prima anime....

f. 75r blank

69.   According to the index on ff. 4v-5v two sections now missing (leaves 41-64 of the original foliation) with the headings *De mortuis* and *De fratre mortuo* were included between arts. 68 and 70.

Arts. 70-80 are unidentified sermons for feast days.

70. f. 76r-v *Dominica in oct. epyphanie.* Remansit puer ihesus in ierusalem [Luke 2.43]. Verbum hoc sumptum est de euangelio beati luce quod quamuis ystorialiter exponatur ... sponsam ornatam monilibus suis.

71. ff. 77r-77v [heading in upper margin:] Dominica. 1x. [text:] Exiit qui seminat seminare ... [Luke 8.5]. Verbum istud sumptum est de euangelio beati luce. Et est uerbum saluatoris eterni genus humanum ... et credentibus exercitantibus se in illo.

72. ff. 78r-79r [heading in upper margin:] Dominica quinquagessime. [text:] Ihesu fili dauid miserere mei [Luke 18.38]. Verbum istud sumptum est de euangelio beati luce et est uerbum illius ceci sedentis secus uiam ... Ad quam patriam ille uos et ... Amen.

73. ff. 79r-80r *Dominica prima xl^e.* Non in solo pane uiuit homo ... [Matthew 4.4]. Verbum hoc sumptum de euangelio beati Matthei est uerbum saluatoris eterni christi s. filii dei temptationi diabolice respondentis ... Venite benedicti patris mei precipite regem ... Seculorum.

74. f. 80r-v *De beato francisco.* Vidi septem candelabra aurea et in medio ... [Apoc. 1.12-13]. In uerbis istis de appocalypse sumptis ad laudem et gloriam beati patris nostri francisci ... caritatis et desiderio martirij.

75. ff. 80v-82v *De passione christi.* Exeamus ad eum extra castra ... [Hebrews 13.13]. Considerans beatus apostolus immensitatem benignitatis christi ... et consedere nos si faceret in celestibus. Amen.

76. f. 82v *De resurrectione.* Venit ihesus ianuis clausis et stetit ... [John 20.26]. Post regis nostri conuiuantis conuiuia post patientis tollerata supplitia ... ad possessiones redire etc. [Four lines of art. 78 at end of this article, crossed out by original scribe.]

77. ff. 82v-83r *De asscensione.* Introiuit ihesus in ipsum celum ut appareret uultui ... [Hebrews 9.24]. Questio facta fuerat sponse a suis sodalibus in canticis 6. Quo abiit dilectus tuus ... Securum accessum habes ... etc.

78. f. 83r-v *De pentecosten.* Quis continuit spiritum dei in manibus suis [Proverbs 30.4]. Spiritus dei ... [Wisdom 1.7]. Tria sunt utilia immo necessaria in enuntiatione diuini eloqui ... dona spiritus sancti de quibus dicitur in ysaya etc.

79. f. 83v *De eodem.* Adduxit dominus deus Spiritum super terram et prohibite sunt pluuie de celo ... [Genesis 8.1-2]. Describere hoc donum spiritus sancti ut gratum et liberale ... Spiritus eius ornauit celos etc.

80. ff. 83v-84r *In ascensione.* Introiuit ihesus in ipsum celum ut supra [Hebrews 9.24]. In maliuolam [*sic*] animam non introibit sapientia ... [Wisdom 1.4]. Sicut ex multis scripture locis colligitur. Sapientia est Res clara ... Introuit ihesus in ipsum celum etc.

Arts. 81-84 consist of passages from the Bible grouped according to subjects (some sections accompanied by short commentary).

81. ff. 84r–85r   *De sacerdote nouo.* Nota quod sacerdotes debent esse. Sanctitate immaculati et puri. Illi enim dicuntur spiritualiter. leu. 21. Sancti erunt domino deo suo ... [five sections on this topic follow].

82. ff. 85r–86r   *De die cinerum.* Cuius uestrum bos aut asinus [Luke 14.5]. Semen cecidit in terram bonam [Luke 8.8]....

83. ff. 86r–87r   *De consecratione ecclesie.* Elegi et sanctificaui locum istum ut sit nomen meum ibi in sempiternum [2 Chronicles 16]....

84. f. 87r–v   *De consecratione altarium.* Altaria tua domine uirtutum rex meus et deus meus [Ps. 83.4]....

85. ff. 87v–105r   *Quedam boetij in libro de consolatione.* Quedam dicta Boetij excepta [*sic*] de libro de consolatione phylosophye de primo libro in primis uersibus. Mors hominum felix que se nec dulcibus annis ... Exultat uiso lapsus et ipse quidem. Almifico deo laudes referimus. Explicit liber quintus Boetij de consolatione philosophie. Gratias deo nostro et domino ihesu christo.

Excerpts from Boethius, *De consolatione philosophiae*; L. Bieler, ed., CC lat. ser. 94 (1957) pp. 1–105.

86. f. 105r–v   Miscellaneous notes (e. g., Nota de diuersis apparitionibus angelorum).

Paper (sturdy but of uneven weight; no watermarks, wavering chain-lines ca. 53 mm. apart), ff. 106, 228 x 148 (182 x 115) mm. Written in 2 columns of 45 lines; ruled in lead, single vertical and horizontal bounding lines full across. Prickings in upper, outer and lower margins.

I^6, II–V^8, VI^8 (+ 1, small leaf, f. 41), VII^8, VIII^4, IX–X^8, XI^6, XII^8, XIII^6 (+ 1 leaf, before f. 90), XIV^{10}. Catchwords below second column, sometimes enclosed on 3 sides by brown and/or red strokes.

Written mostly by one scribe, perhaps over a period of time, in a small gothic bookhand with many abbreviations. Additions by slightly later hands in more or less formal script, e.g. ff. 1v, 3r–5v, 87v–105v.

Initials (3-line), paragraph marks, underlining and strokes on 1-line capitals in red.

Binding: Date? Square, flush boards. Trimmed out turn-ins suggest a late date. Covered in vellum with contents and a compass-drawn circle on lower cover.

Written in Italy in the first half of the 14th century; an early owner made careful marginal notations, for which he added extra rulings in the margin (e.g., ff. 40v, 42r). On f. 1r, in a nearly contemporary hand, "Deputatus ad usum fratris Nicolutij Vingnutij de Fabriano." Belonged to the Convent of St. Francis at Serra S. Quirico, according to a note on f. 1r, in a hand of s. xvi or xvii: "Conuentus S. Francisci Serrae S. Quirici." No. 12 in an unidentified sales catalogue (entry in library files). Given to Yale in 1942 by Dr. Lowell C. Frost, Yale 1905.

secundo folio: Gregorius in

MS 81

Bibliography: Faye and Bond, p. 26, no. 80.

MS 81 England, s. XIII^2
Bible Pl. 18

ff. 204r-473v Order of the contents is as follows (numbers in parentheses refer to prefaces in Stegmüller, v. 1): text begins imperfectly in 3 Ezra 8.86 //omni tempore ut inualescentes...; Tobit (332); Judith (prologue missing, f. 208 cut out); Esther (341 + 343); Job (344, 357); Psalms; Proverbs (457); Ecclesiastes (462); Song of Songs; Wisdom (468); Ecclesiasticus (introduction to Ecclesiasticus considered as prologue: Multorum et magnorum nobis...); Isaiah (482); Jeremiah (487); Lamentations; Baruch (491); Ezekiel (492); Daniel (494); Prologue for Minor Prophets (500), Hosea (507), Joel (511, 510), Amos (515, 512, 513), Obadiah (519, 517), Jonah (524, 521), Micah (526), Nahum (528), Habakkuk (531), Zephaniah (534), Haggai (538), Zechariah (539), Malachi (543), 1 Maccabees (547, 553, 551), 2 Maccabees; Matthew (590, 589); Mark (607); Luke (Luke 1.1-4 treated as a prologue, followed by 620; missing 15.3-17.24, f. cut out after 433); John (624); Romans (677; missing 12.15-16.27, f. 452 cut out); 1 Corinthians (685), 2 Corinthians (699); Galatians (707); Ephesians (715; missing 1.20-6.24); Philippians (prologue and 1.1-2.25 missing, ff. 463-64 cut out); Colossians (736); 1 Thessalonians (747), 2 Thessalonians (752); 1 Timothy (765), 2 Timothy (772; f. 452 cut out); Titus (780); Philemon (783); Hebrews (793), whose text ends imperfectly at 10.11: est tottidie ministrans et easdem sepe offe//

Parchment, ff. i (parchment) + 264 (foliated, s. xv, 204-473) + i (parchment), 185 x 118 (122 x 78) mm., trimmed. Written in 2 columns of 52 lines; single vertical bounding lines with additional double vertical lines in inner and outer margins; 5 sets of horizontal bounding lines, double lines in upper and lower margins as well as at top and bottom of written space, triple lines through center of written space.

I^8 (structure uncertain, f. 208 cut out), II-IX^{24}, X (-8, after f. 411; no loss of text), XI^{24} (-7, f. 434), XII^{24} (-1, f. 452; -12, 13, ff. 463-64; -24, after f. 473). Catchwords, lower right between lower horizontal lines near gutter, on verso. Unidentified marks, in red, in lower margin, at end of each quire and beginning of subsequent quire, perhaps for the binder.

Written in tiny gothic textura by a single scribe.

Good initials for the beginning of each book and prologue, 10- to 4-line, blue or pink, with various shades combined in a single letter, with white highlights, often with prominent floral serifs in blue, pink, red, orange, and yellow, against pink and blue grounds; grounds for body of letter and serifs in opposite colors. Elaborate descenders, ascenders, as serifs, but often with biting dragons. Letters filled with curling floral motifs, often with dragon-head terminals, and biting dragons. The initials on f. 214r (Esther) and f. 220r (Job) are more elaborate than the others. 2-line initials for each chapter, blue or red, with red or blue flourishes. Running headings and chapter numbers in red and blue, with flourishes. Rubrics throughout.

Binding: s. xix. Printed parchment fragment, in large gothic letters, with portion of John 4.

Written in England in the second half of the 13th century; early provenance unknown. Presented to Yale in 1938 by Charles E. Bushnell.

Bibliography: Faye and Bond, pp. 26-27, no. 81.

MS 82 France, s. XIII^{med}
Bible Pl. 10

The codex is probably a normal French Bible (see Ker, MMBL, v. 1, pp. 96-97), but is so badly bound, with lacunae throughout, that we cannot be certain. Numbers in parentheses refer to prologues listed in Stegmüller, v. 1.

1. ff. 11-19   Exodus 2.3-36.15; Leviticus 13.30-23.13 with gaps between ff. 12 and 13, 13 and 14, 15 and 16, 16 and 17, and 18 and 19.

2. ff. 68-164, followed by ff. 1-10   1 Chronicles 15.12 to Ecclesiastes 3.10, with gaps throughout (see collation below). Prologues remaining: 2 Chronicles (327), 1 Ezra (330), Tobit (332), Judith (335), Esther (341 + 343), Job (344, 357), Proverbs (457), Ecclesiastes (462).

3. ff. 20-67   Matthew 7.26 to Hebrews 3.18 (with gaps). All of Thessalonians, Acts, Catholic Epistles, Apocalypse missing. Prologues remaining: Mark (607), Luke (1.1-4 treated as a prologue, followed by 620), John (624), 2 Corinthians (699), Galatians (707), Ephesians (715), Philippians (728), Timothy (765), Philemon (783), Hebrews (793).

Parchment, ff. i (parchment) + 164 + i (parchment), 296 x 197 (197 x 139) mm., trimmed. Written in two columns of 45 lines. Double outer and inner vertical bounding lines, with extra ruling between columns. Horizontal bounding lines, all full across: two in upper and lower margins (some trimmed); three at top, bottom, and center of written space; additional two in upper and lower halves of written space. Ruled in lead; remains of some prickings in outer margins.

Present state of the codex (Roman numerals represent quire signatures of the original scribe): fragmentary quires consisting of one bifolio (ff. 11-12), two bifolios (ff. 13-16), and one bifolio (ff. 17-18 + 19, glued in); XVII^{12} (-1, 9; ff. 68-77), XVIII^{12} (ff. 78-89), XIX^{12} (-6, 7; ff. 90-99), XX-XXIV^{12} (ff. 100-159), XXV^6 (-6; ff. 160-64, no loss of text), XXVI^{12} (-6, 7; ff. 1-10), XXVII-XLI missing, XLII^{12} (only two outer bifolios remaining, ff. 20-23), XLIII^{12} (-5, 8, 9, 10, 12; ff. 24-31), XLIV missing, XLV^{12} (ff. 32-43), XLVI^{12} (-3, 4, 9, 10; ff.

44-51), XLVII[12] (ff. 52-63), XLVIII[12] (two bifolios, ff. 64-67). Signatures located in the center of the lower margin, on verso.

Written by a single scribe in a neat, but slightly round, gothic bookhand, above the top line. Notes for initials and chapter numbers in margins, in an informal cursive script. Numerous corrections between rulings in lower margin; the corrections were then written in a neat gothic bookhand next to the text.

The surviving historiated initials, 8-, 7-, 6-, and 5-line, are of varied design, and are all badly damaged. In type and style they are somewhat comparable to initials in mid-13th century Parisian manuscripts, for example, those assigned by R. Branner to the Mathurin and Grusch ateliers (*Manuscript Painting in Paris during the Reign of St. Louis* [Berkeley, 1977] figs. 167-73, 212-43). For the most part, the initials are red or blue, with white highlights; the body of the letter on a dark blue, pink, or grey ground, with white dots; curling floral and dragon serifs, some with cusps (orange, red, and green); descenders (up to 2/3 of text column) same color as body of letter, with adjoining strips of pink, blue, or grey, often with cusped floral terminals, rampant dragons; all sections thickly edged in black. Other historiated initials, blue or pink, with cusped serifs, against a brown ground with delicate floral filigree in white; thick black edging. Three historiated initials (ff. 25r, 90v, and 117v) in architectural settings, in dark blue, blue, red, pink, and gold, with elaborate floral pendants below. Subjects as follow: f. 9v (Ecclesiastes) Judgment of Solomon; f. 25r (Mark) Mark as scribe; f. 55v (2 Corinthians) Paul with sword and book; f. 59v (Galatians) Paul preaching; f. 61v (Ephesians) Paul preaching; f. 65r (Timothy) Paul with a book; f. 66r (Titus) Paul with a book; f. 66v (Laodiceans) Paul with banderole; f. 66v (Philemon) Paul with banderole; f. 67r (Hebrews) Paul disputes with three Jews, identified by *Judenhutte*; f. 74v (2 Chronicles) Solomon on a throne, virtually effaced; f. 90v (Ezra) King Cyrus; f. 100r (2 Ezra [= 3]) Josias with soldier; f. 106v (Tobit) Tobit and the swallow; f. 111v (Judith) Judith and Holofernes; f. 117v (Esther) King Ahasuerus above, Haman hanging below, Esther outside the initial between the text columns; f. 124v (Job) Job on dunghill; f. 136r (Psalm 1) David harping; f. 140v (Psalm 26) subject illegible, Unction of David[?]; f. 143v (Psalm 38) David pointing to eyes, with nimbed figure of Christ[?]; f. 146v (Psalm 52) Fool; f. 149v (Psalm 68) David in deep waters; f. 152v (Psalm 80) David at carillon; f. 156r (Psalm 97) Cantors at lectern; f. 159v (Psalm 109) Trinity. The historiated initials for two books, f. 1r (Proverbs) and f. 63v (Philippians) were cut out; script and decoration have been restored with unusual care (s. xv): large floral buds (green, orange, yellow, and/or pink) on short green stems against purple or black grounds.

Illuminated initials, 4- to 2-line for prologues, pink or blue with white highlights, occasionally with gold; otherwise, diminutive versions of historiated initial types (f. 63 [Prologue to Philippians] with a small bird); one initial of this type f. 35v (John), originally historiated, has also been restored. 4- to 2-line initials for chapters, set into text columns, red and blue with blue and red penwork flourishes running along column into margins, some with animal-head terminals; some initials in bottom line with unusual penwork pendants. Capitals in text stroked in red. Chapter numbers, red and blue, often with flourishes; running headings, red and blue; rubrics in red throughout; corrections surrounded by undulating red lines, occasionally with trailing penwork flourishes.

Binding: s. xviii–xix, vellum case. Paper boards are composed of fragments of several French legal documents of the 16th and 17th centuries.

Written possibly in Southern France toward the middle of the thirteenth century; early provenance unknown. Inscription on f. 86v (s. xvi): "Jacoby d'Hormier [?]". From the library of Hubert A. Newton (Yale 1850). Gift of Mrs. John Porter in 1949.

Bibliography: Faye and Bond, p. 27, no. 82.

MS 83 France, s. XIV^{in}
Bible Pl. 11

ff. 2r–553v   Order of the contents is as follows (numbers in parentheses refer to prefaces in Stegmüller, v. 1): General prologue (284); Prologue to Pentateuch (285), Genesis, missing 39.4–43.11, Exodus, Leviticus, Numbers, Deuteronomy; Joshua (311); Judges; Ruth; 1 Kings (323), 2 Kings, 3 Kings, 4 Kings; 1 Chronicles (328), 2 Chronicles (327) + Prayer of Manasses; 1 Ezra (330); Nehemiah; 2 Ezra (= 3 Ezra: Stegmüller, no. 94, 1); Tobit (332); Judith (335); Esther (341 + 343); Job (344, 357); Psalms; Proverbs (457); Ecclesiastes (462); Song of Songs; Wisdom (468); Ecclesiasticus (introduction to Ecclesiasticus, Multorum nobis..., considered as prologue); Isaiah (482); Jeremiah (487); Lamentations; Baruch (491); Ezekiel (492); Daniel (494); Minor prophets (500), Hosea (507), Joel (511, 510), Amos (515, 512, 513), Obadiah (519, 517, followed by: *Item alius prologus non est prologus sed glosa*: Asau filius ysaac frater iacob uocatus est ... contra ydumeos ergo loquitur hic propheta), Jonah (524, 521), Micah (526), Nahum (528), Habakkuk (531), Zephaniah (534), Haggai (538), Zechariah (539), Malachi (543); 1 Maccabees (547, 553, 551), 2 Maccabees; Matthew (prologues and beginning of text missing on leaf removed after f. 444; text begins at 2. 16); Mark (607); Luke (620, followed by 1. 1–4 treated as a prologue); John (624); Romans (677); 1 Corinthians (685), 2 Corinthians (699); Galatians (707); Ephesians (715); Philippians (728); Colossians (736); 1 Thessalonians (747), 2 Thessalonians (752); 1 Timothy (765), 2 Timothy (772); Titus (780); Philemon (783); Hebrews (793); Acts (640); Catholic Epistles (809); Apocalypse (839).

Parchment, ff. i (parchment) + 552 (foliation 2–553) + i (parchment) 322 x 223 (196 x 130) mm., trimmed. Written in two columns of 46 lines; single vertical bounding lines with extra line between columns; horizontal bounding lines, all full across: triple at top, bottom, and center of written space, double in upper and lower margins. Ruled in lead. Prickings visible only for guide-lines for some corrections made by original scribe.

I (missing; remains of string), II[12], III[12] (-9, 10), IV-XXXVIII[12], XXXIX[12] (-1), XL-XLVI[12], XLVII[14]. Catchwords lower right, verso.

Written by a single scribe in a neat gothic bookhand. Marginal notes and/or corrections by original scribe and several later ones.

Historiated initials, 8- to 5-line, many excised, with figures (red and blue) in the summary, linear style characteristic of early 14th-century French manuscript illumination; blue or pink with white highlights, with figures against gold grounds; descenders composed of dark blue, blue and red segments, often decorated with gold balls; long cusped floral serifs with gold balls, occasionally with additional trailing foliage, rabbits, birds, etc. Subjects as follow: f. 2r (Epistle of Jerome) Jerome at desk, set within a thick 3/4 bar border composed of red and blue strips heraldically arranged with delicate white-vine filigree and pink and blue strips with geometric highlights, set within thin gold bands, with large, cusped floral terminals sprouting natural foliage and stag, rabbit, birds, and trees in the bas-de-page; f. 5v (Genesis) The seven days of creation, against gold grounds in a full-length framework of intersecting blue and red vines sprouting red trilobe leaves, set against a blue and red ground with white highlights; large spiral vine-terminals against cusped red and gold grounds supporting birds, dogs, rabbits, etc.; f. 25r (Exodus) Moses leading the Jews; f. 43r (Leviticus) Sacrifice of sheep; f. 55r (Numbers) Moses on Mt. Sinai; f. 72r (Deuteronomy) Man and woman at altar; f. 88r (Joshua) initial excised; f. 98v (Judges) Two Jews kneeling in prayer; f. 109v (Ruth) Elimelech, Naomi with one child, 17-line vertical format; f. 112r (1 Kings) Elkanah and Hannah before altar; f. 127v (2 Kings) excised; f. 140v (3 Kings) excised; f. 155r (4 Kings) excised; f. 169v (1 Chronicles) Two Jews disputing with a King; f. 182v (2 Chronicles) Solomon sacrificing sheep; f. 199r (Ezra) Cyrus builds temple, 20-line vertical format; f. 203v (Nehemiah) gold cup; f. 210r (2 Ezra [= 3]) Jew asperging altar; f. 217r (Tobit) excised; f. 221v (Judith) Judith and Holofernes; f. 227v (Esther) Esther and Ahasuerus (vertical format); f. 233v (Job) excised; f. 245r (Psalm 1) David harping; f. 249r (Psalm 26) David points to eye; f. 252r (Psalm 38) David points to lips; f. 254v (Psalm 52) Fool; f. 257r (Psalm 68) God, David in the deep waters; f. 260v (Psalm 80) David at carillon; f. 263v (Psalm 97) Cantors at lectern; f. 266v (Psalm 109) excised; f. 273r (Proverbs) Solomon teaching; f. 283r (Ecclesiastes) excised; f. 286v (Song of Songs) excised; f. 288r (Wisdom) Solomon knighting soldier; f. 295r (Ecclesiasticus) excised; f. 313v (Isaiah) excised; f. 335v (Jeremiah) Lapidation; f. 360r (Lamentations) excised; f. 362r (Baruch) Baruch as scribe; f. 365v (Ezekiel) Vision of the four beasts, Ezekiel in bed; f. 388v (Daniel) excised; f. 398r (Hosea) excised; f. 401r (Joel) excised; f. 402v (Amos) Head of God, Amos with sheep; f. 405v (Obadiah) God appears to Obadiah in bed; f. 406r (Jonah) excised; f. 407r (Micah) Micah with banderole; f. 409r (Nahum) Nahum and collapsing tower [Nineveh]; f. 410v (Habakkuk) Habakkuk as scribe; f. 411v (Zephaniah)

Zephaniah with banderole; f. 413r (Haggai) Haggai with banderole; f. 414r (Zechariah) Zechariah seated with book; f. 417v (Malachi) Malachi standing with scroll; f. 419v (1 Maccabees) Beheading; f. 433v (2 Maccabees) Delivery of letter; f. 458v (Mark) Mark in guise of monk, standing; f. 467v (Luke) Luke as monk at altar; f. 483r (John) John as seated monk; f. 494v (Romans) Paul with sword; f. 500r (1 Corinthians) excised; f. 505v (2 Corinthians) Paul with sword; f. 509r (Galatians) Paul with sword; f. 511r (Ephesians) Paul in tower, angel with scroll; f. 513r (Philippians) Paul with scroll; f. 514r (Colossians) Paul with book; f. 515v (1 Thessalonians) Paul with sword and book; f. 516v (2 Thessalonians) Paul with sword; f. 517v (1 Timothy) Paul with sword; f. 519r (2 Timothy) excised; f. 520r (Titus) Paul with book; f. 520v (Philemon) Paul in tower, angel with scroll; f. 521r (Hebrews) excised; f. 525r (Acts) excised; f. 539v (James) James with book; f. 541r (1 Peter) Peter with key; f. 542v (2 Peter) Peter with book; f. 543v (1 John) John with book; f. 545r (2 John) John with sword; f. 545r (3 John) excised; f. 545v (Jude) Jude with book; f. 546r (Apocalypse) John at desk with the 7 churches of Asia above.

Illuminated initials, 7- to 5-line (larger for *I* initials) for prologues, blue or pink with white highlights, cusped serifs, filled with curling vines, red trilobe leaves, and dragon heads, against red, orange, and gold grounds. 5-, 4-, and 2-line initials for chapters in red and blue with blue and red penwork, with elaborate calligraphic extensions running the full length of the text column; extensions composed either of two thick red lines with a thin blue one in between or two thick blue lines with a thin red line, the arrangement alternating for successive initials; with adjacent superimposed *J*'s, alternating red and blue, also running the full length of column; elaborate vertical terminal flourishes. Compare, for example, the finer calligraphic ornament in Vatican, Vat. lat. 738, or in Paris, B. N. lat. 375, two of a group of manuscripts written and decorated in Avignon in the 1320's, reproduced in A. Dondaine, "La Collection des Oeuvres de Saint Thomas dite de Jean XXII et Jacquet Maci," *Scriptorium* 29 (1975) pp. 127–52, pls. 13c and 14c. The more elaborate calligraphy for initials between ff. 360v and 370v appears to be by a different hand. Chapter numbers in margins, in alternating red and blue figures, with blue and red vertical hatching and red, blue, and occasionally purple flourishes. Running headings in similar manner. Marginal corrections boxed in red; glosses frequently underlined in red.

First folio badly mutilated.

Binding: s. xix–xx. Original sheepskin covering of spine and part of boards, blind-tooled, adhered on a recent binding. Wooden boards also probably original. Stubs of three (originally four) fastening straps, reinforced with vellum, on upper cover.

Written in Southern France at the beginning of the fourteenth century as indicated by the decoration, especially the calligraphic initials; evidence of heavy use in the 14th through 16th centuries includes marginal notes of an early corrector

(e. g., "hunc prologum non correxi quia non inueni correctum" on f. 182r and "Quidam non hunc istum uersum" on f. 539v). Purchased from Dawson's Book Shop, Los Angeles, 7 Dec. 1932, by Henry Fletcher; his gift to Yale in 1950.

secundo folio: et prudentiam

Bibliography: Faye and Bond, p. 27, no. 83.

MS 84 England [?], s. XV
Boethius, De consolatione philosophiae

1. ff. 1r–169r   Carmina qui quondam studio florente peregi. Flebilis heu mestos cogor inire modos ... cum ante oculos agitis iudicis cuncta cernentis. *Explicit*. ff. 169v–170r ruled, but blank

   L. Bieler, ed., CC lat. ser. 94 (1957) pp. 1–105.

2. ff. 170v–171r   Short notes (in Latin and English) on medical recipes, including "Medicyn for the Colyk". f. 171v ruled, but blank

Parchment, ff. iv (contemporary parchment, iv = stub) + 171 + iv (contemporary parchment, i = stub), 100 x 80 (68 x 41) mm., trimmed in a very irregular manner. Written in 12 long lines; single bounding lines full across. Ruled in pale brown ink; remains of prickings (slashes) in outer margins, and occasionally in upper and lower margins.
  I^{10}, II^{12}, III^{12} (–7, no loss of text), IV^8, V–XVII^{10}. A few signatures on recto.
  Written by three scribes in informal gothic scripts. 1: ff. 1r–33v, with running titles, in red, on f. 4v and 28r; catchwords, underlined in red, with paragraph marks preceding each; this is the only section of the text with rubrication. 2: ff. 34r–60v, 112v–169r (in a style of writing verging on Anglicana), catchwords in gutter, often surrounded by rectangles. 3: ff. 60v–112v (many erasures and corrections by 2), no visible catchwords. Marginal and interlinear glosses in several contemporary hands, one of which added the notes on ff. 170v–171r.
  First initial in red penwork, 4-line, with crude portrait of Boethius. Simple red initials to mark sections of text.
  Binding: s. xv, possibly German or Dutch. "Girdle-book." Although early, it is not the original binding. Resewn on three narrow, tawed, double thongs. The endbands do not seem to have laced cores, but a primary sewing may have been sewn to the head and tail of the chemise, underneath the braided secondary endbands. The thongs are laced into grooves in beech boards, the pattern reversed; one horizontal above one *V* lacing on the upper board and a *V* above a horizontal on the lower. The thongs are pegged. The outer wrapper of tawed skin, now grey, is sewn to a tawed, pink, inner chemise around the outer edges of the boards. The wrapper extends about 130 mm. to a Turk's head knot at the tail, about 25 mm. at the head, and has an overlap of about 50 mm. on the upper board. The

edges of the wrapper are turned in and hemmed. The book hung upside down when attached to the girdle by having the knot slipped under it, but was right side up when picked up (still attached to the girdle) to be read. A strap-and-pin fastening, the pin on the upper board, consists of a thick, brown leather strap nailed to the lower board and tacketed to the cover with a leather thong ending in an anthropomorphic brass clasp, the head of which catches on the pin. A glued repair was made before, a sewn one after 1973. Cf. exhib. cat., *The History of Bookbinding, 525–1950 A.D.*, The Walters Art Gallery (Baltimore, 1957) p. 56, no. 130.

Written in England in the 15th century, as is suggested by the style of writing (especially of Scribe 2) and by the recipes in English. It is, however, questionable whether the codex was bound there as well, since "girdle-books" were produced primarily in the Low countries and Rhine Valley; no examples of these bindings seem to survive from England. Evidence of trimming, with some loss of marginalia, may indicate that the codex was written in one place and bound in another. Belonged to A. Edward Newton (*The A. Edward Newton Collection of Books and Manuscripts* [New York, 1941] v. 2, p. 28); his sale (New York, 14 May 1941, no. 105) to C. A. Stonehill. Presented to Yale in 1941 by the Yale Library Associates.

secundo folio: Qui cecidit

Bibliography: Faye and Bond, p. 27, no. 84.
    E.T. Silk, "The Yale 'Girdle-Book' of Boethius," *Gazette* 17 (1942) pp. 1–5 (plate facing p. 1).
    The Secular Spirit: Life and Art at the End of the Middle Ages, exhib. cat. (New York: Metropolitan Museum of Art, 1975) pp. 164–65, no. 183, with 2 plates.

MS 85   France, s. XV[1]
Boethius, De consolatione philosophiae, etc.

1. f. 1r blank, f. 1v   [Title page:] *Anicij manlij seuerinj boecij exconsulis ordinarij atque patricij philosophice consolationis liber primus incipit.*

2. ff. 2r–210v   Carmina qui quondam studio florente peregi Flebilis heu mestos cogor inire modos ... probitatis cum ante oculos agitis iudicis cuncta cernentis. explicit boecius.

   L. Bieler, ed., CC lat. ser. 94 (1957) pp. 1–105.

3. ff. 3r–56v   Excerpts from the commentary of Nicolas Trevet (in margins) on Boethius, Book I.1.1 – II.5.34.

    Parchment, ff. i (parchment) + 210 + i (parchment), 153 x 110 (75 x 48) mm.

Written in 12 long lines (with no verse divisions for poetry); single vertical bounding lines, upper horizontal, single or double, full across. Ruled in pale red ink; prickings along upper, lower, and outer edges.

I^{10}, $II-XXV^8$. Catchwords with decorative flourishes in gutter; remains of leaf signatures (e.g., h1, h2, etc.) on recto.

Written by two scribes in an ornate and elegant gothic bookhand. 1: ff. 1v-154v; 2: ff. 155r-210v. The marginal commentary is in a neat informal bâtarde (ink paler than that used for text).

Plain initial, 3-line, in blue at beginning of text; other initials, 2-line, in red throughout text to mark the beginning of poetry and prose sections. Title page (f. 1v): alternating lines of blue and gold.

Grease stain in margins at end of codex; bottom of f. 81 trimmed.

Binding: s. xix. Brown sheepskin, blind-tooled. Repaired.

Written in France in the first half of the 15th century, with ample margins apparently intended for glossing. Note on f. 1r (s. xvii): "dono domini de la Frezeliere" may indicate that it belonged to Carolus Frezeau de la Frezelière, bishop of La Rochelle in 1673 (d. 1703). Acquired from Goldschmidt's in 1943.

secundo folio: [falla]cem mutauit

Bibliography: Faye and Bond, p. 27, no. 85.
E.T. Silk, "A New Manuscript of Boethius' *Consolatio*," *Gazette* 18 (1944) pp. 46-47.

MS 86
England, s. XIV/XV
Brut Chronicle (in Anglo-Norman), etc.
Pl. 18

1. front and back flyleaves: a paper document of s. xviii, relating to Wiltshire, with Julianna Charter as plaintiff.

2. ff. 1r-12v   Fragments of a Brut Chronicle, in Anglo-Norman. //Rome et oscist touz lez mescreauntz gil poet ... ou il fuist ioyeusement resceu.

    The text of this fragment begins imperfectly in chapter 36 (Constantine) and has several lacunae. Folios 1-4 (the two central conjugate leaves of a gathering) correspond to the English text in F. W. D. Brie, ed., EETS, v. 131 (1906) pp. 40/20 - 67/22 and contain chapters 36-44. Folios 5, 7, 6, 8 (individual leaves in that order) may be from one quire, but one leaf is missing after both 5 and 6; 9-12 are the two outer bifolios of a quire originally consisting of 8 leaves, but the two inner bifolios are wanting after f. 10. Folios 5-10 contain portions of chapters 81-84. The work ends in chapter 86 (beginning on f. 11r) with the thirty-first year of Edward III.

3. f. 13r (a single leaf tipped in)   *Progenies ab Adam usque Henricum IIII Regem Anglie.*

A note stating that King Henry IV was consecrated in 1399 and documenting his descent from Adam.

4. f. 13v *Nomina Regum Anglie quorum cronicke consecuntur.*

A list of 86 kings (each numbered) from Brutus to Edward III. The offset image of an illuminated initial with extensive border indicates that the leaf originally preceded art. 2.

5. f. 14r Names of prisoners captured and killed at the battle of Poitiers (19 Sept. 1356), in Anglo-Norman.

6. ff. 14v-19v Terms of the treaty of Bretigny (8 May 1360), in 40 chapters, numbered in red (Anglo-Norman).

7. ff. 19v-20v *De modo [tenendi] parliamenti.* Hic discribitur modus quomodo parliamentum Regis Anglie et anglorum suorum tenebatur temporibus Regis Edwardi filij Etheldredi Regis ... *De loquela Regis post pronunciacionem* ... ad eius et eorum honores et comoda fore inteligerint et sincierint [changed to sencierint]//

N. Pronay and J. Taylor, *Parliamentary Texts of the Later Middle Ages* (Oxford, 1980) pp. 67-72. According to Taylor, the Yale *Modus* appears to be an early version of the "A" Recension similar in some ways, although not in all, to the group associated with London, B. L. Vespasian B. VII.

Parchment, ff. i (paper, s. xviii) + 20 + i (paper, s. xviii; same document serves as front and back flyleaves), 366 x 245 (275 x 165) mm. The physical format varies somewhat depending upon the text. Folios 1-12, 14r: written in 41 long lines; single or double vertical and horizontal bounding lines full across; ruled in lead; remains of prickings in upper, lower, and outer margins. Folio 13: written in 43 lines, sometimes in 2 columns, with appropriate rulings in lead; the leaf appears to have been slightly trimmed. Folios 14v-20v: written in 41 long lines; single inner and double outer vertical bounding lines, double horizontal bounding lines, full across, with additional ruling in outer margin; ruled in lead; some prickings in all margins, except inner.

For collation of ff. 1-13, see articles 2-3; folios 14-19 are composed of a single gathering of six leaves, plus one added at end (f. 20).

Written in Anglicana bookhand by a scribe who also copied Malmesbury Church, MS 2 (see below).

Decorative initials, blue with red penwork, appear only on ff. 1-12; initial strokes and headings, in red, throughout.

Binding: s. xviii-xix. Stab sewn to a vellum folder made up of a legal document (trimmed with some loss of text) dated 1766 and involving the manors of Whitechurch and Milbourne in Wiltshire. The outside has an inscription, s. xix, "Some leaves of early English History in Norman French supposed to have come from Malmesbury Abbey." A similar inscription occurs on f. i verso.

Written in England at the end of the 14th or beginning of the 15th century; in 1971 N. R. Ker determined that it was copied by the same scribe as two items now belonging to Malmesbury Church (MS 2) in Wiltshire and that all three items were formerly bound together (see Ker, MMBL, v. 3). The original manuscript was acquired by James P. R. Lyell who divided it into three parts and sold each separately (*Lyell Cat.*, p. xxix). One portion (46 leaves) was repurchased by Lyell on 8 April 1942 and presented to Malmesbury Church; Yale acquired the second part (20 leaves in present binding) from Henry Fletcher in 1950; Malmesbury Church bought the final part (41 leaves) in 1961. Papers accompanying the manuscript and now in Beinecke Library files include: 1. unsigned note, s. xix, "These old Parchments were found in Malmesbury Abbey during excavations. They are written in Norman French and are supposed to be part of an Early English History, but they have never been deciphered. The 2 loose pages [now missing from both the Yale and Malmesbury texts] belong apparently to a book of travels, probably Sir John Mandeville's, which were written about 1372"; 2. letter dated 3 Feb. 1882, Ashburton, Devon, "My dear Sparke, Thanks for sending me the curious leaflet which I now return. It is written in Norman French which I unfortunately know very little about and have no books that throw any light on it ... [comments on the 2 lost leaves:] It begins with an account of the Isle of Rhodes altho the first words are 'estre appelle Collos et vncore les Turkes l'appellent ensynt. Et seint Poul en ses pistres estriuoit a eux dicele Isle ad Colocenses. Ceste Isle est bien.' ... It is beautifully written and to anyone who knew Norman French it would be easy to make out ... Yours very Truly, John S. Amery." [The words quoted from the Mandeville text belong to the Insular version, ch. 4; see G. F. Warner's edition for the Roxburghe Club (1889) p. 13/39.] Note (s. xix) in red, inside front cover: "Re Bayliffe/ 33 Anglesea Place/ Clifton/ Bristol."

Bibliography: Faye and Bond, p. 27, no. 86.

MS 87   Italy, s. XV^{med}
Caesar, Opera omnia

1. ff. 1r–79r   *C. Iulii Caesaris Commentariorum belli gallici liber primus incipit feliciter. Iulius Celsus. V. C. emendauit.* Gallia est omnis diuisa in partes tres quarum unam incolunt belge ... Ipse bibracti hiemare constituit his litteris cognitis rhome dierum. xx. supplicatio redditur.

   A. Klotz, ed., Teubner v. 1 (1929) pp. 1–178.

2. ff. 79r–90v   *A. Hircii Commentariorum belli galli gallici epistola primum ad Cornelium Balbum incipit feliciter.* Coactus assiduis tuis uocibus balbe ... cuiusquam existimem posse comparari. Vale. *Incipit eiusdem liber belli gallici Iulius Celsus Constantinus. V. C. emendauit.* Omni gallia deuicta cesar cum a superiore estate

nullum bellandi ... quod sibi spes aliqua relinqueretur iure potius disceptandi quam belli gerendi.

Klotz, *op. cit.*, v. 1, pp. 178-205.

3. ff. 90v-146r   *C. Iulii. Caesaris. Commentariorum belli ciuilis Pompeiani liber primus incipit feliciter Iulius. Caelsus. Constantinus Quintus. consul emendauit.* Litteris a fabio. C. cesaris consulibus redditis egre ab his impetratum est ... indicatis deprehensisque internuntiis a cesare est interfectus.

Klotz, *op. cit.*, v. 2 (1950) pp. 1-159; V. Brown, *The Textual Transmission of Caesar's Civil War* (Leiden, 1972) p. 57 (list of Contaminated Manuscripts: M-N Types).

4. ff. 146v-164r   *C. Iulii. Caesaris. A. Hircii. Commentariorum. belli. Alesandrini. ... emendauit.* Bello Alexandrino conflato Cesar rhodo atque ex siria ciliciaque ... Rebus felicissime celerrimeque confectis Cesar in italiam celerius omnium opinione uenit.

Klotz, *op. cit.,* v. 3 (1966) pp. 1-53.

5. ff. 164r-185v   *A. Hircii. Commentariorum. belli. africani ... emendauit.* Cesar itineribus iustis confectis nullo die intermisso ad xiiii KL. Ian....in portibus cohibeatur ad urbem rhomam uenit.

Klotz, *op. cit.*, v. 3, pp. 59-135.

6. ff. 185v-195v   *A. Hircii. Commentariorum. belli. hispaniensis ... emendauit.* Pharnace superato affrica recepta qui ex his preliis cum adolosccente ... que non solum uobis obsistere etiam celum diruere possent. Quarum laudibus et uirtute. [added in a somewhat later hand:] Explicit Liber comentariorium Iulij Caesaris. Laus deo. f. 196r-v blank

Klotz, *op. cit.*, v. 3, pp 136-67.

Parchment, ff. i (original parchment) + 196, 230 x 162 (154 x 94) mm. Written in 35 long lines; single vertical bounding lines. Ruled in pale ink or lead; remains of prickings in upper and lower margins.

I-XIX[10], XX[6]. Catchwords perpendicular to text along inner bounding line. Written by a single scribe in a small elegant humanistic bookhand.

Fine initials, gold capitals, 9- to 5- line, edged in yellow, filled with white-vine ornament, on blue, green, and red ground, decorated with yellow dots (cf. Pächt and Alexander, v. 2, no. 237: Oxford, Bodl. Lib. D'Orville 209 [Tuscany, s. XV[med]]). Headings in red.

Binding: s. xv. Wound sewing on four slit straps. Colored beaded endbands sewn onto cores of tawed skin laced and nailed into wooden boards. All edges gilt. The sewing straps are laced through tunnels in the edges of the boards and nailed in channels on the outside, protruding well above the face. Covered in dark brown goatskin, blind-tooled with an eight-pointed star and corners filled in with

MS 88 125

rope-tool interlace interspersed with copper-colored dots, in a border of rectangular tools. Four catches on the lower board and stubs of red cloth (velvet?) straps lined with parchment held to the upper with star-headed nails (exhib. cat., *The History of Bookbinding, 525-1950 A.D.*, The Walters Art Gallery [Baltimore, 1957] no. 196; T. de Marinis, *La legatura artistica in Italia nei secoli XV e XVI* [Florence, 1960] v. 1, p. 101 [incorrectly identified as "Yale MS. Richardson 16"]).

Written probably in Florence or Tuscany in the middle of the 15th century; early note on front flyleaf: "Quisto libro e de Baldanto Balducci." Description of manuscript, in Italian (s. xix) pasted inside front cover. Belonged to Sir Thomas Phillipps (no. 12277, note on f. i recto); his purchase from Payne and Foss in 1848 (one of a group of manuscripts from the abbey of Nonantola). Label with "From the Library of George Dunn [1864-1912] of Woolley Hall near Maidenhead." Wilfred Merton collection (booktag inside front cover). Acquired by David Wagstaff (bookplate) from Davis and Orioli in 1942; gift of Mrs. David Wagstaff in 1943.

secundo folio: damnatum penam

Bibliography: Faye and Bond, p. 27, no. 87.

E. T. Silk, "The Wagstaff Collection of Classical and Mediaeval Manuscripts", *Gazette* 19 (1944) pp. 1-5 (plate of f. 1r opposite p. 6).

MS 88 England, s. XV^{med}
Carta de foresta, etc.

1. f. i recto blank; f. i verso   Note in English (s. xv^2) on 1 January as the beginning of each year for the Golden Number, beginning: Euermore prime schal chaunge the furste day of new yere scilicet in circumsisio [*sic*] domini....

2. f. 1r blank; f. 1v [same hand as art. 3:] In marche after the furste C/ loke the prime Where hit be/ the thride Sonday....

   IMEV 1502, couplets on finding the date of Easter.

3. ff. 2r-7v   Graded calendar in red and black, including the following feasts: David (1 March, 9 lessons), Chad (2 March, 9 lessons), "Resurrectio domini" (27 March, in red), Richard of Chichester (3 April, 9 lessons), Translation of Richard of Chichester (16 June, in red), Ethelreda (23 June), Anna (26 July, in red).

4. ff. 8r-17r   [E]dwardus dei gratia Rex ... salutem. Inspeximus cartam domini henrici quondam Regis ... [f. 8v] In primis omnes foreste quas h. annis ... duodecimo die Octobris Anno regni nostri vicesimo quinto. Explicit Carta de fforesta.

   SR, v. 1, Charters of Liberties, pp. 42-44, altered at the end to conform to text printed on p. 36.

5. ff. 17r–20r   *Incipit Sentencia [Excommunicationis] lata super Cartam.* [A]nno domini Millesimo ducentesimo quinquagesimo tercio ydus Maij in maiori aula ... Nos signa nostra presentibus duximus apponenda. *Explicit sentencia lata super Cartam.*

SR, v. 1, pp. 6–7.

6. ff. 20r–26r   [E]wardus dei gratia Rex ... salutem. Dum imbecillitatis humane conspicimus imperfectum ac onera longe lateque diffusa ... apud Westmonasterium xxvij die Maij Anno regni nostri tricesimo quarto.

SR, v. 1, pp. 147–49.

7. ff. 26v–28r   *Statuta de malefactoribus in Parcis.* Ut malefactores in parcis forestis chaceis et Warennis de cetero plus timeant in eisdem intrare ... et secundum consuetudinem regni fuerit faciendum etc.

SR, v. 1, pp. 111–12.

8. ff. 28v–30r   *Incipit ordinacio de fforesta.* Come astimes gentz qui sount hors de fforeste par la purale et par le grant ... en lour baillies en la forme auantdite.

SR, v. 1, p. 144.

9. 30v–33v   *Incipiunt Capitula de regardis faciendis etc.* [V]idenda sunt assarta facta post principium secundi anni primi coronacionis domini henrici Regis ... vel aliquod aliud ingenium ad malefaciendum domino Regi de feris suis etc.

These are the articles in *Calendar of Patent Rolls in Public Record Office* (1225–32) pp. 286–87 (13 Henry III).

10. ff. 34r–36v   *Statutes Edwardi tercij Anno Primo de fforesta.* Et pur ceo que pluseurs gentz sont disherites et destruez par les souereins gardeins ... par vewe de foresters eodem Anno status etc.

SR, v. 1, p. 254; the end of the text differs somewhat from the printed version.

11. ff. 37r–38v   *Statutes de fforesta Anno vij Ricardi Regis.* Item a la greuouse pleint que est ore fait des Ministres ... de hoc in addicione fforeste Anno primo Regis Eduardis tercij capitulo vj^{to}.

12. ff. 39r–46r   *Assisa fforeste.* Si quis fforestarius iuratus facere attachiamenta inuenerit aliquem attachiabilem ... al Roy dj mars etc.

SR, v. 1, pp. 243–45; Latin version ends at n.2 in printed text, p. 244; text continues in French.

13. ff. 46v–57v   *Onus Articulorum foreste super Swanymote tenendum per sacramentum.* First sirs ye shul do vs to Witte yf all tho men that owen to sue to this Swanymote ... And of all other defautes that been forte presente.

Selections similar to those in J. Manwood, *A Brefe Collection of the Laws of the Forest* (London, 1592) pp. 114–20.

14. ff. 58r–67v   [R]egardum factum in fforesta de Rokyngham et de Clyue ab

octauo die Maij Anno regni Regis Edwardi fili Regis Edwardi quintodecimo vsque.... f. 68r blank

Cf. *Lyell Cat.*, p. 80, art. 24.

15. ff. 68v-69r   henricus dei gratia etc. vic. Sutht. salutem precipimus tibi quod sine aliqua dilatione conuenire facias ... Capitula videnda sunt assarta facta in foresta etc.

Breve de regardis faciendis to the Sheriff of Hampshire; cf. *Calendar of Patent Rolls in Public Record Office* (1216-1225) pp. 402-03 (7 Henry III).

Parchment, ff. ii (contemporary parchment) + 68 (foliated 2-69), 115 x 82 (70 x 47) mm.; ff. i-7 smaller in size. Written in 14 long lines; frame-ruled in ink. Numerous prickings for art. 3; prickings in upper, lower, and outer margins for remainder.

I^6, $II-VIII^8$, IX^6. Some gatherings signed with letters of the alphabet under written space, on recto.

Arts. 4-14 written in a neat chancery script with Anglicana influence; arts. 1 and 15 in similar, but less elegant hands; arts. 2-3 are in gothic textura.

Plain initial, in red, with crude ink penwork flourishes on f. 1v; KL monograms and portions of calendar also in red.

Some stains on ff. 2r-7v render text illegible.

Binding: s. xix-xx. Rebinding in quarter pigskin, tanned, not tawed, with a strap-and-pin fastening. The oak boards, cambered on all four outer edges and with rectangular pegs, are probably contemporary with the manuscript. Front pastedown composed of a small fragment of prayers in Latin (s. xv).

Written in England in the middle of the 15th century; early provenance unknown. Inscription (s. xvi) on front pastedown: "Tho. Martin". Unidentified shelf-mark on back pastedown: "AE/ 2095". Slip from an unidentified Sotheby sale catalogue affixed to f. i recto. Gift of David Wagstaff (bookplate) in 1944.

secundo folio: [text, f. 9] et si boscum

Bibliography: Faye and Bond, p. 27, no. 88.

MS 89
Carta de foresta, etc.

England, 1562
Pl. 9

1. ff. 1r-9v blank; f. 10r   [Title page:] *Here begynnethe the Booke named Carta Foreste. 1562.* [ff. 10v-13v blank; text ff. 14r-77v; running title on f. 14r:] *Forest. What thing dothe* make a forest, and how a forest is made ... [text:] *The wourdes be.* Omnes fforeste etc. Now it is to be seen what thing is a fforest ... and what thinges do make a forest, and who may make a fforest ... [f. 77v] the lawe will suffer him after the quantitie of his tenure or grant to us to witt.

A collection of hunting and forestry laws that predates but is similar to those published by John Manwood, *A Brefe Collection of the Lawes of the Forest* (London, 1592) and *A Treatise and Discourse of the Lawes of the Forrest* ... (London, 1598). The writer of MS 89 has left certain portions blank (e. g., ff. 71v, 73r-v) perhaps intending to make later additions. The arrangement of the contents is as follows: Forest, Disaforestacion, Justices, Sommons, Sessions, Purpresture, Assarte Waste, Disafforestacion, Purraylley, Regardours, Regarde, Distresse, Forresters, Swanymote, Attachementes, Verdor, Agistement, Pawnage, Forfeyture, Chasing, Enditementes, Fynes, Rawnsom, Abiuracion, Beastes, Noysaunce, Hawkes, Bees, Hony, Forester of fief, Chiminage, Outelawrye, Suerties, Plees, Verte, Venyson, A warren; Swanimote: The Charge of the Swanymotte, For the verte, For the venyson (2 sections). The material on ff. 74r-78v is another version of that found in Beinecke MS 88, ff. 46v-57v.

2. ff. 78r-85v Collection of extracts, in Latin, all concerning laws of forest. Includes: (ff. 78v-80v) Assisa fforeste [SR, v. 1, pp. 243-45]; (ff. 82v-84v) Statuta de addicionibus fforeste tempore Edwardi primi anno Regni sui xxiiij^{to} [*sic*] [SR, v. 1, pp. 147-49].

Paper (watermarks: unidentified pot), ff. i (contemporary parchment stub) + xiv (i and ii glued together) + 72 (contemporary foliation; modern foliation includes paper flyleaves) + xvi (xv and xvi glued together) + 1 (contemporary parchment stub), 300 x 215 (215 x 128) mm. Written in ca. 29 long lines; frame-ruled in ink, with an additional vertical line in left margin to form column for annotations.

I-VI^{12}.

Written in a well formed secretary hand by a single scribe (see below).

Binding: s. xvi. Endleaves reinforced with vellum, two leaves originally pasted to each board. Sewn on five single, tawed skin thongs laced into paste boards rounded on the outside of the spine edge. Beaded endbands sewn on leather or cane cores but not laced to boards. The spine is square, with traces of adhesive. Covered in dark brown calf, blind-tooled with a triple line border and a small central ornament. Two ribbon fastenings, now wanting. Leather broken at joint, sewing reinforced.

Written in England in 1562 by John Thatcher, who wrote an inscription on f. 1r: "Leonardus danet emitor/ a me Johanne Thatcher/ Londiniensi vicesimo primo/ die mensis martij anno domini/ .1562./ Precio xxs." Collection of Reginald Rawdon Hastings, Esq. (Historical Manuscripts Commission, *Report on the Manuscripts of the Late Reginald Rawdon Hastings*, v. 1 [London, 1928] p. 432; on the Hastings family and collection, see *Guide to British Historical Manuscripts at the Huntington Library* [San Marino, 1982] pp. 78-81). Listed in Maggs Cat. 577, no. 1476, with pl. 32 of f. 60v; and Maggs Cat. 680 (1939), no. 92, with plate of f. 60v facing title page. Purchased from H. P. Kraus by David Wagstaff (bookplate). Gift of Mr. and Mrs. David Wagstaff in 1944.

Bibliography: Faye and Bond, p. 28, no. 89.
   M. G. Wynne, "The Wagstaff Sporting Books and Manuscripts," *Gazette* 20 (1945) p. 11.

MS 90 France, s. XVI
Jean Franchières, La fauconnerie

1. ff. 1r–145r   //Michelin. Cestuy fut tout son temps faulconnier du Roy de chippre ... [text begins:] Selon que dyent les trois maistres de faulconnerye dessusditz Ilz sont sept manieres de faulcons ... Quant vous vouldrez mettre vostre oiseau en mue ... //

   Begins imperfectly in the Prologue and apparently ends at the beginning of Bk. 4, ch. 22. The treatise in MS 90, based on the works of Malopin, Michelin, and Amé Cassian, differs considerably from the early printed editions (e. g., Paris, 1531 [?]).

2. ff. 145r–147r   Miscellaneous notes on the care of falcons, including one recipe glued to f. 147r. ff. 147v–161r blank; signatures and pen trials on f. 161v

Paper (watermarks buried in gutter), ff. iii (paper) + 161 + iii (paper), 213 x 155 (161 x 103) mm. Frame-ruled in hard point, ca. 17 lines.
   Too closely bound to collate.
   Art. 1 written by a single scribe in a sprawling bâtarde. Notes on ff. 145r–147r added by several later writers.
   Major headings in red.
   Loss of text on ff. 145r–146r due to trimming.
   Binding: s. xix. Green goatskin, gold-tooled, by the same binder as MS 467.

Written in France in the 16th century; inscriptions on f. 161v include: Jehan Goels (s. xvi), Monsieur de la Porte (s. xvii). Belonged to Sir John Saunders Sebright (1767–1846; bookplate) and David Wagstaff (bookplate). Gift of Mr. and Mrs. David Wagstaff in 1944.

Bibliography: Faye and Bond, p. 58, no. 90.
   M. G. Wynne, "The Wagstaff Sporting Books and Manuscripts," *Gazette* 20 (1945) p. 12.

MS 91
Mellon Chansonnier

Italy, s. XV^2

1. f. 1r with staves, but no notation or text
2. ff. 1v–2r [Busnois], Bel Acueil.
3. ff. 2v–3r [Busnois], En soustenant vostre querelle.
4. ff. 3v–4r [Caron], Accueilly m'a la belle.
5. ff. 4v–5r Johannes Okeghem, Petitte Camusette.
6. ff. 5v–6v [Busnois], A une damme. f. 7r with staves only
7. ff. 7v–8r Loing de vo tresdoulce presence.
8. ff. 8v–9r Busnois, Est-il merchy.
9. ff. 9v–10r Busnois, Ung plus que tous.
10. ff. 10v–11r G. Joye, Ce qu'on fait a quatimini.
11. ff. 11v–12r Busnois, A qui vens tu tes coquilles.
12. ff. 12v–14r Johannes Regis, Puis que ma damme ne puis voir/ Je m'en voy et mon cueur demeure.
13. ff. 14v–16r [Busnois], Je ne puis vivre ainsy.
14. ff. 16v–17r [Joye], Non pas que je veuille penser.
15. ff. 17v–18v [Busnois], Ja que li ne s'i attende. f. 19r with staves only
16. ff. 19v–20r Busnois, Pour entretenir mes amours.
17. ff. 20v–22r [Busnois], Quant ce viendra.
18. ff. 22v–23r Guillaume Dufay, Vostre bruit et vostre grant fame.
19. ff. 23v–24r Vincenet, Fortune, par ta cruaulté.
20. ff. 24v–25r Johannes Tinctoris, O Virgo, miserere mei.
21. ff. 25v–26r Johannes Okeghem, L'aultre d'antan.
22. ff. 26v–27r Busnois, Le corps s'en va.
23. ff. 27v–28r Se mon service vous plaisoit.
24. ff. 28v–29r Joye, Mercy, mon dueil.
25. ff. 29v–30r Robert Morton, N'aray je jamais mieulx que j'ay?
26. ff. 30v–31r Barbingant, L'omme banny.
27. ff. 31v–32r Vincenet, Ou doy je secours querir.
28. ff. 32v–33r Gilles Binchois, Comme femme desconfortee.
29. ff. 33v–36r Petit Jan, Mon trestout et mon assotee/ Il estoit ung bonhomme.
30. ff. 36v–38r Busnois, Joye me fuit.

31. ff. 38v–40r   Okeghem, Ma bouce rit.
32. ff. 40v–42r   G. le Rouge, Se je fayz dueil.
33. ff. 42v–43r   Hayne van Ghizeghem, De tous biens plaine.
34. ff. 43v–44r   G. Dufay, Dona gentile.
35. ff. 44v–45r   [Morton], Il sera pour vous conbatu/ L'ome armé.
36. ff. 45v–46r   Walter Frye, Tout a par moy.
37. ff. 46v–48r   Caron, S'il est ainsi.
38. ff. 48v–49r   [Busnois], O Fortune, trop tu es dure.
39. ff. 49v–51r   Enfermé suys je en la tour.
40. ff. 51v–52r   [Busnois], Au povre par necessité.
41. ff. 52v–54r   Caron, Mort ou mercy.
42. ff. 54v–55r   [Morton], Paracheve ton entreprise.
43. ff. 55v–56r   [Busnois], A vous sans aultre.
44. ff. 56v–57r   Vincenet, Triste qui sperò morendo.
45. ff. 57v–59r   Vincenet, La pena sin ser sabida. ff. 59v–61r with staves only
46. ff. 61v–63r   Walter Frye, So ys emprentid.
47. ff. 63v–65r   [Bedingham], Gentil madona.
48. ff. 65v–67r   [Bedingham], Myn hertis lust.
49. ff. 67v–69r   Ou lit de pleurs.
50. ff. 69v–71r   Or me veult bein Esperance mentir.
51. ff. 71v–73r   Dufay, Donnés l'assault.
52. ff. 73v–74r   Dufay, Par le regart.
53. ff. 74v–75r   Hora cridar "Oymè".
54. ff. 75v–76r   Puis que je vis le regart.
55. ff. 76v–77r and 50v   Ma dame de nom/ Sur la rive de la mer.
56. ff. 77v–79r   [Frye], "Alas, alas, alas" is my chief song.
57. ff. 79v–80r   A. Basin, Nos amys, vous vous abusés.
58. ff. 80v–81r   Jo. Tinctoris, Virgo Dei throno digna.

A facsimile edition with a detailed commentary has been published by L. L. Perkins and H. Garey, *The Mellon Chansonnier* (New Haven and London, 1979) 2 vols.

Parchment (thin, fine quality), ff. ii (parchment) + 81 + ii (parchment), 191 : 133 (ca. 130 x 82) mm. Written in 7 staves, with or without text below each;

single vertical bounding lines ruled in lead, staves ruled in brown ink, no ruling for text.

I-VII^{10}, VIII^{10} (+ 1 leaf, following f. 80).

Written by one scribe in bâtarde, usually one line below each staff, but sometimes text written on every other line of the staves.

The style of the Chansonnier's initials points to one of the ateliers active in the service of Ferrante I of Naples, in particular to the shop of Matteo Felice, for whom cf. Valencia, Bibl. Univ. 887 (*olim* 662; see Perkins and Garey, *op. cit.*, pp. 26-28 and pl. 9, and *Exhibition Catalogue*, pp. 236-38, no. 62, where the signature of the Valencia MS is incorrectly cited). One 2-line initial (f. 1r) tan, shaded purple and green, with curling floral serifs, blue and puce, filled with curling leaves against burnished gold and blue, with white filigree, against gold ground, framed in blue with white filigree; short, 3-stemmed flowers, gold, with brown hair-spray stems project from upper serif and midpoint; 3 gold dots with hair-spray symmetrically disposed around letter; floral border in outer margin, hair-spray stems with gold and green leaves and flowers, blue, purple, and gold at midpoint and terminals. One-line initials throughout, gold, infilled blue or purple, with white filigree, against irregular grounds, purple or blue, edged in black, with white filigree and two short flowering tendrils, as in border on f. 1v; often with a gold dot with hair-spray adjacent in outer margin.

Binding: s. xix-xx. Brown goatskin, blind-stamped, by Henri Marius-Michel of Paris (1846-1925), whose name is stamped inside the front cover. Not in his usual style. For a photograph of the binding, see Perkins and Garey, *op. cit.*, v. 1, pl. 1. Included in the center front and back panels are monograms of Baron Joseph Vitta (see Provenance).

Written probably at the Aragonese court in Naples in the 1470's, perhaps as a wedding gift for Beatrice of Aragon, who married Matthias Corvinus, King of Hungary, in 1476 (see Perkins and Garey, *op. cit.*, pp. 4-28). Inscription on f. 1r, mostly effaced and not legible even under ultra-violet light or with infrared photography, includes the date 1574. Inscription written over the effaced inscription states that the codex was given to Johan Georg Trigbor by Matteus Rohn [?] of Glatz, in the city of Freudenthal, 3 October 1609. Belonged (s. xix-xx) to Baron Joseph Vitta, a Parisian [?] book collector, for whom it was bound. Acquired from him by an anonymous owner, perhaps in the 1930's. Offered for sale by that owner through A. Rosenthal's of London, in 1939. Given to Yale by Paul Mellon in 1940.

secundo folio: Bel accueil

Bibliography: Faye and Bond, p. 28, no. 91.
Exhibition Catalogue, pp. 236-38, no. 62.
M. Bukofzer, "The Mellon Chansonnier," *Gazette* 15 (1940) pp. 25-28.
For a detailed bibliography, see Perkins and Garey, *op. cit.*

MS 92
Cicero, Epistolae ad familiares (with glosses) Germany, s. XV²

All bibliographical references in parentheses refer to D. R. Shackleton Bailey, ed., *Cicero: Epistulae ad familiares,* 2 vol. (Cambridge, 1977).

1. f. 1r-v   Prefatory notes to first letter.
2. f. 2r-v   To C. Scribonius Curio (v. 1, no. 45, pp. 104-05).
3. f. 2v   To C. Scribonius Curio (v. 1, no. 46, p. 106).
4. ff. 2v-3r   To C. Scribonius Curio (v. 1, no. 47, pp. 106-07).
5. ff. 3v, 5r   To C. Scribonius Curio (v. 1, no. 48, pp. 107-08).
6. ff. 4 and 9   Lists of vocabulary words arranged according to classifications, e.g., Me hercule, castor, ecastor, edepol; Obtestor, obsecro, oro).
7. f. 5r-v   To C. Scribonius Curio (v. 1, no. 49, p. 109).
8. ff. 5v-7r   To C. Scribonius Curio (v. 1, no. 50, pp. 110-12).
9. f. 7r-v   To M. Caelius Rufus (v. 1, no. 90, pp. 175-76).
10. ff. 7v-8v, 10r   To C. Scribonius Curio (v. 1, no. 107, pp. 199-200).
11. f. 10r   To M. Caelius Rufus (v. 1, no. 89, p. 175).
12. ff. 10r-11r   To Q. Minucius Thermus (v. 1, no. 115, pp. 214-15).
13. ff. 11r-12r   To C. Coelius Caldus (v. 1, no. 116, pp. 215-16).
14. f. 12r-v   To Ap. Claudius Pulcher (v. 1, no. 64, pp. 123-24).
15. f. 13r-v   To Ap. Claudius Pulcher (v. 1, no. 65, pp. 124-25).
16. ff. 13v-14v   To Ap. Claudius Pulcher (v. 1, no. 76, pp. 150-51).
17. ff. 14v-17v   Ser. Sulpicius Rufus to Cicero (v. 2, no. 248, pp. 108-11).
18. ff. 17v-19r   To Ser. Sulpicius Rufus (v. 2, no. 249, pp. 111-13).
19. f. 19r-v   To M. Claudius Marcellus (v. 2, no. 229, p. 79).
20. ff. 19v-20r   To M. Claudius Marcellus (v. 2, no. 233, p. 85).
21. f. 20r-v   M. Claudius Marcellus to Cicero (v. 2, no. 232, p. 84).
22. ff. 20v-22r   Ser. Sulpicius Rufus to Cicero (v. 2, no. 252, pp. 116-18).
23. ff. 22r-23r   To C. Antonius (v. 1, no. 5, pp. 36-37).
24. f. 23r-v   To Cn. Pompeius Magnus (v. 1, no. 3, p. 34).
25. ff. 23v-24r   Q. Metellus Nepos to Cicero (v. 1, no. 11, p. 46).
26. f. 24r-v   P. Vatinius to Cicero (v. 2, no. 255, pp. 119-20).
27. ff. 24v-25r   To T. Fadius (v. 1, no. 51, pp. 112-13).
28. ff. 25v-26r   To P. Vatinius (v. 2, no. 241, p. 98).

29. f. 26r-v   To Cn. Plancius (v. 2, no. 241, p. 98).

30. ff. 26v-27r   P. Vatinius to Cicero (v. 2, no. 255, pp. 119-20).

31. ff. 27v-28v   To L. Lucceius (v. 2, no. 252, pp. 115-16). ff. 29r-32v blank

Marginal and interlinear notes accompany the text of each letter (except for that to P. Vatinius appearing on ff. 26v-27v which was copied twice, apparently in error).

Paper (sturdy; watermarks: unidentified letter P in gutter), ff. i (paper) + 32 + i (paper), 214 x 149 (162 x 95) mm. Written in ca. 20 long lines; frame-ruled in lead, often with no horizontal bounding lines.

I-II^{12}, III^8. Catchword (f. 24v) in gutter.

Written by a single scribe in gothic cursive, with a smaller script for glosses.

Simple initials in red at the beginning of each letter; titles preceded by paragraph marks, and underlined, in red.

Binding: s. xix-xx. Vellum case; spine fragile and splitting.

Written in Germany in the second half of the 15th century, probably for use as a school text (vocabulary lists on ff. 4 and 9). Unidentified no. "39906" on back cover, in ink; note inside front cover, in French, gives brief description of volume. Bought from C. A. Stonehill by Henry Fletcher who presented it to Yale in 1946.

secundo folio: Quanquam

Bibliography: Faye and Bond, p. 28, no. 92.

MS 93
Cicero, Orationes, etc.

Italy, s. XV$^{2/4}$

Pl. 25

1. ff. 1r-9v   *De imperio Cn. Pompeii*; P. Reis, ed., Teubner v. 6, 1 (1931) pp. 3-34.

2. ff. 9v-22v   *Pro T. Annio Milone*; A. Klotz, ed., Teubner v. 8 (1918) pp. 13-66.

3. ff. 22v-37r   *Pro Cn. Plancio*; A. Klotz, ed., Teubner v. 7 (1919) pp. 473-536.

4. ff. 37r-49r   *Pro P. Sulla*; F. Richter, ed., Teubner v. 6, 2 (1932) pp. 120-62.

5. ff. 49r-59r   *De haruspicum responsis*; A. Klotz, ed., Teubner v. 7 (1919) pp. 122-58.

6. ff. 59v-66v   *De provinciis consularibus*; A. Klotz, ed., Teubner v. 7 (1919) pp. 334-59.

7. ff. 66v-79r   *Pro M. Caelio*; A. Klotz, ed., Teubner v. 7 (1919) pp. 277-332.

8. ff. 79r-88r   *Pro L. Cornelio Balbo*; A. Klotz, ed., Teubner v. 7 (1919) pp. 361-400.

9. ff. 88v-94r   *In P. Vatinium testem interrogatio*; A. Klotz, ed., Teubner v. 7 (1919) pp. 252-75.

10. ff. 94r-111r *Pro P. Sestio*; A. Klotz, ed., Teubner v. 7 (1919) pp. 161-250.

11. ff. 111v-130v *De domo sua*; A. Klotz, ed., Teubner v. 7 (1919) pp. 41-120.

12. ff. 131r-134v Pseudo-Cicero, *Oratio antequam in exilium iret*; M. Gianascian, *M. Tullius Cicero*, in Scriptorum romanorum quae extant omnia v. 102-03 (Venice, 1968) pp. 160-72.

13. ff. 134v-140r *Orationes cum Senatui gratias egit*; A. Klotz, ed., Teubner v. 7 (1919) pp. 2-24.

14. ff. 140r-143v *Oratio cum populo gratias egit*; A. Klotz, ed., Teubner v. 7 (1919) pp. 26-39.

15. ff. 143v-147r *Pro M. Marcello*; A. Klotz, ed., Teubner v. 8 (1918) pp. 69-81.

16. ff. 147r-151r *Pro Q. Ligario*; A. Klotz, ed., Teubner v. 8 (1918) pp. 84-100.

17. ff. 151v-156r *Pro rege Deiotaro*; A. Klotz, ed., Teubner v. 8 (1918) pp. 101-19.

18. ff. 156v-160r *Pro L. Licinio Archia*; P. Reis, ed., Teubner v. 6, 2 (1932) pp. 165-80.

19. ff. 160r-176r *In L. Catilinam IV*; P. Reis, ed., Teubner v. 6, 2 (1932) pp. 5-68.

20. ff. 176r-187v *Pro P. Quinctio*; A. Klotz, ed., Teubner v. 4 (1923) pp. 4-44.

21. ff. 187v-200r *Pro L. Flacco*; L. Fruechtel, ed., Teubner v. 6, 2 (1932) pp. 182-243.

22. ff. 200r-201r Pseudo-Sallust, *Invectiva in M. Tullium Ciceronem*; M. Gianascian, ed., *C. Sallustius Crispus*, in Scriptorum romanorum quae extant omnia v. 49 (Venice, 1965) v. 1, pp. 83-86.

23. ff. 201r-203v Pseudo-Cicero, *Invectiva in Crispum Sallustium; ibid.*, v. 1, pp. 87-95.

24. ff. 203v-228r *Pro A. Cluentio*; L. Fruechtel, ed., Teubner v. 6, 1 (1931) pp. 37-140.

Parchment, ff. i (parchment) + 228 + i (parchment), 391 x 274 (250 x 173) mm. Written in 33 long lines, double bounding lines full across. Ruled in hard point on the hair side before folding; prickings in the 3 outer margins. I-XXII[10], XXIII[8]. Catchwords in center of lower margin.

Written by a single scribe in a beautiful humanistic script (see below).

Delicately executed gold initials, 7- to 5-line, filled with white-vine ornament (highlights in pale orange) on blue, pale green, and pale orange ground with brown dots, mark the beginning of each oration. Rubrics (modified square capitals) throughout.

Binding: s. xviii. Narrow brown calf spine with brown spattered-paper sides, small vellum corners. Bound for the Convent of San Marco, Florence; rebacked in Yale Library Conservation Studio.

Written in Florence ca. 1430-40 by a careful scribe who was concerned with the accuracy of the text (variant readings neatly recorded in margins; spaces left for words to be inserted later). According to A. C. de la Mare the scribe also seems to have written Florence, Laur. 35, 27, a manuscript of Lucretius with ex-libris of Piero de' Medici, but probably produced for his father Cosimo. Shelf-mark (c. II. a) on f. 1r of the Jesuit scholar Girolamo Lagomarsini (1698-1773; Cosenza, v. 3, pp. 1894-95); belonged to the Dominican convent of San Marco, Florence (rebound in 18th century; no. 253 on spine; see B. L. Ullman and P. A. Stadter, *The Public Library of Renaissance Florence* [Padua, 1972] p. 227, no. 14). From the collection of Friedrich Ludwig von Keller, German scholar of Roman law (1799-1860; stamp on f. 1r); booklabel of Ambroise Firmin-Didot, with date 1850, inside front cover (see *Catalogue illustré des livres précieux manuscrits ... de M. Ambroise Firmin-Didot*, v. 1 [Paris, 1878] p. 4, no. 3). Belonged to William Morris, Kelmscott House, Hammersmith (1834-96; bookplate); his sale (London, 6 Dec. 1898, no. 357). Acquired by Lawrence W. Hodson, Esq., of Compton Hall, Wolverhampton (his sale, London, 3 Dec. 1906, no. 128); acquired by Sir Sydney Cockerell (signature dated 3 Dec. 1906, and notes inside front cover); John Gribbell (1858-1936; bookplate), St. Austell Hall. From the collection of David Wagstaff; presented to Yale in 1945 by Mrs. David Wagstaff.

secundo folio: rerum magna

Bibliography: Faye and Bond, p. 28, no. 93.

MS 94 France, 1396
Compte de la vennerie de Charles VI

Copy of an account book for the hunting expenses of King Charles VI of France. The account is rendered by Philippe de Courguilleroy [?] "chevalier maistre veneur du Roy et maistre de ses canes et forestz" and encompasses November 1395 to 2 February 1396.

Parchment (crude), ff. ii (paper) + 8 + ii (paper partially stuck together), 339 x 290 (257 x 180) mm. Written in 44 long lines, ruled in lead. Format varies.
Composed of 8 individual sheets.
Written in a chancery script by a single scribe.
Binding: s. xviii-xix. Brown mottled and spattered calf with a red label, gold-tooled.

Written in France in 1396. Belonged to Sir Thomas Phillipps (no. 4365; inscription on f. 1r, mutilated tag on spine) who acquired it from the bookdealer Royez in Paris. C. F. G. R. Schwerdt (bookplate; see the catalogue *Hunting Hawking Shooting* [London, 1928] v. 2, p. 319); his sale (Sotheby's, 12 March 1946, no.

2191). Purchased from Goldschmidt's by David Wagstaff (bookplate); gift of Mrs. David Wagstaff in 1946.

Bibliography: Faye and Bond, p. 28, no. 94.

MSS 95-96 Yale Latin American Collection (Sterling Memorial Library)

MS 97 England, ca. 1564
Sir Gilbert Dethick, Book of Arms

1. f. 1r [Dedication:] *To the Quenes* most Excellent Majestie. A Booke of all suche knightes (not beinge of the moste noble ordre of the Garter) as hath ben maid sence the firste yere of your Highnes Reigne, their Armes with thiere Creastes, set fourth by youre majesties most houmble Servante Sir Gilberte Dethicke knight alias Garter your Princypall King of Armes and Chiefe offycer of Armes of youre moste noble ordre of the garter, the Laste daye of Desember in the yere of our Lord 1564.

2. ff. 2r-28r Illustrations of coats of arms, in color, one per folio recto or verso; above each except the first, the name of the bearer, as given below. No mottoes given. (f. 2r) Royal arms of Elizabeth I of England; (f. 2v blank; f. 3r) Knightes of the Bathe, The Lord Darcy of Darcy; (f. 3v) The Lord Sheffelde; (f. 4r) The Lord Darcy of Chiche; (f. 4v) Sir Roberte Ryche; (f. 5r) Sir Roger Northe; (f. 5v) Sir John Souche; (f. 6r) Sir Henry Weston; (f. 6v) Sir Edward Vmpton; (f. 7r) Sir Henry Cary nowe Lord of Honnsdon; (f. 7v) Sir Thomas Leigh, then Lord Maior of London; (f. 8r) Sir Nycholas Bacon Lord Keper of ye great Sealle; (f. 8v) Sir Robert Cattelen Lord Chief Justice; (f. 9r) Sir Nycholas Poynes; (f. 9v) Sir John Barkeley; (f. 10r) Sir George Speke; [at bottom of the folio:] here endeth the Knights of ye Bathe; (f. 10v) Sir Thomas Parrey; (f. 11r) Sir Thomas Gresham; (f. 11v) Sir William Huet then Lord Maior of London; (f. 12r) Sir George Bowes; (f. 12v) Sir Arthur Grey nowe Lord Grey of Wilton; (f. 13r) Sir Barnaby fitzpaterike; (13v) Sir Edward Braye; (f. 14r) Sir William Mallorye; (f. 14v) Sir Edward Lyttelton; (f. 15r) Sir William Babthorpe; (f. 15v) Sir John Conwey; (f. 16r) Sir Walter Aston; (f. 16v) Sir Rychard Newporte; (f. 17r) Sir William ffairefax; (f. 17v) Sir Rychard ffulmerston; (f. 18r) Sir William Harper then Lord Maior of London; (f. 18v) Sir Owen Hopton; (f. 19r) Sir Edward Capell; (f. 19v) Sir Adryan Poynynge; (f. 20r) Sir Thomas Lodge then Lord Maior of London; (f. 20v) Sir John White then Lord Maior of London; (f. 21r) Sir Henry Williams alias Cromwell; (f. 21v) Sir Henry Cheyney; (ff. 22r-27v blank; f. 28r) Sir Gilbert Dethicke alias Garter. f. 28v blank

Parchment (thick and furry), ff. ii (paper) + ii (contemporary parchment) +

28 (interleaved with modern paper, latter not foliated) + ii (paper), 172 x 130 mm. (illustrations ca. 135 x 115 mm.). No ruling.

Impossible to determine the collation, because all leaves are now separate and stitched to stubs of modern paper.

Introduction and labels of illustrations in cursive with loops, by one scribe.

Each shield enclosed in shaded pink border designed to look like worked metal, and surmounted by a jousting helm in profile, mantling gules doubled argent with gold tassels; wreath in colors from shield. Only shields (in up to 17 quarters) and crests vary. Slight variations from this scheme on f. 2r (royal arms) and f. 3r (mantling sable doubled argent). Fair quality of workmanship.

Bookblock detached from the binding. Illustration badly smeared on f. 11r, slightly smeared f. 28r.

Binding: ca. 1873. Gold-stamped red goatskin case.

Written in England in the late 16th century, probably ca. 1564 (see f. 1r); for Sir Gilbert Dethick (ca. 1500-84) see DNB, v. 5, pp. 868-69 and W. H. Godfrey, Sir A. Wagner, and H. S. London, "The College of Arms...," being the sixteenth Monograph of the London Survey Committee (1963) pp. 46-47. Bought by E. Champion Bacon in London in 1844 (signature on third flyleaf; note copied onto verso of first flyleaf). Belonged to Thomas R. Trowbridge in 1873, who had it rebound. Presented to Yale in 1924 by Francis B. Trowbridge.

Bibliography: Faye and Bond, p. 29, no. 97.

MS 98
Diploma (in Lat.)

Italy, 1598

ff. 1r-6v *In Christi nomine amen. Vniuersis* et singulis praesens hoc publicum Doctoratus Priuilegium uisuris, lecturis, seu legi audituris. *Aloysius Brullinus* Forosem proniensis, Iuris Vtriusque Doctor, et in Episcopatu Paduae ... et frequenti copia Testibus omnibus ad premissa vocatis, et rogatis. [followed by autograph signature of Aloysius Brullinus] Franciscus de Oddis Not. Cas. Alm. Vniuersitat. Pat. scriptor scripsit.

Diploma for a doctorate in Theology accorded to Iosephus Prudentius from the University of Padua, June 1598.

Parchment, ff. i (paper) + 6 + ii (paper), 220 x 165 (175 x 121) mm. Written in 18 long lines, single vertical bounding lines ruled in lead; the written space is surrounded by double lines in purple ink.

One quire of 6. One or two syllables as catchwords at lower right of written area on each verso.

Written by Franciscus de Oddis (see below), in an elegant italic.

On f. 1r, a full vine-scroll border, in purple ink with grapes and highlights in gold, outlined in double purple lines; a 5-line initial, gold, with purple and gold vines. Headings and names of persons in humanistic bookhand or square capitals, in gold.

Binding: s. xix. Brown leather wrapper, gold-tooled.

Written in Padua in 1598 by Franciscus de Oddis, notary of the University of Padua; early provenance unknown. Unidentified catalogue entry pasted on front flyleaf: "394 Roman Catholic Ms. in Latin. On 6 leaves of vellum. Bound in russia. Padua. 1598". Bought from Blackman's in 1939.

Bibliography: Faye and Bond, p. 29, no. 98.

MS 99   Germany, s. XVI/XVII
Valentin von Eickstedt, Pommersche Chronik, etc.

1. ff. 1r–458r   *Von etlichen vornemen Steten in Pommern Vineta.* Vor alters dein etliche grosse kund ... Vnnd also ist hie mit de kurstliche [for *kurfürstliche*?] leich Procession geschlossen werden. f. 458v blank, except for later notes

    The order of the contents is as follows: descriptions of some cities of Pomerania, genealogy of the Dukes of Pomerania, the Chronicle proper. Written by Valentin von Eickstedt in 1574; contents correspond closely to those listed in W. Lubuik (*Baltische Studien* v. 3, part 1 [Stettin, 1835] pp. 80–81), but the Beinecke codex has fewer articles. Von Eickstedt (1527–79) usually worked from the same sources as Thomas Kantzow (d. 1542?), author of a chronicle on Pomeranian church history (G. Gaebel, ed., *Pomerania. Eine pommersche Chronik aus dem sechzehnten Jahrhundert* [Stettin, 1908] 2 vols.). The arrangement of the material in the two chronicles is similar, and there is some paraphrasing, but the Beinecke manuscript contains no dedicatory epistle and uses some different material at the beginning.

2. f. 459r blank; ff. 459r–524v   [Colorful and elaborate title page occupies ff. 459v–460r, written sidewise:] *Ex mandato illustrissimi principis ac domini domini [?] casimiri ducis ... parentalia posthuma ... celebrabit Daniel Cramerus, D. Pastor ...* [text:] Si quas mihi hoc ipso die dicendi partes necessitas imperauit ... notisque nostris [crossed out: annis (?)] annuit *Christus Jesus* benedictus in aeternum. *Dixi.*

    Funeral orations for the Dukes of Pomerania, by Daniel Cramer (1568–1637), Lutheran theologian and archdeacon of Stettin (cf. *Allgemeine Deutsche Biographie* v. 4, pp. 546–47, and H. Heyden, *Pommersche Geistliche vom Mittelalter bis zum 19. Jahrhundert*, in Veröffentlichungen der historischen Kommission für Pommern, 11 [Cologne, 1965] pp. 173–79).

Paper (sturdy and rough; watermarks: an unidentified letter *Z* in two concen-

tric circles), ff. iv (paper) + 528 + iii (paper), 310 x 185 (254 x 132) mm. Ca. 25-27 long lines; ruling in red ink, only 2 vertical bounding lines.
Too tightly bound for accurate collation.
Written by several scribes in gothic cursive and italic script.
Headings of gothic textura, square capitals, and a large humanistic script, in reddish brown, green, and black.
Binding: s. xix, after 1861. Brown goatskin Jansenist binding by Chambolle-Duru (Paris).

Written in Germany in the late 16th or early 17th century; inscription at top of f. 1r: "Ex b. viri Andr. Schotti Scabini Gedanensis bibliotheca publica auctionis lege [...] dita hic codex supperlectili librariae adjectus est Joachimi Guilielmi Weickhmann Ged. 1764." On the third flyleaf at the front, "Chronique de Poméranie ecrite en 1570 par Valentin de Eickstetten, Chancellier des Princes de Poméranie. Un abrégé en a été fait en 1728 et imprimé par Balthazar à Gryphiswold in 8°." Belonged to comte Paul Riant (bookplate inside front cover; L. Germon and L. Polain, *Catalogue de la bibliothèque de feu M. le comte Riant* [Paris, 1896] p. 361-62, no. 2486). Given to Yale in 1896 by Mrs. Henry Farnam.

Bibliography: Faye and Bond, p. 29, no. 99.

MS 100 England, s. XVI^{ex}
The Fawkners' Glasse

1. f. 1r blank; f. 1v *The fawkners' Glasse*. 1. Washe your handes alwayes before you feede her ... 16. Vse no Phisick withouthout an apparent cause of a dyesease. [Drawing of a falconer tipped in between ff. 1 and 2; see below.]

   J. E. Harting, *A Perfect Booke for Kepinge Sparhawkes or Goshawkes* (London, 1886) p. 3.

2. ff. 2r-18v *A perfect waie and order to be observed in chosing and keping of sparhawkes*. Theare be certayne tokens wherby a man maye chose them, to have them stronge ... and for a flyinge hawke no better meate to be hadd. [added in a later hand:] A brefe Rule to kepe a hawke ... This is a perfect Booke for kepinge of Sparhawkes or Goshawkes. ff. 19r-20v blank

   Harting, *op. cit.*, pp. 5-35.

3. ff. 21r-22v [Brief passages, most of which have been crossed out:] *Medicens and Practises which I never proved. To Clense a hawke that hath Surfited*. When her mewtes shew her to be surfyted ... *To cause a hawke Mewe be tymes*. Pull her flagges next her Principals ... in Aprile or Maye when the other flagge be home or nere// f. 23r-v blank

   Harting, *op. cit.*, p. 36 (lists only those sections not crossed out).

4. f. 24r – inside back cover   Miscellaneous rules, in several hands, for treating dogs, etc., e.g., *To helpe Spanielles. For Mangines*. Washe the dogg throughly in Cowes pysse 3 or 4 tymes daylye the newer the better.

Parchment, ff. 24, 176 x 141 (147 x 108) mm. Written in ca. 27 long lines; leaves were first frame-ruled in ink, with horizontal lines for text added in lead; prickings in corners of written space.
I–VI^4 (+ 1 leaf added between ff. 1 and 2).
Articles 1 and 2 written by a single person in a careful secretary script; other items added by several contemporary and later hands.
One loose leaf, presently tipped in between ff. 1 and 2, has pen and ink sketch of falconer, with bird and dog; adapted from a woodcut in G. Turberville, *The Booke of Faulconrie* (London, 1575). Inscription above drawing: "Lorde let me not, in Vanitie/ Delight more, then I should in thee."
Binding: s. xvi–xvii. Limp vellum case with title lettered on spine.

Written in England toward the end of the 16th century; early provenance unknown. Belonged to W. A. Tyssen-Amherst, of Hackney (1835–1909; bookplate); his sale (5 Dec. 1908, no. 340). Collection of C. F. G. R. Schwerdt (see catalogue *Hunting Hawking Shooting* [London, 1928] v. 2, p. 327, with plate no. 157 of drawing); his sale (Sotheby's, 12 March 1946, no. 2205). Purchased from Quaritch, 26 Oct. 1946, by the Yale Library Associates, with funds contributed by Mrs. Samuel Milbank.

Bibliography: Faye and Bond, p. 29, no. 100.

MS 101 England, s. XV^{med}
Edward, Duke of York, Master of Game

ff. 2r–51v   //which mygt him most auayle. Now schal y preue þe how an hunter ... common strakyng as is aboue deuysed and seide, etc. Explicit.

W. A. and F. Baillie-Grohman, eds., *The Master of Game by Edward, Second Duke of York* (London, 1904); for a modernized edition of the Prologue, see J. McDonald, *The Origins of Angling* (New York, 1963) Appendix A, pp. 251–58. A table of contents (s. xviii) precedes the text on f. i recto.

Parchment, ff. ii (paper) + i (contemporary parchment) + 50 (foliated 2–51) + i (contemporary parchment) + ii (paper), 268 x 180 (190 x 126) mm. Written in 34 long lines; single vertical and double horizontal bounding lines, full across. Ruled in ink; prickings in all margins, except inner.
I^8 (-1,2), II–VI^8, VII^4. Catchwords in lower margin, verso; remains of leaf signatures (e.g., iij, iiij, etc.) in red, recto.
Written by a single scribe in a careful English secretary script.

Gold initials, 3-line, on blue and dark pink grounds with white highlights mark text divisions. Headings and marginal chapter references, in red, throughout.

Binding: s. xviii. Brown skin, flesh side out, blind-tooled, over paper boards. Front cover detached.

Written in England ca. 1460, according to K. Scott; belonged to John Berners (s. xv/xvi). Inscriptions on f. iii recto concerning John Berners are not in his own hand, but are presumably those of the person who had the volume bound in the 18th century and who made a copy of what was written on the old "cover" (a parchment wrapper?). The inscriptions include: "Iste liber dico, constat homini Generoso/ Si quis queratur, John Berners nominatur" and "Iste liber constat Johanni Nomine Barners/ Qui contradicit, Rusticus est, et Erit." (Another note on Dame Juliana Berners apparently led some later owner to have the binding stamped "Julian Bernes [sic] On Hunting etc. M. S. S."). On f. 5r the signature of J. Lovell (s. xviii); a note by T. Martin (subsequent owner) on f. i recto states "He [J. Lovell] was the last of that Antient [sic] Family in Norf. and dyd at New Buckenham." From the collection of Thomas Martin (1697–1771), antiquary of Palgrave, Suffolk; his signature inside front cover, with shelfmark "B. 2. 15". Inscription of the London bookseller Thomas Payne, 19 July 1770 (f. i recto). Bookplate of Christopher Jeaffreson, Esquire, Dullingham House. Purchased from Bowes and Bowes of Cambridge, England, in 1940 by the Pierpont Morgan Library; according to an undated note in library files David Wagstaff (bookplate) "traded a manuscript of Ovid for it [with the Pierpont Morgan Library]." Presented to Yale by Mr. and Mrs. David Wagstaff in 1944.

Bibliography: Faye and Bond, p. 29, no. 101.

MS 102
Albertano da Brescia, etc.

Italy, s. XIV[1]

1. ff. 1r–13v   *Incipit moralium dogma.* Moralium dogma philosophorum per multa dispersum uolumina tuo quidem instinctu uir optime et liberalis henrice ... [with a table of contents between the prologue and the text] sed rei magnitudo usum quoque exercitationemque quam desiderat. [Followed without a break by the end of Boethius, *De consolatione philosophiae* (5.6):] Aduersamini igitur ... cernentis. Magna nobis est si dissimulare non uultis necessitas indicta probitatis cum ante oculos agitis indicis cuncta cernent. *Explicit liber moralitatis. Deo gratias.*

   For the controversy concerning the authorship of this work see M. T. d'Alverny, *Alain de Lille* ... (Paris, 1965) p. 65, and notes; J. Holmberg, ed., *Das Moralium dogma philosophorum des Guillaume de Conches* in *Vilhelm Ehmans Universitetsfon* 37 (Uppsala, 1929) pp. 5–74. The ending is that of Holmberg's MSS P, Q, U and E.

MS 102

Articles 2-4 also appear together in Marston MS 87.

2. ff. 13v-46v *Incipit liber albertani in primis de amore et dilectione dei et proximi et aliarum rerum et de forma uite hominis. liber .j.* Initium michi tractatus sit in nomine domini a quo cuncta bona procedunt ... *Explicit de amore et dilectione dei et proximi et aliarum rerum et forma uite* ... quem Albertanus causidicus brixiensis de hora sancte agathe conpilauit ac scripsit cum esset in carcere domini imperatoris frederici in ciuitate cremone in quo positus fuit cum esset capitaneus gauardi [?] defendendo locum ipsum ad utilitatem communis brixie. Anno domini .m. cc. trigesimo octauo. Indictione xi. de mense augusti in die sancti alexandri quo obsidebatur ciuitas brixie per eundem dominum imperatorem.

   Albertano da Brescia, *De amore et dilectione Dei.*

3. ff. 46v-63r *Incipit liber consolationis et consilii.* Quoniam multi sunt qui in aduersitatibus et tribulationibus taliter affliguntur et deprimuntur ... Ite in pace et nolite amplius peccare et ita utraque pars cum gaudio et letitia recesserunt. *Explicit liber consolationis et consilii qui albertanus causidicus brixiensis de hora sancte agathe conpilauit sub .m. xl. sexto* [sic] *in mensibus aprilis et maii.*

   Albertano da Brescia, *Liber consolationis et consilii*; T. Sundby, ed., *Albertani Brixiensis Liber consolationis et consilii* ... (London, 1873) pp. 1-127.

4. ff. 63r-67v *Incipit liber de doctrina dicendi et tacendi.* Initio et medio ac fini mei tractatus assit gratia sancti spiritus. Quoniam in dicendo multi erant [sic] ... Deum insuper exora quo michi donauit predicta tibi narrare ut ad eterna gaudia nos faciat peruenire. *Explicit liber de doctrina dicendi et tacendi ab albertano causidico brixiensi compositus et compilatus. sub. m. cc. xlv. de mense decembris. Explicit opus.*

   Albertano da Brescia, *Liber de doctrina dicendi et tacendi*; GKW, v. 1, nos. 531-63; T. Sundby, ed., *Della vita e delle opere di Brunetto Latini* (Florence, 1884) pp. 479-506.

5. ff. 67v-73r *Parabole Salomonis.* Omni tempore diligit qui amicus est et frater in angustiis conprobatur [Prov. 17.17] ... prospities haec tristitia huius mundi yl [wormhole] tumultuosa quietus extrema securus.

6. ff. 73r-80r *Regule Senece.* Auxilia humilia firma consensus facit./ Aut amat aut odit mulier. nihil est medium/ ... Vltionis contumeliosum genus est non uisum esse dignum ex quo petatur ultio. Explicit. f. 80v blank

   Various selections from both the prose and poetry of Seneca that appear to be arranged as follow: a) ff. 73r-74r sententiae; b) ff. 74r-77r extracts from prose works, especially from the *De ira*; c) ff. 77r-80r proverbia, listed in alphabetical order (similar to those printed by Stephan Plannck [Rome, ca. 1500]).

Parchment, ff. 80, 233 x 178 (166 x 122) mm. Written in 2 columns of 38 lines; single vertical and double horizontal bounding lines, full across. Ruled faintly in lead; prominent prickings (slashes) in all margins, except inner.

I-VIII[10]. Catchwords, enclosed by rectangle and flourishes, near gutter.
Written by a single scribe in a precise round gothic bookhand.

Small initials, 4- to 1-line, alternating red and blue, sometimes accompanied by simple penwork designs. Headings, in red, throughout. Some paragraph marks, in red or blue, and strokes on 1-line initials, in red.

F. 1r rubbed, with loss of text.

Binding: s. xiv. Original sewing, wound and catching up the previous threads on three slit, tawed straps laced into edged tunnels in square-edged beech boards and laid in channels on the outer face. Pegged. A thread, tied at one kettle-stitch, runs along the spine, underneath the sewing supports, and is tied to the other kettle-stitch of the second quire. Covered in tawed skin, now a dirty cream color, with corner turn-in tongues. White, tawed straps attached to the upper board with nails and traces of pins on the lower. Traces of five bosses on each board and of a chain near the tail of the upper one. On the inside (only) of this board, at the center near the head and tail are unaccounted for rusty holes. Remains of a small paper label near the head of the lower board. The spine covering and sewing supports are broken and the bosses, fastenings, and chains wanting.

Written in Italy probably toward the beginning of the 14th century; early inscription on back pastedown: "Iste liber est domini Ambrosij." Presented to Yale in 1941 by Carl B. Spitzer who acquired it from Hoepli in Milan for 500 lire [letter in library files].

secundo folio: credere de

Bibliography: Faye and Bond, p. 30, no. 102.

MS 103
Ghatrif; Moamin

Italy, s. XV/XVI

1. ff. 1r–23v [Ghatrif:] Incipit tractatus aujum de doctrina eorum et de medicamjnibus Infirmitatum eorundem qui liber est translatus de persico In latjnum. [text:] Dixit Gatriph persicus Multi persiarum et grecorum sapientes In arte auium rapacium ... plenum aqua umida et bibat si uoluerit.

2. ff. 24r–66v [Moamin:] Incipit liber primus Medicamjni [*sic*] falconerij, translatus de arabico In latjnum per magistrum theodorum phisicum domjni federjci Romanj Imperatorjs Et correctus est per ipsum Imperatorem tempore obsidjonjs fanencie de quo libro sunt tres tractus ... Capitulum primum. Genera volatium viuencium de rapina quibus vtitur gens aucupando ... vapor ad ipsum et sudet et quando sudabjt omnes pediculi cadent. Et finis.

This treatise is divided into 3 sections, all on falconry; the second and third are preceded by lists of the chapters. Missing from the text are the Prologue and "Quartus, natura et medicamen quatrupedum cum quibus venamur."

MS 104 145

For the manuscript tradition of both arts. 1 and 2 see H. Tjernald, *Moamin et Ghatrif* (Stockholm, 1945); Beinecke MS 103 is nos. 21 and 5 on p. 4.

Paper (watermarks similar to Briquet Sirène 13880), ff. iv (paper) + 67 + iii (early paper) + iv (paper), 277 x 206 (230 x 115) mm. Written in ca. 25 long lines. There are no rulings; the page has been folded vertically to delineate the written space.
I^{14}, II^{18}, III^{16}, IV^{20} (-20).
Written by a single person in a sprawling italic.
Binding: s. xix. Three-quarter vellum, gold-tooled, with marbled paper sides. Bound by Domenico Conti-Borbone, Milan (tag inside front cover).

Written in Italy at the end of the 15th or beginning of the 16th century; early provenance unknown. The codex was rebound in Milan during the 19th century. Belonged to Professor Hermann Suchier (1848-1914; bookplate) and C. F. G. R. Schwerdt (bookplate; see catalogue *Hunting Hawking Shooting* [London, 1928] v. 2, p. 330); his sale (Sotheby's, 12 March 1946, no. 2210). Purchased from Goldschmidt's by David Wagstaff (bookplate); presented to Yale by Mrs. David Wagstaff in 1946.

secundo folio: Capitulum de reclamacione

Bibliography: Faye and Bond, p. 30, no. 103.
A. Lupis, "Petrus de l'Astore, Moamyn, Ghatriph: Sulla tradizione dei trattati di falconeria d'epoca federiciana," *Codices manuscripti* 3 (1977) p. 16.

MS 104 Italy, 1515
Venetian Document

Ducale issued in the name of Antonio Grimani, doge of Venice (1436-1523), giving instructions in Latin and Italian to a Venetian governor setting out for the island of Crete. The name of the governor, Petrus Barbarus, is in a 16th-century hand quite different from the scribe's hand that wrote the body of the document and is written over a dirty erasure. The date "Die. 4. Marcij. M. D. XV." and the signature of the scribe "Victor Blanchus Secret^s" on f. 14r may be later additions. f. 14v ruled, but blank

Parchment, ff. 14 + i (original parchment flyleaf), 220 x 146 (172 x 113) mm. Written in 29 long lines; vertical bounding lines in hard point; guide-lines for text in ink; remains of prickings for bounding lines only.
Composed of a single gathering of 16 leaves (-1, 16 = flyleaf). Some leaf signatures, in red, on recto in lower right corner.
Written in an upright humanistic script exhibiting chancery influence.
One crude full border (f. 1r), with inset panels (framed by thick gold bands)

containing the lion of St. Mark stepping out of water and holding an open book, St. Peter, red and black vine ornament against parchment ground, and red and blue vines against tan ground; in lower margin, an effaced coat of arms. One 6-line initial (f. 1r) gold, against a dark pink ground with red vine ornament, as above. The first two lines of the text in red majuscules against a gold ground; the third in blue majuscules. 2-line initials, gold, on f. 1r only. 1-line initials, red, outside text column (painted over guide-letters to rubricator) throughout.

Binding: s. xvii. Brown goatskin blind-tooled and gilt with IHS monogram on both covers. Boards flush. Remains of four green ribbon ties.

Written probably in Venice on 4 March 1515; arms of early owner on f. 1r effaced. From the estate of the Rev. T. Lawrason Riggs in 1944.

Bibliography: Faye and Bond, p. 30, no. 104.

MS 105 England, s. XVI^2
Robert Heron, Argus

Composed of three dialogues, in verse modeled on Vergil, between Argus, a good shepherd of the English Church, and Epicurus, a typical Papist as seen by an Anglican. In the third dialogue Epicurus has finally been converted and is called "Theodidactus".

1. f. 1r-v   Honorabili viro Willielmo Cicilio Domino ac Baroni Burleio huius florentissimi Regni Angliae Thesaurario generali Domino suo obseruantissimo Robertus Heron humilis uerbi Dei Minister ... Cetera tui iudicii candori refero ... Londini quarto kalendarum Februarii. Tuus in omnibus Robertus heron.

    Dedicatory preface to William Cecil, Lord Burghley (1520-98), in which the author claims to be impoverished, a wanderer, and a man with many enemies.

2. ff. 2r-30r   Argumentum in Dialogum Primum. Argus, erat pastor prudens, doctusque minister,/ Qui Domini verbo pascebat ouillia Christi/ ... Dialogus primus incipit. Dic Epicure mihi cuium pecus, Herculis est ne [?] /Epicurus. Non, pecus est Caci, Cacus mihi tradidit ipse/ ... Argus. I prius ecce sequar, domui huic pax esto perennis/ Omnibus atque salus, intra qui haec culmina degunt./ Finis dialogi primi.

3. ff. 30v-42r   Argumentum in Dialogum secundum. Vt dies aduenit, Epicuro prospera cuncta/ Argus poscendo, Patrem sub nomine Iesu/ ... Dialogus secundus incipit. Coloquitores idem. Argus. Sit dies ista tibi foelix Epicure peropto, /Dante deo, cui laus detur pro nocte quieta/ ... Ergo nunc maneo tecum. Deus cepta peropto/ Perficiat, uobis adiutor propitius sit./ Finis Secundi Dialogi.

4. ff. 43r-49v   Argumentum in Dialogum tertium. Hunc Epicurum Argus, heu quo perduxit amice/ Tandem, diuinis studiis, ut nomina mutet,/ ... Dialogus

tertius incipit. Coloquitores Argus et Theodidactus. Argus. Nunc Theodidacte, hic dies est quia gratus ouilli,/ Vmbrosoque pecus nitidum sub tegmine Fagi/ ... Theodidactus. Sit sic, quaeso Deus pergamus ergo precatum./ Finis.

Paper (watermarks: unidentified pot, much worn), ff. viii (paper) + i (original paper flyleaf) + 49 (original pagination 1-96) + viii (paper), 292 x 194 (251 x 129) mm. Written in ca. 26 long lines or lines of verse; frame-ruled in ink with double upper and outer, and single lower and inner bounding lines; additional ruling in outer margin delineates narrow column for explanatory notes.
Composed of a single gathering of 50 folios (includes original front flyleaf). Written in an elegant italic script.
Binding: s. xix. Red goatskin, gold-tooled, by Birdsall and Son of Northampton, probably in the second half of the century.

Written in England sometime between 1572 when William Cecil, Lord Burghley, was appointed Lord High Treasurer of England (see art. 1) and his death in 1598; perhaps in the hand of the author, Robert Heron. Signature of James Sotheby on f. 1r; bookplate of C. W. H. Sotheby. Sale of Col. H. G. Sotheby (24 July 1924) with note on cover of catalogue: "Many of these books have been in the possession of the family since they were purchased by James Sotheby towards the end of the XVIIth Century." Belonged to Prof. Thomas O. Mabbott (signature with "New York, 1946" on second flyleaf) who presented it to Yale in 1946.

Bibliography: Faye and Bond, p. 30, no. 105.

MS 106
France, s. XV$^{3/4}$
Hours, use of Paris

1. f. 1r-v   Office of the Dead, use of Paris. *Antiphona*. Placebo. *Psalmus*. Dilexi quoniam exaudiet dominus ... Conuertere anima mea in requi// [continues in art. 10]

2. ff. 2r-13v   Full calendar, in French. At the end of each month, a note of how many hours in the day and night, in the form *la nuit a* [Roman numeral] *hore le iour* [Roman numeral]. The calendar corresponds closely to that in Perdrizet.

3. ff. 14r-19r   Sequences of the Gospels. Two rubrics are incorrect: that for Matthew (f. 16v) is incomplete, that for Mark (f. 18r) reads *secundum Matheum*.

4. ff. 19r-22v   Prayer to the Virgin. *Oratio*. Obsecro te ... [masculine forms; Leroquais, LH 2. 346-47].

5. ff. 22v-25r   Prayer to the Virgin. *Oratio ad beatam mariam uirginem*. O intemerata ... [Wilmart 488-90].

6. ff. 25r-80v   Hours of the Virgin, use of Paris. *Incipiunt hore beate marie uirginis*. [f. 25v blank] //mis iubilemus ei. Aue maria. Quoniam deus magnus dominus

et rex magnus ... ut beati iohannis apostoli tui et euuangeliste illuminata doctrinis ad dona perueniat sempiterna. Per.

Due to the presence of Psalms 24, 123, and 124 in both Sext and Vespers, the scribe, although he had just finished copying them for Vespers, thought that he was in Sext and thus "returned" to that point in Sext in his copying; all the material from the antiphon "Post partum" on f. 65r up to the beginning of the psalm "In conuertendo" on f. 72v is a duplication of what had already been done on ff. 57v–65r.

7. ff. 80v–95v   Penitential Psalms and Litany [f. 80v, rubric only:] *Incipiunt septem psalmos.* [f. 81r:] //lectum meum lacrimis meis stratum meum rigabo ... et parcere suscipe deprecacionem nostram ut quos delictorum cathena constringit miseracio tue pietatis// Among the 13 martyrs, Dionysius (8), Eustachius (9); among the 5 confessors, Ivo (5).

8. ff. 96r–98v   Short Hours of the Cross. //laudem tuam. Deus in adiutorium meum intende. Domine ad adiuuandum. Patris sapiencia ueritas diuina ... Sis michi solacium in mortis agone. Amen.

9. ff. 98v–100v   Short Hours of the Holy Spirit [f. 98v, rubric only:] *Sequuntur hore sancti* [rest of rubric effaced; f. 99r:] //deus da nobis illam sancti spiritus graciam quam discipulis tuis ... Dixi ut nos uisites inspiracione. Nos uiuamus iugiter celi regione. Amen.

10. ff. 101r–144v   Office of the Dead, use of Paris [see art. 1 for first folio of text]. //em tuam quia dominus benefecit tibi. Quia eripuit ... ut nostre congregacionis fratres sorores parentes amicos et benefactores no//

11. ff. 145r–149v   Fifteen Joys of the Virgin, in French. //biens qui portastes. ix. mois ihesucrist en uos precieux flans et lalaittastes ... pries pour moy et pour tous pecheurs et pour toutes pecherresses dont il ueult estre// [Leroquais, LH 2. 310–11].

12. ff. 150r–152r   Seven Requests, in French. //Biau sire dieux ie uous requier conseil et aide ... Sire si comme ce fut uoir regardes moy en pitie. Pater noster. [Leroquais, LH 2. 309–10].

13. f. 152r–v   Saincte uraye croix aouree. Qui du corps dieu ... [Sonet 1876].
ff. 153r–154v ruled, but blank

Parchment, ff. i (contemporary parchment, ruled but blank) + 152 + ii (contemporary parchment, ruled but blank), 208 x 154 (113 x 66) mm. Calendar written in 17 long lines, text in 15; single vertical bounding lines, full across; ruled in pale red ink.

I^{12} (+ 1 leaf before f. 1; moved from its place in XIII [8] after f. 100), II^8, III^4, IV^8 (-1), V–X^8, XI^8 (-1), XII^8, XIII^8 (-1, 5, 8), XIV–XVIII^8, XIX^8 (-5), XX^6 (-3). Catchwords in lower margin of last folio of quire, slightly right of center in bâtarde script.

MS 106

Liturgical gothic bookhand in two sizes.

The style of the miniature and borders as well as the format are typical of manuscripts produced in Normandy and the Isle-de-France ca. 1450-75 (cf. Delaissé, Marrow, de Wit, *Waddesdon Manor* MS 10, figs. 10-13, especially for the borders). All of the miniatures, with one exception, have been removed. F. 1r (Office of the Dead), a funeral mass, originally followed f. 100. Stubs and breaks in the text, as well as traces left by miniature frames and borders, indicate other miniatures followed ff. 13 (Sequences), 25 (Hours of the Virgin, Matins), 80 (Penitential Psalms), 98 (Hours of the Holy Spirit), 144 (Fifteen Joys), and 149 (Seven Requests). Another miniature probably preceded f. 96 (Hours of the Cross).

The surviving miniature (of poor quality), 13-line, is set in a narrow gold, black, and white arched frame, with a 3/4 bar border, gold and black, surrounded by gold and blue acanthus leaves, flowers, strawberries and black hair-sprays with gold trilobe leaves, all within red bounding lines. Other borders frequently, but not always, traced (3/4 on folios with 4-line initials, confined elsewhere to outer margin) in same manner, the latter without any bar elements. 4-line initials, blue and gold with white highlights, filled with pink and blue trilobe leaves; 3-, 2-, 1-line initials in gold on blue and red with white highlights (2-line initials occasionally with black hair-sprays and gold trilobe leaves extending into margin). Line fillers: ribbons, in blue, red, and gold, and flowers and geometric shapes in blue, red, and white. Rubrics in orange-tinted red. Calendar has 2-line initials for KL monogram; month, dates and important feasts in gold, other feasts alternately blue and crimson.

Binding: s. xvi. Original sewing on four narrow, double, tawed thongs laced into oak boards and pegged or nailed. Plain, wound endbands on vegetable fiber cores, probably laid in grooves, are covered with secondary colored endbands sewn through the spine covering. The edges are gilt, the spine round. Covered in brown goatskin, blind-tooled with a diamond pattern on the spine, each diamond enclosing two small concentric circles, a floral border on the sides enclosing vertical lines of assorted ornaments. A strap-and-pin fastening, the wood cut out for the strap ends, the pins on the lower board. Joints partially cracked, straps wanting, some worm damage.

Written in Northern France in the third quarter of the fifteenth century as indicated by the format, the style of miniature, and the border decoration. Signature of De Lahave on f. 154v, dated "Le Veme decembre 1589". Signature of Mrs. Fenton inside front cover. Armorial bookplates of Edward Wilfrid Fordham and Marinus Willet Dominick. Presented to Yale in 1940 by the Rev. Howard Chandler Robbins.

Bibliography: Faye and Bond, p. 30, no. 106.

MS 107 France, s. XV²
Hours, use of Rouen

1. ff. 1r–2v   Prayers added by a later hand, some with headings in French or Latin. Ihesus soit en ma teste et mon entendement. Ihesus soit en mes yeux...; Quant tu [1 or 2 words rubbed] deuant le crucifix. Salua nos christe saluator per virtutem sancte crucis...; Oratio ad patrem. Pater de celis deus miserere nobis. Oremus. [D]omine sancte pater omnipotens eterne deus qui coequalem...; Oratio ad filium. Filij Redemptor mundi deus miserere nobis. Oremus. Oratio. Domine ihesu christe fili dei viui qui es verus...; Oratio ad spiritum sanctum. Spiritus sancte deus miserere nobis. Oremus. Oratio. Domine spiritus sancte deus qui coequalis ... [HE 124–25]; Quant on veult receuoir le corps de nostre saluator ihesu crist. [D]omine non sum dignus vt intres sub tectum meum sed tu domine...; Quant on la Receu. Vera perceptio corporis et sanguinis tui deus omnipotens non mihi veniat...; Stabat mater dolorosa ... [RH 19416, followed by versicles and the prayer, Interueniat pro nobis]; [A]ue regina celorum, aue domina angelorum ... [RH 2070]; [S]alue regina misericordie ... [RH 18147]; [I]nuiolata integra et casta ... [RH 9094]; [R]egina celi letare ... [RH 17170].

2. ff. 3r–8v   Calendar, in French, with a feast for every day of the year; lacking February, June, July, August, September, and November. Among the entries, Romanus (23 Oct., in gold).

3. ff. 9r–13r   Sequences from the Gospels, that of John beginning defectively and followed by the prayers, Protector in te sperancium ... [Perdrizet, 25] and Ecclesiam tuam quesumus.... f. 13v ruled, but blank

4. ff. 14r–49r   Hours of the Virgin, use of Rouen; beginning lacking for Matins (after f. 13), for Lauds (after f. 22), for Prime (after f. 33), for Terce (after f. 37), for Sext (after f. 39), for None (after f. 41), for Vespers (after f. 43), and for Compline (after f. 45). //Quoniam deus magnus dominus et rex magnus super omnes deos quoniam non repellet dominus plebem suam....

5. f. 49r–v   Ruling of text space ignored; prayers added by the same scribe as art. 1: [G]loriosa passio domini nostri ihesu christi nos liberet a penis inferni...; [O] bone ihesu christe per tuam misercordiam esto michi ihesus...; O crux aue spes unica...; [D]omine Ihesu christe filii dei redemptor mundi deffende me de manu inimicorum....

6. ff. 50r–61r   Penitential Psalms and Litany. //Turbatus est a furore oculus meus inueteraui.... The beginning of the Litany, including the list of martyrs, is lacking. Among the 12 [remaining?] confessors, Mellonus (4) and Romanus (5); among the 15 virgins, Honorina (9) and Austreberta (10). f. 61v ruled, but blank

7. ff. 62r–63v   Short Hours of the Cross. //giri digneris viuis misericordiam et gratiam deffunctis requiem et veniam ecclesie tue....

MS 107

8. f. 64r-v Short Hours of the Holy Spirit. //tus. Septiformis gracia carisma vocatus *antiphona* Veni sancte spiritus. Omnipotens sempiterne. Deus in adiutorium. Dextre dei tu digitus virtus spiritalis....

9. ff. 65r-85v Office of the Dead, use unidentified; imperfect at beginning and throughout. Responses to the lessons at Matins are 1. Credo quod, 2. Qui lazarum, 3. Domine quando, 4. Domine quando, 5. Ne recorderis, 6. Domine secundum, 7. Peccantem me, 8. Requiem eternam, 9. Libera me. ff. 86r-87v were ruled, f. 86r-v had a text in a later hand as did f. 87r-v; both have been so thoroughly erased that nothing is legible, even under ultraviolet light.

10. ff. 88r-91v Fifteen Joys of the Virgin, in French. //tout le monde vendroit en vous. Douce dame priez lui que il veulle venir ... [Leroquais, LH 2.310-11].

11. ff. 91v-94r Seven Requests, in French [Leroquais, LH 2.309-10].

12. ff. 94r-100v Obsecro te ... [masculine forms; Leroquais, LH 2.346-47] and O intemerata ... [Wilmart 494-95].

13. ff. 101r-103v Ruling of text space ignored; prayers added by the same [?] later hand as arts. 1 and 5: [O] Domine iesu christe adoro te in cruce pendentem ... [Leroquais, LH 2.346]; Domine ihesu christe qui hanc sacratissimam carnem ... [Wilmart 378, n.]; Domine ihesu christe Rogo te amore illius gaudij...; Fremuit spiritu Iesus et turbauit se ipsum et dixit Iudeis vbi posuistis Lazarum ... Oremus. Deus cuius vnigenitis assumpte humanitatis probabile argumentum In Resuscitacione lazari...; Avete omnes anime fideles quarum corpora ... Oremus. [D]omine Iesu christe salus et liberacio ... [Leroquais, LH 2.341]; *Oratio ad beatam mariam.* [A]ve domina sancta maria mater dei regina celi...; *Oratio dicenda ante confessionem.* [O]mnipotens et misericors deus quoniam non mortem sed penitentiam desideras peccatorum...; *De sancta susanna.* Victima tu christi virgo susanna fuisti ... [with versicle and prayer]. f. 104 blank, except for the holes and faint outlines (3) of pilgrim's badges once attached

Parchment, ff. 104 + iii (paper), 188 x 127 (101 x 66) mm. Written in 16 long lines per page, ruled in pale red ink; single vertical bounding lines, full across; prickings visible in outer margins.

I^{14} (-4, 8, 9, 10, 11), II^6, (-1, 6), III^6, IV^8, V^6, VI^8 (-1, 6), VII^8 (-1, 4, 7), VIII^6 (-2), IX^8 (-1), X^6 (-2, 4), XI^6 (-1, 5, 6), XII^8 (-1, 3), XIII^6, XIV^6, XV^4, XVI^6, XVII^6, XVIII^4. Remains of catchwords in pale brown ink in the lower right corner of the last folio, on verso.

Written in liturgical gothic bookhand in two sizes, by a single scribe. Prayers (ff. 1r-2v, 49r-v, 101r-103r) added in an informal bâtarde script, apparently by a single person.

The manuscript originally contained the full complement of miniatures; their removal (following ff. 8, 13, 22, 33, 37, 39, 41, 43, 45, 49, 61, 64, and 87) is indicated by stubs, missing bifolios and breaks in the text. The remaining decoration consists of compartmentalized borders typical of late 15th-century Rouen manuscripts (cf., e.g., Paris, Arsenal 562, G. Ritter and J. Lafond, *Manuscrits à peintures de l'école de Rouen* (Rouen, 1913) pls. 66, 67; and Waddesdon Manor MS 14, Delaissé, Marrow, and de Wit, *Waddesdon Manor*, figs. 8-10, 13). One full border (f. 3r) in red bounding lines with pink and blue acanthus leaves on a gold ground, alternating with flowers and strawberries on parchment ground, filled in with black and gold dots; three borders (ff. 4r, 6r, 7r) in outer margin only. 3/4 band borders (with 5- and 4- line initials); single bands in outer margin (with 2-line initials); additional small bands occur when 2-line initial is on a recto. Borders are traced whenever they occur on recto and verso of same leaf; all with blue and gold acanthus leaves, flowers on parchment ground, filler as for full border. Many pages have no border. Initials, 5-, 4-, 2-, and 1-line, gold, on blue and red grounds with white highlights; 4-line initials, blue on a gold ground, filled with red and blue trilobe leaves in lattices; the 2-line initials occasionally with a narrow border in inner margin with flowers, black hair-spray, and gold dots (red bounding lines). Ribbon and quatrelobe line-fillers in gold, blue, and red, highlighted in white. Rubrics in orange-tinted red. Calendar has months, dates, and important feasts in gold; other feasts alternately in blue and red. Most spaces for initials within the added prayers have not been filled.

Binding: s. xvii. Dark red goatskin, gold-tooled, with a smooth spine.

Written in Northern France, probably in Rouen, in the second half of the 15th century; early provenance unknown. Belonged to Sir Charles Frederick, Surveyor General of Ordnance (bookplate designed by W. H. Toms, 1752). Presented to Yale in 1939 by Jonathan Godfrey.

Bibliography: Faye and Bond, p. 30, no. 107.

L. Nemoy, "A Fifteenth-Century *Beatae Virginis Mariae Horae*," *Gazette* 15 (1940) pp. 20-21.

MS 108 France, s. XVI^{in}
Hours, use of Rome Pl. 13

1. ff. 1r-6v   Calendar, in French. Entries include Hilary (13 Jan., in red), Martialis (30 June, in red), Cybard (1 July, in red), Fiacre (30 Aug.), Caprasius (20 Oct.), Anianus (17 Nov.).

2. ff. 7r-14v   Sequences of the Gospels (John 1. 1-14; Matthew 2. 1-12; Mark 16. 14-20; the Passion according to John 18. 1-42; Luke 1. 26-38).

3. ff. 15r-42v   Hours of the Virgin, use of Rome; Short Hours of the Cross and of the Holy Spirit worked in.

4. ff. 42v-50v   Penitential Psalms and Litany. The angels are Michael, Gabriel, Raphael, and Raguel; among the 11 martyrs, Hippolytus et socii; among the 26 confessors, Hilary (14), Medard (22), Eligius (24), and Ludovicus (25); among the 15 virgins, Geneviève.

MS 108

5. ff. 50v-63r Office of the Dead, use of Rome.
6. ff. 63v-64v Prayers to the Virgin, in French, in a later hand. Glorieuse vierge marie mere de Iesucrist le vray dieu tout puissant ... [Leroquais, LH 2.340. In short lines at lower right of f. 64r:] Oraison a la glorieuse vierge marie pour dire tous les jours [text begins:] Glorieuse vierge marie/ A toy me rens et si te prie ... [Sonet 675].

Parchment, ff. ii (paper) + 64 + ii (paper), 143 x 87 (105 x 59) mm. Calendar written in 33 long lines per page, text in 32; single vertical and horizontal bounding lines, full across; ruled in pale brown ink.

Bound too tightly for accurate collation.

Two hands can be distinguished: ff. 1r-6v and 15r-63r are written in a small, even bâtarde; ff. 7r-14v in a rounded gothic script showing some bâtarde characteristics. Folios 7-14 may have been added later (see *Exhibition Catalogue*, p. 264, no. 80); this hypothesis is supported by the difference in the style and color of the miniatures and their placement on the page. Prayers added on ff. 63v-64v in bâtarde, early 16th century.

Sixteen *camaieu-gris* miniatures by three artists, in tondo format, with gold frames inscribed in white capitals. The format, style, and technique recall both the work of Jean Bourdichon of Tours and contemporary Limoges enamels; in neither case has a workshop affiliation been established (see *Exhibition Catalogue*, pp. 263-65). The miniatures are as follow: f. 7r (John) Vision of St. John; f. 8r (Matthew) Adoration of the Magi; f. 9r (Mark) Ascension; f. 10r (Passion) Betrayal of Christ; f. 15r (Matins) The Annunciation; f. 19v (Lauds) The Visitation; f. 24v (Hours of the Cross) Crucifixion; f. 25v (Hours of the Holy Spirit) Pentecost; f. 26v (Prime) Nativity; f. 29r (Terce) Annunciation to the Shepherds; f. 31v (Sext) Adoration of the Magi; f. 33v (None) Presentation in the temple; f. 36r (Vespers) Flight into Egypt; f. 40r (Compline) Coronation of the Virgin; f. 43r (Penitential Psalms) King David; f. 51v (Office of the Dead) The Three Living and the Three Dead. The miniatures on ff. 15v and 19v are by the leading artist; the remainder are by a competent assistant (with the exception of ff. 7v, 8r, 9r, and 10r, which are of inferior quality; see comments under script). 4-, 3-, 2-, and 1-line initials, grey with gold highlights, on a black ground, some with leaves and dots in gold. On ff. 7r-14v the letters are composed of leaf forms. Ribbon line-fillers, geometric and leaf forms, gold, grey, and white on black. Rubrics in pale red. Calendar has KL monogram as 2-line initials, month and dates in red; feasts in blue, major feasts in red.

The black ink of the initials has run on many pages, and has sometimes adhered to the opposite pages.

Binding: s. xviii-xix. Brown goatskin gold-tooled, silver fastenings. On the spine, flowers and the words "Heur en Latin. MSS. S. Velin en Min."

Written probably in Southwestern France (perhaps Limoges?) as is suggested by the calendar and style of decoration, at the beginning of the 16th century. Bookplates of W. H. H. Newman, Buffalo, New York (inside front and back covers; oval tag on spine, no. Z). Purchased from Martin Hago in 1940.

Bibliography: Faye and Bond, p. 30, no. 109.
    Exhibition Catalogue, pp. 263-65, no. 80.
    Yale Library Associates, Reports for 1940-41 (New Haven, 1941) p. 21.
    Gray is the Color: An Exhibition of Grisaille Painting XIIIth-XXth Centuries. Institute for the Arts (Rice University, Houston, Texas, 1973) Item 4, pp. 30-31 (with illus. of ff. 26v and 40r).

MS 109   Flanders [?], s. XV^2
Hours, use of Sarum [?]

This manuscript has nearly the same contents as Beinecke MS 310 and London, Dulwich College MS 25 (Ker, MMBL, v. 1, pp. 46-48).

1. f. ii recto-verso   Catalogue of contents, in Latin, in a later cursive hand.

2. ff. 1r-26v   Hours of the Virgin, probably use of Sarum, but now lacking the beginning of Matins, all of Terce, and the end of Sext through to the Nunc dimittis of Compline. After Lauds, suffrages to the Holy Spirit, the Trinity, Michael, John the Baptist, Andrew, Lawrence, Stephen, Thomas of Canterbury, Nicolas, Mary Magdalen, Catharine, Margaret, All Saints and for peace; Short Hours of the Cross worked in; Compline followed by the Salve Regina with its set of 7 versicles, Virgo mater ecclesie ... and its prayer, Omnipotens sempiterne deus qui gloriose uirginis et matris marie ... [HE 62-63]; [G]aude uirgo mater christi ... *Oremus*. [D]eus qui beatam uirginem mariam in conspectu [sic] et partu ... [HE 63-64]; [G]aude flore uirginali ... [HE 64-65] *Oremus*. [O] clementissime domine ihesu christe pro tua infinita pietatis misericordia.... Leaves at the end of Lauds (f. 16v), Prime (f. 20v) and the Office itself (f. 27r-v) ruled, but blank

3. ff. 28r-34r   Has videas laudes qui sacra uirgine gaudes ... Salve uirgo uirginum ... [a farcing of the Salve Regina, attributed to Bonaventure, *Opera*, 1668 ed., 6. 466-67] and its prayer, Deus qui de beate marie uirginis utero.... f. 34v ruled, but blank

4. ff. 35r-37r   O intemerata ... [masculine forms; Wilmart 488-90]. f. 37v ruled, but blank

5. ff. 38r-41v   Obsecro te ... [masculine forms; Leroquais, LH 2.346-47].

6. ff. 41v-56v   Various prayers. *Quicumque hec septem gaudia* [heading gives 100 days of indulgence from Pope Clement] ... Uirgo templum trinitatis ... [RH 21899]; *Oratio a nostra domina oratio* [sic]. Te precor sanctissima maria mater dei pietate plenissima ... [masculine forms]; *Ad ymaginem christi crucifixi bona*

oratio. Omnibus consideratis ... [verse prayer in 10 parts referring to the wounds of Christ, with the 9th to the Virgin and the 10th to John the Evangelist, attributed to Jean de Limoges; see Wilmart 527 and 584] with its prayer, Omnipotens sempiterne deus qui unigenitum filium tuum....

7. ff. 57r–71r Penitential Psalms and Litany. Among the 12 martyrs, Thomas (9); among the 14 confessors, Bavo (3), Gildard (8), Medard (9), Hubert (11), Ghislain (12); among the 17 virgins, Geneviève (13), Zuwarda (16), and Afra (17).

8. ff. 71v–91r Office of the Dead, use unidentified; the responses at Matins are: 1. Credo quod, 2. Qui lazarum, 3. Domine quando, 4. Heu michi, 5. Ne recorderis, 6. Ne tradas, 7. Peccantem me, 8. Domine secundum, 9. Libera me domine de morte. f. 91v ruled, but blank

9. ff. 92r–102v Commendationes animarum with Ps. 118 only, and the prayer, Misericordiam tuam domine sancte pater...; f. 102 misbound and should follow f. 97.

10. ff. 103r–114v Psalmi de passione, all in full, with Ps. 23 not copied and with the order of Pss. 25 and 26 reversed.

11. ff. 115r–130r Psalterium sancti ieronimi, preceded by the prayer, Suscipere dignare domine deus omnipotens ... [HE 116-22]. f. 130v ruled, but blank

Parchment, ff. iv (paper) + 130 + iii (paper), 111 x 77 (62 x 37) mm., trimmed. Written in 19 long lines, ruled in pale red ink; single bounding lines full across except on ff. 23-27, where the upper horizontal lines are double and the lower single or double; some prickings visible in outer margins.

Bound too tightly for accurate collation.

Written in two sizes of liturgical gothic by two scribes. Scribe 1: ff. 1r–22v and 28r–130r; Scribe 2: ff. 22v–26v. Many later marginal notes throughout, including titles at the top of each page.

One very crude full-page miniature on f. 71v (Office of the Dead): mourners at a bier. Set in a narrow arched frame of gold edged in black, in a border of pink, blue, and green acanthus leaves (concentrated at corners), flowers in same colors, infilled with black ink hair-spray with gold dots; the whole rather carelessly done. 6- and 5-line initials (ff. 57r and 72r): blue with white highlights, on gold ground, infilled with blue, green, and pink trilobe leaves, with segmented bar border (strapwork corners) in blue, white, pink, black, and gold; full border as for miniature. Other illuminated initials (5- to 2-line, as above) with segmented bar borders without strapwork, and full borders as for full-page miniature. 5-line initials (ff. 35r and 38r) gold, on pink and blue ground with white highlights; in inner margin, a simple bar border sprouting black hair-spray with gold leaves at top and bottom. 2-line initials: gold on pink and blue grounds with white highlights. 1-line initials within text sometimes marked with a red stroke. Line fillers: occasionally a red cable after a rubric or, in the litany, oblique red and blue strokes with dots attached (perhaps added later, as colors do not match those of 1-line initials). Rubrics in orange-tinted red.

Mold at bottom of ff. 122-130; text not damaged.

Binding: s. xix. Brown calf, blind- and gold-tooled.

Written in Flanders [?] in the second half of the 15th century, probably for the English market (cf. Ker, MMBL, v. 1, p. 46); early provenance unknown. On f. 27r, "William Harriman his booke." On f. 27v signatures of John Browne and Robert Browen [?]; on f. 11r: "Robert Laing, is my nam and with my pen." Inscription (s. xix?) of J. Kendall (inside cover and on f. 1r). From the Russell G. Pruden collection; donated by Mr. and Mrs. E. A. Prentis in 1949.

Bibliography: Faye and Bond, p. 30, no. 109.

MS 110
Flanders, ca. 1480
Hours, use of Rome (partly in Flemish)

1. ff. 1r-12v   Calendar in Flemish; among the entries, Aldegundis (30 Jan.), Gertrude (17 March), Medard (8 June), Basil (14 June, in red), 10,000 Martyrs (22 June), Amalberga (10 July), Wilgefortis (19 July), Audomar (9 Sept.), Lambert (17 Sept.), Bavo (1 Oct., in red), Gereon (10 Oct.), Hubert (3 Nov.), Lebwin (12 Nov.), Maclovius (15 Nov.).

2. ff. 13r-16r   Short Hours of the Cross. f. 16v ruled, but blank

3. f. 17r blank; ff. 17v-26v   Short Hours of the Virgin, immediately followed by the Seven Joys of the Virgin [HE 64-66] and the prayer, Dulcissime domine ihesu christe qui beatissimam dei genitricem uirginem mariam ... [Leroquais, LH 1. 282]. f. 27r blank

4. ff. 27v-105v   Hours of the Virgin, use of Rome, with psalms designated for the days of the week at Matins; the Advent Office begins at f. 92r. Center bifolium missing in quire 9, with loss of the end of Prime.

5. f. 106r blank; ff. 106v-131r   Penitential Psalms and Litany. Among the 18 martyrs, Nicasius (14); among the 20 confessors, Basilius (12), Amandus (9), Vedast (10), Donatianus (11); among the 20 virgins, Gertrude (11), Aldegundis (12), Petronilla (17). f. 131v blank

6. ff. 132r-176v   Office of the Dead, use of Rome.

7. ff. 177r-178r   Gospel of John 1. 1-14. f. 178v ruled, but blank

8. ff. 179r-185v   *Salutatio ad uirginem*. Obsecro te ... [masculine forms; Leroquais, LH 2.346-47]; *Salutatio ad uirginem*. O intemerata ... [Wilmart 488-90].

9. ff. 186r-207v   Various prayers. *Eene minlic ende zeere deuot ghebet vander maghet marie die min heere sinte bernaert macte.* O domina glorie regina leticie. O fons

MS 110

pietatis...; (f. 187r) *Snuchtes alstu up staes zo teekent hu met den teeke des heilichs crucen.* Gratias tibi ago omnipotens pater qui me in hac nocte custodire dignatus es...; (f. 187r) *Oremus.* Domine sancte pater omnipotens eterne deus qui nos ad principium ... [Leroquais LH 1.100, 183]; (f. 187v) Salua me domine rex eterne glorie...; (f. 188r) Benedicat me deus pater...; (f. 188r) Oremus. *Oratio.* Actiones nostras quesumus domine aspirando preueni ... [Sinclair, p. 407]; (f. 188v) *Dit zijn de viii versen van sinte bernaert. Psalmus.* Illumina domine oculos meos ... [RH 27912]; (f. 189v) *Oremus. Oratio.* Omnipotens sempiterne deus qui ezechie ... [Leroquais, LH 1.32]; (f. 190r) *Vanden heilighen gheest.* Ueni creator spiritus mentes ... [RH 21204]; (f. 191r) *Oremus. Oratio.* Deus qui corda fidelium sancti spiritus illustratione docuisti ... [Lyell Cat., p. 65, art. 9]; (f. 191v) *Desen bedinghe salmen lesen naer sanctus ter eeren vander heiligher triniteit.* Auxiliatrix esto michi sancta trinitas gloriosa ... [Leroquais LH 1.111, 119]; (f. 192v) *Salutacie toot den heilighen sacramente seer deuot.* Aue salus mundi uerbum patris hostia sacra ... [RH 35720]; (f. 193r) *Eene deuot salutatie tot den helighen bloet.* Aue sanguis qui fluxisti de preclara carne christi...; (f. 193v) *De sacramento.* Anima christi sanctifica me. copus [sic] christi salua me ... [RH 1090]; (f. 194r) *Vanden heleghe sacrament.* In presentia ueri corporis et sanguinis tui preciosissimi ... [Leroquais, LH 1.329]; (f. 195r) *Tot den helich sacrament.* Aue principium nostre creationis. Aue precium nostre redemptionis ... [Wilmart pp. 23, 366, 377 n.]; (f. 196r) Oremus. *Oratio* ... Deus qui nobis sub sacramento mirabili passionis ... [Sinclair, p. 255]; (f. 196v) *Dit siin de bedinghe van der passie ons heere ihesu christi.* Mundi creator et redemptor ihesu christe qui ad passionem iturus...; (f. 197v) Deprecor te pijssime domine ihesu christe propter illam...; (198v) Domine ihesu christe per amaritudinem mortis tue...; (f. 199r) Benignissime domine ihesu christe respice super me...; (f. 199v) *Vanden .vij. Woorden die ons heere sprac an t'cruce.* Domine ihesu christe qui septem uerba ... [Prayer of the Venerable Bede; Leroquais, LH 2.342]; (f. 202r) *Dese naer uolghende bedinghen mactet mijn heere sinte gregoris doe ons heere ihesus christus* ... [rubric gives 20 thousand years and 23 days of indulgence by Gregory, confirmed by Pope Calixtus III] Domine ihesu christe adoro te in cruce pendentem ... [Seven Prayers of St. Gregory; Leroquais, LH 2.346]; (f. 203r) *Dese bedinghe maectet mijn heere sinte bernaert ter eeren vander soete namen van ihesus.* O bone ihesu. O dulcissime ihesu. O pijssime ihesu ... [Leroquais, LH 2.345]; (f. 205v) Oremus. *Oratio.* Deus qui manus tuas et pedes tuos et totum corpus tuum ... [Leroquais, LH 1.34]; (f. 206v) *Van sinte baerbele. Antiphona.* Aue martir gloriosa barbaraque generosa ... [RH 1915].

10. ff. 208r–215r   Devotions on the Passion of Christ, in Latin, with rubrics in Flemish. *So wie beghert dat sine bede ghehort oort van gode* ... Adoramus te christe et benedicimus tibi ... [followed by a psalm and an antiphon; this pattern is repeated 4 more times]. f. 215v ruled, but blank

11. ff. 216r–220v   Prayers in Flemish. *Aue maria gratia plena dominus tecum benedic-*

ta tu. O vlietende borne in der eewicheit ... [Meertens 6.293]; (f. 217r) *Dit es een deuote bedinghe van onse lieue vrauwe*. O vrauwe maria moeder gods uwe helighe gratie...; (f. 219v) *Noch een ander van maria*. O maria ghegroet si di in der helegher drie voudicheit...; (f. 220r) *Men vint bescreuen dat onse lieue vrauwe drie weruen reip doe ons lief heere sine cruce drouc* ... Ten eersten male riepsi. O Wee een gheboren sone troost dijn eneghe moeder....

12. f. 221r-v   Apostles' Creed and the Confiteor; the latter incomplete, ending with "consensu tactu uisu". The phrase "ego infelix peccatrix" in the Confiteor indicates that the book was written for use by a woman.

Parchment, ff. i (paper) + 221 + i (paper), 130 x 94 (85 x 56) mm., trimmed. Written in 17 long lines in the calendar, 16 in the text, ruled in pale red ink; single vertical and horizontal bounding lines, full across.

I-II^6, III^8 (+ 1 leaf for miniature after f. 16), IV^6 (-1), V^8 (+ 1 leaf for miniature before f. 28), VI-VIII^8, IX^8 (-4, 5), X-XIV^8, XV^8 (+ 1 leaf for miniature before f. 107), XVI^8, XVII^8 (+ 1 leaf after f. 130), XVIII^8 (3, 4, 5, 6 single leaves), XIX-XXII^8, XXIII^8 (-8), XXIV^8, XXV^6, XXVI-XXVIII^8, XXIX^6.

Written in liturgical gothic bookhand by one scribe.

Three full-page miniatures of mediocre quality: f. 17v (Short Hours of the Virgin) Annunciation; f. 27v (Hours of the Virgin, Matins) Agony in the Garden; f. 106v (Penitential Psalms) Last Judgment. Each miniature set in a narrow frame of gold, black, pink, and white; full border of blue and gold acanthus leaves, red, pink, and blue flowers and strawberries, and black pen flecks. One 7-line historiated initial on f. 216r (Flemish Prayers): Pietà, pink with white highlights on gold; full border as above; text separated from border by a narrow band attached to initial of gold and pink, edged in black. Illuminated 5-line initials with full borders (e. g., ff. 13r, 18r, 28r), pink or blue with white highlights on gold, filled with blue or pink trilobe leaves. 2-line initials, gold on pink and blue with white highlights, one on f. 92r (Advent Office) with a band attached, as above, and small sections of border, as above; one 3-line initial on f. 179r (Obsecro te) in similar manner. 1-line initials, blue with red penwork and gold with black penwork; initials within text washed in yellow. KL monograms as 2-line initials; Latin names of months and important feasts in red. Line fillers: oblique lines with dots attached, stylized plant motifs, dots, etc., in blue or gold. Rubrics in faded red.

Binding: s. xix. Brown, originally black, sheepskin; stamped in gold on the spine: "Psaterium." Red edges.

Written in or near Bruges ca. 1480, according to J. Marrow; early provenance unknown. Signature on f. 1r: "Hanelle" (s. xviii). Belonged to Russell G. Pruden. Gift of Mr. and Mrs. E. A. Prentis in 1949.

Bibliography: Faye and Bond, p. 31, no. 110.

MS 111

MS 111 Italy, s. XIV/XV, XV
Jacobus de Voragine, Legenda aurea, etc. Pl. 22

I. 1. ff. 1r–2v [Prologue, followed by table of contents:] Uniuersum tempus presentis inde in quatuor distinguitur ... usque ad aduentum. *De tempore renouationis.* De aduentu. *.i.* De sancto andrea. *.ij.* ... De inuetione [*sic*] corporis sancte iustine. *.C. lxxiiij.*

2. ff. 2v–289v *De aduentu domini.* Aduentus domini per quatuor septimanas agitur ad significandum ... [ends with De dedicatione ecclesiae:] templum ad honorem dei dedicatum erit ... et regnat deus per omnia secula seculorum. Amen. Expliciunt legende sanctorum.

T. Graesse, ed., *Jacobi a Voragine Legenda aurea* (Leipzig, 1846). The legends in this manuscript occur in the following order (with numbers corresponding to chapters in Graesse): 1–42, Faustinus and Jovita (of Brescia), 43–47 (missing Sophia), Longinus (of Mantua), 49–51 (missing Timothy), 53–63 (missing Fabianus), 65 (missing Apollonia), 67–70 (missing Boniface), 72–126, 130, 127–29, 131, 134–38, 132, 139, 133, 140–82.

3. ff. 290r–291r Three sections on St. Justina of Padua: *De nomine* [Graesse, *op. cit.*, beginning of 142]; *De sancta iustina virgine et martyre.* Beata iustina filia regis uitaliani et regine...; *De inuentione corporis sancte iustine.* Cum paduanorum nobilissima ciuitas.... f. 291v blank except for a few notes

II. 4. ff. 292r–295r *De sancta clara.* Uenerabilis christi sponse deoque dicate uirginis clare natalicium diem fratres ... oramus ad Christum paupercularum pia mater ... est omnis honor et gloria per infinita secula seculorum. Amen.

BHL 1817.

5. ff. 295r–297r *De sancta barbara.* Temporibus maximiani erat uir quidam nomine dyoscorus diues ualde ... Valentinus uero quidam uir uenerabilis ... saluatoreque nostro ihesu christo cui honor est et gloria ... Amen.

BHL 917.

6. f. 297r *De sancto pantaleone.* Pantaleon filius senatoris pagani matris christiane ... arbor que illa repleta est fructu.

Cf. BHL 6442a.

7. ff. 297r–299v *Epistola beati anselmi episcopi de festo conceptionis beate marie uirginis.* Ansellmus cantuariensis archiepiscopus et pastor angulorum [*sic*] ... et matre sua gloriosa uirgine maria uiuet et regnat ... Amen.

Pseudo-Anselm; PL 159.319–24.

8. ff. 299v–300v *De sancto thoma apostolo.* Temporibus calixti pape secun-

di patriarcha yndorum Romam deueniens ... cum clero et populo suo gratias reddidit deo cui est honor ... Amen.

Cf. BHL 8145.

9. ff. 300v-306v *Legenda sancti Willelmi confessoris*. Scripturus uitam serui tui prout tu dederis et inspiraueris ... que oculis nostris conspeximus Vel in nobis ipsis comperimus.

BHL 8923; the life of William, hermit, priest, and founder of the Benedictine convent of Olive-sur-l'Ermitage, Hainaut.

Composed of two manuscripts with different formats:

I. Parchment, ff. 292 (foliated 1-11, 11*, 12-291), 330 x 220 (225 x 145) mm. Written in 2 columns of 40 lines; single vertical bounding lines. Ruled lightly in ink or lead; remains of prickings in upper margins. Round gothic bookhand by a single scribe who made neat corrections, often on lines ruled in the margins. Border decorations (ff. 1r Preface, 2v Beginning of Text, 13v De natiuitate domini, 48v Pars secunda, 76v De resurrectione domini, and 108r De tempore peregrinationis): long stems, inner and top margins or between text columns, in blue, pink, and grey segments divided by small balls, sprouting curling foliage (blue, light blue, and orange), concentrated at corners, with large spiky leaves at terminals and large spiral angular returns filled with mauve or gold in the lower margins; large gold dots tucked under leaves and trailing from the tips of leaves on thin brown pen lines. Initials, 4- to 3-line, attached to stems, pink and grey with white highlights; foliage serifs, as above; letters filled with blue and gold, with some vine work (green and grey), against gold grounds with thick black edging. 2-line initials, set into text columns, blue or red, with very elaborate, minute penwork, blue, red, and occasionally green, built up of small spirals, roundels, and long "caterpillar"-like segments, often extending the full length of text columns; with curling flourishes in margin. 1-line initials in Table of Contents red or blue, with thin vertical strokes in the opposite color; chapter numbers in red. Headings and paragraph marks in blue or red; rubrics throughout.

II. Parchment, ff. 15 (foliated 292-306), 326 x 220 (225 x 148) mm. Written in 2 columns of 41 lines; single vertical and double horizontal bounding lines, full across. Ruled in ink; prickings (oblique slashes) in all margins except inner. Well formed gothic textura. Plain initials, 5- to 3-line, alternating red and blue, with large serifs; one on f. 300v in red and blue. Headings and initial strokes in red.

I-IX^{12}, X^{12} (+ 1 leaf after 10, f. 118), XI-XXIV^{12} (half-leaf inserted after 6 of quire XX, f. 235), XXV^2 (ff. 291-92), XXVI^8, XXVII^8 (-8). I: catchwords, with flourishes, under inner column; II: catchwords along lower edge, under inner column.

Binding: s. xix. Pinkish brown calf case.

Part I was written in Italy at the end of the 14th or beginning of the 15th century; the inclusion of Sts. Faustina and Jovita, Longinus, and Justina (arts. 2, 3), as well as the style of decoration, suggest Northern Italy. Part II may have been written in Hainaut (see art. 9) and added during the 15th century. Acquired by Sir Thomas Phillipps (no. 345; inscription on f. 1r; stamp on f. 3r; label on spine) from the Cistercian abbey of Cambron in Hainaut. Purchased from C. A. Stonehill in 1941 for the Albert H. Childs Memorial Collection.

secundo folio: De sancto paulo

Bibliography: Faye and Bond, p. 31, no. 111.

MS 112   Italy, s. XV^2
Juvenal; Persius

1. ff. 1r–74v   Semper ego auditor tantum numquam ne reponam/ Vexatus totiens rauci teseide codri/ ... Pytagoras cunctis animalibus abstinuit qui/ Tanquam homine et uentri indulsit non esse legumen. *Telos Deo Gratias.*

    Juvenal, *Satirae I–XVI* (with XVI preceding XV); W. V. Clausen, ed., OCT (1959) pp. 37–175. For the *argumenta* of Guarino of Verona see S. Endlicher, *Catalogus codicum philologicorum latinorum Bibliothecae Palatinae Vindobonensis* (Vienna, 1836) p. 116 and Walther, *Initia* 10770.

2. The satires are followed (on f. 74v) by eight lines of unidentified text in alternating lines of red and black: Voma superstitio egipti seruasque nefanda ... Tempora reprehendens iniqua ducesque.

3. ff. 75r–87v   *Flacci Persii uolterrani satirarum prima foeliciter incipit.* Nec fonte labra prolui caballino/ Nec in bicipiti somniasse parnaso/ ... Iam decies redit in rugam depinge ubi sistam/ Inuentus crisippe tui finitor acerui. Amen. *Telos. Flacci Persii satirarum ultima foeliciter explicit.*

    Persius, Prologue followed by *Satirae I–VI*; W. V. Clausen, *op. cit.*, pp. 3–28.

4. ff. 88r–89v   Miscellaneous notes in various hands, including selections from Horace, an epitaph for Persius, and identifications of mythological characters (e.g., Prometheus et Epimetheus fratres fuerunt).

Paper (watermarks: similar to Briquet Enclume 5961 and unidentified horn) and parchment (ff. 1, 10), ff. ii (paper) + 89 + ii (paper), 215 x 145 (151 x 70) mm. Written in 26 lines of verse; double vertical bounding lines, full across; ruled in hard point.

I^{10}, II–VII^{12}, VIII^8 (-8). Catchwords are located in lower margin; some are enclosed in a rectangle or surrounded by flourishes.

Written in poorly formed italic by a single scribe. Marginal and interlinear glosses in several contemporary hands.

Argumenta of Guarino of Verona in red and simple initials in red or black at beginning of most satires. First letter of each line stroked with red.

Many waterstains that sometimes affect the text.
Binding: s. xix. Vellum stays. Half vellum case with blue paper sides.

Written in Italy in the second half of the 15th century; early provenance unknown. Belonged to Henry Allen (acquired ca. 1800; bookplate); Samuel Allen sale (London, 30 January 1920, no. 71). Bought from C. A. Stonehill by Thomas E. Marston, who presented it to Yale in 1946.

secundo folio: Aut diomedeas

Bibliography: Faye and Bond, p. 31, no. 112.

MS 113
Juvenal

Italy, s. XV$^{3/4}$

ff. 1r–81v *Iunii Iuuenalis aquinatis satyrarum liber primus*. Prima refert causas Satyrarum, etc. Semper ego auditor tantum. nunquamne reponam/ Vexatus toties [*sic*] rauci Theseide Codri/ ... Vt qui fortis erit, sit felicissimus idem,/ Vt laeti phaleris omnes, et torquibus omnes. f. 82r-v ruled, but blank

Juvenal, *Satirae I-XVI*; W. V. Clausen, ed., OCT (1959) pp. 37–175.

Parchment (ff. 1 and 40 added in the 17th century to replace lost or mutilated text), ff. i (paper) + i (parchment, s. xvii) + 82 (pagination from 1–162) + i (paper), 194 x 118 (122 x 75) mm. Written in 24 lines of verse; double inner and single outer vertical bounding lines, full across. Ruled in brown ink; some prickings visible at bottom of folio.

I–X^8, XI^2. Quires signed in Roman numerals along lower edge of last folio, verso; catchwords perpendicular to text on inner bounding lines.

Written in a careful round humanistic script by a single scribe.

Fourteen white-vine initials, 6- to 4-line, gold, partially edged in black, against blue, green and pink grounds with white dots; hair-spray and gold dots project into margin from corners and midpoint.

Binding: s. xvii. Brown leather, flesh side out, with the arms of William Laud, Archbishop of Canterbury, gold-stamped on each side. Rebacked.

Written in Rome ca. 1460–1470 by a scribe who frequently worked for Cardinal Bessarion. Among manuscripts attributable to this scribe is Venice, Marc. Lat. XIV. 14 (4235), the Act of Donation of 1468 by which Bessarion gave his library to San Marco, Venice (we thank A. C. de la Mare for this information). Belonged to William Laud, Archbishop of Canterbury (1573–1645), for whom it was bound; given by him to his secretary, William Dell (inscription on f. ii recto: "Will: Dell. 1637. Donum Domini mei honoratissimi Archiepiscopi Cantabrigiensis"). Collection of Charles Kingsley (1819–75; bookplate); his sale (New York, 13 June 1911, no. 64). Presented to Yale in 1948 by Thomas E. Marston (bookplate).

MS 114

secundo folio: Quid referam

Bibliography: Faye and Bond, p. 31, no. 113.

MS 114 Italy, s. XV$^{2/4}$
Lactantius, Opera Pl. 24

1. f. 1r Copy of passage omitted from *Institutiones* VII. 9 and supplied in a later hand, with note "hec praecedencia debebant posita esse libro septimo et capitulo ix...." f. 1v blank

2. ff. 2r-8v [Prefatory material:] De his libris dici potest aliquid habere eos ut consonum qui non precipiendi auctoritate sed proficiendi exercitatione scribuntur a nobis ... [followed by a table of contents:] Quanti sit et fuerit semper cognitio ueritatis et quod nec sine religione sapientia nec sine sapientia sit perturbanda religio. C. j.... Exortatio ut omnes properent ad suscipiendam cum religione sapientiam per quam peruenitur ad beatissimam eterne uite hereditatem C. xxi.

3. ff. 9r-162v [Heading, in a later hand:] Liber Coelij Lactancij et firmiani diuinarum institucionum aduersus gentes primus de falsa religione ad Constantinum Imperatorem feliciter incipit. [text:] Magno et excellenti ingenio uiri cum se doctrine penitus dedissent quicquid laboris poterat impendi ... ac deuicto aduersario triumphantes premium uirtutis quod ipse promisit a domino consequamur. Deo gratias. Firmiani lactantij aduersus gentiles liber septimus et ultimus explicit.

   S. Brandt and G. Laubmann, eds., CSEL v. 19 (1890).

4. ff. 163r-177v [Heading, in a later hand:] Liber Coelij Lactancij firmiani de Opificio dei seu hominis formacione Incipit ad demetrianum. [text:] Quam minime sim quietus etiam [later addition: in] summis necessitatibus extimare [*sic*] ... si labor meus aliquos homines ab erroribus liberatos ad iter celeste deuexerit. Finis Lactantij Firmiani de opificio hominis.

   S. Brandt, ed., CSEL v. 27 (1893) pp. 3-64.

5. ff. 177v-193v [Heading, in a later hand:] Liber Coelij Lactancij de Ira dei ad donatum Incipit. [text:] Animaduerti sepe donate plurimos id existimare quod etiam nonnulli philosophorum putauerunt ... ut et propitium semper habeamus et numquam uereamur iratum. Firmiani Lactantij de ira liber explicit. [later addition:] Laus deo.

   S. Brandt, ed., CSEL v. 27 (1893) pp. 67-132.

Parchment, ff. i (paper) + 193 + ii (paper), 280 x 192 (178 x 116) mm. Written in 39 long lines; single vertical bounding lines. Ruled in hard point or lead; remains of prickings in all margins, except inner.

I⁸, II–XII¹⁰, XIII⁸, XIV–XVII¹⁰, XVIII⁶, XIX–XX⁸, XXI⁶ (-6). Catchwords along lower edge.

Written by a single scribe in a "fractured" gothic script (see below). Marginal notations by several later writers, one of whom made extensive corrections to the text and added Latin translations for the Greek passages.

Ten neat gold initials, 9- to 8-line, infilled and surrounded by white vinework on blue, pale green, and pale red grounds, with white dots and pale yellow highlights (ff. 9r, 33v, 53v, 77r, 100r, 119v, 144r, 163r, 163v, 177v). Greek quotations in red (only for ff. 1r–88r). Capitals and paragraph marks, alternating red and blue for ff. 2r–8v.

Binding: s. xviii. Brown calf case, gold- and blind-tooled with interesting pictorial tools.

Written in Florence ca. 1425–35, according to A. C. de la Mare; arms of unidentified owner effaced (f. 2r). The same scribe copied a whole group of texts in a distinctive fractured gothic hand which has occasionally been thought to be of the 14th century or even earlier (A. C. de la Mare, "Humanistic Script, the First Ten Years," in *Das Verhältnis der Humanisten zum Buch*, ed. F. Kraft, D. Wuttke [Boppard, 1977] n. 35); the texts he copied included Asconius Pedianus, rediscovered by Poggio and friends at St. Gall in 1416 (Florence, Bibl. Laurenziana 50, 4: 2nd part) and speeches of Cicero rediscovered by Poggio in 1417 (Florence, Bibl. Laurenziana 48, 25). He also copied Quintilian (Vatican, Pal. lat. 1557), and the Letters of Pliny (using Coluccio Salutati's manuscript, Florence, Bibl. Laurenziana 47, 34), and further speeches of Cicero (Vatican, Ottob. lat. 1463/1). Belonged to Abate Luigi Celotti (ca. 1768–ca. 1846; see *Phillipps Studies*, v. 3, pp. 50–51); Sir Thomas Phillipps (no. 947; tag on spine). Presented to Yale in 1943 by Thomas E. Marston.

secundo folio: [rati]onem. C. xij

Bibliography: Faye and Bond, p. 31, no. 114.

MSS 115–19 Puebla Manuscripts (Sterling Memorial Library)

MS 120 Latin American Collection (Sterling Memorial Library)

MS 121 France, s. XV^ex
Livre du roy Modus, etc.

1. ff. 1r–58v Au temps que le Roy modus donnoit doctrine de tous deduits Il disoit a ses aprentis ... Aussy est il de la char de lhomme. *Explicit Modus et Ratio*.

MS 121

G. Tilander, ed., *Les livres du roy Modus et de la royne Ratio* in *Société des anciens textes français* (Paris, 1932) v. 1, pp. 12-310.

2. f. 59r-v   Je suis soullart le blond et le beau chien courant/ De mon temps le meilleur et le mieulx parchassant/ ... chie le grand seneschal ou elle [*sic*] sera finee. [Followed by a list of 32 names of dogs, both masculine and feminine forms.] f. 60r-v blank, except for drawing (see below)

G. Tilander, ed., *Jacques de Brézé. La chasse. Les dits du bon Chien Souillard et les louanges de Madame Anne de France* (Lund, 1959) p. 51, MS N; p. 59: reproduction of f. 59r; pp. 56-68; p. 96. C. E. Lutz, "Le bon chien Soullart," *Gazette* 51 (1977) pp. 208-12.

Paper (watermarks: similar to Briquet Tête de cerf 15548, Tête de boeuf 14247, and unidentified unicorn), ff. vi (paper) + 60 + vi (paper), 283 x 202 (224 x 156) mm. Written in ca. 34 long lines (2 columns of verse for ff. 45v-51r); frame-ruled in hard point.
I-VI^{10}.
Written by a single scribe in a running script, with a more formal style of writing for headings.
Penwork drawing (with red added) of the hound, Soullart, on f. 59r; drawing of a lion [?] in same style on f. 60r. Simple decorative initials and headings in red, blue and/or black; some with calligraphic penwork designs and grotesques extending into margins. Paragraph marks, underlining, and highlights, in red.
Binding: s. xix. Half purple leather with textured cloth sides.

Written in France at the end of the 15th century; the watermarks suggest Northern France. Belonged to the antiquary Laurence Nowell (inscription "Laurens Nowell" with the date "1564" on ff. 1r and 59v). The manuscript apparently passed to the Anglo-Saxon scholar William Lambarde, a friend of Nowell, and remained in the Lambarde family until this century when it was sold by William Lambarde (bookplate; London, 18 June 1924, no. 505). For a discussion of the Nowell-Lambarde collection, consult R. Flower, "Laurence Nowell and the Discovery of England in Tudor Times," *Proceedings of the British Academy* 21 (1935) pp. 47-73; however, the antiquary Laurence Nowell is confused with a cousin of the same name, who was Dean of Lichfield. Collection of C. F. G. R. Schwerdt bookplate; see the catalogue *Hunting Hawking Shooting* [London, 1928] v. 2, p. 347); his sale (Sotheby's, 12 March 1946, no. 2235, pl. 164 of f. 1r). Purchased from Goldschmidt's by David Wagstaff; gift of Mrs. David Wagstaff in 1946.

secundo folio: Laprentis

Bibliography: Faye and Bond, p. 32, no. 121.

MS 122   Germany, s. XVII
Lutheran Church, Sacramentarium et Collectae

1. ff. 1r–6v   Prayers and readings for marriage. *Vom Vertrawen und Einsegnen Braut und Breutigam. Andechtigen Lieben Freunde in* Christo dem Herrn Gegenwertige … Der Herr erhebe sein Angesichte über euch und gebe euch Frieden. Amen. Bedencket die armen vmb Gottes willen.

2. ff. 7r–13v   Prayers and readings for baptism. *Das Tauffbuchlein. Vermanung an die so die Kinder zur Tauff bringen. Lieben Freunde in Christo.* Wir hören alle Tage aus Gottes wort erfahrens auch beyde an unserm leben vnd sterben … der sterkke dich mit seiner gnade zum Ewigen Leben. Amen. Der Friede des Herrn sei mit dir. Antwort. Amen.

3. ff. 14r–17v   Prayers and readings for Communion. *Exhortatio vnd vermahnung vom Sacrament des Altars an die Communicanten. Mein allerliebsten.* Uns wird stets durch die Predigt das Evangelij … Christe du Lamb Gottes der du tregst die Sunde der welt Gib uns deinen Frieden. Amen. [Added on f. 17v by a later hand is a prayer for the dying which begins:] Ein gebet welches über den Krancken vor der Communion von den umbstehenden kan gesprochen werden. Almächtiger Gott, Himlischer Vater, sintemal dieser Krancke dir nicht…; [in a different hand are words to be said to the assistants when visiting someone sick:] Eine Vermahnung an die umbstehende wenn man einen Krancken besucht. Lieben Freünde! Demnach wir befinden, daß unser lieber Bruder … [this addition concludes in the lower margin of f. 18r].

4. ff. 18r–19v   Prayers related to Baptism. *Oratio loco Introductionis puerperarum.* [above the first heading, in another hand:] Hie werde hergesetzet das Formular von der Nohttaüffe, die hinten fast am Ende stehet. [text:] *Quando partus foelix, Vel mediocris fuit atque infans accepto Baptismo tunc adhuc viuit.* Lieben Freunde es ist eine Kindelbetterin, die nachgehaltenem…; (f. 18v) *Quando infans Baptismum accepit, Sed ante expletum puerperij tempus decessit: In posteriori parte omittantur ea quae de infante loquuntur.* Dieselbige befihlet sich nun dem frommen…; (f. 19r) *Quando infans in partu difficili mortuus natus.* [2 words crossed out] Wiewohl er ihr in Kindesnöten … seinen Göttlichen Segen. Amen. [Added on f. 19v by a later hand:] *Collecta auf den Sontag Palmarum. Oremus.* Herr Gott himlischer Vater, wir dancken, loben und preisen dich … [followed by:] *Collecta auf Ostern.* Christus ist umb unser Sünde will dahingegeben … [prayer:] Herr Gott himlischer Vater, der du deinen Sohn umb unser Sünde Willen dahingegeben … lieben Sohn unsern Herrn.

5. ff. 20r–42v   Collects for feasts, Sundays, and special occasions. Most are preceded by a note (Num. 18, Num. 20, etc.) which may be a reference to a hymn. After the heading may come the 2 opening lines of a hymn, written by the same or a later hand; these are followed by a prayer. Given below is the heading, the number of the hymn [?], the opening line of the hymn, and

the opening words of the prayer. *Collecta vff das Fest Michaelis*. Num. 20. Der Herr hat seinen Engeln befohlen über dir ... Herr Gott himmlischer Vater, der du deine Engel zum Schutz...; (f. 20v) *Auff Ostern Collecta*. Num. 11. Christus von den Todten erstanden, stirbt hinfürt nimmer ... Almächtiger Gott der du durch den Todt deines Sohnes...; (f. 21r) *Ein Gebet für die Gemeine noth*. Num. 22. Herre handel nicht mit uns nach unsern Sunden ... Herr Allmächtiger Gott, der du der Elenden Schufftzen [?]...; (f. 21v) *Vor ein Gnediges Gewitter oder Regen zu bitten*. Num. 23. Aller augen warten auff dich Herr ... Herr Allmächtiger Gott, der du alles was da ist regierest...; (f. 22r) *Auff das Fest Trinitatis*. Num. 18. Wir loben Gott den Vater, Sohn, und den heiligen Geist ... Allmächtiger Ewiger Gott, der du uns gelehret hast...; (f. 22v) *An Christi Himmelfarts tage*. Num. 13. Christus ist auffgefahren in die Höhe ... O Allmächtiger Herre Gott, [added above: himlischer] Vater, wir bitten dich von hertzen...; (f. 23r) *Collecta auf Pfingsten*. Num. 16. Schaffe in mir Gott eine reines hertze ... Herr Gott, lieber Vater, der du (an diesem Tage) deiner glaubigen Hertzen...; (f. 23v) *Collecta beim begrebnis*. Num. 24. Herr handel nicht mit uns nach unsern Sünden ... O Ewiger Gott und Vater, der du nicht bist ein Gott der Todten...; (f. 24r) *Ein andere Wieder den Schnellen Todt zu Sterbens zeitenn*. Num. 26. Selig sind die Todten die in dem herrn sterben ... Allmächtiger, Barmhertziger Herre Gott Vater wir bitten dich hertzlich du wollest...; (f. 24v) *Ein Andere*. Num. 23. Herr handel nicht mit uns nach unsern Sünden ... Herr Gott himlischer Vater, der du nicht Lust hast an der armen Sünder Todt ... [added below in a later hand:] Mehr collecten zur Sterbenszeit besiehe unten zum beschluß aller collecten, nach dem Fest Michaelis, Num. 21.; (f. 25r) *Collecta auff den Aduent*. Num. 1. Bereitet den Weg dem Herren ... Lieber Herre Gott wecke uns auff...; [added in a later hand at bottom:] Hie wirde auch den Collecte auf den Advent hingesetzt, so nach 3. blätten Zu in den Num. 1-6.; (f. 25v) *Collecta auff Wehenachten*. Num. 2. Das Wort ward fleisch ... [given at side as an alternate hymn:] Ein kind ist uns gebohren ... Hilff lieber Herre Gott daß wir der Newen lieblichen Gebürt...; (f. 25v) *In Die Circumcisionis Domini*. Num. 3. O Herr Gott himlischer Vater wir dancken dir für dein Väterliche Gnaden...; (f. 26v) *Collecta am tage der Tauff Christi*. Num. 7. Herre Gott himlischer Vater der du in der Tauff...; [f. 27r: a large *X* is drawn over the page, and in the upper left-hand corner a later hand wrote, "Haec omittatur."] *Pro pluvia*. Herr handel nicht mit uns nach unsern Sunden ... Herr Allmechtiger Gott, himlischer vater, der du alles was da ist regierst...; (f. 27r) *Pro serenitate*. Herr Allmechtiger Gott, himlischer vater, der du alles was da ist regierst...; (f. 27v) *Beim begrebnis*. Num. 25. Herr handel nicht mit uns nach unsern Sunden ... Almächtiger Ewiger Gott, himlischer Vater, der du durch den todt deines lieben Sohns...; (f. 27v) *Pro pace*. Num. 27. Gott gib friede in deinem lande ... Herr Gott himlischer Vater, der du die heiligen ... gib deinen dienern den fried...; (f. 28r) *Collecta auf den Aduent*. Num. 1.b. Machet die thore weit, und die thür in der Welt hoch ... Herr Gott himlischer Vater wir dancken dir von ganzen hertzen...; (f. 28v) *Collecta auf Weinachten.* Num. 2. Das Wort ward fleish ... [given at side as an alternate hymn:] Euch ist heute der heiland gebohren ... Herr Gott himlischer Vater, Wir dancken dir deiner grossen gnade und Barmhertzigkeit, daß du deinen Eingebohrnen...; [f. 29r; an *X* is drawn through this section] *Collecta auf das Newe Jahr.* O Herr Gott himlischer Vater wir dankken dir für dein Vaterliche gnaden daß du der armen sünder...; (f. 29r) *Eine andere Collecta auf das Newe jahr.* Allmächtiger Ewiger Gott, von dem alle gute Gaben herkommen...; (f. 29v) *Collecta auf Trium Regum.* Num. 5. Herr Gott himlischer Vater der du deinen Eingebohrnen Sohn...; (f. 30r) *Collecta auf Purificationis Mariae.* Num. 6. Herr Gott himlischer Vater der du deinen Sohn uns zum Heylande bereitet hast...; (f. 30v) *Collecta auf Verkündigung Mariae.* Num. 8. Herr Gott himlischer Vater wir dancken dir vor deine unaussprechliche gnade...; (f. 30v) *Collecta Dominicae VII Trinitatis. De peccatrice.* O Jesu du Sohn des lebendigen Gottes der du umb der Sunde...; (f. 31r) *Collecta auf das Leiden Christi zur Fastenzeit.* Num. 9. Christus ist umb unser missethat willen verwundet ... Barmhertziger Ewiger Gott der du deines Einigen Sohns nicht verschonet hast...; (f. 31r) *Eine Andere.* Num. 10. Die straffe lieget auf ihn, auf daß wir friede hetten ... Allmächtiger Vater, Ewiger Gott, der du für uns hast deinen Sohn des Creützes pein lassen leiden...; (f. 31r) *Collecta Dominicae Palmarum.* O herr Gott himlischer Vater, der du aus Vaterlicher gnaden deines Eingebohrnen Sohns...; (f. 31v) *Collecta auf Ostern.* Num. 12. Ich weiß daß mein Erlöser lebet ... Herr Gott, himlischer Vater, der du deinen Eingebohrnen Sohn umb unser Sünde willen hast dahingegeben...; (f. 32r) *Collecta auf himmelfahrt.* Num. 14. Ich fahre auf zu meinen Vater und zu euren Vater ... Allmächtiger herr Gott, verleihe uns, die wir gleüben [?]...; (f. 32r) *Eine Andere.* Num. 15. Herr Iesu Christe, du Sohn des allerhöchsten Gottes der du nun forthin...; (f. 32v) *Collecta auf Pfingsten.* Num. 17. Herr Iesu Christe, du Sohn des Allmächtigen Gottes, wir bitten dich, du wollest durch dein Wort...; f. 33r-v blank; (f. 34r) *Dominica iii. Epiphaniae.* [rest of f. 34r blank]; (f. 34v) *Collecta Dominicae post circumcisionem. De Fuga Christi.* Allmächtiger und Barmhertziger Gott himlischer Vater wir dancken dir hertzlich, daß du deinen lieben Sohn...; (f. 34v) *Collecta Dominicae ii Epiphaniae.* Herr Gott himlischer Vater wir dankken dir, daß du mit deiner gegenward...; (f. 35r) *Gemeine Collecten.* [added: *Dominica 4 post Trinitatem*]. Herr handele nicht mit uns nach unsern Sünden ... Allmächtiger Herr Gott Vater der du bist ein beschützer...; (f. 35r) *Eine Andere.* [added: *Dominica 3 post Epiphaniam*]. Herr handele nicht mit uns nach unsern Sünden ... Allmächtiger Herr Gott Vater verleihe uns einen bestendigen glauben...; (f. 35v) *Eine Andere.* [added: *Dominica Quasimodo geniti*]. Herr handele nicht mit uns nach unsern Sünden ... Herr Gott himlischer Vater der du aus Väterlicher Liebe uns armen Sündern...; (f. 35v) *Eine Andere.* [added: *Dominica Laetare*]. Herr handele nicht mit uns nach unsern Sünden ... Herr Gott himlischer Vater von dem wir ohn unterlaß...; (f. 36r) *Eine Andere.* [added: *Dominica 7 post Trinitatem*]. Herr handele nicht mit uns nach unsern Sünden

... Verschone Herr, verschone unser Sünde...; (f. 36r) *Eine Andere.* [added: *Dominica 4 post Epiphaniam*]. Herr handele nicht mit uns nach unsern Sünden ... Allmächtiger Ewiger Gott der du durch deinen heiligen Geist...; (f. 36r) *Eine Andere.* [added: *Dominica 5 post Epiphaniam*]. Herr handele nicht mit uns nach unsern Sünden ... Herr Gott himlischer Vater wir bitten dich du wollest deinen heiligen Geist in unser hertzen...; (f. 36v) *Eine Andere.* [added: *Dominica 3 post Trinitatem*]. Herr handele nicht mit uns nach unsern Sünden ... Allmächtiger Ewiger Gott Vater der du sehen lessest das Liecht...; (f. 36v) *Eine Andere.* [added: *Dominica 19 post Trinitatem*]. Herr handele nicht mit uns nach unsern Sünden ... Herr Gott himlischer Vater, wir bitten dich, du wollest durch deinen heiligen Geist uns also leiten...; (f. 37r) *Eine Andere.* [added: *Dominica Jubilate*]. Herr handele nicht mit uns nach unsern Sünden ... Allmächtiger Ewiger Gott Vater, der du aus Väterlicher Wollmeinung...; (f. 37r) *Eine Andere.* [added: *Dominica Rogate*]. Herr handele nicht mit uns nach unsern Sünden ... Allmächtiger Ewiger Gott der du dürch deinen Sohn Vergebung...; (f. 37v) *Eine Andere.* [added: *Dominica 17 post Trinitatem*]. Herr handele nicht mit uns nach unsern Sünden ... Herr Gott himlischer Vater wir bitten dich du wollest durch deinen heiligen Geist uns also Regieren...; (f. 37v) *Eine Andere.* [added: *Dominica Sexagesima*]. Herr handele nicht mit uns nach unsern Sünden ... Wir dancken dir herr Gott himlischer Vater von grund unsers hertzens...; (f. 38r) *Eine Andere.* [added: *Dominica Oculi*]. Herr handele nicht mit uns nach unsern Sünden ... Herr Gott himlischer Vater der du uns deinen Sohn geschencket...; (f. 38r) *Eine Andere.* [added: *Dominica Inuocavit*]. Herr handele nicht mit uns nach unsern Sünden ... Herr Gott himlischer Vater der du deinen Sohn unsern Herrn Jesum Christum in diese Welt...; (f. 38v) *Eine Andere.* [added: *Dominica 19 post Trinitatem*]. Herr handele nicht mit uns nach unsern Sünden ... Allmächtiger Herr Gott Vater, wir bitten dich du wollest unsere Sünde gnädiglich...; (f. 38v) *Eine Andere.* [added: *Dominica 21 post Trinitatem*]. Herr handele nicht mit uns nach unsern Sünden ... Allmächtiger Herr Gott wir bitten dich hertzlich, du wollest unsern glauben...; (f. 38v) *Eine Andere.* [added: *Dominica 18 post Trinitatem*]. Herr handele nicht mit uns nach unsern Sünden ... Herr Gott himmlischer Vater Wir bitten dich du wollest deinen heiligen Geist in unsere hertzen geben...; (f. 39r) *Von der Nothtauffe.* Wen das kindlein in der noth daheime getauft ist...; (f. 40r) *Eine andere gemeine Collecta.* [added: *Dominica Reminiscere*]. Herr handele nicht mit uns nach unsern Sünden ... Allmächtiger Herr Gott, der du bist ein trost der traurigen...; (f. 40r) *Eine Andere.* [added: *Dominica 1 post Trinitatem*]. Herr handele nicht mit uns nach unsern Sünden ... Allmächtiger Ewiger Gott ein beschützer aller die auf dich hoffen...; (f. 40r) *Eine Andere.* [added: *Dominica Cantate*]. Herr handele nicht mit uns nach unsern Sünden ... Herr Gott himlischer Vater wir bitten dich du wollest uns den Geist der Warheit...; (f. 40v) *Eine Andere.* [added: *Dominica 11 (post) Trinitatem.*] Herr handele nicht mit uns nach unsern Sünden ... Barmhertziger Ewiger Gott der du deines Eigenen Sohns nicht verschonet hast...; (f. 40v) *Eine Andere.* [added: *Dominica 13* (post) *Trinitatem.*] Herr handele nicht mit uns nach unsern Sünden ... Allmächtiger Herre Gott gib uns den rechten Warhaftigen glauben...; (f. 40v) *Eine Andere.* [added: *In die para Sceves* (sic)]. Allmächtiger Ewiger Gott der du für uns hast deinen Sohn des Creutzes...; (f. 41r) *Eine Andere.* Herr handele nicht mit uns nach unsern Sünden ... Allmächtiger Ewiger Gott, himlischer Vater, wir bitten dich, du Wollest dich deines Volcks...; (f. 41r) *Eine Andere.* Herr handele nicht mit uns nach unsern Sünden ... Allmächtiger Ewiger Herre Gott, der du den Irrenden das Liecht...; (f. 41r) *Eine Collecta auf die Zehen Geboth.* [added: *Dominica 6 et 18 Trinitatis*]. Lehre mich, herr, daß ich bewahre dein gesetze ... Herr Allmächtiger Ewiger Gott, der du das gottlose wesen hassest [?]...; (f. 41v) *Eine Collecta auf den Christlichen Glauben.* [added: *Dominica 3 Epiphaniae, Dominica Reminiscere, Dominica 21 post Trinitatem*]. Dem gleübigen wird sein glaube gereihnet zur gereihtigheit ... Herr Allmächtiger Gott, von dem alle gute und vollkommene gaben...; (f. 41v) *Eine Collecta auf das Vater Unser.* [added: *Dominica Vocem Iucunditatis item. Dominica XI post Trinitatem*]. Das verlangen der Elenden Hörestu herr ... [given as an alternate hymn:] Ehe sie ruffen, wilich antworten ... Herr Gott himlischer Vater du weissest daß wir in so mancher...; (f. 42r) *Eine Collecta auf das heilige Nachtmal.* [added: *In die Viridium*]. So oft ihr von diesen Brodt esset, und von diesen Kelch trincket ... [given as an alternate hymn:] Welcher unwürdig von diesen Brodt isset, oder von dem Kelch des herrn trincket ... Ach du Lieber Herre Gott, der du uns bey diesen...; (f. 42r) *Eine Collecta auf die Tauffe.* [added: *Dominica 4 Adventus*]. Wer da gleübet und getauffet wird, der wird selig werden ... Herr Barmhertziger Gott, der du uns deinen Lieben Sohn Iesum Christum geschencket hast...; (f. 42v) *Eine Collecta vom jüngsten Tage.* [added: *Dominica 2 Adventus, Dominica 25, 26, 27* (post) *Trinitatem*]. O herr Iesu Christe, der du zukünftig bist...; (f. 42v) *Eine Collecta auf das heilige predigampt.* [added: *Dominica Misericordiae Domini*]. O Barmhertziger Gott der du gelehret hast die hirten ... dürch Iesum Christum unsern Herrn.

Paper (lightweight and brittle; watermarks buried in gutter and obscured by text), ff. 42 + ii (paper), 190 x 160 (ca. 145 x 120) mm. 15-27 long lines. Not ruled. I^{10} (-1), II-III^6, IV^{10} (-9?), V^4, VI^8 (-1?), VII^2.

Written in gothic textura and cursive by many scribes. Scribe 1 (ff. 1r-17v) writes in a large gothic textura. Scribe 2 (ff. 18r-27r) writes in an even cursive script. Other cursive hands make notes and additions on ff. 1r-27r, and are intermingled in the text of ff. 27v-42v.

Elaborate capitals on ff. 1r-17v, all by the first scribe, in brown ink. On ff. 18r-26v, headings in gothic textura, square capitals, or humanistic script, above the cursive text. Musical notation on a 5-line staff on ff. 15r-16v (the Lord's Prayer).

Most of the folios are now detached from the binding; some attempt was made to repair this, using paper strips. Margin of f. 1 repaired; does not affect the text

MS 123

Binding: s. xix. Vellum case, blind-tooled.

Written in Germany in the 17th century, judging from the script; many later additions and corrections. Early provenance unknown. Note inside front cover: "Aus dem Nachlass des Abts D. Thiele für AGrube [*sic*], Braunschweig d 9. Oct. 1886."; probably Heinrich August Ludwig Thiele (1814–86), Lutheran theologian and Abbot of the monastery of Riddagshausen (*Allgemeine Deutsche Biographie* v. 38, pp. 750-53). Presented to Yale in 1948 by Maybelle M. von Kalinowski.

Bibliography: Faye and Bond, p. 32, no. 122.

MS 123 Latin American Collection (Sterling Memorial Library)

MS 124
Italy, s. XV^{ex}
Mathias Mercader, Practica de citreria

1. ff. i–ii ruled, but blank; ff. iii recto – vi verso [Table of contents:] *Prohemio dellautore a. Carta. I ... Ad panno che uene ali occhi. a. Carta. Lxviiii.* ff. vii–viii ruled, but blank

2. ff. 1r–68r *Practica de Citreria breuemente facta ad petitione et Comandamento del serenissimo et inuictissimo Principe et Signore lo Signore Re Don Ferrando* [King Ferdinand of Naples] *per la diuina gratia Re de Sicilia Hierusalem et Hungaria Facta et composta per lo Reuerendo Misser Mathia Mercader Archidiacono de Valentia.* [S]erenissimo et Inuictissimo Signore. Multe et diuerse volte per la Maiesta uostra me stato dicto et comandato ... Facto in la uostra citta de napole lo primo di de Iunio M CCCC LXXV. Finis.

   Cf. J. E. Harting, *Bibliotheca accipitraria* (London, 1891) p. 131.

3. ff. 68v–69r [Two unidentified short selections:] *Medicina experimentata per Iuliano ciurczo Ad male de chioui di falconi o daltro ucello. Farriti allaczare la uena della cossa che sta ... Ad panno che uene alli occhi di falcone o de altro ucello. Pigliarite la herba chiamata Virga pastoris et caczaritene lo suco....* ff. 69v–72v ruled, but blank

Parchment, ff. ii (paper) + 78 (numbered i–viii, modern hand; I–Lxviiij, by original scribe; 1–72, modern hand), 142 x 100 (82 x 61) mm. Written in 16 long lines; single vertical bounding lines, full across; lightly ruled in ink.
I–X^8. Catchwords perpendicular to text along inner bounding line, accompanied by lateral embellishments.
Written by a single scribe in a fine round humanistic script.
Space left for initial on f. 1r; headings, small initials, and entries for table of contents, in red.

Binding: s. xviii-xix. Vellum case. Fine paste paper flyleaves and pastedowns.

Written in Italy at the end of the 15th century; early provenance unknown. Belonged to the Rev. Walter Sneyd (booklabel; T. Phillipps, *Catalogus manuscriptorum Magnae Britanniae* [Middle Hill, 1850] p. 15, no. 215) who may have acquired it from Abate Matteo Luigi Canonici. Collection of C. F. G. R. Schwerdt (bookplate; see catalogue *Hunting Hawking Shooting* [London, 1928] v. 2, p. 346); his sale (Sotheby's, 12 March 1946, no. 2233) to Goldschmidt's, from whom it was acquired by David Wagstaff (bookplate). Gift of Mr. and Mrs. David Wagstaff in 1946.

secundo folio: Vostra Maiesta

Bibliography: Faye and Bond, p. 32, no. 124.
  A. Lupis, *La sezione venatoria della Biblioteca Aragonese di Napoli* ... (Bari, 1975) p. 32.

MS 125
Wycliffite New Testament

England, s. XIV/XV

ff. 1r–97v   //locustis and hony of þe wode þanne ierusalem wente out to him and al Iude and al þe cuntre aboute iordan ... þe grace of oure lord ouer aboundid with feiþ and loue þat is in crist ihesu a trewe word//

Begins imperfectly in Matthew 3.4 and breaks off at 1 Timothy 1.15; also missing Romans 9.22 to 1 Corinthians 1.23 (2 bifolios lost after f. 73). Contains the Gospels without prologues, and the Epistles with prologues. The text has been altered in places by a nearly contemporary hand that has written over erasures. Since the alterations correspond to those adopted in the later edition of John Purvey, MS 125 may reflect an intermediate stage between the Wycliffite Bible and Purvey's version. See J. Forshall and F. Madden, eds., *The Holy Bible ... by John Wycliffe and His Followers* (Oxford, 1850) v. 1: MS W, no. 168, p. lxiv (the editors comment that "the scribe not infrequently makes gross errors") and v. 3: text; C. Lindberg, "The Manuscripts and Versions of the Wycliffite Bible," *Studia neophilologica* 42 (1970) p. 336.

Parchment (thick, furry), ff. i (paper) + 97 + i (paper), 284 x 180 (222 x 132) mm. Written in 2 columns of 49 lines; double outer and single inner vertical bounding lines; usually double or single upper and lower horizontal bounding lines, full across; additional pair of lines in upper (for running titles) and lower margins. All rulings in ink; some have smeared.

I^8 (-1), II–IX^8, X^8 (-3 through 6), XI^8, XII^6, XIII–XIV^4. Structure of final 14 leaves is uncertain due to binding repairs. Catchwords between horizontal lines in lower margin, under inner column. Remains of original leaf signatures on ff. 40r and 41r: the letter *f* with *i* and *ij* below.

Written in a neat gothic bookhand by a single scribe who carefully corrected his errors; changes by at least one nearly contemporary and one later writer.

Blue initials, 10- to 4-line, with extensive penwork designs in red, introduce each chapter. Headings, running titles, and underlining in red; paragraph marks in red or blue.

Bookblock chewed by rodent in upper right corner; margins of many leaves trimmed resulting in some loss of text, marginalia, and catchwords.

Binding: s. xviii. Red spattered edges. Brown leather, flesh side out, blind-tooled. A black calf spine, gold-tooled, added.

Written in England ca. 1400, the codex bears evidence of much use. Signature of William Massey (Quaker scholar born in 1691?) on f. 94v and 7r (effaced). Notes of the typographical historian William Herbert (1718-95) on front pastedown: "W. Herbert 17th March 1766" and "Besides the above Testimony, I have examined it by W. Lewis's compleat History of the several Translations of the Holy Bible and New Testament into English, and find it agree [later addition: nearly] with his Quotations against which I have put a [drawing of a hand] in the Margin." Belonged to the antiquary Richard Gough (1735-1809) at whose sale (April 1810) the codex was purchased by the Rev. H. H. Baber (1775-1869). Acquired from Thorpe in 1836 by Sir Thomas Phillipps (nos. 7220 and 9302; tags on spine, inscription on f. 1r and inside front cover); sold (London, 28 June 1938, no. 455) to Robinson's. Purchased by Henry Fletcher; his gift to Yale in 1944.

Bibliography: Faye and Bond, p. 32, no. 125.
Exhibition Catalogue, pp. 216-17, no. 42.
R. J. Menner, "A Manuscript of the First Wycliffite Translation of the Bible," *Gazette* 19 (1945) pp. 37-44, with pl. of f. 69r.

MS 126 Italy, s. XII^2
Bible, with glossa ordinaria (fragment)

ff. 1r-66v //appetitur. adducet eam ad sacerdotem et offeret oblationem pro illa decimam partem ... que precepit dominus per manum moisi ad filios israel in campestribus moab super iordanem contra Iericho.

Book of Numbers (begins imperfectly at 5.14) with glossa ordinaria (Stegmüller, v. 9, no. 11784; PL 113. 390-446).

Parchment, ff. ii (paper) + 66 + ii (paper), 314 x 202 (size of written space varies; written space of biblical text when no gloss present: 192 x 124; when gloss in three margins: 192 x 55 mm.). Text of Numbers written in ca. 21 widely spaced lines suitable for interlinear notes; gloss in 49 lines (but never in lower margin). Single vertical bounding lines for both text and gloss. Ruled in hard point or pale brown ink; prickings in upper, lower, and outer margins.

I–VII[8], VIII[10]. Catchwords near lower edge of folio.
Written by a single scribe in two sizes of carolingian minuscule.
Binding: s. xx. Vellum case with brown paper sides.

Written in Italy in the second half of the 12th century; early provenance unknown. Belonged to Edward Duff Balken (bookplate). Unidentified note from a sale catalogue (no. 41) pasted inside front cover. Presented to Yale in 1950 by Henry Fletcher.

Bibliography: Faye and Bond, p. 32, no. 126.

MS 127 Italy, s. XIV
Moamin, etc.

1. ff. 1r–30r *Incipit tractatus primus de rethorica* [sic] *huius artis continens Capitula xiij. Capitulum primum de genere uolatilium et moribus eorum.* Generum uolatilium uiuencium de rapina quibus utitur gens aucupando ... uapor ad ipsam et sudor et quando sudabit omnes pediculi cadent. *Explicit tercius tractatus libri falconarie magistri oxamini arabiti.*

   This treatise by Moamin (Oxaminus may be a variation of his name) is divided into three sections, all on falconry; the second and third are preceded by lists of chapters. Missing is the prologue. The fourth section appears later in the volume (see art. 6). For the manuscript tradition: H. Tjernard, *Moamin et Ghatrif* (Stockholm, 1945); Beinecke MS 127 is no. 22 on p. 4.

2. ff. 30r–35r *Incipit alius.* Dancus rex stabat in suo palacio et ante eum stabant discipuli sui ... et liga eum et fac ita cottidie Et sic sanabitur.

   Treatise of Dancus rex; G. Tilander, ed., *Dancus Rex, Guillelmus falconarius, Gerardus falconarius* (Lund, 1963) MS Y, p. 45; pp. 48–116.

3. ff. 35r–37v *Verba de magistro et medicinis perfectis.* Iste magister non fuit mendax sed uerax. Iste medicine sunt bone et perfecte et multum probate. Guilielmus falconerius qui fuit nutritus in curia regis ... Et si uult capere grues opportet habere duodecim ysmerlos. *Explicit liber falconum et Rapacium auium.* f. 38r-v blank

   Treatise of Guillelmus falconarius; Tilander, *op. cit.*, pp. 134–68.

4. ff. 39r–46v *Ad dolorem pedum equorum.* Ad dolorem pedum equorum qui euenit occasione percussionis martelli uel lapidum aut alterius rei ... et pone super uermem et liberabitur si deo placuerit probatum est. *Liber compositus de medicinis equorum.*

   Anonymous treatise on horses, begins imperfectly?

5. ff. 47r–67r *Incipit liber de medicamine equorum et primo de medicamine equi habentis calorem.* Cum equs [sic] habet calorem pendet caput in terra et non potest ip-

sum leuare ... [ends with a table:] *Sinonima super medicaminibus equorum. Amila id est alba pasta ... Togenu palati tantum ualet quantum palatina.*

Anonymous treatise on horses.

6. ff. 67v-73r *Incipit tractatus de dispositionibus naturalibus et accidentalibus canum et rapacium quadrupedum. Continens. vi. Capitula.* [followed by list of chapters] ... *Capitulum de numeratione primum rapacium quadrupedum et proprietate canum.* Huius autem operis professores sufficienter non tractauerunt de canibus ... de fece ferri puluerizata et laua loca illa et conualescent. *Explicit liber tractatus Canum.*

Moamin, part 4, on dogs (see art. 1).

7. ff. 73r-75v *Incipit liber Guicennatis de arte versandi.* Si quis scire desiderat de arte bersandi in hoc tractatu cognoscere poterit ... cum illis tanto meliores erunt et precipue quando post bonas bestias equitabis. *Explicit liber rapacium auium. Equorum et canum.* Explicit liber rapacium auium. Equorum et canum deo gratias. *Amen.*

G. Tilander, ed., *Guicennas de arte bersandi* (Upsala, 1956) MS D, pp. 13, 18-28; K. Lindner, ed., *De arte bersandi* (Berlin, 1966) MS D, pp. 14, 24-36.

Parchment, ff. i (original parchment flyleaf) + i (paper tipped in) + 76, 195 x 128 (143 x 87) mm. Written in 31 long lines; single vertical and double upper horizontal bounding lines full across. Ruled in lead; remains of prickings in all margins except inner.

I-II^8, III^6, IV-VIII^8, IX^6, X^8. Catchwords (Scribe 1 only) decorated with lines and flourishes (some in red) along lower edge.

Written in a small round gothic bookhand by two scribes. Scribe 1: ff. 1r-37v, 67v-75v; Scribe 2: ff. 39r-67r.

One 6-line initial, red and blue, filled with red and blue penwork in a floral pattern. 4-, 2-, and 1-line pen initials, red, with long trailing serifs and blue calligraphic flourishes. 2- and 1-line initials outside text column. On f. 1r, arms of the duchy of Austria (crudely executed; later addition?):, or, two eagles palewise displayed and crowned sable (Hungary), impaled with barry of 6 gules and argent; supported by griffins passant gules; the whole set between thick pink bands. Linefillers red undulating lines. Rubrics throughout.

Binding: s. xvi. Sewn on three supports, the two outer ones leather, the central one tawed skin, laid and nailed in channels in wooden boards. Plain wound primary endbands sewn on a tawed core at the head and a leather one at the tail, laid in grooves and nailed, with a secondary embroidery added. The square spine is lined with vellum between supports. Covered in dark red goatskin, blind-tooled, with four brass catches on the lower board. Leather cracking along joints, clasps wanting.

Written in Italy in the 14th century; the arms of the Duchy of Austria appear to be a later addition. Unidentified shelf-mark on f. 1r: "T/ 175". Belonged to

C. F. G. R. Schwerdt (bookplate; see the catalogue *Hunting Hawking Shooting* [London, 1928] v. 2, pp. 349-50); his sale (Sotheby's, 12 March 1946, no. 2241) presumably to David Wagstaff (bookplate); gift of Mrs. David Wagstaff in 1946.

secundo folio: Cum uero incipit

Bibliography: Faye and Bond, p. 32, no. 127.
 A. Lupis, *La sezione venatoria della Biblioteca Aragonese di Napoli* ... (Bari, 1975) pp. 36-37.
 Idem, "Petrus de l'Astore, Moamyn, Ghatriph: Sulla tradizione dei trattati di falconeria d'epoca federiciana," *Codices manuscripti* 3 (1977) p. 16.

MS 128 Spain, s. XVI^{ex}
Hernán Pérez de Oliva, Historia de la invención de las Yndias

ff. 1r-33v   Historia de la inuencion de las Yndias, y de la conquista de la nueua España que escreuia el maestro Fernan Perez de Oliva natural de Cordoua ... [f. 1v blank; f. 2r:] *Narracion primera. Cristoual Colon, Genoues, natur*al de Saona, fue ombre de alto animo ... *a los hijos de los Reyes, para que en las fiestas las cantassen, y destos las oyan los otros. Fin de la ystoria de Colon.*

 J. J. Arrom, ed., *Hernán Pérez de Oliva, Historia de la Inuención de las Yndias* (Bogota, 1965) pp. 39-126. L. Olschki, "Hernán Pérez de Oliva's 'Ystoria de Colón'," *Hispanic American Historical Review* 23, no. 2 (1943) pp. 165-96. J. J. Arrom, "A Sixteenth-Century Account of the Voyages of Columbus," *Gazette* 19, no. 2 (1944) pp. 21-22.

 Paper (thin and brittle, with a slight gloss; watermarks: Briquet Croix latine 5678), ff. ii (later paper) + 33 + i (later paper), 210 x 155 (170 x 100) mm. Written in 28 long lines, frame-ruled in hard point.
 I-III^8, IV^8 (+ 1 at end, f. 33). Catchwords for each folio below written space, at right.
 Written in italic by one hand.
 Headings on ff. 1r and 2r in square capitals and round humanistic, executed in brown ink, as text.
 The ink has eaten through the paper at some points, but has not seriously affected the text.
 Binding: s. xix-xx. Narrow spine of mottled brown leather with marbled paper sides. Printed on the upper cover: "Fernan Perez de Oliva. Narracion Cristobal Colón. Historia inédita muy interesante. 1583."

Written in Spain, probably in the last quarter of the 16th century, judging from the watermarks (Briquet gives examples of this type for 1576 and 1579); there appears to be no mention in the manuscript itself of the date 1583, printed on the front cover, although Arrom considers it accurate ("An Early Unpublished

Manuscript on the Discovery of America," *Texas Quarterly* 3, no. 2 (1960) p. 170).
Note in cursive (s. xx) inside front cover: "If lost please return to G. S. Hellman, 331 W. 71st." (probably George Sidney Hellman, author born in New York, N.Y., 14 Nov. 1878, who often served as a consultant on rare books for the Morgan, Widener and Schiff collections). Presented by Frank Altschul in 1944, in memory of Prof. William Lyon Phelps.

Bibliography: Faye and Bond, p. 32, no. 128.

MS 129 (2 vol.) Flanders, s. XV$^{3/4}$
Petrus Comestor, Historia Scholastica, Fr. tr. Guyart des Moulins

1. f. 1r [Table of contents:] *Cy aprez sensieuent les liures historiaux de la bible quy en ce present volume sont translatez et tout par histores. Les escollastres ... Et premiers [E]n ce present volume est translate le livre de Genesis ... les euvangilles exposees selon histoire.* f. 2r-v blank

2. f. 3r *Cy commence le prologue. En pallais de Roy ou dempereur appartient a auoir trois mansions ...* [Vol. 2:] *Et ce qui ensieut iusques en la fin du liure est translate de ledition theodoce. Explicit.*

    Missing the beginning of Numbers (v. 1, one folio following f. 115), the beginning of 3 Kings (v. 1, one folio following f. 236), and part of Luke (v. 2, one folio following f. 260). See S. Berger, *La Bible française au moyen-âge* (Paris, 1884) pp. 166 and *passim*.

    Parchment, two volumes, v. 1: ff. ii (paper) + 266 + ii (paper); v. 2: ii (paper) + 294 + ii (paper). Both volumes 424 x 332 (267 x 184) mm., trimmed. Written in two columns, 35 lines. Ruled in red or violet ink. For the text, 4 vertical bounding lines, 2 for each column; between columns, three full-length bounding lines. 3 horizontal bounding lines, 2 at top and 1 at bottom of written space; for the glosses, 2 additional vertical bounding lines in outer margin, outer full across (on many folios, several additional lines); 2 lines full across in upper margin for running headings; 2 in lower margin for catchwords. On some folios, single lines doubled.
    V. 1: 1^2, II-XIII^8, XIV^6 (+1 leaf, f. 105), XV^8, XVI^8 (-3 following f. 115), XVII-XXX^8, XXXI^8 (-5 following f. 236), XXXII-XXXIII^8, XXXIV^8 (+1 leaf, f. 264), XXXV^2. V. 2: I-XXXII^8, XXXIII^8 (-5 following f. 260), XXXIV-XXXVI^8, XXXVII^6 (+1 leaf following f. 293). Catchwords at the end of nearly all quires. Traces of original quire markings and folio numbers, lower right verso.
    Written in a formal bâtarde with some loops by one scribe. Marginal glosses in a similar but smaller script by the same hand. Corrections by a later hand (s. xv) in brown ink.

Miniatures and decoration by the same artist as the *Cité de Dieu* (French translation of Raoul de Presles) made for Anthony of Burgundy and dated 1466 by the scribe. The codex was divided in 1720: the part in Turin, Bibl. Naz. MS L. I. 6 was almost completely destroyed in the fire of 1904; the other part is Turin, Archivio di Stato MS *b*. III. 12 J (see A. de Laborde, *Les Manuscrits à peintures de la Cité de Dieu de Saint Augustin* [Paris, 1909] v. 2, pp. 371-87 and v. 3, pls. XXIIIa-XXVIIa and XLII-XLIII; we thank J. Marrow and A. van Buren for assistance with this manuscript). Miniatures in v. 2 by an assistant. One large, 2-column miniature, 18-line, f. 3r, of three scribes, set in a wide (25 mm.) frame, brown, decorated with a continuous garland of flowers in gold, green and white, outlined on both inner and outer edges with bands of pink, gold and blue, highlighted in white. Text surrounded by a 3/4 band of pink and gold with white highlights, edged in black. Full border: curling sprouts of blue, gold and some red and light blue acanthus on green stems, largely confined to the corners and centers of the border, with blossoms containing animals, devils, knights; the intervening spaces filled with trailing vines of green and gold leaves with varied flowers in red, blue, light blue, strawberries, grapes and beans as well as denser vines in black ink with leaves in gold and green, with flowers, as above; the entire border densely filled with pen flecks, black, with gold dots.

Historiated initials (one column, 8-line), for the Seven Days of Creation (ff. 4v, 5r, 5v, 6v, 7v, 8v and 10r), roundels, with circular frames, brown with garlands as above, in some cases with the top and bottom of the roundel lopped off, set against a field of acanthus and/or flowers, as above, and set between two thin gold bands, edged in black. Short, thin borders of acanthus, vines, and flowers as above, divided from text by gold and pink bands, edged in black. Other miniatures (11- or 10-line), v. 1: f. 49r (Genesis) The Selling of Joseph; f. 63r (Exodus) Moses with the Children of Israel; f. 101r (Leviticus) Sacrifice of Burnt Offerings; miniature for Numbers missing (following f. 115); f. 166r (Joshua) Joshua's Dream; f. 176v (Judges) Battle Scene; f. 196r (1 Kings) Presentation of Samuel in the Temple; f. 217v (2 Kings) The execution of a soldier; miniature for 3 Kings missing (following f. 236). V. 2: f. 1r (4 Kings) Elijah in the fiery chariot; f. 41v (Job) God the Father enthroned addressed by the Devil; f. 43r (Tobit) Death of Tobit; f. 50r (Daniel) Daniel interprets Nebuchadnezzar's dream; f. 70r (Judith) Judith decapitates Holofernes; f. 100v (1 Maccabees) Scene of an Army; f. 126r (2 Maccabees) Four soldiers on horseback; f. 142r (3 Maccabees) Four soldiers on horseback leaving a city; f. 153v (Gospels) Birth of John the Baptist; f. 285v (Jeremiah) Jeremiah seated at a writing desk with Jerusalem in the background; f. 289v (John) John the Evangelist holding the poisoned chalice, with three men, one with short wings attached to his head. Diagrams (in purple ink) of the tabernacle in lower margins of ff. 87v and 166v. Each miniature with a 5-, 4- or 3-line initial, blue with white highlights, filled with strapwork and blue and pink ivy with white highlights, on irregular gold ground (cf. Waddesdon Manor, MS 9, ff. 226-88, a Book of Hours made in Bruges ca. 1450-75, reproduced in Delaissé, Marrow and de Wit, *Waddesdon Manor*, figs. 16-18). 2-line initials throughout, gold filled with red set against a blue ground or vice versa, trailing black hair-spray with gold, red and blue dots. Initials cruder in v. 2. Linefillers in both text and glosses in similar fashion. Running headings (in v. 1 only), and keys for glosses in red throughout. Traces of tabs in outer margins.

Binding: 1981. Bound in a brown, linen buckram case in the Yale Library Conservation Studio to replace an 18th-century brown calf binding. One board of this binding retained in box.

Written in Flanders (perhaps Bruges, judging from the miniatures) in the third quarter of the 15th century; early provenance unknown. Belonged to Capt. John Harrison-Broadley of Welton House, Brough, East Yorks; sold at Sotheby's (13-14 Feb. 1922, no. 33; with illustration of v. 1, ff. 63r and 217v). Sold by Maggs (1928, catalogue 500, no. 31). Presented in 1949 by Louis M. Rabinowitz.

secundo folio: [of text, f. 4] Cest a dire

Bibliography: Faye and Bond, p. 33, no. 129.
    Exhibition Catalogue, pp. 242-43, no. 67, and pl. 23 (v. 1, f. 3r).
    T. E. Marston, "The Comestor Manuscript," *Gazette* 34 (1950) pp. 172-73.
    Clive R. Sneddon, "The 'Bible du XIIIe Siècle': Its Medieval Public in the Light of Its Manuscript Tradition," in *The Bible and Medieval Culture*, ed. W. Lourdaux and D. Verhelst, in *Mediaevalia Lovaniensia*, Series 1, Studia 7 (Louvain, 1979) p. 130, n. 8.

MSS 130-32 Latin American Collection (Sterling Memorial Library)

MS 133   Italy, s. XV$^{3/4}$
Plutarch, Vitae, Lat. tr. Leonardo Bruni   Pl. 25

1. ff. 1r-33v *Marci Catonis vita per Leonardum Arretinum e Plutarcho in Latinum traducta incipit feliciter*. Catonis genus principium dignitatis et glorie sumpsit a proauo catone ... Sequenti uero tempore se bruto coniungens cum fidem et studium in bello ostendisset in philippis et ipse mortuus est. *M. Catonis vita per Leonardum Arretinum e Greco in Latinum traducta explicit feliciter. Deo gratias*.

    V. R. Giustiniani, "Sulle traduzioni latine delle 'Vite' di Plutarco nel Quattrocento," *Rinascimento* 2^a ser., 1 (1961) p. 36, no. 20, b.

2. ff. 33v-55v *Pyrrhi regis Epirrhotarum vita per Leonardum Arretinum e Plutarcho in Latinum traducta incipit feliciter*. Thesprotis et Mollossis post diluuium phetonta primum imperasse tradunt unum ex ijs ... Erga amicos quoque pyrri benignus fuit castro atque exercitus uniuersi potitus. *Pyrrhi regis Epirrhotarum vita explicit feliciter*.

Giustiniani, *op. cit.*, p. 30, no. 14, a.

3. ff. 55v–75r *Pauli Emilii vita e Greco in Latinum traducta per Leonardum Arretinum uirum eloquentissimum feliciter incipit.* Emiliorum familiam in urbe roma patriciam sane ac uetustam fuisse plurimi tradunt ... Tales mores uitaque pauli emilij fuisse dicuntur. *Pauli Emilii uita e Plutarcho in Latinum traducta per Leonardum Arretinum explicit feliciter. Deo gratias.*

Giustiniani, *op. cit.*, p. 28, no. 11, b.

4. ff. 75r–76v *.L. Arretini uiri eloquentissimi prefatio in uitam Quinti Sertorii uiri prestantissimi ad Antonium Luscum uirum doctissimum e Plutarcho in Latinum traductam per eundem Leonardum feliciter incipit.* Credo nonnunquam tibi euenisse antoni carissime mihi nanque ipsi sepius quam uellem ... huius quoque uiri exemplo temeritatem contendentium perfringere et segnitiem nostri temporis obiurgare possis. Vale. *Explicit prefatio.*

Dedicatory epistle of Leonardo Bruni to Antonio Loschi; H. Baron, *Leonardo Bruni Aretino humanistisch-philosophische Schriften* (Leipzig, 1928) pp. 123–25.

5. ff. 76v–91r *.Q. Sertorii uita e Plutarcho in Latinum traducta per Leonardum Arretinum incipit feliciter.* Non est fortasse mirandum per infinitum tempus alibi aliter fortuna influente res humanas ... hic enim siue latens siue neglectus in quadam barbarie uilla inops inuisusque consenuit. *.Q. Sertorii uita e Plutarcho in Latinum traducta per Leonardum Arretinum feliciter explicit.*

Giustiniani, *op. cit.*, p. 31, no. 15, a.

6. ff. 91r–103r *Demosthenis oratoris prestantissimi uita per Leonardum Arretinum e Greco* ... Demosthenis pater Demosthenes ut theopompus historicus tradit in primis ... quod soepe [sic] predicenti demostheni credere noluerat. *Demosthenis oratoris uita e Plutarcho ... feliciter explicit.*

Giustiniani, *op. cit.*, p. 38, no. 22, b.

7. ff. 103v–105r *Prefatio Leonardi Arretini in uitam Marci Antonii incipit.* Marci Antonii uitam multiplici ac uaria historiarum serie contextam et uel magnitudine rerum uel mutabilitate fortunae admirandam ... Sed haec plura et iam quam satis nunc ipsum antonium uideamus. *Explicit Prefatio.*

Dedicatory epistle of Leonardo Bruni to Coluccio Salutati; Baron, *op. cit.*, pp. 102–04.

8. ff. 105r–145v *.M. Antonii uita e Greco* ... Marco Antonio auus fuit antonius orator quem syllanas partes secutum .C. marius necauit ... nec multum abfuit quin flagitijs et amentia romanorum subuerteret imperium quartus ab antonio per gradus successor. *.M. Antonii uita e Greco ... feliciter explicit.*

Giustiniani, *op. cit.*, p. 40, no. 23, b.

9. ff. 145v–155r *Tyberii Gracci uita per Leonardum Arretinum e Plutarcho in Latinum conuersa feliciter incipit.* De agide et cleomene que dicenda fuerunt superius enar-

ratis nunc in romanorum parte non minores ... quod antea fecerat nunquam et ipse ad maledicta in plebem irritatus est de quibus in scipionis uita sigillatim diximus. *.T. Gracci uita e Greco ... explicit feliciter.*

Giustiniani, *op. cit.*, p. 29, no. 12, b.

10. ff. 155r–163v   *.C. Gracci uita per eundem* ... Caius autem gracchus siue inimicos ueritus siue ut inuidiam illis accumularet statim post mortem tiberij fratris ... sed in cadendo moderationem animi ferentis aduersa non aufert. *.C. Gracci uita per Leonardum Arretinum ... explicit feliciter.*

Giustiniani, *op. cit.*, p. 29, no. 12, b.

11. ff. 163v–164v   *Prefatio in uitam Marci Tullii Ciceronis* ... Ocioso mihi nuper ac lectitare aliquid cupienti oblatus est libellus ... ciceronis honor ut uehementer exoptem a multis de hoc ipso scribentibus superari.

Dedicatory epistle of Leonardo Bruni to Niccolò Niccoli; Baron, *op. cit.*, pp. 113–14.

12. ff. 164v–188v   *Marci Tullii Ciceronis uita* ... Tulliorum familia que et ciceronis postea cognomentum accepit e municipio arpinati ... Ita omnes ciceronis inimici misere tandem ignominioseque perierunt. *Finis. .M. Tullii Ciceronis uita per Leonardum Arretinum uirum doctissimum edita feliciter explicit. Deo gratias.*

Giustiniani, *op. cit.*, p. 38, no. 22, b.

Parchment, ff. ii (paper) + 188 + ii (paper), 223 x 153 (146 x 90) mm. Written in 27 long lines; double upper and single lower horizontal bounding lines, double vertical bounding lines, all full across. Ruled in hard point on the hair side; remains of prickings for bounding lines only.
I–XVII^{10}, XVIII^{8}, XIX^{10}. Catchwords in center of lower margin accompanied by clusters of dots and/or flourishes.
Written in an upright italic by a single scribe.
Small, 4-line, white-vine initials, one to commence each work, gold, infilled with pink and green with white dots, all on a blue ground; gold dots and hairsprays.
Binding: s. xviii. Green goatskin with red labels on spine. Delicately gold-tooled.

Written in Florence in the third quarter of the 15th century according to A. C. de la Mare; early provenance unknown. Belonged to David Wagstaff; presented to Yale in 1943 by Mrs. David Wagstaff.

secundo folio: ludere uellent

Bibliography: Faye and Bond, p. 33, no. 133.

MS 134 Germany, s. XV[1]
Prayers (in Ger. and Lat.), for Augustinian use

1. ff. 1r–6r [Prayers on the flyleaves] Oratio ad Deum Patrem. Benedico te Pater celestis Pater Domini mei Jesu Christi...; (f. 3r) Soe wer dese 3 Pater Noster 3 Dagan ein ander spricht in der H. Missen met gefallden sienden ... [text begins:] O liebe Herr Jesu Christe ierstete dat Pater Noster offeren ich dir zur werdicheit...; (f. 5r) O Heere Jesu Christe sone vanden leuen den godt gont my.... f. 6v ruled, but blank

2. ff. 7r–21r *Hier begint ein boechelgen van gebettergen daglichen zu gebruchen und wie man des morgens sal verhalden wan man auffstehet.* Das heilige Euangelium sagt von funff weÿsen vnd den funff Torchten Jungfrawen also....

3. ff. 21v–82v [Prayers to God and Christ] *Gebett so isst men ontwachget zu Gott dem herren.* O Gott almechtich vatter der barmhertzicheit vnd alles troestes...; (f. 24v) *Des morgens auffopfferung seiner selbst vnd aller seiner werck.* Almectiger Ewiger Gutiger vnd Barmhertziger gott ich danke dir...; (f. 29v) *Auffopfferung einer Gottliebbenden Seel zu Morgens fruhe sehr nutzlich zu verrichten.* Almechtiger ewiger Got ich wie wol deines Gottlichen Angesichts der aller Vnwurdigste dancke dir...; (f. 33r) *Eÿn gebett von rew vnd leydt der sunden.* Es ist mir schmertzlich leÿdt O herr Jesu christi...; (f. 36v) *Gebett.* Almechtiger ewiger Gott Vatter Sohn vnd heÿliger Geist ich dein vnwurdige Creatur N. bekenne die...; (f. 38v) *Drÿ gebetger wie du Gott alle tag dinen glauben soltest befelhlen am morgen zu sprechen.* Ich befelhe heut meinen Glauben der almechtichkeit Gottes Vatters...; (f. 40v) *Mit disen 3 gebettger hat die h. Brigitt daglich angeroiffen gott.* O Lieber herr Iesu Christe ein sohn des lebendigen gottes vnd aller welt erloeser komme mir zu hulff...; (f. 42v) *Wan eyn mensch alle tag sinen willen apoffer der h. dryfeldicheit als hÿ dede in syner profession der wirt vntfencklichen [?] der seluer gnade de hÿ op dem tag seiner profession vntfinck.* O Herr Gott hymmelscher vader ontfanck mich nach deinen wortten vnd ich sal leue...; (f. 45v) *Drÿ schone gebetger in den namen Jesu Christu zu bitten.* Gott vatter von himmel ich bitten dich in dem Namen Jesu christi nazareni...; (f. 47r) *Dit synt de acht versen S. Bernardo vmb eyn seligs end zu bitten.* O Herr erleuchte mir meine Augen ... [the 8 Verses of St. Bernard, Illumina oculos meos ... (RH 27912)]; (f. 49r) *Hir beginnen die 7 sloissger.* O Gewarre ewiger Gott beslous myn arme seel nu...; (f. 51v) *Dreÿ gebettlein mit 3 pater nosterchen mein Crucifit vnserchen pater noster.* O lieber herr ich opffer dir dis pater noster zu lob vnd zu ehren...; (f. 55r) *Dreÿ Schoene gebettlein von leÿden Christi.* O lieber herr Jesu christe diss Pater Noster opffer ich dir...; (f. 57v) *Vier schoene gebettlein von h. lÿden Christi.* O Lieber herr Jesu Christe ich ermahne dich des Schreckens...; (f. 62r) *Dit syn die 3 Todt Stossen vns lieben herren.* O Herr Jesu christe ich erman dich vnd danck dir...; (f. 67v) *Eyn gebett zu der wonde der scholder vns lieben herren..* O Herr Iesu Christe Ich grutzen die gebenedÿde wonde...; (f. 68v) *Dit gebett batt S. Gregorius doe hie vnsen lieuen herren sag mit sÿnen wonden.* O Herr vnd barmhertziger vader Schencke mich in die dieffheit dÿner h. wonden...; (f. 70v)

Eyn gebett zu vnsen lieuen herren. O Lieue herr du hast mit deiner h. bloit sturtzung vntbonden de benden meiner sunden...; (f. 72v) *Trage ein sonderliche hertzliche Andacht zu den h. wunden christi Suche in denselben Medicin fur alle kranckheiten deiner Seelen vnd sprich.* O Mein verwundter Jesu durch deine aller heÿligst wunden...; (f. 78v) *Zu ehren der v. wunden Kusse v. mal die Erdt vnd sprich.* O Mein Jesu durch die verdeinsten deiner Ersten wunden...; (f. 81r) *So wer desse dÿrfluss* [sic] *vns herren bett mit drÿ pater noster xxx tag der hat ein bede an vnsem lieben herren Pater noster.* O Lieue herre ich bitten dich durch den floss deiner h. tranen....

4. ff. 82v–93v *Van der broderschaff des sussen namen Jesus Des Sondags lest den Magnificat dan den hymnus* Jesu nostra ... [includes a Litany].

5. ff. 93v–167r [Prayers, mostly to the Virgin] *Funff gebeder dat du van Gott nit gescheiden werdes.* O Lieue herr Jesu christe ich begere dat dyn h. Name seÿ myn leste wort...; (f. 95r) *Hier folgen nach etliche gebetter zu der moder Gottes Wer maria eÿgen begert* ... O Du allerliefte Jungfrawe maria ich ergeue mich dir gantz vnd gar zu eÿgen...; (f. 98v) *3 gebett zu der moder gottes vm genadt zu erhalden deine 3. Gelobten zu leisten.* O Maria du allergehorsamste dochter des ewigen himmlichen Vatters...; (f. 100v) *Hie volgen xv Salue regina zur ehren der moder Gottz vmb eyn siliges endt zu bidden.* O Du gnadenriche vnd werdige Junffer...; (f. 117v) *Mit disen gebet offer der moder gottes die xv Salue regina mit andacht.* Eÿa du tzarte moder aller gnaden vnd barmhertzicheit...; (f. 122r) *Dit sÿnd die zweÿtz wehtzich Aue maria zu der moder gotz Sehr Nutzlichen zu sprechen.* O Genedige moder der barmhertzicheit. Ich bitten dich...; (f. 137r) *Ein gebett zu maria eines Sunders der sich bekeren wil.* O Du allersuessest Junfraw maria Ich bitt dich...; (f. 146r) *Dit is dat korngen* [sic] *von der moder gotts ersten lest den hÿmnus Aue maris stella.* Gegrutz sÿstu maria du bis ein einige dochter des ewigen vatters...; (f. 152r) *Credo.* O Gloriose Junffer maria ontfanck zu ehren der genoemder h. drÿueldicheit 12 aue maria 3 pater noster...; (f. 153r) *Dit sint die x duechen maria.* Gegrutz sÿstu aller wÿeste Junffer maria du bÿs vol genaden der herr...; (f. 154v) *Dit sint vii hertzer der moder gotz.* O Gloriose Jonffer maria ich grutzen dyn gebenedide hertz...; (f. 156v) *Dit is ein gebett zu der seel maria.* O Gloriose Jonffer maria ich grutzen dyn allerhillichste hertz...; (f. 158r) *Dit is der Namen man psalm Maginfica* [sic]. O Maria ein middelerm tuschen gott vnd den meschen...; (f. 158v) *psalm ad donium* [sic]. O Maria ein hulperin in allen enxden vnd noeden kom mir zu hulpen...; (f. 159r) *Psalm Rettibue* [sic] *ser.* Retribue seruo tuo viuifica me...; (f. 162r; no rubric) O Maria ein weder brengerin der verlorener genaden weder brenge mir...; (f. 162r) *psalm In conuertendo.* O Maria ein verluchterin die dar geboren haiß dat ewiger Licht...; (f. 162v) *psalm ad te leua.* O Maria eyn vursprecherin aller ellendiger menschen...; (f. 163r) *Dit is den gulden reÿffen maria.* O Maria moder der barmhertzigheit ich beuellen dir mein Lief...; (f. 165v) *Eyn gebett zu der moder gottes.* O Gloriose Jonffer maria moder aller genaden vnd barmhertzicheit ich bitten dich....

6. ff. 167r–173v *Letaneÿ zu der moder Gottes* [no saints mentioned by name].

7. ff. 174r-189r   Prayer and Litany to one's Guardian Angel. Prayer begins: O Mein h. engel Ich dancke dir von hertzen das mir dise....

8. ff. 189v-209v   *Litaneÿ zu den patronen.* Includes: Lawrence, Cassius and Florentius, Dionysius, Augustine as "Eyn funderer vnsers Ordens" (f. 196r), Theresa and Monica.

9. ff. 209v-245r   [Prayers to Christ, the Virgin, for after Communion, etc.] *Gebett.* O Suester her Jesu Christe myn geliebster Nazarener...; (f. 211r) *Wie du dich an dem dag wan man bichten sal verhalten sollest.* [text underlined throughout in red:] *Am morgens froe Gottoitmoedelich bitten dat er mir gnadt wolle geben mich zu erinneren...*; (f. 213r) *Gebetter fur der bicht.* O Du h. Geist der du de lieb bis Ich bitten de mutiglich gib mir...; (f. 215r) *Schuss gebettlein.* Wesche mich O herr ab von meinen sunden mit dinen kostbarlichen Blut...; (f. 219r) *Wie du dich in vnd nach der bicht verhalden soll.* In der bicht nichts verschweigen alles demutig bekennen...; (f. 220v) *gebett.* O Gott meiner Seelen der du nit ophoerest taglich...; (f. 221v) *S. Augustini gebett So offt du es andechtig lisest verdienstu achtzig tausent Jahr ablass wans ... ablass den Bonifacius viii ...* O Gott der du fur der welt heÿl hast wollen...; (f. 224r; no rubric) Gegrust seÿstu h. haupt vnsers Seligmechers Jesu Christi...; (f. 229r) *Eyn schon vbung vnd lehr wie du dich zu dem h. S. bereÿden solles.* Eerstelich sollestu zuvor viertag dir starck fur setzen ob du es thun wollest...; (f. 238r) *Nach ein Ermahnung vor der h. Communion.* Erstlich nach einer wahren vnd reinen Bicht soltu dich behutsamlich...; (f. 239v) *Gebett.* Ach mein hertzlieber herr Jesu Christe sihe hie erscheine ich...; (f. 242v) *beger von deinen h. patronen das seÿ vor dich bitten beÿ gott ...* O Mein geliebter verleÿhe mir gnad mich auff das best zu diser Communion zu bereiten....

10. ff. 245r-248r   *Wei ein Bettler herumbgehen vnd von Allen etwas erbitten.* O Gott Vatter Sohn vnd heiliger Geist erbarm dich meiner nach deiner grossen barmhertzigheit ... [includes invocations to the Virgin, Angels, Joseph and Patriarchs, Peter and the Apostles and Evangelists, Lawrence and the Martyrs, Augustine and the Confessors and Bishops, and Barbara and the Virgins].

11. ff. 248v-285r   [Various prayers] *Vor der Communion kanstu ein klein kronlein auss 12 Tugenden deinem Geliebten im h. Sacrament auffopffern.* O Mein Iesu ich komme zu dir deiner zugeniessen zu deiner Ehren vnd meiner Seeligkeit...; (f. 252v) *Begere durch die furbit der moder gottes rew vnd leid vber dein sunden vnd verzeÿhung.* O Allerheiligste Jungfraw maria ich bitte dich durch dein Reinigkeit von allen sunden erwerbe mir...; (f. 256v) *Beghere von deinem geliebten so bald du in empfangen den segen.* O Mein geliebter vater allen gebenedeÿt segne vnd benedeÿe meyn hertz...; (f. 258v) *Nach der Communion sage ihm danck.* O Mein allerliebster Jesu O du geliebter meins hertzens...; (f. 265r) *Auffopfferung deiner selben zu allen wolgefallen deines Geliebten.* O Mein allergutigster Jesu du hast dich mir gantz geben...; (f. 268r) *Begert von deinen geliebsten was dir sonderlich an der Seelen vnd des leibs von noehten ist.* O Mein Jesu O Jesu meines hertzens was kan mir ietzt mangelen...; (f. 273v) *Drÿ vnd drissig schutz gebetter fur de 33. Jaren des leben christ.*

O guede Jesu du bist dat wort des vatters bekiere mich...; (f. 278r) *Etliche Abens gebetter.* O Herr Jesu christe des lebendiger Gottes Sohn mein eynniger heÿland...; (f. 281v) *Grusse de Seligste Jungfraw mit drÿ aue maria op de weiss welche de mutter Gottes selb de h. Mechtildis gelehret hatt* ... O Ehrentreiche Fraw O h. Maria gelich wie Gott der Vatter....

12. ff. 285r-287r *Zu den patronen.* O Mein h. patronen meinen h. schutzengels ... [invocations to Joseph, Peter, Lawrence, Augustine, Ursula, Barbara, Catharine, Mary Magdalen, Monica, and Theresa].

13. ff. 287r-300v [Various prayers] *Dan Examennir dyn gewissen.* O Unendliche Gute dir sag ich danck vmb alle deine gutthaten...; (f. 289v) *Folgende gebetlein konte man hinzusetzen.* O Ewiger hymmelscher Vatter durch das leben vnd Todt deines lieben Sohn...; (f. 291v) *Gebet zu Ehren des h. leinwathr.* O Gott der du vns in deinen h. Leintwat dar in dÿn allerheilligster lieb...; (f. 292v) *Ein gebett von den h. blut.* O Gutiger pellican herr Jesu Christi reinige mein vnsaubers hertz...; (f. 295v) *Vnse lieuer herr sprach op ein zeit zu einer h. Junffer begerstu mir* ... Zu dem ersten kneende in de gedechteniss des vnmessichens lÿdens...; (f. 298r) *Eyninige oeffeninge vnd heÿst der crutz ganck met christen* van der passien christi ... De I. v pater noster vnd aue maria sal man sprechen algaende....

14. ff. 300v-307v and inside back cover [Prayers in later hands including:] Dreij Gebett fuglich nach der bicht zu sprechen. O Herr Jesu christe, ich grose sunder ermane dich...; (f. 304r) Precatio Ante Litanias. Miserere mihi misero peccatori misericors Trinitas Sancta....

Paper (watermarks trimmed; unidentified), ff. iv (paper; foliation begins on first flyleaf) + ii (contemporary paper) + 293 + i (contemporary paper) + vi (paper; foliated through last flyleaf), 79 x 48 (57 x 33) mm., trimmed. Written in 14 long lines; single vertical bounding lines ruled in pale brown ink; horizontal bounding lines, single at bottom and single or double at top, ruled in lead, all full across; some prickings at sides.

I-IV^8, V^8 (-6), VI-XII^8, XIII^4, XIV^8, XV^6, XVI-XXII^8, XXIII^6 (+1 leaf after f. 175), XXIV-XXIX^8, XXX-XXXI^4, XXXII-XXXIV^8, XXXV^8 (-1), XXXVI^8, XXXVII^8 (-8), XXXVIII-XXXIX^8, XL-XLI^4. Tops of a few signatures visible on first folio of quire, recto, in lower right-hand corner.

Text written in formal gothic by one scribe. Prayers added on the flyleaves, front and back, by several later hands in italic of the 17th century and later.

2- and 1-line initials in blue-grey or orange-tinted red. 1-line initials within the text, with red stroke. Extensive rubrication in orange-tinted red.

Binding: s. xvi-xvii. Sewn on three single, round, vegetable fiber cords laced into wooden boards. "Made" endbands glued on and extending onto the outer face of the boards. Red edges and numerous place marks of vellum or tawed skin on the fore-edge. The spine rounded and lined. Covered in dark brown calf with two brass catches on the upper board and brass clasps hinged to the lower. The lower board is detached and one clasp and some leather at head and tail of the spine are wanting.

Written probably in Southern Germany in the first half of the 15th century for Augustinian use (cf. arts. 8, 10 and 12). Signature of Werner Hapthauser [?] inside front cover. Given by Charles Stonehill in 1943.

secundo folio: ihren vngebutzten

Bibliography: Faye and Bond, p. 33, no. 134.

MS 135
Treatises on rhetoric (in Lat.)　　　　　　　　　　　　　　Germany, s. XVI/XVII

1. pp. 1-207　*Quaestiones rhetoricae quibus legitima artis praecepta exemplis facilimis demonstrantur.* Quid est Rhetorica? Est ars benè dicendi. Quid nominis? Ρητορική deducitur a ῥέω vel ... Tantum de ijs quae de praeceptis Rhetorices legitimis dici debent etsi alicubi commonefactiones aliae quoque sunt aspersae quae tamen studia puerilia in hoc genere iuvant. Τέλος. pp. 208-220 blank

   The treatise follows roughly (with numerous examples added) the text printed in P. la Ramée, ed., *Audomari Talaei rhetorica* [Omer Talon, ca. 1510-1562] (Paris, 1572).

2. pp. 1-81　*Commonefact[i]ones de quibusdam alijs praeceptis quae a rhetoribus in arte ponuntur.* Nonne plura sunt Rhetorices praecepta, qu** [trimmed] ea, quae superius sunt proposita. Multa equidem recensentur sed partim ex ill** [trimmed] intelliguntur ... Exempla. Exempla Methodi artificiosa sunt Ciceronis Philippica 7 Phil: 8. Phil: 11. Phil: 12. Phil: 13 & 14. τῷ θεῷ Δώξα. pp. 82-98 blank

   This unidentified work consists of a series of questions and answers arranged thematically and accompanied by examples from classical authors.

Paper (unidentified watermarks similar in design to Briquet Tour 15937), pp. viii (i = front pastedown) + 220 + 98 (the codex is paginated 1-207 and 1-81) + iv (iv = back pastedown), 159 x 88 (136 x 68) mm. Written in 16-29 long lines; frame-ruled in ink, red for the first treatise, red or black for the second.
I^8 (pastedown, ff. i-vii), II-VII^8, VIII^6, IX-XV^8, XVI^6, XVII-XXI^8, XXII^{10}, XXIII^4 (4 = pastedown). Signatures on recto (Aa, Bb, Cc, etc.).
Written by two scribes in italic script; Scribe 1: pp. 1-207, Scribe 2: pp. 1-81 (second treatise). Some headings in red.
Trimming at beginning of second part has resulted in loss of text.
Binding: s. xvii. Covered in alum-tawed pigskin over pasteboards with a different panel stamp of the Passion of Christ on each. Initials "P. S." in panel on upper board. Edges colored red and green in wide crosswise stripes.

Written in Germany at the end of the 16th or beginning of the 17th century, presumably as a school text; inscription on f. i recto: "Sebastianus Hornung/ Anno Epochae Christianae/ 1603." Presented to Yale in 1945 by David D. Marsden.

Bibliography: Faye and Bond, p. 33, no. 135.

MS 136   Italy, s. XV
Giordano Ruffo, Marescalcia equorum

1. ff. 1r–2v blank; ff. 3r–35r *Marescalcia equorum secundum marescalciam domini federici Regis quondam imperatoris secundi.* Cum inter cetera animalia summo rerum opifice euidenter creata usui humani generis ... necnon totus guttur uniuersaliter grossum uel inflatum habuerit difficile subuenitur. Hoc opus conposuit Jordanus rufus de calabria miles et familiaris Federici imperatoris secundi ... *Explicit.*

   The text differs considerably from that in Beinecke MS 161.

2. f. 35r–v Recipes for curing the ailments of horses, partly written by the original scribe, in Latin; partly by a later hand, in Italian. f. 36r–v blank

Paper (watermarks: unidentified, in gutter; outer and inner bifolios reinforced with parchment strips), ff. 36, 217 x 152 (157 x 101) mm. Written in 36 long lines for ff. 3r–9r, 2 columns of ca. 31 lines for ff. 9r–36v; single vertical bounding lines. Ruled in crayon; remains of prickings in upper and lower margins. I^{20}, II^{16}.

Written by one person in round gothic bookhand; additions by a later hand.

Small plain initials, in red, mark beginning of each section; headings, paragraph marks, some strokes on initials in red.

Binding: s. xv. Sewn on two tawed, slit straps laid in a channel and nailed in square, flush wooden boards. The spine is square. Covered in reddish brown leather with corner turn-in tongues. Decorated with a blind-tooled panel of interlaced rope work and green dots in circles inside concentric borders. A catch on the lower board and a cloth strap [velvet?] attached to the upper with star-headed nails. Strap wanting, otherwise intact.

Written in Italy in the 15th century; early provenance unknown. Belonged to David Wagstaff (bookplate); presented to Yale by Mrs. David Wagstaff in 1943.

secundo folio: [la]queari debet

Bibliography: Faye and Bond, p. 34, no. 136.

MS 137
Lorenzo Rusio, Marescalcia equorum (It. tr.)

Italy, s. XV

ff. 1r-44v *Della natura dellj cauallj Capitolj .j.* El cauallo e di calda natura estimasj che sia tenperato, el calore si dimostra per la legereza ... a. iij. giornj in quantita dj due o iij lib. per ciascuna volta e fia churato// [breaks off in middle of section headed *Contra febre di chaualli Capitolj Clxiij*; the manuscript seems to have been misbound with one of the later leaves inserted as f. 2]

This anonymous Italian translation differs considerably from that published by P. Delprato, *La mascalcia di Lorenzo Rusio* (Bologna, 1867) v. 2, pp. 7-403.

Paper (brown; watermarks similar to Briquet Balance 2401), ff. i (paper) + 44 + i (paper), 285 x 212 (200 x 158) mm. Written in ca. 33 long lines, frame-ruled in hard point or crayon.

Extensive repairs to binding make it impossible to collate the codex; original quires may have consisted of six leaves. Remains of catchwords in center of lower margin.

Written in a cursive notarial script by one person who also foliated the manuscript.

Uninspired initials, alternating red and blue, the former with purple parallel penwork designs, the latter with red. Rubrics throughout.

Most leaves stained and repaired.

Binding: s. xix-xx. Limp vellum case.

Written in Italy during the 15th century; early provenance unknown. Presented to Yale in 1948 by Mrs. Samuel Milbank.

secundo folio: [f. 3] un poco

Bibliography: Faye and Bond, p. 34, no. 137.

MS 138
Juan de Sant-Fahagun; Pedro López de Ayala, etc.

Spain, s. XV^2
Pl. 21

1. ff. 1r-2v [Preface of Juan de Sant-Fahagun:] *Este es el libro iohan de sant fagun caçador de nuestro señor el rrey* ... En el nonbre del padre et del fijo et del spiritu santo dize et amonestanos el apostol ... de comò han de ser curadas por sus melezinas en el qual ay çinquenta et tres capitulos.

   Table of Contents for Book I on f. 2r-v; a second table for Books II-III occurs on ff. 55r-58r.

2. ff. 2v-80v [Text:] *Capitulo primero del falcon nebli comò se ha de rregir et governar et conosçer su plumage.* De comò deueys conosçer la fermosura del falcon por el plumage et por las façiones ... et entrepetar comò a la vestra señora plogujere

et por bien tomere. [followed on ff. 81r-87v by:] Las propiedades de la medçanas ya dichas son estas que se syguen. momjia fina. [in margin:] Caliente y seca en el segundo grado ... sangre de drago. [in margin:] Caliente en el primo grado seco en el secundo.

3. ff. 1v-77r [Commentary of Don Beltran de la Cueva, Duke of Alburquerque, in margins surrounding text:] En este libro de iohan de sant fagun fizo escriuir el muy yllustre señor don beltran de la cueua duque de alburquerque conde de huelma las espiriencias que en los falcones de su señoria espirimento ... ha muerto falcones girifaltes y sacres y neblis.

E. Lafuente and P. de Gayangos, eds., *El libro de las aves de caça del Canciller Pero López de Ayala con las glosas del duque de Alburquerque* (Madrid, 1869) pp. 171-95. Beinecke MS 138 contains a much fuller commentary than that printed in this text.

4. ff. 88r-89r [First preface of Pedro López de Ayala, *Aves de caça*:] En el nonbre del padre et del fijo et del spiritu santo amen. dizenos et amonestanos ... et señales dellos et rremedios et melezinamjentos para ellos.

J. Gutierrez, ed., *Libros de cetrería* (Madrid, 1879) v. 1, pp. 139-43.

5. ff. 89r-90r [Second preface:] Nuestro señor dios quando crio el mundo et fizo el omme todas las anjmalias ... algunas cosas prouechosas para ayuda de la dicha arte.

Gutierrez, *op. cit.*, pp. 143-46.

6. ff. 90r-91v [Table of contents:] Capitulo primero de las aues que son llamadas de rrapina asi comò açores ... Capitulo. xlvij. de quales cosas et melezinas deue andar ... et traer consigo.

Gutierrez, *op. cit.*, pp. 146-49.

7. ff. 91v-150r [Text:] *Capitulo primero de la aues que son llamadas de rrapina asi como açores falcones* ... De cada dia ujeron los ommes comò naturalmente vnas aues toman a las otras ... poluas para la vña del falcon en el capitulo xxv et son buenos para feridas de la caça.

Gutierrez, *op. cit.*, pp. 151-344.

8. ff. 150r-152r [Unidentified text, chapters i-xiiii:] *El primero capitulo es de comò deue melezinar el gaujlan et el açor* ... Dezimos asi que si el gaujlan oujere alguna enferme dar ... et vanar lo has nueve dias al ssol caliente et asi sero sano. deo gratias. f. 152v blank

Paper (watermarks: similar to Briquet Main 11154), ff. 152 + i (paper), 300 x 216 (202 x 125) mm. Written in 31 long lines; double vertical bounding lines; ruled in hard point.

The binding is too damaged to permit accurate collation.

Written by a single scribe in a neat humanistic bookhand, with a somewhat smaller script for the surrounding commentary.

Two initials (both f. 1r), the first, 5-line, for the rubric, purple with red penwork; immediately below, the second, for the text, 9-line, the upper portion red, filled with purple penwork, the lower portion purple, filled with red; attached to a thick bar border (side and lower margins) of red and purple vine scrolls in pen, with touches of light brown. One 7-line initial (f. 88r) red, with purple penwork, with exuberant loops and flourishes extending into top and side margins. Depictions of various implements, in black, within text (ff. 37v, 72v, 114r, 115r, 125r, 127r, and 137r). 3-line initials, paragraph marks, and headings in red throughout (except f. 1r, on which, in keeping with the initials, some of the paragraph marks are purple).

Binding: s. xvii-xviii. Limp vellum case; title, now illegible, on spine. Front and back pastedown and back flyleaf contain extensive Latin legal references (s. xvii).

Written in Spain in the second half of the 15th century; unidentified note (in English, s. xix) inside front cover: "This volume containing Two Treatises — Iohan de Sant Fagun de las Aves que Caçan — and Petri Lupi de Ayala de Re Accipitraria, is particularly described by Nicolas Antonio, as being in his time, in the Royal Library at Madrid, see Biblioth. Hispana Vetus, edit. Matrit., 1788, fol. vol. ii. p. 193. note. It is ascribed by Antonio to the fifteenth century." Collection of David Wagstaff; gift of Mr. and Mrs. David Wagstaff in 1944.

secundo folio: rregla

Bibliography: Faye and Bond, p. 34, no. 138.

M. G. Wynne, "Wagstaff Sporting Books and Manuscripts," *Gazette* 20 (1945) p. 11 (reproduction of f. 1r opposite p. 11).

MS 139 Byzantium, s. XV, 1606
Divine Office (in Greek)

1. ff. 1r-225v [Hymns and Prayers for the Office:] ὕμνος τριαδικὸς σὺν εὐχῇ, εἰς τὸ μεσονυκτικόν· λέγεται δὲ εἰς τὴν ἀρχὴν, μετὰ τὸ εἰπεῖν τὸν τρισάγιον. ἢ μετὰ τὸ πιστεύω εἰς ἕνα θεόν, καὶ ἔτι μετὰ τὸν τρισάγιον. ἐκ τῶν δογμάτων τοῦ ἁγίου διονισίου τοῦ ἀρεοπαγίτου, ἐκλογὴ καὶ σύνταξις θηκαρᾶ μοναχοῦ· καὶ τὸ ἰδοὺ ὁ νυμφίος καὶ ἕτερα. Δόξα τῇ ἀπειροτάτῃ καὶ παναιτίῳ καὶ ζωαρχικῇ βασιλείᾳ σου ... [explicit, in hand of Scribe 2:] Τέλος τῶν θείων καὶ ἱερῶν ὕμνων.

2. ff. 226r-315r [Canons and Laments for Vespers for each day of the week; title, in black and red:] κανὼν παρακλητικὸς εἰς τὸν κύριον ἡμῶν ἰησοῦν χριστὸν οὗ ἡ ἀκροστιχὴ θρηνῶν ἄδωσι, πρῶτον οἰκτίρμον μέλος. ᾠδὴ α, ἦχος α, ᾠδὴν ἐπινίκιον. [in margin:] τῇ κυριακῇ ἑσπέρας [text begins:] Θεὲ ὑπεράγαθε πάτερ

MS 139

καὶ λόγε καὶ πνεῦμα τὸ ἅγιον ... ἐπὶ πάντας τοὺς ἐπικαλουμένους τὸ ὄνομά σου ἐν ἀληθείᾳ· ὅτι ... ἀμήν.

3. ff. 315r-318v [Prayer for Saturday Vespers; text begins, after rubric stating occasion for use:] Ἡ χάρις σου δέδωκέ μοι τὸ λαλεῖν πρὸς σὲ κύριε ... δοξάζων καὶ εὐλογῶν τὴν ἀπειροδύναμον σου ἀγαθότητα ... ἀμήν. [colophon of Scribe 2:] δόξα σοι ὁ θεός· ἡ μου δο [remainder illegible] ἐγράφη. ζριδ. σωφρονίου ἱερομοναχοῦ.

Paper (watermarks similar to Harlfinger Ancre 67), ff. iii (paper) + 318 + i (paper), 210 x 145 (145 x 88) mm. Written in 19 long lines; single horizontal bounding lines at top, double at bottom; triple vertical at sides; ruled in hard point.

I-VIII^8, IX^8 (-5), X-XL^8. Signatures at top of first folio of each quire, recto: a cross in the center, a letter of the Greek alphabet at right.

Written in angular Greek minuscule mainly by one copyist. A second scribe, Sophronius, wrote ff. 315v-318v and made additions elsewhere; he dated the manuscript on f. 318 to 1606 (see art. 3 for colophon). Marginal notes in several hands.

Headpieces in red and black. 2-line capitals with floral motifs above and below, in orange-tinted red. Same color for 1-line capitals and to mark headings and sections of the text; many spaces for rubrics were not filled in. Punctuation added in red over the original black.

Discoloration from mold on ff. 303-318.

Binding: s. xvi. Wound sewing on three round, vegetable fiber cords laced into beech boards and frayed out on the inside of them. Beaded, colored endbands are sewn on what is probably the spine lining but are not tied down through the quires. The spine is square, with a coarse, hand-woven cloth lining extending on the inside across more than one third of the boards. Covered in dark, red-brown goatskin with the turn-ins pasted over the pastedowns. A central medallion of the crucifixion very heavily impressed in the center of the upper board within concentric borders, all blind-tooled. A barely visible different design using the same border tool on the lower board. Two strap-and-pin-fastenings, the pins in the edge of the upper board, the triple strands of the clasps laced through the lower board to the inside of the pastedown. One strand broken.

Written in Byzantium in the 15th century and supplemented in 1606 by Sophronius. Brought by Archbishop (Kurios) Manasses from Moscow in February 1668 (note on f. i recto; various other marginal notes of the 17th century also refer to Moscow). Sold by Maggs (Catalogue 542: *The Art of Writing* [London, 1930] no. 158, pp. 278-79, with plate). Acquired by C. A. Stonehill in 1936. Purchased 18 January 1937 as a gift of the Yale Library Associates.

Bibliography: Faye and Bond, p. 34, no. 139.

MSS 140-42 Latin American Collection (Sterling Memorial Library)

MS 143 Italy, s. XV^2
Tacitus

1. ff. 1r-82v   *Fragmentum. libri. undecimi. cornelii. taciti. feliciter. incipit.* Nam ualerium asiaticum bis consulem fuisse quondam adulterum eius credidit ... post lentitudinem exitus graues cruciatus afferens conuersus in demetrium. f. 83r-v ruled, but blank

   Annales XI-XVI; E. Köstermann, ed., Teubner v. 1 (1936) pp. 200-382.

2. ff. 84r-218v   *Initium* mei operis Ser[g corrected to u]ius galba iterum titus iunius consules erunt. Nam conditam urbem octigentos ... arma in germania mouit que mutianus in syria aponius in moesia flauianus in pannonia. *Finis eius quod cornelii taciti reperitur.* ff. 219r-220v blank

   Historiae I-V; E. Köstermann, *op. cit.*, v. 2 (1936) pp. 1-219.

Parchment, ff. i (parchment) + ii (contemporary parchment) + 220 (modern foliation, upper right recto, is correct through f. 110 and then continues in lower right recto) + i (parchment), 263 x 190 (171 x 112) mm., trimmed. Written in 26 long lines; double vertical bounding lines. Ruled in hard point, for the most part on the hair side, traced in lead or pale ink on the flesh side.
I-XXVII^8, XXVIII^4. Quires signed by Scribe 1 in the middle of the lower edge; by Scribe 2 in the center of the lower margin.
Written by two scribes; Scribe 1: ff. 1r-126r in a neat, slightly rounded gothic bookhand; Scribe 2: ff. 126v-218v, in a neat humanistic bookhand.
Full border, f. 1r, attributed to Nicola Rapicano (cf. Paris, B. N. lat. 12947, reproduced by P. d'Ancona, *La miniature italienne* ... [Paris and Brussels, 1925] pl. LXXXIX): white vine, infilled blue, red, and green, with white dots; framed and divided into panels by thin gold bands, the inner frame with a second band in two shades of purple, with white highlights. Outer and lower margins divided by band of fruit, in the outer margin, black with gold highlights, in the lower margin, red with green and gold highlights; divided into sections and at corners by English frets, infilled blue or green with white dots. In center of outer margin, a medallion after a classical coin or cameo, bust of a man in profile with a laurel wreath against a blue ground with fine white filigree; in center of lower margin, coat of arms of Alfonso II, Duke of Calabria, King of Naples (quarterly, first and fourth paly of 4 or and gules [Aragon], second and third argent, a cross potent sable [Calabria]), in a gold and purple quatrilobe frame, a gold diadem above, against a blue ground, as above, supported by four putti. Putti, birds (including a large peacock, center of inner margin), insects, and a bowl of fruit, symmetrically arranged in corners and around swags, often overlapping or passing behind decorative elements. Both inner and outer frame broken by text and marginalia,

suggesting that the border is a later addition. Two lines of gold capitals open the text on f. 1r. On f. 136v, a 5-line white vine initial, gold, infilled red, green, and blue, against a blue ground, of inferior execution compared to f. 1r. Two 3-line initials, ff. 25v and 40v, gold or blue with purple or red penwork; each with guide-letters for illuminator.

Binding: s. xix^{ex} or xx. Dark brown goatskin, blind-tooled with rope work interspersed with copper-colored dots in Italian style (s. xv) by Léon Gruel (active under his own name between 1891 and 1923).

Written in Naples in the second half of the fifteenth century possibly for Alfonso II, Duke of Calabria, King of Naples, as indicated by his arms on f. 1r (see T. De Marinis, *La Biblioteca napoletana dei re d'Aragona* [Milan, 1947-52] v. 4, pl. 233 of f. 1r). Bought from Maggs in 1940 with the income of the Altschul Fund.

secundo folio: inter coniugalem

Bibliography: Faye and Bond, p. 34, no. 143.
C. W. Mendell, "Tacitus: Yalensis III," *Gazette* 15 (1940) pp. 70-77.

MS 144
Tacitus

Italy, s. XV$^{3/4}$

1. ff. 1r-91v [N]am ualerium asiaticum bis consulem fuisse quondam adulterum eius credidit ... prae lentitudine exitus graues cruciatus afferente obuersis in demetrium [in margin:] Deficit multum.

   Annales XI-XVI; E. Köstermann, ed., Teubner v. 1 (1936) pp. 200-382.

2. ff. 92r-205v [I]nitium mihi operis seruius galba iterum T. uinius. consules erunt. Nam post conditam urbem octingentos ... Arma in germania mouit quae mutianus in syria aponius in moesia flauianus in parma.

   Historiae I-V; E. Köstermann, *op. cit.*, v. 2 (1936) pp. 1-219. Note on front flyleaf "Codex continet verba (Historiae. I. 67-75, et I. 86 - II. 2) quae desunt in Mediceo 68.2."

Parchment, ff. i (parchment) + 205 + i (parchment), 310 x 229 (206 x 141) mm. Written in 26 long lines; double vertical and horizontal bounding lines, full across; ruled in hard point on hair side.

I-XX^{10}, XXI^5 (structure uncertain). Catchwords perpendicular to text between inner bounding lines.

Written by a single scribe in an elegant humanistic script.
Spaces left for decorative initials and headings.
Binding: s. xix. Vellum case with brown labels on spine.

Written by a scribe who was probably active in Naples in the third quarter of the 15th century, according to A. C. de la Mare; early provenance unknown.

Discovered in an unidentified location by Joseph Martini of Lugano (notes inside front cover and on first flyleaf). Purchased by Branford College (Yale University) in 1940.

secundo folio: [sen]tentiam et scipio

Bibliography: Faye and Bond, p. 34, no. 144.

MS 145 Italy, ca. 1475
Corvinus Tacitus

1. ff. 1r–82v [Added later:] Annal. L. xi. [text:] *Nam* Valerium asiaticum bis consulem fuisse quodam adulterum eius credidit ... graues cruciatus afferente obuersis in demetrium. [at side, slightly smaller:] Hic multum deficit.

   Annales XI–XVI; E. Köstermann, ed., Teubner v. 1 (1936) pp. 200–382.

2. ff. 83r–191r [Added later:] Historiarum L. i. [text:] *Initium* michi operis seruius galba iterum Titus Iunius consules erunt. Nam post conditam urbem ... quae mucianus in syria aponius in moesia flauianus in parma. [in slightly smaller script, same hand:] gratias ago deo. f. 191v blank, except for a Greek inscription (= "The illiterate man is like a barren tree") and an erased Latin inscription, illegible.

   Historiae I–V; E. Köstermann, ed., *op. cit.*, v. 2 (1936) pp. 1–219.

Parchment (thin, good quality), ff. ii (contemporary parchment) + 191 (including 67 *bis* and 105 *bis*) + i (contemporary parchment), 261 x 192 (180 x 113) mm. Written in 28 long lines; ruled in ink; double vertical bounding lines, full across. Prickings at upper edge.

I–XXIII^8, XXIV^8 (+ 1 leaf, f. 191). Catchwords, accompanied by delicate flourishes, perpendicular to text between inner bounding lines.
Written by a single scribe in a well formed humanistic script.
Twelve initials, 7- to 2-line, at beginning of each book (2 at the beginning of the *Annales*), gold edged in black, with white-vine ornament, against a panelled ground of blue, green and mauve, with white dots, outlined with one or two thin white and one black line; ivy, drawn or pen, with triangular gold leaves or dots, projecting from corners into margins. On f. 1r, the initial includes a putto in the vinework; in the lower margin, coat of arms of Corvinus, type A (quarterly, first and fourth barry of 8 gules and argent [Hungary]; second and third gules, a lion rampant and queue-fourché argent [Bohemia]; an inescutcheon azur with raven sable holding an annulet or, with bordure or [Hunyadi family]; K. Csapodi-Gárdonyi, *Bibliotheca Corviniana* [New York and Washington, 1969] notes to pl. 49). Workmanship of fair quality; style Northern Italian?
Binding: s. xv. Sewn on three tawed, slit straps laid in channels in beech boards. The straps are pegged and the channels filled in with plaster as are the endband

grooves and the edge channels cut out for the clasps. The primary endband is plain, wound, and sewn on a tawed core and the secondary is beaded and colored. The core is laid in a groove and pegged. The square spine is given a slightly round shape by the bevelling of the boards and is lined with a tawed skin. Covered in dark, brick-red goatskin with a cusped shield azur, charged with a crow sable [Hunyadi family], in the center of each board; blind-tooled rope work, punch dots and other ornamentation gilt, gold-tooled or painted. "Cornelius Tacitus" is tooled along the head of the lower cover and is also written down the fore-edge with black ink. There are four fastenings, the brass catches on the lower board, with three of them covered over with added leather. The clasps are the same color as the cover and are reinforced with parchment. They are pegged in channels at the edges of the board, underneath the cover. The clasps and a little leather of the spine and the upper board are wanting. Described and reproduced *The History of Bookbinding, 525-1950 A.D.*, The Walters Art Gallery (Baltimore, 1957) pp. 91-92, no. 205, pl. XXXIX; cf. I. Schunke, "Vom Stil der Corvineneinbände," *Gutenberg Jahrbuch* (1944/49) p. 213, Abb. 2.

Written for King Matthias Corvinus of Hungary (1458-90; arms on binding and f. 1r), ca. 1475, perhaps by Italians at his palace of Buda. Removed from Buda by Jacob Spiegel (b. 1483), apparently when he visited the palace in 1514. Spiegel's gift in 1518 to Beatus Rhenanus (1485-1547), who used it for his printed edition of 1533. Notes of Beatus Rhenanus in the text and on f. 1r include, "Beati Rhenani sum, nec muto dominum. Ex dono Iacobi Spingellii Iureconsulti. An. Salut. M. D. XVIII. Hic liber sumptus est ex Bibliotheca Budensi..."; hence the name Budensis formerly used for this manuscript. Two inscriptions (the second badly rubbed) dated 1534 appear on last flyleaf, verso, in cursive: "Victoria Philippi Hessorum Lentgrauii restituentis Udalricum Ducem Wirtenbergensem accidit die 13 Maij Anno 1534, cedente exercitu Ferdinandi regis," and "Andreas Tasenprat Thras// et Weneslaus Prudensis [?] bd tr// hc enus fuerunt hic in re**rh// dij An: 1534 in vigilia Ascension// quae erat decimo quinto die Maij." Belonged to J.-P. Dorsner (b. 1750), who gave it to Jeremias Oberlin (1735-1806) by whom it was used in 1801 to revise J. Ernesti's edition of Tacitus (see W. Allen, Jr., "The Yale Manuscript of Tacitus (Codex Budensis Rhenani)," *Gazette* 11 [1937] p. 85). Acquired in 1805, in Strasbourg, by Sámuel Teleki (1739-1822), Lord Chancellor of Transylvania, for his library of Marosvásárhely (no. 140 A/2, square tag on spine; see *Bibliotheca Corviniana*, no. 96, p. 61). Obtained from the Teleki family in 1934 by Gabriel Wells of New York. Bought from him with funds collected by Mrs. Edward S. Harkness and a group of alumni, and presented to Yale in 1935.

secundo folio: Nam cuncta

Bibliography: Faye and Bond, no. 145, pp. 34-35.
Exhibition Catalogue, p. 235, no. 60.

W. Allen, Jr. "The Yale Manuscript of Tacitus (Codex Budensis Rhenani); Its History and Affiliations," unpublished D. Phil. dissertation (Yale, 1936).

Idem, "Beatus Rhenanus, Editor of Tacitus and Livy," *Speculum* 12 (1937) pp. 382-85.

Idem, "The Four Corvinus Manuscripts in the United States," *New York Public Library*, 1938, pp. 3-11.

Idem, "Tacitus, Histories IV, 46-53," *Yale Classical Studies* 6 (1939) pp. 31-38.

K. Csapodi-Gárdonyi, ed., *Bibliotheca Corviniana* (New York and Washington, 1969) p. 61, no. 96, and pl. 49, with extensive bibliography.

MS 146 Italy, ca. 1480
Theological and Pastoral Tracts, etc. (in Lat. and It.)

The manuscript is composed of many selections and excerpts, the organization of which is not always clear. In at least two cases the same passage is repeated (f. 69r-v and f. 76r-v; f. 86v and f. 91v).

1. ff. 1r-11v Postquam aliqua dicta sunt de trinitate dei de creatura mundi et corruptela peccati restat nunc aliqua breuiter dicere de incarnatione uerbi ... suam liberalissimam prouidentiam et prouidentissimam largitatem. Amen.

    Leaf with text missing between ff. 6-7; Bonaventure, *Breviloquium* Bk. 4; Stegmüller, *Sent.* 117.

2. ff. 12r-16v Hora est iam nos de somno surgere ad Ro. 13. Volentes aliqua de uirgine gloriosa predicare ab eius immaculata conceptione sumemus ... Hora est igitur ut a tanta cecitate surgamus.

3. ff. 17r-29r *Circha precepta decalogi secundum Alexandrum de ales.* Circa primum notandum quod preceptum est iussio uel imperium faciendi aliquid uel non faciendi ... sicut dicit dominus Diligens proximum tuum sicut teipsum.

4. ff. 29r-53r *Incipiunt quedam questiones super euangelia Quadragesime. Feria quarta cinerum.* Cum Ieiunatis nolite fieri sicut ypocrite tristes [Matt. 6. 16]. Hic queritum inter doctores theologicos Quid sit maioris meriti ... et de hoc habetur in euangelio hodierno. Expliciunt questiones introductionum euangelorum xlme. Finis.

5. f. 53r-v *Epistola Sancti Ambroxij.* Dilecte fili dilige lacrimas noli differre eas ... Vide quisquis hec legis ne quod legendo respicis uiuendo contemnas finis.

    De novae vitae institutione usually attributed to Valerius Abbas Bergidensis or to Ambrose, as in this manuscript. See PL 17. 749-52 and M. C. Díaz y Díaz, *Index scriptorum latinorum medii aevi hispanorum* (Salamanca, 1959) v. 1, no. 383.

6. ff. 53v-55r *Incipit quoddam interrogatorium seu confessionale uulgari sermone pro paruulis et alta non ascendentibus.* Incomenza vno interrogatorio confessionale in uulgare per satisfare a le persone ydiote et simplice [followed by 10 regulae and a con-

cluding section] ... Da tu la decima o sey da cordio [?] con lori. Se tu aparechiato quando fusti rechiesto.

7. ff. 55r-76v *Incipiunt interrogationes et primo circha precepta decalogi*. A tu amato dio superiore ogni cosa. A tu amato piu te medesimo che dio ... et quantum ad haec dicitur libera nos a malo et cetera....

8. ff. 77r-92r Various passages from the Bible and patristic excerpts (e.g., Cyprianus de uoluntate dei ait: Voluntas dei est quam christus fecit et docuit, humilitas in conuersatione stabilitas in fide...).

9. f. 92v Three medical prescriptions: Tempore pestis utantur hijs pillulis [Thorndike and Kibre, 1558], Pro splene, Electuarium pro catharo. ff. 93r-96r ruled, but blank

10. f. 96v Aue maria immaculata e sancta/ Dolçe madre del fiolo de dio/....
Unidentified hymn to the Virgin, in It.

11. ff. 97r-98v Various short recipes, in Lat. and It.: Aqua perfectissima da ochij, Pillule imperiales, Pillule subtiles et salse, Puluis ad sustinendum catharum, Pro voce fortificanda et restauranda, Ad retinendum et ad ingrosandum catarum, Pillule confortantes stomacum, Pillule bicherchie que tenentur sub lingua ... [4 recipes].

12. f. 99r-v Four short epistolary forms: 1. Recomendatio; 2. Forma cedule discreti fiendi; 3. Forma littere discreti; 4. Forma obedientie guardianorum.

Items 1-3 mention the place "S. Maria apud Castrumarquatum"; no. 3 also gives the date 1480. The letters seem to have been written for Franciscan use.

Paper (watermarks: unidentified bird above mountain [?], trimmed), ff. ii (contemporary parchment) + 100 + ii (contemporary parchment), 150 x 97 (100 x 68) mm. Written in 32 long lines; single vertical bounding lines; ruled in lead. I^{10} (-7, a stub foliated 6a), II^2, $III-XI^{10}$. Catchwords along inner ruling.

Written in a tiny humanistic script with many abbreviations, by a single person who added to the volume at various times.

Headings and paragraph marks, in red, for ff. 1r-92r.

Binding: wanting. Marks of wide sewing tapes and fastening straps on first and last flyleaves. Sewn on one leather and two tawed slit straps.

Written in Italy for Franciscan use probably at the "Castrumarquatum" (Arquà? There are several Italian towns by this name) mentioned in art. 12. No. 21 in the collection of W. H. H. Newman, Buffalo, New York (label on f. i recto; bookplate). Presented to Yale in 1941 by Martin Hago.

secundo folio: Circa uerbum

Bibliography: Faye and Bond, p. 35, no. 146.

MS 147 Italy, ca. 1420
Valerius Maximus Pl. 23

ff. 1r-149v *Valerij maximi dictorum factorum memorabilium ad tiberium cesarem domesticarum exterarumque gentium liber primus incipit. i. De religione capitulum primum ... Urbis Rome exterarumque gentium* facta simul ac dicta memoratu digna ... *De religione. Capitullum primum Rubrica i.* Maiores statis solemnesque cerimonias pontificum ... caput imperio clementer iminens iusto impendere supplitio coegit. Explicit liber valerij. Deo gratias. Amen.

C. Kempf, ed., Teubner (1966) pp. 1-472.

Parchment, ff. i (paper) + 149 + i (paper), 283 x 223 (170 x 112) mm. Written in 33 long lines; single (sometimes double outer) vertical bounding lines. Ruled in lead; remains of prickings at lower edge of leaf.

I-XVIII^8, XIX^5[?]. Catchwords with penwork embellishments in center of lower margin.

Written by a single scribe in a precise round gothic bookhand.

Illuminated by Cristoforo Cortese ca. 1420, according to C. S. Huter; cf. Oxford, Bod. Lib., Canon. Misc. 251 (Venice, 1424) in Pächt and Alexander, v. 2, no. 443; see also C. S. Huter, "Cortese at Oxford," *Apollo* 3 (1980) pp. 10-17. Fine historiated initial (12-line) on f. 1r, the author seated at a lectern, pink, purple, green, red, and blue foliage on a gold ground, edged in black, with delicate white highlights; an exuberant vine and foliage border in three margins; the upper margin with a bar, gold and blue, with white highlights. Eight illuminated initials (9- or 8-line) on ff. 14v, 29v, 45r, 61r, 79r, 98v, 115r, 132r in the same style, borders in outer margin. Fine penwork initials throughout, blue with red penwork or vice versa (7- to 4-line). Several lines following initials written in ornate majuscules widely spaced on every other line, filled in with sepia penwork (some left unfinished, especially near end of manuscript). 2-line initials, blue with red or red with blue penwork, less ornate than above. Rubrics missing for major text divisions; paragraph marks in red or blue.

Borders cut out on ff. 1r, 45r, and 79r, replaced with parchment, with initials and borders partially restored.

Binding: s. xviii-xix. Mottled calf case, gold-tooled.

Written in Northern Italy ca. 1420; early provenance unknown. Belonged to Prince Marco Antonio Borghese (bookplate; see P. Borghese, *Bibliotheca burghesiana* [Rome, 1842] v. 1, pp. 679-80, no. 4563). Acquired by David Wagstaff (bookplate); presented to Yale in 1943 by Mrs. David Wagstaff.

secundo folio: figulus

Bibliography: Faye and Bond, p. 35, no. 147.

E. T. Silk, "The Wagstaff Collection of Classical and Mediaeval Manuscripts," *Gazette* 19 (1944) p. 1 (reproduction of f. 1r appears as frontispiece).

D. M. Schullian, "A Preliminary List of Manuscripts of Valerius Maximus," *Studies in Honor of Ullman...*, ed. L. Lawler, D. Robathan and W. Korfmacher (St. Louis, 1960) p. 88.

Idem, "A Revised List of Manuscripts of Valerius Maximus," *Miscellanea Augusto Campana* in *Medioevo e Umanesimo* 45 (Padua, 1981) p. 712.

MS 148 Latin American Collection (Sterling Memorial Library)

MS 149 Italy, s. XV^{ex}
Xenophon, De venatione, Lat. tr. Leonicenus Omnibonus

ff. 1r–28v [Incorrect title, in a later hand:] Xenophontis de Venatione Libellus Francisco Aretino Interprete Ad Malatestam Novellum [followed by dedicatory epistle to John Tiptoft:] [N]uper legebam princeps Illustrissime. Xenephontis de uenatione libellum in quo ... [text begins:] [V]enatio et canes deorum inuentio fuit apollinis atque diane ... Verum etiam foemine quibus haec deus tradidit. Ut diana athlanta procris et si qua alia fuit. Finis.

Xenophon's *De venatione* translated into Latin by Leonicenus Omnibonus and preceded by a dedicatory epistle to John Tiptoft; *Xenophontis philosophi et historici clarissimi opera* ... (Basel, 1534) pp. 217–32.

Paper (highly polished; watermarks similar in design to Briquet Oiseau 12127), ff. i (paper) + 28 + i (paper), 210 x 140 (130 x 95) mm. Written in 22 long lines; frame-ruled in lead on one side of each bifolium, with horizontal bounding lines full across; prickings in upper and lower margins.

I^{12}, II^{16}. Catchword (first gathering) in center of lower margin; first leaves of each quire signed with Roman numerals in lower right corner.

Written in a well formed italic by a single scribe.

Spaces left for rubrics and initials.

Binding: s. xix. Paper case with paste paper sides. Rebound in Yale Conservation Studio in 1982.

Written in Italy at the end of the 15th century; early provenance unknown. Belonged to C. F. G. R. Schwerdt (bookplate; see his catalogue *Hunting Hawking Shooting* [London, 1928] v. 2, p. 355); his sale (Sotheby's, 12 Mar. 1946, no. 2253) to Goldschmidt's, from whom it was acquired by David Wagstaff (bookplate); presented to Yale in 1946 by Mrs. David Wagstaff.

secundo folio: [V]enatio et canes

Bibliography: Faye and Bond, p. 35, no. 149.

MS 150 (2 vol.) Byzantium, s. XI[1]
Seymour Gospels (in Greek)

Vol. 1:
1. ff. 1r–67v [Text begins in the middle of Matthew 5. 17] [κα]//ταλῦσαι ἀλλὰ πληρῶσαι ἀμὴν γὰρ λέγω ὑμῖν. Ἕως ἄν ... πάσας τὰς ἡμέρας. ἕως τῆς συντελείας τοῦ αἰῶνος ἀμήν. f. 68r blank; portrait of Mark on f. 68v
2. ff. 69r–115v [In gold uncials:] Εὐαγγέλιον ἐκ τοῦ κατὰ μάρκον. [text begins:] Ἀρχὴ τοῦ εὐαγγελίου Ἰησοῦ Χριστοῦ υἱοῦ τοῦ θεοῦ. ὡς γέγραπται ἐν ... καὶ τὸν λόγον βεβαιοῦντος. Διὰ τῶν ἐπακολουθούντων. σημείων. ἀμήν.
3. ff. 116r–117r [Table of chapter headings for Mark, written in red uncials:] τοῦ κατὰ μάρκον εὐαγγελίου τὰ κεφάλαια. α. περὶ τοῦ δαιμονιζομένου. β. περὶ τῆς πενθερὰς πέτρου ... μη. περὶ τῆς αἰτήσεως τοῦ κυριακοῦ σώματος.

Vol. 2:
1. ff. 1r–3r [Table of chapter headings for Luke, written in red uncials:] τοῦ κατὰ λουκᾶν εὐαγγελίου τὰ κεφάλαια. α. περὶ τῆς ἀπογραφῆς. β. περὶ τῶν ἀγραυλούντων ... τοῦ σώματος τοῦ κυρίου. πγ. περὶ τοῦ κλεόπα. [portrait of Luke on f. 3v]
2. ff. 4r–86r [Heading in gold uncials, badly rubbed:] Εὐαγγέλιον κατὰ Λουκᾶν [text begins:] Ἐπειδήπερ πολλοὶ ἐπεχείρησαν ἀνατάξασθαι διήγησιν περὶ τῶν ... ἐν τῷ ἱερῷ αἰνοῦντες καὶ εὐλογοῦντες. τὸν θεὸν ἀμήν. f. 86v blank
3. f. 87r [Table of chapter headings for John, written in red uncials:] τοῦ κατὰ ἰωάννην εὐαγγελίου τὰ κεφάλαια. α. περὶ τοῦ ἐν κανᾶ γάμου.... ιη. περὶ τῆς αἰτήσεως τοῦ σώματος τοῦ κυριοῦ. [portrait of John on f. 87v]
4. ff. 88r–147v [Heading in gold uncials, badly rubbed:] Εὐαγγέλιον τὸ κατὰ Ἰωάννην [text begins:] Ἐν ἀρχῇ ἦν ὁ λόγος. καὶ ὁ λόγος ἦν πρὸς τὸν θεόν ... οὐδὲ αὐτὸν οἶμαι τὸν κόσμον χωρῆσαι. τὰ γραφόμενα βιβλία ἀμήν. f. 148r-v ruled, but blank

C. R. Gregory, *Textkritik des neuen Testamentes* (Leipzig, 1900–1909) v. 3, p. 1173, no. 1701; K. W. Clark, *A Descriptive Catalogue of Greek New Testament Manuscripts in America* (Chicago, 1937) pp. 194–95, pl. XXXVI. For the text of Vol. 1, arts. 1–2 and Vol. 2, arts. 2 and 4, see E. Nestle and K. Aland, *Novum Testamentum Graece*, ed. 26 (Stuttgart, 1979) pp. 10–319.

Parchment, Vol. 1: ff. i (parchment) + 117 + i (parchment); Vol. 2: ff. i (paper) + 148 + i (paper). Both volumes exhibit the same physical format and were clearly bound together at an earlier date: 172 x 139 (114 x 78) mm., written in 20 long lines, ruled in hard point on the hair side before folding; double vertical bounding lines for written space, additional pairs of guide-lines in upper, lower, and outer margins (the upper pair were used for running titles, in red; the area between the two sets of lines in outer margin was used for notations; the lower pair are usually left empty); prickings consisting of horizontal slits in lower margin.

Vol. 1: I–VIII^8, IX^4 (4, f. 68 with portrait of Mark, seems to have been sewn in later, though the binding is too tight to determine precisely the composition of the quire), X–XIV^8, XV^8 (+ 1 additional leaf).

Vol. 2: I^3 (bound in separately in front of text; f. 3 with portrait of Luke), II–XI^8, XII^4, XIII–XX^8, XXI^8 (–6). There are no signatures or catchwords present in either volume.

Written by a single copyist in minuscule script, with headings and tables of chapters in uncials; writing runs through guide-lines rather than sitting on them.

Full-page portraits of Mark, Luke, and John; all are depicted on gold. Mark holds a codex in his left hand and touches his chin with the right. Luke (f. 3v, Vol. 2) writes in an open codex he is holding in his lap, while John (f. 87v, Vol. 2) holds a scroll bearing the opening phrases of his gospel. Illuminated headpieces and ornamental initials in gold with stylized foliage, before each book (except Mark); red initials at beginning of first, tenth, and twentieth lines of text. The style of decoration shows many similarities with a series of Gospel Books of the tenth through the eleventh centuries. See K. Weitzmann, exhib. cat. *L'art byzantin, art européen* (Athens, 1964) no. 334; G. Vikan, exhib. cat. *Illuminated Greek Manuscripts from American Collections* (Princeton, 1973) pp. 74–75, no. 9, fig. 14.

Bindings: Volume 1, ca. 1904. Vellum case, gold-tooled. Volume 2, 1961. Orange goatskin gold-tooled, bound by Sidney Cockerell.

Written in Byzantium in the first half of the 11th century; early provenance unknown. Vol. 1: Belonged to private owners in Serres, Macedonia. The Gospel of Matthew was purchased by Professor Thomas Day Seymour in 1903 through Dr. John Henry House, an American missionary with the Thessalonika Agricultural and Industrial Institute in Salonika. Professor Seymour then purchased the Gospel of Mark from a second, unidentified source. The two portions were bound together by him in modern vellum, ca. 1904 (bookplate of Prof. Seymour inside front cover). The volume passed to his daughter, Mrs. George C. St. John, in 1914 and was then presented to Yale by Mrs. St. John and her family in 1947.

Vol. 2: Purchased by H. P. Kraus in 1960 from Sotheby's, where it had been consigned "by a lady" (Kraus, *Catalogue 100: Thirty-Five Manuscripts* [New York, n.d.] no. 2; idem, *Catalogue 107: A Selection of Rare Books and Manuscripts* [New York, n.d.] pp. 36–37, no. 42). Bought by Yale in 1967 with the Beinecke Rare Book Endowment Fund.

The history of the reuniting of these two volumes is given by T. E. Marston, *Gazette* 42 (1968) pp. 211–14.

Bibliography: Faye and Bond, p. 35, no. 150.

Exhibition Catalogue, pp. 182–83, no. 8, pl. 2.

T. E. Conrad, "The Seymour Gospels," Private edition, University of Chicago Libraries (Chicago, 1942) [Discusses Vol. 1 only].

MS 151 Italy, s. XV^{med}
Aristotle, Ethica (It. tr.) Pl. 26

1. ff. 1r–6r [Prologue of Leonardo Bruni:] *Proemio. di. messere. lionardo. darezo. nel ethica. daristotile. tradocta. di greco in latino. et. di latino. tradocta. in. uolgare. in. firenze. ad petitione. di messere. nugnio gusmano. spagniolo.* Io ho nuouamente ordinato e libri delletica daristotile tradurgli in latino ... questi libri latini con cio sia cosa che inanzi non fussino.

2. ff. 6r–7r [Dedicatory epistle to Pope Martin V:] *Proemio. di messere. lionardo. darezzo. nel ethica. daristotile. mandato. ad papa martino.* Egli e manifesto beatissimo padre non essere cosa nuoua ... pero inanzi per discussione dessi ho iscripto certo cose.

3. ff. 7r–180v *Incomincia. il. primo. libro. del. ethica. daristotile. tradotta. da. messer. lionardo darezo. di. greco in latino. et. di latino. facta uolgare. in. firenze.* Ogni arte et ogni doctrina et similmente ogni acto et electione pare che ... sia ordinata et con che leggi et con che costumi. *Finis.* [erasure: *Finisce*] *il decimo et ultimo. libro. del ethica. daristotile.*

An anonymous Tuscan translation made for Nuño de Guzman from the Latin translation of Leonardo Bruni.

Parchment, ff. i (paper) + 180 + i (paper), 260 x 180 (164 x 113) mm. Written in 27 long lines; double vertical bounding lines; ruled in ink.
I-XVIII^{10}. Catchwords perpendicular to text between inner bounding lines, on verso. Remains of signatures in lower right corner (e.g., f 1, f 2, etc.), on recto.
Text written in a well formed humanistic bookhand by a single scribe; the rubrics, in majuscules, by another scribe who used excessive punctuation.
The decoration is by Gioacchino de' Gigantibus (see below). A gold initial, 5-line, on f. 1r embedded in white-vine ornament, extending into sides, top, and lower margin, filled in with green, red, and blue, with small section at regular intervals filled with gold; a green bird near the initial; in lower margin, an empty laurel wreath supported by putti filled later with a coat of arms (unidentified) in pen, now effaced; a few gold dots with hair-spray in brown ink. Other initials, gold, 5- to 4-line, on ff. 7r, 93v, 106v, 126r, 161v, in same manner, but with gold infilling.
Significant stains in margins of first few leaves.
Binding: s. xviii. Edges gilt. Green calf with tan, gold-tooled label.

Written in Florence by a scribe who seems to have specialized in copying vernacular texts; the rubrication is by a different scribe identifiable as "Sinibaldus C." who worked for Vespasiano da Bisticci; the codex was decorated by Gioacchino de' Gigantibus, probably in Florence before 1453 when he moved to Rome (we thank A. C. de la Mare for this information). Probably from the collection of Count Carlo Archinto of Milan (1669–1732) as suggested by the characteristic binding; Archinto sale (Paris, 21 March 1863; this catalogue not available to us). Note on f. 155r: "In the Possession of Mr. Manson/ August 31. 1809." Leighton cat., 1912, no. 9. Belonged to Coella L. Ricketts; his sale (New York, 1942, no. 37). Acquired by David Wagstaff (bookplate); gift of Mrs. David Wagstaff in 1943.

secundo folio: in que libri

Bibliography: De Ricci, v. 1, p. 651, no. 216; Faye and Bond, p. 35, no. 151.

MS 152 Italy, s. XV[1]
Cicero, Tusculanae disputationes Pl. 22

ff. 1r–66v Cum deffensionum laboribus senatorijs muneribus aut omnino aut magna ex parte ... et undique circumfusis molestijs alia nulla potuit inueniri leuatio. *Marci Tulij ciceronis Tuschulanarum disputationum liber quintus et ultimus explicit. deo gratias amen. Scriptus eugubii per Petrum visnadellum cremonensem.*

M. Pohlenz, ed., Teubner (1918) pp. 217–459.

Paper (watermarks: similar to Briquet Huchet 7682 and Briquet Monts 11719), ff. i (paper) + 66 + i (paper), 270 x 203 (200 x 105) mm. Written in 37 long lines; double vertical bounding lines, with additional single lines in upper, inner, and outer margins; upper horizontal bounding line full across. Ruled in lead; remains of prickings in upper margins.
I^{14} (-1), II^{12}, III^{10}, IV–V^{12}, VI^{7} (structure uncertain). Catchwords in center of lower margins surrounded by dots and flourishes, and preceded by red paragraph mark.
Written in fere-humanistic script by Petrus Visnadellus Cremonensis who added neat marginal notes (see contents for colophon).
Large ornamental pen-and-ink initial on f. 1r, with drawing of scribe seated at desk; foliage border, also in pen-and-ink, extends into upper and inner margins. Red penwork initials mark beginning of Books II–V; rubrics throughout. Paragraph marks, in red; many letters stroked in red, ff. 1r–14r.
Binding: s. xix–xx. Vellum stays in center and outside of quires. Rigid vellum case.

Written in Italy probably in the first half of the 15th century at Gubbio by Petrus Visnadellus Cremonensis; early provenance unknown. Tag with number "33" inside front cover. Belonged apparently to the Marquis de Bou (note on end flyleaf not verified). Collection of Henry Allen (acquired ca. 1800, bookplate); Samuel Allen sale (London, 30 Jan. 1920, no. 54) to Quaritch. Coella L. Ricketts (note inside back cover: "This ms. was in the library of C. L. Ricketts, Chicago, great collector, scholar, successful businessman, master scribe in the 19-20th centuries — extraordinary American civilized man. — Feb. 1942. Note by one who knew and understood his greatness."). Parke-Bernet sale (22-23 April 1942, no. 134, notice pasted to front fly-leaf). David Wagstaff (bookplate); gift of Mrs. David Wagstaff in 1943.

secundo folio: dicendi studium

Bibliography: De Ricci, v. 1, p. 651, no. 221; Faye and Bond, p. 32, no. 152.

MS 153 Netherlands, s. XV/XVI
Ritual (in Dutch)

1. ff. 1r–50r   *Vp onser vrauwen lichtmesse dach Ter processien. Eerst zo seit de priester dominus vobis etc.* Onder wijst bidden wy heere hu volc en dwel ke ghy vutwendelic gheest ... sekerer vryht mach dienen Ouer.

2. ff. 50r–97v   *Vp den palmsondach. Matheus.* In dien tiden Seide ihesus zinen iongheren Ghi ... [includes Matthew 26.1–27.66, Mark 14.1–15.46, Luke 22.1–23. 53, and John 18.1–19. 42] graf daer bij was so hebben zijt daer gheleidt. *Deo gracias.* ff. 88r–89v, between the selections from Luke and John, blank

3. ff. 98r–150r   *Van der cleedinghe der susteren Eerst zuntmen veni creator.* Comt scepper gheest visentere dine dienaers inwendicheit uervulle met hemelscher gracien ... gheeste. *Requiescat in.* Dy moeten rusten in vrede Amen.

4. ff. 150r–153v   *Hier volghen marien .vij. ween.* O Ghebendide maghet maria moeder gods almachtich Ic biddu duer dat nee en droufheit ... en moet werden maer tot uwen gheselscepe moet commen. Amen.

5. ff. 154r–231v   Psalter with prologue and prayers. *Hier volghet een zuuerlic bouxkin gheheeten marien sauter prologus.* Hier beghint onser lieuer vrawen sauter der salligher maghet marien der moder ons heeren...; (f. 154v) *Eermen den sauter beghint oratio.* Heere doet vp minen mont te louene dinen alder helichsten...; (f. 155r) *Oracien tot marien.* O coninghinne des hemels ontfanghe den lof zanck die ic dy met ghetrauwer herte...; (f. 156v) *Pater noster Aue maria Ps. j.* Salich es die ghene die dinen name lief hebben ... [includes Psalms 1–150]; (f. 231r) *Pater Offerande.* O hemelsche coninghinne maria ontfanct goedertierlic desen sauter ... bystandicht inde huere mijnder doot Amen.

6. ff. 231v–244v   *Hier volghen die cantiken vander saligher maghet marien.* Ic sal dÿ belyden ower de vrawe. Want duer hu es de heere ... enn vaste ghelooue die en mach niet salich werden.

7. ff. 244v–250v   *De letanÿen. Heere ontfaermt dÿ onsere Christe ontfaermt dÿ* ... [invokes Father, Son, Trinity, and the Virgin Mary by various names] commende quade periculen Ouer. *Hier hendt det sauterkin der glorioser maghet marien.*

8. ff. 250v–251r   *Een offerande vp den souter van marien.* O hemelsche coninghinne maria ontfanct goedertierlic desen souter die ic dÿ offere ... enn bystandicheit in die huere mijnder doot. Amen.

9. ff. 251r–269r *Hier beghint een deuote oufeninghe ten .vij. ghetijden van dat medeliden der glorioser maghet marien ghemaect bÿ sente bonauentura. Vp de passie christi. Te mattenenen.* Heere ghÿ sult open doen mine leppen Enn minen mont sal boodschepen dijn lof. God zijt gheneghen [3 lessons at Matins] ... ontfaermherticheit gods mocten rusten in vreden Amen. *Hier hendt date beleedt Der compassien van marien.*

10. ff. 269r–272v *De paus innocencius de vierde gheuet den ghenen die dese aue marien enn dese woorden spreken alle daghe* [rubric gives 6666 days of indulgence] ... O vlietende borne der eeuwicheit Hoe bestu dus versleghen ... [Meertens 6.293]; (f. 269v) *Men vint bescreuen det onse lieue vrauwe drie waerf riep doen ons lieue heere zijn cruce drouch Ten eersten riep zij.* O wee eenighe gheboren zone troost dijn eenighe moedere...; (f. 269v) *Die dese .v. aue marien daghlijcx leest met aendachte die weet in zinen drucghe troost ooc waert een nonne diese daghelics las vander pinen der hellen en des vagheiuer verlost.* O coninghinne der hemelen en vrawe der inghelen. Ic die ellendich en bedrucht...; (f. 270v) *Aue. Ter eeren van .x. sonderlinghe preuilegie enn duegden van maria suldi lesen .x. Aue marien daer Alexander die seste paus groote ... Deerste prudencia.* Weest ghegroedt O alder wijste enn daerste moeder ... [Sections also devoted to *humilitas, castitas, charitas, Graciarum actionis, obediencia, paciencia, paupertas, fides, martirium*]; (f. 272v) *Een buelinghe voor eenen goeden mensche om smorghens voor alle dijnc te ouffenen Oratio.* O alder helischste maria moeder gods moeder ons liefs heeren Ic beuele heden uwer moedeliker herten ... euenmensche ende ter salicheit van mijnder ziele. Amen.

Paper, ff. iii (paper) + 272 (unidentified watermarks in gutter, upper margin, trimmed; including, on ff. 90–98 [quire XII], an unidentified hand) + ii (paper), 139 x 100 (97 x 69) mm. Written in ca. 20 long lines, frame-ruled in lead. Remains of prickings in upper, lower and outer margins.

I–VI^8, VII^8 (-7, cut out after f. 54), VIII^8, IX^{10}, X–XIX^8, XX^8 (-6, after f. 152), XXI–XXXIV^8.

Written by three people in what Lieftinck calls *Littera brevitura* (cf. *Maatschappij*, pl. VI. b). Scribe 1, ff. 1r–87v and 98r–153v, writes in a large and rather careless hand; 2, ff. 90r–97v, in a small even hand; 3, ff. 154r–272v, in a large uneven hand.

Calligraphic initials, 5- to 3-line, in green or red with red or grey flourishes, often extending the length of the written area. Initials, 3- to 1-line, underlining, strokes on 1-line initials, and headings in red.

Binding: s. xvi. Original sewing on three double, tawed supports laced into the wooden boards. The spine is heavily rounded, with the sewing supports well defined by blind-tooled lines. Covered in dark brown calf with a panel of the Annunciation (similar to J. B. Oldham, *Blind Panels of English Binders* [Cambridge, 1958] pl. XI, BIB. 5), in a border of birds, animals and flowers blind-stamped on each board inside outer frames of lines. There is a brass catch on the upper board and a long, thin brass clasp on a leather strap attached to the lower with a brass plate. The leather is slightly torn at the head of the spine but otherwise the book is in fine condition, with no trace of sophistication. Front and back pastedowns from a 15th-century Latin liturgical manuscript.

Written in the Netherlands in the late 15th or early 16th century, possibly for a nunnery (see art. 3). Signature of M. De Laudegum [?] (in a cursive hand of the 16th or 17th century, on the first flyleaf), along with the words "les 4 euangille et les 7 douler". Belonged to Edward Gordon-Duff; sold by Sotheby's (16 March 1925, no. 106) to H. Stevens. Signature of William L. Clements of Bay City, Michigan (first flyleaf; described as his property in De Ricci). Purchased from C. A. Stonehill in 1942.

secundo folio: [woen]sten noch

Bibliography: De Ricci, v. 2, p. 1132, no. 7; Faye and Bond, p. 36, no. 153.

P. E. Webber, "The Need for a Closer Description of the Medieval Netherlandic Manuscripts in American Libraries: Specific Cases in Point," *Archives et Bibliothèques de Belgique* 46 (1975) p. 285.

MS 154   England, s. XII^2
Robert of Bridlington   Pl. 17

1. ff. 1r–50v   //*Propter quod tradidit illos deus in desideria* ... *Anselmus* Item uindicta. Tradidit deus ideo dicit quia nichil absque eius permissione fit ... per quod uernaculo hebreorum sermone uera et fidelia esse que scripta sunt ostendit. *Explicit epistola ad Romanos.*

    Robert of Bridlington, Catena on Romans, begins imperfectly at 1.24; Stegmüller, v. 5, no. 7382; missing Romans 9.17-21 (and portions of 9.16, 22).

2. ff. 51r–71v   *Incipit epistola prima ad corinthios cuius argumentum. l. abbreuiatio talis est. Ieronimus.* Corinthij sunt achaici. Et hij similiter ab apostolo sunt conuersi sed ... id est confirmare que predicta sunt nisi intellexerit predicationem. *Explicit epistola prima ad corinthios.*

    Robert of Bridlington, Catena on 1 Corinthians; Stegmüller, v. 5, no. 7382, 1; missing 7.39-15.44.

3. ff. 72r–96r   *Incipit argumentum secunde epistole ad corinthios. Ieronimus.* Post actam penitentiam scribit eis epistolam consolatoriam a troade ... de meritis baptistarum inuidebant. Animositates habebant quando//

    Robert of Bridlington, Catena on 2 Corinthians; Stegmüller, v. 5, no. 7382, 2; ends abruptly at 12.20.

Parchment, ff. ii (parchment) + i (paper: title page) + i (parchment) + 96 + i (parchment), 350 x 239 (268 x 181) mm. Written in two columns of 47 lines; widely spaced double upper and lower horizontal bounding lines, full across; double outer and single inner vertical bounding lines, with additional ruling between columns and at top of folio for running titles. Ruled in crayon; prickings prominent in all margins.

I^4 (-1, 2; beginning of text lost), II–IV^8, V^8 (-2), VI^8, VII^8 (+ 1 leaf after 7, f. 49), VIII–IX^8, X^8 (-1, 2, 3, before f. 67), XI–XIII^8 (+ 1 leaf at end). Single signature (.I.) on f. 2v.

Written in a neat gothic bookhand by three scribes. Scribe 1: ff. 1r-2v; 2: 3r-22v, 51r-71v; 3: ff. 22v-50v, 72r-96v.

Large elegant initial, 26-line, in red penwork, on f. 72r; smaller similar initial, 16-line, in green with red highlights, also on f. 72r; simple decorative letters, 14- and 6-line, green and red respectively, on f. 51r. Quotations from Bible and marginal notes referring to authors cited, in red. Modern illuminated title page inserted as f. iii: "Catena Commentariorum S. S. Patrum, in Epistolis ad Romanos et Corinthios. M. S. Saeculi XIV".

Binding: s. xix. Pink calf with large bosses (different on upper and lower covers) and strap-and-pin fastening. Blind-tooled.

Written in England in the second half of the 12th century; early provenance unknown. Inscription of the 18th century [?] on f. 25v: "Alexr Campbell Bookseller Carlisle". Bequeathed in 1896 by Adam Watters "Merchant Grocer" of Quebec to his son, Frank S. Watters (autograph note of the latter in library files). Purchased by Henry Fletcher from Dawson's Book Shop, Los Angeles; his gift to Yale in 1950.

Bibliography: De Ricci, v. 2, p. 1670, no. 1; Faye and Bond, p. 36, no. 154.

MS 155 Germany, s. XV^{med}
Seneca, etc.

1. f. 1r *In nomine domini nostri ihesu cristi Amen. Sanctus iheronimus de seneca in Cathologo sanctorum* [uirorum illustrium]. Lucius Annaeus Seneca cordubensis ... a nerone interfectus est.

   PL 33. 629.

2. ff. 1r-2v *Epistole senece neronis imperatoris magistri ad paulum apostolum et pauli apostoli ad Senecam. Seneca paulo Salutem.* Credo tibi paule nunciatum esse ... perpetuam animam parit ad dominum istinc properantem. Vale Seneca carissime nobis. *Expliciunt epistole.*

   Fourteen letters between Seneca and St. Paul in the same order as F. Haase, ed., Teubner (1872) v. 3, pp. 476-81.

3. f. 2v *Incipiunt* [sic] *epitaphium Senece.* Cura labor meritum ... reddimus ossa tibi. *Explicit epithaphium senece.*

   Haase, *op. cit.*, p. 482.

4. ff. 2v–6r *Incipiunt capittula supra singulas epistolas eiusdem ad lucilium prima capitula primi libri.* De colligenda ut sistenda fuga temporis et non esse ... bonum in nullo nisi in quo ratio est. *Capitula xxij. libri Expliciunt.*

22 numbered chapters, for art. 5.

5. ff. 6r–167v *Incipiunt epistole mentis Colonus et cultorum morum lucius anneus seneca et moralis philosophie emulatorum studiosissimus et beatissimo paulo apostolo mira familiaritate coniunctus ad amicum suum lucilium has morales fecit epistolas per libros distinguens mira exhortacione vitam moralem continentes. Incipit liber primus de colligenda et sistenda fuga temporis et non esse pauperem cui esse modicum sat* [sic] *est. Seneca lucilio suo salutem.* Ita fac mi lucilli vendica te tibi ... quom intelleges felicissimos [sic] esse felices. Vale. *Explicit epistularum liber amici lucij senece xxij.*

L. D. Reynolds, ed., OCT (1965) 2 v. The letters are arranged in the following order (Roman numerals refer to the book divisions as they appear in the manuscript and Arabic numbers to the letters in Reynolds): I. 1–10; II. 11–19; III. 20–28; IV–V. 29–44 (portions of letters 33–36 missing along with the beginning of Book V); VI. 45–50; VII. 51–57; VIII. 58–65; IX. 66–69; X. 70–72; XI. 73–76; XII. 77–79; XIII. 80–82; XIV. 83–85; XV. 86–87; 88 treated separately, see art. 7; XVI. 89 (divided into two letters, the second of which begins "Haec lucili uirorum optime") –92; XVII. 93–95; XVIII. 96–100; XIX. 101–06; XX. 107–19; XXI. 110–17; XXII. 118–24.

6. ff. 168r–170v *Incipit prologus in librorum senece de remedijs fortuitorum.* Hunc librum composuit Seneca nobilissimus orator ... *Explicit prologus. Incipit liber Senecae de remedijs fortuitorum ad gallionem.* Licet cunctorum poetarum carmina gremium tuum ... Vides autem quam domi sit ista felicita [sic] rara. *Explicit liber de remedijs fortuitorum annei lucij senece.*

Haase, *op. cit.*, pp. 446–57.

7. ff. 170v–174r *Incipit liber eiusdem de vij liberalibus artibus ubi docet de eis singulis quod animi* ... De liberalibus studiis quid sentiam scire desideras. Nullum ... ne hoc quidem nobis reliquerunt nihil scire. *Explicit liber annei lucij de vij. liberalibus artibus.*

Letter 88 of Seneca's *Epistolae*; cf. art. 5 (Reynolds, *op. cit.*, v. 1, pp. 312–23).

8. ff. 174r–177r *Incipit tractatus eiusdem de Quatuor virtutibus.* Quatuor virtutum species multorum sapientium studijs diffinite sunt quibus animus humanus componi ... deuitet insaniam aut deficientem puniat ignauiam. *Explicit tractatus de iiij^{or} virtutibus annei lucij Senece.*

Formula vitae honestae of Martin of Braga, C. W. Barlow, ed., *Martini episcopi bracarensis opera omnia* (New Haven, 1950) pp. 237–50.

9. ff. 177r–215v *Incipit primus liber eiusdem ad nouatum Senecam meli felicis suo declamationum. Seneca nouato senece me. fi. salutem.* Exigitis rem magis iocundam mihi quam

facilem ... bono exemplo dampnatus est proditor malo inuentus. *Explicit liber x. annei lucij Senece declamationum ad nouatum. Senecam meli filios.*

Seneca the Elder, *Controversiae*, divided into ten books; A. Kiessling, ed., Teubner (1872) pp. 57-525.

10. ff. 216r-222v *Seneca de verborum Copia. Quisquis prudentiam* sequi desideras tunc per rationem ... Turpissima iactura est que pro negligentiam sit. *Explicit Seneca de uerborum Copia. Incipit ludus Seneca//* [the next text is wanting]

For a discussion of this spurious text see Barlow, *op. cit.*, pp. 208-09.

Paper (sturdy; unidentified watermarks, much worn), ff. i (paper) + 222 + i (paper), 282 x 210 (210 x 121) mm. Frame-ruled in lead, with lines full across; prickings at upper, outer and lower edges.

I-II^{12}, III^{12} (-11), IV-XVIII^{12}, XIX^{12} (-8 through 12).

Written by one scribe in small, even cursive with some loops.

9- to 2-line initials, in red; the larger ones split. 1-line capitals stroked with red, rubrics throughout.

Binding: s. xvii-xviii. Limp vellum case with tan calf, gold-tooled label. Ribbon ties, now missing. In ink on upper cover: "1442. Epistola Senecae ad paulum et pauli ad Senecam". In poor condition; many quires detached.

Written in Germany in the mid-15th century, possibly in 1442 as noted on cover; early provenance unknown. Unidentified round paper label with "1007", on spine. Belonged to the Jesuit College at Agen (note at top of f. 1r: "Collegij Agen Societatis Jesu Catal-Ins."). Sold by Thorpe (cat. 1836, no. 1156) to Sir Thomas Phillipps (no. 9072; note inside front cover); his sale (London, 1897, lot 689) to Little. Sale by Anderson (New York, 4 Dec. 1903, no. 399) to Caxton. Presumably acquired by Adolph Lewisohn (listed in De Ricci) through V. G. Simkhovitch (see the *Catalogue of the Private Library of Mr. Adolph Lewisohn* [New York, privately printed, 1923] p. 82). Belonged to David Wagstaff (bookplate); gift of Mrs. David Wagstaff in 1944.

Bibliography: De Ricci, v. 2, p. 1720, no. 5; Faye and Bond, p. 36, no. 155.

MS 156
Lactantius, Divinae institutiones

Italy, s. XV^{med}

ff. 1r-130v *Firmiani lactantil.* [sic] *Aduersus gentiles Institutionum liber primus incipit feliciter.* Magno et excellenti ingenio uiri cum se doctrine penitus dedissent quicquid laboris poterat impendi ... iustos se esse tamen ac prudentes uideri uolent ceci et hebetes et rerum et ueritatis ignari// [ends abruptly in Book 5]

S. Brandt and G. Laubmann, eds., CSEL v. 19 (1890).

Parchment, ff. ii (contemporary parchment) + 130 + ii (contemporary parchment), 276 x 192 (178 x 116) mm. Written in 30 long lines; single vertical bounding lines; ruled in ink.

I–XIII[10]. Remains of catchwords along lower edge, on verso; signatures for first half of quire (A.1, A.2, etc.), on recto.

Written in a well formed humanistic bookhand by a single scribe who omitted Greek quotations, but did add Latin glosses in each space.

One modest and rubbed gold initial (f. 1r), 9-line, filled and surrounded by white-vine ornament on blue, green, and pink ground; gold-colored highlights added to vinework. Smaller gold initials, 6-line (ff. 34v, 62r, 120r; space left for one, f. 91v) on green, dark pink, and/or blue grounds with yellow and/or white highlights. Headings in red.

Binding: s. xviii–xix. Edges gilt, green calf, gold-tooled, with lion rampant on each cover. Rebacked.

Written probably in Florence in the mid-15th century (we thank A. C. de la Mare for the attribution). Unidentified shelf-mark on f. i recto: ΔΔΔ/III/37; note on back cover: "(6720)/ Codice del sec. XV di carte 130". (Unverified references: Leighton cat., 1912, no. 196; W. J. Leighton sale [London, 27 Oct. 1919, III, no. 2422]). Sold at Maggs (Cat. 395, 1920, no. 57 and Cat. 404, 1921, no. 64; pl. xxxix reproduces a portion of f. 1r). Purchased by David Wagstaff (bookplate); gift of Mrs. David Wagstaff in 1943.

secundo folio: disputatio. Nam

Bibliography: De Ricci, v. 2, p. 1901, no. 1; Faye and Bond, p. 36, no. 156.
E. T. Silk, "The Wagstaff Collection of Classical and Mediaeval Manuscripts," *Gazette* 19 (1944) p. 1.

MS 157 Belgium, s. XIII/XIV, XIV[2]
Aelred of Rievaulx, De amicitia, etc.

> I. 1. ff. 1r–6r *Incipit liber beati augustini de amicicia.* Cum essem adhuc puer in scolis et sociorum meorum me gratia plurimum ... Ita a sancto illo amore quo amplectitur amicum ad illum conscendens quo amplectitur christum spiritualem amicicie fructum capit. *Explicit liber de amicicia.*
>
> Aelred of Rievaulx, *De amicitia*. The treatise, an abridged compendium of the *De spirituali amicitia* which circulated from the 13th century as the *De amicitia* of St. Augustine, is printed with spurious works attributed to him in PL 40. 831–44. (See A. Hoste, *Bibliotheca Aelrediana* in Instrumenta Patristica (Steenbrugg, 1962) p. 70; *idem*, "Le traité pseudo-augustinien *De amicitia*," *Revue des études augustiniennes* 6 (1960) p. 157.
>
> II. 2. ff. 6v–7r *Liber siue Sermo sancti Augustinj de humilitate et obediencia.* Nichil deo sic placet quomodo obediencia. Cayn maledictus fuit et post multa

secula manet ... qui habet aures audiendi audiat in christo ihesu domino nostro. Amen.

PL 40. 1221-24. This work may perhaps be attributed to Geoffrey of Bath; see J. P. Bonnes, "Une des plus grands prédicateurs du XIIe siècle," *Revue bénédictine* 56 (1945) p. 175 ff.

III. 3. ff. 7v-22v *Tulij Ciceronis Lelius. Uel de amicicia liber incipit.* Quintus mucius augur multa narrare de G. lelio socero suo memoriter et vicunde [sic] solebat ... amicicia esse non potest ut ea excerpta nichil amicicia prestabilius putetis. *Finit liber ciceronis de amicicia.*

Cicero, *Laelius de amicitia*; K. Simbeck, ed., Teubner (1917) v. 14, 46c-86c.

Composed of three distinct sections, all of thick parchment ca. 203 x 147 mm: I: ff. 1r-6r (151 x 112) mm. 42 long lines; single vertical and double upper horizontal bounding lines. Ruled in lead; prickings visible in all margins except inner. Written in informal gothic bookhand by one scribe who signed the first sheets of the gathering with Roman numerals, in red. Small initial, 4-line, blue with red penwork (beading) on f. 1r; other plain initials, alternating red and blue. Rubrics throughout; many letters stroked with red.
II: ff. 6v-7r (151 x 105) mm. 2 columns of 42 lines; single vertical and double horizontal bounding lines full across. Ruled in crayon, same arrangement of prickings as in Part I. Neat gothic bookhand, with simple initial and rubric at beginning of text; first initial of each sentence stroked with red.
III: ff. 7v-22v (140 x 95) mm. Written in 31 long lines; frame-ruled in ink; remains of prickings on ff. 7-12 (as established for gathering by first scribe). Gothic bookhand by a third person who made marginal notations underlined in red.
I^{12}, II^{10}. Catchword (of third scribe) along lower edge near gutter.
Binding: s. xx. Red velvet case.

Written in Belgium in three stages: Part I at the end of the 13th or beginning of the 14th century; Parts II and III were copied in the second half of the 14th century by or for someone who already owned one treatise on friendship and who wanted two additional works on the same subject. Belonged to Guglielmo Libri; his sale (London, 28 March 1859, no. 106) to Sir Thomas Phillipps (no. 16244; note on f. 1r); his sale (London, 1897, no. 197) to Tregaskis. Collection of Walter A. Copinger, Manchester (bookplate); sale by Sotheby's (2 Aug. 1929, no. 1526) to Last. David Wagstaff (bookplate); presented to Yale in 1944 by Mrs. David Wagstaff.

secundo folio: inde suscipiunt

Bibliography: De Ricci, v. 1, p. 1901, no. 2; Faye and Bond, p. 36, no. 157.

MS 158 Italy, ca. 1450-60
Cicero, De officiis

ff. 1r-95r *M. T. C. De officiis liber primus incipit*. Quamquam te marce fili annum iam audientem ... Karissimum sed multo fore cariorem si talibus ornamentis preceptisque letabere. Deo gratias Amen. *Explicit*. Finis. f. 95v blank

   C. Atzert, ed., Teubner (1949) pp. 1-123.

   Parchment, ff. ii (parchment) + 95 + ii (parchment), 230 x 150 (148 x 88) mm. Written in 26 long lines; single vertical bounding lines; ruled in ink.
   I-IX^{10}, X^6 (-6). Catchwords perpendicular to text along inner bounding line. Written by one scribe in a neat humanistic script.
   One initial (f. 1r), 5-line, filled and surrounded by white-vine ornament on a blue, green, and pink ground, with white dots, extending into left and upper margins; gold balls and hair-sprays. In lower margin, an unidentified coat of arms (or, a chief argent with a rose [?] vert), set within a wreath supported by two putti seated on white-vine ornament, as above. Smaller initials, 2-line, in blue, throughout text (guide-letters for illuminator for each initial in brown ink, in margins). Cf. Pächt and Alexander, v. 2, no. 294: Oxford, Bod. Lib. D'Orville 161 (Florence, s. XV$^{3/4}$).
   Binding: s. xix-xx. Brown goatskin, blind-tooled, by Thebaron.

Written in Florence ca. 1450-60 (we thank A. C. de la Mare for establishing the date); early provenance unknown (unidentified coat of arms on f. 1r). Belonged to Henri Leclerc (Paris, ca. 1900; stamp inside front cover; not in his sale catalogue). Acquired by David Wagstaff (bookplate); his inscription inside front cover: "Said to be written on woman's skin" is apparently based upon a note in the library files by "J. G." written in French (19th century) which asserts that the skins of young innocent women were much prized for their fine quality. Presented to Yale in 1943 by Mrs. David Wagstaff.

secundo folio: multa uero

Bibliography: De Ricci, v. 2, p. 1901, no. 3; Faye and Bond, p. 36, no. 158.

MS 159 Italy, s. XV$^{3/4}$
Cicero, De officiis, etc.

1. ff. 1r-92r Quamquam te marce fili annum iam audientem Cratippum ... Sed multo fore cariorem si talibus monumentis praeceptisque laetabere. Finis. τελος.

   C. Atzert, ed., Teubner (1949) pp. 1-123.

2. f. 92r *Silus*[?] *Italicus in Ciceronis laudem*. Tullius gratas raptabat in agmine turmas/ ... Par decus eloquio cuiquam sperare nepotum. f. 92v miscellaneous notes

Walther, *Initia* 8719 (with four extra verses and rubric at beginning).

Parchment, ff. iii (paper) + 92 + iii (paper), 227 x 147 (147 x 90) mm. Written in 26 long lines; single vertical bounding lines. Ruled in hard point; some prickings along lower edge.
I-VIII[10], IX[12]. Catchwords perpendicular to text.

Written by one scribe in round humanistic script; a second contemporary hand corrected the text and added marginal and interlinear notes/corrections in both Latin and Greek, as well as the poem on f. 92r. One initial (f. 1r), a 5-line gold capital filled and surrounded with white-vine ornament on a blue, red, and green ground with white dots, extending into the left and top margins (cf. Pächt and Alexander, v. 2, no. 335: Oxford, Bod. Lib. Laud Lat. 48 [Rome? 1450]). Other initials 3-line capitals alternating red and blue, throughout.

Binding: s. xix. Dark purple goatskin quarter case, gold-tooled. Textured paper sides.

Written probably in the third quarter of the 15th century in Northeastern Italy (we thank A. C. de la Mare for the attribution); early ownership by a scholar familiar with Greek. Erased inscription in lower margin of f. 1r. Belonged to David Wagstaff (bookplate); presented to Yale by Mrs. David Wagstaff in 1943.

secundo folio: sint in philosophia

Bibliography: De Ricci, v. 2, p. 1901, no. 4; Faye and Bond, p. 36, no. 159.

MS 160 Italy, s. XV[3/4]
Cicero, Tusculanae disputationes

f. 1r ruled, but blank; ff. 2r-127r *M. T. C. in tusculanarum questionum libros prefatio.* Cum defentionum laboribus senatorijsque muneribus aut omnino aut magna ex parte ... Nostris quidem doloribus varijsque undique circumfusi molestiis alia nulla poterit inueniri leuatio. τέλος. f. 127v ruled, but blank

M. Pohlenz, ed., Teubner (1918) pp. 217-459.

Parchment, ff. i (parchment) + 128 (numbering does not include first leaf) + i (parchment), 200 x 138 (123 x 77) mm. Written in 24 long lines; single vertical bounding lines; ruled in ink.
I[10] (with one leaf added at beginning), II-XII[10], XIII[8] (-8). Catchwords, in lower margins, often accompanied by four flourishes.

Written by one scribe in a neat humanistic script. Marginal notations by several later scribes, one of whom supplied running titles, foliation, and headings.

One gold initial, 6-line, embedded in white-vine ornament on a green, blue, pale red, and gold ground with white dots; extends into inner margin. Many other gold initials, 7- to 5-line, on red, blue, green grounds, with yellow and white

highlights. Spaces left for rubrics that were supplied by later hand.
Binding: s. xix. Green goatskin, gold-tooled.

Written in Italy, perhaps in either Rome or Florence, in the third quarter of the 15th century; early provenance unknown. Belonged to the Rev. Edward Craven Hawtrey; his sale (London, 4 July 1853, no. 537) to Boone, who sold it to Sir Thomas Phillipps (no. 25368; mutilated tag on spine, signature inside front cover). Phillipps sale (London, 1908, no. 185) to W. J. Leighton (Cat. of mss. 1912, no. 68); his sale (London, 28 Oct. 1919, no. 2103) to Maggs (Cat. 404, 1921, no. 43). Collection of David Wagstaff (bookplate); gift of Mrs. David Wagstaff to Yale in 1944.

secundo folio: nos futuros

Bibliography: De Ricci, v. 2, p. 1902, no. 5; Faye and Bond, p. 36, no. 160.

MS 161 Italy, 1454
Giordano Ruffo, Marescalcia equorum

1. ff. 1r–2r *Tabula libri quarti de generatione equorum.* De generatione natiuitate et nutritura pullorum. Cap. j. de laqueatione pullorum. Cap. 2 ... de cognitione equorum et pulcritudine et tempora. cap. 83. f. 2v blank

2. ff. 3r–86r *Incipit liber de generatione equorum et de necessitate pullorum et nutritura. Anno domini. 1454. Pirani.* Cum inter cetera animalia uiui hominis deputata equus sit nobilius ... *De generatione natiuitate et nutritura pullorum Rubrica. Capitulo primo.* Equus debet gigni in stalone assidue studiose ac diligenter custodito ... ut subito dolore et angustia testiculorum procedat. Curantur equi restiuj si ipsorum testiculj abscindantur.

   The text differs considerably from that in Beinecke MS 136.

3. f. 86v Miscellaneous obituary notices (mostly illegible) dated ca. 1695.

Parchment, ff. i (paper) + 86 + i (paper), 200 x 140 (146 x 85) mm. Written in 32 long lines; frame-ruled in crayon; prickings at corners of written space. I^2, II–III^{12}, IV^{10}. Catchwords, with penwork decorations, in center of lower margin.

Written by Ieronimo Sandei in fere-humanistica for the introduction and rubrics, and in informal humanistic for the text (see below for scribe).

Historiated initial on f. 3r, 9-line, St. George and the dragon, curling foliage, mauve, red, and green, with gold and white and yellow highlights, on gold ground, edged in black, in a loose and painterly style. 3- and 2-line initials, blue or red with elaborate red or light purple penwork respectively. Paragraph marks in red or blue. Rubrics throughout.

Binding: s. xvii–xviii. Covered in brown leather, blind-tooled with concentric borders. Four clasp-and-catch fastenings. Modern paper pastedowns and flyleaves, the former covering an unidentified printed text in German.

Written in Pirano (near Pola) in 1454 by Ieronimo Sandei, who incorporated his name, as well as the place and date, into the penwork border decoration of an initial on f. 26r (see also article 2 above); perhaps the same scribe as *Colophons*, v. 2, no. 7181, Hieronymus de Sandellis. Obtained from Harper's by David Wagstaff (bookplate); his gift to Yale in 1944.

secundo folio: [table, f. 2] de inflatura crurium
  [text, f. 4] mansuete tractetur

Bibliography: De Ricci, v. 2, p. 1902, no. 7; Faye and Bond, p. 36, no. 161.
  M. G. Wynne, "The Wagstaff Sporting Books and Manuscripts," *Gazette* 20 (1946) p. 12.

MS 162 France, 1502
Arthelouche de Alagona, etc.

1. ff. i recto – ii recto Several notes and pen trials; f. ii verso: coat of arms (partially effaced) and inscription (see below).

2. ff. 1r–37v Sensuit ung petit liuret fait et compose par messire Artelouche de alagonne seigneur de meirargues conseillier et chamberlan du roy de cecille ... [text:] Austour et tersol naist an region chaude ... et aux mues tous le xv Jours. Et aux sors tous les xx Jours. Deo gracias. *Si finist le present liure de faulconnerie lequiel se nomme Artelouche, Escript et illumine par Moy Vincent philippon davignon Lan de grace Mil et V^c et ij. Et fust acheue en Camarges le darnier Jourt de septembre de lad* [sic] *annee. Vray luy seray Ami* [with M composed of a love knot] *Philippon*.

    Text is defective from ff. 32v–33r; leaf missing after f. 32. First printed in Poitiers in 1567; other editions date from 1585, 1602, 1604 [?], 1607, 1618, and 1621.

3. f. 38r Recipe for curing an asthmatic bird, in It. (later hand). f. 38v blank

Parchment, ff. ii (original parchment flyleaves) + 38, 175 x 126 (100 x 71) mm. Written in 26 long lines; single vertical and single or double horizontal bounding lines, full across; ruled in red ink.
I–IV^8, V^8 (-1, 8).
Written by Vincent Philippon in elegant upright bâtarde (see colophon and below).
One undistinguished miniature (f. 1r), a falconer standing on a shallow ground, with some blue tinting for sky, set between blue and red columns with gold highlights; a blue and red band above inscribed in gold: "VRAI LVI SERAI AMI." A large coat of arms on f. ii verso (possibly a later addition and now effaced) supported by two angels with a miter above, in brown ink. One blue and red initial

(f. 1r), 3-line, against a gold ground. 6- to 1-line initials throughout, brushed gold against blue or red grounds; line-endings, blue or red with gold highlights. Rubrics throughout.

Binding: s. xvi–xvii. Original sewing on three tawed, slit straps laced in and out of the boards. The spine is square. Covered in brown calf, blind-tooled with vertical lines of square and diamond shaped tools in a border of flowers in squares. Two ribbon fastenings. The upper board is broken down the center and sewn together. Half the lower board, endbands, ties and leather around the edges of the boards wanting.

Written and illuminated in Camargue in 1502 by Vincent Philippon d'Avignon who also produced Paris, B. N. fr. 2005 (1509) and Arles, Bibl. mun. 133 (1521); cf. *MSS datés*, v. 6, p. 35, pl. 159. Early inscription on f. ii verso with arms: "Francischus Fauzonus episcopus mon^{lis} Pertuis [?]"; this does not appear to be the same person who added art. 3 on f. 38r. Purchased from E. Nourry, Paris, by David Wagstaff; his gift to Yale in 1944.

Bibliography: De Ricci, v. 2, p. 1902, no. 8; Faye and Bond, p. 36, no. 162.
J. Thiébaud, *Bibliographie des ouvrages français sur la chasse* (Paris, 1934) v. 1, p. 46.

MS 163 England, s. XV^{med}; XIV
Wagstaff Miscellany (in Lat. and Eng.) Pl. 20

I. 1. ff. 1r–14v   Apud Romam fuit quidam imperator qui dioclicianus vocabat uxorem duxit et ex illa vnum filium genuit ... [ends with the tale bearing the rubric *Narracio filij imperatoris*:] ... Ipse nos ab omnibus insidijs malefactorum defendat et det nobis et ad finem venerabilem attingere valeamus. Amen. *Explicit Whittokysmede* [? rubric has been partially effaced].

Historia septem sapientum Romae; Beinecke MS 163 begins in a manner similar to G. Blomquist, ed., *Schacktavelslek och Sju vise mästare* (Stockholm, 1941) pp. 265–92.

2. ff. 14v–15v   Medical recipes, charms and prognostications, in English and Latin, including: A medicine for a ffelon approvyd, Optima medicina pro palesye probatus est, Bona medicina pro ouibus que patiunter þe pokks the Rede evyll and the clayfykes, Medicina bona pro flewme, Prouerbium bonum secundum antiquos.

3. ff. 15v–16r   Coniuracio contra latrones. Almyghty god in trenite fadir and sone and holy gost ... Ihesu lorde grannte me this as wysse as þu art in hevyn blisse Amen. [followed immediately by Latin prayers:] Saluator mundi salua me qui per crucem tuam...; Ihesus nazarenus Rex iudeorum fili dei miserere nobis....

For the charm against thieves see IMEV, no. 242.5; C. F. Bühler, "Middle English Verses against Thieves," *Speculum* 33 (1958) pp. 371-72; J. D. Vann, III, "Middle English Verses against Thieves: A Postscript," *Speculum* 34 (1959) pp. 636-37.

4. ff. 16r-23r   *De modo* [tenendi] *parliamentum.* Hic describitur modus quomodo parliamentum Regis Anglie et Anglorum suorum tenebatur temporibus Regis Edwardi filij Ethelredi Regis ... [ends abruptly with the rubric:] *Cancellarius per mandatum Regis respondit quod protestacio illa irrotulari debet in parliamento* [corrected from parliamentum] *autoritate parliamenti cum autem sicut fuit tempore suo et temporibus progenitorum et modo ampliori etc.*

N. Pronay and J. Taylor, eds., *Parliamentary Texts of the Later Middle Ages* (Oxford, 1980) MS c of Recension A, pp. 67-72, 197-201; the final two portions of the text are in Middle English.

5. f. 23r-v   Medical recipes, in English, including: A meddyson ffor a Wonde þt suellyth or þt ys ffusterd, A mettyson for the hert suellyng, For to Restore þe lyuyr, For þe Wynde yn þe Stomake, For þe dropsy, A good Salve, For the eyes.

6. ff. 24r-28v   *Incipit liber distincionum* [?] *secundum Aristotulum. Ianuarius.* Qui natus fuerit in signo aquarij est honoratus in vno tempore sanitatem in alio tempore infirmitatem ... [ends in December:] *et venus mali vero dies mars mercuria veste nigra vtatur. Explicit. Explicit. Explicit.*

Thorndike and Kibre, 1209.

7. f. 28v   Dies nabugodonosor Regis omnis enim populus tradebat ei sompna que videbat ut solueret Daniel propheta ... luna xxx^a infra tres dies videns quod sompniasti. *Expliciunt lune distinccionum.*

From the interpretation of dreams attributed to the prophet Daniel, cf. *Lyell Cat.*, p. 89, and Thorndike and Kibre (under Daniel).

8. f. 29r-v   *Nota.* Ryght as poverte causeth sobrenesse/ ... [IMEV, 2820]; *Nota bene.* The Wyse man his sone forbede ... [IMEV, 3693]; *De versibus Salerni.* Anglorum Regi scripsit tota scola salerni/ ... [S. De Renzi, ed., *Collectio Salernitana* (Naples, 1852) v. 1, p. 445, lines 1-5; followed by selected verses on eating, drinking and digestion].

9. ff. 30r-31v   O scacci camera locus est mirabilis ille/ ... In qua si danda desint chekemata patebit. Explicit.

R. L. Poole, "Verses on the Exchequer in the Fifteenth Century," *English Historical Review* 36 (1921) pp. 58-67.

10. f. 31v   Medical recipe, in English, For the palsy.

11. f. 32r-v   [Index to art. 12:] De generatione et natiuitate et nutritura pullorum/ De laquiacione ... De nutritura.

12. ff. 32v-49v   [Preface:] Cum inter cetera animalia vsui hominis

deputata equs sit nobilius ... [text:] *De generatione et natiuitate.* Equs debet gingi a stallone assidue studiose et diligenter custodito ... a carne separato cum spatula cato imponatur ita foramen catonis in medio scissure fit.

Giordano Ruffo, *Marescalcia equorum.*

13. f. 49v   Medical recipe, in English, in a later hand: For an hors that hath the malanndyr.

14. ff. 50r–55v   Carefully organized selections on the care of horses, beginning: "Take a lyne and leye hit to the louest here above the hoof and so alonge up to the legge" and including advice on the following topics: For to knowe hov þt a colt schalle preve in Wexying, For to knowe a hors and for to knowe Wyche propirteys þt be best þt longeth to a hors old or yonge, A sadde Sorell is best next, A ppulle grey is next best; ... For to tame a Wilde hors, For to teche a hors Ambyll, For to make a hors to folowe his maister, For make a hors to seme yonge, For to make a horse ffatte; ... For a kanker yn the Wedeissond, For the morning of the chyne.

15. f. 55v   Medical recipes for horses added by a later hand, in English, including: For to breke the Glaunders, For þe wynys, A medyson to breke a boche [*sic*] w^{t}yn vj yorsse, A medyson to hele the paynnys that growyth in a horsse hellys, A meduson ffor þe Glandurs.

16. ff. 56r–57r   [Index to art. 17:] Here bygynnyth the chapters of divers makyng and dy3tyng of potagis and flesch ... Canabens/ Canabens with bacon/ ... Hote mylke of almondz/ Colde mylke of almonndz.

17. ff. 57r–76v   Take caules and stryp hem from the stalkes and betes borage anans vyolet malues parsely ... [ends in section with rubric *Colde mylke of almondys*:] till they be hard and serve hem forth yn another disch with the mylke. *Explicit.*

According to C. Hieatt, who intends to edit these recipes, the text in MS 163 corresponds most closely to those in London, B. L. Sloane 7 (ff. 93v–111v) and 442 (ff. 6r–25v), but neither of these is as full. This list of ca. 185 recipes includes some devoted to: Caboches, Hare in cyve, Conyngys in clere brothe, Chykens in bruett, Pyke in sauce, Salmon rostyd in sauce, Creme boyled, Perys in composte, Peyrs in syrypp, Colde bruet of rabets, Quayle rostyd, Storgeon, Perche boyled.

18. ff. 76v–82v   *Here may men se þe vertues of herbes* which ben hoot and which been coold and for how many thinges they be gode. Quynte foyl and .v. leef ... [text concludes with two recipes *For þe scabbes*, the second of which is:] Vngatur ungento salso in palmis ... et debebitur scabies sicca.

For an edition of the text from a different manuscript tradition see P. Grymonprez, ed., *Here Men May Se the Vertues off Herbes* [Oxford, Bod. Lib. 483] in *Scripta* 3 (Brussels, 1981); H. Hargreaves, "Some Problems in Indexing Middle English Recipes" in *Middle English Prose: Essays on Bibliographical Problems*, ed. A. S. G. Edwards and D. Pearsall (New York, 1981) pp. 91-113. This same treatise also appears in Yale Medical Library MSS 27 (unfoliated) and 40, ff. 62r-66r.

19. ff. 82v-99r   Collection of medical recipes, beginning with the head and continuing downwards, followed immediately by remedies for wounds.

20. ff. 99r-101v   Incipit liber de diuersis aquis [brief table of chapters on f. 99r:] De aqua preciosa herbarum/ Aqua preciosa de radicibus herbarum/ ... For to make aqua vite yn the beste maner. Tractus mirabitur aquarum quem compuit petrus hispanius ... [text begins:] *Aqua mirabilis ad visum conseruandum ... and all thes thynges wittnesseth ypocras. Explicit.*

Petrus Hispanus, *Tractatus mirabilis aquarum*; Thorndike and Kibre, 119. Text begins in Latin and changes to English after the recipe *Ad partum mulieris*; thus only the final section is in English.

21. ff. 101v-102v   Miscellaneous medical recipes, in English, including: A fayr medysyn aʒenst pestylence, A fayre medyson aʒenst þe axcesse, A medysyne ffor þe bryst yevyll, A medson prouyde ffor þe schakyng off þe axsys, A medyson ffor the laske [two recipes], For the palssye.

22. ff. 103r-112v   Here begynnyth the Boke of astronomye conciued and ymade of the wyseste philosoferes and Astronomyers that euyr were ... hir good dayes ben moneday thursday and Fryday tuysday and Saturday euyll. *Explicit.*

This treatise on astronomy is a common one, often found in collections of scientific writings (e. g., it appears in London, B. L. Royal 17 A. xxxii). There is also an abbreviated version in San Marino, Huntington Library HM 64 (ff. 52r-61v) which is apparently similar to that printed by J. Krochalis and E. Peters in *The World of Piers Plowman* (Philadelphia, 1975) pp. 3-17 [from Cambridge, University Library Ll. 4. 14].

23. f. 113r   Tot vides gentes que sunt auersa loquentes/ Per totum mundum nescio ... Fama repleta malis per vicibus volat alis. *Explicit.*

Unidentified poem, in 34 verses.

24. ff. 113v-115r   Various short selections (e. g., the 10 ages of man, 15 signs of judgment day, 4 elements of the world, 7 joys).

25. ff. 115r-122v   Augustinus in libro de fide ad petrum dixit miraculum est quid arduum vel insolitum super facultatem hominis ... [mentions the date 16 Dec. 1323, the city Alesti, and Frater Johannes Gobi] residuum penitentis sue compleuit in purgatorio. *Requiescant anime fidelium in pace.*

De spiritu Guidonis; for the English version see G. Scheich, ed., "The Gast of Gy," *Palaestra* 1 (Berlin, 1898) pp. i-lxviii and 1-230. The Latin version also occurs in Zurich, Stiftsbibliothek MS Car. C 110, ff. 59r-66v, and San Marino, Huntington Library HM 28174, ff. 144v-151r.

26. ff. 122v-124r   Wine recipes, in English, including: For Wyne þt begynneth to boyle aȝen, For Wyne þt is longe and ffatte in the mouthe to make hit shorte, For Wyne þt is to Grene, For Wyne þt Wolle notte hold colour, For Wyne þt is ffoyste, For Wyne þt saveryth of the vessell as it Were rotyn, For to make of reede Wyne White, For Wyne þt hath lost his myght wyth travayle, For to amende wyne þt is sowre. Followed by a short passage beginning "Mundus modo ponitur totus in errore/ Ratus non diligitur a suo genitore/...".

27. f. 124r-v   Medical recipes, in English, including: Water for the yes, An nother for the Clensing of the yes [and another], Fayr medycyne aȝenst pestylence, And Fayr medycyne aȝenst the axcesse.

28. ff. 125r-134r   Thu that art a gentilman/ And gentilmanys game wylt lere/ ... [second part, beginning on f. 131v:] Now of gosehauk kepying I have ȝou tolde ... I pray to god bothe nyȝth and daye/ Alle fauconerys he saue fro drenkelyng Amen. *Explicit modus occupandum* [?]. [Followed by a "medicen for the pooke" in another hand.]

A poem on hawking: IMEV, 3693; B. Danielsson, "The Percy Poem on Falconry," *Stockholm Studies in Modern Philology* 3 (1970) pp. 5-60.

29. ff. 134v-178v   [Index:] Here bygynnyth the table of the chapytres that bethe conteynyd yn the boke of huntyng the weche ys callyd maister of game ... the hare and of hys nature/ of the hert and of his nature/ ... [prologue, f. 135r:] To the honoure and reuerence of ȝou my worshupfulle and drede lorde h.... [text, f. 138v:] The hare is comyn beste ynow and there fore me nedyth not to telle of here ... comyn strakying as ys aboue deuysed ordeigned and also pleyndly ynow I seyde and rehersed. Laus tibi sit christo ihesu liber explicit iste. *Explicit*. [Horn signals marked in red on ff. 171r-178v.]

Edward, Duke of York, *Master of Game*; W. A. and F. Baillie-Grohman, eds., *The Master of Game by Edward, Second Duke of York* (London, 1904). For a modernized edition of the Prologue see J. McDonald, *The Origins of Angling* (New York, 1963) Appendix A, pp. 251-58.

30. f. 179r   Medical recipe, in English, "for tympanyetes".

31. ff. 179r-183v   *Confessio*. I knowlich me to my lorde ihesu cryst and to his blessid moder oure ladi seynt marie and to all his seyntis and to the prest my gostly fader of all thatt ych haue trespassed ... ye shul nott excuse your selfe butt lame you and telle the naked trowthe.

For similar forms of confession see P. S. Jolliffe, ed., *A Check-list of Middle English Prose Writings of Spiritual Guidance* (Toronto, 1974) pp. 69-73;

P. Revell, ed., *English Prayers and Meditations: A Descriptive List of Manuscripts in the British Library* (New York, 1975) nos. 346-48. This confession appears to be an abbreviated version of one found in Beinecke MS 317, ff. 42v-50v.

32. f. 184r   Medical recipe, in English: "To make oyle Exceter [?]" for various remedies.

33. f. 184v   Miscellaneous notes and verses, in Latin; including: Meum est propositum in taberna mori ... [lines 1-6 only; L. Laistner, E. Brost, W. Bulst, eds., *Carmina Burana* (Heidelberg, 1974) pp. 116-19]; Qui uult esse bonus frater bibat semel bis ter quater ... [Walther, *Initia* 15745].

34. ff. 185r-186r   Lists corresponding to those in *The Booke of Hauking huntyng and fysshyng*, attributed to Dame Julianna Berners (London [1561]). "The Companyes of beastes and foules" followed by "Termes to speake of brekyng or dressyng of diuers beastes and foules, etc.". See also the modern edition of W. L. Braekman, *"The Treatise of Angling" in the Boke of St. Albans (1496)* in *Scripta* 1 (Brussels, 1980), and R. Hands, *English Hawking and Hunting in the Boke of St. Albans* (Oxford, 1975).

35. f. 186r-v   Seven lines of English verse on hunting: "An herte if he chased he woll desyre/..."; "A meddyson for þe stoune yprouyde"; nine lines of Latin poetry [incomplete?] concerning the Judgment of Paris: "Pallas Iuno Venus nemorosem vallibus Ide/..."; four-line English devotional prayer: "Sitte [?] hathe wonder that reason nat telle canne/..."; ten-line poem in Latin: "Sunt tria que vere faciunt me sepe dolere/..." [Walther, *Initia* 18886]; recipe for a sick horse [without heading]; recipes "For a hefy purgacyon" and "A medicine for the fflyxe".

II. 36. ff. 187r-193r   [Written perhaps a century earlier than the rest of the text] Lists of emperors, kings, and archbishops and their sees. They appear to have been compiled in 1288 (the date 20 November 1288 occurs on f. 193r), but the date of writing is probably mid-14th century. Composed of 10 leaves (-5, 9, 10) added later.

37. f. 193v   Yhesu lorde þt maydyst me and wt thy precyus blode hast bousthe ... helpe me lady and all myne and shelde vs all fro hell pyne.
   Hymn of Richard de Caestre; IMEV 1727.

Parchment composed of 2 parts, both of uneven quality, ff. 193:
I. ff. 1-186. 291 x 200 (217 x 135) mm. Written in ca. 31-44 long lines or lines of verse; frame-ruled in hard point. I^8, II^6, III^{10} (-1, after f. 14; lower part of 8, f. 21, cut off), IV^6 (-1, after f. 23), $V-VI^4$, $VII-VIII^6$, IX^{10}, X^8, XI^6, XII^8, $XIII-XIV^6$, XV^{10} (lower part of 10, f. 102, cut off), XVI^6, $XVII-XVIII^8$, XIX^4, $XX-XXI^6$, XXII^8, $XXIII-XXVIII^6$. Catchwords below written space at right, with blue or red line on 2 sides. Quires V-VIII signed below catchword by original

scribe (signed as II–VIII, with the present quire VI marked iiij at beginning and v at end). Written in Anglicana, by 2 main scribes, with abundant notes and texts added in margins and blank spaces by other hands. On ff. 179r–181r the scribe begins in Anglicana formata but lapses into a more cursive grade. Initials (3- and 2-line), underlining, rubrics and slashes at ends of sentences in red. From ff. 103r–140v, 3- and 2-line initials in blue with red penwork and long flourishes; on ff. 30r–31v (on the exchequer), checkerboards in blue, red and black in upper and lower margins. Water stains on ff. 1–2, only affecting a few words of the text.

II. ff. 187–193. 255 x ca. 165 (209 x ca. 155) mm. Written in 3 columns of ca. 35 lines; ruled in lead, single or double vertical bounding lines at left side of each column, single horizontal bounding lines, no guide-lines for text. One quire of 10 (-5, 9, and 10, after ff. 190 and 193). Written by one scribe in an uneven 14th-century Anglicana. Three-line initial on f. 187r not filled in. Outer column of f. 187 cut off.

Binding: s. xvi–xvii. Limp, flush boards are made up of fibrous, felted material [paper?] sandwiched between two layers of vellum, which extend across the spine. This case is glued and tacketed to the bookblock with three tackets consisting of at least six threads each. Stitches go through the spine linings around three threads at head and tail. Covered with tawed skin, originally pink, the turn-ins glued over the pastedowns. The cover extends in fore-edge and envelope flaps. Some rodent damage on the upper board and part of the envelope cut away. Discoloration and traces of adhesive on three outer edges of envelope flap.

According to J. J. Smith the Middle English in Beinecke MS 163 lies somewhere between " 'colourless' regional writing" and "writing with a regional basis which includes forms from Chancery Standard" (see M. L. Samuels, "Spelling and Dialect in the Late and Post-Middle English Periods," in M. Benskin and M. L. Samuels, eds., *So meny people langages and tonges: Philological Essays in Scots and Mediaeval English Presented to Angus McIntosh* [Edinburgh, 1981]); a number of non-standard, dialectically restricted forms suggest the Southwest Midlands as a probable area of provenance. Part I of the codex written in England in the mid-15th century. The name "Whittokesmede" occurs in red on ff. 59r and 101v, and has been effaced from f. 14v; the same hand wrote "Explicit" at the end of several sections. The final quire, written probably in the 14th century, was bound in with the first 186 ff. in the 16th or 17th century. Early provenance unknown, but the codex shows signs of heavy use: there are extensive early additions and marginal notations (e. g., regarding the efficacy of the recipes). Probably belonged to Henry Percy, 9th Earl of Northumberland (1564–1632), of Petworth House; sold by his descendant, Lord Leconfield (Sotheby's, 23–24 April 1928, no. 84). Bought by Edwards. Belonged to David Wagstaff (bookplate); gift of Mrs. David Wagstaff in 1943.

secundo folio: quod si eam

Bibliography: De Ricci, v. 2, pp. 1902–03, no. 9; Faye and Bond, p. 36, no. 163.

A. A. Horwood, "Manuscripts of the Right Honourable Lord Leconfield, at Petworth House, Co. Sussex," Great Britain, *Historical Manuscripts Commission Report No. 6* (London, 1877) item 8, p. 289.

E. T. Silk, "The Wagstaff Collection of Classical and Mediaeval Manuscripts," *Gazette* 19 (1944) pp. 1-9.

MS 164   Italy, s. XV
Cornelius Nepos

ff. 1r-89r   *Emilius probus de Illustribus ducibus exterarum gentium.* Non dubito fore plerosque Attice qui hoc genus scripture leue et [added in a later hand: non] satis dignum ... Sepultus est iuxta uiam apiam ad quintum lapidem in monumento Q. cecilij auunculi sui. [followed by a table of contents on f. 89v:] Emilius probus de Illustribus ducibus exterarum gentium. Melciadis atheniensis uita ... Pomponij attici uita et mores.

P. K. Marshall, ed., Teubner (1977) pp. 1-101; *idem, The Manuscript Tradition of Cornelius Nepos* in Bulletin Supplement — University of London Institute of Classical Studies no. 37 (London, 1977) p. 70.

Paper (unidentified watermarks in gutter), ff. iii (paper) + 89 + ii (paper), 203 x 143 (129 x 82) mm. Written in 25 long lines; single vertical bounding lines. Ruled in lead for vertical lines, ink for horizontal; prickings in lower margins.

I-IV^{16}, V^{24} (+ 1 leaf tipped in at end, f. 89). Catchwords in center of lower margin; leaf signatures in lower right corner, on recto (a 1, a 2, etc.).

Written in round humanistic script for ff. 1r, 89v, running titles, and chapter headings; in informal humanistic for ff. 1v-4v, and in a style in between the two for ff. 4v-89r.

Plain initials, in bright red, mark text divisions; headings and running titles, in dull red, throughout.

Binding: s. xix. Dark purple calf, gold- and blind-tooled.

Written in Italy in the 15th century; early provenance unknown. Sold by Leighton (Cat. II, 9 [ca. 1925] no. 300); notice pasted on f. ii recto of J. T. Adams sale (London, 7 Dec. 1931, no. 64); Dobell (*The Ingatherer*, no. 22, Feb. 1932, no. 6). Unidentified rectangular tag with "73" inside front cover. Belonged to David Wagstaff (bookplate); gift of Mrs. David Wagstaff in 1944.

secundo folio: cognitum

Bibliography: De Ricci, v. 2, p. 1903, no. 11; Faye and Bond, p. 36, no. 164.

MS 165
Terence, Comoediae

Italy, s. XV$^{3/4}$
Pl. 27

See R. Kauer and W. M. Lindsay, eds., OCT (1926) for arts. 1-6.

1. ff. 1r-19r   *Publij Tirentij Afri Andria incipit. Natus in excelsis tectis cartaginis* ... leget sic puto cautus erit [Walter, *Initia* 11627]. *Prologus. Sororem falso* ... coniugem. *Argumentum. Poeta cum primum animum ad* scribendum appulit id sibi negotij ... si quid est quod restat. Vos ualete et praudite [*sic*]. Ego caliopius recensui. *Publij Terenthij Afri Andria explicit.*

2. ff. 19r-40r   *Eunuchus feliciter incipit. Acta ludis Megelensibus* ... *Meretrix adolescentem* cuius ... inluditur. *Sororem* falso dictam ... audiente parmenone seruo suo. *Prologus*. Si quisquam est qui se studeat placere bonis ... Ite hac, vos valete et plaudite ego caliopius recensui.

3. ff. 40r-60r   [*Heautontimorumenos*] *Acta ludis megalensibus* ... *Argumentum. In militiam profisci gniatum* ... clitipho uxorem accipit. *Prologus. Ne cui* sit uestrum mirum cur partes seni poeta dederit ... fiat. Vos valete et plaudite caliopus recenssui.

4. ff. 60r-77r   *Pvblij Terrentij Afri Incipit adelfos. Acta ludis funebribus* ... *Duos cum haberet* Demea adolescentulos ... patre duro demea. *Prologus*. Posquam [*sic*] poeta sensit scripturam suam ab iniquis ... Istuc recte est. Valete....

5. ff. 77r-93r   [*Hecyra*] *Acta Ludis Romanis* ... *Argumentum. Uxorem duxit Pamphilus* phylomenam ... pamphylus cum filio. *Prologus*. Hechyra est huic nomen fabule hec cum hec data est ... ante hunc diem umquam valete et praudite....

6. ff. 93r-112r   *Acta Ludis Romanis* ... *Formio. Cremetis frater* aberat peregre ... a patruo agnitam. *Prologus. Postquam poeta* vetus poetam non potest retrahere a studio et tradere hominem socium ... Iam faxo aderit. *Vos valete* ... *Finis. Finis.*
   f. 112v blank

Parchment, ff. i (paper) + i (parchment) + 112 + ii (parchment) + i (paper), 195 x 120 (130 x 73) mm. Written in 31 long lines; double vertical bounding lines; ruled in ink.

I-X^{10}, XI^{12}. Catchwords along lower edge of verso near gutter; remains of leaf signatures, in red, on recto.

Written by a single scribe in well-formed italic.

On f. 1r an elaborate floral border, with large bulbous flowers and broad leaves in blue, red, yellow, and green sprouting symmetrically from tall stalks, with birds, dogs, putti, and harpies in pairs; in the lower corners two busts softly modelled of a man (profile) and woman (3/4 view) on blue grounds and lobed gold frames; in lower center a wreath for a coat of arms (effaced) supported by two putti, the entire border filled with gold dots and fine brown hair-spray. Also on f. 1r, two 6-line initials in gold, with white-vine ornament infilled with pink and green, on blue grounds decorated with white dots; and one 3-line initial in gold, filled with pink and green, on a blue ground. 4- to 2-line initials in blue.

Lower part of f. 112 (with colophon?) cut off, and replaced with modern parchment.

Binding: s. xix. Brown diced calf, blind- and gold-tooled.

Written in Florence ca. 1465-75 by a scribe who also wrote Oxford, Bod. Lib. D'Orville 161 (we thank A. C. de la Mare for this information); effaced arms of early owner on f. 1r. Unidentified shelfmark inside front cover: "II: C: 164". No. 331 in a sale catalogue. Unknown Sotheby sale: partially erased note on front flyleaf has not been completely deciphered "15 May 19 [?]". Belonged to Charles Butler; his sale (London, 19 July 1921, no. 522) to Edwards. J. T. Adams sale (Sotheby's, 8 Dec. 1931, no. 270) to Davis and Orioli (cat. 56, Feb. 1932, no. 236) from whom it was purchased by David Wagstaff. Gift of Mrs. David Wagstaff in 1943.

secundo folio: iusta et clemens

Bibliography: De Ricci, v. 2, pp. 1903-04, no. 12; Faye and Bond, p. 36, no. 165.
  E. T. Silk, "The Wagstaff Collection of Classical and Mediaeval Manuscripts," *Gazette* 19 (1944) p. 1.

MS 166 Italy, s. XV^1
Statius, Thebais, etc.

1. f. 1r Various notes and pen trials, including "Dic mihi quid feci nisi non sapienter amaui" and "Duc manum leue si uis scribere bene." The central portion of the page gives, in another hand, three lines of text with astrological rules concerning the nature of the signs of the zodiac and their correspondence with the planets. The three lines are followed by a chart/horoscope, or Nativity, of the standard form, which was probably drawn at Padua in the 15th century (inscription in center of chart: "Ad meridianum patauii per astrolabium raptim factum"). This horoscope is difficult to date because of the variations from the traditional usage of one sign for each house whereby one can reckon the given figures for each planet in right ascension. (We thank R. Lemay for his assistance with this art. and the following one.) f. 1v blank

2. f. 2r Full-page detailed phlebotomy table according to astrological rules. ff. 2v-4v blank

3. ff. 5r-173r [F]raternas acies alternaque regna profanis/ decertata odiis sontesque euoluere tebas/ ... Mox tibi si quis adhuc pretendit nubila liuor/ Occidit et meriti post me referantur honores. Sursuli papinii statii liber Tebaidos xii explicit.

    Statius, *Thebais*; A. Klotz and T. C. Klinnert, eds., Teubner (1973) pp. 1-475; the text is accompanied by extensive marginal and interlinear glosses, some lost due to trimming (see R. D. Sweeney, *Prolegomena to an Edition of the Scholia to Statius* [Leiden, 1969] p. 28).

4. f. 173v [Two summaries, in verse, of the *Thebais*, the second of which also appears in the lower margin on f. 5r:] 1. Uoluitur in primo fratrum concordia libro/ denegat et fedus repetit que regna secundus/ ... Vltimus oggigias dat tesea uincere tebas. 2. Associat profugum tidea primus polinicem/ Tidea legatum mictit insidias que secundus/ ... Argiam flentem memorat duodecimus ignem. [Walther, *Initia* no. 1630]

5. f. 174r [Unidentified poem (28 verses):] [?]ic fontis breuis unda latens demersa tenetur/ Ignote et uigiles esse putantur aque/ ... Et oportet fortare uoca coripe disce mone. f. 174v blank

6. f. 175r Complete tabular alphabet of Greek and Latin equivalents, including diphthongs. Followed by some verses in Italian, and some that are Italian transliterated into Greek. ff. 175v–177r blank

7. f. 177v Large pen-and-ink drawing of a knight in armor, surrounded by various notes, e. g., "Sepe rogare, Rogata tenere, Retenta docere: Hec tria faciunt discipulum superare magistrum."

Paper (watermarks: similar in design to Harlfinger Ciseaux 43, for ff. 1–4; Briquet Cercle 3134 and unidentified fleur-de-lis, for remainder), ff. ii (paper) + 177 + ii (paper), 295 x 215 (215 x 117) mm. Written in ca. 30 lines of verse; double upper and single lower horizontal bounding lines full across; double or triple vertical bounding lines, and often additional single lines in upper, lower, and/or outer margins. Ruled in lead or hard point; remains of prickings in all margins except inner.

I^4 (later addition), II^{10}, III^{12}, IV^{10}, V^8, VI^{14}, VII^{12}, VIII^{10}, IX^{14}, X^{12}, XI-XIII^{10}, XIV-XV^8, XVI^6, XVII-XVIII^8, XIX^3 (structure uncertain).

Written by multiple scribes in careless fere-humanistic scripts. Each scribe uses a different style of catchword and decorates his section according to personal whim (some folios have no decoration). Extensive glosses in many hands. The first two leaves, written by another scribe in italic, appear to be later additions.

Binding: s. xix. Brown diced leather, blind- and gold-tooled.

Written in Italy probably toward the beginning of the 15th century for use as a school text. A note on f. 1r, previously deciphered as "Karolus de Fortro ... ys arnio caps [?]" is now virtually illegible. Unidentified tag (s. xviii) pasted to f. 1r: "No. 24/ Statius". Sold by Thorpe (Cat., 1836, no. 1226) to Sir Thomas Phillipps (no. 9089; tag on spine, note on f. i recto). The following information appearing in De Ricci (v. 2, p. 1904) has not been verified: "[probably in his sale, London, 1908, n. 704 to Corton (bought in?)]; his sale (London, 1910, no. 758) to Leighton; W. J. Leighton sale (London, 27 Oct. 1919, III, no. 2754) to H. Davies (Leighton, Cat. II, 1 [June 1920], n. 329); Cat. II, 9 [ca. 1925] n. 844."

Belonged to J. T. Adams; his sale (Sotheby's, 8 Dec. 1931, no. 264) to Dobell (*The Ingatherer*, no. 22, Feb. 1932, no. 18). Acquired by David Wagstaff (bookplate); gift of Mrs. David Wagstaff in 1944.

secundo folio: Seruantem

Bibliography: De Ricci, v. 2, p. 1904, no. 13; Faye and Bond, p. 36, no. 166.
E. T. Silk, "The Wagstaff Collection of Classical and Mediaeval Manuscripts," *Gazette* 19 (1944) pp. 3-5.

MS 167 Italy, s. XV^2
Pseudo-Phalaris, Epistolae, Lat. tr. Francesco Griffolini of Arezzo

1. ff. 1r-3v [Dedicatory epistle to Malatesta Novella of Cesena] *Francisci aretini in phalaridis tyranni agrigentini epistolas ad illustrem principem Malatestam novellum de malatestis. proemium incipit.* Vellem malatesta novelle princeps illustris tantam mihi dicendi facultatem dari ... exemplar dabitur particulis illis correctis ad praestantiam tuam mittam. Sed iam phalarim audiamus.

2. ff. 3v-43r [Letters, numbered 1-138] *Phalaris Alciboo.* Polycletus Messenius quem proditionis apud ciues tuos insimulas morbo me incredibili liberauit ... quae talem uirum tulerit ciuitatem quam qui miserit laudem consecuturam.

3. f. 43r-v [Dedicatory epistle to King Alfonso I of Naples] *Franciscus aretinus Diuo Alfonso Regi.* Quattuor phalaridis epistolas quas nuper in alio libro inuentas in latinum traduxi ... libens felicissimo nomini tuo dedicabo.

4. ff. 43v-44v [Letters, numbered 139-142] *Phalaris Ariphanti et Thrabulo.* Quas uobis pecunias dedimus Teucro ... sed summae bonitatis praemium accepissent. Vale. τέλος σὺν τῷ θεῷ.

There is no modern edition of these letters. An early printed text (Treviso, 1471) contains another dedicatory epistle to Francesco Pellato.

Paper (watermarks: similar in design to Briquet Tête de boeuf 14579-80), ff. i (paper) + 44 (modern foliation in lower margin 91-133, with 126 bis) + i (paper), 209 x 146 (158 x 95) mm. Written in 27 long lines; single vertical bounding lines, upper horizontal full across. Ruled in ink; remains of prickings along upper edge.

I-II^{10}, III-IV^{12}. Catchwords under written space near gutter.

Written in humanistic script by a single scribe who also numbered the letters of Phalaris in red.

Plain red initial, 4-line, on f. 1r; headings and initials at beginning of each epistle, in red.

Binding: s. xix. Half brown calf, gold- and blind-tooled. Paste paper sides.

Written in Italy in the second half of the 15th century as part of a larger volume;

early provenance unknown. Probably from the collection of Abate Matteo Luigi Canonici that was sold in 1835 to the Rev. Walter Sneyd (booklabel; T. Phillipps, *Catalogus manuscriptorum Magnae Britanniae* [Middle Hill, 1850] p. 14, no. 102); Sneyd sale (London, 18 Dec. 1903, no. 614) to Greene; Leighton, Cat. II, 9 [ca. 1925] no. 712. Belonged to J. T. Adams; his sale (Sotheby's, 8 Dec. 1931, no. 194) to Dobell (*The Ingatherer*, 22 Feb. 1932, no. 14). Acquired by David Wagstaff; gift of Mrs. David Wagstaff in 1944.

secundo folio: adnotat. Eius

Bibliography: De Ricci, v. 2, p. 1904, no. 14; Faye and Bond, p. 36, no. 167.

MS 168 Italy, s. XV$^{3/4}$
Justinus, Epitome in libros Pompeii Trogi

ff. 1r–116v *Justini Epithomatis in libros quatraginta quatuor Pompeii Trogi Prohemium incipit feliciter.* Cum multi ex romanis etiam consularis dignitatis uiri res romanas greco peregrinoque ... legibus ad cultiorem uite usum traductum in formam prouincie redegit. *Iustini Epithoma in quatragesimum quartum et ultimum Pompeii Trogi librum feliciter explicit. Deo gratias. Amen.*

F. Rühl, ed., Teubner (1886) pp. 3–248. Portions of the text in the first gathering are lacking; some leaves are misbound (see collation).

Parchment, ff. ii (parchment) + 116 + ii (parchment), 239 x 151 (151 x 92) mm. Written in 29 long lines; double vertical bounding lines; ruled in pen.
I^{10} (-3, 5, 6, 8; 4 and 7 misbound [now ff. 8, 9]), II^{10} (composed of ff. 5-7, 10-16), III-XI^{10}, XII^{12} (-11, 12 with no loss of text). Quire VI (ff. 57-66) occurs after VII (ff. 47-56). Catchwords perpendicular to text between inner bounding lines, on verso; remains of signatures (e.g., g 1, etc.), on recto.
Written in neat italic by a single scribe who also added frequent marginal notes.
One fine 6-line initial (f. 1r), gold, with white-vine ornament, on blue, pink, and green ground decorated with white, gold, and blue dots extending into side and upper margins, the vines inhabited by birds, insects, and putto; gold dots and brown hair-sprays. A coat of arms in lower margin (effaced and blotted out) supported by a winged putto, set in ornament similar to above. Large blue capitals, 5- to 4-line, in blue, throughout. Headings and Roman numerals for books (in upper margin of recto), in red, for ff. 1r–35r.
Binding: s. xix. Tan goatskin, gold-tooled, by C. Lewis (1800–40); his note regarding binding, in Latin, on f. ii recto.

Written in Florence ca. 1450–70 (we thank A. C. de la Mare for the attribution); effaced arms of early owner, f. 1r. Belonged to the Rev. Henry Drury (1778–1841); his sale (London, 3 March 1827, no. 2440) to Payne and Foss (Cat., 1827, Suppl. [May], no. 520; Cat., Feb. 1830, no. 1113). Collection of Henry Allen (bookplate;

acquired ca. 1800); Samuel Allen sale (London, 30 Jan. 1920, no. 67) to Young. J. T. Adams sale (Sotheby's, 7 Dec. 1931, no. 134) to Davis and Orioli (Cat. 56, Feb. 1932, no. 235), from whom it was acquired by David Wagstaff (bookplate). Gift of Mrs. David Wagstaff in 1943.

secundo folio: semiramide

Bibliography: De Ricci, v. 2, p. 1904, no. 15; Faye and Bond, p. 36, no. 168.
   E. T. Silk, "The Wagstaff Collection of Classical and Mediaeval Manuscripts," *Gazette* 19 (1944) p. 1.

MS 169   Italy, s. XV^2
Cicero, Tusculanae disputationes

ff. 1r-162r   *M. Tull. Ciceronis ad M. Brutum Tusculanarum disputationum Liber I incipit feliciter. Prologus.* Cum defensionum laboribus senatoriisque muneribus aut omnino aut magna ex parte ... Nostris quidem acerbissimis doloribus variisque et vndique circumfusis molestiis alia nulla potuit inueniri leuatio. *M. Tull. Ciceronis ad M. Brutum Tusculanarum disputationum liber quintus et ultimus explicit feliciter.* f. 162v blank

M. Pohlenz, ed., Teubner (1918) pp. 217-459.

Parchment, ff. i (parchment flyleaf) + 162 + i (parchment flyleaf), 172 x 120 (95 x 55) mm. Written in 25 long lines; double vertical bounding lines; ruled in hard point.

I-XIX^8, XX^{10}. Catchwords, surrounded by dots and flourishes, to the right in lower margin.

Written in fine humanistic script by a single scribe who also made careful marginal annotations, in red, and less often black ink (e.g., Hector; scutum, gladius, galea; Dubius hic textus).

One initial (f. 1r), 6-line, a gold capital filled with white-vine ornament on a blue, green, and pink ground, with white highlights. Ivy, blue and pink with berries and gold leaves, trails from the corners. In the upper margin, an IHC monogram, surrounded by purple penwork; in the lower margin, a coat of arms (effaced) and initials "F. C." also with purple penwork (later additions?), surrounded by curling vines with flowers, as above. Eight other smaller initials in the text (ff. 4r, 44v, 67r, 69r, 96r, 98v, 125r, and 128v) in the same style (cf. Pächt and Alexander, v. 2, no. 716: Oxford, Bod. Lib. Auct. T. 4. 16 [Lombardy, s. XV^{med}]; no. 730: Oxford, Bod. Lib. Canon. Pat. Lat. 162 [Lombardy, 1461]). Headings, running titles, marginal notes, in red, throughout.

Stains at end of codex sometimes affect marginalia.

Binding: s. xvi. The backs of the quires are cut in at the sewing stations. Original wound sewing on three tawed, slit straps laid in beech boards; the endband cores laid in grooves. The spine is very slightly rounded and the cover adhered to it. Covered in dark brown calf, blind-tooled in concentric borders, the central panel containing a rope interlace diamond and square tools, with an *agnus dei*, also in squares, in rows above and below. Borders of flowers and rope tools. Four fastenings, the catches on the lower board, the clasps of brown leather nailed to the upper. Endbands, some spine leather, corners and clasps wanting. Sewing breaking and some slight repairs to boards.

Written in Milan during the middle or third quarter of the 15th century, according to A. C. de la Mare; arms of the original owner (f. 1r) effaced and the letters "F.C." probably a later addition. Signature with date on f. i recto: "1535/ Gio. Batt. Fliscus [Fieschi]". Unidentified shelf-marks (f. i recto): "C. 99" and "L. 1" (in red). Belonged to E. P. Warren, Esq., at Lewes; his sale (London, 28 Oct. 1929, no. 47) to Lubrano. Collection of David Wagstaff (bookplate); presented to Yale in 1943 by Mrs. David Wagstaff.

secundo folio: anno ante

Bibliography: De Ricci, v. 2, p. 1904, no. 16; Faye and Bond, p. 36, no. 169.

MS 170 Italy, s. XV
Cicero, De officiis

1. pp. 1-169 [Q]uamquam te Marce filij annum iam audientem Cratippum idque athenis abundare oportet ... Sed multo fore cariorem si talibus monimentis preceptisque letabere. Excellunt libros cunctorum philosophorum Isti quos fecit tres tulius officiorum.

   C. Atzert, ed., Teubner (1932) pp. 1-123.

2. p. 169 De Cicerone. Ille super gangem super exauditus et indos/ ... cuiquam sperare nepotum.

   Walther, *Initia* 8719

3. p. 170 [Beginning of Cicero, *De amicitia*:] [Q]uintus Mucius Augur Sceuola multa narrare de C//

Parchment, ff. ii (paper) + 85 (paginated 1-170) + ii (paper), 200 x 137 (135 x 98) mm. Written in 25 long lines; single vertical bounding lines ruled in lead; horizontal lines in ink.
I-VI^8, VII-VIII^{10}, IX^8, X^{10} (-10). Signatures (letters of alphabet) by a modern hand.
Written in well formed humanistic script by a single scribe who often did not write on the final two guide-lines; some marginal notes by a contemporary hand (also responsible for article 2).

Spaces left for decorative initials.
Binding: s. xix–xx. Red goatskin, gold-tooled.

Written in Italy in the 15th century; early provenance unknown. Tag with no. "74" inside front cover. Belonged to Henry Allen (acquired ca. 1800; bookplate); Samuel Allen sale (London, 30 Jan. 1920, no. 32) to Tregaskis; Maggs (Cat. 404, 1921, no. 44). Sotheby sale (London, 8 April 1925, no. 578) to Dobell (Cat. 62, Dec. 1926, no. 86). Belonged to J. T. Adams; his sale (Sotheby's, 7 Dec. 1931, no. 50) to Dobell (*The Ingatherer*, no. 22, Feb. 1932, no. 3; notice pasted on first front flyleaf). Collection of David Wagstaff (bookplate); gift of Mrs. David Wagstaff in 1943.

secundo folio: ea quae de officijs

Bibliography: De Ricci, v. 2, p. 1905, no. 17; Faye and Bond, p. 36, no. 170.

MS 171 England, s. XV
The Treatise of Fishing with an Angle

pp. 1–20 Saloman in hys paraboles seith þat a glad spirit maket a flowryng age that ys to sey a feyr age ... In octobre take þe same for þey be especiall baytes for þe trowyt all tymys//

For a modern critical text, facsimile of the Beinecke manuscript, and discussion of the attribution of the treatise to Dame Juliana Berners, see J. McDonald, *The Origins of Angling* (New York, 1963); see also W. L. Braekman, "The Treatise of Angling" in the Boke of St. Albans (1496) in *Scripta* 1 (Brussels, 1980). A comparison of Beinecke MS 171 with the 1496 edition of Wynkyn de Worde (*The Book of St. Albans*) indicates that the manuscript is missing three leaves between pages 10 and 11 and seven leaves at the end.

Paper (watermarks: unidentified hand), ff. 10 (paper) + 10 (paginated 1–20, with modern paper interleaved) + 2 (paper), 190 x 145 (ca. 172 x 125) mm. No lines or prickings visible.
Collation impossible; each leaf is glued to a modern stub.
Written by a single scribe in a bold English secretary script.
Simple flourishes and initial strokes, in red.
Stains throughout, some obscuring text. Severe trimming has resulted in loss of marginalia.
Binding: s. xix. Brick-red calf, gold-tooled by C. Lewis in 1823. Rebacked.

Written in England during the 15th century; early provenance unknown. Belonged to William Herbert (1718–95). Passed to the Rev. John Brand (1744–1866); his sale (London, 6 May 1807, no. 72). Presented in 1821 by George Isted to John Haslewood (bookplate) who arranged the codex in its present format with three illuminations (coat of arms, title page, painting of a fisherman adapted from a woodcut in the 1496 edition) followed by his preface, and his transcription of the text interleaved with the original folios. The whole was rebound at Haslewood's request in 1823. Haslewood sale (London, 16 Dec. 1833, no. 462) to Edward Jesse (1780-1868); his sale (Nov. 1868) to Alfred Denison (bookplate) for forty-five shillings. Correspondence between Thomas Satchell and Denison, now in library files, indicates that the manuscript was examined by W. W. Skeat who believed it to have been written in "1450 or even earlier". Denison sale (London, 17 July 1933, no. 63) to Rosenbach. Purchased by David Wagstaff (bookplate) and given to Yale in 1946 by Mrs. David Wagstaff.

secundo folio: w^t thornes

Bibliography: De Ricci, v. 2, p. 1905, no. 18; Faye and Bond, p. 36, no. 171.
  E. F. Jacob, "The Book of St. Albans," *Bulletin of the John Rylands Library* 28 (1944) pp. 115-17.

MS 172 Italy, s. XV^2
Vergil, Bucolica, etc.

1. ff. 1r-14r *Incipit liber Bucolicorum Virgilij maronis Ad Pollionem*. Titire tu patule recubans sub tegmine fagi/ Siluestrem tenui musam meditaris auena/ ... Iuniperi grauis umbra nocent et frugibus umbrae/ Ite domum sature uenit hesperus ite capellae. *Publij uirgilij maronis Buccolicorum liber explicit.*

   R. A. B. Mynors, ed., OCT (1969) pp. 1-28.

2. ff. 14r-48v *Publij uirgilij maronis Georgicorum liber primus incipit feliciter.* Quid faciat letas segetes quo sidere terram/ Vertere mecenas ulmisque adiungere uites/ ... Carmina qui lusi pastoram audaxque iuuenta/ Tityre te patule cecini sub tegmine fagi. *Finis Amen. Publij Virgilij Maronis Georgicorum quartus et ultimus explit* [sic] *feliciter. Deo gratias Amen.* f. 49r blank

   Mynors, *op. cit.*, pp. 29-101. Each book is preceded by the Pseudo-Ovidian arguments in four lines.

3. ff. 49v-50r [Two short summaries of the *Aeneid*, followed by one of the *Georgics*, all in verse:] Primus habet libyam ueniunt ut troes in urbem/ ... Vltimus imponit bello turni nece finem; Eneas primo libiae depellitur oris/ ... Excidium troiae iussus narrare parabat; Qualis buccolicis quantus tellure domandi/ ... Contineat que quisque liber lege carmina nostra.

   Walther, *Initia* 14661, 580, 15117.

4. ff. 50r-202v Arma uirumque cano troiae qui primus ab oris/ Italiam fato profugus lauinaque uenit/ ... Feruidus ast illi soluuntur frigore membra/ Vitaque cum gemitu fugit indignata sub umbras. *Finis libri duodecimi et ultimi Publij Virgilij*

Maronis Eneidos liber explicit Deo Gratias Amen. Mantua me genuit calabri rapuere tenet nunc/ Partonope cecini pascua rura duces.

Mynors, *op. cit.*, pp. 103-422; for the epitaph see Walther, *Initia* 10656. Each book of the *Aeneid* is preceded by several lines of verse attributed to Ovid (Walther, *Initia* 8699).

Parchment, ff. i (parchment) + 202 + i (parchment) 250 x 165 (167 x 104) mm. Written in 32 lines of verse; double vertical bounding lines full across. Ruled in hard point on the hair side for bounding lines, mostly in ink for the written space; remains of prickings along upper, lower, and outer edges.
I-IV^{10}, V^8 (+ 1 leaf at end, f. 49), VI-XVIII^{10}, XIX^8, XX^{12}, XXI^4 (-4). Catchwords perpendicular to text between inner bounding lines, accompanied by dots and flourishes.
Written by one scribe in neat round humanistic script.
Two initials (ff. 1r, 50r), 8-line, gold capitals, embedded in white-vine ornament on a green, blue, and dark red ground with white dots; the former initial extending into inner margin. On f. 50r bar border in the lateral margins, red, green, and gold, divided into segments by quatrelobes, with dense flower-spray terminals, blue, green and dark red, and gold dots which fill the upper and lower margins. Effaced arms within a laurel wreath at bottom center. Many other gold initials, 7- to 2-line, on red, blue and green grounds, with yellow and white highlights; small initials in red or blue. Rubrics throughout.
Binding: s. xvii. Dark brown calf with spine gold-tooled and a red-brown label added.

Written in Central Italy in the second half of the 15th century; original owner's arms effaced from f. 50r. Although white-vine decoration is characteristic of Florence, the style of the flower-sprays as well as the bar borders suggest Emilia Romagna, perhaps Ferrara. For the flower-sprays cf. Oxford, Bod. Lib. Canon. Liturg. 131 and 383, both attributed to Ferrara by Pächt and Alexander (v. 2, nos. 396, 433); for the white-vine initials, Oxford, Bod. Lib. Canon. Class. Lat. 229, Ferrara, 1461 (*ibid.*, no. 391). Clues concerning its early provenance include: signature "priuli" (barely visible on f. 202v); "GG 16" on f. 1r; "A 21" on f. 1r and inside front cover. Belonged to Wilfred M. Voynich; sale by Sotheby's (London, 5 March 1934, no. 15) to Quaritch. Belonged to David Wagstaff (booklabel); gift of Mrs. David Wagstaff in 1944.

secundo folio: Ti. Ante

Bibliography: De Ricci, v. 2, p. 1905, no. 19; Faye and Bond, p. 36, no. 172.

MS 173 Italy, s. XV
Seneca, Tragoediae

1. ff. 1r–27v   Soror tonantis. hoc enim michi solum/ Nomen relictum est. semper alienum iouem/ ... Restituet armis. ista te alcide uocat/ Facere innocens terra quae superos solet.

   Hercules furens; R. Peiper and G. Richter, eds., *Tragoediae*, Teubner (1902) pp. 3–48.

2. ff. 27v–50v   [Q]uis me furor nunc sede ab infausta abstrait/ Auido fugaces ore captantem cibos/ ... Hijs puniendum te tradunt mea/ Te puniendum liberis trado tuis.

   Thyestes; Peiper and Richter, *op. cit.*, pp. 281–318.

3. ff. 50v–61v   [C]eci parentis regimen ac fexi unucum/ Patris leuamen nata quamquam tanti est mihi/ ... Patriam penates coniugem. flammis dare/ Imperam pretio quolibet constant bene.

   Phoenissae; Peiper and Richter, *op. cit.*, pp. 93–115.

4. ff. 62r–83v   [I]te umbros eingnite [*sic*] siluas/ Summaque motis iuga cicropij/ ... Ratem retatat ne det oblicum latus/ Currus gubernat ora nunc pressis trahit//

   Hippolytos; Peiper and Richter, *op. cit.*, p. 157 and following (the text ends abruptly at line 1075).

   According to A. MacGregor, Beinecke MS 173 appears to be closely related to Osimo, Collegio Campana MS XLIX. 17 and may be a direct descendant from it; the Yale codex, like all manuscripts belonging to the vulgar (A) tradition, is dependent upon Vatican, Vat. lat. 2829 (see A. MacGregor, "The MS Tradition of Seneca's Tragedies: *Ante renatus in Italia litteras,*" *Transactions of the American Philological Society* 102 [1971] pp. 327–56).

Paper (watermarks: similar to Briquet Étoile 6045 [but with cross] and similar in design to Monts 11706), ff. i (paper) + 83 + i (paper), 288 x 212 (159 x 87) mm. Written in 25 lines of verse; single vertical and horizontal bounding lines full across. Ruled in lead; prickings along outer edge of leaf.

I^{14} (–1, no loss of text), II–VI^{14}. Catchwords in center under written space.

Text written in awkward fere-humanistic script; interlinear and marginal notes (ff. 1r–29r) in a less formal style of writing.

One inelegant initial on f. 1r, 8-line, dark red, crimson, dark green, dull brown foliage on gold rectangular ground, edged in black; with borders of same design and colors in upper and lower margins. Gold dots, surrounded by penwork designs and squiggles, in all margins, except outer. Space left for decorative initials at beginning of other tragedies.

Binding: s. xviii–xix. Edges daubed with pink and green. Rigid vellum; rebacked.

Written in Italy in the 15th century; the poor quality of the decoration and the numerous peculiar readings in the text suggest that it is a product of a provincial workshop. Two inscriptions [s. xviii?] on f. 1r: "Queste sono uarie Tragedie de Seneca [followed by erasure]"; and "Con. S. A. Neapoli". Tregaskis, Cat. 969 (June 1929) no. 152. Belonged to J. T. Adams; his sale (London, 8 Dec. 1931, no. 220) to Dobell (*The Ingatherer*, no. 22, Feb. 1932, no. 17). Acquired by David Wagstaff (bookplate); gift of Mrs. David Wagstaff in 1944.

secundo folio: Parum est

Bibliography: De Ricci, v. 2, p. 1905, no. 2; Faye and Bond, p. 36, no. 173.
  E. T. Silk, "The Wagstaff Collection of Classical and Mediaeval Manuscripts," *Gazette* 19 (1944) p. 1.

MS 174 Germany, s. XV^{ex}
Ovid, Remedia amoris, etc.

1. f. 1r-v Prefatory material including: notes from Horace concerning Heroici, Satirici, Lirici, Elegiaci, Comici, Tragici, Fabulosi; Epitaph of Ovid, beginning: Quisquis lege versus oculo properante viator/ ... [Walther, *Initia* 16190]; passage on the life of Ovid, beginning: Presens autor prenomine publius nomine Ouidius...; short selections entitled: De Qualitate carminis, De intencione autoris, Continuacio textus.

2. ff. 2r-18r Publij Ouidij Nazonis sidmonensis amoris de remedio elegiaticum opus incipit. Legerat huius amor titulum nomenque libelli/ ... Carmine sanati femina uir [*o* crossed out] que meo. P. Oui Na [*sic*] de Remedio amoris liberi [*sic*] expliciunt. f. 18v blank

   E. J. Kenney, ed., *Remedia amoris*, OCT (1961) pp. 205-37; text is accompanied by marginal and interlinear glosses.

3. ff. 19r-23r Opusculum perutile et breue continens compendiose Quod Oui [*sic*] in 3bus libris in de arte amandi dispendiose conscripsit. Si quem forte iuuat subidi sapienter amori/ ... Plenus hic ameno carmine doctus erit. Et tantum de arte amandi sequitur de remedio ouidij.

   Pseudo-Ovid; E. J. Thiel, "Mittellateinische Nachdichtungen von Ovids 'Ars amatoria' und 'Remedia amoris'," *Mittellateinisches Jahrbuch* 5 (1968) pp. 168-77.

4. f. 23r Ex stacio et prudencio. Maior in exiguo regnabit corpore virtus [Walther, *Sprichwörter* 14274]. Simicus patricius. Omnis ostendacio non tacet suspicionem mendacij....

5. ff. 23r-24r Nosse primum decet quantum sit femina turpis/ ... Nec petat hanc rursus nec petat inde magis. Et tantum de remedio amoris et finit feoliciter [*sic*] etc. ff. 24v-25v blank

   Pseudo-Ovid; Thiel, *op. cit.*, pp. 177-80.

6. ff. 26r-29v Pseudo-Vergil. Short poems, all of which are accompanied by marginal and interlinear glosses:

a. f. 26r De vino et venere: [N]ec veneris nec tu bachi capiaris amore/ ... [Walther, *Initia* 11706].

b. f. 26r-v De liuore seu invidio liuor tabificum malis fenenum [*sic*]/ ... [Walther, *Initia* 10378].

c. ff. 26v-27r De lucro: Sperne lucrum vexat mentes vesana libido/ ... [Walther, *Initia* 18488].

d. f. 27r De sole et die: Clarus inoffenso procedat lumine titan/....

e. f. 27r-v De fortuna. Fortuna potens tantum/ iuris atrox que vendicas/ ... [Walther, *Initia* 6810].

f. ff. 27v-28r Hortulus: Adeste muse maximi proles iouis/ ... [Walther, *Initia* 518].

g. f. 28r De seipso et humero: Mellifluum quisquis romanum nescit homerum/ ... [Walther, *Initia* 10873].

h. f. 28r-v De uiro sapiente et bono: Vir bonus et sapiens qualem vix reperit ullum/....

i. ff. 28v-29r De est et non est: Est et non cuncti montasaba [written above: monisilba] non frequetant/ ... [Walther, *Initia* 5658].

j. f. 29r-v De littera Y: Littera pitagore discrimine secta bicorni/ ... [Walther, *Initia* 10361].

k. f. 29v De orpheo: Threicius quondam vates et fide creditur canora/ ... [Walther, *Initia* 19280].

Articles 7-9 and 12-18, composed by Johannes Fabri de Werdea (b. 1450), are listed by J. Stohlmann in *Verfasserlexikon: Die deutsche Literatur des Mittelalters*, Band 2, Lieferung 3 (Berlin, 1977) 690-95.

7. ff. 29v-30v Quorundam notabilium questionum [Walther, *Initia* 16104/5].

8. ff. 30v-32r De musis [Walther, *Initia* 11936/7, 9951].

9. ff. 32v-33r De moribus studentum et beanorum [Walther, *Initia* 382].

10. f. 33v Prefatory material on Vergil the poet.

11. ff. 34r-36v [I]am nox hibernas bis quinque peregerat/ ... Atque agit in segetes et terre condit aratrum/ finis.

Pseudo-Vergil, *Moretum*; W. V. Clausen *et al.*, eds., OCT (1966) pp. 158-63.

12. ff. 36v-38v Carmen de philosophia [Walther, *Initia* 2436]. f. 39r-v blank

13. ff. 40r-43v Carmen de fine et vtilitate posis [Walther, *Initia* 9927].

14. ff. 43v-45r Carmen de tribus deabus fatalibus [Walther, *Initia* 4170].

15. ff. 45r-46r Carmen de beate virginis visitatione [preceded by a short selection, an introductory paragraph, in prose].

16. ff. 46v-49r Carmen de vtilitate poesis [Walther, *Initia* 4403].

MS 175   237

17. ff. 49v-50r   Carmen de bonis moribus [title lacking; Walther, *Initia* 6100].
18. ff. 50r-52r   Carmen questionum utrum scire malum sit [title lacking]. f. 52v blank

Paper (watermarks: similar to Briquet Balance 2411, and similar in design to Piccard Ochsenkopf XII. 732-735 and Briquet Tête de boeuf 14552), ff. ii (paper) + 52 + ii (paper), 320 x 212 (280 x 108) mm. Written in ca. 25 lines of verse; double vertical bounding lines and additional rulings in inner and outer margins to delineate columns for marginal annotations; ruled in hard point.
I-II^{12}, III-IV^{14}.
Written in running script exhibiting bâtarde influence for both text and commentary.
Plain 2-line initial, in red, on f. 2r. Some underlining and initial strokes, in red, for ff. 1r-6r only.
Some of marginalia lost in gutter.
Binding: s. xix. Half red-brown goatskin, gold-tooled. Marbled paper sides. Emblem and motto ("Endure fort") on front cover.

Written in Germany toward the end of the 15th century; early provenance unknown. Pencilled note on flyleaf: "Said to be in the handwriting of Melancthon [Philip, 1479-1560?]", but does not resemble printed facsimiles of his hand. Obtained from Dobell (*The Ingatherer*, no. 22, Feb. 1932, no. 13) by David Wagstaff (bookplate). Gift of Mrs. David Wagstaff in 1944.

secundo folio: Publij Ouidij

Bibliography: De Ricci, v. 2, p. 1906, no. 21; Faye and Bond, p. 36, no. 174.

MS 175   Italy, s. XIV^2
Boethius, De consolatione philosophiae

ff. 1r-37v   //Set tempus est medecine quam querele uero tum intenta in me totis luminibus ... non sunt uera bona si uideantur esse appetuntur quasi sunt uera bona//

Bk. 1.2.1-3.10.38; L. Bieler, ed., CC lat. ser. 94 (1957) pp. 4-55.

Paper (sturdy; watermarks: similar to Briquet Fruit 7397), ff. ii (paper) + 37 + i (paper), 230 x 143 (158 x 108) mm. Written in ca. 28 long lines or lines of verse; frame-ruled in lead; prickings at corners of written space.
Extensive repairs do not permit an accurate collation.
Written in crude bâtarde by one scribe.
Binding: s. xviii-xix. Narrow, green, straight-grained calf spine, vellum corner tips and paste paper sides.

Written in Italy in the second half of the fourteenth century as part of a larger book; early provenance unknown. Tag with number "85" on f. i verso. Belonged to Henry Allen (acquired ca. 1800; bookplate); Samuel Allen sale (London, 30 January 1920, no. 10) to Dobell (*The Ingatherer*, no. 22, Feb. 1932, no. 2), from whom it was purchased by David Wagstaff (bookplate). Gift of Mrs. David Wagstaff in 1944.

Bibliography: De Ricci, v. 2, p. 1906, no. 22; Faye and Bond, p. 36, no. 175.

MS 176
Juvenal (fragment)

Italy, s. XV

//Ostrea callebat primo deprendere morsu/ ... Contennunt mediam temeraria lina charybdim//

Satires 4.142-5.102; W. V. Clausen, ed., OCT (1959) pp. 65-69.

Parchment, ff. 2 (bifolium), 237 x 159 (157 x 100) mm. Written in 29 lines of verse; double [?] bounding lines ruled in hard point; horizontal rulings in ink; remains of prickings at top and bottom of folio.
Written in a neat humanistic hand.
The bifolium was removed from a binding for it is rubbed, stained, creased, and mutilated.

Written in Italy in the 15th century; early provenance unknown. Purchased from Maggs (1931) by Thomas E. Marston who presented it to Yale in 1937.

Bibliography: De Ricci, v. 1, p. 155, no. 1; Faye and Bond, p. 36, no. 176.

MS 177
Vitae sanctorum

Germany, s. XV

1. ff. 1r-16r   *Vita basilij. Amphilochij episcopi ichonij in uita et miraculis sancti patris nostri basilij archiepiscopi capodocie*. Dilectissimi non erit indecorum fideles filios patris contristari defunctione ... ac uiuifico spiritu nunc et perpetuam et in secula seculorum. Amen. *Explicit uita magni et persancti basilij.*

    Amphilochius, Life of St. Basil, Lat. tr. Euphemius; BHL 1023.

2. ff. 16r-17r   Brief notes on: St. Gregory the Great, St. John Chrysostom, St. Possidius, St. Hilary of Arles, St. Cyril, St. Ephrem, St. John IV "the Faster," St. Fulgentius, St. Gregory Nazianzen, St. Ignatius of Antioch "Theophorus". ff. 17v-18r ruled, but blank

3. ff. 18v-42r   [Heading on f. 18v:] *Incipit uita Sancti Augustini yponensis episcopi patris nostri Conscripta ab possidio episcopo* ... [heading on f. 19r:] *Incipit uita beati*

episcopi Augustini patris nostri per omnia laudabilis. Anministrante [*sic*] rem publicam theodosio gloriosissimo ac uictoriosissimo imperatore ... dei promissis cum eodem perfruar ... *Explicit uita sancti augustini episcopi. Et hic indicium omnium librorum eius.* Contra paganos uel achademicos libri iiij ... et nunc est quoniam mortui audient uocem liber j. [followed by notes, in a later hand]

BHL 787 (text), BHL 786 (index).

4. ff. 43r–68v   Prefacio sequentis operis. *In uitam sancti Iohannis elemonisinarij.* Cogitanti ac diu tacite solliciteque mecum consideranti quid in domo dei commodius ac dignius operari potuissem ... cum sancto spiritu gloria honor imperium nunc et perpetuam et in secula seculorum. Amen. *Expliciunt acta sancti iohannis elemonis* [?] *Que quidem pretermissa fuerant*.... f. 69r-v ruled, but blank

Leontius, Life of St. John the Almsgiver, Lat. tr. Anastasius; BHL 4388–89, PL 73. 337–84.

5. ff. 70r–97r   Incipit prologus bernardi abbatis in vitam beati malachie episcopi et confessoris. Semper quidem opere pretium fuit illustres sanctorum describere vitas ut sint in speculum et exemplum ... et cum ipso pariter regnaturi in secula seculorum. Amen.

Bernard of Clairvaux, Life of St. Malachy; BHL 5188, PL 182. 1073–118.

6. f. 97r   *Hymnus beati bernardi abbatis de sancto malachia episcopo et confessore.* Nobilis signis, moribus suauis....

RH 12000, PL 182. 1118.

7. ff. 97v–109v   *Incipit prologus seueri in uitam sancti martini* [followed by long blank space] *Incipit uita sancti martini.* Seuerus desiderio fratri karissimo salutem. Ego quidem frater vnanimis libellum quem de vita sancti martini ... vt spero habebit premium a deo non quicumque legerit sed quicumque crediderit.

BHL 5610, PL 20. 159–76.

8. ff. 109v–110v   [plus half-leaf bound in after f. 109 with omitted text] *Incipit epistola sulpicij seueri ad aurelium diaconum de obitu beati martini episcopi.* Hesterna die cum ad me plerique monachi venissent inter fabulas iuges ... Vnde intelligat quisquis haec legerit non temptatum quidem illo martinum periculo sed probatum.

BHL 5611, PL 20. 175–78; heading is incorrect and should read Epistola ad Eusebium presbyterum.

9. ff. 110v–111v   Posteaquam a me mane digressus es eram residens solus in cellula ... eadem tibi ex quadam nostri confabulacione prestaret carta solacium.

Epistola Sulpicij Seueri ad Aurelium diaconum; BHL 5612, PL 20. 178–80.

10. ff. 111v–113v   *Epistola sulpicij seueri de obitu sancti martini ad basulam.* Sulpicius seuerus basule parenti venerabili salutem. Si parentes vocari in ius liceret ex-

pilaciones furtique ream ad pretoris tribunal ... Martinus Abrahe sinu letus excipitur. Martinus hic pauper et modicus celum diues ingreditur.

BHL 5613, PL 20. 181-84.

11. ff. 113v-114v Opere pretium est eciam illud inserere lectioni qualiter eius corpusculum in locum vbi ... adiuuante domino nostro ihesu christo qui cum patre et spiritu sancto uiuit et regnat per omnia secula seculorum amen.

Gregory of Tours, Life of St. Martin of Tours; BHL 5623.

12. ff. 114v-115v Igitur post excessum beati martini turonice ciuitatis episcopi summi et incomparabilis viri ... cui est gloria honor laus imperium vna omni coeterno patris et spiritu sancto in secula seculorum. Amen.

Gregory of Tours, Life of Brictius of Tours from his *Historiae* 2.1; BHL 1452, PL 71. 188-91.

13. f. 115v Short selection, in a later hand, from Vincent of Beauvais, *Speculum historiale*, ch. 25.

14. ff. 115v-142v *Incipit prologus euagrij presbiteri in translatione vite sancti Antonij.* Presbiter euagrius innocentio karissimo filio in christo salutem. Ex alia in aliam linguam ad verbum ... *Incipit prologus athanasij episcopi in vitam beati Antonij.* Optimum fratres inistis certamen aut equare egipti monachos aut superare ... acque eiciant deceptores scilicet hominis et totius corruptionis artifices. Finit vita beati antonii ab athanasio episcopo greco eloquio edita ab euagrio presbitero in latinum translata. f. 143r ruled, but blank

BHL 609, PL 73. 125-70.

15. f. 143v Table of contents, in a later hand (s. xvii-xviii). f. 144r-v ruled, but blank

Paper (watermarks: unidentified unicorn, in gutter), ff. i (paper) + 144, 211 x 140 (154 x 95) mm. Written in 41 long lines; frame-ruled in ink; prickings for bounding lines.

Binding is too tight to permit accurate collation. Remains of signatures (a 3, a 4, etc.) for ff. 70-142.

Written by a single scribe in a neat running hand. Rubrics (often omitted), in a more formal gothic script, appear to be later additions (instructions for rubricator along outer edges of leaves).

Plain initial with modest penwork designs, in red, on f. 1r. Small initials, 3- to 2-line, headings, and initial strokes, in red, throughout.

Binding: s. xvi [?]. The backs of the quires are cut in at the sewing stations and coarsely woven cloth stays are adhered in the center of each. Sewn on five tawed, slit straps laced into wooden boards. Endbands, sewn on vegetable fiber cores, are covered with the covering leather which is backstitched. The wooden boards are flush, or nearly so. The spine is rounded and lined with cloth extending onto the outside of the boards. Covered in dark brown calf with a diamond

MS 178

pattern drawn on each board with a pointed instrument. A rectangular space for a label [now missing] is cut out of the upper board near the head. There are marks of four round, brass bosses on the lower board and the remains of two strap-and-pin fastenings, the pins on the upper board. The brown calf straps are attached with metal plates. Some mold damage to the bookblock. Rebacked. Bosses and fastenings wanting.

Written in Germany in the 15th century; early provenance unknown. Purchased in 1949 from C. A. Stonehill by Thomas E. Marston (bookplate); his gift to Yale in 1952.

secundo folio: eubolum Erat

Bibliography: Faye and Bond, p. 36, no. 177.

MS 178 Italy, s. XIV[1]
Antiphonal Pl. 21

1. ff. 1r–235v   Proprium de tempore, for the full liturgical year.

2. ff. 236r–245v   Ten settings for the Venite exultemus.

Parchment, ff. ii (bifolium from a 17th-century antiphonary, with offices from the sanctorale) + 245 + ii (bifolium from the same 17th-century antiphonary), 512 x 355 (480 x 245) mm. Written in 10 long lines of text with staves, ruled in brown crayon; single vertical bounding lines full across. Prickings in lower margin.

I–III[8], IV[6], V[8], VI[10], VII[8], VIII[10], IX–XIV[8], XV[10], XVI–XVII[8], XVIII[12] (-12, cut out after f. 151), XIX–XXII[8], XXIII[2], XXIV[4], XXV[6] (-6, cut out after f. 194), XXVI[4], XXVII[2], XXVIII–XXX[8], XXXI[8] (portion of f. 194v covered with paste-in), XXXII[4] (-1 after f. 235), XXXIII[10]. Catchwords centered in lower margin, verso.

Written in two sizes of round liturgical gothic script by several scribes: Scribe 1, ff. 1r–235r; Scribe 2, f. 235r–v, and Scribe 3, ff. 236r–245v.

Three fine historiated initials, 4- to 2-line: ff. 32r (Nativity), 152r (Three Marys at Tomb), and 179r (Pentecost); shaded pink and/or green, with blue, yellow, green and orange foliage and knots, with gold dots and orange frame; figures against blue ground. 3- to 2-line calligraphic initials, divided, red and blue with red penwork, with blue and red penwork flourishes. 1-line initials red or blue with blue or red penwork, sometimes with black and green; some initials with guide-letters in outer margin. 1-line initials with yellow. Square notes on 4-line red staves. Rubrics throughout, with notes to rubricator in margins. One very crude 4-line initial (s. xvii) on f. 1r, in red, yellow, blue, green and purple.

Binding: s. xviii. Rebound in brown cowhide [?], blind-tooled, with numerous metal bosses. Pastedowns from the same 17th-century antiphonary used as flyleaves.

Written in Italy, probably Florence, in the 1330's, according to C. Gilbert; early provenance unknown. Bought in 1933 from C. A. Stonehill by Thomas E. Marston; his gift to Yale in 1953.

secundo folio: iam totam

Bibliography: Faye and Bond, p. 37, no. 178.

MS 179
Cicero, etc.

Italy, s. XV

I. 1. ff. 1r–30v   *Mar. Tulius Cicero de amicitia*. [Q]uintus mucius Augur sceuola multa narrare de C. lelio socero suo memoriter et iocunde solebat ... Nam quid ego de studijs cognoscendi semper aliquid// f. 31r–v, a later addition, blank

De amicitia; K. Simbeck, ed., Teubner (1917) pp. 46c–85c. Text ends abruptly in 26.104; also lacking a small portion of 9.32 [scribal error?].

II. 2. ff. 32r–53v   *Marci tulii ciceronis de senectute*. [O] tite si quid ego adiuto curam ueleuasso [*sic*] que nunc te coquit ... ut ea que ex me audiuistis re experti probare positis. M. T. Ciceronis. De senectute Liber explicit Feliciter. ff. 54r–63v blank, except for a few notes

De senectute; Simbeck, *op. cit.*, pp. 3c–43c.

III. 3. ff. 64r–90v   Cicero meo ut cernis et ipsum [?]. Cicero Lucio Uenturio suo salutem. Collegi ea que pluribus modis dicerentur quo uberior promptiorque esset oratio ... [3 columns] Vociferatur/ uitare uellatur/ Operitur prestolatur. Finis. f. 91r–v blank; f. 92r–v miscellaneous quotations

Pseudo-Cicero, *Synonyma*; GKW, v. 6, nos. 7031–40.

IV. 4. f. 93r–v   Per leonardum Aretinum Basilii Prologus et S. Collucio. [E]go tibi hunc librum Colucij ex media vt aiunt Grecia delegi ... in quo animaduerte queso quanta grauitas sit. Vale.

Dedicatory epistle of Leonardo Bruni to Coluccio Salutati; H. Baron, ed., *Leonardo Bruni Aretino humanistisch-philosophische Schriften* (Leipzig, 1928) pp. 99–100.

5. ff. 94r–105v   [Heading in a later hand:] Diui Basilij Capadocie Aepiscopi ad Nepotes suos de liberalibus studijs et de ingenuis moribus liber. [text:] Multa filij sunt que me hortantur ad ea uobis consulenda ... quod uos nunc non paciamini recta consilia aspernentes. Finis.

Basil, *De libris gentilium legendis*, Lat. tr. of Leonardo Bruni; GKW, v. 3, nos. 3700-18.

Composed of four separate manuscripts:

I. Paper (watermarks: unidentified arrow, much worn), ff. 30 + i (f. 31, modern paper, tipped in), 209 x 145 (134 x 78) mm. Written in 24 long lines; single horizontal and double vertical bounding lines; ruled very faintly in hard point. I-III^{10}. Clumsy humanistic script by a single scribe. Spaces left for headings and decorative initials; some letters stroked in red.

II. Paper (watermarks: similar in design to Briquet Tête de boeuf 14803 and unidentified mountain), ff. 32 (numbered 32-63), 210 x 145 (130 x 75) mm. Written in 27 long lines; double vertical and horizontal bounding lines, full across; ruled in hard point. I-II^{10}, III^{12}. Catchwords in center of lower margin. Inelegant fere-humanistic script. Heading and one plain initial in red (later additions?).

III. Paper (watermarks: similar to Briquet Flèche 6285), ff. 28 (numbered 64-91), 210 x 144 (136 x 105) mm. Arranged in 3 or 4 columns of 23 lines; single vertical and horizontal bounding lines, full across. Ruled in lead; some prickings in upper and lower margins. I-II^{10}, III^{8}. Catchwords in center of lower margin. Italic script. Initial strokes, in red, for ff. 64-83.

IV. Paper (watermarks: unidentified balance in a circle), ff. 14 (numbered 92-105), 210 x 143 (124 x 85) mm. Written in 22-23 long lines; double vertical and horizontal bounding lines, full across; ruled in hard point. A single gathering of 14 leaves, written in an angular humanistic bookhand.

Binding: Date? Resewn on three tawed, slit straps laid in beech boards bevelled on the inside. Quarter covered in dark brown goatskin. Two clasp-and-catch fastenings. The boards do not fit the bookblock very well, the off-printing on them does not match the writing on the first and last leaves, and the marginal notes have been partially cut away. Edges of paper tinged with red.

Written in Italy at various times in the 15th century; all four sections owned, at the end of that century or the beginning of the next, by an individual whose notes, in a careful italic, appear throughout. Unidentified circular label with perforated edge on spine: "S II J/ Cicero/ MS XV/ 4º 69503". Purchased in 1949 from C. A. Stonehill by Thomas E. Marston (bookplate); his gift to Yale in 1952.

secundo folio: [f. 2] [dispu]tantem Quia
              [f. 33] obripit
              [f. 65] Adiscite
              [f. 94] Multa filij

Bibliography: Faye and Bond, p. 37, no. 179.

MS 180 Italy, s. XV^2
Claudian, De raptu Proserpinae

ff. 1r–20v *Claudiani poetae clarissimi liber primus de raptu proserpine feliciter incipit.* Inuenta secuit primus qui naue profundum/ Et rudibus remis sollicitauit aquas/ ... Antra procul sillea petit, canibusque reductis/ Pars stupefacta silet, pars mundum exterrita latrat. *Explicit liber Claudiani de raptu proserpine.*

The order of the verses is confused, but is not due to misbinding: 1.1–2.320; 3.45–170; 2.321–3.44; 3.294–448 (3.171–293 now lost). According to J. B. Hall, ed., *Claudian De raptu Proserpinae* (Cambridge, 1969), Beinecke MS 180 belongs to that class of manuscripts which is free from all lacunae (MS y in his sigla; p. 32).

Parchment, ff. i (paper) + 20 + i (paper), 216 x 130 (148 x 85) mm. Written in 27 lines of verse; double vertical bounding lines. Ruled in ink; prickings (often two spaced closely together) along upper and lower edges.

I–II^{10}. Catchwords perpendicular to text.

Written by a single scribe in neat humanistic script.

Crude initials in red, some with red and/or blue penwork designs; rubrics throughout.

Binding: s. xix–xx. Brown paste-paper case with a blank paper label. (See also MSS 184 and 194.)

Written in Italy in the second half of the fifteenth century; early provenance unknown. Belonged to the German landscape painter and engraver Friedrich von Schennis (1852–1918; bookstamp on f. 1r). Bought in 1949 from C. A. Stonehill by Thomas E. Marston (bookplate) who presented it to Yale in 1951.

secundo folio: Coniurant

Bibliography: Faye and Bond, p. 37, no. 180.

MS 181 England, s. XII^2
Eusebius Gallicanus, etc.

An anonymous catena of Eucharistic proof texts that also occurs in Salisbury, Cathedral Library MS 61. Cf. A. Wilmart, "Un developpement patristique sur l'Eucharistie dans la lettre de Pascase Radbert à Fredigard," *Analecta reginensia*, in *Studi e Testi* 59 (1933) pp. 267–78; J. Geiselmann, "Die Eucharistielehre der Vorscholastik," *Forschungen zur Christlichen Literatur und Dogmengeschichte* 15, 3 (1926) pp. 1–459; Parkes, *Keble College*, MS 22, p. 69.

1. ff. 1r–4r *Incipit liber Sancti eusebii De corpore christi.* Magnitudo celestium beneficiorum angustias humane mentis excedit ... nos in corpus inmortalitatis assumat ... piis nos operibus preparare dignetur qui uiuit et regnat in secula seculorum. Amen.

Eusebius Gallicanus; J. Leroy, ed., CC lat. ser., v. 101 (1970) no. xvii, pp. 195-208.

2. ff. 4r-5r   *Uos nunc qui inter patrem* et filium uoluntatem ingerunt unitatem inter[added above: ro]go ... in se patrem habeat cum uiuat ipse per patrem.

Hilary, *Liber de Trinitate*, Bk. 8.13-14.16; PL 10. 246-47, 249; P. Smulder, ed., CC lat. ser., v. 62A (1980) pp. 325-28.

3. f. 5r-v   *Audiuimus* ueracem magistrum diuinum redemptorem hunc manum saluatorem commendantem nobis precium nostrum sanguinem suum ... Dixi uobis quod nemo uenit ad me nisi cui datum fuerit a patre meo.

Augustine, *Sermo* 131.1-2; PL 38. 729-30.

4. ff. 5v-6v   [I]*dcirco credo* quia hoc tam aperte cum uiuentibus ac nescientibus agitur ... Si ante mortem deo hostia ipsi fuerimus.

Gregory, *Dialogorum liber* 4.59-60; PL 77. 425-29.

5. ff. 6v-10r   [H]*is abluta* plebs diues insignibus ad christi altaria dicens Et introibo ad altare dei ... tamen in illo letitia secularis in te autem iocunditas est spiritualis.

Ambrose, *De mysteriis* 8.43-55 and 58; *De sacramentis* 4.13-14, 19-28; 2.5-8; O. Faller, ed., CSEL, v. 73 (1955).

6. f. 10r-v   *Sicut uerus* est dei filius dominus noster ihesus christus non quemadmodum homines per gratiam sed quasi filius ex substantia patris ... Et tuus homo uetus in fontem dimersus peccato crucifixus est sed deo surrexit.

Ambrose, *De sacramentis* 6.1-4; O. Faller, ed., CSEL v. 73 (1955) pp. 72-74.

7. f. 10v   [C]*um fugeret* dauid persecutorem saul inquiens ita et efferebatur manibus suis hoc uere quomodo fieri potest ... enim illud corpus in manibus suis.

Cf. Augustine, *Enarrationes in Psalmos* (Ps. 33.10); E. Dekkers and J. Fraipont, eds., CC lat. ser., v. 38 (1956) pp. 280-81.

8. f. 10v   [R]*ecte ergo* sub ara martyres collocantur ... consequantur functionemque sacerdotis accipiant.

Pseudo-Augustine, *Sermo* 221; PL 39. 2154-55.

9. ff. 10v-11r   [T]*unc enim* et sacrifici [erasure] munda est oblatio et misericordie sancta largitio ... a quibus contra id quod accipitur disputatur.

Leo, *Sermo* 91.3; A. Chavasse, ed., CC lat. ser., v. 138A (1973) p. 566.

10. f. 11r   [Q]*uomodo peccata* mundi tollat inquit quo ordine iustificet impios apostolus petrus ostendit qui ait ... sed fidelium ore suam sumitur in salutem.

Bede, *Homilia* 1.5; D. Hurst, ed., CC lat. ser., v. 122 (1955) pp. 105-06.

11. f. 11r-v   [N]*ecessarie* igitur et hoc adicimus annuntiantes filii dei idem ihesu christi ... propriam eius factam qui propter filius hominis est factus et uocatus.

Cyril, *Epistola Synodica*; PG 84. 569.

12. f. 11v [A]*dorate* scabellum pedum eius quem sanctum est. Sanctus Augustinus in exposicione eiusdem uersiculi ita dicit Videte fratres quid iubeat ... tale scabellum domini et non solum peccamus adorando.

Augustine, *Enarrationes in Psalmos* (Ps. 98.9); PL 37. 1264; E. Dekkers and J. Fraipont, eds., CC lat. ser., v. 39 (1956) p. 1385.

13. ff. 11v-12r [Q]*uid dicit* omnis homo terra quando accipit sanguinem christi amen dicit Quid est amen. Verum est ... per illum tua tibi dimitti peccata.

14. f. 12r [Q]*ui* autem anima christiana quae ascensura es ex sacratissimo fonte ... qui pro uobis fundetur in remissionem peccatorum.

15. ff. 12r-13r [S]*acerdotii* autem de quo loquimur aspice dignitatem. Agitur quidem in terra ... sed tota funditus interiret nisi magnum gratie dei esset auxilium.

16. f. 13r-v [N]*am eum qui* pro omni [erasure] ciuitate quid autem dico ciuitate immo pro omni mundo legatione fungitur ... quod ad tale ministerium me nitebaris inducere.

17. ff. 13v-16r [N]*emo qui* sanctorum uitas et exempla legerit ignorare poterit quo spe hec mistica corporis et sanguinis sacramenta ... et fide uberius requiratur interius in eadem quod exterius conspexit.

Paschasius Radbertus, *De corpore et sanguine Domini* 14.2-168; B. Paulus, ed., CC Cont. Med. 16 (1969).

18. f. 16r Hec diligenter adtende prudenter intellige sollicite inquire diuina tibi misteria declarantur ... et eo tempore arma orationis assumas quo solet incursare temptator.

19. f. 16r-v *Dicit ille* populus nationum ille in prima electione despectus qui renouatus est ... mihi ille panis dei descendit de caelo qui uitam dat huic mundo.

20. ff. 16v-23v [S]*icut ante nos dixit* quidam sapiens cuius sententiam probamus licet nomen ignoremus intuentes inquiens apostoli sententiam qui dicitur ... At autem corpus christi spiritualis alimonia pertinens potius ad interiorem hominem ... Conclusio liquet igitur non obnoxium secessui esse. *Explicit liber.*

Gerbertus, Pope Sylvester II, *De corpore et sanguine Domini*; PL 139. 179-88.

21. f. 23v [Processional antiphon, with neumes:] Quam pulcra es et quam decora carissima in deliciis ... [RH 32196; followed by:] Et autem corpus christi spiritualis alimonia pertinens potius ad interiorem [repeated from art. 20?].

The antiphon is written in a script of French aspect slightly distinct from those of the main manuscript. According to K. D. Hartzell the musical notation is probably the work of the text scribe. It has been proficiently entered *in campo aperto* with a minimum of diastematy.

Parchment (thick, furry), ff. iii (paper) + 23 + iii (paper), 154 x 108 (132 x 75) mm. Written in 33 long lines; double vertical and horizontal bounding lines, full across. Ruled in hard point; remains of prickings in upper and outer margins. I^8 (-7), II-III^8. Signed with Roman numerals in center of lower margin, on recto.

Written by several scribes, perhaps at different times, in early gothic bookhand.
Plain initials in red or green (spaces left for others), followed by rustic capitals. Heading, in red, on f. 1r. Simple schematic drawings to explicate the text of art. 20 (ff. 21r, 22r).

Some loss of text due to trimming on f. 23v.

Binding: s. xix. Brown goatskin, blind- and gold-tooled.

Written in England in the second half of the twelfth century; early provenance unknown. Inscriptions as follow, s. xvii: (f. 2v) Iohannis Staycye; (f. 4v) Tho. Stacye; (f. 6r) Martin Bretland; (f. 6v) Tho. Bretland Liber eius anno Incarnationis Dominica; (f. 7r) Benjamin Bretland His Booke 1693/4; (f. 7r) Tobias [partially erased]; (f. 10v) Samuel, Francis Sitwell; (f. 12r) Ex libris John Bretland; (f. 14r) Benjamin; (f. 15v) Samuel Bretland; (f. 23v) London John S. Unidentified notice from sale catalogue indicates that it was part of the collection of Guglielmo Libri (1802-69); we have been unable to verify this. Belonged to Thomas B. Strong, Vice Chancellor of Oxford (signature and date 1897 on f. i verso). Signature of Frederick Fox Bartrop with date 1937 (f. i verso). Bought from H. P. Kraus in 1947 by Thomas E. Marston who presented to Yale in 1951.

secundo folio: Dei nature

Bibliography: Faye and Bond, p. 37, no. 181.

MS 182
Herodian, Sp. tr. Diego Guillén de Ávila Spain, s. XV/XVI

1. f. 1r Title page, in a modern hand; ff. 1v-3v a prologue "en el que se registra un dialogo entre la Reina Isabel de Castilla y el Marqués de Villena." f. 4r-v blank

2. ff. 5r-112r Siguise la epistola de angelo policiano al papa ynocencio octabo et la traducion de la estoria de erodiano del griego en latyn la qual diego Guillén de avila ... traslado de latín a Romançe ... [preface:] Capitulo primero. Estando yo agora en Romà agora ha tres años ... [heading for Book I, f. 6r:] Libro primero de la ystoria de errodiano ... [text:] Aquellos que las cosas antiguas declararon a los venjideros [?] y qui se estudiaron ... al ymperio Romano siendo por todos [?] declarado princeps. f. 112v blank

   Unpublished translation by Diego Guillén de Ávila (active 1487-1516), from Politian's Latin translation of Herodian.

Paper (sturdy; watermarks somewhat similar to Briquet Main 10793), ff. i (paper) + 113 + i (paper), 300 x 205 (235 x 110) mm.; deckle edges appear on some folios. Not ruled.

Bound too tightly for accurate collation. Catchwords (rare) below written space, at right.

Written by three scribes, in gothic cursive (*cortesana*) script. Scribe 1 (ff. 1v-3v) uses a large, sprawling hand; Scribe 2 (ff. 5r-86v) a compact, regular one; Scribe 3 (ff. 87r-112r) a large and sprawling one.

Binding: s. xix. Worn red velvet with 2 brass clasp-and-catch fastenings.

Written in Spain in the late 15th or early 16th century. Early provenance unknown. Bought from Parke-Bernet's (30 Nov. 1948, no. 348) by Thomas E. Marston (bookplate); his gift to Yale in 1951.

Bibliography: Faye and Bond, p. 37, no. 182.

MS 183
Ovid, Ars amatoria

Italy, s. XV

ff. 1r-42v //Profuit et tenui uentos mouisse flabello/ Et caua sub tener [hole in page] edem/ ... vt quondam iuuenes ita nunc mea turba puelle/ inscribant folijs Naso magister erat. *Explicit liber nasonis de arte amandi felliciter amen. Amen.* ff. 43r-44v blank, except for random scribblings (e.g., Omnia uincit amor et non [*sic*] cedamus amori)

E. J. Kenney, ed., *Amores*, OCT (1961) pp. 119-200. Yale MS 183 begins abruptly at Book 1.161 and exhibits frequent lacunae and interpolations (e.g., the text skips from 1.198 to 263, and inserts two lines between 1.331 and 332).

Paper (watermarks: unidentified balance, in gutter), ff. iii (paper) + 44 + iii (paper), 220 x 143 (140 x 99) mm. Written in 24 lines of verse; double vertical bounding lines. Ruled in lead or ink; prickings in outer margin.

I^{10} (-1, 2), $II-IV^{10}$, V^6. Catchwords along lower edge, in gutter.

Written by a single scribe in humanistic script; marginal notes in italic.

Crude initials on ff. 15r and 30v, 8-line, outlined in black and filled with various shades of red and yellow; the first initial incorporates a grotesque. Smaller plain initials, some paragraph marks, and initial strokes, in red. Spaces left for headings.

Stained and/or repaired throughout; loss of text on f. 1.

Binding: s. xx. Grey paper case with a dark brown calf label, gold-tooled.

Written in Italy in the 15th century; early provenance unknown. Belonged to Baron Horace de Landau (1824-1903, bookplate inside front cover; see his *Catalogue des livres manuscrits et imprimés* [Florence, 1890] v. 2, p. 102, no. 206 bis); sale (Geneva,

MS 184   249

1948, no. 101). Acquired from C. A. Stonehill in 1948 by Thomas E. Marston (bookplate) and presented to Yale in 1951.

Bibliography: Faye and Bond, p. 37, no. 183.

MS 184   Italy, s. XIV^{ex}
Pseudo-Seneca, etc.

1. f. 1r-v Unidentified table of medical problems. De effimera et eius cura ... De fistula./ De cura./ De quiaria [?]/ De cura.

2. ff. 2r-5v Quatuor Virtutum species multorum sapientum sentencijs diffinite sunt quibus animus humanus comptus ad honestatem ... aut mente compos ipse deuiet insaniam aut definientem puniet ignauiam. Explicit liber senece de iiij uirtutibus.

   Early printed text by Konrad Hist (Speier, ca. 1500); the *Formula vitae honestae* of Martin of Braga, C. W. Barlow, ed., *Martini Episcopi Bracarensis opera omnia* (New Haven, 1950).

3. ff. 5v-8r Incipit liber senece de remedijs fortuniorum [*sic*]. Licet cunctorum poetarum carmina gremium tuum semper illustrent aliquando deliberans hoc tibi opusculum ... felix est non qui alijs uidetur sed qui sibi. Vides autem quam domi sit ista felicitas rara. Explicit liber senece de remedijs fortuitorum amen. f. 8v blank

   F. Haase, ed., Teubner (1872) v. 3, pp. 446-57.

Parchment (palimpsest with unidentified text, in two columns, from the 13th [?] century), ff. i (paper) + 8 (early foliation 116-23) + i (paper), 191 x 132 (157 x 117) mm. F. 1 written in 2 columns of 32 lines; ff. 2-8 in 33-39 long lines. Remains of prickings and ruling from lower text only.
   Composed of a single gathering of eight leaves.
   Written in gothic bookhand for f. 1; an academic cursive for the remainder (cf. Thomson, *Latin Bookhands*, pl. 72).
   Plain red initial, 1-line, on f. 2r; initial strokes in red for f. 2r.
   Binding: s. xx. Paste paper case with blank and inscribed labels. (See also MSS 180 and 194).

Written in Italy toward the end of the 14th century, originally as part (ff. 116-23) of a longer manuscript; early provenance unknown. Unidentified circular paper label with perforated edge on front cover: "S. III. 5/ Seneca/ MS XV/ 4º. 75429". Bought in 1949 from C. A. Stonehill by Thomas E. Marston (bookplate); his gift to Yale in 1951.

Bibliography: Faye and Bond, p. 37, no. 184.

MS 185 Italy, s. XV^{ex}
Terence; Cicero (with glosses)

1. f. 1r   Natus in ectelsis [*sic*] tectis carthaginis alte ... leget sic puto cautus erit.

   Life of Terence; Walther, *Initia* 11627.

2. ff. 1r–47r   *Argumentum Andrie*. Sororem falso ... coniugem. *Prologus*. Poeta cum primum animum ad scribendum appulit. Id sibi negotij ... Si quid est quid restat. Vos ualete et plaudite. Ego caliopius recensuj. *Explicita Andria*.

   Terence, *Andria*; R. Kauer and W. M. Lindsay, eds., OCT (1926).

3. ff. 47v–98r   *Incipit Enuchus* [sic]. Acta ludis megalemsibus ... *Argumentum*. Meretrix adolescentem cuius ... illuditur. *Argumentum Eunuchj*. Sororem falso creditam ... audiente hic loquitur. *Prologus*. Si quisquam est qui se placere studeant bonis ... Ite hac. Valete et plaudite. Casiopolus recensuj. Vale. *Explicit Eunuchus*.

   Terence, *Eunuchus*; Kauer and Lindsay, *op. cit.*

4. ff. 98r–112v   *Incipit Eaphtomtimorumenon* [sic]. Acta ludis megalensibus ... *Argumentum*. In milicias proficisci gnatum ... Clitipho uxorem accipit. *Prologus*. Ne cuj uestrum sit mirum. Cur partes seni poeta dederit ... Nam uos iamdudum expectat senex//

   Terence, *Heautontimoroumenos*; Kauer and Lindsay, *op. cit.*

All bibliographical references in parentheses for articles 5–24 refer to D. R. Shackleton Bailey, ed., *Cicero: Epistulae ad familiares* (Cambridge, 1977) 2 vols.

5. ff. 113r–115r   Martij Tulj Ciceronis Epistolarum Liber primus Incipit; to P. Cornelius Lentulus Spinther (v. 1, no. 12, pp. 46–48).

6. ff. 115r–116v   To C. Scribonius Curio (v. 1, no. 45, pp. 104–05).

7. f. 116v   To C. Scribonius Curio (v. 1, no. 46, p. 106).

8. ff. 117r–118r   To C. Scribonius Curio (v. 1, no. 47, pp. 106–07).

9. ff. 118r–119r   To C. Scribonius Curio (v. 1, no. 48, pp. 107–08).

10. f. 119r–v   To C. Scribonius Curio (v. 1, no. 49, p. 109).

11. ff. 119v–122v   To C. Scribonius Curio (v. 1, no. 50, pp. 110–12).

12. ff. 122v–124v   To C. Scribonius Curio (v. 1, no. 107, pp. 199–200).

13. ff. 124v–125v   To M. Caelius Rufus (v. 1, no. 90, pp. 175–76).

14. ff. 125v–126v   To M. Caelius Rufus (v. 1, no. 85, pp. 168–69).

15. ff. 126v–128r   To M. Caelius Rufus (v. 1, no. 95, pp. 182–83).

16. f. 128r–v   To M. Caelius Rufus (v. 1, no. 89, p. 175).

17. ff. 128v–129v   To Q. Minucius Thermus (v. 1, no. 115, pp. 214–15).

MS 185

18. ff. 129v-131r   To C. Coelius Caldus (v. 1, no. 116, pp. 215-16).
19. ff. 131r-132v   To Ap. Claudius Pulcher (v. 1, no. 64, pp. 123-24).
20. ff. 132v-133v   To Ap. Claudius Pulcher (v. 1, no. 65, pp. 124-25).
21. ff. 133v-134v   To Ap. Claudius Pulcher (v. 1, no. 76, pp. 150-51).
22. ff. 134v-138r   Ser. Sulpicius Rufus to Cicero (v. 2, no. 248, pp. 108-11).
23. ff. 138r-140r   To Ser. Sulpicius Rufus (v. 2, no. 249, pp. 111-13).
24. ff. 140r-142r   To M. Claudius Marcellus (v. 2, no. 230, pp. 80-82) ... qui essent auderem scribere nisj te intelligere considerem// f. 142v blank
25. ff. 143r-144v   Commentary, partly in Italian, on the first letter of Cicero to Lentulus Spinther (some loss due to trimming). Ego omni officio argumentum huius [struck out: tale est] epistola tale est quicum tolomeus rex egictj per prouinciales de regno ... et numquam me sibi esse iratum ostendi ac decansa moriens ipse in*** tes benedictiones mihi donauit// ends at section 2, line 12 (Shackleton Bailey, *op. cit*, v. 1, no. 12, pp. 46-47).
26. ff. 144v-145v   Short letters, first in Italian and then in Latin (some loss due to trimming): Scipio to Lentulus; Rex Federicus P. A. S. D. (only in Italian and incomplete); Paul to John; Tulius S.D. Precetori [*sic*].

Paper (unidentified watermarks buried in gutter include horn, mermaid in a circle; two distinct birds in circles similar to Briquet Oiseau 12203 and 12220), ff. viii (i = front pastedown; paper) + 145 + vi (vi = back pastedown; paper), 195 x 141 (142 x 85) mm. Written in ca. 17 long lines; single bounding lines, sometimes full across. Ruled in lead; remains of prickings in outer margins.

I-X^{10}, XI^8, XII^8 (-5, 6, 7, 8 after f. 112), XIII^{10}, XIV-XV^8, XVI^8 (-5, 6, 7, 8), XVII^4 (-4). Catchwords in lower margins.

Written by multiple scribes in various styles of round humanistic and gothic scripts. One hand supplied most of the glosses on Terence and Cicero and the texts on ff. 143r-145v in italic.

Crude initials mark beginning of each section; rubrics throughout; many letters stroked in red.

Binding: s. xvii. Limp vellum case with title lettered in ink down the spine.

Written in Italy at the end of the 15th century presumably for use as a school text; early provenance unknown. Round label with perforated edge on spine: "S II J [or F?]/ Terentius/ Cicero/ Ms. XV./ 4º 74457". Bought in 1949 from C. A. Stonehill by Thomas E. Marston (bookplate) who presented it to Yale in 1952.

secundo folio: in andriam ex

Bibliography: Faye and Bond, pp. 37-38, no. 185.

MS 186
Tibullus; Catullus

Italy, s. XV^2

1. ff. 1r–40v [Life of Tibullus] Albius Tibullus eques regalis insignis forma cultuque ... Obijt adolescens ut indicat epigrama inscriptum. *Epitaphyum tibulli.* Te quoque uirgilio comitem non equa tibulle/ ... Aut caneret forti regia bella pede. *Epystola prima dandam operam amori obmissis ceteris officijs.* Diuitias alius fuluo sibi congerat auro/ Et teneat culti iugera magna soli/ ... Crimina non hec sunt magno sine facta dolore/ Quid miserum torques rumor acerbe tace. *Finis. Amen. Albii tibulli equitis romani feliciter explicit Amen.*

   F. W. Lenz and G. C. Galinsky, eds., *Albii Tibulli aliorumque carminum libri tres* (Leiden, 1971); life of Tibullus: pp. 171–72; epitaph: p. 171; text: pp. 51–170.

2. ff. 41r–88r *.Q. Catulli Veronensis liber incipit Ad cornelium.* Qui dono lepidum nouum libellum/ Arido modo pumice expolitum/ ... Contra nos tela ista tua euitamus amicta/ At fixus matres tu dabis suplicium. [followed by verses of Guarino of Verona:] Ad patriam uenio longis a finibus exul/ ... Cuius sub modio clausa papirus erat. *Quinti Catulli Veronensis poete celeberimi liber feliciter explicit. Amen.* ff. 88v–90r ruled, but blank

   H. Bardon, ed., Teubner (1973) pp. 1–144; verses of Guarino of Verona: Walther, *Initia* 413.

3. f. 90v Various notes, in Lat. and It., dated 1585 at top of folio.

Paper (watermarks similar to Briquet Fleur 6690, Harlfinger Fleur 108 [lower example], Harlfinger Fer à cheval 5 [but with cross], Briquet Tour 15865, Harlfinger Monts 78; unidentified watermarks: mountain, ladder, full-bodied unicorn, letter R), ff. i (paper) + 90, 210 x 142 (142 x 80) mm. Written in 25 lines of verse; ruled in hard point.
I–IX^{10}.

Written by two scribes in humanistic script. Scribe 1: ff. 1r–20v (single vertical bounding lines, catchwords perpendicular to text along innermost bounding line); Scribe 2: ff. 21r–88r (double vertical bounding lines, catchwords in center of lower margin, accompanied by dots and flourishes, in red and black). Marginal notations in several contemporary hands.

Two inelegant black initials (ff. 1r, 41r) with vine-work ornament on red and blue ground. Simple red initials, some with penwork designs, mark the beginning of each poem. Headings and initial strokes, in red, throughout.

Many leaves stained and/or repaired.

Binding: s. xix. Brown calf spine and small corners with marbled paper sides.

Written in Italy, probably in the second half of the 15th century, as is suggested by the watermarks. The pattern of waterstains in the codex indicates that ff. 21–90 were copied after damage occurred to ff. 1–20. Belonged to Gustavo Cammillo Galletti of Florence (1805–68; bookstamp on f. 1r). Collection of Baron Horace de Landau (1824–1903; bookplate inside front cover; see his *Catalogue des livres manuscrits et imprimés* [Florence, 1890] v. 2, p. 102, no. 206); his sale (Geneva, 1948, no. 202). Acquired from C. A. Stonehill in 1948 by Thomas E. Marston (bookplate) and presented to Yale in 1952.

secundo folio: At uos exiguo

Bibliography: Faye and Bond, p. 38, no. 186.

MS 187 Byzantium, s. XIII
Lectionary, etc. (in Greek)

A collection of liturgical readings mainly from the Old Testament, but including some readings from the Gospels and Epistles, together with prayers and hymns for the office. Text begins abruptly: //κάζεσαι· διὸ πρὸ τέλους βόησον χριστῷ τῷ θεῷ· ὡς τὸν ἄσωτον δέξαι με υἱὸν ... καὶ θείαν ὁμήγυριν· τῶν ἁγίων πάντων· εὐερ// The texts on f. 5r relate to the Sunday of the ἀποκρέου (two weeks before Lent), those on f. 189v to the Sunday of All Saints (eight weeks after Easter).

K. Aland, *Kurzgefasste Liste der griechischen Handschriften des Neuen Testaments* (Berlin, 1963) p. 299, Gregory-Nr. 1686; K. W. Clark, *Descriptive Catalogue of Greek New Testament Manuscripts in America* (Chicago, 1937) pp. 6–7.

Parchment (thick; many leaves palimpsest: Greek liturgical text of the tenth century, in uncial script, still visible), ff. 193, 215 x 161 (178 x 122) mm. Written in 2 columns of 38–40 lines; single vertical bounding lines (often full across), sometimes with an additional line between the columns and along outer edge of outer column. Ruled in hard point with a heavy hand; prickings visible at top, bottom, and sides of page.

I^8 (-1, 2, 7), II^4, III^{10} (2 unnumbered leaves sewn in between 12 and 13 after foliation was added in upper right corner), IV^8 (-1), $V-VI^8$, VII^8 (-6), $VIII-X^8$, XI^8 (-8, followed by a bifolium cut out, + 1 leaf sewn in), $XII-XIII^8$ (+ 1 leaf), XIV^8, XV^8 (-1 and 8, f. 101), XVI^8, XVII^4, XVIII^8 (-1), XIX^8 (-6), XX^8, XXI^8 (-8), XXII^8, XXIII^6, XXIV^8 (-5, 8), XXV^8, XXVI^8 (-8), XXVII^6, XXVIII^8 (-5, 6, 8), XXIX^8 (-1, 2, 8). Gatherings signed (Greek notation) on first and last leaves in lower margin.

Written in a clear but informal minuscule by a single scribe who does not follow the guide-lines that were originally drawn for the lower text of the palimpsest.

Numerous small red initials throughout.

The manuscript was apparently in a fire, since ff. 36–58 are severely charred and the edges of all leaves have been blackened.

Binding: s. xvi. Resewn with heavy thread (fine cord?), three sewn-in chains linking the quires. Two strands of sewing cord cross over to the horizontal bars of a Z lacing, the diagonals of the lacing visible through the pastedowns of the inside of the flush wooden boards, the horizontal lacing protruding under the leather of the cover. The edges of the boards are concave at head and tail. The smooth, round spine is lined with a coarse, blue-green cloth extending almost to the center of the boards on the outside. The endbands which straddle the boards are laced through them. Covered in dark red, now brown, calf faintly blind-tooled with diamonds with crosses in circles at the intersections. A strap-and-pin fastening, the pin in the edge of the upper board, two holes for the strap in the lower. Sewing slightly repaired, some leather on the spine replaced. Front cover is lined with a parchment leaf from a 15th-century Greek liturgical manuscript.

Written in Byzantium in the 13th century; early provenance unknown. According to library files Dr. John Henry House of Salonika obtained the codex on Mt. Athos (see provenance of MS 150); his sale to Prof. Thomas Day Seymour of Yale ca. 1899. Bequeathed to his daughter, Elizabeth Day Seymour Angel in 1907, in whose memory it was presented to Yale in 1952 by her husband, John Angel.

Bibliography: De Ricci, v. 2, p. 1652, no. 1; Faye and Bond, p. 38, no. 187.

MS 188
Pope Pius II, etc.

Germany and Italy [?], s. XV^2

Articles 1-3 are printed texts that were bound together with the manuscripts (arts. 4-21) in the 16th century:

I. 1. ff. 1r-36v Bulla retractationum; De curialium miseria: printed by Ulrich Zell (Cologne, ca. 1470); Hain 260 and 194. ff. 37r-38v blank

2. ff. 1r-16v Epistolae de laude poeticae, de differentia inter scientiam et prudentiam et de poetis, de laude litterarum, cur libri cumulentur: printed by Printer of "Dictys" (Cologne, ca. 1470-71); Hain 186b (in part).

3. ff. 1r-8v Epistola ad procopium de fortuna: printed by Printer of "Dictys" (Cologne, ca. 1471); Hain 192.

II. 4. f. 1r [title:] Bulla pape pij secundi contra turcos [f. 1v blank; text on ff. 2r-9v:] Pius episcopus seruus seruorum dei ... Vocauit [nos] pius et misericors dominus ad sacram beati petri sedem ... Datum Rome apud sanctum petrum. Anno incarnationis dominice M°cccc lviij iij idus octobris pontificatus nostri anno primo, etc.

Pius II (Aeneas Silvius Piccolomini) *Epistulae in pontificatu editae* (Milan: Antonius Zarothus, 1481) a1-14 verso; Hain 169.

III. 5. f. 10r [heading:] Bulla in qua Sigismundus dux Austrie ac certi textes ... denunciantur ... [text:] Pius Episcopus seruus seruorum dei ... Salutem et Apostolicam benedictionem infructuosos palmates de vnica ... desuper confecte continetur in hac forma.

MS 188

6. ff. 10r–18r [heading:] Bulla constittucionis [*sic*] pape pij quod deinceps non debet appellari ad futurum consilium. [text:] Pius Episcopus seruus seruorum dei ... Execrabilis et priscis temporibus manditis tempestate nostra ... Rome aput sanctum petrum Anno Incarnacionis dominice Millesimo quadringentesimo sexagesimo quarto Nona Nouembris pontificatus nostri anno Tercio.

7. ff. 18r–21v [heading:] Breue missum ad herbipolensiscatensis [?] Bambergensis, etc. Episcopos et certas communitates etc. Pius papa secundus. [text:] Dilecti filij salutem et apostolicam benedictionem. Saluator humani generis in hunc veniens mundum ... Datum Rome ... die xviij Octobris Anno MCCCC lx pontificatus nostri Anno tercio.

8. f. 21v [heading:] Appellacio Gregorij heimburg etc. [text:] Vis consilij expers mole ruit sua vim temperatam mi sublime// Catchword: prouehit deus.

IV. 9. f. 22r [pen trials and title:] Varie epistole et copie bullarum. f. 22v blank

10. ff. 23r–28r Six short letters between Pope Pius II and Louis XI, king of France, all dated 1463. ff. 28v–37v blank

The first letter (beginning: Pius et misericors deus qui te regem constituit et in vertice...) corresponds to that in Vat. Urb. lat. 404, f. 163v.

V. 11. ff. 38r–46v [heading:] Epistola ad exterminacionem tyrannidis et suasionem iusticie et magnanimitatis et expulsionem hostium. a R. blodelli. [text:] Eo regum et potentum maiestates illustrissime princeps in altissimo gradu subuecte ... Si antiquos hostes expellas, furentem tyrannidem oppresseris, et deperditam libertatem restitueris. ff. 47r–49v blank

VI. 12. ff. 50r–61r [heading, in a different hand:] Copia bulle confirmationis gestorum per dominum felicem. [text:] Nicolaus Episcopus seruus seruorum dej. Ad futuram rei memoriam. Vt pacis qua nichil desiderabilius in vniuersali ecclesia ... Datum Spoleti Anno Incarnationis dominice Millesimo quadringentesimo quadragesimo nono. Quarto decimo Kalendas Julij Pontificatus nostri Anno Tertio. f. 61v blank

VII. 13. ff. 62r–66v [heading, in a different hand:] Copia bulle Maledictionis die iouis sancta publi^{ta}. [text:] *Paulus* episcopus seruus seruorum dei ad perpetuam rei memoriam excommunicamus et anathematizamus ex parte dei omnipotentis ... Omnes hereticos gazaros, Patarenos, pauperes de Lugduno ... Datum Lateranj Anno Incarnacionis dominice. Millesimo quadringentesimo sexagesimo sexto. Tercio Nonas Aprilis Pontificatus nostri Anno secundo. Explicit. f. 67r–v blank

VIII. 14. ff. 68r–77r [heading:] Thimotheus Mafeus Veronensis Canonicus Regularis cunctae Italie principibus Salutem. [text:] Deum inmortalem sepe numero precatus sum ... A perditissimorum hominum scelere deffendat. Valete Ex Bononia 1453. [epilogue:] Thimothei Veronensis Canonici finit epistola qua cunctos italie principes ... suis copijs in barbarum mature contendant qui nuper Constantinopolitana ciuitate potitus est. ff. 77v-79v blank

Timoteo Maffei, *Epistola*; cf. Vat. lat. 1946, ff. 163v-179v, and B. Pez and P. Hüber, eds., *Thesaurus anecdotorum* (Augsburg, 1729) v. 5, pp. 367-78.

IX. 15. ff. 80r-82v   Paulus Episcopus seruus seruorum dej. Ad perpetuam rei memoriam. Ineffabilis prouidentia summi patris qui pro redemptione ... Datum Rome apud sanctum petrum Anno incarnationis dominice Millesimo quadringentesimo Septuagesimo tercio decimo Kalendas Maij Pontificatus nostri anno Sexto. f. 83r-v blank

X. 16. f. 84r   *Pij Pape .ij. circa finem vite sue in Ancona tussi et febre laborantis Oratio* ... Pja dei genetrix quamuis tua potestas nullis coartatur finibus et totum implet orbem ... Interim hoc munus accipito mee seruitutis signum.

Followed by a brief note on Pius II's death (1464) and burial.

17. ff. 84v-92v   [Epitaphs for Pius II:] *Tumuli inscriptio talis est.* Pius .ij. pontifex maximus natione Tuscus fuit patria ... et hic conditus. *Franciscus Cardinalis Senensis Auunculo sanctissimo f.f.*; (f. 85r) *Pio .ij. Maximo pontifici Leodrisius Cribellus* [Cosenza, v. 2, p. 1145]. *Epitaphium.* Hic inuicta patris capiunt veneranda quietem/ Uiuenti ignotam principis ossa pij/...; (f. 85r) *Antithei Anguigene Philelphi in Pium Pontificem summum.* Quo magis ingratus nemo fuit alter et idem/ Qui dici uoluit impietate Pius/...; (f. 85v) *De origine et moribus Antithei Anguigene Philelphi in pium pontificem summum inuecti. Bartholomei Sulmonensis* [Cosenza, v. 1, p. 441] *opus.* Uertice parnasi phebus phitona sagittis/ Perculit et pestem sustulit ... [arranged as a dialogue between Manes, Megera and Lathesis]; (f. 90v) *Epitaphium Antithei Philelphi.* Hic iaceo putrida et stigia de fece deorum/ Vipereaque satus stirps inimica ioui/...; [f. 91r, a preface to the next epitaph:] Sic uolumus reliquis nequeas implere quod optes/ Mens mala pro uoto manca sit..., *Responsio in Epitaphium Antithei Philelphi.* Sepe *Philelphe* tue numos petiere tabelle/ Abnuit is fetido chremata ferre viro/...; (f. 92r) *Dominus P. Candidus* [Petrus Candidus Decembrius, Cosenza, v. 2 pp. 1196-204]. Hic nouus *Alcides* felix *Sulmonis* alumnus/ Qui monstrum domuit ... Nec rabiem sordesque trucis timuit nebulonis. f. 93r-v blank

XI. 18. ff. 94r-103r   *Oracio Ambrosij Vignati legati ducis sabaudie ad beatissimum pontificem maximum Paulum .ii.* Experior nunc, nunc cerno ipsis oculis, dum hec loquor pater sancte, illud Satyri ita verum ... suae sanctae vniuersalis ecclesiae diutissime et feliciter conseruare dignetur. Amen. f. 103v blank

Ambrosius de Vignate, *Oratio*.

XII. 19. ff. 104r-110r [heading:] Fratris paracliti cornetani ordinis Fratrum hermitarum sancti Augustini in capitulo generali tolentini celebrato de eligendo priore generali etc. [text:] Et si michi priusquam hunc locum conscenderem [?] amplissimus orandi annis fuit ... et si magna cum victoria hostium castra fudisset. Torquatus quoque consularis dignitatis eximius dum// ff. 110v-115v blank

XIII. 20. ff. 116r-121r [heading, in a later hand:] Ad sublimem et preclarum virum d. franciscum Sega Illu. d. venetiarum cancellarium. B. Saccensis apostolice Camerae clericus in Stephanum portium sacrilegum impiissimum. Oratio. [text:] *Solent* plerique homines sublimis vir optimeque pater ... Vale mihi et me ut solet ama. Ex urbe Idus Ianuarij 1453º. Explicit opusculum. Carmen eiusdem ad sacrilege patibulum ... Accipe jam dignis pro factis premia tantis. ff. 121v-122v blank

Bartolomeo Platina (1421-81), *Oratio*.

XIV. 21. ff. 123r-129v [title, f. 123r:] Oratio per Johannem Alouisium ad summum Pontificem pium Secundum. [f. 123v blank] *Ad Summum Pontificem Pium papam secundum Per Johannem Alouisium Tuscanum etc.* Cimba tenella tremit pelagus conscendere vastum/ Qua vix per riuos ducere sciret itere/ Quare ... vt prior eneas romanam condidit vrbem/ Sic pius eneas protegat iste fidem. Explicit oratio per iohannem Alouisium ad pontificem pium secundum etc. *Deo gratias*. f. 130r-v blank

Johannes Tuscanus Aloisius, *Oratio*.

The manuscript section of the codex is divided into 13 sections, all of paper, ff. iii (paper) + 65 (printed texts, foliated 1-41, 1-16 and 1-8) + 130 + iv (paper), 207 x 145 mm.

II. ff. 1-9. Watermarks: unidentified chariot, in the gutter. Written space: 135 x 82 mm. Ca. 25 long lines, not ruled. One quire of 10 (-1 or 2). Hasty cursive with loops by one scribe. Crude 9-line initial on f. 2r, in brown and red; red strokes on 1-line capitals. Stains on f. 1r suggest that it was once bound separately.

III. ff. 10-21. Watermarks similar to Briquet Lettre P 8608. Written space: 125 x 75 mm. 19-20 long lines, frame-ruled in hard point. One quire of 12; catchword f. 21v, in inner margin. Even cursive hand with loops, by one scribe. Calligraphic initials in brown and red; paragraph marks and strokes on 1-line capitals in red.

IV. ff. 22-37. Watermarks: unidentified fleur-de-lis. Written space: 160 x 100 mm. Ca. 30 long lines, frame-ruled in lead. One quire of 16. Hasty cursive, by one scribe. Calligraphic initials, stroked with red; red for paragraph marks and strokes on 1-line capitals. Stains on ff. 22r and 37v suggest they were once the cover or flyleaves.

V. ff. 38-49. Watermarks similar to Piccard Ochsenkopf VII.127. Written space: 147 x 82 mm. Ca. 31 long lines, frame-ruled in lead. One quire of 12.

Written by one scribe in a cramped running hand. 2-line initial, paragraph mark and strokes on 1-line capitals in red.

VI. ff. 50-61. Very light-weight paper, watermarks similar to Briquet Ciseaux 3668. Written space: 130 x 73 mm. Ca. 25 long lines, frame-ruled in hard point. One quire of 12. Written by one scribe in small cursive. 5-line initial at beginning and strokes on 1-line capitals in red. Stains on f. 61v suggest this section was once bound separately.

VII. ff. 62-67. Watermarks buried in gutter. Written space: 152 x 92 mm. 26-27 long lines, ruled in hard point. One quire of 6. Written by one scribe in a cursive hand. 3-line initial on f. 62r in brown, with much red, followed by the rest of the word in large gothic textura; 1-line capitals stroked with red. On f. 67v, in large brown capitals by a later hand: ".I.W.G.".

VIII. ff. 68-79. Watermarks: unidentified hatchet. Written space: 170 x 90 mm. Ca. 40 long lines, frame-ruled in hard point. One quire of 12. Very small cursive script by one person. 2-line initial by the scribe, with some red; 1-line capitals stroked with red.

IX. ff. 80-83. Watermarks buried in the gutter. Written space: 180 x 90. Ca. 41 long lines; frame-ruled in hard point. One quire of 4. Written by one scribe in small cursive with loops. 3-line initial by the scribe, with some red; 1-line capitals stroked with red.

X. ff. 84-93. Watermarks similar to Briquet Licorne 10001. Written space: 110 x 74 mm. 24 long lines or lines of verse; single bounding lines in hard point, full across, guide-lines for text in lead. One quire of 10. Written by one scribe in neat humanistic script. 5-line initial, paragraph marks and strokes on 1-line capitals, in red.

XI. ff. 94-103. Watermarks similar to Piccard Horn VII.106. Written space: 119 x 74 mm. 25 long lines, ruled in lead; single vertical bounding lines, full across. One quire of 10. Written by one scribe in elegant italic. Heading in square capitals; paragraph marks and strokes on 1-line capitals in red.

XII. ff. 104-115. Watermarks: unidentified dragon. Written space: 139 x 85 mm. Ca. 32 long lines, frame-ruled in lead. One quire of 12. Written by two hands in gothic cursive with some bâtarde shading. Paragraph marks and strokes of 1-line capitals, in red.

XIII. ff. 116-122. Watermarks buried in the gutter. Written space: 171 x 96 mm. Ca. 36 long lines, frame-ruled in hard point. One quire of 8 (-7, blank). Written by one scribe in very small, cramped gothic cursive. 3-line initial outlined by the scribe, followed by a word in modified square capitals, with red; paragraph marks and strokes on 1-line capitals, in red.

XIV. ff. 123-130. Watermarks buried in gutter. Written space 130 x 80 mm. 22 lines of verse, ruled in hard point, double vertical and horizontal bounding lines, full across. One quire of 8. Written by one hand in gothic cursive with a few loops. Heading in a larger form of the same script; 1-line initial and strokes of 1-line capitals in red.

Binding: s. xvi. There are vellum stays from a 15th-century humanistic manuscript in the center of the quires. Original sewing on three double, twisted, vegetable fiber cords laced into square wooden boards. Plain wound endbands, also laced, and covered with the covering leather which is back-stitched around them. Covered in brown leather with corner tongues, blind-tooled with six-petalled flowers at the intersections of diamonds within a linear border. Brass clasp-and-catch fastening, the catch on the upper board. Rebacked, clasp and strap wanting.

Written in Germany and Italy [?] at different periods in the second half of the 15th century; the codex is composed of many small booklets in different hands, apparently bound together with the printed texts (arts. 1-3) in the 16th century. Early provenance unknown. Erased note on f. 93r in humanistic script, not legible under ultraviolet light. Unidentified shelf-mark "B XXI" on front cover, in ink, perhaps contemporary with the binding. Unidentified shelf-mark "H.III.27" inside front cover. Unidentified paper tag on spine, with notation "Za 74a". Bought from Lathrop C. Harper (bookdealer) as the gift of Edwin J. Beinecke in 1953.

Bibliography: Faye and Bond, p. 38, no. 188.

MS 189 England, s. XII[ex]
Hugo de Folieto, Moralitates de avibus, etc. Pl. 17

1. ff. 1r-10v [First line and a half erased; rubric partially rubbed] //*Gallus alis se percutiens est doctor alijs exemplum prebens. De gallo. Intelligentia galli prouidentia magistrj.* Quis dedit gallo intelligentiam. De gallo queritur a quo ei intelligentia tribuatur ... Qui ad petram rostrum acuit dum se ipsum christo per bonam operationem conformem reddit.

   Moralitates de avibus; PL 177. 33-55 (for a comprehensive list of manuscripts containing this work see F. Ohly, "Probleme der mittelalterlichen Bedeutungsforschung und das Taubenbild des Hugo de Folieto," *Frühmittelalterliche Studien* 2 [1968] pp. 198-201; see also N. Häring, "Notes on the 'Liber avium' of Hughes of Fouillay," *Recherches de théologie ancienne et médiévale* 46 [1977] pp. 53-83, no. 37). The first gathering of Beinecke MS 189 is misbound, with two folios missing; the order of the chapters is: Book 1.36 (beginning), 42 (preceded by the end of 41), 43, 44 (incomplete), 36 (end of text), 37-40, 41 (incomplete), 46 (end of text), 47-53, 55-56.

2. f. 10v *Incipiunt capitula libri de medicina anime. i.* De homine qui microcosmus. id est minor mundus appelatur ... *xxi.* De capillis cadentibus. *xxij.* De dolore frontis.

3. ff. 10v-14v *Incipit prologus de medicina anime.* Cogis me frater karissime ut ea que de medicina anime ... et quod diu distuli debitum petitori reddam. *Explicit prologus. Incipit liber de medicina anime de homine qui microcosmus. i. minor mun-*

dus appellatur primum. Homo microcosmus id est minor mundus appellari ab antiquis solet ... et unum medium. Vt ignis superiorem habet extremitatem [followed by erasure]//

PL 176. 1184-92 (Chapters 1-7, incomplete at end). Both works are often attributed to Hugh of St. Victor in manuscripts; they are printed with his works in PL. See R. Goy, *Die Überlieferung der Werke Hugos von St. Viktor* (Stuttgart, 1976) pp. 491-92.

Parchment (thick, furry), ff. ii (paper) + 14 + ii (paper), 275 x 190 (224 x 146) mm. Written in 2 columns of 35 lines; single vertical bounding lines, sometimes with an additional line between columns; double horizontal bounding lines, full across. Ruled in lead; remains of prickings along upper edge.
I^8 (-1, 8 with text missing), II^8.
Written by one scribe in bold gothic bookhand.
Eighteen colored drawings of birds, many of which have been retouched by a later hand: f. 1r rooster, f. 2r stork, f. 2r blackbird, f. 2v horned owl, f. 3r ostrich, f. 5r vulture, f. 5v crane (damaged), f. 6r kite, f. 6r swallow, f. 7r heron, f. 7r caladrius, f. 7v phoenix, f. 7v quail (coturnix), f. 8r quail (perdix), f. 8v hoopoe, f. 8v swan, f. 9r peacock, f. 9v eagle. Well drawn initials in red or blue, with penwork designs of the other color, mark the beginning of each chapter; rubrics throughout. See W. B. Clark, "The Illustrated Medieval Aviary and the Lay Brotherhood," *Gesta* 21/1 (1982) pp. 63-74; *idem, The Medieval Book of Birds* (forthcoming).
Most folios are stained and have been repaired, but with little loss of text.
Binding: s. xx. Red goatskin, gilt, by Zaehnsdorf. Marks and small holes along outer edges of leaves suggest that an earlier binding had two fore-edge clasps.

Written in England in the last quarter of the 12th century as part of a larger book; early provenance unknown. Belonged to Sir Thomas Phillipps (no. 3691; listed in Munby, *Phillipps Studies*, under "Ex Bibliotheca M. Allard, & de Paris"); purchased from W. H. Robinson (notes on first and last flyleaves) in 1962 as the gift of William Robertson Coe, Yale 1949 Hon.

Bibliography: Faye and Bond, p. 38, no. 189.
Exhibition Catalogue, p. 189, no. 17.

MS 190 Flanders, s. $XV^{3/4}$
Hours, use of Rome Pl. 14

1. ff. 1r-12v   Calendar. Among the saints, Gudula (8 Jan.), Walburga (23 Feb.), Valeric (1 April), Bernardinus of Siena (20 May), Basilius (14 June, in red), 10,000 Martyrs (22 June), Eligius (25 June and 1 Dec.), Bertin (5 Sept.), Remigius and Bavo (1 Oct., in red), Donatianus (14 Oct., in red), Hubert (3 Nov.).

2. f. 13r blank; ff. 13v-20r   Short Hours of the Cross. f. 20v ruled, but blank
3. f. 21r blank; ff. 21v-27r   Short Hours of the Holy Spirit. f. 27v ruled, but blank
4. f. 28r blank; ff. 28v-34v   Mass of the Virgin. Introit: Salue sancta parens.
5. ff. 35r-39v   Sequences of the Gospels; Mark rubricated "secundum lucam" (f. 39r).
6. ff. 40r-46v   Suffrages to Michael [beginning lacking], John the Baptist, Peter and Paul, James, Sebastian, Nicolas, Antony abbot, Anna, Mary Magdalen, Catharine, and Barbara [end lacking].
7. ff. 47v-124r   Hours of the Virgin Mary, use of Rome, with different Psalms for the days of the week at Matins. Advent Office begins on f. 115v. ff. 47r, 67r, 79v-80r, 86r, 91v-92r, 108r, 114v-115r, and 124v are blank
8. f. 125r blank; ff. 125v-146v   Penitential Psalms and Litany. Among the martyrs, Servatius, Protasius; among the doctors, Augustine; among the monks and hermits, Benedict, Paul, Nicolas, Antony, Bernard, Francis, Dominic, and Alexius; among the virgins, Monica.
9. f. 147r blank; ff. 147v-192v   Office of the Dead, use of Rome.
10. ff. 193r-199v   Obsecro te ... [masculine forms; Leroquais, LH 2.346-47]; O intemerata ... [Wilmart 488-90].

Parchment, ff. i (modern parchment) + 199 + i (modern parchment), 147 x 102 (71 x 49) mm. Written in 17 long lines per page; ruled in pale red ink; single bounding lines; prickings often occur near edges of folios.
I-II^6, III^8 (+ two leaves, ff. 13, 21), IV^8 (+ one leaf, f. 28), V^8, VI^8 (-1), VII^8 (+ one leaf, f. 47), VIII^8, IX^8 (+ one leaf, f. 67), X^8 (+ one leaf, f. 80), XI^8 (+ one leaf, f. 86), XII^8 (+ one leaf, f. 92; another addition, after f. 96, now missing), XIII^8 (an addition, after f. 100, now missing), XIV^8 (+ 2 leaves, ff. 108, 115), XV^8 (+ one leaf, f. 125), XVI-XVII^8, XVIII^8 (+ one leaf, f. 147), XIX-XXIV^8. Tops of some catchwords still visible.
Written in round gothic script, by one scribe.
Twelve full-page miniatures on the verso of tipped-in leaves (blank on recto), rather routine and careless, in the style associated with the so-called "Willem (or Guillaume) Vrelant group", active in Bruges from 1454-1481/2 (see J. D. Farquhar, "The Vrelant Enigma: Is the Style the Man?," *Quaerendo* 4 [1974] pp. 100-08): f. 13v (Hours of the Cross) Crucifixion; f. 21v (Hours of the Holy Spirit) Pentecost; f. 28v (Mass of the Virgin) Virgin and Child; f. 47v (Matins) Annunciation; f. 67v (Lauds) Visitation; f. 80v (Prime) Nativity; f. 86v (Terce) Annunciation to the Shepherds; f. 92v (Sext) Adoration of the Magi; miniatures for None and Vespers originally following ff. 96 and 100 cut out; f. 108v (Compline) Flight into Egypt; f. 115v (Advent Office) Coronation of the Virgin; f. 125v (Penitential Psalms) King David kneeling; f. 147v (Office of the Dead) mourners around a coffin. Miniatures are set in a narrow gold, black, and white arched frame;

the whole set in a border of thin, spiky acanthus leaves in black, grey, and gold with touches of white, among blue, purple, and mauve flowers. [Cf., e.g., the borders on the pages added to MS 9, Waddesdon Manor (Bruges, ca. 1460), Delaissé, Marrow and de Wit, *Waddesdon Manor.*] Each miniature facing a 6-line initial, black, with white highlights, on a gold ground, filled with blue and black trilobe leaves. Ten historiated initials, in the same style as the illuminated ones, illustrating the suffrages: f. 40r, John the Baptist; f. 40v, Peter and Paul; f. 41v, James; f. 42r, Sebastian; f. 43r, Nicolas; f. 43v, Antony; f. 44r, Anna; f. 45r, Mary Magdalen; f. 45v, Catharine; f. 46v, Barbara; each initial with a border, as above. 2-line initials, gold on red and blue grounds with white highlights; some (on rectos) with black ink hair-spray with blue and gold flowers. 1-line initials, blue, with red penwork, or gold, with black penwork. Rubrication for headings and to mark antiphons, verses etc.; also for dates and major feasts in calendar.

Binding: s. xvi. The backs of the quires are cut in on either side of the sewing supports and at the kettle stitches. Original sewing on five supports attached to wooden boards. Edges gilt and gauffered. Covered in dark brown calf with a panel stamp of two sets of horizontal inhabited vines within text borders, divided by a line of fleurs-de-lis and flowers in diamonds. The four panels are enclosed by the inscription: "Ora pro nobis sancta dei genitrix ut digni efficiamur promissione Christi". Spine lining, endbands and silver [?] clasps and catches added when the book was rebacked. One joint cracked. (See *Exhibition Catalogue*, pp. 249-50, no. 72; Weale, *South Kensington*, pp. 165-66, nos. 314-16.) According to J. Marrow a binding with same stamps and inscription occurs also on a Bruges Book of Hours in the Boston Public Library, MS q. Med. 137.

Written in Bruges in the third quarter of the 15th century; belonged to Count Axel von Kalckreuth and Alva B. (Mrs. Bernard F.) Gimbel (bookplates). Given to Yale by Mrs. Gimbel in 1956 and often referred to as the "Gimbel Hours".

Bibliography: Faye and Bond, p. 38, no. 190.
Exhibition Catalogue, pp. 249-50, no. 72.
T. E. Marston, "The Gimbel Manuscripts," *Gazette* 30 (1956) p. 152.

MS 191 Germany, s. XII^{ex}
Psalter, etc.

1. ff. 1r-175v   Biblical psalter beginning defectively in Ps. 9.11 and missing Pss. 51.1-53.1 after f. 56, and Pss. 67.29-68.4 after f. 72; text occasionally interrupted by "Gloria patri. Sicut." as, e.g., after Pss. 9.19, 17.25, 36.26. Several later 15th-century hands have traced over faded portions of the text and added antiphons (some with neumes) and ferial divisions in the margins.

2. ff. 175v-194r   (no break in text) Six ferial canticles (Audite celi [f. 182v] is divided at "Ignis successus est"), Benedicite, Benedictus, Magnificat, Nunc

dimittis ("Canticum Simeonis"), Te deum ("Ymnus Ambrosij"), Quicumque uult ("Fides catholica").

3. ff. 194r-198v Litany and prayers; in the first set of 27 martyrs Pantaleon (18), Gereon (26); in the second set of 11 martyrs Ewald (2), Lambert (4), Nabor and Felix (9, 10), Oswald (11); among the 26 confessors Eucharius (12), Valerius (13), Maternus (14), Willibrord (15), Cunibert (16), Heribert (17), Ludger (18), Suitbert (19), Benedict (20), Maurus (21), Columban (22), Gallus (23), Simeon (25); among the 19 virgins Walburgis (15), Ursula (18), Cordula (19), 11,000 Virgins (20).

4. ff. 199r-207v Hours of the Virgin, use unidentified (large portions of the text have been effaced, and others have been written over in a later hand, s. xv); antiphons and capitula at Prime and None are [ant. at Prime erased]: Ego sapiencia [rewritten?], Sub tuum presidium, Transite ad me.

5. ff. 207v-210v Office of the Dead; lessons and responses at Matins are: *Lectio I.* Ne des alienis honorem, *Resp.* Credo quod; *Lectio secunda.* Melius est nomen bonum, *Resp.* Qui lazarum; *Lectio iii^a*, Memento creatoris tui; *Resp.* Domine quando.

Parchment (ff. 56v-57r palimpscst?), ff. i (later paper) + 210 + ii (later paper), 189 x 120 (147 x 94) mm. Written in 16 long lines; double vertical and horizontal bounding lines, full across; ruled in lead.
I-VII^8, VIII^8 (-1, 2), IX^8, X^8 (-3), XI^8, XII^{10}, XIII-XIV^8, XV^{12} (-3, no loss of text), XVI^{10} (-3, no loss of text), XVII-XX^{10}, XXI^4, XXII-XXIII^8, XXIV^8 (-7), XXV^{10} (-1), XXVI^6 (-4, 5, 6).
Written by a single scribe in well formed late caroline minuscule, above the top line. Marginal notes, some with neumes above them (e.g., ff. 63v, 65r), in several later hands have been partially lost due to trimming.
Initials for text divisions, 11-line (f. 115r: Ps. 101) and 7-line (f. 22r: Ps. 26, f. 40r: Ps. 38, f. 93r: Ps. 80, f. 112v: Ps. 97, f. 133r: Ps. 109), gold, with symmetrical gold tendril ornament, occasionally with dragon-head terminals, against green and mauve panelled grounds covered with dense red cross-hatching set in red and mauve frames. 7- to 2-line initials for other Psalms, red or green with red and/or green flourishes. 1-line initials for verses, alternating red and green. Headings in red and/or green throughout.
Binding: s. xvi. Resewn on four tawed, slit straps. Wooden boards chamfered and indented. Edges gilt. The spine is square and now lined with cloth. Covered in dark brown calf, blind-stamped with portraits of saints (one of whom may be Rochus) and fleurons in concentric panels [?]; very little of the earlier cover remains. Clasp-and-catch fastening, the catch on the upper board, the brown leather straps attached through metal plates to the lower. Rebacked with one half of the leather on the boards replaced with old leather from another book. Catches and clasps wanting. Upper sewing supports broken.

Written in the Rhineland at the end of the twelfth century; the saints in the litany indicate with near certainty that the manuscript is from the diocese of Trier. An inscription from the 16th century inside front cover: "Diss boich is Marien Van Der ie [? partially covered by paper] genant Erlenbach" suggests the book belonged to a member of the important family von der Ecken, prominent in Trier from the 15th to the 17th century; perhaps she was a member of a Trier convent. [We thank J.-C. Muller and J. Schiffhauer for this information.] Unidentified bookstamp on f. 1r: "G. W. B. I." Purchased from Bernard Rosenthal by Thomas E. Marston who presented it to Yale in 1955.

secundo folio: [inpi]us incenditur

Bibliography: Faye and Bond, p. 38, no. 191.

MS 192 (olim Zi.3692)   Italy, s. XV^2
Jacobus Utinensis

ff. 1r–4v *Supplicatio oratoria D. Iacobi Utinensis de duobus canonicatibus pro nepote.* Pollicitus fui praeclara gesta Sanctitatis tuae litteris mandaturum ... plena est promissi gratia nostri et illud consecutus sum tantopere concupiuj//

Paper (watermarks: unidentified bird), ff. 4, 199 x 144 (135 x 82) mm. Written in 22 long lines; single vertical bounding lines; ruled in hard point.
Composed of one gathering of four leaves.
Written in italic with heading of modified square capitals.
Plain initial, 3-line, in brown, at beginning of text; heading in red.
Unbound, but with a manuscript fragment as binding reinforcement in the center of quire.

Written in Italy in the second half of the 15th century; formerly bound in at the end of Cicero, *Synonyma*, edited by Paulus Alexius Sulpitianus and printed by Stephan Plannck (Rome, 1491); GKW 7034. Presented to Yale by Louis M. Rabinowitz in 1946.

Bibliography: Faye and Bond, p. 38, no. 192.

MS 193   France, s. VIII^{in}
Bible (fragment)

//Misit in renibus meis filias faretrae suae/ ... Oculus meus depredatus// [a large portion of the verso is covered by a fragment of a 15th-century German manuscript glued to the leaf in an attempt at repair]

Lamentations, 3.13–51 [52–56 obscured]. Fifteen folios from the original codex survive; for bibliography on the Beinecke fragment and for information concerning its relationship to the other leaves see CLA, v. 11, p. 35, no. 1337 (eleven fragments listed; four leaves appeared in the sale catalogue of Sotheby Parke-Bernet and Company, *Catalogue of Twenty Western Illuminated Manuscripts from the Fifth to the Fifteenth Century* [1982] pp. 16-19).

Most of the verses have received neumes. According to K. D. Hartzell these were certainly added much later than the leaf's own date. The ink is a medium brown which has been rubbed here and there. The neumes on the verso are much fainter than those on the recto. They were written in an unknown center by a scribe who practiced a mixed style, possibly in the eleventh century. No examples of climacus or porrectus are present. The virga's head turns to the right in the Lorraine manner, but the punctum is not the Lorraine form. The clivis is closer to the French style than the German, but the torculus is decidedly Germanic. The podatus, made in one stroke, resembles that in a Gradual-Lectionary from St. Bertin (St. Omer, Bibliothèque Municipale MS 252; *Palèographie musicale*, III, pl. 184b). The result is thus eclectic. Although he probably learned to write neumes from a German, the scribe modified his script under French influences.

Parchment, 1 f., 326 x 262 (265 x 212) mm. 2 columns of 29 lines. Rulings in hard point on the flesh side barely visible.

Written in elegant Luxeuil minuscule, with headings in uncials.

Large initial at beginning of each verse filled with yellow, red, and/or green; headings in green or red.

Removed from a bookbinding; text suffers from holes, stains, creases, and repairs.

Written at Luxeuil or one of its affiliated houses at the beginning of the 8th century. Most of the remaining fragments (except for those in Munich which are from the binding of CLM 17738 from Stadtamhof near Regensburg [see CLA, v. 9, p. 29, no. 1337]) may be traced to the Benedictine abbey of Admont in Austria. The handwritten inventory of J. Wichner (*Catalogus codicum manu scriptorum Admontensis* [1889] p. 330, no. 12) contains a marginal notation that three leaves: "Fragmenta Ezechielis et Jeremiae, Perg. VIII" were acquired by Goldschmidt's of London in 1936. The Yale fragment was presumably one of these since it was bought from Goldschmidt's in 1938 by Clarence Mendell who presented it to the Branford College Library of Yale University. Deposited in the University Library in 1953.

Bibliography: Faye and Bond, p. 39, no. 193.

MS 194 Italy, s. XV
Historia Alexandri Magni (It. tr.), etc.

Vol. I: ff. 1r-55v *Historia Alexandri Magni* compiled largely from the version of Archpresbyter Leo, translated into Italian. //tto[?] sapeuano la misura della terra distingieuano londe del mare e chonosceuano le chose cielestialj ... finissce alexandro che ttuto e detto del suo nasscimento insino alla fine. ff. 33v–34r blank; f. 44 has notes, but no text

This is not the Italian translation found in GKW, v. 1, nos. 880–83.

Vol. II: ff. 1r–59r   Leonardo Bruni, *De primo bello punico*, translated into Italian. [Preface:] //antiche auendo per materia preso a sscriuere della prima guerra punicha la quale per lunghezza de tenpo era gia dimentichata e spenta ... Et che primamente ebbono nauilj. Et primamente chonbatterono per mare. [text:] //fue intral popolo Romano e i chartaginesi grandissima per mare e per terra ebbe principio da cierte nouita di messina ... E non molto da poi tolto loro le posessionj chostrettj furono in gran parte il paese. E chosi fue loro fine per la superbia e arroghanza loro. ff. 9v–10r, 59v blank

GKW, v. 5, no. 5604; L. Bruni, *La prima guerra punica*, ed. A. Ceruti (Bologna, 1878) pp. 1–246.

Composed of two volumes formerly bound as one, with original foliation remaining: Vol. I: ff. 1–55; Vol. II: ff. 56–115 (66 omitted).

Paper (sturdy; watermarks similar in design to Briquet Chapeau 3369–70, unidentified mountain), ff. 114 (each volume has a modern paper flyleaf at beginning and end), 285 x 216 (ca. 225 x 160) mm. Some leaves are frame-ruled in lead or hard point (prickings at corners of written space), others have no visible guide-lines.

Vol. I has been repaired so extensively that the original gatherings cannot be distinguished. Vol. II: I–V^{10}, VI^8 (+ 1 leaf added at end).

Written by a single scribe in careless notarial script.

Blank spaces for headings that would have also included the first few words of text.

Binding: s. xx. Brown decorated paper cases with blank and inscribed labels. (See also MSS 180 and 184.)

Written in Italy in the fifteenth century by a scribe who apparently worked in some haste (blank leaves were left in the middle of both works) and who was producing the codex for his personal use. Early inscriptions in Vol. I: f. 1r, "Petrus Franciscus de Genninis"; in another hand the date "31 di Iuglio 1520"; f. 44r, "Lorenzzo Hilippilipo Strozzi" (with partial drawing of a face). Unidentified circular labels on spine (perforated edges): "S. III 8-9./ Alexander/ Magnus/ s. xv/ fol. 43342" and "S. III. 8-9./ Polybius/ s. xv./ fol. 43343". Unidentified stamp [of the Strozzi family?] with motto "Expecto" on f. 1r. Purchased from C. A. Stonehill and presented by Thomas E. Marston (bookplate) in 1951.

secundo folio: chosi fisamente

Bibliography: Faye and Bond, p. 39, no. 194.

MS 195 England, 1576-1579/80
Nathaniel Bacon

Account book, being a record of Stiffkey mill belonging to Nathaniel Bacon (1546?-1622) for the time period 8 December 1576-1579/80. Contains weekly statements of George Brigges, John Wilson, Thomas Shorten, William Fether, Robert Merkyn, and Henry Corye.

A. Hassell Smith, ed., *The Papers of Nathaniel Bacon of Stiffkey* (Norwich, 1979) pp. xxxi, 238.

Paper (watermarks: unidentified pot), ff. vi (paper) + i (parchment of the 13th century) + 21 + i (parchment of the 13th century) + x (paper), ca. 305 x 205 mm. Tabular format.
Collation impossible due to tight binding.
Written by several individuals in informal cursive scripts.
Most folios are wrinkled, torn; some have been mended.
Binding: s. xix. Half green goatskin with green cloth sides, gold- and blind-tooled. Leaves of a didactic theological text (Germany, s. XIII^{med}) bound at beginning and end; probably a bifolium. Parchment; 291 x 196 (220 x 155) mm., 2 columns, 43 lines; double outer, single inner vertical bounding lines, ruled in lead; prickings (slashes) in upper, lower, and outer margins. Written above top line in a small gothic bookhand. Initials in red or green with penwork designs of the other color. Stained, but with little loss of text.

Written in England 1576-1579/80; the signature of Nathaniel Bacon appears in several places, apparently as examiner of entries. Part of lot 300, Sotheby's, 19 Dec. 1911. Purchased from Tregaskis in 1913 by Philadelphia jurist Samuel W. Pennypacker; his note, dated December 1913, on first flyleaf: "From 1740 to 1865 four generations of my forefathers in the paternal line were millers. Therefore the record of a mill, kept in 1577 by the brother of Lord Verulam the great Chancellor, and carrying us through its manuscript binding into the more distant past, finds its place at Pennypacker's Mills on the Perkiomen [creek in Southeastern Pennsylvania]." Presented to Yale in 1955 by Mrs. Leonard Bacon.

Bibliography: Faye and Bond, p. 39, no. 195.

MS 196 Lower Rhine, s. XV^2
Devotions to the Blessed Virgin Mary Pl. 16

1. ff. 1r-12v   Calendar in Latin, including the feasts of Basilius (1 Jan.), "Anniuersarium patrem et matrem ordinis nostri" (6 Feb.), Translation of Augustine (28 Feb.), Suitbert (1 March), Heribert (16 March), Translation of Monica (9 April), Monica (4 May, in red), Conversion of Augustine (5 May, in red), Michael archangel (8 May), Canonization of Nicolas of Tolentino (5 June),

"Anniuersarium fratrum et sororum ordinis nostri" (7 July), "Festum niuis" (5 Aug.), Augustine (28 Aug., in red), Octave of Augustine (4 Sept.), Nicolas of Tolentino (10 Sept., in red), Michael archangel (29 Sept., in red.), Translation of Augustine (11 Oct.), 11,000 Virgins (21 Oct., in red), Cordula (22 Oct.), Cunibert (12 November).

2. ff. 13r–83r *Hyer begijnt die prologijus van onser liever vrouwen pselter. Den der heilige leirre Sanctus Bernardus gemacht hait* ... *Here doe op myn typpen ind mynen mont zo louer dynen abren helichsten ind onsprechlichsten naeme* ... *Primo nocturno. O Ioncfer marja salich is die mynsch die lieff hait* ... [the 150 Psalms], *Desen te deum hait gemacht petrus damyanus. Dich moder gotz louen wir* ... [followed by a litany to the Virgin and 2 prayers]. f. 83v ruled, but blank

3. ff. 84r–95r *Dyt is onser lijever uer[?] pselter den begynt mon op onser liever vrouwen dath als ir der engel die baetschaff bracht Ind der salmen vort alle wechen eyns up den selven dach dat onser lieuer vrouwen dach dat Iaer* ... *Dyt Nae volgende gebet Mater sij pijssima ad me miseram Gebet. O alre mijlste moder godes neige zo min onseliger dyn oren* ... [followed by the pericope from Luke, Missus est angelus Gabriel, in Ripuarian language, and then by prayers]. f. 95v ruled, but blank

4. ff. 96r–113v *Hyer begynt der gulden Pselter den der gloriose vader Sanctus Augustinus gemacht hait* ... *Ind he hait ander half hondert verssen Ind zo cynne eicklichen versse salmen eyn ave maria sprecchen* ... *Gegruetzet sijstu Iuncfrouwe eyn holtz des leuens werdich alles loues du hais gehalden dyn geloifde* ... [150 short prayers, beginning in like fashion, each preceded by an Ave Maria and with Pater Noster added in the margin by a different hand after every 10 prayers]. f. 114r–v ruled, but blank

5. ff. 115r–177v *Hyr begynt eyn suuerlich gebet van onser lieuer vrauwen Ind is van al yrem heiligen leuen Ind van den leuen yrs lieuen kyndes* ... *Tzo loue ind zo eren der glorioser Iuncfferen ind moder godes Maria. Die eyn moder is des uubeuleckden lemgens ihesus christus* ... [numerous prayers, each followed by an Ave Maria, divided into groups for the days of the week]. f. 178r–v ruled, but blank

6. ff. 179r–220v *Hyer begynnet die kroen des loefs marien Der alre glorioster koenynckynnen des hemels ind der erden Wylche yi tzo offeren is* ... *O ewerdighe mich Dych tzo louen Beheiliche maget Maria myt onsen heren ihesum christum Der gebenedider vrucht dyns buychs* ... [numerous prayers arranged in 2 sections and quoting many authorities: Ubertinus, Franco abbas luginensis, Bernardus, Anselmus, Johannes gerson, Augustinus, ex horologio sapiencie, Salomonis, Petrus blesensis, Hugo de sancto victore]. f. 221r–v ruled, but blank

7. ff. 222r–238v *Hyer Begynnent die gulden getzijde van onser liever vrauwen seer suuerlichen.* Maria Ioncfer Ontfanck die groisse die der van dem heren by dem heiligen engel gabriel ... [an office for the Virgin; hymn at matins; Laist ons syngen dat goede ind dat suesse woert die engelsche groitze...]. f. 239r–v ruled, but blank

MS 196

8. ff. 240r–256v *Dijt syn die vii Pselmen van onser lieuer vrauwen Die Ierste pselm.* O Vrauwe Maria almechtich In der verbolgent heit gotz en verhenge ons ... [Penitential "psalms" and litany of the Virgin]. f. 257r–v ruled, but blank

9. ff. 258r–266r *Dijt is onser lieuer vrouwen krantz op die liter das namen Maria.* Gegruet sijstu sterne des mers hoge godes moder ... [translation in Ripuarian of 5 hymns, canticles or psalms, beginning with Ave maris stella and the Magnificat, each followed by 2 prayers]. f. 266v ruled, but blank

10. ff. 267r–273r *Hyer Begynt dat gebet van den hondert. Ave.* O Maria suesse maget ich vermanen dich der groisser vrouden Eeren ind werdicheit ... [10 prayers to the Virgin beginning in like fashion, to be said after 10 Hail Marys]. f. 273v ruled, but blank

11. ff. 274r–297r *Hyer begynt eyn ynnych getzüde Van dem gloriosen paschlichen hoechtzijde. Antiphona.* O Heilige dach Ind eirlichen West gegruest ewelichen In wijlchen dagen got verwonnen hait die helle ... [an office for Easter; hymn at matins: O here dyr si lof ind eere du die vur ons betzaelt heues den ewigen vader...]. f. 297v ruled, but blank

12. ff. 298r–320r *Hyer begynt eyn ynnych getzijde Van der ewiger wijsheit* ... Min siel hait dich begert in der nacht Ind myn geist in dem ynresten myns hertzen ... [office of the Eternal Wisdom; hymn at matins: Ihesus soisse gedencknisse du geues waer achtige blijtscaf des hertzen...]. ff. 320v–321v ruled, but blank

13. ff. 322r–352v [Prayers as follow:] *Dyt gebet sal men sprechen err men die xxv benedixcien begint.* O werde moder gotz des almechtigen konynchs gewerdige dich tzo intfangen ... *Hier begynen die xxv benedixcien van onser lieuer vrouwen ... Ave maria.* Gegrutzet systu Maria vol gnaden sich erlichen wael vol ind gebene dyt vol van gracien ... [each of the 25 benedictions preceded by an Ave Maria]; (f. 331v) *Men seget soe wie dese xv blijtschaffen alle dage leset xv dage lanck* ... West gegruet in verblijt O Conynckynne des hemels blynckende da gerat ... *Ave maria gracia.* Verblijt dich heilige tempel godes serr blynckende vas vol alre daechden ... [an introductory prayer, then 15 others, beginning in like fashion to be said before an image of the Virgin]; (f. 334v) *Hyer begynnen die getzüde van den rouwe onser lieuer vrauwen. Ave.* O alre heilichste Ioncfer maria om dat swaer versuchten daer dyn hertze ... [a prayer for each of the canonical hours]; (f. 339r) *Eyn schoen gebet van unser lieuer vrauuen der hemelscher konnyckyne.* Gegroit sijstu schone hemelsche konynckynne Edel Ionffrauwe Maria vol genaden eynbeslossen garden alre welden...; (f. 348r) *Hier begynt eyn schon Gebet van onser lieuer vrouwen* ... O Gloriose vrouwe Ind alre suesste maget heilige Maria moder gotz vol alre god diensticheit.... f. 353r–v ruled, but blank

14. ff. 354r–376r [Prayers as follow:] *Soe wer dit Gebet myt ynnicheit syns hertzen van eynen Satersdach zoe dem anderen leset Der hait eyn bede an onser lieuer vrouwen der suysser marien.* Ich bidden dich heilige Ionffrouwen suysse maria dorch die groisse genade die dir got gedaen hait ... [4 prayers beginning in like fashion, each

followed by a Magnificat and a Pater Noster; the rubric at the end reads:] *End nu leyst magnificat inde pater noster Inde nompt die sach die du begerste myt gansszen betrouwen Ind sy sal dyr gegeuen werden Amen*; (f. 357r) *Alsus plach der suysse leirre Bernart zoe sprechen zoe den mynlichen hertzen der glorioser Ionfferen Marien* ... Ich sprechen zoe dynen reynen hertzen O werdige Ionffer maria Inde anbeden dat als eynen heiligen tempel godes...; (f. 360r) *Dyt is eyn suuerlich Gebet van onser lieuer vrouwen der hemelsche konnynckynnen.* O Mylde Ionffrouwe maria alre heilichste moder Eyn konnynckynne der engelen...; (f. 362v) *Dyt is Eyn schoen Gebet van onser lieuer vrouwen marien Inde hait gemacht onse heilige vader Sanctus Augustinus.* O lieue selige inde heilige gebenedide Ionffrouwe maria du dochter des vaders du moder des sones...; (f. 365r) *Eeyn schoen gebet van unser lieuer vrouwen.* O Gloriose vrouwe inde mylde maget O heilige konnynckynne der hemelen vrouwen der engelen Inde eyn moder des leuendigen godes...; (f. 367r) *Dyt gebet hait Sanctus Bernardus gemacht ind is van unser lieuer vrouwen.* Godt groisse dich maria eyn maget dei heiliger driueldicheit...; (f. 368r) *Hier begynt eyn schoyn Gebet van onser lieuer vrauwen der suesser moder.* O Maria hoege loefde gebenedide hemelsche konynckgynne ich arme sun dich unnutze sundersche offer dir...; (f. 370v) *Wanne eyn mynsche sunderlynge sachen begert die sal hie he nomen Gebet.* O Maria vol genaden bewijse mir dyn oueroloidige genade want ich sicherlichen weis...; (f. 371v) O Maria du op brechende rode morgen van wilchen vort komen is die ewiche clair sonne der gotheit...; (f. 375r) *Dyt is eyn suuerlich Gebet van onser lieuer vrauwen der suesser moder.* Got gruys dich mynnentliche maget o moder alre genaden des paradijs suyssicheit.... ff. 376v–380v ruled, but blank

Paper (watermarks similar to Briquet Armoiries 1656) and parchment for leaves heavily illuminated, ff. ii (original paper, i verso and ii recto ruled in ink for 19 lines, but blank) + 376 + iv (original paper), 131 x 102 (93 x 61) mm., trimmed. Written in 20 long lines; single vertical and double horizontal bounding lines, full across. Ruled faintly in lead; a few prickings along outer edge.

Two original paper fly-leaves, connected to original parchment pastedown; I^{12}, II–IV^8, V^8 (-4, following f. 40), VI–XI^8, XII^{10}, XIII^8, XIV^{12} (-8, following f. 116), XV–XXI^8, XXII^{12} (-1, following f. 186), XXIII–XXVI^8, XXVII^{10}, XXVIII–XXX^8, XXXI^{12} (-1, 10, following folios 253 and 261), XXXII–XXXIV^8, XXXV^{10}, XXXVI–XLIV^8, XLV^{10} (-1, following f. 367), four original paper fly-leaves connected to original parchment paste-down.

Text written in varying bookhands, most with bâtarde influence; more formal scripts for some rubrics and portions of text on parchment.

Two historiated initials, 12- and 10-line, on parchment bifolios: f. 15r (*Primo nocturno*) Mary as child before altar, and f. 84v (Prayer to the Virgin) Kneeling angel with harp, the letters gold and blue with brown and red penwork, the figures crudely drawn in pen and colored brown, blue and green, against bright red grounds with white highlights; brown and red calligraphic flourishes with red, green, blue and yellow dots extending along upper and side edges of written space.

12-, 10-, and 9-line initials (ff. 13r, 96r, 115r, 179r, 222r, 258r, 322v) gold (or red for ff. 258r, 322v) and blue, filled with brown floral penwork designs with calligraphic flourishes and dots, as above. Floral borders for each 12- through 9-line initial (except ff. 15r and 258r), red, blue, and green flowers with gold dot centers, connected by brown ink stems, arranged in rows or spirals; ff. 13r and 84v with a vase and bird in the margins. Two 9-line initials, ff. 274r and 298r, on parchment bifolios, in a markedly different style, green and blue respectively, with yellow and white highlights, against gold grounds, filled on f. 274r with a large flower, blue and red, on f. 298r with short sections of curling pink and green acanthus. Borders large blue or red flowers with gold dots and centers or short sections of blue and red acanthus on spiraling brown stems with small green teardrop leaves. Numerous 7- through 2-line initials, red and/or blue, with brown penwork and flourishes, as above. *I*-initials, up to 13-line, red or blue throughout. Some capital *W*'s in text in blue or red. 2-line *KL* monograms, alternating red and blue. Some portions of the text, including proper names, underlined in red. Notes for rubricator in gutter, perpendicular to text.

Binding: s. xvi. Original sewing on four supports attached to wooden boards. Covered in dark brown calf with corner turn-in tongues. Blind-tooled with concentric borders, an *X*, roses and small flowers in the central panel, roses and rampant lions in the outer borders. Two clasp-and-catch fastenings, the catch on the upper board. Rebacked and the endbands probably added. Straps replaced. Covers lined with fragments of unidentified scientific text, in Latin (s. XV).

Written in Cologne/Lower Rhine (Ripuarian language area) in the second half of the 15th century for Augustinian use (see art. 1); early provenance otherwise unknown. Belonged to Henri-Auguste Brölemann (bookplate inside front cover; polygonal label, white with blue edging and "A N° 212/9x1" inside back cover); collection formed during the early part of the 19th century by Brölemann and sold by order of his great grand-daughter Madame Etienne Mallett (Sotheby's, 4-5 May 1926, no. 175). Booktag of the bookseller Menno Hertzberger of Amsterdam. Acquired by Henry Fletcher and presented to Yale in 1955 by Mrs. Henry Fletcher.

Bibliography: Faye and Bond, p. 39, no. 196.

MS 197
Petrarch; Pope Pius II

Germany, s. XV^2

1. ff. 1r–7r *Incipit epistola domini francisci petrarche poete laureati Ad dominum iohannem florentinum poetam de constantia griseldis mulieris maxime constantie et pacientie in preconium omnium laudabilium mulierum.* Librum tuum quem nostro materno eloquio vt opinor olim iuuenis edidisci ... rusticana hec muliercula passa est. *Explicit epistola domini ffrancisci petrarche laureati poete ad dominum Iohannem florentinum*

poetam de constancia Griseldis mulieris maxime constancie et paciencie in preconium omnium laudabilium mulierum.

Petrarch, *Boccacii Griseldis historia (Rer. senil.*, 18, 3); I. B. Severs, *The Literary Relationships of Chaucer's Clerkes Tale* (New Haven, 1942) pp. 254-92.

2. ff. 7v-10r   *Incipit Epistola Enee siluij poete Laureati siue pij pape secundi de amoris remedio.* Eneas siluius etc. Ipolito mediolanensi salutem plurimam dicit. Querebaris mecum nocte preterita quod amori operam dares ... quod tibi damno est auertere stude. Ex uiena secundo calendas Ianuarij Anno domini M° quadringencesimo quadragesimo tercio. *Explicit Epistola Enee siluij poete laureati Siue Pij pape secundi de amoris remedio:*

Pope Pius II, *Epistola*; R. Wolkan, ed., *Der Briefwechsel des E. S. Piccolomini* in *Fontes rerum austriacarum* 67 (Vienna, 1912) pp. 33-39.

3. ff. 10v-14v   *Francisci petrarche ad nicholaum de azaiolis de florentia magnum regni cecilie senescallum epistola.* Iam tandem vir clarissime perfidiam fides auariciam largitas et superbiam vicit humilitas ... velocior ad sedes ethereas prouolabit. Vale patrie decus ac nostrum. *Explicit ffrancisci petrarche ad Nicholaum de azaiolis de florencia magnum regni cecilie senescallu[m] epistola. Deo gracias.*

Petrarch, *Famil. rerum*, 12, 2; V. Rossi, ed., *Le familiari* (Florence, 1933) v. 3, pp. 5-17.

4. ff. 15r-21r   *Pij pape secundi Bulla retractacionum omni dudum per eum in minoribus adhuc agentem pro consilio et Basilien. et contra Eugenium summum pontificem scriptorum Incipit feliciter.* Pius episcopus Seruus seruorum dei delectis filijs Rectori et universitati scole Colonien.... In minoribus agentes nondum sacris ordinibus ... Iudicia reuocamus atque omnino respuimus. Datum Rome apud sanctum petrum. vi. Kal. Maias Millesimo quadringentesimo sexagesimo tercio. *Pij pape secundi Bulla retractationum ... finit feliciter. Deo gratias semper.*

Pope Pius II, *Bulla retractationum*; F. Gaude, ed., *Bullarum Diplomatum et Privilegiorum* (1860) v. 5, pp. 173-80.

5. ff. 21v-26v   *Incipit Epistola Enee poete De fortuna ad dominum Procopium militem.* Eneas Siluius poeta S. P. D. domino Procopio de Rabeynsteyn milici litterato et prestanti. Noctu preterita priusquam me quieti committerem ... holus Epicurei ac pictagore legumen. Ex Vienna. *Explicit epistola Enee poete. De Fortuna Ad dominum Procopium de Rabensteyn militem.*

Pope Pius II, *Epistola de fortuna*; Wolkan, *op. cit.*, 61 (Vienna, 1909) pp. 343-53.

Paper (watermarks in gutter), ff. i (paper) + 26 + i (paper), 207 x 142 (166 x 93) mm. Written in 36 long lines; single vertical and double horizontal bounding lines full across. Ruled in hard point or lead; prickings in outer margin with two for the top lower horizontal bounding line.

I-II^{12}, III^2.

Written by three scribes in similar styles of informal gothic scripts (bâtarde influence). Scribe 1: ff. 1r–7r; 2: ff. 7v–14v; 3: ff. 15r–26v.

One calligraphic initial, f. 1r, 4–line, blue with white floral motifs; infilled with red penwork floral designs tinted with green; penwork trails into inner margin, with plain green dots. Four initials, ff. 1v, 7v, 10v, 21v, red ink, 6– to 2–line. Paragraph marks in red. Numerous capitals stroked in red; rubrics throughout; explicits underlined in red.

Binding: s. xx. Vellum spine (verso of an unidentified manuscript) with "Petrarcae et Aeneae Silvii Epistoles" written in brown ink; grey-blue paper sides.

Written in Germany in the second half of the 15th century; early provenance unknown. Purchased from C. A. Stonehill in 1952 with income from the Altschul Fund.

secundo folio: erat Itaque

Bibliography: Faye and Bond, p. 39, no. 197.

MS 198
Italy, s. XIV^2
Nicolas Trevet, Commentarius in Boethium

ff. 1r–118v [First prologue:] Explanationem librorum boetij de consolatione philosophica [much of f. 1r badly rubbed and illegible] ... [f. 2r, second prologue:] Consolationes tue letificauerunt animam meam. psalmo nonagesimo tertio. Inter letari et letificari hoc interesse uidetur ... [f. 3r, Commentary:] Carmina. Volens igitur Boetius agere de consolatione phylosophica ... Et sic terminatur liber quintus continens prosas vi et metra vi. et sunt uniuers*** libro toto prose xxxviiij. et metra totidem. deo gratias.

R. J. Dean, "The Life and Works of Nicholas Trevet," unpublished D. Phil. dissertation (Oxford, 1938).

Parchment (thick, mottled), ff. ii (paper) + 118 + ii (paper), 270 x 195 (208 x 149) mm. Written in 2 columns of 38–40 lines; single vertical bounding lines; ruled in hard point on flesh side.

I–XIV^8, XV^6. Catchwords between bounding lines in center of lower margin, some enclosed in decorative rectangles.

Written in neat round gothic by one scribe who also made corrections to the text.

Large initial, f. 1r, in red, with black penwork designs (worn). Plain initials and paragraph marks, in red, throughout. Spaces left for rubrics.

Several folios, including first and last, are illegible in sections due to rubbing.

Binding: s. xix. Brown, hard-grained goatskin, blind- and gold-tooled.

Written in Italy in the second half of the 14th century; early provenance unknown. Presented to Yale in 1954 by Robert J. Barry.

secundo folio: dirigens

Bibliography: Faye and Bond, p. 39, no. 198.

MS 199 France [?], s. XIV^{med}
Guillaume de Saint-Amour

1. ff. 1r–157v [Heading, in a later hand:] Gulielmus de Sancto amore contra ordines mendicantium. [text:] Sapienciam antiquorum omnium exquiret sapiens in prophetis vacabit narrationem virorum ... Cui data est omnis potestas in celo et in terra ... seculorum. Amen. Explicit bouberch.

    Published as "Collectiones catholicae et canonicae scripturae" in *Opera omnia* (Constance, 1632) pp. 111–487.

2. f. 158r–v [Table; heading lacking:] [Q]uod predicant non missi uel non canonice missi ... Quod procurant se per maiorum epistolas commendari contra doctrinam apostoli et exemplum.

    Published as "Tabula de signis per quae pseudo-praedictores discerni possunt a veris" in *Opera omnia, op. cit.*, pp. 487–90.

Parchment (thick, furry), ff. iii (paper) + 158 + iii (paper), 239 x 170 (178 x 130) mm. Written in 2 columns of 32 lines; single vertical and horizontal bounding lines full across. Ruled in crayon; some prickings in upper and lower margins.
I–XIX^8, XX^6 (structure uncertain due to extensive repairs). Remains of signatures, in red, often at top and bottom of folio, on recto; catchwords under inner column, on verso.
Written in gothic textura by a single scribe, who listed the authors quoted in the margins and added occasional running headings. Marginal and interlinear notations by several later hands.
Initials, probably added in the Netherlands (s. XV^2), 6- to 3-line, edged in black, filled with blue or red, with white filigree spirals, against square or cusped red or blue grounds, with white highlights, edged in black, often with black hairspray at corners. Paragraph marks and intermittent underlining, in red, throughout.
Binding: s. xviii. Edges spattered with red. Brown spattered calf, gold-tooled, with a red label.

Written in Northern France or possibly the Netherlands in the middle of the 14th century; Bouberch may possibly be the name of the scribe (see art. 1). Initials appear to have been painted later in the Netherlands (s. XV^2); early provenance otherwise unknown. Number 106 in an unidentified French catalogue (note pasted on f. iii recto); unidentified bookplate with motto "Forte fide pugnat uigilat". Purchased from Goldschmidt's in 1940 by Henry Fletcher; gift of Mrs. Henry Fletcher in 1953.

secundo folio: [nesci]unt subvenire

Bibliography: Faye and Bond, p. 39, no. 199.

MS 200 (olim Uzn 25.561bc) England, s. XVI
Hunting Calls

Seventeen hunting calls with hunting codes for the horn. Instructions in English: "To call the Company in the Morninge ... The Mount is from partie to partie every Note repeated thrice."

Paper (watermarks: unidentified pot similar in design to Heawood 3637-38), a single sheet measuring 390 x ca. 281 mm.
Written in well formed English secretary script.

Removed from a copy of *The Booke of hawking, huntyng and fysshyng* attributed to Dame *Juliana Berners* (London, [1561]). Signature of Thomas Parker on verso. The volume containing this sheet was formerly in the libraries of Thomas Faxon (signature on title page) and Joseph Haslewood (bookplate; his sale 16 Dec. 1833). Belonged to Edward C. Lowe who presented it to Ely Cathedral Library in 1879 (booktag; see C. W. Stubbs, *In a Minster Garden* [London, 1901] pp. 117-22). Acquired by James P. R. Lyell (bookplate) from whom it was apparently purchased by Davis and Orioli and sold to David Wagstaff (bookplate). Presented to Yale in 1945 by Mrs. David Wagstaff.

Bibliography: Faye and Bond, pp. 39-40, no. 200.

MS 201 Reclassed as Zi.6937.6

MS 202 Reclassed as Zi. + 2073

MS 203 France, s. XV^2
Petrarch, De remediis utriusque fortunae Pl. 13

ff. 1r-177v [Prologue missing] Etas florida est multum superest vite. *Racio*. En prima mortalium spes vana que multa hominum ... fateri oportet non felicius que enim ista felicitas non sencientis seu saxi seu saxo abditi alioquin si//

Opera (Basil, 1554) pp. 7-253.

Parchment, ff. ii (parchment) + 177 + ii (parchment), 308 x 218 (210 x 152) mm. Written in 2 columns of 37-38 lines; single vertical and horizontal bounding lines, full across. Ruled in pale red ink; remains of prickings in outer and lower margins.

I^8 (-1, 2, 3, 7), II–VI^8 (-4), VII^8 (-4), VIII–XI^8, XII^8 (-4, 5), XIII–XIV^8, XV^8 (-4), XVI–XXI^8, XXII^6, XXIII^8 (+9, 10, 11). Catchwords along lower edge near gutter, on verso; leaf signatures (e.g., gi, gij, etc.), on recto.

Written by a single scribe in beautiful bâtarde script characterized by calligraphic flourishes (some stroked with yellow) in upper and lower margins.

4-line initial on f. 1r, blue with white highlights, on a gold ground, with a coat of arms (effaced) against burgundy ground with gold floral sprays; short floral border, pink and blue flowers on green stem, infilled with gold dots with black hair-spray. 6-line initials on ff. 84r and 87r green with yellow highlights, on gold ground, with a love-knot connecting E (brown with gold highlights) and N (blue) against silver ground, borders as above. 2-line initials at beginning of chapters, gold with black penwork and flourishes; 1-line initials (*R* for *Racio*, and *G*, *S*, *D*, *M*, for the other interlocutors) blue or gold, with red or black penwork.

On ff. 1r and 8r three quarters of the page was ruled, but left blank, presumably for miniatures.

Binding: s. xix. Red velvet case, much worn.

Written in France in the second half of the 15th century for unidentified owner(s) whose initials E and N are incorporated into initials on ff. 84r and 87r. Two leaves currently preserved in the Philadelphia Free Library, Lewis European MSS T 188 and T 189, also belong to this codex. T 188 contains text from the Prologue, which was previously the third leaf in the first gathering of Beinecke MS 203; T 189, with portions from Bk. 1. 5-8, was formerly the seventh folio. (We thank D. Dutschke for his assistance in locating these leaves.) Belonged to Prince Odescalchi (bookplate) and B. G. Odescalchi (Denver, Colorado). Pencil note on Odescalchi bookplate reads "Bersohn, Robt." Purchased from C. A. Stonehill in 1953 with income from the Altschul Fund.

secundo folio: ille durus

Bibliography: De Ricci, v. 1, p. 152, no. 1; Faye and Bond, p. 40, no. 203.

Ullman, no. 57, and the forthcoming revision of D. Dutschke.

N. Mann, "The Manuscripts of Petrarch's *De remediis utriusque fortunae*: A Checklist," *Italia medioevale e umanistica* 14 (1971) p. 70.

MS 204
Frère Laurent, Somme le Roi France, s. XV$^{3/4}$

1. ff. 1r-5v [Table of contents:] Ci commence le mirroir du monde Et premierement des .x. commandemens de la loy, dont les trois premiers nous ordennent a dieu et les aultres vij. a noz proismes *I* ... De sobriete .*CC*. Des degrez sobriete *CC* et .*I*.

2. ff. 6r-312r *Cy commence le mirroir du monde* ... Li premiers commandement que dieux commanda si est teulz. Tu nauras mie diuers dieux ... La ou est par durable vie Amen. Amen, chascun en dit. Ung frere Iacobin qui cest liure ordonna Pour le grant Roy Phellipe ... Riens ny a contenu. Ne soit verite pure. Explicit. [in a later hand: "1263. Vide Baring Tab. 17"; added below in the original hand:] Cy fait des vices la somme/ ... Que. Ia. sa mere ne sendueille. [f. 312v ruled, but blank; contemporary inscription on f. 313r:] Ce liure fut a feu Madame agnes de Bourgoigne en son viuant duchesse de bourbonn Et dauuergne. ff. 313v-315v blank

E. Brayer, "Contenu, structure et combinaisons du 'Miroir du Monde' et de la 'Somme le Roi'," *Romania* 79 (1958) pp. 1-38, 433-70; the Beinecke codex appears to follow most closely "Rédaction X" (pp. 467-68).

Paper (watermarks: ff. ii-5, Briquet Armoiries 1876; ff. 6-315, similar to Briquet Lettre P 8527), ff. i (paper) + 316 (foliated ii, 1-315, in lower right corner; earlier pagination in upper left) + i (paper), 277 x 207 (192 x 132) mm. Written in 25 long lines, single vertical, single upper horizontal, single or double lower horizontal bounding lines, all full across. Folios 1-5 ruled in lead; the remainder in violet ink. Remains of prickings along outer edge.

I^6 (ff. ii, 1-5); the codex seems to be composed of gatherings of ten (sometimes of eight), but it is too closely bound to be certain. Catchwords along inner ruling perpendicular to text (Scribe 2 only).

Written by two scribes in bâtarde script. Scribe 1: ff. 1r-100v, 131r-217v; Scribe 2: ff. 101r-130v, 217v-312r, 313r.

At the beginning of each book there are spaces (9 to 13 lines) left blank for miniatures. 4- to 2-line initials for each book and for a few chapters, gold against blue and red grounds with silver or white filigree, with coarse gold ivy and black hair-spray. 2-line initials in blue or red for chapters; 1-line initials, blue or red, in table of contents. All initials with guide-letters. Chapter numbers and paragraph marks in red. Rubrics throughout.

Binding: s. xviii. Edges red. Brown calf, spine gold-tooled, with a red label: "Miroir du Monde M. S. S. Antiq."

Written in Northern France ca. 1470 presumably for Agnes of Burgundy, Duchess of Bourbon, who died at Moulins-sur-Allier in 1476 (see art. 2). Unidentified shelfmark on f. 1r: "N. 39. L. 2"; ownership inscription at top of same folio struck out. Note concerning the author and text in an unidentified hand (s. xix) on f. 315r (see art. 2). In the sale of the bookdealer W. J. Leighton (Sotheby's, 27 October 1919, no. 2428). Presented by Mrs. Charles A. Stonehill and Robert J. Barry in memory of Charles A. Stonehill in 1955.

Bibliography: Faye and Bond, p. 40, no. 204.

T. E. Marston, "*Le Miroir du Monde,*" *Gazette* 30 (1956) pp. 153-54.

MS 205 Germany, ca. 1440
Processional, Dominican use (partly in Ger.) Pl. 15

1. ff. 1r-62v   Noted processions for Palm Sunday, Maundy Thursday with services for the washing of the altars (antiphon to Catharine of Alexandria; altars of the Virgin, John the Evangelist, the Apostles, the 10,000 Martyrs, Sigismund) and for the washing of feet, Good Friday, Easter, Ascension, Corpus Christi, Dedication of a church, Purification, Assumption, Reception of legates and prelates, and of secular princes (includes an Antiphon to Dominic). f. 63r blank, with only vertical bounding lines.

2. ff. 63v-66r   *Ordinarius de communione infirme* [running title]. *Von der communion einer siechen swester*. Wenne ein siche swester die heiligen communion empfahen sol ... denne das das sacrament gottes leichnam hin wider getragen wurde.

3. ff. 66r-76v   *Ordinarius de extrema vnccione* [running title]. *Von der heiligen olunge*. Wenne ein swester das heilige oley enpfahen sol ... vnd angesanck sprechen Subuenite sancti dei et cetera als hernoch geschriben ist.

4. ff. 76v-84r   *Ordinarius de transitu sororis* [running title]. *Von der hinfart der swester*. Wenne ein swester gentzlichen zu dem tode nehet ... Libera me domine et cetera mit gesange.

   Litany in this art. also includes several additions by a slightly later hand: Peter as the last martyr; among the confessors: doubling of Dominic, Thomas in the original hand, addition of Vincent, Bernard, Henry, Louis, Beroald; among the virgins: Anna, doubling of Catharine, Barbara, Ursula in the original hand, addition of Elisabeth.

5. ff. 84r-111v   *De commendacione anime* [running title]. *Commendacio anime Responsarium*. Subuenite sancti dei. Occurrite angeli domini suscipientes animam eius ... nach dem als der priorin vnd swestere andacht denne vrteilt zetunen.

6. f. 111v-138v   *Ordinarius de officio sepulture* [running title; the burial service is noted]. *Von dem ampt der begrebnusse*. Wenne ein gestorbenne swester sol zu grabe getragen werde ... Sanctificat tibi domine. Oremus deus noster pro et cetera. Als hie vorgeschriben stet et cetera.

Parchment, ff. i (contemporary parchment) + 138, 165 x 120 (108 x 78) mm.

Written in ca. 17 long lines; single vertical bounding lines, widely spaced double upper and lower horizontal bounding lines and two additional rulings in upper margin for running titles (ff. 63v-138v), all full across; ruled in ink. Prickings in upper margin.

I-XVII⁸, XVIII². Catchwords along lower edge near gutter.

Written by a single scribe in well formed gothic textura. Articles 1 and 6 have 4-line staves, in red, and black square notes.

Uninspired blue initial, 2-stave, on f. 1r, infilled and surrounded by red penwork flourishes with blue accents. Similar plain initials, 2-line, alternate in blue, red, and black with red, throughout. Running titles and headings in red.

Binding: s. xvi. Resewn, using original sewing holes, on three double vegetable fiber cords laced into back-cornered and indented oak boards. Endbands embroidered on a strip of vellum and adhered, the vellum extending onto the outside of the boards. The spine is square and lined all along with manuscript fragments extending to the inside of the boards. Covered in vellum blind-tooled with concentric borders containing heads in oval frames among foliage in the outer, and busts of saints in the inner. Two brass fastenings, the catch on the upper board, straps attached to the lower with a metal plate. Straps wanting and a slight crack in one joint. See *Festschrift Ernst Kyriss* (Stuttgart, 1961) p. 182, pl. 5, and H. Helwig, *Handbuch der Einbandkunde* v. 1, (n.p., 1953) pp. 74-75, pl. 75 for similar bindings from Wittenburg, Augsburg and Nuremberg late in the 16th century.

Written apparently in Southern Germany as a gift for Barbara Pfintzing, who entered a nunnery in 1441 at the age of 16; inscription on f. i verso: "Item ich swester barbara pfinczingin würd geporn noch unsers lieben herren ihesu christi gepurt. M. CCCC. und in dem xxv Iar am achten tag vor weihen nahten. Vnd kom in das kloster an sant Erharsz tag. M. CCCC. und in dem xlj iar." The text (see articles 1 and 4) indicates that the manuscript was produced for use in a Dominican house of nuns; liturgical directions are written in German (the feminine forms in the antiphons and prayers often bear suprascript masculine endings, in red). Acquired by Henry Fletcher from Dawson's Book Shop, Los Angeles; gift of Mrs. Henry Fletcher in 1953.

secundo folio: dicens ite

Bibliography: Faye and Bond, p. 40, no. 205.

MS 206 France, s. XIII^ex
Bible Pl. 11

ff. 1r-450v Bible, in the following order (numbers in parentheses refer to Stegmüller, v. 1): General prologue (284); Pentateuch (285), Genesis, Exodus (leaf missing between ff. 21-22), Leviticus, Numbers (leaf missing between ff. 46-47), Deuteronomy (leaf missing between ff. 60-61); Joshua (311, leaf missing between ff. 73-74); Judges (leaf missing between ff. 82-83); Ruth; 1 Kings (323; leaf missing between ff. 93-94), 2 Kings (leaf missing between ff. 105-106), 3 Kings (leaf missing between ff. 115-116), 4 Kings; 1 Chronicles (leaf missing between ff. 139-140), 2 Chronicles (327) + Prayer of Manasses; 1 Ezra (330); Nehemiah; 2 Ezra (= 3 Ezra, Stegmüller no. 94, 1; leaf missing between ff. 174-175); Tobit (332); Judith (leaf missing between ff. 184-185); Esther (341 + 343); Job (leaf missing between ff. 194-195); Psalms (leaf missing between ff. 204-205); Proverbs (2 leaves missing between ff. 224-225); [folios 231-253 have been misbound:] Ecclesiastes (ff. 236-237; beginning missing); Song of Songs (f. 238; beginning missing); Wisdom (ff. 239-243; beginning missing); Ecclesiasticus (ff. 244-253, 231-235; beginning missing) Isaiah (leaf missing between ff. 253-254); Jeremiah (leaf missing between ff. 271-272); Lamentations (leaf missing between ff. 293-294); Baruch (491); Ezekiel (492); Daniel (494); Minor Prophets (500): Hosea (507), Joel (511, 510), Amos (515, 512, 513), Obadiah and end of Jonah missing (leaf lost between ff. 334-335), Micah (526), Nahum and beginning of Habakkuk missing (leaf lost between ff. 336-337), Zephaniah (534), Haggai (538), Zechariah (539), Malachi (543); 1 Maccabees (547, 553, 551), 2 Maccabees; Matthew (590, 589), Mark (607), Luke (620, followed by Luke 1.1-4 treated as a prologue), John (624); Romans (677), 1 Corinthians (leaf missing between ff. 414-415), 2 Corinthians (699), Galatians and beginning of Ephesians missing (several [?] leaves missing between ff. 421-422), Philippians (728), all of Colossians and beginning of 1 Thessalonians missing (several [?] leaves missing between ff. 423-424), 2 Thessalonians (752), 1 Timothy (765), beginning of 2 Timothy and all of Titus missing (several leaves [?] missing between ff. 425-426), Philemon (783), Hebrews (793); Acts (leaf missing between ff. 429-430); Catholic Epistles (809; leaves missing between ff. 413-414, 444-445); Apocalypse (beginning missing between ff. 444-445).

Parchment, ff. 450, 224 x 157 (162 x 111) mm. Written in 2 columns of 51 lines; single vertical bounding lines full across, double horizontal rulings in upper margin for running titles. Ruled in lead; prickings in lower margins.

A precise collation is impossible due to extensive repair of the binding; the contents given above indicate where leaves appear to be wanting. Remains of signatures along center of lower edge, on verso, do not reflect current construction of codex.

Written by a single scribe in small, neat, gothic bookhand; note in his hand on f. 209r, too trimmed to be legible.

Approximately half the historiated initials have been excised. The initials, 51- to 9-line, painted gold, red and blue with white highlights and punctuated with gold dots, terminate in spiralling floral serifs, often with biting animal heads, with long projecting stems against cusped grounds. The figures are red, blue, orange and grey, against red or blue grounds, some of them diapered and decorated with groups of three white dots and gold dots. The subjects of those surviving are as

MS 206

follow: f. 1r (Prologue) Three scribes; f. 4r (Genesis) Creation, with only six days; f. 37r (Leviticus) Jews before an altar; f. 92r (Ruth) Elimelech, Naomi and two children; f. 128r (4 Kings) Ahaziah on deathbed; f. 151r (2 Chronicles) Solomon praying; f. 166v (1 Ezra) Cyrus building tower; f. 180v (Tobit) Tobit and swallow; f. 190r (Esther) Esther, Ahasuerus and Haman; f. 207r (Psalm 26) Annointing of Samuel; f. 209v (Psalm 38) The Devil tempting the psalmist (an unusual iconography, for which compare a Psalter, Paris, B. N. nouv. acq. lat. 3104, Northern France, ca. 1270, f. 84v, reproduced in *Manuscrits à peintures offerts à la Bibliothèque Nationale par le comte Guy du Boisrouvray* [Paris, 1961] no. 7, pp. 39-40 and pl. 18); f. 212r (Psalm 68) David in the deep waters, God the Father above; f. 214v (Psalm 80) David at carillon; f. 217r (Psalm 96) Cantors; f. 219v (Psalm 109) Christ in Majesty; f. 295r (Baruch) Baruch as scribe; f. 298r (Ezekiel) The Vision of the Tetramorph; f. 318v (Daniel) Daniel in the lions' den; f. 328v (Hosea) Hosea and Gomer on throne; f. 331v (Joel) Joel with two Jews; f. 333r (Amos) Amos as Shepherd; f. 335v (Micah) Micah before city; f. 338r (Zephaniah) Zephaniah seated; f. 339r (Haggai) Haggai standing with king; f. 340r (Zechariah) Annunciation to Zechariah; f. 344r (Malachi) Malachi with two Jews; f. 345v (1 Maccabees) Execution of the idolatrous Jew, who holds a pig's head; f. 359r (2 Maccabees) Delivery of letter; f. 368r (Matthew) Tree of Jesse; f. 381r (Mark) Mark with lion; f. 389r (Luke) Luke censing altar, winged man; f. 402r (John) John with eagle; f. 419r (2 Corinthians) Angel with scroll, man in bed; f. 423r (Philippians) An execution; f. 424v (2 Thessalonians) Paul with sword and standing man; f. 425r (Timothy) King with two soldiers; f. 426r (Philemon) Paul in tower and standing man; f. 426r (Hebrews) Paul with two Jews; f. 443r (James) Standing man.

Illuminated initials, 51- to 5-line, occasionally for books (f. 74v [Joshua] and f. 175r [Nehemiah]), for the most part for the prologues, similar to the historiated initials, except infilled with interwining and angular vines with biting head terminals, red and/or blue against red or blue grounds with gold dots and set in frames of painted gold. 2-line calligraphic initials for chapters, red or blue with blue or red penwork, each attached to a column of superimposed *I*'s, red and blue, running the full length of the text column, with penwork flourishes, especially at the terminals. Capitals for verses stroked in red. Running headings and chapter numbers in alternating red and blue letters or numbers.

Binding: Date? Resewn on four single, round, vegetable fiber cords which are frayed out and adhered inside the oak boards. There are no endbands, but traces of alum tawed endband cores and sewing supports remain in the holes in the boards. The spine is square. Some lettering in ink on the fore-edge. Covered in red-brown calf, with an exceptionally large stamp of the Virgin and child in an aureole within concentric frames, one with an inscription, on the upper board and diamonds filled with crosses, roses and IHS in circles on the lower. The latter ornaments are also stamped on the turn-ins underneath the pastedowns. Rebacked and edges repaired. Upper board detached. Not the original and possibly not an early binding. Rebacked in the Yale Conservation Studio in 1982. The upper and lower covers are lined with single leaves, pasted down, of a missale plenum (s. XI?). Portions of Dominica VI post Pentecosten, Feria IV of that week (upper cover), an unidentified mass of the Sanctorale, Dominica III post Pentecosten (lower cover). Where they occur, the texts of the proper chants are notated in German neumes *in campo aperto*. Some of the chants are cited by incipit; these are usually not noted. The Alleluia for DMC III is Domine in virtute; that for DMC VI is Eripe me. (We thank K. D. Hartzell for his assistance with these fragments.)

Written probably in Northern France toward 1300; note of a corrector along lower edge of f. 21v (partially trimmed) suggests that the manuscript travelled to Avignon: "feci auinion. Non. Septembro anno domini .M. CCC. xxii in ecclesia [?] fratrum augustinorum." Notes by at least 2 hands of the 15th century. Unidentified booklabel, gold on pale blue, inside front cover; unidentified paper label with "393" inside back cover. Gift of Mrs. Bernard F. Gimbel in 1955.

secundo folio: [perscrip]ta sunt breuiter

Bibliography: Faye and Bond, p. 40, no. 206.
T. E. Marston, "The Gimbel Manuscripts," *Gazette* 30 (1956) p. 152.

MS 207 France, ca. 1270
Thomas Aquinas, In tertium librum Sententiarum Petri Lombardi

1. ff. 1r–132v [Added by scribe in upper margin:] In nomine patris et filii et spiritus sancti amen. [text:] Ad locum vnde exeunt flumina reuertuntur ut iterum fluant. ecclesiastes i. ex verbis istis duo possumus accipere ... et uirtutes perficit quibus ad uitam peruenitur eternam in qua cum christo viuamus per omnia secula seculorum amen. Explicit tertius fratris. T. de aquino ordinis predicatorum.

    M. F. Moos, ed., *Scriptum super III libros Sententiarum* (Paris, 1933) v. 3.

2. ff. 133r–135v [Table of contents, in a later hand:] *Incipiunt tituli libri tertij sancti thomae*. Vtrum deum incarnari fuerit possibile./ Vtrum fuerit congruum./ ... Quid per .x. corda psalterij intelligatur./ Explicit.

Parchment, ff. i (parchment) + i (contemporary parchment) + 135 + i (contemporary parchment) + i (parchment), 325 x 210 (226 x 163) mm. Ff. 1r–132v written in 2 columns of 55 lines; single bounding lines, upper horizontal full across; ruled in lead; prickings visible for bounding lines only. Art. 2: 3 columns of 55 lines; double outer and single inner vertical bounding lines; double upper and lower horizontal bounding lines full across, with an additional pair of lines in lower margin. Ruled in lead; prickings for all guide-lines.

I-XI¹², XII³ (structure uncertain). Catchwords near gutter, enclosed by rectangle.

Written in neat gothic textura by a single scribe *secundum pecias* (notations along bottom of leaves, mostly trimmed).

Small decorative initials in red and/or blue with penwork designs of either or both colors; notes for illuminator in margins. Paragraph marks alternating red and blue throughout; running headings in red and blue.

Some folios mended with chartreuse thread.

Binding: 1899. Quarter leather over wooden boards, blind-tooled, with a gold-tooled label and brass clasps. Bound by Douglas Cockerell (stamp with date inside back cover).

Written in Paris ca. 1270; copied from an exemplar vended by Gulielmus Senonensis, stationer on the rue St. Jacques (see P. M. J. Gils, "Codicologie et critique textuelle pour une étude de MS. Pamplona, Catedral 51," *Scriptorium* 32 [1978] pp. 221-30, plates 17-19, especially pl. 18e of the note in MS 207 on f. 46r: "Nota confundatur stacionarius qui me fecit deturpari librum alicuius probi uiri"). Evidence of early use includes: table of contents added on ff. 133r-135v; *divisiones* and *distinctiones* added in a semi-cursive hand; marginal notes suggesting a later collation of the text. Belonged to the Cistercian monastery of Royaumont in the diocese of Senlis: inscription of the 14th century on f. ii verso "Iste liber pertinet monasterio Regalismontis ordinis Cisterciensis siluanetensis diocesis" (noted by J. Leclercq, "Textes et manuscrits cisterciens dans les bibliothèques des États-Unis," *Traditio* 17 [1961] p. 164). Belonged to Sir Thomas Phillipps (no. 772, inscription on f. ii recto); his purchase from the Chardin Library, Paris (see *Phillipps Studies*, v. 3, p. 23). Collection of Albert May Todd (1850-1931; bookplate). Acquired by Henry Fletcher and presented to Yale in 1950.

secundo folio: reducere. Si

Bibliography: Faye and Bond, p. 40, no. 207.

Exhibition Catalogue, p. 193, no. 21.

E. T. Silk, "The Fletcher Manuscript of St. Thomas on the 'Sentences' of Peter Lombard," *Gazette* 25 (1950) pp. 60-62.

C. E. Lutz, "Manuscripts Copied from Printed Books," *Gazette* 49 (1975) p. 262 (reprinted in her *Essays on Manuscripts and Rare Books* [Hamden, 1975]).

MS 208 Italy, s. XVI^med
Ptolemy, Harmonicorum libri III (in Greek) Pl. 31

1. f. 1r [Table of Contents, for Book I only:] Κλαυδίου πτολεμαίου ἁρμονικῶν πρῶτον. Κεφάλαια. περὶ τῶν ἐν ἁρμονικῇ κριτηρίων ... πόσα ἐστὶ τὰ συνηθέστερα ταῖς ἀκοαῖς γένη καὶ τίνα.

2. ff. 1v-65v *Κλαυδίου πτολεμαίου άρμονικῶν πρῶτον· περὶ τῶν ἐν ἁρμονικῇ κριτηρίων.* Ἁρμονικὴ ἐστὶ δύναμις καταληπτικὴ τῶν ἐν τοῖς φόφοις ... πρὸς ἥλιον καὶ διὰ πάντας ἐπὶ σφαλείς [sic]. Κλαυδίου πτολεμαίου ἀρμονικῶν τῶν εἰς τρία τὸ τρίτον. τέλος.

I. Düring, ed., *Ἁρμονικά* (Göteborg, 1930) pp. 2-111.

Paper (unidentified watermarks are faint and have been obscured by ink), ff. i (paper) + 65 + ii (paper), 333 x 231 (210 x 120) mm. Written in 30 long lines, lightly ruled in hard point; single bounding lines that do not always extend to edges of folio.

I-VI[10], VII[4] (+ 1 added at end, f. 65). Catchwords are perpendicular to text in lower margin along inner bounding line.

Written in a neat Greek minuscule by Camillus Venetus (see below).

Book and chapter headings and 3-line initials in red. Many delicately drawn diagrams illustrating the text: tones, harmonics, scales, modes, the zodiac.

Binding: s. xvi. Original sewing with two strands of thread on five single supports adhered to the inside of the boards. Plain wound endbands are sewn on vegetable fiber cores which are laced into pasteboards. The square spine is lined all along with vellum. The edges are lavender. Covered in black goatskin, blind-tooled with a large diamond in concentric borders made up of flowers, foliage and heads in medallions. Two ribbon fastenings now wanting, as is some spine lining and leather.

Written in Northern Italy in the middle of the 16th century by Camillus Venetus, who was also responsible for Beinecke MSS 270 and 271. According to Karpozilos (p. 68) the scribe was associated with or a student of Andreas Darmarius; Knox attributes MSS 270 and 271 to Andreas Darmarius himself (*Ziskind Catalogue*, pp. 44 and 53). However, a close inspection of the hand reveals that all three manuscripts were written by Camillus Venetus (we thank P. Canart for his assistance in attributing the Beinecke codices). Unidentified shelf-mark "N. 46" on f. 1r. Library of the Santa Iglesia del Pilar, Saragossa, Spain (Graux and Martin, p. 212, no. 416; Olivier, pp. 52-57). Gift of the Yale Library Associates in 1954.

Bibliography: Faye and Bond, pp. 40-41, no. 208.

"Eight Medieval Manuscripts," *Gazette* 29 (1955) pp. 108, 112.

T. Mathieson, "Towards a Corpus of Ancient Greek Music Theory: A New *Catalogue raisonné* Planned for RISM," *Fontes artis musicae* 25, no. 2 (1978) pp. 129-32.

MS 209
Precepts for Students

Germany, s. XV²

1. ff. 1r-8r *Compendiosa de modo studendi preceptio. Prefatio.* [E]x re profecto discipulorum videbitur esse si ad capescendas bonarum artium disciplinas debitum legendi modum ac ... [text:] *Preceptum primum.* Cum omnium virtutum dux sit Religio et omnis sapientie ... [concludes after 34 precepts:] Oderunt peccare mali formidine pene. Oderunt peccare boni virtutis amore.

    Accompanied by extensive marginal annotations including references to Bernard, Seneca, Boethius, Quintilian, Augustine, Jerome, Plato, and Cicero.

2. ff. 8v-10v *Carmen Statuta Comprehendens modumque viuendi honestum scolarium siue studentum.* [E]xpedit in cunctis mores seruare decentes. Nam solet auctorem mos redimire bonus ... Primum statutum mandat latinitatem a scolaribus obseruandam ... [concludes after 7 statutes:] huic puto suspensor iure magister erit.

    Interlinear and marginal glosses (ending with the 5th precept).

Paper (watermarks: unidentified bull's head buried in gutter), ff. i (contemporary paper) + 10 + i (contemporary paper), 206 x 145 (140 x 83) mm. Written in ca. 18 long lines or lines of verse. Vertical rulings delineate main text as well as an inner and outer column for commentary; frame-ruled in hard point.
Composed of a single gathering of 12 leaves.
Written by one scribe in a small running script, with a more formal style of writing for headings.
Some loss of marginalia due to trimming.
Binding: s. xx. Fragment of a 16th-century choirbook from Germany (four-line staves, in red; square notes, in black).

Written in Germany in the second half of the 15th century; early provenance unknown. Acquired from Goldschmidt's in 1927 by the Rev. Anson Phelps Stokes (bookplate) who sold it to Yale in 1956.

Bibliography: De Ricci, v. 2, p. 2276, no. 3; Faye and Bond, p. 41, no. 209.

MS 210
Bible, with glossa ordinaria (fragment)

Italy, s. XII^{med}

ff. 1r-22v //et huic nouissime dare sicut et tibi. Ann [*sic*] licet michi facere quod uolo ... mandaui uobis et ecce ego uobiscum sum usque ad consummationem seculi.

Matthew 20.14-22.10; 25.11-28.20, with glossa ordinaria ending: qui diuina mansione sint [corrected from sunt] digni (Stegmüller, v. 9, no. 11827; PL 114. 150-78). Crayon notes throughout in an unskilled hand, now mostly erased.

Parchment, ff. 22, 240 x 146 (written space for text of Matthew: 160 x 52; for text with gloss: 160 x 126) mm. Text written in 20 widely spaced lines; gloss in ca. 40 lines arranged in single columns on each side of the text. Single vertical and horizontal bounding lines full across; ruled in crayon for the vertical bounding lines of the central column and in hard point, on hair side, for all other lines. Prickings in upper, lower, and outer margins.

I^6, II-III^8 (gathering missing between I and II).

Written in fine carolingian minuscule of two sizes, the smaller script with tall ascenders; marginalia added in several later hands. Early Arabic numerals in upper right corner indicating chapter number.

Binding: s. xx. Plain vellum wrapper.

Written in Italy in the middle of the 12th century. Evidence of use and ownership in the 13th century includes inscription on f. 22v: "Iste matheus concessus est fratri Ottolino de busco ordinis fratrum heremitarum qui est natione Cremonensis." Belonged to Henry Fletcher; gift of Mrs. Henry Fletcher in 1953.

Bibliography: Faye and Bond, p. 41, no. 210.

MS 211
Psalter, etc.

Germany, s. XIII^2
Pl. 15

1. ff. 1v-2r Calendar, all entries in black (4 folios containing March through October cut out); among those listed: Pantaleon (18 Feb.), Willibrord (7 Nov.), Othmar (16 Nov.), Peter, bishop and martyr (25 Nov.; instead of St. Catharine of Alexandria), Barbara (4 Dec.).

2. ff. 2v-111v Biblical psalter adapted to liturgical use through the addition of antiphons in the margins (missing 40.7-43.6 after f. 35, 61.6-77.38 after f. 49; Pss. 148-50 run on).

3. ff. 111v-123v Six ferial canticles, Benedicite, Benedictus, Magnificat, Nunc dimittis ("Canticum symeon"), Te deum, Quicumque uult ("Fides catholica").

4. ff. 123v-125r Litany (with three entries on f. 123v erased, including one later addition "Bertilia" visible under ultraviolet light; undetermined number of leaves appear to be missing between ff. 123 and 124), followed by prayers, the final ones written in a slightly later hand after f. 125 was glued to back cover.

Parchment (sturdy), ff. 125 (125 = back pastedown), 196 x 141 (128 x 89) mm. Written in 20 long lines; double horizontal bounding lines, single vertical, all full across. Ruled in ink; prickings (slashes) in upper, lower, and outer margins.

I^6 (-2, 3, 4, 5), II^{10}, III^8, IV^8 (+1 leaf at end), V^8 (-1, 8), VIII-X^8, XI^{10} (-10, no loss of text), XII-XVI^8, XVII^3 (1 tipped in; 2 and 3 conjugate, with 3 pasted to back cover).

Written by a single scribe in bold, early gothic bookhand. Notes by several later scribes, some of which have been erased.

Full page initial *B* (f. 2v) in blue with pink and blue interior vine-stem patterns, on gold ground surrounded by red rectangular frame outlined in black. Smaller gold initials, 10- to 8-line, for Psalms 26, 38, 51, 52, 80, 97, 101, 109 (ff. 21r, 33v, 43r, 43v, 53v, 68r, 70r, 83r), of similar design, on blue ground with vine-stem patterns of olive green, white, and red, and rectangular frame of red and white. Other psalms introduced by gold initials, 9- to 3-line, outlined in red, infilled and surrounded by blue penwork designs; headings and first letter of each verse in red. Most decorative initials are severely rubbed.

Trimming of outer margins on ff. 8 and 122 affects text.

Binding: s. xvi-xvii. Resewn with three strands of thread on four round, twisted, vegetable fiber cords laid in forked grooves and laced in and out of flush oak boards. The cords are pegged twice: from outside to inside and vice versa with almost square pegs. The vegetable fiber endband cores are laced into the boards, the endbands themselves wanting. The spine is rounded, with traces of adhesive. Covered in tawed skin, once white, now tan and white. The turn-ins are sometimes turned in over small fragments of a parchment manuscript, in other cases, under, and the corners cut square. There is some inscribed parchment on the outside of the upper board, probably part of a spine lining. The discoloration on the endleaves does not match the present turn-ins. There are traces of four round bosses on each board and of a pin in the center of the upper one. The white, tawed strap, most of which is now wanting, is attached to the lower board through a metal plate. One corner of the upper board is cut away and the covering of the spine and part of the boards wanting. A messy, somewhat primitive binding.

Written in Germany in the second half of the 13th century, perhaps in Trier. Unidentified round tag on front cover with notation "HSS 1021." Belonged to Professor Leander van Ess of Marburg (signature on f. 2r; booklabel inside front cover) who is known to have acquired manuscripts from St. Maximinus of Trier following its secularization during the French Revolution. See H. Schiel, "Erwerb von zwei Mattheiser Handschriften des 11. und 12. Jahrhunderts für die Stadtbibliothek Trier," *Vierteljahrsblätter der Trierer Gesellschaft für nützliche Forschungen* 1 (1955) pp. 6-9; for van Ess in general, N. Adler, "Leander van Ess und seine Übersetzung des Neuen Testaments," *Archiv für mittelrheinische Kirchengeschichte* 14 (1962) pp. 575-76 and H. Becker, "Der Nassauische Geheime Kirchen- und Oberschulrat Dr. Johann Ludwig Koch (1772-1853)," *Archiv für mittelrheinische Kirchengeschichte* 15 (1963) pp. 147-79. Some of the unusual saints in the calendar (Pantaleon [Feb. 18] and Peter, bishop and martyr [25 Nov.]) occur in a few Trier manuscripts of the 10th through 14th centuries (see P. Miesges, "Der Trierer Festkalender," *Trierisches Archiv, Ergänzungsheft* 15 [Trier, 1915]). (We thank J.-C. Muller and J. Schiffhauer for this information.) Van Ess sale to Sir Thomas Phillipps (no. 485; stamp and inscription on f. 1r; see *Phillipps Studies*,

v. 3, pp. 29-33). Acquired by Yale in 1955 from V. G. Simkhovitch.

secundo folio: [text, f. 4] qui tribulant

Bibliography: Faye and Bond, p. 41, no. 211.

MS 212 France, s. XV$^{4/4}$
Salic Law

1. ff. 1r-37r *Incipit lex salica.* R. Theodericus rex francorum cum esset cathalones elegit viros sapienter qui cum in regno suo legibus ... [text:] *De mamnire* [sic]. R. Si quis ad malum legibus dominicis mannitus fuerit et non uenerit si eum ... [ends in the section entitled:] *De eo qui filiam alienam acquisierit et se retraxerit.* Si quis filiam alienam ... et dimidium culpabilis iudicetur. *Explicit hic liber legis salice.*

2. f. 37r-v [contemporary addition:] Si vero .l. porcos furatus fuit ... et pleraque alia in lege salica passim corrupta reperiuntur. [in a later hand:] .917.

   K. A. Eckhardt, ed., *Pactus Regis Salicae* in *Monumenta Germaniae Historica* (Legum sectio I, Regum nationum germanicarum 4, 1) (Hanover, 1962) pp. 18-234.

Parchment, ff. i (contemporary parchment) + 37 (pagination, s. xvii, 1-74) + i (contemporary parchment). Written in 22 long lines; single horizontal and vertical bounding lines, full across. Ruled faintly in red; prickings in all margins. I-IV^8, V^4 (+ 1, f. 37). Remains of original leaf signatures (e.g., bij), on recto. Catchwords perpendicular to text on inner bounding line.

Written in a neat bâtarde by a single scribe who also made interlinear and marginal notes. Corrected by at least one later hand.

One full compartmentalized border, f. 1r, divided into diagonal bands, outlined in red ink, blue and beige curling acanthus against a plain parchment ground and flowers, red and blue, on stems with green leaves, against a beige ground. One 4-line initial (rubbed), f. 1r, red with gold highlights on a blue ground with white highlights; 2- and 1-line initials throughout, painted in brushed gold against red or blue grounds. Line endings red and/or blue, with gold highlights. Rubrics throughout.

Binding: s. xv-xvi. Original sewing, including pastedowns, on four tawed, slit straps which are laced into wooden boards. Red and olive green endbands. Covered in brown calf, blind-tooled with concentric borders, the center filled in with vertical lines of animals facing in opposite directions. There are two catches on the lower board and attachments, presumably for a metal clasp hinge, on the upper. Rebacked.

Written in Northern France probably in the last quarter of the 15th century; inscription and date on f. i recto: "En Vsu et scriptura 1573." Inscription inside front cover, in hand of 16th century (visible under ultraviolet light): "Dono possideo/ G Selb DX [?]". Signature of "Jac. Roch" with date "20 Aprilis 1793" on f. 1r; later inscription "Bought of Mr. Roche of Cork [probably identifiable as James Roche, 1770-1853; DNB, v. 17, p. 69]." Belonged to Sir Thomas Phillipps (no. 3899; stamp and notation inside front cover; tag on spine). From the library of George Dunn of Woolley Hall near Maidenhead (1865-1912, booklabel and inscription "δβλ/ G D./ May 1903" inside front cover; his sale at Sotheby's, 2 Feb. 1914, no. 1573). Two unidentified entries from sales catalogue pasted inside front cover and on first flyleaf. Belonged to Henry Fletcher; gift of Mrs. Henry Fletcher in 1953.

secundo folio: qui clauem

Bibliography: Faye and Bond, p. 41, no. 212.

MS 213
Collection of legal documents

Italy, 1541

A collection of copies of grants and concessions made to Jacobo Probo, conte di Pianelle, from Francesco Gonzaga, Marquis of Mantua (1466-1519), and his son Federico II (1500-40), all of which are in Latin. The three documents of Francesco are dated 1496 (ff. 8r-10r), 1514 (ff. 6v-7v), 1516 (ff. 1r-2r); the two of Federico are dated 1519 (ff. 2v-5r) and 1526 (ff. 5v-6r). On f. 10v there is a statement by the notary "Castantius [*sic*] Iottus" authenticating these copies (dated 18 Oct. 1541). Two documents of Ferdinand II of Aragon, King of Sicily (1452-1516) confirming title to the property in question (ff. 11r-14r) seem to have been added later by another writer. f. 14v blank

Parchment, ff. iv (contemporary paper) + 14 (13, 14 actually flyleaves conjugate to ff. iii, iv in front) + ii (contemporary paper: conjugate leaves to the front flyleaves), 195 x 150 (ca. 140 x 130) mm. Folios 1r-10v written in 26 long lines; ff. 11r-14r in ca. 30 lines. Ruled in hard point. Single vertical (and sometimes horizontal) bounding lines, full across; prickings at corners of written space.

I^{12} (the final two documents continue onto back flyleaves).

Written in inelegant italic for ff. 1-10; a sprawling running hand for ff. 11-14.

Binding: s. xvi. Levantine? A single gathering backstitched to the vellum lining of a semi-limp pasteboard folder covered with red-brown goatskin with corner tongues. Blind-tooled with a cross on a pedestal in a border on the upper board and an *X* on the lower. The design made up of fleurs-de-lis, diamonds with concave sides and flowers, the flowers bordering the turn-ins. Two ribbon fastenings, missing. Some mold and worm damage.

Written in Italy in 1541, with later additions; early provenance unknown. Presented to Yale by Carl B. Spitzer in 1955.

Bibliography: Faye and Bond, p. 41, no. 213.

MS 214 France, 1229
Petrus Comestor, Historia Scholastica, etc. Pl. 2

1. f. 1r [Title-page in half-uncials, rows alternating orange and blue:] *In nomine patris et filii et spiritus sancti amen. anno ab incarnatione domini millesimo ducentesimo uicesimo nono petrus monachorum omnium minimus obtulit istum librum beatissimo martiri quintino. Si quis eum abstulerit in die iudicii ante conspectum domini nostri ihesu christi ipsum sanctissimum martirem contra se accusatorem sentiat.*

   A colophon, also by Petrus, is recorded in a record of a manuscript given to Mont-Saint-Quentin in 1206, Paris, B. N. lat. 12692, f. 208v (see W. B. Clark, "Art and Historiography in Two Thirteenth-Century Manuscripts from North France," *Gesta* 17 [1978] pp. 37–48, especially p. 38, n. 11.)

2. ff. 2v–180v *Incipit prologus epistolaris ad guillelmum tunc senonensem postea uero remensem archiepiscopum ... Item prefatio magistri petri manducatoris in hystoria ueteris et noui testamenti.* [Adapted slightly for use as incipit in orange and blue half-uncials at the bottom of the second text column; text of preface:] *Imperatorie maiestatis est in palatio habere mansiones. auditorium uel consistorium in quo iura decernit ... Et nota differentiam translatus enoch subuectus est helias ascendit ihesu propria scilicet uirtute. Expliciunt evangelia.*

   Stegmüller, v. 4, nos. 6543–64. Text missing at beginning of 2 Kings (one folio following f. 85), and at end of 2 Kings and beginning of 3 Kings (one bifolium following f. 90).

3. ff. 181r–203r *Incipiunt actus apostolorum. huc usque ystoriatus est magister petrus. Ab hinc dissipuli* [sic] *eius. Anno nonodecimo imperij tyberij cesaris adhuc procuratore iudee pilato ... et in loco magis honorabili scilicet in cathacumbis. Explicit liber actuum apostolorum.* f. 203v blank.

   Stegmüller, v. 4, nos. 6565 and 6785, attributed to Petrus Pictaviensis.

Parchment, ff. iii (parchment) + 203 + iii (parchment), 450 x 305 (314 x 203) mm., trimmed. Written in two columns of 47 lines, single vertical bounding lines, three lines between text columns, triple horizontal bounding lines at top, center, and bottom of written space, all full across. Ruled in crayon. Prickings in inner and lower margins.

I^8 (1, 8 cut out and trimmed, then reinserted on new stub, suggesting perhaps that title-page is not in its original position), II–X^8, XI^8 (-6), XII^8 (-4, 5), XIII–XXV^8, XXVI^6. Quire signatures (.i., .ii., etc.) center verso. (Collation in Clark, *op. cit.*, note 2, is incorrect.)

Written in bold, early gothic bookhand by one scribe (see art. 1 and below). Writing above top line, with tall ascenders in upper margin. Various corrections in a different hand (s. xiii). Guide-letters for illuminator throughout. Scattered short marginal glosses (brown ink) in a similar but smaller hand (s. xiii). Transcriptions of rubrics in a 15th-century hand.

Richly illuminated in early gothic style by the same workshop which produced its probable companion volume, Brussels, Bib. Roy. MS 9178-87, a collection of secular chronicles and genealogies (see Clark, *op. cit.*). The half-uncial presentation text is set inside a double frame of orange and blue strips, the latter decorated with orange dots; the entire page crowned by an elaborate architectural canopy above four trilobe arches supported at the side of the frame by columns, in blue. There are twenty-three historiated initials orange or blue, decorated with stylized foliage in white, occasionally with biting dragon and curling vine serifs, set in or above orange frames, on gold grounds: f. 2r (two initials) Petrus Comestor presenting his book to William of Champagne, Archbishop of Sens, and Petrus copying the book; f. 3r a Genesis initial, an elaborate armature structure, orange, blue, and green on gold, with the seven days of Creation and the four rivers of Paradise (comparable to those in three Channel-style Bibles of the Mainerius group, Paris, B. N. lat. 8823, f. 1r; B. N. lat. 11535, f. 6v; and Bib. Ste. Geneviève, MS 8, f. 7v; f. 30r (two initials) a scribe portrait and the Finding of Moses (Exodus); f. 46r a scribe portrait; f. 46v Sacrifice of a sheep, a bull, and doves (Leviticus); f. 62r a scribe portrait; f. 62v Moses expounding the tablets (Deuteronomy); f. 66r Joshua at Jericho (Joshua); f. 70r Joshua made leader, the army departs (Judges); f. 76r Ruth removes kinsman's shoe (Ruth); f. 77r Presentation of Samuel (1 Kings); leaf with miniature missing following f. 85 (2 Kings); f. 116v Tobit, Raphael, Tobias (Tobit); f. 118v Jeremiah and the People (Jeremiah); f. 119v Ezekiel eats the scroll (Ezekiel); f. 121r (two initials) scribe portrait and Daniel in the Lions' Den (Daniel); f. 129v scribe portrait; f. 130r Decapitation of Holofernes (Judith); f. 134r Esther receives scepter (Esther); f. 139r Mathathias slays apostate Jew (Maccabees); f. 149r (two initials) Zechariah receives prophecy, Annunciation (Gospels); f. 181r Ascension of Christ (Acts).

Six large foliate initials, in a style dependent on Channel-School models: tight pink and blue vine scrolls with dragon terminals, in some cases on a green trellis, set in light orange frames, edged in black, against gold grounds; on f. 2v an *I* running the full length of the page (Preface); f. 66r (Joshua); f. 77r (Prologue, 1 Kings); f. 127r (Story of Susannah), f. 134r (Esther) and f. 144r (2 Maccabees), blue capitals with white highlights, filled with vine scrolls and framed as above, against gold grounds. 6- and 3-line initials, red and blue, with blue or red penwork respectively; a few (e.g., f. 98v) in a more elaborate manner with penwork in both colors. On some pages a single column of text is further divided by a vertical guilloche pattern in orange ink. Rubrics in orange throughout.

Some pages sewn; some bleeding of orange ink; upper right corner of f. 190 cut out. Text not damaged.

Binding: s. xix-xx. Gilt, gauffered edges. Brown goatskin blind-tooled, with elaborate bosses and fastenings, by Lortic.

Written in or just before 1229 in Northeastern France for the Abbey of Mont-Saint-Quentin, as indicated on the title-page (see art. 1) and given by Petrus, who is possibly to be identified with a "Petrus monachus sancti quintini de monte" commemorated on August 10 in the obituary of Corbie (Paris, B. N. lat. 16776, f. 177r). The same Peter gave Brussels, Bib. Roy. MS 9178-87 to Mont-Saint-Quentin in 1227, according to a colophon (now lost) recorded by the Burgundian chronicler Aubert le Mire (*Donationum belgicarum* [Antwerp, 1629] I, 71). See Clark, *op. cit.*, and *Exhibition Catalogue*, no. 18, pp. 189-90. A note (s. xv?), f. 203v, reads, "Liber iste est de monte sancti quintini prope perronam." Belonged to Octave Godechon, Mont-Saint-Quentin. Collection of Ambroise Firmin-Didot (book label, with date 1850, inside front cover; *Bibliothèque Ambroise Firmin-Didot, manuscrits et imprimés* [Paris, 26 and 31 May 1879] no. 13). Owned by Léon Gruel, Paris, 1937. Library of André Hachette (his sale catalogue, Paris, 16 Dec. 1953, no. 10 and *Times Literary Supplement*, 22 Jan. 1954). Sold by Laurence Witten to Louis M. Rabinowitz, who presented it to Yale in 1954.

secundo folio: [f. 2r blank; f. 3r:] *De prima*

Bibliography: Faye and Bond, p. 41, no. 214.
    Exhibition Catalogue, pp. 189-90, no. 18, pl. 6 of f. 3r.
    E. Quantin, ed., *Notice sur l'Abbaye du Mont-Saint-Quentin et description d'un manuscrit exécuté en 1229* (Péronne, 1885).
    Chefs d'oeuvre de l'art français, International Exposition (Paris, 1937) no. 748.
    C. Nordenfalk, book review in *Zeitschrift für Kunstgeschichte* 7 (1938) pp. 353-55.
    T. E. Marston, "A Thirteenth-Century Manuscript of Comestor's *Historia Scholastica*," *Gazette* 30 (1955) pp. 60-63.

MS 215 (4 vol.)   France, s. XV^{in}
St. Augustine, De civitate Dei, Fr. version of Raoul de Presles   Pl. 12

V.1, f. 1r [Prologue:] A vous tres exellent prince charles le quint Roy de france ... [v. 4, f. 211v] et que nostre mere Sainte eglise en tient. *abte de ceste translacion.* Cest translacion fu achevee le premier jour de Septembre lan de grace mil. ccc. Soixente et Quinze. *Explicit.*

See *British Museum General Catalogue of Printed Books*, v. 8, col. 518.

Composed of 4 volumes, originally bound as 2, of parchment. Vol. 1: ff. ii (paper) + i (contemporary parchment) + 219 + ii (paper); vol. 2: ii (paper) + 187 + iv (contemporary parchment, with iii and iv glued together) + ii (paper); vol. 3: ii (paper) + iv (contemporary parchment, i and ii stubs) + 146 + ii (paper); vol. 4: ii (paper) + 211 + iv (contemporary parchment, i = stub) + ii (paper). All volumes 345 x 253 (250 x 172) mm., trimmed. Written in 2 columns, 42-44 lines; single bounding lines, full across; ruled in pale brown ink.
    Vol. 1: I-XIII^{12}, XIV^{10}, XV-XVII^{12}, XVIII^7 (originally 12, now divided between v. 1 and 2); vol. 2: I^5 (five loose leaves glued in; originally part of final

quire in v. 1), II–XV^{12}, XVI^{14}; vol. 3: I–XII^{12}, XIII^2; vol. 4: I^{10}, II–XVII^{12}, XVIII^{10} (–10). Quires marked in lead, s. xx, lower right recto: v. 1: A–S; v. 2: S–Z, 2A–2K; v. 3: 2L–2Z; v. 4: 3A–3Q; no J, U, or W. Catchwords lower right verso, first letters often stroked in red.

Written in an informal bâtarde by one scribe who also added proper names in the margins.

The miniatures are dry and unoriginal copies of rather average quality. The illustrations of Bks. 1–10, the original first volume (now vols. 1–2), are by an associate of the Boethius Master and depend upon the cycle created for the *Cité de Dieu* by the Virgil Master (see S.O.D. Smith, "Illustrations of Raoul de Praelles' Translation of St. Augustine's 'City of God' between 1375 and 1420," Diss. New York University, 1974, p. 126, no. 54; pp. 133–37, 219–22). The mediocre illustrations of Bks. 11–22, by workshop assistants, used other models. Other manuscripts to which the miniaturist of the present vols. 1–2 contributed (Smith, *op. cit.*, p. 135) are: New York, Pierpont Morgan MS 804; Brussels, Bib. Roy. MS 9475; Grenoble, Bib. Pub. MS 870; Camarillo (California) St. John's Seminary, Doheny Memorial Library, *Bible Historiale*; London, B. L. Lansdowne 1178; Oxford, Bod. Lib. Douce 202. Another *Cité de Dieu* from the Boethius Master's workshop is Paris, B. N. fr. 20–21.

One large 2-column miniature of the Two Cities at the beginning of Bk. 1 (f. 5r) in a thin gold frame; on 3 sides a bar-border with pink, orange, and blue plant scrolls on a gold ground, surrounded by a full border of dense ivy in pink, red, orange, blue, and gold, with white highlights; interspersed with gold balls with hair-sprays. Before the Prologue and all the remaining books, miniatures, 19- to 18-line (vols. 1–2) or 16- to 15-line (vols. 3–4), in thin frames, pink and blue, with white highlights, set within a gold band, with 3/4 bar borders in red, blue, and gold, highlighted in white, and a full ivy border, as described above (no orange). These miniatures are as follows: v. 1: f. 1r (Prologue) Presentation of the work to Charles V; f. 37r (Bk. 2) Messala and Cassius with musicians; f. 88v (Bk. 3) Seizure of Rome by the Gauls; f. 166r (Bk. 4) Ptolemy and Pompey; v. 2: f. 1r (Bk. 5) Wheel of Fortune and Nigidius; f. 46r (Bk. 6) Varro and Apuleius; f. 69v (Bk. 7) Berecynthia; f. 105r (Bk. 8) Aristippus in a boat; f. 140r (Bk. 9) Monotheism; f. 160r (Bk. 10) The Old Law; v. 3: f. 2r (Bk. 11) Christ with Mary; f. 21r (Bk. 12) Fall of the Rebel Angels; f. 36r (Bk. 13) Original Sin; f. 50r (Bk. 14) Four Philosophers; f. 74r (Bk. 15) Cain and Abel; f. 108v (Bk. 16) Tower of Babel; v. 4: f. 1r (Bk. 17) a man and woman on horseback (Abraham and his wife on their way to Egypt?); f. 29r (Bk. 18) The Last Judgment; f. 80r (Bk. 19) Philosophers Discussing; f. 111r (Bk. 20) Musicians; f. 145r (Bk. 21) The Devil Seated on a Rock between Two Philosophers; f. 177v (Bk. 22) Christ seated, with two angels, greets two men. Many of the folio numbers given in A. de Laborde (*Les manuscrits à peintures de la Cité de Dieu de Saint Augustin* [Paris, 1909] pp. 301–05, no. 25) are incorrect.

Beneath each miniature there is a large initial, 7- to 5-line, blue or pink with scrolls and geometric forms in white highlighting, on blue or pink grounds respectively, set within thin gold frames, or blue and/or pink on a gold ground; both types filled with red and/or blue ivy scrolls with white highlights (in one case, v. 4, f. 74r, there is also a dragon terminal). Initials, 3- to 2-line, at the head of each chapter, gold edged in black, on pink and blue grounds with white highlights. Paragraph marks and book numbers, top center of each folio, recto and verso (which in v. 4, ff. 152r–54r read XXII instead of XXI) in the same manner. Ribbon line-fillers (in v. 3–4 only) red and blue, with gold dots or lozenges and white highlights, edged in black. Chapter headings and numeration in red (orange occasionally).

There are some stains, abrasions, and irregularities in the parchment throughout; none obscure text or miniatures.

Binding: s. xix. Marbled and gilt edges. Blue goatskin heavily gold-tooled. Bound for Count Justin MacCarthy-Reagh. Spines mislabelled: II labelled IV, III labelled II, IV labelled III, I labelled correctly.

Written in Paris, ca. 1415. A *terminus ante quem* of 1409, first suggested by Laborde (*op. cit.*, p. 302), and based upon the presumed ownership of Jean II de Montagu, the *grand maître d'hôtel* of Charles VI, need no longer be assumed; the inscriptions on which it depends ("Monsieur de Montagu", v. 1: f. 1r; v. 3: f. 1r) seem to be of a later period (s. xvi?). As the Boethius Master was active ca. 1414–1418/20 (M. Meiss, *The Limbourgs*, pp. 369–70), the Yale manuscript may be dated ca. 1415. Belonged to Duc de Brancas (sale G. de Bure, *Catalogue d'une collection de livres choisis provenant du Cabinet de M**** [Paris, 1770] no. 49). Library of Count Justin MacCarthy-Reagh, Toulouse (see binding; sale G. de Bure, *Catalogue de livres rares et précieux de la bibliothèque de feu M. le Comte de ...* [Paris, 1825] no. 547). Collection of Sir Thomas Phillipps (no. 4359; P. Durrieu, "Les manuscrits à peintures de Sir Thomas Phillipps à Cheltenham," *Bibliothèque de l'école des Chartes* 50 [1899] p. 392). Bequeathed to his grandson, M. T. Fitzroy Fenwick, Thirlestaine House, Cheltenham. Purchased in 1946 by William H. Robinson, Ltd., London. Acquired from Dudley M. Colman through C. A. Stonehill in 1954 as the gift of the Yale Library Associates.

secundo folio: [v. 1, f. 2r] a ceste parlong
              [v. 3 (originally 2)] lune que

Bibliography: Faye and Bond, p. 41, no. 215.
   Exhibition Catalogue, pp. 217–18, no. 43.
   "Eight Medieval Manuscripts," *Gazette* 29 (1955) pp. 105, 109, with illustration of v. 1, f. 6r.

MS 216 France, s. XV²
Raoul LeFèvre, Le Recueil des histoires de Troies

1. ff. 1r–5v [Table of contents:] Cy commence la table des Rubriches dung chacun chappitre de ce present Volume intitule le Recueil des hystoires de troyes ... que hercules estoit mort a cause de son ignorance.

2. ff. 6r–262r [Author's Prologue to Philip the Good, Duke of Burgundy:] Quant Je Regarde et congnois les opinions des hommes nourris en aucunes singulieres hystories de troyes ... [text:] *Cy demonstre la genealogie du Roy saturne* ... Tous les filz de noe espartz par les climatz les regnes et les estranges habitacions des siecles ... par la grace de dieu duc de Bourgoigne et cet. quen gre vueille mon Rude labour recepuoir. Amen. f. 262v blank

Paper (watermarks: similar in design to Briquet Lettres et Monogrammes 9747), ff. ii (paper) + i (contemporary paper) + 262 + ii (paper), 275 x 205 (189 x 135) mm. Written in 31 long lines, single vertical and horizontal bounding lines, full across; ruled in crayon.
I⁶ (1 = contemporary paper flyleaf), II–VII¹², VIII¹¹ (too tightly bound to determine which leaf is missing). Catchwords along inner bounding line perpendicular to text (Scribe 1) or along lower edge of folio (Scribe 2).
Written in bold bâtarde by two scribes. Scribe 1: ff. 1r–125r; Scribe 2: 125r–262r.
On f. 6r, a 4-line initial in red and black, crude. 3- to 1-line plain initials and paragraph marks, in red. Rubrics, sometimes with calligraphic flourishes extending into margins, throughout.
Binding: s. xviii. Yellow edges. Blue diced calf, gold-tooled, with red labels.

Written in France probably in the second half of the 15th century; early provenance unknown. Unidentified shelf-mark: round paper tag with "1655" on spine. Belonged to John Towneley (1731–1813, bookplate); sold by Evans, 8 June 1814. Sold by Saunders (13 April 1818) to Sir Thomas Phillipps (no. 8385, on spine). Acquired in 1956 from Hans P. Kraus with income from the Altschul Fund.

secundo folio: [f. 2, table] Comment Iupiter
[f. 7, text] leua ung

Bibliography: Faye and Bond, p. 41, no. 216.

MS 217 France, s. XV²
Iours Pl. 12

1. ff. 1r–12v Calendar in French, with an entry for most days; among those listed: Honobert (5 Jan.), Agricola (26 Feb.), Liphard (3 June), Cirycus and Julitta (in gold, 16 June), Aredius (in gold, 16 Aug.), Andochius (24 Sept.).

2. ff. 13r-18v   Sequences of the Gospels.

3. ff. 18v-22v   *Oratio deuota*. Obsecro te ... [masculine forms; Leroquais, LH 2.346-47].

4. ff. 22v-24r   O intemerata ... [Wilmart 488-90]. f. 24v ruled, but blank

5. ff. 25r-78v   Hours of the Virgin, use unidentified; the hymn at Matins is Quem terra pontus ethera; ant. at Prime, Ave Maria gratia plena; capit. at Prime, Virgo dei genitrix; ant. at None, Ortus conclusus; capit. at None, Felix namque es sacra uirgo.

6. ff. 79r-82v   Short Hours of the Cross.

7. ff. 83r-86v   Short Hours of the Holy Spirit.

8. ff. 87r-102v   Penitential Psalms and Litany. Among the 13 martyrs, Leodegar (13); among the 15 confessors, Fiacre (7), Majolus (9), Arigius (12), Maurus (13), and Lupus (14); among the 13 virgins, Geneviève (8), Julitta (12), and Radegundis (13).

9. ff. 103r-131v   Office of the Dead, use unidentified; the responses to the lessons at Matins are: 1. Qui lazarum 2. Redemptor meus 3. Beati mortui qui.

10. ff. 131v-137v   Fifteen Joys of the Virgin [Leroquais, LH 2.310-11].

11. ff. 138r-140v   Seven Requests [Leroquais, LH 2.309-10].

Parchment (very stiff), ff. ii (parchment) + ii (paper) + iii (contemporary parchment) + 140 + iv (contemporary parchment) + ii (parchment), 208 x 140 (102 x 65) mm. Written in 16 long lines, single bounding lines full across; ruled in pale red ink.

I^8, II^6, III^8, IV^4, V-VIII^8, IX^4, X-XI^8, XII^2, XIII-XIX^8, XX^6. Catchwords in lower margin on verso.

Written in liturgical gothic verging on bâtarde, by one scribe.

Crude miniatures by two artists whose compositions, figure types, and painterly technique reflect faintly the work of Jean Colombe, active in Bourges in the late fifteenth century: f. 13r (Sequences of the Gospels) John on Patmos; f. 25r (Matins) Annunciation; f. 37r (Lauds) Visitation; f. 48r (Prime) Nativity; f. 54r (Terce) Annunciation to the Shepherds; f. 58v (Sext) Adoration of the Magi; f. 63r (None) Presentation in the Temple; f. 67v (Vespers) Flight into Egypt; f. 74r (Compline) Coronation of the Virgin; f. 79r (Short Hours of the Cross) Crucifixion; f. 83r (Short Hours of the Holy Spirit) Pentecost; f. 87r (Penitential Psalms) David and Goliath; f. 103r (Office of the Dead) a funeral service; f. 132r (Fifteen Joys) stock portrait of the owner, a woman in grey, kneeling before the Virgin and Child; f. 138r (Seven Requests) Gnadenstuhl Trinity. The miniatures by the first artist (all except ff. 74r and 138r) are in arched frames, in purple or crimson ink, occasionally with black cusping on the arch, tangential or close to upper bounding line, set within a 3/4 strip, either beige with alternating blue and pink flowers and black flecks, edged in black, or gold with blue and red trilobe leaves.

Traced full or 3/4 borders, one (f. 25r) compartmentalized in gold and blue, with an angel bearing the arms of the Coquille family (azure, 3 escallops or [Coquille], impaled with ermine [Garnier]), red bounding line, filled with blue and green acanthus, flowers, strawberries, grotesques, gold balls, and pen flecks. Initials accompanying miniatures, 4- and 3-line, pink and blue with white highlights on gold, filled with a flower on a beige ground. The miniatures by the second artist (ff. 74r and 138r), probably an assistant to the first, are in thick crimson frames, with 3/4 borders as above, except with finer and stiffer acanthus, each with an initial, 4- or 3-line, gold on blue and crimson with white highlights. Calendar with zodiac signs and occupations of the months set within 3/4 borders, as above. 2-line initials, *KL* monograms, as above; name of month, dates, major feasts in gold, other feasts alternately in blue and red. Rubrics in crimson or in blue.

Binding: s. xix. Tan calf case, heavily gold-tooled spine and doublures. Bound by C. Lewis (leading figure in English binding 1800–40). Dark red-brown cover (s. xvi–xvii) inset on sides.

Written in central France in the second half of the 15th century, as indicated by the saints in the Calendar and Litany as well as by the style of the miniatures. An inscription (s. xvii) on f. 25r, below the Coquille arms, reads: "Dame Charlotte Garnier, vefve de feu Gilbert Coquille, Sieur des espoisses, pere de Maitre Anthoine Coquille, a fait faire ces heures-cy dieu leur face Misericorde". Writing on the flyleaves at front and back records events and the births of various Coquille children, mainly at Nevers, from 1610 to 1683. On f. vii verso, a later inscription reads, "Dono datum a Domino francisco clement canonico de Cenon [?] domicellae Joannae morot cognatae suae uxoris Grunonis Viellard patroni aeduae commorantis anno D 1713." Library of Philip Henry Kerr (1882–1940), 11th Marquess of Lothian (note inside front cover reads "Library Blickling *CHS*"); his sale in 1932 (Anderson Galleries, New York, 27 Jan. 1932, no. 19) to Louis W. Dommerich. Presented by Mrs. Louis W. Dommerich in 1956.

Bibliography: Faye and Bond, p. 41, no. 217.

MS 218 Flanders, ca. 1470
Hours (in Low Ger.) Pl. 14

1. ff. 1r–14v Penitential Psalms and Litany. Among the 19 martyrs Erasmus (7), Lebwin (12), Maurice (14), Boniface (16); among the 21 confessors Servatius (9), Ulric (10), Bernard (16), Bernardinus (18), Alexius (20), Remigius (21); among the 20 virgins Odilia (8), Walburga (14), Gertrude (15).

2. ff. 14v–17v *Dyt naschreuen beth Sancti Augustinus* [sic] *het In latine Summe sacerdos dat he maket to der bereydinge des Sacramentis.* O du hogeste prester vnde ware bisschopp Ihesu criste.... f. 18r ruled, but blank

3. ff. 39r-48v (quire V), 19r-38v   Hours of the Passion in Low German, beginning defectively in Sext.

4. ff. 49r-118r [Various prayers] *Hijr begynnet sich eyn schon gebed van demm liden christi. Dat selden ane gnade wert gesproken.* O Enedige vnnd barmhertige here ihesu christe Ik bidde dy...; (f. 73v) *Hijr na begynnet sick eyn schone bed van der marter vnnsis heren Ihesu christi.* Eya sote Ihesu ewige cruczigede wyszheit myn herte vormanet dy...; (f. 81r) *To der Iuncfrowen Marien.* Gegrutet sistu konigynne gegrutet sistu maria du czarte muder Ik vormane dy ... [including a Salve regina in Latin, f. 86r-v]; (f. 90r) *Hijr na folget eyn ynige betrachtinge der wapen vnd des lidens vnnses heren ihesu christi.* In deme Sondage sculle wij vnse herte dorch grauen...; (f. 96r) *Hijr na volget eyn bed van den ledematen christi vnses heren.* Gegrutet sy dat erwerdige benedyde hovet vnses leuen heren ihesu christi...; (f. 98v) *Van deme namen Ihesu.* O Gude Ihesu. O Sote ihesu. O ihesu der iuncfrouwen zone vul barmhertighet vnnd warheit ... [Achten-Knaus, p. 148]; (f. 101r) *We desse nagescreuenne vijff bede vnnd to eynem issliken eyn pater noster ... alse he sunte gregorio restheyn [?] to Rome in der Capelle Ierusalem under der missen, de vordynet xx dusent vnnd xx. Iar. vnnd xxiiii daghe afflates de sunte Gregorius hefft gegeven vnnd ander pawese van synen tyden wente to Calixto de de sulve pawes Calixtus bestediget hefft, Vnnd is gefunden in deme anderen boke syner registere in deme cweyhunderden derden vnnd dritteynden blade.* Here ihesu christi ik bede dy an, an deme cruce hangende ... [translation of the Seven Prayers of St. Gregory, Leroquais LH 2. 346; Meertens, 6, p. 16]; (f. 103r) *Vnnse here got lerede synen frundenn veffteyn pater noster, vnnd xv. ave maria, we de sprekt, de schal daruan entfangen grote salicheit, Vnnd vnse here god sprak also, dorch des gebedes willen wil ik lozen veffteyn selen vth deme vegefure ... den ik den andern nicht geuen wil die des nicht vordynet. Sequitur. Dat erste pater noster sprik.* Dat erste pater noster hebbe ik gesproken to loue leue here alle dyner lidinghe wente...; (f. 114v) *Hijr na volget eyn kort gebed sunder ed hefft grote gnade in sick we dat mit ynnicheit sprikt.* O leue here ihesu christe des leuendigen goddis sone...; (f. 114v) *Men leset in deme leuende sancti Bernhardi dat ...* O herre vorluchte myne ogen vp dat ik nimmier enslape in deme dode ... [translation of the verses of St. Bernard, RH 27912]. f. 118v ruled, but blank

5. ff. 119r-172r [Prayers to the Virgin] O du aller soteste Iuncfrowe maria ik arme sunder valle othmodichlike to den voten dyner hilligheit...; (f. 126v) *Van den frouden vnser frowen.* Maria Ik vormane dik der ouerflodigen stoude ere vnnd werdicheit de dyn zele...; (f. 134v) *Hijr na volget de krone vnnser leuen frowen marien.* Mit frouden latet vns hilligen vnnd werdigen de gedechtnisse des namen der Iuncfrouwen marien...; (f. 145v) *Van der bodeschop marien de antyphona. Hec est dies quinque.* Dit is de dagh den de here gemaket hefft hute hefft de here angesehn...; (f. 147v) *Eyn ander bed van der Iungfrouwen marien volget.* O du werdighe ewige Iungkfrowe maria du sote beschermerynne des mynschliken geslechtes...; (f. 154r) *Van vnser leuen frouwen bodeschopp volget hijr na eyn gud gebeth.* O hemmelsche konigynne maria werdige godis muder ... [the scribe made

several errors in the first 7 lines on f. 154v; he crossed out all the lines with red ink and began again on 155r]; (f. 157r) *Item volgen hijr na De Souen word de unse leue frouwe sprak under deme cruce. Pater noster.* O du uth fletende borne der ewigheit wu bistu my alsus gar vorsegen ... [Achten-Knaus, p. 60]; (f. 158r) *Hijr na volget eyn schone gebed van vnnser leuen frowen vnnd sunte Iohanse ewangelisten.* O Vmbefleckede gnedige sunderlike iuncfrowe vnd moder goddis maria ... [translation of O intemerata..., Wilmart 488-90]; (f. 165r) *Hijr begynnet sik de Rossenkrantz der Eddeln hochgeloueden Iuncfrowen marien.* Gegrutet sistu maria ful gnaden de herre is mit dy....

6. ff. 172v-186r   Prayers to all the Angels, all the Saints, all the Apostles, Anna (Hersame frouwe aller frouwen de werdigiste...), Andrew, Barbara, Maurice, Angels. f. 186v ruled, but blank

Parchment, ff. ii (contemporary parchment) + 186, 120 x 90 (70 x 52) mm., trimmed. Written in 13-14 long lines, ruled in black ink. Double horizontal bounding lines with 2 or more lines of text between, single vertical, all full across; except ff. 49r-68v (quires VI-VII), which are frame-ruled. Prickings at all but inner edges.

I^{10} (-4), II-XVIII^{10}, XIX^{8}. The volume has been misbound; quire V should follow quire II. Catchwords in lower margin near gutter, on verso; signatures (letters of the alphabet, probably added later), in lower right-hand margin, on recto.

Written in a neat bâtarde by two scribes: Scribe 1, ff. 1r-17v; Scribe 2, ff. 19r-186r.

Fourteen good full-page miniatures of typical Southern Netherlandish production of the late 15th century (cf. Pächt and Alexander, v. 1, no. 329: Oxford, Bod. Lib. Buchanan e. 5 [Hainaut? s. XV$^{3/4}$]): f. 1v (Penitential Psalms) Last Judgment; f. 18v (Hours of the Virgin) Virgin and Child on a crescent; f. 24v (Vespers) Deposition; f. 32v (Compline) Entombment; f. 45r (None) Crucifixion; f. 95v (Prayer *van den ledematen christi*) St. Veronica holding the cloth; f. 102v (Prayers of Gregory) Mass of Gregory; f. 119v (Prayer to the Virgin) "portrait of the owner", a woman in grey, worshipping the Virgin and Child; f. 127v (Prayer to the Virgin) the Risen Christ appearing to the Virgin; f. 145v (Prayer to the Virgin) Annunciation; f. 159r (Prayer to the Virgin and John) Virgin and St. John standing at the foot of the Cross; f. 165v (*Rossenkrantz der Eddeln ... marien*) Virgin and Child enthroned; f. 177v (Prayer to Anna) another "portrait of the owner", a woman in grey, this time kneeling before the Virgin and Child and Anna; f. 181v (Prayer to Barbara) Barbara beside the tower, holding an open book and a palm branch; f. 183v (Prayer to Maurice), Maurice, wearing armor and a red and blue cape, holding a gold cross. The miniatures (except those on ff. 1v, 18v, 159r) are painted over ruling for a normal text page and are set in wide arched frames of gold and black, within a full border of blue, gold, pink, and pale orange acanthus leaves, with red, purple, and blue flowers.

Illuminated initials, 7-, 5-, or 4-line, with full borders on ff. 1r, 96r, 127r, 146r, 158r, 166r, and 177r: blue with white highlights filled with red, blue, and green trilobe leaves on a gold ground, borders as for miniatures. The text is set off from the border by a narrow black, gold, white, and red frame not joined to the initial. Nine illuminated initials, 5- or 4-line, with three-quarter borders: gold on pink and blue, with white highlights, borders as for miniatures. 6-, 5-, 3-, and 2-line initials in gold on pink and blue, with white highlights; black ink hair-spray, with gold trilobe leaves and flowers, attached. 1-line initials in blue with red penwork or gold with black penwork; within the text, a black initial occasionally marked with a red stroke. Line-fillers in Litany only; leaves, cables, oblique lines with dots attached, etc., in blue or gold. Rubrics in orange-tinted red or crimson.

Binding: s. xvii. Resewn on three twisted vegetable fiber cores laced into wooden boards. The colored, beaded endbands are embroidered on a piece of material, probably parchment, which extends to the outside of the boards. The spine is round and lined with parchment; the edges gilt and with a faintly discernible honeycomb pattern. Covered in light brown calf, extensively gold-tooled. There are two fastenings, the catches on the upper board, brass clasps attached to leather straps which are nailed to the lower board through metal plates. The lower joint has cracked and all the spine leather is detached from the bookblock, creating the effect of a case binding.

Written in Flanders ca. 1470. (For other codices made in Bruges, but with text in Low German, see H. J. Leloux, *Mittelniederdeutsche in den Niederlandern entstandene Manuskripte und Frühdrucke*, Nachbarn 23 [Bonn, n. d. ca. 1980]. We thank J. Marrow for this reference.) Signatures of the 16th century on second flyleaf: "Gasper Vant' Lantenach [?]" and "Gaspar Van Santen". Belonged to Philip Henry Kerr, 11th Marquess of Lothian (1882–1940; Anderson Galleries sale, New York, 27 Jan. 1932, no. 18). Collection of Louis W. Dommerich. Presented to Yale by Mrs. Dommerich in 1956.

Bibliography: Faye and Bond, p. 42, no. 218.

MS 219 Germany, s. XV^2
Das Leiden Ihesu Christi, etc.

1. ff. 1r–63r *Hebt sich ann ein schoner passion kurczlichen das leiden ihesu christi darÿnen zw betrachten*. Da zw dem erstenn driualtigklichen per institutionem Sacramentorum per efussionem sudorum per inpositionem peccatorum ... vergissen nit an vns verlorn lass werden. Amen.

The scribe has noted in the opening lines that "per inpositionem peccatorum" should be placed before "per institutionem Sacramentorum".

2. ff. 63r-76r *Ein schone dancksagung zw vnsserm lieben heren ihesum christum vmb sein pÿtters leiden vnnd sterben vnnd plutt vergissen vnnd vmb sein grosse liebsprich also.* O du aller liebster here ihesu christe ich arme Sunderin sag dir meinem hercz lieben got ... Amen. *pater noster*; (f. 66r) O here mein got ich erman dich vnnd danck dir von ÿnickert meines herczens ... Amen. *pater noster*; (f. 68r) O du mein aller liebster here Ihesu christe ich sag dir meinem got den hochsten danck ... *pater noster*; (f. 71r) O mein here ihesu christe pis ermant mit herczlicher danckperikeit vmb den schmerczen ... Amen; (f. 73r) O du aller liebster here ihesu christe mein erlosser vnnd hochste zw versicht ich sag dir lob ... Amen.

These prayers are for the use of a woman.

3. f. 76r-v *Item ein schon gepett wie sich ein mensch mit got dem sun sol auffopffern got seinen himelischen vater solches gepett auch sanct Bernhardt hat gethan.* O lieber here ihesu christe gottes Sun vnnd der Iunckfrawen Marie Ein warer mitler ... dan dich aller menschen//

Paper, ff. ii (paper) + i (contemporary paper flyleaf) + 76 + ii (paper), 150 x 108 (102 x 63) mm. Written in 17 long lines; frame-ruled in ink and lead with upper horizontal bounding line full across.
The binding is too tight to permit accurate collation.
Written in upright informal bâtarde by a single scribe.
Ordinary blue initials, 2-line, on ff. 1r and 76r, with crude penwork designs in red. Plain 1-line initials, paragraph marks, headings, and letter strokes, as well as some corrections, in red.
Binding: s. xvi-xvii. Wooden boards, slightly cut in at the fore-edge for two catches on the upper cover and covered in brown calf, blind-tooled in a curvilinear design, are probably early. The rest of the stab-sewn, rebacked binding obviously is not. Upper board detached, fastenings wanting.

Written probably in Southern Germany in the second half of the 15th century; early provenance unknown. Unidentified paper tag on front cover "17069"; note with the contents in an unidentified hand (s. xix) pasted inside front cover. Purchased from Robert F. Metzdorf in 1956 with funds from the William Lyon Phelps Memorial.

secundo folio: die sundt

Bibliography: Faye and Bond, p. 42, no. 219.

MS 220 England, s. XIV^{in}
Psalter, etc.

1. f. 1r-v Portions of unidentified prayers, in Latin, beginning imperfectly and ending "thus wrot Ion". //a periculo mortis et a diabolicis insidiis amen. Sanc-

te gabriel sancte michael omnes sancti angeli et archangeli ... [a version of the prayer printed in HE 125]; oracio. Succurre michi virgo virginum intercessionibus tuis sacris ... michi peccatrici ... Elysabet famulam suam....

2. f. 2r blank, with miscellaneous notes; f. 2v Medical advice associated with the signs of the zodiac (e.g., Aries tenet capud et faciem. Taurus gutter et collum ... Pisces pedes. Nota quod luna moratur in qualibet signo...).

3. f. 3r Astrological table in red and black with title, but no text: Tabula magistri petri de datia dicti philomena....

Thorndike and Kibre, 53.

4. f. 3v Astrological notes attributed to Bede: Dicit Beda quod tres sunt dies in mense februarii in quibus si quis masculus natus fuerit ... hec uera sunt obseruet ea qui uult.

5. ff. 4r-9v Calendar, in red and black; has a large number of columns (12) giving computation information. Includes entries for Oct. S. Thomas (5 Jan.), Wulstan (19 Jan.), Queen Bathildis (30 Jan.), King Edward "the Martyr" (18 March), Cuthbert (20 March), Resurrectio domini (27 March), Elphege (19 April), Dunstan (19 May), Ethelbert (20 May), Aldhelm (25 May), Augustine of England (26 May), translation of Edmund Rich (9 June, in red), Botulph (17 June), translation of King Edward (20 June), Alban (22 June, in red), Ethelreda (23 June), translation of St. Thomas of Canterbury (7 July), translation of Swithin (15 July), Kenelm (17 July), Anna (26 July, in red), Cuthburga (31 Aug.), translation of Cuthbert (4 Sept.), translation of Edward the Confessor (13 Oct.), Edmund archbishop (16 Nov.), Edmund King (20 Nov.), Thomas of Canterbury (29 Dec.). f. 10r inscriptions, see below; f. 10v blank

6. ff. 11r-75v Biblical Psalter, with no later antiphons. Missing Psalms 50.6-53.3, 100.5-102.6, 108.9-110.9.

7. ff. 75v-82r Six ferial canticles, Te deum, Benedicite, Benedictus, Magnificat, Nunc dimittis, Quicumque uult.

8. ff. 82v-85r Litany and prayers. Among the 23 martyrs: Austremonius (6), Thomas (10), Edmund (13), Leodegar (18); among the 26 confessors: Dunstan (14), Philibert (17), Columban (18), Odo (20), Majolus (21), Odilo (22), Hugo (23), Germar (24), Gerald (26); among the 19 virgins: Cyrilla (8), Ethelreda (11), Walburga (13), Florencia (14), Consortia (15), Daria (16).

9. ff. 85r-94v Office of the Dead, use unidentified, with spaces left for musical notation. Responses at matins: 1. Credo quod, 2. Qui lazarum, 3. Domine dum, 4. Subuenite sancti, 5. Heu mihi, 6. Ne recorderis, 7. Peccantem me, 8. Requiem eternam, 9. Libera me ... de morte.

10. f. 95r [Indulgence *de ueronica*] Fac mecum signum in bono ... Deus qui nobis signatis lumine uultis tui ... [Leroquais LH 2. 58]; [added in a later hand:]

[D]eus cui proprium est misereris semper et parcere ... [*Lyell Cat.*, p. 372, no. 85].

11. ff. 95v-96r   Two prayers, in a later hand. Deus cuius misericordie non est numerus suscipe pro animabus famulorum ... [*Sarum Missal*, p. 435]; Domine ihesu christe qui hanc sacratissimam carnem ... [HE 72, 177]. ff. 96v-98v blank, except for scribbles

12. f. 99r [back contemporary flyleaf]   2 prayers added in different 15th-century hands: Per verum omnium sanctorum angelorum archangelorum patriarcharum prophetarum ... meritum intercessionem...; Deus in cuius manu corda.... f. 99v blank

Parchment, ff. 99 (the last a contemporary parchment flyleaf), 115 x 76 (80 x 52) mm. Written in 2 columns of 28 lines; double upper, central, and lower horizontal bounding lines full across, single vertical bounding lines; two additional rulings in all margins except inner. Ruled in ink; prickings in upper, lower, and outer margins, often at the intersecting points of additional pairs of guide-lines. I^{10}, II^{12}, III^{12} (-12), IV^{12}, V^{12} (-12), VI^{12} (-6), VII-VIII^{12}, IX^8 (-8). Catchwords in lower margin near gutter, sometimes between horizontal rulings in lower margin.

Written by two scribes in tiny gothic textura. Scribe 1: ff. 2v-91v; Scribe 2: ff. 91v (last folio of quire 8) - 95v. Several later hands have added scribbles, prayers, and inscriptions on ff. 1r-2r, 10r, 95v, 96r, 97v, 98r, 99r.

Small (6-line) and rather crude historiated initials: f. 1r (Psalm 1) David harping; f. 21r (Ps. 26) David points to his eye; f. 28r (Ps. 38) David points to his lips; f. 40v (Ps. 68) David in the deep water; f. 49r (Ps. 80) David at carillon; and f. 56r (Ps. 96) Cantors at lectern. The initials for Ps. 52 (the Fool) and Ps. 109 (the Trinity) are missing. In each initial, the figure drawn in black and colored pink, green, and/or blue on a gold ground; the initials attached to cusped, tapering bar border, blue, red, and gold, with white highlights, with ivy terminal, black with red and green leaves. Gold and blue calligraphic initials (2-line), with blue and red penwork respectively; 1-line initials, alternating red and blue. *KL* monograms, gold on red and blue, with white highlights. Because the initial *I* was placed in the margin without an inset space in the text, the illuminator often missed it (e.g., for Ps. 70 on f. 42r; for Ps. 113 on f. 62r, and for Ps. 125 on f. 68v).

Binding: s. xv-xvi. Resewn on three two-layered tapes of tawed skin attached to wooden boards. The endband cores are of tawed skin with a tawed skin braid at the head, a new endband added at the tail. The spine is square and the cover adhered to it. Covered in tawed skin, originally pink, with corner tongues. Cover repaired at spine and two corners and two silver clasps added. In a flexible grey leather pouch.

Written in England at the beginning of the 14th century. The manuscript presents evidence of extensive use: prayers added in several English hands (mostly of the

15th century, e.g., art. 1) and signatures from the 16th century on f. 10r: K. Dunbar, Thomas Saunders, gent., Edmaunt [?] Parke. Belonged to George Dunn (1865-1912) of Woolley Hall, Maidenhead; his note, in pencil, on f. 2r: "English Work/ Late 13th Century/ Original Binding/ Silver fastenings, but one clasp gone/ δπγ GD/ Jan. 1902." His sale (Sotheby's, 11 Feb. 1913, v. 1, no. 630) to Dobell. Davis and Orioli, Cat. 32 (1922) no. 3 (notice pasted inside back cover). Sold by A. H. Reynolds (21 Dec. 1924) to Dawson's Book Shop, Los Angeles, from whom it was purchased by Henry Fletcher. Gift of Mrs. Henry Fletcher in 1953.

secundo folio: [text, f. 12] Neque habitabit

Bibliography: De Ricci, v. 2, p. 1670, no. 2; Faye and Bond, p. 42, no. 220.

MS 221   Italy, s. XV^{in}
Valerius Maximus   Pl. 24

1. f. 1r blank, f. 1v   Miscellaneous notes, in Latin (16th century), with references to various classical authors.

2. f. 2r-v   [Table of contents:] *Liber j. De religione. De neglecta religione ... Liber x. De prenomine.*

3. ff. 3r-126r   *Valerij maximi factorum et dictorum memorabilium ad Tiberium cesarem liber primus incipit. j. de religione. ij.... Prohemium.* Urbis rome exterarumque gentium facta simul ac dicta memoratu digna ... *De Religione. C. j.* Maiores statas solennesque cerimonias pontificum scientia ... Animaduerto enim in consulum fastis perplexum usum prenominum et cognominum fuisse dictum postumium cominum aruntum et postumium ebutium eluam. *Explicit liber decimus de prenomine.*

C. Kempf, ed., Teubner (1966) pp. 1-472 (lacks spurious Book 10).

Parchment, ff. 126 + i (original parchment), 286 x 210 (167 x 132) mm. Written in 2 columns of 32 lines; single vertical bounding lines. Vertical lines (full across) ruled in ink, horizontal in lead; prickings in all margins except inner, also four (arranged in a rectangle) for running book notations, in upper margin. I^2, II-XIII^{10}, XIV^4. Catchwords in center of lower margins.

Written by a single scribe in fere-humanistic script. Marginal and interlinear notes in several contemporary and later hands.

On f. 3r, a good historiated initial, 7-line: the author in armor, holding his book; thick, curling foliage forms, pink, orange, blue, and green, on an irregular gold ground, edged in black. Nine illuminated initials (ff. 16r, 29v, 43r, 57r, 72r, 85v, 98r, 111v, and 126r) to open Books 2-10, composed of foliage, as above, and striated color strips, in vibrant blue, orange, crimson, mauve, green, and occasionally yellow, highlighted in white and variations of the same basic hues.

4-, 2-line initials, blue with red penwork or vice versa. Book numbers at top of page, red and blue; rubrics throughout. Remains of guides for rubricator.

Binding: s. xv-xvi. Resewn on four tawed, slit straps laced through the edge of wooden boards and nailed in channels which are filled in with plaster. There is a piece of leather at the exit from one tunnel and what may be the tips of nails just inside the channel so earlier supports may have been of leather, nailed twice. The endbands, sewn on twisted leather cores laid in grooves, were tied down through a leather spine lining, the embroidery with three beads. The edges are gilt with a design scratched on them, the spine square. Covered in dark brown goatskin with corner tongues, blind-tooled with a star in a circle with wide rope interlace panels above and below, inside concentric outer borders. Small diamonds and dots on the spine. Four brass catches on the lower board and stubs of velvet straps nailed to the upper. One joint cracked and repaired and one endband added.

Written in Italy (probably Florence) in the early 15th century in a script that shows the influence of Coluccio Salutati; early provenance unknown, but the manuscript was heavily used as is indicated by the variety of marginal notes. Unidentified shelf-mark inside front cover: "n. 298.27." Presented to Yale in 1953 by Thomas G. Bergin.

secundo folio: [table, f. 2] liber j.
               [text, f. 4] uidentur

Bibliography: Faye and Bond, pp. 42-43, no. 221.
    D. M. Schullian, "A Preliminary List of Manuscripts of Valerius Maximus," *Studies in Honor of Ullmann*, ed. L. B. Lawler, D. M. Robathan and W. C. Korfmacher (St. Louis, 1960) p. 88.
    Idem, "A Revised List of Manuscripts of Valerius Maximus," *Miscellanea Augusto Campana* in *Medioevo e Umanesimo* 45 (Padua, 1981) p. 712.

MS 222
Boccaccio, Filostrato, etc.

Italy, 1415, s. XIV
Pl. 4

I. 1. ff. 1r-78v [Heading:] Filostrato el titolo di questo libro e la cagione e per cio che ottimamente si confa tal nome chol efetto de libro ... [prologue:] Molte fiate gia nobilisima donna auenne che io il quale della mia puerizia ... [text, f. 4r:] [Q]ui inchomincia la prima parte de libro chiamato Filostrato de lamorose fatighe di troiolo ... [poetry begins:] [A]lchuni di gioue sogliono il fauore/ ... e con sposta a me lieta tu riui. Qui finisce e libro del filostrato conposto per lo nobile poeta misser Giouannj bocchaci da ciertaldo fiorentino. Scritto per me Nicholo di giouannj cinuzi da siena al primo di settenbre 1415 in ferara. Ed e di Niccholo azonj cittadino di siena. ff. 79r-90v ruled, but blank

Boccaccio, *Filostrato*; V. Branca, ed., *Tutte le opere di Giovanni Boccaccio* (Verona, 1964) v. 2, pp. 15-228.

II. Articles 2-35 and 38-39 consist of a collection of Italian *canzoni* by various authors as well as anonymous poems, all of which have been published from this codex by R. Mignani, *Un canzoniere italiano inedito del secolo XIV* (Florence, 1974). The pages cited following each entry refer to this edition.

2. f. 91r [C]osi mi parto doloroso e lasso/ ... et mal si tien chui lungo assedio accinge.

Anonymous *canzone*, pp. 100-01.

3. f. 91v [S]pente la cortesia spente larghessa/ ... e sensa spada con ragion difesa.

Pietro de' Faitinelli, *canzone*, pp. 102-04.

4. f. 92r Vienne la maiestate imperatoria/ ... che tosto aura buon uento sua nauicola.

Fazio degli Uberti [?], *canzone*, pp. 106-09.

5. f. 92r-v Di uento pasci chi techo si gloria/ ... Onde per lor mal fructa cotal arbaro.

Anonymous *canzone* in response to the *canzone* attributed to Fazio degli Uberti on f. 92r; pp. 110-13.

6. ff. 92v-93r [N]e lintellecto nuouo pensier formasi/ ... ben che sij nata qui fra lafra el teuere.

Ser Ciano del Borgo San Sepolcro, *canzone*, pp. 114-17.

7. f. 93r-v Cento fiate nel pensier mi rutola/ ... el seruo quando col signor sincorpora.

Ser Ciano del Borgo San Sepolcro, *canzone*, pp. 118-21.

8. ff. 93v-94r Io sono a te mandata padre santo/ ... amor richiama scritto a la rinuerso.

Anonymous *canzone*, pp. 122-25.

9. ff. 94r-95r Vertu celeste in titol triumfante/ ... contastar non pora a [with dot below] lultimo grido.

Maestro Antonio da Ferrara (Antonio Beccari), *canzone*, pp. 126-28.

10. f. 95r Era di stelle il cielo ancor dipinto/ ... e peggio e sensa fama hom chanim[ale: lost due to trimming].

Anonymous *canzone*, pp. 130-32.

11. f. 95v [O] pouerta cosi ti strugga idio/ ... questo ragiona oue tu sij vdita.

Manettino da Firenze [?], *canzone*, pp. 133-35.

12. f. 96r-v   La gran fama signor di uertu carca/ ... come uuol cannoscensa et honorata.

Anonymous *canzone*, pp. 138-41.

13. ff. 96v-97r   Auegna amicho che la nostra barcha/ ... chabbaglieresti a sua parola ornata.

Anonymous *canzone*, pp. 142-45.

14. f. 97r-v   [F in margin has been crossed and replaced by:] Morte poi chio non trouo a chui mi doglia/ ... quell anima gentil di chui Io sono.

Iacopo Cecchi, *canzone*, pp. 146-48.

15. f. 97v   Se mia uertute exprimer potesse/ ... che non fa chi mai quinde non recede//

Anonymous *canzone*, vv. 1-39 (see art. 19 for concluding verses), pp. 149-50.

16. f. 98r   Laspro tormento che consuma et sface/ ... et allor fa che dichi il tuo talento.

Anonymous *canzone*, pp. 44-46.

17. f. 98v   [S]u[ss crossed out]bbitamente amor con la sua fiaccola/ ... mi troueresti facto escha di uermine.

Anonymous *canzone*, pp. 47-49.

18. f. 98v   [S]i come il cigno quando a morte uene/ ... che contra me//

Anonymous *canzone*, vv. 1-13 (see art. 21 for concluding verses), p. 50.

19. f. 99r   //Apresso e da ueder del exercitio/ ... per cha cercato la preditta uita.

Anonymous *canzone*, beginning "Se mia uertute..." vv. 40-84 (see art. 15 for opening verses), pp. 150-51.

20. f. 99r-v   La uerita malletta et dice pensa/ ... pero che uerita uolentier uesto.

Anonymous *canzone*, pp. 152-54.

21. f. 100r   //fedele/ uçato auete com io ueggio chiaro/ ... che la mersede omai piu non mi neghi.

Anonymous *canzone*, beginning "Si come il cigno..." vv. 13-82 (see art. 18 for opening verses), pp. 50-52.

22. f. 100r-v   Poi che da uoi fortuna e rampognata/ ... pero che forse ne perdresti honore.

Giannozzo Sacchetti, *canzone*, pp. 53-55.

23. ff. 100v–101r   Qual fie si duro cuor domo o di donna/ ... costui per chui rimaso e il mondo ciecho.

Anonymous *canzone*, pp. 57–59.

24. f. 101r–v   Mentre che uisse il mio dilecto spoço/ ... chelli e disposto ad fare dei guelfi caccia.

Anonymous *canzone*, pp. 60–62.

25. ff. 101v–102r   [L]o degno et dolce amor del natio loco/ ... et poi tamanta di perfecta pace.

Anonymous *canzone*, pp. 63–64.

26. f. 102r–v   Ai pisa uitopero delle gente/ ... pero sta mecho et non andare altroue.

Anonymous *canzone*, pp. 65–66.

27. f. 102v   Per che saccenda nel cor uolontade/ ... per tucto luniuerso ondella [with dot under a] a bando.

Anonymous *canzone*, pp. 67–68.

28. ff. 102v–103r   Sio potesse ridir come comprese/ ... e i pie faciano andando picciole orme.

Fazio degli Uberti [?], *canzone*, pp. 69–70.

29. f. 103r–v   Souente nel mio cor nasce un pensero/ ... e i suoi contrari auran danno e uergogna.

Fazio degli Uberti [?], *canzone*, pp. 71–73.

30. f. 104r–v   I guardo i crespi e i biondi capelli/ ... fuor che ui mancha un pocho di pietade.

Fazio degli Uberti, *canzone*, pp. 74–76.

31. ff. 104v–105r   [A] donna grande possente et magnanima/ ... et tu ne se ricepto et tabernachulo.

Fazio degli Uberti, *canzone*, pp. 79–81.

32. f. 105r–v   Nel primo punto quando amor percosse/ ... cosi la malaspina in me sinpruna.

Fazio degli Uberti [?], *canzone*, pp. 83–85.

33. ff. 105v–106r   [L]asso che quando immaginando uegno/ ... che certa sij chio non auro mai pace.

Fazio degli Uberti, *canzone*, pp. 86–88.

34. f. 106r   De qual sera che si rallegri omai/ ... pregando ogni ora che ti dia uictoria.

Anonymous *canzone*, pp. 91–93.

35. f. 106r-v   Tanto son uolti i cieli di parte in parte/ ... et uendicar manfredi et curradino.

   Fazio degli Uberti, *canzone*, pp. 94-97.

36. f. 107r-v   Amor se uuoi chio torni al giogo anticho/ ... lassando trista e libera mia uita.

   Petrarch, *Rerum vulg. fragm.*, no. 270; G. Contini, ed., *Canzoniere* (Turin, 1966) pp. 341-44.

37. ff. 107v-108r   Di pensier in pensier di monte in monte/ ... qui ueder puoi limaggine mia sola.

   Petrarch, *Rerum vulg. fragm.*, no. 129; Contini, *op. cit.*, pp. 179-81.

38. f. 108r-v   Le stelle uniuersali e i cieli rotanti/ ... chassai son presso a priuarmi dellessere.

   Maestro Antonio da Ferrara (Antonio Beccari), *canzone*, pp. 160-62.

39. f. 109r   Questa aulente rosa colorita et frescha/ ... Di me misero/ che non mi raueggio.

   Anonymous *canzone*, pp. 164-66.

40. ff. 109v-110v   Various accounts, pen trials, drawings, prayers (including notes of a priest from Pisa and its environs) with dates ranging from 14 Nov. 1369 to 22 March 1373. In August of 1371 this priest was in the service of "Azone" (f. 110r) who is perhaps a relative of Niccolò Azzone, an owner of Part I (see colophon on f. 78v).

The codex is composed of two manuscripts; the pattern of stains suggests they were originally bound separately.

Part I: Paper (watermarks similar to Briquet Monts 11678), ff. i (paper) + i (contemporary parchment) + i (contemporary paper) + 90, 298 x 210 (229 x 120) mm. Written in ca. 40 lines of verse per page; frame-ruled in lead, often with upper horizontal bounding line only. I^{18} (1 = front contemporary paper flyleaf), II-IV^{20}, V^{20} (-13 through 19). Quire signatures (1-5) in upper left and lower right corners, on recto. Written by a single scribe in a bold upright notarial script.

Part II: Paper (coarse, brown; watermarks similar to Briquet Ciseaux 3737), ff. 20 (misbound; early arabic foliation runs 9-15, 1, 16, 2-8, 17-20) + ii (paper), 298 x 210 (235 x 168) mm. Written in 41-46 lines per page (with 2-3 verses per line); frame-ruled faintly in lead. Structure of original gatherings unclear due to repairs and misbinding. Written in a clear notarial script by a single scribe; later writers have added the initials, offset in margins, for the major sections of text (sometimes inaccurately) and the notes on ff. 109v-110v. Crude drawings include a falconer with birds, f. 103v, and a ghost [?], f. 103r. Stained throughout; some ink blotches affect text.

Binding: s. xix. Brown calf over wooden boards, blind-tooled. Red-brown, gold-tooled label. Parchment reinforcements between quires.

Written in two stages. Part II was copied in the mid-14th century (before 1369) in Tuscany, possibly in Pisa (see art. 40). Part I was copied by Niccolò di Giovanni Cinuzi da Siena in Ferrara, Italy, by 1 Sept. 1415 (colophon in art. 1). During the latter part of the 14th century Part II was owned by an unidentified priest in the pay of the Azzone family; in 1415 Part I was owned by Niccolò Azzone who may have bound together the two sections. Belonged to Richard Heber (1773-1833); his sale to Thorpe (Cat. 1836, Pt. 2, no. 186) from whom it was purchased by Sir Thomas Phillipps (no. 8826, tag on spine). Acquired by Yale from Laurence Witten in 1956, as the gift of Edwin J. and Frederick W. Beinecke.

secundo folio: piena

Bibliography: Faye and Bond, p. 42, no. 222.
   Exhibition Catalogue, pp. 213-14, no. 39.
   Ullman, no. 58, and the forthcoming revision of D. Dutschke.
   S. J. Pacifici, "A Manuscript of Boccaccio's *Il Filostrato*," *Gazette* 31 (1956) pp. 20-27.

MS 223
Jacobus Mediolanensis, Stimulus amoris, etc.

England, s. XV[1]

1. ff. 1r-2v   [Table of contents for art. 2:] *Here bigynneth a tretys or a book called Stimulus amoris that is to say the prikke of loue of oure lorde ihesu crist ... And now atte begynnynge be write the chapitres of all the hool book.* How a man or womman oweth gladly to have the passion of crist ihesu in mynde *cap. primum* ... Of the staat of blessed soules in heuenly ierusalem. *Capitulum xliiij.*

2. ff. 2v-106v   How a man or womman oweth gladly to haue the passion of crist ihesu in mynde. Cap. primum. Alle forwondred of oure selfe auʒte vs for to be ʒif we bethougte vs inwardly ... and so mut oure tretys enden in louyng of god so that all blissed spirites mote louen oure lorde, in the blisse of heuene. Amen. *Here endeth the tretys, that is called the prikke of loue. Made bi a frere menour Bonauenture that was a Cardynal of the Courte of Rome.*

   Stimulus amoris, translated into English by Walter Hilton from a Latin devotional text often attributed to Bonaventure. According to H. Kane, who is preparing a critical edition of the text and of the 16th-century commentary accompanying it in this manuscript, the Beinecke codex contains five chapters that are not known in any other manuscript (nos. 6, 9, 10, 26, 32).

3. ff. 106v-108r   How a man shal knowe, whiche is the speche of the flesshe in his herte and which is of the werde ... and tempered with wekenes, it is spekyng of god and not of thi selfe.

MS 223

P. S. Jolliffe (*A Check-list of Middle English Prose Writings of Spiritual Guidance* [Toronto, 1974] p. 82, F. 12) does not list the Yale copy of this anonymous devotional work. The treatise also follows the English translation of the *Stimulus amoris* in Stratton on the Fosse, Downside Abbey 26542, and Cambridge, Trinity College B. 14. 19. For a modern version see C. Kirchberger, ed., *The Coasts of the Country: An Anthology of Prayer Drawn from the Early English Spiritual Writers* (London, n. d.) pp. 75-77.

Parchment (thick, furry), ff. iii (paper) + 108 + iii (paper), 226 x 163 (149 x 102) mm. Written in 28 long lines; single vertical and horizontal bounding lines, full across. Ruled in ink; prickings (slashes) in all margins except inner.

I–XIII^8, XIV^4. Catchwords occur in carefully drawn scrolls, highlighted with yellow.

Written by a single scribe in bold, upright gothic textura; commentary added in an inelegant cursive (s. xvi).

One 4-line initial (f. 2v) gold, edged in black, against a blue and red cusped ground with white filigree, attached to a bar border in outer margin, gold, blue, and pink, with white highlights and leafy sprouts at divisions and terminals, orange, blue, red, and gold; the leaves with black hair-spray vines, both straight and in spirals, with small gold leaves and touches of green, filling upper, outer, and lower margins. Six initial *I*'s (ff. 7v, 31v, 36v, 38v, 61v, 83v), 11- to 7-line, gold against blue and red grounds with white filigree and straight hair-spray vines, as above. 2-line gold initials, against blue and/or pink grounds, with white filigree and hair-spray, as above. Gold or blue paragraph marks with blue or red penwork and flourishes. Gold and blue line-fillers, straight, zig-zag, and wavy, some up to 3/4 of a line long. Headings, occasional underlining, and crossing out, in red.

Trimming has affected some marginal commentary; f. 108 badly mutilated with loss of text. Leaves at beginning and end of codex stained and repaired.

Binding: s. xix. Red edges. Brown goatskin, blind- and gold-tooled.

Written in England in the first half of the 15th century; owned in the 16th century by a scholar who frequently added passages of commentary. Inscription (s. xviii) on f. 98v: "This Book is all damned nonsense./ Hugh Montgomerie." Belonged to John Borthwick of Crookston (signature with date "October 1856" on f. 1r); apparently his note on f. i verso: "Number in Catalogue XIII." Purchased from C. A. Stonehill by Thomas E. Marston (bookplate) who presented it to Yale in 1956.

secundo folio: [table of contents, f. 2] How a man
[text, f. 3] [py]ne his flesshe

Bibliography: Faye and Bond, p. 42, no. 223.

MS 224 Germany, s. XV^{med}
Jacobus de Voragine, Legenda aurea, etc.

1. front pastedown: Prima die eriget se mare xl cubitus super altitudinem moncium ... hec signa scripsit ysidorus xv.

Brief description of the 15 days before judgment; Stegmüller, v. 7, no. 10333.

I. 2. ff. 1r–52r Aduentus domini per quatuor septimanas agitur ad significandum ... Mox se terra aperuit et cunctos illos degluttiuit Reliqui uero ad eum sunt conuersi.

T. Graesse, ed., *Jacobi a Voragine Legenda aurea* (Leipzig, 1846). The legends in Beinecke MS 224 occur in the following order (with numbers corresponding to chapters in Graesse): 1–11, 21–23, 28, 37, 45.

3. ff. 52r–54v Castissimum marie virginis vterum clausum ventris sponse cubiculum signatum pudorem cenaculum plenissime ... saluatoris domini nostri ihesu christi qui cum deo patre viuit et regnat ... Amen. [followed by a short note beginning: Balthasar fuit etatum annorum centum et xvj annos. Melchior...]. ff. 55r–59v blank

Pseudo-Augustine, *Sermo de annuntiatione beatae virginis mariae*; PL 39. 2107–10. This is perhaps the work of Ambrosius Autpertus (see L. Scheffczyk, *Das Mariengeheimnis in Frommigkeit und Lehre der Karolingerzeit* [Erfurt-Leipzig, 1959] pp. 48–53).

4. f. 60r–v In diebus rogacionum. [H]elyas orauit ut non plueret super terram in die beati marci letania mayor peragitur ... laudate peregit etc. in christo quieuit [ends imperfectly?].

A similar selection on the litany appears in Munich, Universitätsbibliothek 2º Cod. MS 128, f. 154.

II. 5. ff. 61r–182v [no heading] De septem donis spiritus sancti de quibus prius scire debes ... Ad que inerrabilia bona eterne glorie perducat dominus noster ... seculorum secula. Amen.

Unidentified treatise, begins imperfectly? Includes the rubrics: *De statu ecclesie, De penitencia, De discipulo inobediente, De tribus hostibus nostris, Ambidexter, De pace, De amore violento, De vita contemplativa, De deo et efficibus eius, De purgatorio.*

6. ff. 182v–186r [Alphabetical index to preceding treatise:] Accessus hominis ad deum. 2º/ Abusio, de abusionibus. 7./ ... Christifideles et maxime Religiosi in vno statu permanere non possunt 29. et ultra.

7. ff. 186v–192v Uidens pijssimus et misericordissimus deus hominem quem ad sui ipsius fruicionem formauerat ... Eterna gaudia et inferni eterna supplicia valent ad resurrectendis peccatis.

MS 224

This work (entitled elsewhere *Tractatus de reparatione hominis lapsi*) also occurs in Klosterneuberg MS 205 (see H. Pfeiffer and B. Černík, *Catalogus codicum manu scriptorum qui in bibliotheca canonicorum regularium S. Augustini Claustroneoburgi asservantur* [Vindobonae, 1922] v. 1).

8. back pastedown: A bifolium from an unidentified 15th-century German manuscript on paper, beginning: Zu dem raben dw solt mir chwnden vnd sagen wo hestu den herren werleichen ... [one leaf: 148 x 103 (93 x 60) mm., written in 14-15 long lines].

Composed of two distinct sections:
I. Paper (watermarks: unidentified bull's head), ff. 60, 207 x 147 (152 x 109) mm. 2 columns of ca. 30 lines; frame-ruled in lead; remains of prickings. I–V^{12}. Written in a neat running script by three scribes: 1: ff. 1r-52r; 2: ff. 52r-54v; 3: f. 60r-v. Small, crude initials in red, some with simple penwork designs; initial strokes in red.

II. Paper (sturdy; watermarks buried in gutter), ff. 132 (contemporary foliation: 1-132; modern foliation: 61-192), 208 x 146 (165 x 105) mm. Folios 61r-182r: written in ca. 32 long lines; ff. 182v-192v: 2 columns of ca. 33 lines. Frame-ruled in ink; remains of prickings. I–XI^{12}. Quire signatures (primus, secundus, etc.) in center of lower margin, on verso. Written by a single scribe in an elegant running script. Portions of the marginal notes by original scribe have been lost due to trimming. Headings, paragraph marks, and initial strokes, in red, throughout.

Binding: s. xv-xvi. Original sewing on three thick, double, vegetable fiber cords laced and pegged in grooves in wooden boards. The grooves for the endband cores, which are also vegetable fiber, start on the spine edge of the boards. The spine of the bookblock is cut off at an angle at head and tail so the braided endbands extend very little beyond the edges. The spine is square and lined all along with tawed skin which extends to the inside of the boards. Covered in tawed skin, originally pink, with two labels at the head of the upper board; on the first, "Passionale ad aduentum domini usque ad festum mathie sancte [?] sermonum collectio [?]," on the second, "G.27". Five round bosses on each board and two strap-and-pin fastenings, the pins on the upper one. Lower board detached, bosses and fastenings wanting.

Written in Germany in the middle of the 15th century; early provenance unknown (see remarks on binding). Unidentified label on spine and notation on f. 1r: "252/P5". Stamp of the Kingsley Trust Association (f. 1r) which presented it to Yale in 1951.

secundo folio: ire parum

Bibliography: Faye and Bond, p. 42, no. 224.

MS 225 Bohemia, 1422
Scholar's Notebook Pl. 4

The following list of contents follows the table written inside the front cover of the codex; this table was apparently added when the manuscript was owned by the Carthusians at Erfurt (see below).

1. ff. 1r–29v   Auctoritates siue Flores totius philosophie naturalis moralis et logice.

    Includes: 12 sections de metaphisicis; 8 de physicis; 4 de celo et mundo; 2 de generacione; 4 de metroris [sic]; 3 de anima; 1 de sensu et sensatu; 1 de memoria et reminiscencia; 1 de sompno et uigilia; 1 de longitudine et breuitate vite; 1 de iuuentute et senectute; 1 de morte et vita; 19 de animalibus; 1 de causis; 10 de ethicis; 1 de bona fortuna; 1 de yconomica; 3 de politicis; 3 de rethoricis Aristotelis; 1 de poetica Aristotelis; Epistola Aristotelis ad allexandrum; 1 de regimine principum; 1 de morte uel de pomo Aristotelis; Epistola Senece ad lucillium; 1 de moribus senece; 1 de fortuna uel moribus vite senece; 1 de beneficijs senece; de remediis fortuitorum senece; 5 sections headed Boecius de consolacione philosophie; 1 headed Auctoritates boecii de disciplina scolarium; 1 headed liber appulei de deo socratis; 2 based on Porphyry and Aristotle.

2. ff. 29v–30v   Cantilogium siue aliquid de musica.

    Unidentified selection on monochords followed by a religious text, mostly rubbed and illegible.

3. ff. 31r–42v   Passages dealing primarily with Aristotle's *Meteorologica* (at least one leaf missing between ff. 42–43).

4. f. 43r–v   Miscellaneous notes added.

5. ff. 44r–263r   Puncta pro gradu magisterii [apparently the notes of Jacobus de Paradiso; see Provenance, below].

    The major divisions in the text are: f. 44r *Iste liber de celo et mundo cuius subiectum est Ens mobile...*; f. 44v *Diffinicio philosophie naturalis*; f. 85r Iste est liber de generacione et corrupcione; f. 111v Metaphysica; f. 124r Brief notes de physica, de meteorologica (f. 130v blank); f. 131r Physica (ff. 150r–v, 157v blank); f. 158r [C]irca inicium paruorum naturalium; f. 198r Circa inicium libri de memoria et reminiscencia; f. 208v Circa librum de sompno et vigilia; f. 219v De sompnis et diuinacione; f. 225v Circa inicium libri de longitudine et breuitate vite; f. 235v Circa libellum de morte et vite; f. 243v Circa principium libri de respiracione et inspiracione; f. 248v Circa inicium libri de iuuentute et senectute; f. 252v Circa inicium phisonomie Aristotelis.
    Colophon on f. 263r: *Finis disputatorum Paruorum naturalium reportatorum post Reuerendum Magistrum Paulum de Worczin in studio Craconien. Anno domini M⁰ cccc⁰ xxij⁰, feria iiij ante festum sancti michaelis.* ff. 263v–264v blank

6. ff. 265r-266r Descriptiones terminorum moralium; Ibidem aliquid in Geometrica. ff. 266r-267r blank

7. ff. 267v-278r Aliqua puncta circa primos sex libros Ethicorum.

8. ff. 278v-279v Aliquid modicum circa libros politicorum.

9. ff. 280r-294r Aliqua notata [on the *Parua naturalia*]. ff. 294v-295v blank

10. back pastedown: Upper half of a leaf from a liturgical manuscript (Germany, s. XII^1) written in long lines, with the number "clxxxxiij" added at the top in a later hand. Strips of parchment, probably from the same manuscript, appear in the center of each quire.

Paper (thick, rough; watermarks: unidentified bull's head), ff. 295, 217 x 150 (ca. 165 x 120) mm. Format varies considerably from one article to the next; most leaves are frame-ruled; prickings in all margins except inner.

I^{12} (-1, 2), II-III^{10}, IV^{12} (undetermined number of folios lost at end; the gathering [ff. 31-42] is composed of paper noticeably different from the rest of the codex), V^{14} (-14, no loss of text), VI-VIII^{12}, IX^{14}, X^{12}, XI^{16} (-3, 4, 16, no loss of text), XII^{12}, XIII^{16} (-1), XIV-XXI^{12}, XXII^{12} (-11, no loss of text), XXIII^{16}, XXIV^{16} (-15, no loss of text). Remains of catchwords.

Written primarily (ff. 44-294) by a single person in a cramped running script, with many abbreviations and in a more elegant display script for some headings and colophon (see colophon in art. 5 and below); several other writers are responsible for arts. 1-4.

Plain initials, headings, and paragraph marks, in red, for ff. 1r-29v. Spaces left for initials and rubrics on ff. 44r-294r.

Binding: s. xv. Original sewing on three double, twisted, tawed thongs which are laced into wooden boards of unequal shape and thickness. Plain, wound endbands sewn on tawed cores are laced into the boards from the spine edge. The cover is adhered to the square spine and kermes pink placemarks to the fore-edge. One quarter covered in brown calf, blind-tooled with lines forming triangles, and very small flowers. One fastening, the catch on the upper board, the brown calf strap attached to the lower with a metal plate. Parchment labels at head of front board. Lower joint repaired, strap wanting.

The main portion of the codex (arts. 5-9, with contemporary signatures 1-20 in upper left corner, on recto) was written in Cracow in 1422 by a student of Magister Paulus de Worczin. Belonged to the Carthusians of Salvatorberg, Erfurt; no. 42 in the 15th-century catalogue of the library (see P. Lehmann, *Mittelalterliche Bibliothekskataloge Deutschlands und der Schweiz* [Munich, 1928] v. 2, p. 488, no. 42). According to this catalogue these are the notes recorded by Frater Jacobus de Paradiso (Jacobus de Jüterbogk) who studied and taught in Cracow and came to the Carthusians at Erfurt in 1442; presumably he is the scribe responsible for ff. 44-294. The remaining portions of the text seem to have been added, the codex bound, and an index pasted to the inside of the front cover at Erfurt, sometime in the 15th century. Ownership inscription (s. xv) inside front and back covers: 'Hic liber est domus carth. prope Erfford." Belonged to A. Franck of Paris (ca. 1850-60; booktag); obtained in 1931 from Goldschmidt's by the Rev. Anson Phelps Stokes (bookplate). Purchased by Yale in 1956 with the Penniman Fund.

secundo folio: per se potest

Bibliography: De Ricci, v. 2, p. 2276, no. 2; Faye and Bond, p. 42, no. 225.

MS 226 Flanders, 1476
Caesar, Commentarii de Bello Gallico, Fr. tr. Jean Duchesne Pl. 8

1. ff. 1r-10r [Table of contents:] Cy commence la table de ce present volume ... Et premiers. Le prologue de translateur. Prologue general du premier chappitre *I* ... La conclusion du translateur de ce present volume ... *lxx^e*. Cy prent fin la table de tout ce present volume. f. 10v blank

2. ff. 11r-261v *Le prologue du translateur des commentaires de Julle cesar*. Tres hault tres puissant tres excellent victorieux et christien prince Mon tres redoubte seigneur Charles ... Atribuant les biens auz composeurs non pas a lindigne escripuain qui de tel los se cognoist non coulpable. *Explicit*. Cy prent le xe darrenier livre des commentaires de cesar fin [partly erased] translatez en la ville de lille, lan mil CCCCxxiii^e par Jehan du chesne humble et indigne. Copie a loriginal par hellin de burchgraue, a la Requeste de honnourable homme et saige jaques donche, conseillier de mon tres redoubte seigneur, monseigneur le duc de bourgogne, son Watregraue et moermaist re de flandres et maistre de la chambre aux deniers de madame la duchesse de bourgogne et cetera en lan mil iiij^e soixante seize.

G. Doutrepont, *La littérature française à la cour des ducs de Bourgogne* (Paris, 1909) p. 180; R. Bossuat, "Traductions françaises des *Commentaires* de César à la fin du XVe siècle," *Bibliothèque d'humanisme et Renaissance*, v. 3 (Paris, 1943) pp. 253-373; R. H. Lucas, "Medieval French Translations of the Latin Classics to 1500," *Speculum* p. 45 (1970) p. 235.

Paper, with parchment bifolios interspersed, ff. ii (paper) + 261 (watermarks similar to Briquet Armoiries: Trois fleurs de lis 1741) + ii (paper) 369 x 265 (ca. 256 x 190) mm., trimmed. Written in 2 columns, 35 lines; single bounding lines. Ruled in pale lavender ink; prickings in outer margin of f. 214 (parchment).

I^{10}, II-V^{12} (outer bifolios are parchment); ff. 59-239 too tightly bound to be collated; ff. 240-49^{10}, 250-261^{12} (6-7 parchment). The description of the construction given in the *Exhibition Catalogue*, no. 75, is inaccurate.

Written in neat bâtarde script by Hellin de Burchgrave (see contents for colophon, f. 261v).

The compositional types of the miniatures recall the work of Loyset Liédet; the style that of the "Vrelant" circle. According to J. Marrow, another manuscript by the same artists is a copy of Jean Mansel's *La Fleur des histoires* in Brussels, Bibl. Roy., MS IV 669 (see *Cinq années d'acquisitions, 1969-1973* [Brussels: Bibliothèque Royale, 1975] pp. 93-99, with 2 illus.). One might also suggest comparisons with miniatures from the circle of the Master of Louis de Bruges (*Exhibition Catalogue*, no. 75, p. 255). The thirteen miniatures in the Beinecke codex closely resemble compositions found in the cycle of twenty-three miniatures in London, B. L. Royal 16 G. VIII, ca. 1470 (see G. Keach, "Two Flemish Manuscripts of Caesar's Commentaries," M.A. Thesis, Yale University, 1969).

Ten half-page miniatures, each in an arched frame composed of two thin bands, gold and red highlighted with white, edged in black, the arch with tiny cusps; beneath, initials, 6-, 4-, or 3-line, blue or blue and red with white highlights on a gold ground of irregular shape conforming to the letter, edged in black, with serifs protruding into the left margin; filled with green and/or red and crimson trilobe leaves on curling stems with white and/or yellow highlights, or with a blue, green, crimson, and gold diapered ground with white highlights. These miniatures are as follow: f. 11r (Prologue) Presentation of the work to Charles, Duke of Burgundy; f. 67r (Bk. 2) The Three Parts of Gaul and the Battle near the Saône; f. 89r (Bk. 3) The Romans battle the Nervii; f. 102r (Bk. 4) Roman Ships on the Marne and the Ruse of Titurius Sabinus against the Venelli; f. 113v (Bk. 5) Caesar Crossing the Rhine; f. 127r (Bk. 6) The Arrival of the Roman Fleet in Britain; f. 147r (Bk. 7) Gaius Trebonius leads the Attack outside Atuatuca; f. 163r (Bk. 8) The Surrender of Alesia and the Flight of the Mandubii; f. 197r (Bk. 9) The Surrender of the Aquitanians; f. 214r (beginning of Bk. 10) Caesar's Embarkation for Thessaly. Three smaller miniatures, 12- or 14-line, occasionally cut off at the upper edge so as to fill only part of a line of text; frames rectilinear, otherwise identical to those described above: f. 25r (Bk. 1) The Birth of Caesar; f. 218r (Bk. 10, ch. 6) Caesar Crossing the Rubicon; f. 256r (Bk. 10, ch. 68) The Assassination of Caesar. Beneath, 2-line initials, blue, with white highlights, filled with trilobe leaves, as above, once (f. 25r) with one leaf of spiky acanthus added, and once (f. 256r) with a pink ground with gold filigree. There is a blank space on f. 27r for another miniature of this type. Other decoration consists of 2-line calligraphic initials, paragraph marks, line fillers (spirals and heraldic dragons), page and chapter headings, all executed in red. The first one or two lines of some books (as well as occasional lines within the text) are underlined in red.

A few folios have tears in the margins.

Binding: s. xviii. Spattered and gilt edges. Red goatskin, gold-tooled, with the arms of Eugène of Savoy on cover and his monogram on spine.

Written for Jacques Donche, counselor of Charles the Bold of Burgundy (K. G. Van Acker, "Jacob Donche, Raadsheer Bij de Raad van Vlaanderen, Baljuw van

Dendermonde," *Handelingen der Maatschappij voor Geschiedenis en Oudheidkunde te Gent*, Nieuwe Reeks 36 [1982] pp. 93 n. 19, 94, 95; J. Bartier, *Légistes et gens de finances au XVe siècle; les conseillers des ducs de Bourgogne* ... [Brussels, 1955] p. 325) by Hellin de Burchgrave in 1476 (colophon on f. 261v; *Colophons*, v. 2, p. 341, no. 6291). Another manuscript owned by Donche is in the library of Claremont Colleges (California), Denison Library, MS Kirby 1 (we thank J. Marrow for this information). The decoration suggests that the Yale copy was made in Bruges. Belonged to Prince Eugène of Savoy, 1663-1736 (arms and monogram on binding). Sir Thomas Phillipps (no. 4739, tag on spine; P. Durrieu, "Les manuscrits à peintures de la bibliothèque de Sir Thomas Phillipps à Cheltenham," *Bibliothèque de l'école des Chartes* 50 [1889] 404); Phillipps sale (Sotheby's, 1 July 1946, no. 25). Acquired from Dudley M. Colman through C. A. Stonehill in 1954 as a gift of the Yale Library Associates.

secundo folio: Coment cesar se prepara

Bibliography: Faye and Bond, p. 43, no. 226.
Exhibition Catalogue, p. 255, no. 75.
"Eight Medieval Manuscripts," *Gazette* 29 (1955) pp. 99, 107, 110 (with illustration of f. 113v facing p. 115).
Exhib. cat. *The Waning Middle Ages* (J. L. Schrader, The University of Kansas Museum of Art, 1969) pp. 23-24, no. 20.

MS 227
Arthurian Romances

France, 1357
Pl. 3

1. ff. 1r-11r   Nostre sires auoit mult danemis et auersaires contre luy. Et si auoit pau de deciples ... et de ciaus quil auoit en iauoit il un piour que mestiers ne li fust ... Et se ie la laissoie atant nus ne sauroit que toutes ces choses seroient deuenues ne pour quel senefianche ie les aroie de parties. f. 11v blank

    Robert de Borron, *Joseph d'Arimathie*. See A. E. Knight, "A Previously Unknown Prose *Joseph d'Arimathie*," *Romance Philology* 21, no. 2 (Nov., 1967) pp. 174-83; G. Weidner, *Der Prosaroman von Joseph von Arimathia* (Oppeln, 1881); and R. F. O'Gorman, "An Edition of the Prose Version of Robert de Borron's *Joseph d'Arimathie*" (unpublished dissertation, Univ. of Penn., 1962). Knight assigns the Yale "Joseph" to O'Gorman's "y group", the stemma of which he alters slightly in order to accommodate it.

2. ff. 12r-140v   Ci qui la haute ce et la seignorie de si haute estoire com est cele du graal met en escript par le commandement du grant mestre mande tout premierement saluz ... Einsit com mesires robert de borron le trest en listoire en la tranlata de latin en romans par la piere monseignour gautier de montbeliart en cui seruise il estoit au iour de lors et commence dun conte en tel maniere mult fu irez ennemi.

MS 227

Robert de Borron, *Lestoire de Saint Graal*. See H. O. Sommer, ed., *The Vulgate Version of the Arthurian Romances* (Washington, 1909) v. 1, pp. xxvii–xviii, and Knight, *op. cit.*, pp. 181–82.

3. ff. 141r–316v   *Si commence la vie Merlin*. Mout fu iries li anemis quant nostre Sires out este en enfer et il en ont gete adam et Eve ... En cel maniere fu Artus esleu a roy de par nostre seignour iheucrist [*sic*] et de par Mellin. Et tient le roiaum de logres mes ce ne fu mie longement em pes. *Ci apres trouueres conment li rois artus si deffendi contre les larronsdon pais qui ne uoloit pas quil fust rois mes melins li aida molt durement sa guere a maintenir.* [The text continues f. 172v with the Vulgate Continuation:] Ci endroit dist li contes que apres la mi aoust que li rois artus fu couronnes. que il tint court merueilleuse ... et ce fu celui qui le trai comme mauuais traiteur et desleal. et par qui il perdi le noble chastel que trebes auoit non quil auoit moult chier. *Ein si comme li contes le deuisera ca auant en la marche degaule le quart liure. Cis liures fu parescripit lan mil. ccc. lvij. le premier samedi de guillet et le fist Jehan de loles escriuen nes de hainnaut pries pour lui et ce que vous en dires puissiez vous auoir soit bien soit mal.*

Robert de Borron, *Lestoire de Merlin*; see A. Micha, "Les manuscrits de *Merlin*," *Romania* 79 (1958) p. 174. According to Knight, *op. cit.*, pp. 182–83, the Yale "Merlin" belongs in the z family of alpha.

Parchment, ff. i (parchment) + 316 (16th-century foliation 1–317, no f. 173) + i (parchment); 423 x 300 (305 x 206) mm., trimmed. Written in three columns of 47–49 lines, each with single vertical bounding lines full across; single or double horizontal bounding lines at top only, full across; ruled in brown ink. (A similar three-column format occurs in a "Roman de Merlin," London, B. L. Add. MS 10292.) Prickings in outer, upper, and lower margins.

I^{12} (-12, following f. 11), II–XVI^8, XVII^6, XVIII^4 (-1, following f. 137), XIX–XXXIX^8, XL^6, XLI^2. Catchwords, some embellished with lightly drawn faces. Remains of leaf signatures on ff. 7r–10r and 12r–52r.

Written by five scribes in gothic textura. Scribe 1: ff. 1r–11r (*Joseph d'Arimathie*). Scribes 2: ff. 12r–83v and 3: ff. 84r–140r (*Lestoire de Saint Graal*). Scribe 4: ff. 141r–317v (*Lestoire de Merlin*), except ff. 149r–156v, the second gathering, written by Scribe 5. [See Knight, *op. cit.*, p. 176.] Scribe 4 is identified as Jehan de Loles from the colophon. [See art. 3.] Guides for rubrics written in lower or inner margin. Inscriptions adjoining miniatures in 14th-century cursive, brown or black ink, are possibly either later identifications or instructions to the minaturist.

The decoration, the work of four hands, is of relatively poor quality (see *The Waning Middle Ages*, The University of Kansas Museum of Art [1969], no. 2, p. 8, pl. 3 [ff. 210r and 211r] and *Exhibition Catalogue*, no. 34, pp. 208–09) and is comparable to the miniatures by the less competent of two hands in a *Bible Historiale*, olim Henry Yates Thompson Collection MS LXXV (*Illustrations from One Hundred Manuscripts in the Library of Henry Yates Thompson* [London, 1916] v. 6, pl. L). Three large miniatures, 11- to 13-line and two column: f. 1r (*Joseph d'Arimathie*) Arrest of Christ, Deposition, Entombment; f. 12r (*Lestoire de Saint Graal*) Monk prostrate beside altar with angel above, Priest performing mass before three kneeling men; f. 141r (*Lestoire de Merlin*) Harrowing of Hell, Monk, woman and child before enthroned man; blue and/or red frames, gold squares in corners, surrounded by a thin gold band, with gold ivy leaves on black hair-lines at midpoints and corners. Miniatures accompanied by 3/4 bar borders, red, blue and gold, with white highlights; dragon and ivy terminals, with additional ivy extending from the gold segments. 182 small miniatures, 8-line, one column, most in bottom margin, suggesting execution after the original illumination had been completed: thin gold, red, and blue frames, single gold ivy leaf on hair-line stem at each corner; gold and diapered grounds. Due to the relatively poor quality of the decoration and its repetitious character, the subjects of the miniatures have not been listed. One historiated initial, f. 186v, 3-line, red against a blue and gold ground, knight and three men outside tent. Illuminated initials, 6- to 4-line, for books and chapters, red against irregular blue grounds with white highlights; gold dots in cusps at corners, infilled with blue and red ivy against gold. 2-line initials (guide-letters remain), gold, against irregular blue, orange, and red grounds with white highlights; black hair-lines at corners. Rubrics in red throughout, with guides for rubrics written in lower or inner margin.

Binding: s. xvi [?]. Worn purple velvet over boards, with massive brass corner pieces and fastenings; plaque with arms removed from front cover. Made possibly for Henri, comte de Clermont-Tonnerre (see Knight, *op. cit.*, p. 175).

Lestoire de Merlin was copied in France in 1357, by Jehan de Loles, as indicated by the colophon (art. 3). The other two works are probably contemporary, but rubbing on the first folio of each work suggests that they were once bound separately. Early provenance unknown. Belonged to Henri, comte de Clermont-Tonnerre (d. 1573 [*Dictionnaire de la Noblesse* v. 5, pp. 865-66). Collection of Charles Yarnold (his sale by Evans, 6 June 1825, no. 855). Acquired by Sir Thomas Phillipps (no. 1045; inscription on front pastedown and stamp on front flyleaf, verso; Sotheby's sale, 1 July 1946, no. 14). Owned by Dudley Colman of Hove, Sussex. Purchased from C. A. Stonehill in 1954 as the gift of Arthur M. Rosenbloom, Yale 1925.

secundo folio: [f. 2r, *Joseph d'Arimathie*] del uaissel
　　　　　　　[f. 13r, *Lestoire de Saint Graal*] auait esprigie [?]
　　　　　　　[f. 142r, *Lestoire de Merlin*] suer que

Bibliography: Faye and Bond, p. 43, no. 227.
　Exhibition Catalogue, pp. 208-09, no. 34.
　"Eight Medieval Manuscripts," *Gazette* 29 (1955) pp. 104-05 and 110.

MS 228 Portugal [?], ca. 1465
Dives and Pauper, etc.

1. ff. 1r-199r [Heading:] Primum preceptum. [text:] Off holy pouert *Capitulum primum. Diues et pauper obuiauerunt sibi utriusque dominator est dominus prouerb. xxij⁰.* Thise ben þe wordis off Salamon þus mych to sey en englissh ... in þe kynges courte of heuen þe wych blysse he bryng us þat for us died on þe crosse. Amen. [added by Scribe 2:] Deo gracias et sue Matri marie amen. 1465 Sancta katherina in lixboa/ 12 [a later addition:] and þer bith writyn wᵗ þe calander iiᶜ x lebir.

For a modern critical edition see P. H. Barnum, ed., *Dives and Pauper* in EETS 275 and 280 (Oxford, 1976 and 1980) v. 1, parts 1 and 2 (part 2 has plate of f. 199r facing p. 325); v. 3 forthcoming. Barnum attributes Beinecke MS 228 to Group B (*op. cit.*, pp. xii-xiv); we thank her for advice concerning the manuscript.

2. f. 199v Business accounts for "blew medley" in English, in tabular format [later addition].

Paper (watermarks: unidentified flower similar in design to Briquet Fleur 6654-56), ff. i (parchment stub) + iii (paper) + 199 + i (paper) + i (parchment stub), 298 x 209 (214 x 146) mm. Written in ca. 40 long lines; lightly frame-ruled in ink; prickings in corners of written space.

I-XII¹⁶, XIII⁷ (structure uncertain; two leaves detached, 8 stubs). Remains of signatures and catchwords along lower edge near gutter.

Text written in sprawling English secretary by two scribes, who added notes to mark sections in the margins.

Several crude initials and line-fillers in red and brown. References to and quotations from the Bible, as well as running headings and marginalia, underlined in red.

Water stains on many folios at front and back, not affecting text.

Binding: s. xvii. Red spattered edges. Brown spattered calf, blind-tooled.

Written, presumably in Portugal, by a scribe trained in England; the note on f. 199r indicates that it belonged to the monastery of St. Catharine in Lisbon in 1465. The business accounts on f. 199v suggest that it was owned by a cloth dealer, possibly an English merchant trading with Portugal. Belonged to Philip Emily [or Smily?]; his signature and the date "July 4 1614" on f. 1r, smeared and struck out. The gift of Humfrey Barbour to Edward Rowden (note of s. xvii-xviii on f. ii recto: "Edw. Rowdon. his booke being the guift of Humfrey Barbour Cle"). Signature (s. xix) of William Brydges, Esquire, on front parchment stub. Sold by Maggs to C. A. Stonehill, from whom it was acquired in 1954 for the Albert H. Childs Memorial Collection.

Bibliography: Faye and Bond, p. 43, no. 228.
"Eight Medieval Manuscripts," *Gazette* 29 (1955) pp. 108, 112.

MS 229 France, s. XIII^{ex}
Arthurian Romances Frontispiece

1. ff. 1r–186r Chi en droit dist li contes que quant Agrauains se fu partis de ses compaignons si come vous aues oit ... tant assembles la veille de pentecouste quil nest nus qui les veist qui ne sen peust esmerueillier. Chi fenist maistre Gautier mape son liure, et commence del graal. f. 186v blank

   Le livre de Lancelot du Lac, part III; H. O. Sommer, ed., *The Vulgate Version of the Arthurian Romances* (Washington, D. C., 1910) v. 5, pp. 3-409.

2. ff. 187r–272v A la veille de pentecouste quant tout li compaignon de la table reonde furent venu a kamaalot ... Et quant Bohort eut contees les auentures du Graal teles com il les avoit veues. Si furent mises en escrit et gardees en labeie de salesbieres dont Maistre Gautier Map les traist a faire son liure du saint Graal por lamor du roi heinri son signor qui fist lestoire translater de latin en francois. Si se taist a tant li contes que plus nen dist des auentures du saint Graal.

   La queste del Saint Graal; Sommer, *op. cit.*, v. 6 (1913) pp. 3-199.

3. ff. 272v–363r Apres ce que Maistre Gautier Mappe ot tretie des auentures du saint Graal soffisaument si com il li sambloit ... Mais a tant se taist ore li contes a parler de lestoire de lancelot du lac car bien a tout mene a fin mestre Gautier maples selonc les choses qui auienrent et define si son liure et si outreement que apres ce ne porroit nus reconter chose quil ne mentist. Explicit la mort au Roi artus et de lancelot du lac et des compaignons de la table reonde.

   La mort au Roy Artus; Sommer, *op. cit.*, v. 6 (1913) pp. 203-391.

Parchment, ff. i (paper) + 363 + i (paper), 475 x 343 (325 x 220) mm. Written in two columns, 39-40 lines, single vertical bounding lines on either side, full length, double horizontal bounding lines at top, center, and bottom of written space, full across. Ruled in lead. Prickings in outer margin; on some folios, an additional pricking in outer margin for the upper of the two horizontal bounding lines at the bottom of the written space.

I-IX^8, X-XII^{10}, XIII-XIV^8, XV^8 (-4, following f. 115), XVI-XLV^8, XLVI^4. Quires signed at center of lower margin, of the first recto (e. g., a, b, c ... a2, b2, etc.). Leaf signatures (e. g., ai, aii, aiii) remain in XXI, XXVI, and XL between the lower horizontal bounding lines, in XXXIII (a, b, c) in the lower margin. Catchwords in brown ink (partially flaked off) between two short ruled lines, lower right verso. Catchword for XVI rewritten above the partially trimmed original in a cursive script (s. xv).

Written in elegant gothic textura by one scribe, with a few interlinear corrections in later hands (s. xiv and xv).

The decoration of this lavishly illuminated manuscript consists of seventy-seven large column miniatures, fifty-one smaller miniatures, and thirty-six historiated initials. Miniatures and historiated initials by at least two artists, the scale and quality of whose work distinguish the manuscript from contemporary and most fourteenth-century Arthurian manuscripts. [See *Exhibition Catalogue*, no. 25, pp. 197-99, and E. Simmons Greenhill, "A Fourteenth-Century Workshop of Manuscript Illuminators and Its Localization," *Zeitschrift für Kunstgeschichte*, v. 40 (1977).] A manuscript in Paris, B. N. fr. 95, which contains, among other non-Arthurian texts, *Lestoire del Saint Graal* and the *Lestoire de Merlin*, may be a pendant of the Beinecke *Lancelot* (see R. S. Loomis, *Arthurian Legends in Medieval Art* [New York, 1938] pp. 95-97 and M. Montpetit in *Art and the Courts*, exhib. cat. [Ottawa, 1972] p. 88, no. 17) or a closely related product of the same shop (see M. A. Stones, "Secular Manuscript Illumination in France," *Medieval Manuscripts and Textual Criticism*, University of North Carolina, Chapel Hill, Dept. of Romance Languages, Symposia, no. 4, ed. C. Kleinhenz [Chapel Hill, 1976] pp. 83-102 and figs. 3, 11 and 13, of ff. 187r, 126r and 290v respectively). Various features of Paris, B. N. fr. 95 (size, format, script, *mise-en-page*, and the type of decoration) are exceedingly close to the Beinecke *Lancelot*. Other manuscripts possibly from the same workshop are Brussels, Bibl. Roy. MS 10607, Psalter of Gui de Dampierre; Marseilles, Bibl. Mun. MS 111, Book of Hours; and Paris, B. N. lat. 1076, Psalter (see Stones, *op. cit.*, p. 91, figs. 12 and 16); Florence, Laur. Ash. 125; Bruges Seminary 45/144. Large miniatures, 12- to 11-lines, one column, framed and usually divided into two registers by thin bands, gold, red and/or blue with white highlights, edged in black, sometimes with arched canopies, often with architectural elements protruding (a few frames composed of thicker bands); figures in black pen against burnished gold (occasionally with painted gold diaperwork), blue or black grounds; chief colors: light blue, dark blue, grey, light brown, white, maroon, with some orange, green and gold. Borders on folios with large miniatures of a variety and inventiveness that defy strict classification: gold, red, and blue bands, edged in black, also running between, below and/or above text columns, terminating in dragons, dragon or human heads, grotesques or, most commonly, floral spirals, some with frets, blue and red with white highlights and orange and green dots, against gold, blue and/or maroon cusped grounds, often with pinwheel-like projections. The borders are populated with magnificent grotesques and marginalia in the same style as the miniatures, many of them of a narrative or satirical character (see L. Randall, "The Snail in Gothic Marginal Warfare," *Speculum* 37 (1962) pp. 338, 367 and *idem, Images in the Margins of Gothic Manuscripts* [Berkeley and Los Angeles, 1966] *passim*); some of these incorporate coats of arms (see Provenance). Small miniatures, 5- to 6-line, 1/2 text column, often with a 2-line initial inserted in upper right corner, otherwise as above, with border decoration on a smaller scale and unattached to miniature. Historiated initials, 5-line (letters without ascenders or descenders) to 13-line, red and/or blue, with geometric motifs in paler shades of red and blue, white, with touches of orange, against gold grounds, edged in black, with long dragon and floral serifs, as above, against cusped gold grounds; figures in same style as miniatures, against gold grounds. The subjects of the miniatures are as follow; in parentheses are given page and line number of corresponding text in Sommer's edition. The symbols LM, SM, and HI indicate large miniature, small miniature and historiated initial. We thank M. A. Stones for her assistance with this sequence of scenes. The subjects of these illuminations are *not* included in the General Index.

f. 1r (3:1) Agravain meets the bandaged knight and the weeping damsel; Agravain takes his leave. [HI]

f. 3v (9:33) Guerrhes meets a peasant leading a donkey loaded with firewood; Guerrhes attacks the ten knights. [LM]

f. 11v (29:34) The knight in the fourth pavilion drags his wife out of bed by the hair. [HI]

f. 14r (35:20) Gaheriet meets a damsel in the woods at vespers. [HI]

f. 15v (38:29) Gaheriet unhorses one of Guinas' knights. [HI]

f. 18r (44:4) Gaheriet and Guidan in combat. [HI]

f. 23v (55:8) The Seneschal breaks his lance and is wounded by Agravain. [HI]

f. 24r (56:9) Agravain set upon by the ten knights. [HI]

f. 25r (59:1) Lucan addresses the King; the Queen with Elysabel; the Queen asleep. [HI]

f. 27v (63:20) Bohort and Lionel leave the court; Lancelot and a damsel on horseback; the Queen asleep. [LM]

f. 29r (67:14) Lancelot, with new armor, leaves the old damsel; Lancelot exchanges greetings with a damsel on horseback. [LM]

f. 31r (70:39) Head of the damsel who brings news of Lancelot [?]. [HI]

f. 31r (71:3) Head of Lancelot [?]. [HI]

f. 31r (71:6; miniature illustrates previous section) The Queen leads to the king the damsel who has told her of Lancelot. [LM]

f. 31r (71:6) Lancelot and the old damsel leave the convent; Lancelot and the old damsel join the banquet of the knight and two damsels. [LM]

f. 31r (71:6) Head of Lancelot's guide [?]. [HI]

f. 39v (89:13) Hector meets a damsel in the woods; Hector and Tercian in combat. [LM]

f. 40v (91:23) The Queen of Sorestan and her suite find Lancelot asleep; the enchanted Lancelot is carried away by litter. [LM]

f. 43r (96:11) Lancelot and the knight in the bed. [HI]

f. 48r (106:23) Lancelot attacks the serpent in the tomb. [HI]

f. 50r (111:23) Lancelot discovers the identity of Pelles' daughter. [HI]

f. 52r (116:28) Lancelot takes his leave despite the knight's warnings. [HI]

f. 56r (124:18) Ywain leaves the friars; Ywain and Bohort fight over the dwarf's dog. [LM]

f. 62v (138:25) Bohort and the damsel arrive at Galvoie; Bohort and Mariales in combat. [LM]

f. 66r (147:37) Gawain leaves the hermit; Gawain overtakes a damsel and squire. [LM]

f. 66v (148:28) The damsels caroling; the enchanted chessboard. [LM]

f. 75r (168:17) Lancelot and the damsel leave the hermitage; the knights of the Round Table in battle with the knights of Baudemagus. [LM]

f. 83r (187:3) Bohort attacks Gaheriet. [HI]

f. 85v (192:29) Unidentified: a man in bed and 3 men before King Arthur; the Queen gives Lancelot the ring of the Lady of the Lake. [LM]

f. 88r (197:28) Two knights set fire to the "castel de la blanche espine". [HI]

f. 92v (206:40) Lancelot and Tercian fight with swords. [HI]

f. 94v (210:30) Lancelot follows the damsel; Lancelot kills the knight in the wood. [LM]

f. 98r (219:3) Gawain takes his leave of Arthur and Guenever; Gawain arrives at the castle of the "quens del parc". [LM]

f. 99r (ca. 220:26; text varies from Sommer) The knights meet at the "castel de trepas"; the squire is dispatched to Carduel. [LM]

f. 99v (222:6) Lancelot picks the rose in Morgan's garden; Lancelot escapes and gives his message to the porter. [LM]

f. 100v (223:38) Lancelot meets a damsel and a dwarf; Lancelot and the wounded knight in a litter. [LM]

f. 104v (231:32) The Scottish King Heliser converted by Joseph of Arimathea is given food by the porter of the abbey; Heliser finds his son beside him on awakening. [LM]

f. 106v (235:8) Lancelot and the wounded Lionel received by the friars; Lancelot rides by the cross of Clochides, talks to the hermit in his hut, climbs towards the castle, with Gawain (identifiable by his bandaged head) and the other imprisoned knights at the battlements. [LM]

f. 109r (240:10) Bohort and Lancelot embrace. [HI]

f. 110v (243:20) Lancelot takes his leave; Lancelot greets the prisoners. [LM]

f. 110v (244:13) Lancelot meets the dwarf who tells him of the dangers of the perilous forest; Lancelot fights the lions guarding the tomb; Lancelot lifts the head out of the boiling water, shows the head to the hermit who points to the tomb, and opens the tomb which contains a headless body. [LM]

f. 112r (247:19) Lancelot asks the hermit what he knows of his past. [HI]

f. 113r (250:8) Lancelot kills the knight who insists on a joust. [HI]

f. 115r (253:33) Lancelot speaking to Sarras after unhorsing Belias. [SM]

f. 119r (263:26) The black knight wounds Lancelot in the shoulder; the followers of the black knight set upon Lancelot as the black knight flees to his castle. [LM]

f. 120v (265:34) Lancelot unfetters Mordret. [HI]

f. 126r (277:37) Lancelot and Mordret see the stag and the lions; two knights seize the horses of Lancelot and Mordret. [LM]

f. 128r (281:31) Mordret unhorses a knight. [SM]

f. 132v (290:5) Hector and Lionel recognize Mordret among the wounded knights; Mordret taken to the castle in a litter. [LM]

f. 133v (292:11) Bohort and Lancelot see a fire; Bohort sees two men dragging a damsel by the hair while others beat a knight clad only in his shirt. [LM]

    f. 135r (299:16) Bohort overwhelmed by a hail of arrows. [SM]

    f. 137v (303:33) Lancelot enters the pavilion with two candles, where a damsel lies on a bed watched by a dwarf; Lancelot fights the damsel's second knight. [LM]

    f. 139r (306:15) Lancelot kills the black knight by his pavilions. [HI]

    f. 140v (308:21) Lancelot unhorses one of the knights who mistakes him for Kex. [HI]

    f. 141v (309:37) Lancelot unhorses Gawain. [HI]

    f. 143v (312:13) Gawain retrieves the shield discarded by Lancelot; the four companions ride toward Camelot. [LM]

    f. 147r (317:25) Gawain and other knights with a squire carrying lances for jousting. [HI]

    f. 147r (318:11) Gawain knocks both Lancelot and his horse to the ground. [HI]

    f. 148v (320:14) Brumant burns in the perilous seat. [HI]

    f. 153v (ca. 330:25; text varies from Sommer) Claudas' fleet. [HI]

    f. 154v (332:8) Arthur summons the companions of the quest to relate their adventures. [LM]

    f. 156v (ca. 337:14; text varies from Sommer) The attack of Patrides. [HI]

    f. 160r (349:40) The battle against the Romans. [SM]

    f. 164r (358:17) The battle against the Romans. [SM]

    f. 164v (359:27) King Carados and his division. [HI]

    f. 165r (ca. 360:27; text varies from Sommer) The battle for the standard. [HI]

    f. 167r (ca. 364:20) Bohort and Hector with Claudius' horse. [SM]

    f. 168r (366:16) Claudin with his escort of forty knights outside Gawain's pavilion. [SM]

    f. 169r (369:15) Arthur threatens the squire; Arthur blows his horn to call his suite. [LM]

    f. 174v (381:11; miniature illustrates previous section) The demented Lancelot in the woods. [LM]

    f. 175r (381:11) The King, Helaine [?], and Bohort reproaching the Queen; Bohort, Hector, and Lionel meet Mellic del Terte near a cross. [LM]

    f. 177v (388:10) Perceval strikes the knight into the water. [SM]

    f. 178r (389:35) Hector and Perceval fight together. [SM]

    f. 180r (393:29) Having found a lance, shield, and sword suspended on a stake outside a pavilion, Lancelot strikes the shield with the sword; Lancelot asleep inside the pavilion with Bliant and the damsel outside. [LM]

    f. 181r (396:6) Bliant and Celinant tie up Lancelot. [SM] [inset initial missing]

    f. 183v (404:3) Hector and Perceval ask the damsel with a hawk about the castle on the Island of Joy; Perceval, Lancelot, and Helaine at a banquet [?]. [LM]

    f. 184v (406:8) Lancelot in black armor charges against Perceval. [SM]

    f. 187r (3:1) Pelles arrives at Camelot; Pelles departs with Lancelot. [LM]

    f. 194v (20:31) Galahad arrives at the abbey of the white friars; a white knight wounds Baudemagus. [LM]

f. 197v (27:1) The fiery devil emerges from the tomb. [SM]

f. 199r (31:1) Melain sees the golden crown on a chair by an empty table; having carried off the crown, Melain is wounded in the left side by another knight. [LM]

f. 201r (35:15) Galahad fights the seven knights. [SM]

f. 202v (37:27) Gawain arrives at the abbey where Galahad left Melain; the seven brothers fleeing from Galahad attack Gawain, Gaheriet, and Ywain by the Castle of the Maidens. [LM]

f. 204r (40:26) Galahad meets Lancelot and Perceval and unhorses Lancelot; Galahad unhorses Perceval with a blow to the head. [LM]

f. 209r (52:3) Perceval returns to the recluse; Perceval's aunt explains the three tables to him. [LM]

f. 213v (63:18) Perceval rides into the forest. [HI]

f. 214v (65:34) A knight kills Perceval's palfrey. [SM]

f. 215r (66:38) The damsel brings Perceval the black charger. [HI]

f. 217v (71:21) Perceval and the ship draped in white samite. [SM]

f. 220r (76:32) Perceval and the beautiful damsel in the ship. [SM]

f. 222v (83:1; miniature illustrates previous section) Perceval sets sail. [LM]

f. 223r (83:1) The hermit preaches to Lancelot for three days; Lancelot meets the squire who reproaches him for having remained unmoved at the sight of the Holy Grail. [LM]

f. 225r (87:14) The nephews of the count try to burn the old man's clothes. [HI]

f. 231r (100:11) Lancelot comes to a castle where a tournament is in progress. [SM]

f. 233r (105;12) Gawain meets Hector; Gawain and Hector asleep in the chapel with their horses outside. [LM]

f. 235r (109:6) Gawain fights the knight who challenges him and Hector. [SM]

f. 238r (116:15; miniature illustrates previous section) Gawain and Hector on horseback. [LM]

f. 238r (116:15) Bohort meets an old friar on an ass; Bohort and the old man eat bread and water together. [LM]

f. 241v (124:22) Bohort and Priadan in combat. [HI]

f. 242v (126:18) Bohort rescues the damsel. [SM]

f. 248r (138:16) The flame from heaven comes between Bohort and Lionel. [SM]

f. 248v (140:14) Galahad meets Gawain in a tournament and strikes him on the head; Galahad leaves the hermitage and rides with the damsel through the forest of Celibe. [LM]

f. 250r (143:13) Galahad, Perceval, Bohort, and the damsel on the ship. [SM]

f. 250v (145:8) Galahad, Perceval, Bohort, and the damsel board Solomon's ship. [SM]

f. 253r (151:11) Adam and Eve eat the fruit of the forbidden tree; the sacrifices of Cain and Abel (Eve spinning and Adam delving in the margin). [LM]

f. 255r (155:19) Cain kills Abel. [SM] [inset initial missing]

f. 257v (161:23) Galahad, Perceval, and Bohort find the ship built by Solomon with the three staves fashioned from the Tree of Life; the three knights and the damsel sail away. [LM]

f. 258v (163:38) Galahad, Perceval, and Bohort in the castle of Count Ernols. [SM]

f. 260v (168:37) Galahad, Perceval, and Bohort fight the knights of the castle. [SM]

f. 262r (173:9) Galahad and Perceval find the castle in ruins and all of its inhabitants slaughtered; Galahad and Perceval part ways at the edge of the wood. [LM]

f. 262v (174:10) Lancelot, holding Perceval's scroll ("cest le seur percheual le galoi"; cf. Sommer, 175:18), in the ship with the damsel on the rich bed; the ship arrives at a rock with an old man in a chapel. [LM]

f. 264v (178:30) Lancelot's ship arrives at the castle guarded by two lions. [SM]

f. 267r (184:28; miniature illustrates previous section) Lancelot returns to court. [LM]

f. 267v (184:28) King Mordrian dies in Galahad's arms and his soul is received by angels; Galahad and Perceval on horseback. [LM]

f. 269v (190:23) Christ (looking like a bishop) gives the host to the kneeling Galahad. [SM]

f. 272v (203:1) King Henry requests Walter Map to translate the *Death of Arthur*; Arthur and his knights set out for Winchester. [LM]

f. 276r (211:22) The Tournament of Winchester. [SM]

f. 277r (214:1) Gawain and Gaherret meet two squires carrying a dead knight; Gawain and Gaherret arrive at Winchester. [LM]

f. 282v (225:21) The knight of Escalot at Lancelot's bedside and the arrival of the damsel of Escalot; the tournament at Taneborc. [LM]

f. 287r (234:34) The King and his suite lose their way in the woods; Arthur arrives at the castle of Morgan. [LM]

f. 289r (239:14) Morgan with King Arthur. [SM]

f. 290v (242:4) Lancelot and the two young knights of Escalot approach Camelot; Gawain speaks with the Queen and Lancelot is told the Queen is ill. [LM]

f. 293r (247:36) Arthur returns from Morgan's castle to Camelot; Gaheris de Kareheu killed by the poisoned apples. [LM]

f. 294r (250:9) Lancelot struck by the huntsman's arrow; Lancelot rides to the hermit. [LM]

f. 295r (252:9) The tournament at Camelot; Bohort speaks with Arthur before leaving Camelot. [LM]

f. 297v (257:19) The arrival of the body of the maiden of Escalot. [SM]

f. 298v (259:20) Lancelot finds a knight sleeping at a fountain; Lancelot and Hector take leave of the hermit. [LM]

f. 300v (263:4) Arthur and Gawain welcome Bohort and Hector; Bohort with the Queen. [LM]

f. 303r (267:27) Mador and Lancelot in combat. [SM]

f. 307r (276:2) Lancelot drags Tanaguis' body into the Queen's chamber. [SM]

f. 308r (277:25) Guerrehes and Mordret take the Queen prisoner; Lancelot kills Agravain and the Queen stands by the fire. [LM]

f. 311r (284:6) The squire tells Arthur that Lancelot has carried off the Queen, and Mordret arrives to confirm the news; Arthur laments over his dead knights. [LM]

f. 313r (288:30) Gawain being cared for in bed. [SM]

f. 315r (293:7) Arthur and his host assemble at Camelot; Arthur's camp pitched by Lancelot's castle. [LM]

f. 318r (299:27) Fighting before La Joyeuse Garde. [SM]

f. 320v (304:22) Encounter between the vanguards of Gawain and Bohort. [SM] [inset initial missing; guide-letter remains]

f. 321r (306:2) Arthur and his knights attack Lancelot and his followers. [SM]

f. 325r (314: ca. 14; text varies from Sommer) Lancelot and his 400 knights leave La Joyeuse Garde by ship; Lancelot and his knights arrive at Benoye. [LM]

f. 326r (310:29) Arthur says farewell to the Queen at the port; Arthur's troops pitch camp in Gaul. [LM]

f. 329r (321:11) A squire presents Mordret's letter to the Queen; Mordret pretends to faint with grief while the Queen mourns. [LM]

f. 332r (327:6) Mordret lays seige to the Tower of London. [SM]

f. 333r (328:18) Arthur asks Gawain how to end the war; Arthur, Gawain, and Carados meet Lancelot, Bohort, and Hector. [LM]

f. 337v (335:24) The exchange of gages. [SM]

f. 339r (337:27) Gawain and Lancelot in combat. [SM]

f. 341v (342:6) Gawain and Lancelot fight with swords. [SM]

f. 345r (348:6) Arthur kills the Emperor. [SM]

f. 346r (351:22) Mordret's seige of the Tower of London; a messenger announces Arthur's return. [LM]

f. 347r (353:6) The Queen leaves the Tower accompanied by two damsels on palfreys and two squires with packhorses; the Queen arrives at the abbey (the second scene badly rubbed). [LM]

f. 348r (355:14) Arthur returns to Dover with the dying Gawain; the death of Gawain. [LM]

f. 350r (360:1) Arthur sets out against Mordret; Arthur's vision of Gawain with the poor. [LM]

f. 352v (ca. 365:15; text varies from Sommer) The Knights of Arcaus and Ywain in combat. [SM]

f. 352v (365:21) Ywain's division in combat with the Saxons. [SM]

f. 353v (367:23) Ywain's division in combat with the Irish. [SM]

f. 356r (text varies from Sommer) The Battle on Salisbury Plain. [LM]

f. 356v (374:25) King Arthur and Mordret in combat. [SM]

f. 357r (375:12) King Arthur charges at Mordret to avenge Galegantin. [SM]

f. 357v (ca. 365:66; text varies from Sommer) Arthur kills Mordret. [LM]

f. 359r (ca. 376:20; text varies from Sommer) Lucan and Gifflet find Arthur in the Black Chapel; Gifflet throws Excalibur into the lake where it is brandished by the hand rising from the water. [LM]

f. 359v (381:15; text given in Sommer, no. 9M) Arthur and his horse board Morgan's ship. [SM]

f. 360v (384:23) Bohort sails to Great Britain; the Battle of Winchester. [LM]

f. 361r (385:13) Lancelot pursues the sons of Mordret. [SM]

f. 361v (ca. 387:2; text varies from Sommer) Lancelot greeted by two priests. [SM]

f. 362r (387:24) Bohort enters Winchester; Hector and Lancelot at the hermitage. [LM]

f. 363r (390:10) The burial of Lancelot. [SM]

f. 363r (390:30) Bohort tells the archbishops of the last years of Lancelot's life. [SM]

Illuminated initials, 3- to 1-line, gold, with globular serifs, edged thickly in black, against irregular red and blue grounds, also edged in black, with white floral filigree or heraldic birds, in white; flowers touched in with orange. (Cf. the illuminated initials in Brussels, Bibl. Roy. MS 18295, C. Gaspar and F. Lyna, *Les principaux manuscrits de la Bibliothèque Royale de Belgique* [Paris, 1937, 1945] pp. 162–63, pl. XXXIIId.) On ff. 1v–2r only, 2-line initials, gold, with red penwork; on f. 7v only, a gold initial, 3-line, with red and blue penwork in a different style. On folios without miniatures (except ff. 2v–8v), a thin gold band runs along the left side of each text column, interrupted by initials, with a thin red pen-line on either side; adjacent, to the left, a column of *I*'s each 3-line and blue and red alternately, with small spiral and curlicue flourishes, terminating in large flourishes in red or blue on alternate openings, each with pinwheel-like arms projecting from a central spiral with small petals and flourishes in blue and red; design of the terminal flourishes varies from one gathering to another; some with naturalistic leaves and flowers or fleurs-de-lis; terminals on ff. 1v–2r by the same hand as penwork initials on those folios. Line-fillers of varying design: two pairs of blue and red tapering bands, heraldically arranged and joined at center by red flower; undulating red line with red and/or blue balls under and over each crest and trough; red zigzag with blue infilling and spiral flourishes at terminals; alternating red and blue flowers; red and blue dots, etc.

Some folios stained; f. 253 slashed in margin; f. 361 cut right across and glued together.

Binding: s. xviii. Light brown calf blind- and gold-tooled. Sewing holes in inner margins.

Written in Northern France toward the end of the 13th century, as indicated by the style of the decoration; M. A. Stones suggests Therouanne as the likely provenance. The marginal decoration incorporates several true coats of arms which may have some bearing on the original ownership, as all are those of important Flemish nobility. Arms of Guillaume de Termonde (1248-1312), the second son of Gui de Dampierre, count of Flanders from 1278 to 1305 (or, a lion sable, a bend gules), on f. 187r and (without gold ground) on ff. 66r and 260v; identified by Stones, *op. cit.*, p. 87. Arms of Gui de Dampierre (or, a lion sable) on ff. 23v, 100v, 126r and 260v. Five arms appear which also appear in the Psalter made for Gui de Dampierre (Brussels, Bibl. Roy. MS 10607, all identified by Gaspar and Lyna, *op. cit.*; cf. *Exhibition Catalogue*, pp. 198-99): those of Gruythuse of Bruges (or, a cross sable), on ff. 1r and 126r; those of Bergen (or, a lion gules), Mortaigne (or, a cross gules) and Court [?] (argent, a lion gules), all on f. 100v; and those of Northwyck, Bouchorst, Crechy or Fiennes (argent, a lion sable), on f. 347r. An unidentified coat of arms (or, a bend cottised gules) on f. 15v. Apparently belonged to Sir Isaac Heard (1730-1822), but we have been unable to confirm this. Bought from Royez by Sir Thomas Phillipps (according to *Phillipps Studies* v. 3, p. 145, n. 1; his no. 130, stamp and inscription inside front cover and tag on spine). Sold by Sotheby's (1 July 1946) to William Robinson, Ltd. Bought from Dudley M. Colman by C. A. Stonehill in 1954. Purchased from C. A. Stonehill in 1955 as the gift of the Yale Library Associates.

secundo folio: a tant

Bibliography: Faye and Bond p. 43, no. 229.
Exhibition Catalogue, pp. 197-99, no. 25, and pl. 10 (f. 209r).
"Eight Medieval Manuscripts," *Gazette* 29 (1955) pp. 99-112 and frontispiece (f. 238r).
G. Evelyn Hutchinson, "Zoological Iconography in the West after A. D. 1200," *American Scientist* 66 (1978) p. 680, fig. 7 (f. 94v).

MS 230 Flanders, ca. 1485
Honoré Bonet, L'Arbre des batailles, etc.

1. ff. 1r-4v [Prologue, *Des droits d'armes*:] *Cy commence le prologue de ce present traittie Intitule des drois darmes* a la loenge de dieu nostre benoit createur a lonneur des princes ... Quod nobilis est ille quem nobilitat sua vertus.

2. ff. 4v-9r Table of Contents (ff. 4v-6v: *Des droits d'armes*; ff. 7r-9r: *L'Arbre des batailles*). f. 9v ruled, but blank

3. ff. 10r-11r Es saintes couronnes de iherusalem et de France au iourdhui par lordonnance de dieu regne loys de charles cousin ... Et sur cestui arbre feray la quarte partie de mon livre ainsy comme veoir le pourrez es choses qui sont aprez.
   Prologue, *L'Arbre des batailles*.

4. ff. 12r-116v Maintenant puis que vous veez comment sur larbre de dolour

sont deux entrees lesqueles est grande discorde ... et conduie a la sienne sainte gloire de paradis. Amen. ff. 117r-v ruled, but blank

Honoré Bonet, *L'Arbre des batailles*. See E. Nys, ed., *L'Arbre des Batailles d'Honoré Bonet* (Paris, 1883) and, for sources and a partial list of manuscripts, G. W. Coopland, *The Tree of Battles of Honoré Bonet* (Cambridge, Mass., 1949) pp. 217-25.

5. ff. 118r-144v *Cy commence un petit traittie de noblesse compose par [jacques de valere en langue despagne et nagueres translate en francoys par maistre] hugues de salues preuost de furnes*. Lors que ie me trouuay a par moy et deliure de toutes pensees ... au long traitie comment elles se doiuent entendre et blasonnes.

Jacques de Valère, Diego de Valera, *Espejo de verdadera nobleza*, Fr. tr. Hugues de Salve. Portion of heading in brackets reconstructed on basis of Paris, B. N. fr. 1280; see H. J. Horn, "Honoré Bonet's *L'Arbre des batailles* and Jacques de Valère's *Traité de noblesse*: A Late Fifteenth-Century Manuscript in the Yale University Library" (M.A. Thesis, Yale University, 1968, p. 7). For the French text, see the edition of 1497, published in Paris by Antoine Vérard; for the original Spanish text, see J. A. de Balenchana, *Epístolas y otros varios tratados de Mosen Diego de Valera* (Madrid, 1878). Horn (*op. cit.*, pp. 6-10) lists six other manuscripts of the *Traité de noblesse*: Brussels, Bib. Roy. MS II 7057; Paris, B. N. fr. 1280, written for Louis of Bruges, who composed one of the treatises in *Des droits d'armes* (see art. 6-vii); Paris, B. N. fr. 5229 (the only manuscript listed here that is without illustrations); Phillipps 10396, present location unknown, described in Coopland, *op. cit.*, p. 303; Vienna, Öst. Nationalbib. Cod. 2616, written for Adolph of Cleves; and a manuscript, present location unknown, formerly in the book-trade, described in Hess Antiquariat, *50 Fine Books, Manuscripts ... and Bindings*, Cat. I (Bern, 1937) p. 35. Cahn and Marrow, *Exhibition Catalogue*, no. 76, p. 256, list one further manuscript in the book-trade, H. P. Kraus, *Catalogue 126* (New York, n.d.) no. 11, pp. 9-12. As in the Yale manuscript, Bonet's *L'Arbre des batailles* occurs in the Kraus manuscript as an interpolation.

6. ff. 144v-196v Seven short treatises, known in conjunction with art. 5 as *Des droits d'armes*. i) f. 145r *La table des xij chapittres du blason darmes*; ii) f. 153r *Comment on fait de nouuel vn empereur par election*; iii) f. 163v Thomas, Duke of Gloucester: *La manière de faire champ a oultrance*, dedicated to Richard II; iv) f. 170v *Les ordonnances aux gaiges de bataille en champ ferme* [an ordinance of Philip IV of France]; v) f. 179r *La premiere institucion des roys darmes et heraulx et des seremens et promesses quilz font a leur creation*; vi) f. 186v *La Manière de faire tournoiz et behours...*; vii) f. 192r Louis of Bruges, section begins without rubric: Pour mettre fin et conclusion a ce present traittie Intitule loffice darmes et noblesse.... f. 197r-v ruled, but blank

See J. van Praet, *Recherches sur Louis de Bruges* (Paris, 1831) pp. 190-97. These

MS 230

seven treatises occur in conjunction with the *Traité de noblesse* in three manuscripts: Paris, B. N. fr. 1280; H. P. Kraus, *op. cit.*, and Vienna, Öst. Nationalbib. Cod. 2616.

7. ff. 198r–206v *Cy contient comment le roy darmes des francoiz fut premierement cree et puis nomme mon Joye et la facon de son noble couronner les seremens quil fait aussy les droiz et ce quil est tenu de fere.* Comme il soit vray selon les anciennes escriptures nous trouuons ... de ceste tres noble ordonnance perdue ia longtempz a.

This treatise, as well as that in art. 8, occur in the manuscript once owned by Hess Antiquariat, *50 Fine Books, op. cit.*, as well as in H. P. Kraus, *op. cit.* and Phillipps 10396 (see Coopland, *op. cit.*, p. 303).

8. ff. 207r–210v Status royaulx touchant le fait de la guerre prins en la chambre du tresorier a paris par philippe sans terre quant il se vint marier a madame margueritte de flandres ... ses mareschaulx et autres de son conseil en lan de grace vii^c lxix.

Ordinances relating to the armies and marshals of France.

Parchment, ff. ii (parchment) + 209 + ii (parchment), 345 x 243 (227 x 158) mm. Written in two columns of 33 lines, each with single vertical bounding lines; single horizontal bounding lines, top and bottom of written space, full across. Ruled in red ink.

I^4 (+ 2 leaves glued in at beginning), II^2 (+ 1 leaf glued in at end), III–XV^8, XVI^4, XVII–XXVI^8, XXVII^8 (+ 4 additional leaves glued in).

Written in formal bâtarde script. Folios 7r–9r, also in formal bâtarde, but in a different hand.

The fine miniatures are by the Master of Bruges of 1482, named for the frontispiece in a manuscript of the *Livre de la propriété des choses*, London, B. L. Royal 15 E III. The cycle of miniatures in the Yale manuscript closely resembles the series in the Kraus manuscript (*op. cit.*, p. 10, pl. of f. 169r on p. 11), by the Atelier of the Edward IV manuscripts; the Yale cycle, however, does not appear to be by the Edward IV shop as stated by Kraus, nor is the Kraus manuscript by the Master of 1482 as stated in *Exhibition Catalogue* (p. 258). In addition to the manuscript in London for which he is named and the Yale manuscript, the Master of 1482 contributed miniatures to an *Ovide moralisé*, Copenhagen, Royal Library, Thott 399; Frederick II of Hohenstaufen's *De l'art de la chasse des oyseaux*, Geneva, Bib. Publ. et Univ. fr. 170; Caesar's *Gallic Wars* (French translation by Jean Duchesne), London, B. L. Egerton 1065; and Oxford, Bod. Lib. Douce 208; and perhaps to a *Decameron*, The Hague, Kon. Bib. 133 A 5. The miniatures, in arched frames composed of thin gold and pink bands, are as follow: one full-page miniature, f. 11v The Tree of Battles; ten half-page miniatures, f. 1r The Shame of Noah, f. 10r Honoré Bonet presents the *L'Arbre des batailles* to Maximilian I of Austria in the presence of Frederick III, Holy Roman Emperor (see H. J. Horn, "Two Rulers, One Throne: An Illumination by the Master of Bruges of 1482," *Essays in Northern European Art* presented to E. Haverkamp-Begemann on his 60th Birthday [Dvornspijk, 1983] pp. 110-12, with pl. 1 of f. 10r; pl. 5 of f. 153v); f. 118r Maximilian I awarding the Golden Fleece to person kneeling before him and Marie of Burgundy gives gold collar to lady; f. 145r The author delivers his treatise to Nobles and Heralds; f. 153v The Coronation of an Emperor; f. 164r A Battle *à l'outrance*; f. 187r Tournament; f. 192r Funeral Procession; f. 198r Crowning of the King of Arms of France; f. 207r A Marshal of France, with followers, before a military encampment; and one small column miniature (11-line), f. 179r Institution of a Herald in his Office. Between ff. 147r and 152r there are sixty-three painted armorial bearings, perhaps a later addition (s. XVI?) as indicated by the type of pigment, the occasional lack of correspondence with the original preparatory drawings, and the fact that some drawings were never overpainted. 5-, 4-, 3-, and 2-line initials, gold, edged in black, against irregular blue and red grounds with white highlights. 1-line initials in the table of contents, red and blue, with guide-letters to illuminator; ff. 7r-9r (the section for the *L'Arbre des batailles*) in darker shades and without notes, suggesting, as does the change of hand, that this section of the table as well as the portion of the text to which it refers were added to the manuscript in a second stage of its production. Paragraph marks, 1-line, red and blue. Pages foliated in red, upper right recto. Headings in red throughout.

Binding: s. xix. Edges gilt. Purple goatskin case with brilliant gold tooling and elaborate doublures.

Written in Bruges ca. 1485. A statement on f. 196v, "il le fault imputer au tempz qui regne de present qui est lan mil iiij^c iiij^{xx} j." referring to the decline of courtesy, provides a *terminus post quem* of 1481 for the compilation of the text. The relation of the text as well as the miniatures to manuscripts produced for the court circles of Maximilian I and Louis de Bruges, Seigneur de la Gruthuyse, clearly suggests an origin in Bruges in the mid-1480's. Belonged to George Hibbert (Evans Sale, 30 March 1829, no. 2707); Sir Thomas Phillipps (no. 3873); William Robinson, Ltd. Collection of Dudley M. Colman, 1946; sold by Colman in 1954 to C. A.Stonehill. Acquired from C. A. Stonehill in 1955 as a gift of the Yale Library Associates.

secundo folio: aprez. Ceste figure

Bibliography: Faye and Bond, pp. 43-44, no. 230.

Exhibition Catalogue, pp. 256-58, no. 76, pl. 27 of f. 198r.

"Eight Medieval Manuscripts," *Gazette* 29 (1955) pp. 106-07, 109-10, pl. of f. 164r.

J. L. Schrader, *The Waning Middle Ages*, exhib. cat. (The University of Kansas Museum of Art, 1969) no. 19, p. 23, pl. XXXVIII (f. 164r).

The Secular Spirit: Life and Art at the End of the Middle Ages, exhib. cat. (New York, The Metropolitan Museum of Art, 1975) no. 277, p. 276.

B. Gagnebin, *L'Enluminure de Charlemagne à François Ier. Manuscrits de la Bibliothèque publique et universitaire de Genève*, exhib. cat. (Geneva, Musée Rath, 1976) p. 168.

A. J. Vanderjagt, "Qui a sa vertu anoblist: The Concepts of *noblesse* and *chose publique* in Burgundian Political Thought," D. Phil. dissertation (Groningen, 1981) pp. 117-18 and pls. 18-19 (of ff. 1r and 118r).

MS 231   Italy, s. XV
Sallust

1. f. i recto-verso ruled, but blank; ff. 1r-29v [Title, in a later hand:] Conjuratio Catalinae. [text:] Omnis homines qui student sese praestare coeteris animalibus summa ope niti decet ... ita uarie per omnem exercitum letitia meror luctus atque gaudia agitabantur.

   Catilinae conjuratio; A. Kurfess, ed., Teubner (1968) pp. 2-52.

2. ff. 29v-89r [Title, in a later hand:] Bellum Iugurthinum. [text:] Falso queritur de natura sua Genus humanum quod imbeccilla atque eui breuis sorte potius ... Ea tempestate Spes atque Opes Diuitatis in illo sitae sunt. [added below by a later hand:] Finis 1430 Finis Belli Jugurthini. ff. 89v-90v ruled, but blank

   Bellum Jugurthinum; A. Kurfess, *op. cit.*, pp. 53-147.

Parchment, ff. i (parchment) + i (paper) + 91 (foliated i, 1-90) + i (paper) + i (parchment), 245 x 125 (180 x 68) mm. Written in 33 long lines; double vertical bounding lines. Ruled in crayon; prickings in upper and lower margins. I^{10} (+ 1 at beginning), $II-IX^{10}$. Catchwords in center of lower margin, accompanied by four dots and/or flourishes; remains of leaf signatures (e.g., e/2. e/3, etc.) on recto.
Written by a single scribe in neat sloping italic; notes and corrections in several later hands.
Two gold initials, 5- and 4-line, of indifferent quality on ff. 1r and 29v, embedded in white vine ornament extending into margins on green, red, and blue grounds, decorated with white dots; gold dots and brown hair-spray. On f. 1v, a coat of arms, unidentified (per pale, azure, a bend or with 3 stars of the field, between 2 fleur-de-lis or; gules, a lion rampant argent, overall a bendlet vert), supported by two putti, set in a panel of white vine ornament, as above. 2-line initials, gold or blue, throughout.
Binding: s. xix. Edges gilt. Blue goatskin, gold-tooled by Ramage.

Written in central Italy in the 15th century; early provenance unknown (unidentified arms on f. 1r). Belonged to Henry Huth (1815-78; bookplate; see *The Huth Library* [London, 1880] v. 4, p. 1291) and to Albert May Todd (1850-1931; bookplate). Sold by Parke-Bernet Galleries, 14 Nov. 1941, to Henry Fletcher; gift of Mrs. Henry Fletcher in 1953.

secundo folio: [ple]rique delicta

Bibliography: Faye and Bond, p. 44, no. 231.

MS 232
Andrea Bragadin, Magister aucupatoris

Italy, s. XIV/XV

1. ff. i recto – iii verso *Incipid tabula istius libri.* De genere auium rapacium uolatilium ssilicet capiencium allias aues ... De medicamine apostematis nascenciarum. Capitulum *.118. Explicit tabula totus istius libri continens capitulla. 118.* f. iiii recto–verso blank

2. ff. 1r–58v *Prologus.* Antiqui philosophi quorum intellectus adeo excelso jnlustratus est ut utillitas humano generi cognoserentur intelligentes quecumque sunt sub cello ad utillitatem honium [*sic*] esse creata ... Vollo quid liber iste uocatur vere Magister Aucupatoris. *Incipit liber primus de teoricha huius artis. Continens capitulla. 27. Capitulum. I. de genera auium* ... Genera uolatilium uiuencium de rapina quibus utuntur gens ssunt quinque et quatordecim species ... et laua loca illa et sanentur. Exsplicit liber quarto. et ultimo. scripto et conpilato per me Andreas bragadino. Nobilis Veneciarum Ciuij. Curendo anni domini nostri. hiessu christi. Millesimo trecentessimo. Septuagessimo. die ultimo menssis Iunij. I uenecijs. In contrata sancti geminiani. in domo patris meis. qui hodie uiuit. Et uocatur domino Iacobo bragadino. Nobilis veneciarum Ciuij. Et est valde sapiens homo. *Finiti sunt isti quatuor libri in unum conpilatum. Refero gracia Ad domino yehsum christum natum.* [added in a small notarial script (cf. article 3):] sono charte scrite. 58. senza la tolla [tabula?]. che sono carte.
3. f. 59 blank, with a few scribblings, including a later notation concerning author, title, and date of the treatise

   It has not been possible to locate a printed text of this work nor is it mentioned by J. E. Harting, *Bibliotheca accipitraria* (London, 1891).

3. back pastedown: Recepta dela stizza di cani In primis. Vno bichiero de olio da mangiare ... e uolse menare intorno Vn poco. At bottom of leaf, enclosed in a rectangle, is a short Greek passage transliterated into Roman letters, by the same notarial hand responsible for the final line on f. 58v

Parchment, ff. 64 (foliated i–iv, 1–60, with 60 as back pastedown), 302 x 202 (223 x 159) mm. Written in 2 columns of 30 lines, table of contents in 30 long lines; single vertical bounding lines. Ruled in lead; remains of prickings in upper and lower margins.

I–II^2, III–IX^8, X^4 (4 = pastedown). Catchwords in middle of lower margin on verso; signed with arabic numbers in same location, on recto.

Written by a single person in large, ungainly round gothic bookhand.

Numerous initials of poor quality, 7- to 2-line, in blue with red penwork designs and borders. Rubrics throughout; paragraph marks and initial strokes in red or blue.

Lower portion of f. 58 trimmed.

Binding: s. xvi-xvii. Wound resewing on three tawed supports. Beaded, colored endbands sewn on tawed cores which extend onto corners of pasteboards. The spine is square, with a paper lining all along. Covered in goatskin, originally black, now brown blind-tooled with concentric borders, the center panel filled in. Four fastenings of tawed skin. Cover coming loose from bookblock.

Written in Italy (perhaps in Northeastern Italy) at the end of the 14th or beginning of the 15th century (author's copy?); early provenance included one scholar familiar with Greek (see art. 3). Inscription on back pastedown, s. xv, now mostly illegible, begins "Ego Ioannes...". Belonged to Prince Alexander Dietrichstein at Schloss Nikolsburg; his sale (Lucerne, Nov. 1933, no. 703; Pl. 38, f. 58v). From the collection of C. F. G. R. Schwerdt (see catalogue *Hunting Hawking Shooting* [London, 1928] v. 4, p. 115, with colored folding plate of ff. 1r and 58v); his sale (London, 12 March 1946, no. 2187). Acquired from Goldschmidt's by David Wagstaff; gift of Mrs. David Wagstaff in 1952.

secundo folio: [table, f. ii] de medicamine
[text, f. 2] aliqui habentes

Bibliography: Faye and Bond, p. 44, no. 232.

MS 233 Germany, s. XV^2
Pietro de' Crescenzi, Liber ruralium commodorum

1. ff. i recto – v verso [Prologue:] Uenerabili in christo patri et domino spirituali viro summe religionis ac sapientie fratri Aymerico de placencia ... vermiculosis pomis in qua multa inueniuntur iocunda. [followed by table of contents:] Incipit liber ruralium commodorum a petro de Crescencijs ciue Bononiense ad honorem dei omnipotentis et serenissimi Regis domini Karoli compilatus. Incipit liber primus de locis habitabilibus eligendis ... Incipiunt Regule libri Decimi de Ingenijs pluribus capiendi animalia fera ... Expliciunt Rubrice libri Ruralium commodorum.

2. ff. v verso – 173v [Dedicatory epistle to Charles of Anjou precedes text:] Excellentissimo principi domino Karolo secundo dei gratia Iherusalem et Sicilie regi illustri ... in omnibus obedire bene placitis et mandatis. *Incipit liber Ruralium comodorum a Petro de crescencijs Ciue Bononiense ... Sequitur ergo Thema.* Cum ex virtute prudencie que inter bonum et malum caute discernit humanus informetur animus ... Item capiuntur aues auibus rapacibus domesticatis et retibus diuersis ac visco et similibus. Et sic est finis. *Sit laus et gloria Cristo per infinita secula.*

There appears to be no modern edition of this work; for early printed texts see GKW, v. 7, nos. 7820–25.

Paper (sturdy; watermarks similar to Briquet Lettre P 8526), ff. ii (paper) + 178 (numbered i-v, modern hand; 1-173, in Roman numerals, by original scribe) + ii (paper), 297 x 212 (202 x 128) mm. Written in 44 long lines; frame-ruled in lead; prickings along outer edges.

I-IV¹², V¹² (-7, no loss of text), VI-XIV¹², XV¹² (-1, no loss of text). Catchwords at bottom of leaf near gutter.

Written by a single scribe in a neat running hand for the text, and in a more formal script for major headings (in red or blue).

Large initials, 11- to 9-line, of intertwining penwork patterns, in red and/or blue, mark text divisions; numerous smaller plain initials, in red or blue. Paragraph marks, foliation, headings, initial strokes in red throughout. Drawing of an incubator for eggs labelled "furnus" appears on f. 139r.

Binding: s. xix. Rigid vellum case, gold-tooled. Remains of original fore-edge leather tabs at beginning of each book.

Written in Germany in the second half of the 15th century; from the library of the Capuchin monastery at Offenburg (inscription with date 1663 on f. i recto). Unidentified bookplate composed of the monogram "C" on verso of second front flyleaf. Belonged to C. F. G. R. Schwerdt (bookplate; see catalogue *Hunting Hawking Shooting* [London, 1928] v. 2, p. 320); his sale (Sotheby's, 12 March 1946, no. 2198). Acquired by David Wagstaff (bookplate); gift of Mrs. David Wagstaff in 1952.

secundo folio: de aere

Bibliography: Faye and Bond, p. 44, no. 233.

MS 234
Aristotle, Porphyry, etc. (in Greek)

Byzantium, s. XIV

I. 1. ff. 1r-51r Ἀριστοτέλης. περὶ οὐρανοῦ. [Ἡ] περὶ φύσεως ἐπιστήμη σχεδὸν ἡ πλείστη φαίνεται. περὶ τὰ σώματα. μεγέθη καὶ τὰ τούτων οὖσα πάθη ... περὶ μὲν οὖν βαρέος καὶ κούφου καὶ περὶ αὐτ[ὸ σ]υμβαινόντων ἀφωρίσθω τοῦτον [ἡμῖν] τὸν τρόπον. ἀριστοτέλους περὶ οὐρανοῦ δέλτα. f. 51v blank

Aristotle, *De caelo*; I. Bekker, ed., *Aristotelis Opera* (Berlin, 1831) v. 1, 268a1-313b23.

II. 2. ff. 52r-63v [Heading in red, crossed out:] Ἀριστοτέλους. περὶ ζώων μορίων. [heading, in brown:] ἀριστοτέλους. περὶ ζώων πορείας. Περὶ δὲ τῶν χρησίμων μορίων τοῖς ζώοις πρὸς τὴν κίνησιν τὴν κατὰ τόπον ἐπισκεπτέον ... τούτων δὲ διωρισμένων ἐχόμενον ἔστι διωρίσαι περὶ ψυχῆς. περὶ ζώων πορείας.

Aristotle, *De incessu animalium*, with marginal notes drawn from Michael of Ephesus; Bekker, *op. cit.*, v. 1, pp. 704a4-714b23.

3. ff. 64r-80r   Aristotle, texts from the *Parva naturalia*, with marginal notes drawn from Michael of Ephesus.

A. ff. 64r-66v   [In a later hand:] ἀριστοτέλους. περὶ μακροβιότητος καὶ βραχυιότητος. [Π]ερὶ δὲ τοῦ τὰ μὲν εἶναι μακρόβια τῶν ζώων ... τούτων γὰρ διωρισθέντων τέλος ἂν περὶ τῶν ζώων ἔχοι μέθοδος. περὶ μακροβιότητος καὶ βραχυβιότητος.

Aristotle, *De longitudine vitae*; Bekker, *op. cit.*, v. 1, 464b19-467b9.

B. ff. 67r-80r   περὶ νεοτήτος καὶ γήρως. καὶ ζωῆς καὶ θανάτου [added in black:] καὶ ἀναπνοῆς. Περὶ δὲ νεότητος καὶ γήρως καὶ περὶ ζωῆς καὶ θανάτου λεκτέον νῦν ... σχεδὸν τελευτῶσιν εἰς τὰς ἀρχὰς τὰς ἰατρικάς. περὶ γήρως καὶ νεότητος καὶ ζωῆς καὶ θανάτου καὶ ἀναπνοῆς. f. 80v blank

Aristotle, *De iuventute*; Bekker, *op. cit.*, v. 1, 467b10-480b30.

III. 4. ff. 81r-88v   πορφυρίου εἰσαγωγή. Ὄντος ἀναγκαίου χρυσαόριε καὶ εἰς τὴν τῶν [added above later] παρὰ ἀριστοτέλει κατηγοριῶν διδασκαλίαν τοῦ γνῶναι τί γένος ... ὁ δὲ ἄνθρωπος ἐπὶ μόνων τῶν ἀτόμων, καὶ τὸ χρεμετιστικὸν ἐπὶ μόνου τοῦ ἵππου, καὶ τῶν κατὰ μέρος//

Porphyry, *Isagoge*, with marginal notes; A. Busse, ed., *Porphyrii Isagoge et in Aristotelis Categorias Commentarium* (Berlin, 1887) pp. 1-14.

IV. 5. ff. 89r-114r   ὁμώνυμα λέγεται ὧν ὄνομα μόνον κοινὸν ... οἱ δὲ εἰωθότες λέγεσθαι σχεδὸν ἅπαντες κατηρίθμηνται. τέλος σὺν θεῷ τῶν κατηγοριῶν.

Aristotle, *Categoriae*; Bekker, *op. cit.*, v. 1, 1a1-15b33.

V. 6. ff. 114r-127v   περὶ ἑρμηνείας. πρῶτον δεῖ θέσθαι [above is added ὁρίσασθαι] τί ὄνομα καὶ τί ῥῆμα. ἔπειτα τί ἐστιν ἀπόφασις καὶ κατάφασις. καὶ ἀπόφανσις καὶ λόγος ... καὶ τοῦτο εἰς ἄπειρον· καὶ πάλιν μουσικὸς βαδίζων// [sic; λευκὸς βαδίζων is added in the margin]

Aristotle, *De interpretatione*, with marginal commentary of Michael of Ephesus; Bekker, *op. cit.*, v. 1, 16a1-21a1.

7. ff. 128r-129v   ἀλλὰ τοῦ μὲν ἀληθὲς εἰπεῖν ἔστι λευκὸν εἴτε μὴ λευκὸν, ὁ αὐτὸς τρόπος ... οὐ ταυτό δ' ἐστὶ, τὸ οὐκ ἔστιν//

Aristotle, *Analytica priora*; Bekker, *op. cit.*, vol. 1, 52a29-52b32.

8. ff. 130r-176r   [Π]ᾶσα διδασκαλία καὶ πᾶσα μάθησις διανοητικὴ ἐκ προυπαρχούσης γίνεται γνώσεως ... ἀλλ' οὐδ' ὅτι οἱ δύο κύβοι, κύβος. οὐδ' ἄλλη ἐπιστήμη//

Aristotle, *Analytica posteriora*, with marginal commentary derived from Themistius and Philoponus; Bekker, *op. cit.*, v. 1, 71a1-75b14.

9. f. 176v   [Anonymous letter; text begins:] //σὺ μὲν οὖν ἄχρι τίνος ἐνταυθοῖ καθεδοῖσθαι τεκμαιρόμεθα ... αἰσχρὸν γὰρ ἀφανῆ παθήματα προκρίνειν καὶ ἰᾶσθαι πεπιστευμένον. οὕτω φανερὰ [α corrected to ῳ] μὴ στόχεσθαι δύνασθαι. [In the lower left margin another hand has added: ἐν ἱπποκρατείοις.]

Cf. P. Moraux, "Unbekannte Galen-Scholien," *Zeitschrift für Papyrologie und Epigraphik* 27 (1977) p. 1, with note.

10. ff. 177r–198v //μέρος ἔργα· τὸ δὲ αὐξάνεσθαι καὶ τρέφεσθαι, φυσικῆς ... τὸ γὰρ ἓν ἀμετάβλητον εἰς ἕτερον.

Scholia to Galen, *De naturalibus facultatibus, De locis affectis, De elementis secundum Hippocratem*; Moraux, *op. cit.*, 1–63.

The work is divided into five distinct parts, all of paper: ff. ii (paper) + 198 + ii (paper), 230 x 151 mm.

I: ff. 1r–51v. Paper (heavy, no watermarks), written space 155 x 120 mm. 24–26 long lines; no ruling or prickings visible. Quires signed in Greek notation on verso. Written in a rather careless Greek minuscule by two scribes: Scribe 1, ff. 1r–16v; Scribe 2, ff. 17r–51v. Some marginal and interlinear notes by a later hand. Diagrams, labelled by the original scribe: syllogisms, consisting of geometrical figures and other groups of curved or straight lines. One simple 2-line initial in red; line-fillers and heading also in red.

II: ff. 52r–80v. Paper (heavy, no watermarks), written space 163 x 76 mm. 28–31 long lines; frame-ruled in hard point. No signatures or catchwords. Written in minuscule, large and rather careless, by Scribe 2 of part I; marginal and interlinear notes by same hand. Contains a few diagrams of syllogisms. Title in red crossed out and rewritten in blackish-brown; one 2-line initial in red.

III: ff. 81r–88v. Paper (thin, no watermarks), written space 162 x 72 mm. Ca. 28–31 long lines per page; ruled in hard point, single vertical bounding lines, full across; an additional vertical bounding line in outer margin for notes; guidelines for text extend across column for notes. Greek minuscule, small and very neat (tops of letters close to but not touching ruling), by Scribe 3; marginal and interlinear notes in red by original scribe; notes in brown by a different hand. Four-line initials in red, with floral ornaments; red also used for headings, notes of original scribe, and diagrams of syllogisms.

IV: ff. 89r–129v. Paper (thick and rough), written space varies greatly. 1–25 long lines of text, depending on number of notes included; no ruling. Quires signed in Greek notation in upper right-hand corner or first folio recto of quire and at left in upper and lower margins of last folio verso of quire. Written in minuscule, large and rather careless, by Scribe 4, who adds flourishes in the margins; a few marginal notes by a later hand. Many diagrams of syllogisms with labels by the original scribe; some doodles in the margins.

V: ff. 130r–198v. Paper (thick and coarse), written space ca. 180 x ca. 115 mm. 5–32 long lines of text, depending on number of notes included; no ruling. Quires signed in Greek notation in lower margin of last folio of quire, verso, slightly left of center. Written in minuscule by several scribes: Scribe 5 (ff. 130r–176r), a small neat hand; Scribe 6 (ff. 177r–198v), a large and progressively more careless hand; f. 176v by a small, neat later hand. A few notes in margins by a later hand. Spaces left for initials within the text were never filled.

MS 235

I-VI⁸, VII⁸ (-5, 6, 7, 8), VIII-X⁸, XI⁶ (-4, 5, 6), XII², XIII⁸, XIV⁸ (2 ff. after f. 89 numbered 90), XV-XVIII⁸, XIX², XX-XXIV⁸, XXV⁸ (-8), XXVI⁸, XXVII⁸ (-8), XXVIII⁸ (-1).

Water damage on ff. 9r-16v and ff. 161-174; Parts I and III eaten by worms. The pattern of the damage suggests that the parts of the manuscript were not originally bound together.

Binding: s. xviii-xix. Brown calf blind- and gold-tooled. Cloth label attached to the spine reads "ARISTOTELIS OPERA VARIA G. M-S."

Written in Byzantium in the 14th century; early provenance unknown. Belonged to Abate Luigi Celotti (signature on first flyleaf, verso); his sale to Sir Thomas Phillipps (no. 890, number and stamp on f. ii recto). Purchased from Laurence Witten with funds from the Jacob Ziskind Charitable Trust in 1957 (MS 6).

Bibliography: Faye and Bond, p. 44, no. 234.
Ziskind Catalogue, p. 45.

MS 235
John Chrysostom, Sermons, etc. (in Greek)

Byzantium, s. XIV

I. 1. ff. 1r-4r [Unidentified sermon, large portions of which have been obscured by binding tape and waterstains:] //*λ*εις τα ὅμ**** τῷ ἀχράντῳ δακτύλῳ τοῦ τυφλοῦ ... ταῦτα καὶ τὰ τοιαῦτα τοῦ δεσπότου λέγοντος [tape] αὐτῷ, ὁ, ἐν αὐτῷ ἠνωμένος ἀδάμ· καὶ συνανίσταται εὔα. ἀλλὰ καὶ πολλὰ σω [tape] ἀνέστησαν, τῶν, ἀπ' αἰῶνος κεκοιμημένων, αἰνοῦντες καὶ ἐπαιωοῦντες χριστὸν τ[ῷ ἡ] δόξα καὶ ... ἀμὴν [end incomplete].

2. ff. 4r-v [Three Meditations:] Θεωρία εἰς τὸ παίζει γὰρ λόγος αἰπὺς ἐν ἑ [tape; text:] Καθ' ἕτερον δὲ τὸ προχείμενον ἄπορ[ο]ν διασκοποῦντες τρόπον ... [end of the third Meditation:] κατὰ τὸ πρακτικόν φημι τοῦ λόγου δυνάμεως νοητῶς παρατασσόμενος.

3. ff. 5r-23r [Unidentified interpretation of the Gospel of John, to chapter 10; later title, in brown:] εἰς τὸ κατὰ ἰωάννην εὐαγγέλιον. μέχρι κεφαλαῖον ι'. [beginning lost:] //τοῦ πνεύματος δωρεὰν καὶ διὰ τὴν ἀπὸ τῆς καταλλαγῆς γενομένης παρρησίαν ... [text ends incomplete, not lost:] τίνος δὲ ἕνεκεν ἐπὶ τῶν προβάτων τούτων ὄπισθεν αὐτῶν ἀκολουθούντων τῶν ποιμένων, ἐπὶ τῶν νοητῶν φησὶν ἔμπροσθεν αὐτῶν πορεύεσθαι τὸν ποιμένα. f. 23v blank, except for notes

4. ff. 24r-29v [Anonymous philosophical definitions and extracts on various topics, including:] Περὶ ἕξεως, Περὶ ψυχῆς, Ἐρώτησις ἁδριανοῦ βασιλέως πρὸς τὸν κυνικὸν σεκοῦνδον.

5. ff. 30r-69r [Title, added in brown by a later hand:] ἀναστασίου ἐρωτήσεις

[text:] //ἐκείνων ἐπιτυχόντα τῶν ἀγαθῶν καὶ γενόμενον υἱὸν θεοῦ ... καὶ καθὼς παρέδωκα ὑμῖν τὰς παραδόσεις ἃς παρελάβετε εἴτε διὰ λόγου, εἴτε δι' ἐπιστολῆς.

Anastasius of Sinai, *Quaestiones*; PG 89.311-823.

6. ff. 69r-70v [Title, by Scribe 1:] ἐρωτήσεις διαφόρων κεφαλαίων τοῦ ἀββᾶ ἀναστασίου [text:] ἐρώτησις .α΄. τὸ ὅλως ἔχειν τὸν ἄνθρωπον ἐν ἑαυτῷ ὅτι πράττει τί ἀγαθόν ... οὐδὲ στέφανοι καὶ μισθοὶ δίδονται.

Selections from Anastasius of Sinai, *Quaestiones diversae*; PG 89.311-823.

7. f. 70v [Title:] Ἑρμηνεία ἰωάννου τοῦ χρυσοστόμου εἰς τὸν πατέρα ἡμῶν. [text:] Πατέρα λέγεις ἄνθρωπε τὸν θεόν; καὶ καλῶς λέγεις ... σκέπασον ἡμᾶς ἐν σκέπῃ τῶν πτερύγων σου.

John Chrysostom, *Interpretatio Orationis Dominicae*; PG 59.627-28.

8. ff. 70v-71r [Title:] Διάλογος βασιλείου καὶ γρηγορίου. [text:] βασίλειος: τί ἐστιν ἀρχή ... οὐδὲ οἱ ἐν ᾅδου ἀπεκρύβησαν.

Anonymous, *Dialogus inter S. Basilium et S. Gregorium Nazianzenum*; N. Krasnoselzev [sic], *Anecdota Graeco-Byzantina* (Odessa, 1898) cannot be located but is cited by C. Baur, *Initia Patrum Graecorum* (Vatican City, 1955) v. 2, p. 504.

9. ff. 71r-74v [Maxims from several authors; title:] Γνῶμαι καὶ ἀποφθέγματα κατ' ἐκλογὴν καὶ κατὰ στοιχεῖον διαφόρων σοφῶν. [text:] Ἄριστον καὶ πρῶτον μάθημα ἐστὶν ἐν ἀνθρώποις πάντα τὰ χρηστά ... ὅτι οὐκ ἔστι λυπηθῆς. ἀρχὴ τοῦ φ. Φ// [text worn; breaks off in mid-sentence].

10. ff. 75r-109v [Title, added by a later hand in brown:] Ἰωάννου τοῦ χρυσοστόμου εἰς ματθαῖον. ὁμιλίαι ιγ [sic] [text of Homily 1 incomplete at beginning:] //ὁ δὲ πέτρου μαθητὴς ὤν, μετὰ ἰωάννου καὶ ματθαίου τὰ εὐαγγέλια ... ἐπὶ τὴν ἐκείνων μετέβαινεν ἐπιμ**ειαν· ποικίλλων τὲ ὁμοῦ//[text of Homily 15 incomplete at end of leaf]

St. John Chrysostom, *Homiliae in Matthaeum* 1-15. Text for all 15 Homilies: PG 57.16. 29-223. 19. Hom. 1, ff. 75r-77v; Hom. 2, ff. 77v-80v; Hom. 3, ff. 80v-83r; Hom. 4, ff. 83r-87v; Hom. 5, ff. 87v-89v; Hom. 6, ff. 89v-92v; Hom. 7, ff. 92v-95r; Hom. 8, ff. 95r-97r; Hom. 9, ff. 97r-99v; Hom. 10, ff. 99v-101v; Hom. 11, ff. 101v-104r; Hom. 12, ff. 104r-106r; Hom. 13, ff. 106r-108r; Hom. 14, ff. 108r-109v; Hom. 15, f. 109v.

11. ff. 110r-133v [Title:] Τοῦ ἐν ἁγίοις πατρὸς ἡμῶν βασιλείου ἀρχιεπισκόπου καισαρείας καππαδοκίας, ἀσκητικὴ προδιατύπωσις. κύριε εὐλόγησον. [text:] Καλὰ μὲν τοῦ βασιλέως πρὸς τοὺς ὑπήκοους τὰ νομοθετήματα. μείζονα δὲ καὶ βασιλικώτερα τὰ πρὸς τοὺς στρατιώτας παραγγέλματα ... τὸ μίαν ἐν πᾶσι καρδίαν εἶναι καὶ θέλημα ἕν// [incomplete at end?]

St. Basil, *Ascetica*; PG 31.520, 1509, 700-869, 881-888.

MS 235 343

II. 12. ff. 134r–136r [Title:] Ὀνειροκριτικὸν κατὰ ἀλφάβητον νικηφόρου τοῦ ἁγιωτάτου πατριάρχου κωνσταντινουπόλεως διὰ στίχων ἰαμβικῶν. [text begins, in two columns, to be read *ab ab*:] Ἄρχε πρὸ πάντων, καὶ παθῶν καὶ κοιλίας [col. b:] καὶ δάκρυον στάλαξον ἐκ τῶν ὀμμάτων ... [col. a:] ὡὰ φαγεῖν ἐφθὰ πρὸς πλοῦτον φέρει. [col. b:] πέρας ἔλαβεν ἡ τῶν ὀνείρων λύσις.

Nicephorus, *Onirocriticon*; F. Drexl, "Das Traumbuch des Patriarchen Nikephoros," in A. M. Koeniger, ed., *Beiträge zur Geschichte des christlichen Altertums und der byzantinischen Literatur* (Bonn-Leipzig, 1922) pp. 100–118.

13. ff. 136r–223v [Title:] διήγησις παρὰ τοῦ βουλγαρίας εἰς τὸ εὐαγγέλιον τοῦ [*sic*] κατὰ ματθαῖον. [text:] Οἱ μὲν πρὸ τοῦ νόμου ἐκεῖνοι θεῖοι ἄνδρες, οὐ διὰ γραμμάτων καὶ βιβλίων ἐδιδάσκοντο ... ξένον γενόμενον τῆς ἄνω πατρίδος συνεισήγαγε. τουτέστι συνεισ// [obscured by tape; incomplete at end]

Theophylactus of Bulgaria, *Enarratio in Evangelium Matthaei*; PG 123.144–433.

III. 14. ff. 224r–228v [Title:] Νικολάου τοῦ ἁγιωτάτου ἐπισκόπου μεθώνης πρὸς λατίνους περὶ τοῦ ἁγίου πνεύματος, ὅτι ἐκ τοῦ πατρός, οὐ μὴν καὶ ἐκ τοῦ υἱοῦ ἐκπορεύεται. εὐχὴ τάξ[εως]. [text:] Βασιλεῦ οὐράνιε· παράκλητε ἀγαθέ· προσκυνητὲ θεέ· τὸ πνεῦμα τῆς ἀληθείας ... κατὰ τὸ ἄζυμον καὶ τὴν ζύμην κεφάλοι*******//

Nicolaos of Methone, *De processione Spiritus Sancti*; K. Simonides, ed., Ὀρθοδόξων Ἑλλήνων Θεολογικαὶ Γραφαί, ed. 2 (London, 1865) pp. 1–39.

This codex is composed of three distinct sections. Part I: ff. 1–133; Part II: ff. 134–223; Part III: ff. 224–228. All three parts are written on sturdy brown paper measuring ca. 260 x 190 mm. with no identifiable watermarks.

Part I: ff. i (parchment flyleaf from a Greek liturgical manuscript of the 12th century) + ii (paper) + 133, with a written space of 205 x 147 mm. Written in ca. 44 long lines; frame-ruled in hard point; prickings at corners of written space. I^4, II–III^8, IV^4 (-4), V–VI^6, VII^{10}, VIII^8 (-1), IX^8, X^6, XII–XIII^4, XIV^6 (+1), X^6, XI^{10} (-10), XII–XIII^8, XIV^4, XV–XVIII^8. Quires signed by a later hand in Greek notation in lower margin, on recto. Written by two scribes. Scribe 1 copied ff. 1r–133v in a neat scholarly hand characterized by extensive abbreviations; Scribe 2 added notes on f. 4 in a more cramped minuscule. Small initials and chapter headings, in red.

Part II: ff. 90, (190 x 160) mm. Folios 134r–136r written in 2 columns of 25 lines; folios 136v–223v in 26 long lines. I–IV^8, V^{10}, VI–VII^8, VIII^6, IX^8, X^{10}, XI^8. Signatures in a later hand. Completed by a single scribe in minuscule, using pale brown ink. Some rubrication.

Part III: ff. 5 + ii (paper) + i (contemporary parchment), with a written space of 243 x 165 mm. 52 long lines by a single scribe in tiny minuscule similar to that of Scribe 1 in Part I. I^6 (-1). Signature added later.

The codex is stained throughout; mending tape and worm holes frequently render the text illegible.

Binding: s. xvi–xvii. Four chain-stitched supports link the quires and are laced into square-edged, flush, wooden boards with grooved edges. Colored, beaded endbands are sewn on fine cords attached to the boards. There are two twisted thread placemarks attached to the headband. The edges are bright yellow; the spine round and smooth with a spine lining extending across about one third of the outside of the wooden boards. Covered in dark brown goatskin, blind-tooled with an *x* surrounded with diamond-shaped tools stamped at random, within an outer border. One board is mended and both have small lumps in corners and center where bosses would normally be, underneath the present cover. There are traces of plaster where the leather is worn through over the lumps. There are two pins in the edge of the upper board, three corresponding holes going through both board and pastedown in the lower. Straps wanting. Rear flyleaf of the 11th century from a Latin liturgical manuscript.

Written in Byzantium in the 14th century. Ownership note (15th century) of "Manolli [?] Notaras de sancta andrea" on f. 26r. Belonged to the Jesuit College of Clermont, Paris (no. 225; table of contents on f. iii verso and note on f. 1r: "Paraphe au desir de l'arrest du 5. juillet 1763. Mesnil."). Acquired by Gerard and Johann Meerman, ca. 1773 (see *Bibliotheca Meermanniana*, v. 4, p. 22, no. 148, where it is described as "Mutilus, mucidus, squallidus et vermibus valde laceratus."); sale to Sir Thomas Phillipps (8 June – 3 July, 1824; stamp with no. 6758 on f. ii recto, tag on spine). Purchased from Laurence Witten with funds from the Jacob Ziskind Trust in 1957 (MS 24).

Bibliography: Faye and Bond, p. 44, no. 235.
Ziskind Catalogue, p. 48.
R. Carter, *Codices Chrysostomi Graeci* (Paris, 1970) p. 18, no. 15.

MS 236   Crete [?], s. XVI[1]
Pseudo-Augustine, Soliloquia (in Greek), etc.

1. ff. 1r–103v   //φυγή μου καὶ ῥύστα μου. βοηθέ μου. πύργος ἰσχύος. καὶ ἐν τῇ θλίψει μου ... [text ends with a prayer on the Holy Trinity:] ποιῶν πάντα τὰ ὀστᾶ μου. καὶ ὡς ἀετοῦ ἀνανεοῦσθαι τὴν πολιάν μου.

   Pseudo-Augustine, *Soliloquia*, translated into Greek by Demetrius Cydonius; first leaf missing.

2. ff. 103v–106v   *σύμβολον τοῦ ἁγίου ἀθανασίου.* Ὅστις ἂν βούληται σωθῆναι πρὸ πάντων χρὴ ... ἣν ἐὰν μήτις πιστῶν πιστεύσῃ σωθῆναι οὐ δυνήσεται. [δόξα τῷ πατρὶ, etc.]

   Creed of St. Athanasius; PG 28.1586–88, Formula 3.

3. ff. 106v-183v Various prayers and hymns, some by John of Damascus and Macarius, but most anonymous. ff. 184r-186v blank

Paper (watermarks: Harlfinger Chapeau 74), ff. ii (contemporary paper) + 186, 153 x 105 (102 x 62) mm. Written in 16 long lines; double outer and single inner bounding lines, often with an additional ruling in upper, lower, and outer margins. Ruled in hard point, on verso.
I^8 (-1), II-XXIII^8, XXIV^4 (4 pasted to back cover). Signed in Greek notation below written space toward outer edge, on recto.
Written by a single scribe in tall, upright minuscule.
Decorative initials, 6- to 5-line, in red with simple floral designs; rubrics throughout.
Binding: s. xvi-xvii. Three original chain-stitched supports, the thread laced into square-edged, flush, wooden boards grooved on the edges. The beaded, colored endbands are sewn on cords which are attached in holes in the edges of the boards. The edges are painted with a red and black interlace design, the spine smooth and round. Covered in brown goatskin, blind-tooled with concentric borders, different on each board, the central panels filled with flowers and small diamonds. One pin hole in the edge of the upper board, three holes for a strap in the lower. Rebacked. According to A. R. A. Hobson, the binding originated in Crete.

Written probably in Crete in the first half of the 16th century to judge from the paper and appearance of the script; early provenance unknown. Belonged to Richard Heber (1773-1833); acquired by Thorpe at the Heber sale and sold to Sir Thomas Phillipps (no. 9551, tag on spine). Purchased from Laurence Witten with funds from the Jacob Ziskind Charitable Trust in 1957 (MS 26).

Bibliography: Faye and Bond, p. 44, no. 236.
Ziskind Catalogue, p. 48.
"Creeds and Confessions," *International Standard Bible Encylopedia* (1979) v. 1, p. 810, reproduction of f. 210v.

MS 237 Byzantium, s. XII/XIII [?]
Joannes Climacus, Scala Paradisi (in Greek)

1. f. 1r //ἔρρωσο ἐν κυρίῳ τιμιώτατε πάτερ.
   Letter of Joannes Raithunus to Joannes, of which only last line remains; PG 88. 624-25.

2. ff. 1r-2v ἐπιστολὴ ἀμοιβαία ἰωάννης ἰωάννῃ χαίρειν. Ἀπεδεξάμην ὡς πρέπουσαν τῷ σεμνῷ σου ... ἀλλὰ θερμότητι προαιρέσεως τοὺς μίσθους ὁ θεὸς ἀποδίδωσι.

Letter of Joannes to Joannes Raithunus; PG 88. 625-28.

3. f. 2v-215v Λόγος ἀσκητικὸς τοῦ ἀββᾶ ἰωάννου τοῦ καθηγουμένου τῶν ἐν τῷ σινᾶ ὄρει μοναχῶν ὃν ἀπέστειλε τῷ ἀββᾶ ἰωάννῃ τῷ καθηγουμένῳ τῆς ῥαιθοῦ· διήρηται δὲ κεφαλαίοις τριάκοντα· βαθμίσι κλίμακος ὁμοίοις ἀπὸ τῶν χθαμαλωτέρων ἐπὶ τὰ μετεωρότερα τοὺς ἑπομένους ἀνάγουσι. παρὸ καὶ κλίμαξ ἡ βίβλος ὠνόμασται. πλάκες τὸ βιβλίον πνευματικαί. περὶ τῆς τοῦ ματαίου βίου βιαίας ἀποτάσεως λόγος α ... Τοῦ ἀγαθοῦ καὶ ὑπεραγάθου καὶ παναγάθου ἡμῶν θεοῦ ... ᾧ τὸ πάντων ἀγαθῶν αἴτιον ἔνεστι καὶ ἦν καὶ ἔσται εἰς ἀορίστους αἰῶνας. ἀμήν.

Joannes Climacus, *Scala paradisi*; PG 88. 632-1161. This codex does not contain scholia given in PG 88.1161-64.

4. ff. 216r-217r [Labels on diagrams of ladders, all in red:] ἀγάπης θεοῦ ... φυγῆς τῆς πρώτης

Parchment, ff. ii (paper) + 218. 130 x 98 (104 x 69) mm. Written in 20 long lines, ruled in hard point; double vertical bounding lines, full across; pricking at outer edges.

I-II^8, III^8 (-6), IV-VIII^8, IX^8 (4, folio between 66 and 67, not numbered), X-XIII^8, XIV^{10} (-2, 8), XV-XX^8, XXI^4 (-1, 2), XXII^8, XXIII^6, XXIV^{10}, XXV-XXVIII^8, XXIX^2. Quires marked by later hand in Arabic numerals, upper right corner of first folio recto (below foliation).

Greek minuscule, regular and well formed, written so that the tops of the letters hang from the ruled lines.

On f. 216r, a ladder drawn in blue and red, with explanations of each step in red; similar ladders and explanations on ff. 216v and 217r, entirely in red. Initials before each step in red, with small linear designs sprouting from them. Rubrics for incipits and explicits of the steps.

F. 1 cut at the edges. Many folios patched with modern paper, sometimes covering a portion of the text.

Binding: s. xv-xvi. Two chain-stitched supports, the thread laced into flush wooden boards without a visible edge groove. The endband cores are tied with three groups of thread which straddle the boards, the endbands embroidered in a beaded herringbone pattern. There are loops of thread around the edges of the quires at head and tail. The spine is smooth and round with a lining extending over about one quarter of the board. Covered in very dark brown goatskin, blind-tooled with two concentric line borders joined at the corners. The fore-edge turn-ins are cut in a notched pattern. Two pin holes in the edge of the upper board, two leather straps with two ends each laced through the lower. Straps wanting except ends inside boards.

Written in Byzantium probably at the end of the 12th or beginning of the 13th century; early provenance unknown. Acquired from Thorpe by Sir Thomas Phillipps (no. 4289 in his collection). Purchased from Laurence Witten with funds from the Jacob Ziskind Charitable Trust in 1957 (MS 59).

Bibliography: Faye and Bond, p. 44, no. 237.
Ziskind Catalogue, p. 53.
Exhibition Catalogue, pp. 199-200, no. 26.
C. E. Lutz, "Johannes Climacus' Ladder of Divine Ascent," *Gazette* 47 (1973) pp. 224-27.

MS 238   Byzantium, s. XVI
Anastasius of Sinai, et al., **Passages on Asceticism** (in Greek)

1. ff. 1r-32r   Λόγοι ἀσκητικοὶ τῶν ἁγίων πατέρων διαφοροί. σημεῖα καὶ ἐνεργήματα τῆς ἀγάπης τοῦ Θεοῦ. Ἡ ἀγάπη τοῦ Θεοῦ θέρμη ἐστι τῇ φύσει ... καὶ παρ' αἰγυπτίοις τῶ φαραῶ ὀνόματι. ff. 32v-33v ruled, but blank

   Anonymous, Excerpts on Asceticism, drawn from John Chrysostom, Basil, Isidore, Theodoretus, Maximus, Nilus and others; no text of this collection has yet been published.

2. ff. 34r-42v   τοῦ ἁγίου Φιλοθέου· λόγος περὶ τῶν ἐντολῶν τοῦ κυρίου ἡμῶν Ἰησοῦ Χριστοῦ· ὅτι τῇ τῆς καρδίας φυλακῇ, συνμφυλάττονται [sic], καὶ αἱ θεῖαι ἐντολαὶ τοῦ Χριστοῦ. Ὁ κύριος ἡμῶν Ἰησοῦς Χριστὸς ἡ τοῦ πατρὸς τοῦ ἀιδίου σοφία καὶ δύναμις, φησὶν ... καὶ ἀειδίω καὶ μακαρία ζωῇ, ἐν Χριστῶ ... ἀμήν.

   Philotheus, patriarch of Constantinople, *De mandatis D. N. Jesu Christi sermo*; PG 154. 729-41. No loss of text, but the treatise was left without the final section by the scribe and divided into four parts, each with a title.

3. ff. 43r-55v   ἐπιστολῆς Συμεὼν μητροπολίτου Εὐχαίτων· πρός τινα μοναχὸν ἔκλειστον. Τρία μέρη λέγουσιν οἱ πατέρες ἔχειν τὴν λογικὴν ἡμῶν ψυχὴν ... καὶ ἐν ἰσχύσει εἰς τὸ ἅγιον αὐτοῦ θέλημα. ὦ ἡ δόξα, ἀμήν. [text of prologue begins f. 55r, after an explanatory note:] Ἐδεξάμην πάτερ πνευματικὲ θεοφιλεῖ σου ταύτην γραφὴν ... τέλος τοῦ προλόγου.

   Symeon Euchaita, excerpts from *Epistola ad monachum quendam*; no text has yet been published.

4. ff. 55v-68v   τοῦ ἀββᾶ πέτρου τοῦ Δαμασκηνοῦ. Ὁ βουλόμενος παντῶν τῶν παθῶν ἐλευθερωθῆναι ... τοῦ συνετῶς ψάλλοντας ἐν κυρίω. αὐτῷ ἡ δόξα εἰς τοὺς αἰώνας, ἀμήν.

   Petrus Damascenus, *Excerpta ascetica*; no text has yet been published.

5. ff. 68v-73v   τοῦ αὐτοῦ· συμβουλία, νοὸς πρὸς τὴν ἑαυτοῦ ψυχήν. Ἄκουε ψυχὴ λογική, κοινωνὲ τῶν ἐμῶν βουλευμάτων· εἰς ζωὴν αἰώνιον εὑρήσει αὐτήν· ὦ ἡ δόξα ... ἀμήν.

   Marcus Eremita, *Consultatio intellectus cum sua ipsius anima*; PG 65.1104-09.

6. ff. 74r-86v   ἐν τῶ γεροντικῶ. λόγοι ὠφέλοι [sic] περὶ τοῦ μὴ κατακρίνει τῶν πλήσιον, τοῦ ἀββᾶ μακαρίου. Ὁ ἀββᾶς μακάριος πειραζόμενος ὑπὸ τοῦ διαβόλου

παρεσκεύασε τινά δαιμονιζόμενον ... και ου δύναται το δένδρων// Text left incomplete in the middle of a page; ff. 87r–89v blank, except that on f. 87r the scribe began to copy the next text, then stopped abruptly.

Anonymous, *Excerpta e Gerontico*; text not included in published collections.

7. ff. 90r–128v ἐρωτήσεις καὶ ἀποκρίσεις περὶ διαφόρων κεφαλαίων ἐκ διαφορῶν προσώπων, πρὸς τὸν ἀββᾶν Ἀναστασίον τοῦ ἁγίου ὄρους σινᾶ· ὧν τὰς λύσεις ἐποιήσατο ἐκ τῶν ἀναγνωσμάτων τῶν ἁγίων πατέρων. [text of question 79 begins:] Ἐάν τις ἄπιστος ἢ ἰουδαῖος ἢ σαμαρείτης ποιήση πολλὰ ἀγαθὰ ... καὶ ἔγγιζε πρὸς τὸν θεόν σου διὰ παντός.

Anastasius of Sinai, *Quaestiones* (selections); PG 89. 311–823.

8. ff. 129r–137v [title:] τοῦ ὁσίου Μάρκου, περὶ τοῦ ἁγίου βαπτίσματος ἐρωτήσεις καὶ ἀποκρίσεις. [text:] Ἐπειδὴ οἱ μὲν τέλειον εἶναι λέγουσι τὸ ἅγιον βάπτισμα ... ὅπερ ἐστὶ τὸ ἐνδότατον καὶ ἀπόκρυφον καὶ εἰλικρινὲς τῆς καρδίας χώρημα.

Marcus Eremita, *Quaestiones de baptismo*; PG 65. 985–1028.

9. ff. 137v–139r περὶ ἀνεξικακίας καὶ πραότητος. Ἰωάννου δὲ τοῦ κολοβοῦ καθημένου μετὰ τῶν ἀδελφῶν ... ἠκολούθησεν αὐτῷ γέγονε δὲ καὶ μοναχός.

Anonymous, *Excerptum de patientia*; text not included in published collections.

10. ff. 139r–140v σύνοψις σαφεῖς [sic] καὶ σύντομος· καὶ διάγνωσις τῆς πίστεως ἡμῶν τῆς ἁγίας τριάδος. Ὀφείλομεν πιστεύειν ὡς ἐβαπτίσθημεν ... ἐν τρισὶ γνωριζομένην καὶ προσκυνουμένην ὑποστάσεσιν.

Anastasius of Sinai, *Fidei notitia*; J. B. Pitra, *Juris ecclesiastici Graecorum Historia et Monumenta* (Rome, 1864–68) v. 2, pp. 271–74. The text of MS 238 diverges substantially from the printed text.

11. ff. 140v–170r Περὶ διαφορῶν ἀρετῶν. Ἐλάβομεν ἐντολὰς παρὰ αὐτοῦ τοῦ Χριστοῦ καὶ θεοῦ ἡμῶν ... καὶ στῆσαι τὴν κυμαινομένην θάλασσαν. τέλος καὶ τῷ θεῷ χάρις. [Colophon:] ἐτελιόθη τὸ πάρον σύταγμα διαχειρὸς ὑπ' ἐμοῦ τοῦ ἐλαχίστου καὶ ἁμαρτωλοῦ· καλλίστου· τάχα ἱεροδιακώνου.

Anonymous, *Excerpta et Quaestiones Asceticae* from Basil, Athanasius, Anastasius of Sinai, Maximus the Confessor, and others; no text of this collection has apparently been published.

Paper (polished, except for ff. 129–136; unidentified watermarks: anchor in circle), ff. i (early parchment) + 170 + i (contemporary parchment), 154 x 103 (119 x 77) mm. Written in 18 long lines; double vertical bounding lines with an additional horizontal ruling in upper and lower margins; ruled in hard point.

The volume is too closely bound to collate. Catchwords for all folios, verso and recto, are located directly below the written space to the right.

Written by a single scribe who signed himself "Callistus the holy deacon" (perhaps to be identified with Vogel and Gardthausen, p. 227, a. 1523; see art. 11 for colophon).

Simple headpieces on ff. 1r, 34r, 58r, 60v, 74r. Initials and headings, in red, for each new passage. Crudely drawn angel hovers over top of initial, f. 34r; birds perch on others. Folios 129-136 are not rubricated.

Binding: Date? Pastedowns sewn with bookblock. Three chain-stitched supports. Endbands attached to the square-edged, flush wooden boards. Loops of thread around the edges of the quires at head and tail. The spine is square and lined all along with vellum extending onto the inside of the boards and there seem to be lining strips extending on the outside of the boards also. Two pin holes with stubs of iron pins in them in the edges of the upper board and two holes for each strap on the lower. Rebacked. Covered with 13th-century Greek manuscript fragment containing musical notation, with front flyleaf from the same manuscript, and back flyleaf from a 12th-century Greek liturgical text (all badly rubbed).

Written in Byzantium in the 16th century. A Greek note (19th century?) on f. 1r states that it came from the monastery of Mt. Lebanon. Ownership inscription, in Latin on f. 169v, has been crossed out by a later hand; only the date April 1623 is legible. The notation "c. v. 14." appears inside front cover. Acquired in 1861 by Sir Thomas Phillipps (no. 15867, on spine) from Puttick. Purchased from Laurence Witten with funds from the Jacob Ziskind Charitable Trust in 1957 (MS 27).

Bibliography: Faye and Bond, pp. 44-45, no. 238.
Ziskind Catalogue, p. 48.

MS 239
Manuel Chrysoloras, Erotemata (in Greek)

Italy, s. XV
Pl. 30

1. f. 1r [Full-page inscription:] ἐρωτήματα τοῦ κυρίου μανουὴλ τοῦ χρυσολουρᾶς τῶν ὀκτὼ τοῦ λόγου μερῶν. ἐμοῦ τοῦ πέτρου τοῦ λ***μου [badly rubbed] ἰατροῦ φλορεντίνου τῶν [?] ου πάντων καὶ τῶν ἑαυτοῦ φίλων. Followed by short prayer. f. 1v blank

2. ff. 2r-33v Ἐρωτήματα κυρίου μανουὴλ τοῦ χρυσολουρᾶς τῶν ὀκτὼ τοῦ λόγου μερῶν. Εἰς πόσα διαιροῦνται τὰ εἰκοσιτέσσαρα γράμματα Εἰς δύο ... ἔστεισο, ἔστητο, ἐστείμεθον, ἔστεισθον, ἐ//

The manuscript is incomplete at end of quire; the text is the abridged version of Guarino of Verona, GKW, v. 6, nos. 6696-700; there is no modern printed text.

Parchment, ff. ii (contemporary parchment, foliated i, 1) + 40 (contemporary foliation, in red; modern foliation is incorrect; the total number of leaves was originally 60 according to a contemporary note on f. 1r), 189 x 137 (125 x 82) mm. Written in 20 long lines, ruled in hard point mostly on the flesh side; single bounding lines that do not extend into margins, except on ff. i and 1.

I-IV¹⁰. No catchwords or signatures.

Written by a single scribe whose name may be that on the title page (second front fly-leaf) which is now erased and partly illegible in the critical portion of the text.

Capitals and headings in red throughout.

Binding: s. xv. Probably Tuscan according to A. R. A. Hobson. One set of sewing holes only. Sewn on four tawed, slit straps laced through tunnels in beech boards and nailed. The endband cores, now wanting, were also nailed. Covered in brown calf, originally a brick red, with corner tongues. Blind-stamped with a rope interlace cross in a rope interlace border. Two fastenings. Rebacked.

Written in Italy in the 15th century by a Western scribe ["Petrus Iatrus Florentinus" mentioned on the title page?]. Unidentified bookstamp consisting of the initials "A. N." enclosed in a double circle, outer thick and inner thin. Collection of Abate Luigi Celotti; his sale through Payne and Foss to Sir Thomas Phillipps (no. 4202, on f. i recto and spine). Purchased from Laurence Witten with funds from the Jacob Ziskind Charitable Trust in 1957 (MS 21).

Bibliography: Faye and Bond, p. 45, no. 239.
Ziskind Catalogue, p. 47.

MS 240 Italy, s. XV¹
Aristotle, Ethica Nicomachea (in Greek) Pl. 29

ff. 1r-132v Ἀριστοτέλους ἠθικῶν νικομαχείων ἄλφα. [text:] πᾶσα τέχνη καὶ πᾶσα μέθοδος. ὁμοίως δὲ πρᾶξις ... καὶ τίσι νόμοις καὶ ἔθεσι χρωμένη λέγομεν οὖν ἀρξάμενοι. [explicit:] τέλος τῶν ἠθικῶν νικομαχείων. Ἀριστοτέλους φιλοσόφου δόξα θεῷ.

B. M. W. Knox has listed variant readings between Beinecke MS 240 and the OCT for 1094a to 1097a (*Ziskind Catalogue*, pp. 45-46); I. Bekker, *Aristotelis opera* (Berlin, 1831) v. 2, 1094a1-1181b23.

Parchment, ff. ii (nearly contemporary paper) + 132 + ii (nearly contemporary paper), 209 x 144 (151 x 92) mm. Written in 27-28 long lines, ruled with hard point on hair side; double vertical and horizontal bounding lines, full across; prickings in outer and upper margins.

I-XII¹⁰, XIII¹². Catchwords in center of lower margin; quires signed in Roman numerals along lower edge (many have been trimmed).

Written by two scribes. Scribe 1: ff. 1r-120v; Scribe 2: ff. 121r-132v. On paleographical grounds, Scribe 1 can perhaps be identified as a pupil of Manuel Chrysoloras. D. Harlfinger, *Die Textgeschichte der pseudo-aristotelischen Schrift* ... (Amsterdam, 1971) p. 420, identifies the hand of Scribe 1 in Beinecke MS 240 with that of a manuscript in Florence, Laurentian Conv. Supp. 47 (= AF 2755).

MS 241 351

For the hand of Chrysoloras and Palla Strozzi, see R. Barbour, *Greek Literary Hands 400-1600 A.D.* (Oxford, 1981) p. 24.

Headings in red. Latin interlinear glosses in red (ff. 1r-25v), in humanistic cursive script.

Folio 1r is rubbed and barely legible.

Binding: s. xix. Rigid vellum case, in the same manner as Beinecke MSS 257 and 264.

Written in Italy in the first half of the 15th century; according to P. Moraux it was acquired by Guillaume Pellicier probably between 1539 and 1542, then in 1573 by Claude Naulot. Belonged to the Jesuit College of Clermont, Paris (no. 247; notes on f. 1r: "Coll. Paris. Societatis Jesu," and "Paraphe au desir de l'arrest du 5. juillet 1763. Mesnil"). Acquired by Gerard and Johann Meerman, ca. 1773, *Bibliotheca Meermanniana* v. 4, p. 46, no. 291 (on spine); sale to Sir Thomas Phillipps (8 June - 3 July 1824; stamp with no. 6764 on f. i recto). Purchased from Laurence Witten with funds from the Jacob Ziskind Charitable Trust in 1957 (MS 7).

Bibliograpy: Faye and Bond, p. 45, no. 240.
Ziskind Catalogue, pp. 45-46.

MS 241 Byzantium, s. XIII/XIV
Catena on Isaiah (in Greek)

ff. 1r-435v Ἡσαίας ὁ προφήτης [ornamental border below heading, then Isaiah, 1. 1:] ["Ο]ρασις ἣν εἶδεν ἡσαίας υἱὸς ἀμῶς ἣν εἶδε κατὰ τῆς ἰουδαίας καὶ ... [Isaiah, 66. 24:] αὐτῶν οὐ σβεσθήσεται καὶ ἔσονται εἰς ὅρασιν πάσῃ σαρκί. [beginning of catena, from St. Basil's *Commentary*:] Τῶν παρ' ἡμῖν αἰσθητηρίων τῶν ἐναργεστάτην τὴν κατάληψιν ἔχον αἰσθητῶν ὅρασις ἔστιν οὔτε γὰρ τὰ φοβερὰ δι' ἀκοῆς δυνατόν ἐστι γνωρίσαι ὡς δι' ὁράσεως ... [end of catena, from Eusebius and Cyrillus, badly mutilated:] τοῦ αὐτοῦ [Cyrillus:] ... κὲς τῆς τιμωρίας, διὰ τούτων δεδήλωκε. καὶ τὸ πῦρ ἄσβεστον καὶ ὁ σκώληξ. τελεύτη. ταύτην ἠπείλησεν. ἐκείνοις τὴν τιμωρίαν οὐκ ἐκείνοις μόνοις, ἀλλὰ καὶ τοῖς τοὺς θείους αὐτοῦ παραβαίνουσι νο[μους]. [Eusebius:] Ὁ δὴ τέλος τῶν ἀσεβῶν ὡρίζ[ετο] (ἰοσῃ). [p. 437, inscription, in same hand as text:] βιβλίον/ κατηχομένων τῆς ἁγίας [λά]/ βρας τοῦ ἁγίου// [page cut off] [p. 438, inscription in another hand:] τοῦτο τὸ βιβλίον δίδοται εἰς τὴν λαύραν παρὰ ἀθανασίου μοναχοῦ ὑπὲρ σωτηρίας ἑαυτ[οῦ] καὶ τ[ῶ]ν ψυχῶν Ἡσαίου μοναχοῦ καὶ καλ****ἠλ καὶ μαρίας. καὶ οἱ ἀναγινώσκ[ον]τες. εὔχεσθε ὑπὲρ αὐτῶν διὰ τὸν κύριον.

Two later scribes, apparently heeding Athanasius' request, added brief notes, the first in red ink (ca. s. xv), referring to books which Athanasius brought; the second, in black (ca. s. xvi), requesting intercession for him and his relatives.

With few exceptions the text corresponds closely to the "Stichproben zu Isaias" printed by M. Faulhaber, *Die Propheten-Catenen* (Freiburg, 1899) pp. 203-08, and taken from Vatican, Ottob. gr. 452. None of the five prologues he lists is in Beinecke MS 241, and the text breaks off just before the end of the catena, omitting the last note cited by Faulhaber and most of the preceding one (cf. R. Devreesse, *Introduction à l'étude des manuscrits grecs* [Paris, 1954] p. 179).

Paper, ff. iv (paper) + 437 (nos. 433-443 are page numbers; the preceding numbers are for folios) + iv (paper), 257 x 165 (202 x 120) mm. Written in ca. 29 long lines (ff. 354r-356r, copied in a smaller script, have 41 lines), ruled in hard point in no uniform format. Sometimes the leaves appear to have been used sideways with the script intersecting the guide-lines rather than sitting on them (see ff. 303-04).

I^6, $II-XIV^8$, XV^8 (1 f. missing and replaced by blank paper; previously numbered 118), $XVI-XXII^8$, XXIII^8 (there are two folios numbered 178), $XXIV-XXIX^8$, XXX^8 (1 f. missing), $XXXI-XXXVI^8$, XXXVII^6, $XXXVIII-XLII^8$, XLIII^6, $XLIV-XLV^8$, XLVI^8 (1 f. missing), $XLVII-LVI^8$, + 1 additional folio. Because of the tight binding it is not possible to collate the manuscript more accurately. Signatures are later than text.

Written by a single scribe in a bold minuscule for the text of Isaiah, and in a smaller, more compact script for the commentary.

One crude decorative headpiece in black and red on f. 1r. Initials in red at beginning and end of text.

Binding: s. xx. Brick-red goatskin, title gold-tooled.

Written in Byzantium in the late 13th or early 14th century. Gift of Athanasius to an unidentified monastery at the time of the completion of the manuscript (mutilated inscription on p. 438; see contents for complete text). Belonged to Frederick North, 5th Earl of Guilford (1766-1827; no. 9, in sale catalogue and at bottom of f. iii recto); to Sir Thomas Phillipps (no. 4930, tag on spine) through Thorpe. Purchased from Laurence Witten with funds from the Jacob Ziskind Charitable Trust in 1957 (MS 14).

Bibliography: Faye and Bond, p. 45, no. 241.
Ziskind Catalogue, p. 47.

MS 242   Italy, ca. 1560
Aelian, De instruendis aciebus (in Greek)

ff. 1r-17v [Heading, in red:] **αἰλιανοῦ τακτικὴ θεωρία**. [followed by border in red across top of page, and by a rubric that was then crossed out by the original scribe:] *περὶ στρατηγῶν ὀνομάτων τε καὶ τάξεων, τοῦ αἰλιανοῦ*: [text begins:] Τὴν παρὰ τοῖς Ἕλλησι τακτικὴν θεωρίαν ἀπὸ τῶν ὁμήρου χρόνων τὴν ἀρχὴν ... ἱππεῖς .ιε. ἢ καὶ .ιβ. τοῦ εἰσέρχεσθαι ἕνεκεν καὶ ἐξέρχεσθαι τοὺς πολεμοῦντας. τῷ θεῷ χάρις. ff. 18r-20v blank; with f. 18r-v blank, but ruled

H. Köchly and W. Rüstow, eds., *Griechische Kriegsschriftsteller* 2, 1 (Leipzig, 1855). The scribe attempts to establish the correct text from a defective exemplar. For example, on f. 2v there is a note, in red, referring the reader to the proper portion of the text on f. 7v. There are several such corrections as well as marginal notes giving variant readings.

Paper (watermarks: Harlfinger Couronne 25 from two manuscripts copied in Venice by Camillus Venetus, and dated 1561 and 1562), ff. iii (contemporary paper) + 20 + iii (contemporary paper), 217 x 146 (150 x 85) mm. Written in 24 long lines, ruled in hard point on verso; single bounding vertical lines.

I–II^8, III^4. Signatures consist of letters of the alphabet placed in center of lower margin on recto of first folio of gathering.

Written in a highly calligraphic Greek minuscule by Angelus Vergecius.

Decorative floral headpiece and initial, in red, on f. 1r; headings and marginal notations, in red. A number of beautifully executed diagrams, in black and red, often extend well into the margins.

Binding: s. xviii–xix [?]. Limp vellum wrapper, with the title on spine and "Aelianus Angeli Vergecij" on cover.

Written probably in Northern Italy ca. 1560 by Angelus Vergecius who was active in Paris during the mid-16th century. See Omont, no. 2; a list of those manuscripts copied by Vergecius appears in E. Legrand, *Bibliographie hellenique*, v. 1 (Paris, 1885) p. clxxv. Beinecke MS 242 is listed in de Meyier, p. 259, no. 2. Unidentified "1190" on front cover. Andrew Fletcher (1655–1716; signature on back pastedown). Purchased from Laurence Witten with funds from the Jacob Ziskind Charitable Trust in 1957 (MS 1).

Bibliography: Faye and Bond, p. 45, no. 242.
Ziskind Catalogue, p. 44, with plate of f. 1r for frontispiece.

MS 243　　　　　　　　　　　　　　　　　　　　　　　　Italy, s. XVI^{med}
Confession Manual (in Greek)

ff. 1r–222r 'Αρχὴ τῆς ἐξομολογήσεως. Περὶ τοῦ πῶς δεῖ ἐξομολογεῖσθαι τὸν πάσα [sic] ἄνθρωπον. λαμβάνει δεῖ τὸν θέλοντα ἐξομολογηθῆναι ἐν τῷ ναῷ ... διὰ τῆς μακαρίας μακροθυμίας καὶ ταπεινώσεως. τέλος τῶν θανατήσιμων ἁμαρτημάτων. [brief table, f. 222v, on the Seven ages of man: infant, child, etc.]

The work includes prayers and materials for examination of conscience, such as lists of mortal sins, canonical obligations, and similar texts.

Paper (sturdy; watermarks: Briquet Ancre 531), ff. ii (paper) + 222 + i (paper), 152 x 112 (106 x 62) mm. Written in 16 long lines; double vertical bounding lines. Ruled in hard point, on verso; no prickings visible.

I-V⁸, VI¹⁰ (plus bifolium bound between 7 and 8, ff. 48-49), VII-XXVII⁸ (+ 2 at end). Signed in Greek along lower edge of verso; some lost due to trimming.

Written by a single copyist in an archaizing script reminiscent of the 13th century.

Simple and crudely executed headpieces mark the beginning of each new section of text; many small initials in red throughout.

Binding: s. xvi. Greek (according to A. R. A. Hobson); original sewing, presumably a chain stitch, on three supports laced into square-edged, flush wooden boards without edge grooves but with blind-tooled lines along the edges. The plain, wound endbands are covered with a bright yellow, beaded, secondary embroidery (traces only). Covered in dark brown calf, blind-tooled with concentric borders, different on each board, and three diamonds and flowers in the center panel. Two pins in the edge of the upper board and two sets of three holes for fastening straps on the lower.

Written probably in Italy (Northern?) in the mid-16th century to judge by the watermarks; early provenance unknown. Unidentified tag with "CCLII" on spine. Belonged to the Greenway family in Devonshire (18th-century bookplate). Dr. Adam Clarke (1762?-1832); at his sale (20 June 1836) it was acquired by Thorpe, who sold it to Sir Thomas Phillipps (no. 9516, on spine). Purchased from Laurence Witten with funds from the Jacob Ziskind Charitable Trust in 1957 (MS 43).

Bibliography: Faye and Bond, p. 45, no. 243.
Ziskind Catalogue, p. 51.

MS 244 Italy, s. XV^{med}
Xenophon, De re equestri (in Greek)

ff. 1r-17v ξενοφῶντος ῥήτορος περὶ ἱππικῆς. Ἐπειδὴ διὰ τὸ συμβῆναι ἡμῖν πολὺν χρόνον ἱππεύειν. οἰόμεθα ἔμπειροι ἱππικῆς ... ἃ δὲ ἱππάρχῳ προσῆκεν εἰδέναι τε καὶ πράσσειν, ἐν ἑτέρῳ λόγῳ δεδήλωται. τέλος.

Knox has collated Beinecke MS 244 with the OCT for Chapters 1-8 (*Ziskind Catalogue*, pp. 54-56).

Paper (watermarks: balance within a circle, surmounted by three small circles and a star, is not similar to those in Briquet and Harlfinger), ff. ii (paper) + 17 + xxxiv (paper), 210 x 136 (152 x 92) mm. Written in 23 long lines; frame-ruled in hard point.

I¹⁰, II⁸ (-8). No catchwords or signatures.

Text is written by a single scribe.

Title and first letter of text in red.

Binding: s. xix. Tan calf with gold-tooled title and arms of Henry Drury, by C. Lewis (worked 1800-40).

Written in Italy in the mid-15th century; early provenance unknown. Supposedly from the Meerman Library (the codex does not appear in the *Bibliotheca Meermanniana*, v. 4). Collection of Henry Drury (1778-1841; arms on cover and signature on f. i recto); his sale (Evans, Feb. - March 1827, lot 4678, on spine) to Thorpe for Sir Thomas Phillipps (no. 3337; stamp on f. i recto). Purchased from Laurence Witten with funds from the Jacob Ziskind Charitable Trust in 1957 (MS 61).

Bibliography: Faye and Bond, p. 45, no. 244.
Ziskind Catalogue, pp. 54-56.

MS 245 Italy, s. XV^{med}
Aristotle, Mechanica (in Greek) Pl. 30

ff. 1r-37v Ἀριστοτέλους μηχάνικα. Θαυμάζεται τῶν μὲν κατὰ φύσιν συμβαινόντων, ὅσον [corrected to ὅσων] ἀγνοεῖται τὸ αἴτιον ... μένει δὲ τὸ κέντρον μόνον. ἄπαντα ἀνάγκη εἰς τοῦτο διαθρίζεσθαι.

B. M. W. Knox has collated Beinecke MS 245 with Bekker's text, *Aristotelis opera* (Berlin, 1831) v. 2, 847a11-858b31, in the *Ziskind Catalogue*, p. 45.

Parchment, ff. i (paper) + i (contemporary parchment) + 37 + i (paper), 208 x 128 (112 x 66) mm. Written in 20 long lines, ruled in pale brown crayon or ink; single horizontal and vertical bounding lines, full across.
I-IV^8, V^6 (-6; last flyleaf glued to f. 37v).
Greek minuscule, compact and neat, with a large admixture of uncial forms; tops of letters hang from ruled lines. J. Wiesner has identified the scribe as the Manuel whose hand appears in Vat. Pal. gr. 258 (illustrated in Harlfinger, *Specimina griechischer Kopisten der Renaissance* [Berlin, 1974] v. 1, pl. 4). Harlfinger attributes the marginalia in this manuscript to Juan Páez de Castro (ca. 1545), whose hand he illustrates on Tafel 4 of *Die Textgeschichte der Pseudo-Aristotelischen Schrift* ... (Amsterdam, 1971) p. 415.
On f. 1r, title in red minuscule by original scribe. Author and title in Latin, brown ink, by a later scribe. 5-line initial in red, with simple floral designs. Initials within text sometimes set outside bounding lines, enlarged and elaborated slightly. Numerous diagrams of geometrical figures in margins.
Binding: s. xix. Blue edges. Tan calf, blind- and gold-tooled, with title on spine.

Written in Italy in the mid-15th century by the scribe Manuel; marginalia added in the 16th century by Juan Páez de Castro (see also above). Augusto Mariotti (*ex libris* on third flyleaf, recto; Cosenza, v. 3, p. 2183). Belonged to Frederick North, 5th Earl of Guilford (1766-1827; bookplate; no. 177 in his catalogue); sold to Payne. Sir Thomas Phillipps (no. 7488; tag on spine). Purchased from

Laurence Witten with funds from the Jacob Ziskind Charitable Trust in 1957 (MS 5).

Bibliography: Faye and Bond, p. 45, no. 245.
Ziskind Catalogue, p. 45.

MS 246
Acts of the Apostles and Revelation (in Greek)

Flanders [?], s. XVI[1]
Pl. 31

1. ff. 1r–61v Πράξεις τῶν 'Αποστόλων. Τὸν μὲν πρῶτον λόγον ἐποιησάμην περὶ πάντων ὦ Θεόφιλε ὧν ἤρξατο ... καὶ διδάσκων τὰ περὶ τοῦ κυρίου 'Ιησοῦ μετὰ πάσης παρρησίας ἀκωλύτως. Πράξεις τῶν 'Αποστόλων εὐτυχῶς συντετελεσμέναι. τῷ θεῷ χάρις. ff. 62r–64v ruled, but blank

    Acts of the Apostles; E. Nestle and K. Aland, eds., *Novum Testamentum Graece*, ed. 26 (Stuttgart, 1979) pp. 320–408.

2. ff. 65r–95v 'Αποκάλυψις τοῦ ἁγίου 'Ιωάννου τοῦ θεολόγου. 'Αποκάλυψις 'Ιησοῦ χριστοῦ ἣν ἔδωκεν αὐτῷ ὁ θεός. δεῖξαι τοῖς δούλοις ... ἔρχου κύριε 'Ιησοῦ. 'Η χάρις τοῦ κυρίου ἡμῶν 'Ιησοῦ χριστοῦ μετὰ πάντων ὑμῶν. Ἀμήν. [explicit:] *Τέλος. Τῷ θεῷ χάρις καὶ δόξα*. f. 96 ruled, but blank

    Revelation; Nestle and Aland, *op. cit.*, pp. 632–80.

Paper (mutilated watermarks consisting of column [?] flanked by fleur-de-lis), ff. 96, 143 x 95 (103 x 69) mm. Written in 22 long lines, ruled in ink; double [?] vertical bounding lines, prickings at lower edge.

I–XII[8]. Quire missing at beginning of manuscript. Catchwords located at lower edge, verso; signatures, on recto, in lower right corner for first four folios of gathering, consisting of majuscule letter for quire number plus minuscule letter for leaf number and preceded by a paragraph mark in pale red.

Written by a single person in a small neat minuscule script.

Initial on f. 1r painted in blue and outlined in red. Illuminated initial on f. 65r in gold, on blue square serving as background; partial border at bottom of page: pink flowers in gold rectangle outlined in black. Running titles throughout.

Binding: Probably ca. 1530. Bruges? See Weale's description of a very similar binding, *South Kensington*, v. 2, p. 195–96, no. 419, and also p. 18, no. 91; p. 264, no. 702. Sewn on four single, tawed thongs laced twice in and out of pasteboards. The tawed cores of the beaded endbands are also laced twice. Half bands divide the end sections of the spine. The bookblock is remarkably clean and the leaves flat. Covered in brown calf with panel stamps of Saint John the Baptist and Saint Michael in arches with a line of dancing figures and a piper in between. Heavily repaired.

Written in Flanders [?] in the first half of the 16th century; early provenance unknown. Belonged to Sir Thomas Phillipps (no. 4527, on spine; his purchase

MS 247 357

from Pierre-Philippe-Constant Lammens, librarian of the University of Ghent). Purchased from Laurence Witten with funds from the Jacob Ziskind Charitable Trust in 1957 (MS 17).

Bibliography: Faye and Bond, p. 45, no. 246.
Ziskind Catalogue, p. 47.
K. Aland, *Kurzgefasste Liste der griechischen Handschriften des Neuen Testaments*, v. 1 (Berlin, 1963) p. 200, Gregory Nr. 2619 (where MS 246 is dated to s. XVIII).

MS 247 Byzantium, s. XV^{in}
Pseudo-Pythagoras, Carmina aurea, etc. (in Greek) Pl. 29

1. ff. 1r–3r [Π]υθαγόρου τὰ χρυσᾶ ἔπη. [Π]υθαγόρου σαμίοιο ἔπη τάδ' ἔνεστι τὰ χρυσᾶ. ['Α]θανάτους μὲν πρῶτα θεοὺς νομῷ ὡς διάκεινται τίμα. καὶ σέβου ὅρκον ... ἔσσεαι ἀθάνατος θεὸς ἄμβροτος. οὐκέτι θνητός. f. 3v blank

   Pseudo-Pythagoras, *Carmina aurea*; Knox lists the variant readings from the critical edition of P. C. Van Der Horst (*Ziskind Catalogue*, p. 53).

2. ff. 6r–92v ['Ι]εροκλέους φιλοσόφου εἰς τὰ πυθαγορικὰ ἔπη ὑπόμνημα. φιλοσοφία ἐστὶ ζωῆς ἀνθρωπίνης κάθαρσις καὶ τελειότης. κάθαρσις ... τῆς ἀπ' αὐτῶν ὠφελείας ὀψὲ γοῦν ποτε κτήσασθαι.

   Hierocles, *Commentary on Pythagoras*; F. Koehler, ed., *Hierocles in aureum Pythagoreorum carmen commentarius* (Stuttgart, 1974) MS C (p. xvi), pp. 5–122.

Parchment, ff. i (paper) + i (parchment) + ii (contemporary parchment) + 90 + i (contemporary parchment) + i (parchment) + i (paper). The foliation, by an early owner, begins on the third front flyleaf. 173 x 117 (117 x 71) mm. Written in 20 long lines, ruled in hard point on hair side before folding; double vertical bounding lines, full across; with additional single guide-lines, in upper, lower, and outer margins, prickings in all margins except inner.

I–XI^8, XII^4. Signatures consist of miniscule letters located in the center of the lower margin on first and final folio of each gathering.

Written by a single copyist whose writing becomes more compact and more abbreviated in the latter portion of the codex.

The manuscript is incomplete, since the initials for headings and text are lacking.

Binding: s. xix. Dark blue goatskin, gold-tooled and with the arms of Henry Drury. Bound by C. Lewis (worked 1800–40).

Written apparently in Byzantium at the beginning of the 15th century. The parchment flyleaves bound with the manuscript bear inscriptions roughly contemporary with the main text. If the obituary notice written on f. 93r was originally bound with the main text, the manuscript was written before 25 July 1333 A.D. Henry Drury (1778–1841; arms on cover; according to the description in the auction catalogue, the manuscript was obtained in Italy); his sale (Evans, Feb. – March 1827, no. 3630) to Thorpe for Sir Thomas Phillipps (no. 3397, on spine). Purchased from Laurence Witten with funds from the Jacob Ziskind Charitable Trust in 1957 (MS 56).

Bibliography: Faye and Bond, p. 45, no. 247.
Ziskind Catalogue, p. 53.

MS 248　　　　　　　　　　　　　　　　　　　　　　　　　Byzantium, s. XIV
New Testament; Eusebian Canons, etc. (in Greek)

1. ff. 1r–32v   Calendar for the liturgical year; the incipit, explicit, and title (if any) are all illegible.

2. f. 33r   Miscellaneous prayers added in the fifteenth century.

3. f. 33v   [Heading:] πόθεις κανόνων τῆς τῶν εὐαγγελιστῶν συμφωνίας. [text begins:] εὐσέβιος καρπιανῷ ἀγαπητῷ ἀδελφῷ ἐν κυρίῳ χαίρειν· ἀμμώνιος ... εὑρήσεις. ἔρρωσο ἐν κυρίῳ.

   Letter of Eusebius to Carpianus; E. Nestle and K. Aland, eds., *Novum Testamentum Graece* ed. 26 (Stuttgart, 1979) pp. 73*–74*.

4. ff. 34r–36v   [Eusebian Canons; text begins:] Κανὼν α: Ἐν ᾧ οἱ δ ... τέλος τῶν .ι. κανόνων.

   Nestle and Aland, *op. cit.*, pp. 74*–78* (in Lat.).

5. ff. 37r–168r   [Title, in blue:] Ὑπόθεσις τοῦ κατὰ ματθαῖον εὐαγγελίον. [beginning of text is illegible] ... καὶ ἔρχου κύριε ἰησοῦ ἡ χάρις τοῦ κυρίου ἰησοῦ χριστοῦ μετὰ πάντων τῶν ἁγίων, ἀμήν.

   Novum Testamentum; Nestle and Aland, *op. cit.*, pp. 1–680.

6. ff. 168r–173r   [Title, underlined in red:] τοῦ ἐν ἁγίοις πατρὸς ἡμῶν ἐπιφανίου ἀρχιεπισκόπου κύπρου εἰς τὴν θεόσωμον ταφὴν τοῦ κυρίου ἡμῶν ἰησοῦ χριστοῦ· καὶ εἰς τὸν ἰωσὴφ τὸν ἀπὸ ἀριμαθίας· καὶ εἰς τὴν ἐν ἄδει κατάβασιν. Τί τοῦτο; σήμερον σιγῇ πολλῇ ἐν τῇ γῇ ... ἀμήν.

   Epiphanius of Cyprus, *In Sabbato Magno*; PG 43.440–64.

7. ff. 173r–183r   [Heading, underlined in red:] Ὅτι θεὸς κατὰ φύσιν τὸ πνεῦμα. καὶ ἐκ τῆς οὐσίας τοῦ πατρὸς ... πρότασις· ὡς ἐκ τῶν δι' ἐναντίας. Εἰ διὰ τὸ λέγεσθαι φησὶ παρὰ ταῖς θείαις ... εἴπερ οὐκ ἔστι θεὸς κατὰ τὴν τινῶν ἀβουλίαν. [Several responses are given for each proposition, usually introduced by ἄλλο.]

   Unidentified disputations on theological matters.

8. ff. 183r–188v   ἰωάννου μοναχοῦ καὶ πρεσβυτέρου τοῦ δαμασκινοῦ. λόγος περὶ τῶν ἐν πίστει χριστοῦ κεκοιμημένων ... Τὰ τῶν βρωμάτων ἡδέα καὶ τίμια προτιθέμενα

πολλάκις ... οἱ φυλάξαντες τὴν ὀρθόδοξον πίστιν καὶ τῶν ἀγαθῶν ἐμφορηθῆναι πάντων.
[text breaks off just before end of the sermon, at the bottom of column 2]

John Damascene, *De dormientibus in fide*; PG 95.248-77.

Parchment, ff. i (paper) + 188 + i (paper), 168 x 128 (124 x 90) mm. Written in 2 columns, 41-60 lines per column, ruled in hard point; double bounding lines at top, single at sides and bottom, all full across; triple vertically through center; prickings at sides and top.

I^6, II-III^8, IV^{10}, V-XV^{12}, XVI-XVIII^8. Signatures (letters of the Greek alphabet) on last folio of quire, verso, and first folio of quire, recto, at right or left or both, added by a later hand.

Written throughout in an extremely small Greek minuscule, by five scribes: Scribe 1, ff. 1r-32v and 171r-173r; Scribe 2, ff. 33v-68v; Scribe 3, ff. 69r-168r; Scribe 4, ff. 168r-170v; Scribe 5, ff. 173r-188v. Notes added on f. 33r (originally blank) and in margins by various later hands; in some of the notes on f. 33r Latin letters are used for Greek words.

Two headings and title of Matthew in blue (f. 37r). Initials in red with simple floral ornament. Extensive rubrication. Headpieces and bars between sections in red, blue, green and yellow (all faded). Eusebian Canons done with compass and ruler, in red and blue.

Several folios originally had holes, which have been written around.

Binding: Date? Original sewing on three chain supports laced in a Z pattern into square, flush wooden boards, grooved on the edges. Two pin holes in the edge of the upper board and three holes for each strap in the lower. Traces of rectangular plates [?] at the fore-edge near the head of the upper board and the tail of the lower. Rebacked and the sides covered with cloth.

Written in Byzantium in the 14th century; early provenance unknown. Belonged to Frederick North, fifth Earl of Guilford (1766-1827; no. 546, on tag on spine, on bookplate, and in sale catalogue; part of a note in his hand pasted inside cover; Greek letters chi and gamma stamped in gold on spine); sold to Payne (bookdealer; his name inside front cover). Sir Thomas Phillipps (no. 7682; tag on spine and note on bookplate). Purchased from Laurence Witten with funds from the Jacob Ziskind Charitable Trust in 1957 (MS 16).

Bibliography: Faye and Bond, p. 45, no. 248.
Ziskind Catalogue, p. 47.
C. R. Gregory, *Textkritik des Neuen Testaments* (Leipzig, 1900) v. 1, p. 212, no. 680 (where MS 248 is assigned to the 11th century).
K. Aland, *Kurzgefasste Liste der griechischen Handschriften des Neuen Testaments* (Berlin, 1963) v. 1, p. 97 (Gregory Nr. 680).

MS 249 Byzantium, s. IX/X, XIII/XIV
Psalmi et Odae cum Catena, etc. (in Greek)

I. 1. ff. 1r-7r   Ἰωάννου τοῦ Ψελλοῦ ἐξ ἐπιταγῆς τοῦ αὐτοκράτορος μιχαὴλ υἱοῦ τοῦ δούκα. Οὐκ ἔστι τὸ ψαλτήριον δέσποτά μου βιβλίον ὡς οἱ πολλοὶ ... καὶ γράψω σοι τὴν ἄρρητον· τῶν ψαλμῶν θεωρίαν.

Michael Psellus, *De Psalmorum titulis*; see G. Parassoglou, "A New Manuscript of Psellos' 'On the Titles of the Psalms'," Ἑλληνικά 25 (1972) pp. 440-42, for a list of variant readings based on the printed text of E. Kurtz and F. Drexl, eds., *Michaelis Pselli Scripta Minora* in *Orbis Romanus, Biblioteca dei texti medievali a cura dell' Università Cattolica del Sacro Cuore* 5 (Milan, 1936) v. 1, pp. 389-400.

2. ff. 7v-10v   κοσμᾶ ἰνδικοπλεύστου. πρόλογος εἰς τοὺς ψαλμούς. Μετὰ τὸν μωυσέα καὶ τὸν τούτου διάδοχον ἰησοῦν τὸν τοῦ ναυῆ ... μάθεται καλὸν ποιεῖν καὶ μάλα εἰκότως ἐπήγαγεν ὁ μακάριος δαυίδ.

Cosmas Indicopleustes, *Prologus in Psalmos*; PG 88.248-49, at which point the text deviates from the printed version.

3a. ff. 11r-28v   Δαβὶδ προφήτου καὶ βασιλέως μέλος. ψαλμὸς πρῶτος. Μακάριος ἀνὴρ ὃς οὐκ ἐπορεύθη ἐν βουλῇ ἀσεβῶν ... βέλη εἰς φαρέτραν. Τοῦ κατατοξεῦσαι ἐν σκο// [the text breaks off abruptly. Commentary on *Psalms* 1.1 begins:] Ἔστι μὲν οὖν τὸ κυρίως καὶ πρῶτος μακαριστὸν τὸ ἀληθῶς ἀγαθόν ... [The scribe stopped copying the commentary in the sixth psalm.]

II. 3b.ff. 29r-307v   //τομήνη τοὺς εὐθεῖς [τῇ κ]αρδίᾳ. Ὅτι ἃ σὺ [κατηρ]τίσω αὐτοὶ ... παρ' αὐτοῦ μάχαιραν ἀπεκεφάλισα αὐτόν. Καὶ ἦρα ὄνειδος ἐξ υἱῶν ἰσραήλ. [Commentary ends on f. 306v at the conclusion of Psalm 150:] πᾶσαν ἡλικιάν πρὸς ὑμνῳδίαν καὶ δοξολογίαν αὐτὸς κινῶν. τέλος.

Psalms 1.1-10.2; Psalms 10.2-90. Folios 29 and 30 are misbound; they contain the text of Psalms 37.8-15 and 44.3-9. On f. 31r the text picks up where it ended on f. 28v, but portions are lost throughout the codex due to the placement of binding tape over the written space. Text for the Psalms: A. Rahlfs, ed., *Septuaginta*, ed. 7, v. 2 (Stuttgart, 1935) pp. 1-164. Text for the commentary on the Psalms: no reliable edition is available. Cf. R. Devreesse, "Chaines exégétiques grecques," in *Dictionnaire de la Bible*, Supplément I (Paris, 1928) pp. 1114-39.

4. ff. 308r-331v   [*Odae*:] ᾠδὴ μωυσέως ἐν τῇ ἐξόδῳ. Ἄσωμεν τῷ κυρίῳ ἐνδόξως γὰρ δεδόξασται ἵππον καὶ ἀναβάτην ... τοῦ κατευθῦναι τοὺς πόδας ἡμῶν εἰς ὁδὸν εἰρήνης [Commentary on *Odae:*] α. τοῦ ἁγίου βασιλείου. ᾠδή ἐστιν. ὅσα θεωρίας ἔχεται ψιλῆς καὶ θεολογίας ... ἐπίλαμψιν ἐποιήσατο ἐπὶ πάντα τὰ ἔθνη.

The text of the *Odae* corresponds to the "Novem Odae ecclesiae graecae" in Rahlfs (*op. cit.*, pp. 164-78) except that his eighth is divided in two in MS 249, after v. 56, and two additional Christian verses are added after

v. 88 (f. 328v): Εύλογεΐτε απόστολοι προφήται και μάρτυρες κυρίου τον κύριον ... and Εύλογοΰμεν πατέρα και υιόν και άγιον πνεύμα τον κύριον.... No reliable edition of this catena has yet been published. For discussion, see R. Devreesse, *op. cit.*, pp. 1139-40.

Beinecke MS 249 is composed of two distinct parts, the first of which was added at a considerably later date to replace lost or damaged leaves at the beginning of the codex. Part I: ff. 1-28; Part II: ff. 29-331.

Parchment, ff. 331 + i (paper), 185 x 136. Written in 2 columns, ca. 39 lines (the main text occupies only 17 lines of the inner column [85 x 53 mm.] and the accompanying commentary completely surrounds it, often covering the folio from top to bottom). The scribe of the older portion (Part II) ruled the parchment in hard point, on the hair side before folding, with double vertical bounding lines. The second scribe (Part I) preserved the format established by his predecessor. Prickings are sometimes visible in Part II along the outer edge.

The codex seems to have been composed originally of quires of 8, but the rebinding is so close and poorly done that it is impossible to collate it accurately. There are no catchwords or signatures, probably due to the severe trimming that has also affected lines of the commentary.

Part I written in a heavy round minuscule; Part II in a fine regular hand with an admixture of uncial forms.

Crude headpiece (f. 11r), headings and small initials in red; some minor initials in gold.

First leaf is rubbed and illegible in many places.

Binding: s. xix. Edges spattered with red. Half tan calf, blind- and gold-tooled with marbled paper sides.

Written in Byzantium ca. 900 and supplemented ca. 1300. Eighteenth-century ownership note of Basil Katzeskyriakos (f. 9r). Belonged to Frederick North, 5th Earl of Guilford (1766-1827; bookplate and handwritten note of contents inside front cover; no. 450 on bookplate, spine and in sale catalogue; Greek letters chi and gamma stamped in gold on spine); sold to Payne. Sir Thomas Phillipps (no. 7713, on spine). Purchased from Laurence Witten with funds from the Jacob Ziskind Charitable Trust in 1957 (MS 15).

Bibliography: Faye and Bond, pp. 45-46, no. 249.
Ziskind Catalogue, p. 47.

MS 250 Italy, s. XV^2
Polyaenus, Strategemata (in Greek)

f. 1r-2r blank; ff. 2v-3v Table of contents for first chapter; ff. 4r-166r *Πολυαίνου στρατηγικά βιβλίον πρώτον. τήν μέν κατά των περσών και παρθυέων νίκην ιερώτατοι βασιλείς ... τούς μέν δή καθείρξαι οι σπαρτιάται. αί θυγατέραις τών//*

Each chapter of the text is preceded by a table of contents, in red; ff. 113v-117r are blank, as in other manuscripts of this text. Beinecke MS 250 omits a passage in Book 6, chapters 29 through 45, and the text ends abruptly in the middle of a sentence. See E. Woefflin and J. Melber, eds., *Polyaeni strategematon libri VIII* (Stuttgart, 1970) pp. 3-425; F. Schindler, *Die Überlieferung des Strategemata des Polyainos*, in *Österreichische Akademie der Wissenschaften, Sitzungsberichte Philosophisch-Historische Klasse* 284, 1 (Vienna, 1973) esp. pp. 133, 137-139, siglum Y.

Paper (watermarks similar to Briquet Ange 660), ff. i (modern paper) + 170 + i (modern paper). The present foliation begins on f. 2, so that there are only 169 numbered leaves. 309 x 215 (220 x 119) mm. Written in 24 long lines, ruled in hard point; single vertical bounding lines full across.

I^4, $II-XIV^{10}$, XV^8, XVI^{10}, XVII^8, XVIII^{10}. Catchwords perpendicular to text along binding edge; signatures are letters of the alphabet on recto in center of lower margin, in red.

Written by a single scribe in a compact calligraphic minuscule.

Tables before each chapter, headpieces, headings, small initials and some marginal notations are in red.

Binding: Date? Pink paper case with an inked label.

Written in Northern Italy (Venice?) in the late 15th century, possibly by a member of the circle of Michael Glynzunios (Schindler, *op. cit.*, p. 139). Signature of John Price (1600-1676?), who became Professor of Greek at the University of Pisa, on f. 2r: "Joannes Pricaeus. Venetijs. 1637." Unidentified inscription (s. xviii) on f. 1r: "Al. S. Manusso Chrisi." Belonged to Sir Thomas Phillipps (his acquisition from an unknown source; no. 10452, on spine, and stamp on f. i). Purchased from Laurence Witten with funds from the Jacob Ziskind Charitable Trust in 1957 (MS 52).

Bibliography: Faye and Bond, p. 46, no. 250.
Ziskind Catalogue, p. 52.

Indices

I. Manuscripts by Places and Periods   365

II. Dated Manuscripts   367

III. General Index   368

IV. Illuminators and Scribes   392

V. Provenance   393

VI. Other Manuscripts Cited   398

VII. Incipits   400

Numbers in the index entries refer to the manuscript number rather than to the page number.

Index I

Manuscripts by Places and Periods

ARMENIA:
s. XV, 3 (no. 45)

BELGIUM:
s. XIII/XIV, 157
s. XIV, 157

BOHEMIA:
s. XV, 225

BYZANTIUM:
s. IX/X, 249
s. X, 187
s. XI, 150
s. XII, 235
s. XII/XIII [?], 237
s. XIII, 187
s. XIII/XIV, 241, 249
s. XIV, 234, 235, 248
s. XV, 139, 187, 247
s. XVI, 238
s. XVII, 139

CRETE [?]:
s. XVI, 236

DENMARK:
s. XV, 39

DENMARK [?]:
s. XVI, 31

ENGLAND:
s. XII, 154, 181, 189
s. XIII, 21, 25, 81
s. XIV, 3 (nos. 47, 52), 22, 60, 62, 220
s. XIV/XV, 86, 125
s. XV, 3 (no. 34), 10, 15, 27, 88, 101, 163, 171, 223
s. XV/XVI, 25
s. XVI, 89, 97, 100, 105, 195, 200
s. XVII, 40, 45, 74, 75
s. XVIII, 11

ENGLAND [?]:
s. XIII-XIV, 3 (no. 39)
s. XV, 84

FLANDERS:
s. XV, 16, 110, 129, 190, 218, 226, 230

FLANDERS [?]:
s. XIII/XIV, 3 (no. 29)
s. XV, 109
s. XVI, 246

FRANCE:
s. VIII, 193
s. XI [?], 206
s. XII, 3 (nos. 2, 4)
s. XIII, 3 (nos. 1, 5, 37), 26, 82, 206, 207, 214, 229
s. XIII/XIV, 19
s. XIV, 3 (no. 33), 18, 19, 33, 83, 94, 227
s. XIV/XV, 38
s. XV, 3 (nos. 28, 44), 17, 85, 106, 107, 121, 203, 204, 212, 215-17
s. XV-XVIII, 46-54
s. XVI, 3 (nos. 16, 46, 53), 18, 82, 90, 108, 162
s. XVII, 82

FRANCE [?]:
s. XIII/XIV, 3 (no. 29)
s. XIV, 199

GERMANY:
s. XII, 191, 225
s. XIII, 3 (nos. 3, 27), 195, 211
s. XIV-XV, 3 (no. 8)
s. XIV/XV, 3 (no. 31)
s. XV, 3 (nos. 10, 12), 5, 7, 8, 20, 24, 41,

s. XV, 3 (nos. 10, 12), 5, 7, 8, 20, 24, 41, 73, 77, 92, 134, 155, 174, 177, 188, 197, 205, 209, 219, 224, 233
s. XVI, 9, 28, 209
s. XVI/XVII, 99, 135
s. XVII, 122
GERMANY [?]:
s. XIII–XIV, 3 (nos. 39, 42)
s. XVI, 31

ITALY:
s. XII, 126, 210
s. XIV, 3 (nos. 7, 30), 6, 13, 57, 80, 102, 127, 175, 178, 184, 198, 222
s. XIV/XV, 3 (no. 38), 111, 232
s. XV, 2, 3 (nos. 11, 50), 4, 12, 37, 42, 43, 57, 58, 61, 63–68, 70–72, 76, 87, 91, 93, 111-14, 124, 133, 136, 137, 143–47, 149, 151, 152, 156, 158–61, 164–70, 172, 173, 176, 179, 180, 183, 185, 186, 192, 194, 221, 222, 231, 239, 240, 244, 245, 250
s. XV/XVI, 1, 103
s. XVI, 3 (nos. 40, 41), 56, 59, 98, 104, 208, 213, 242, 243
s. XVI/XVII, 30
s. XVII, 36, 37

ITALY [?]:
s. XII, 55
s. XV, 3 (no. 13), 14, 69, 188
s. XV/XVI, 3 (no. 17)

LOWER RHINE:
s. XV, 196

NETHERLANDS:
s. XV, 32
s. XV/XVI, 153
NETHERLANDS [?]:
s. XIV, 199

PERU:
s. XVIII, 34A
PORTUGAL [?]:
s. XV, 228

SPAIN:
s. XV, 34, 138
s. XV/XVI, 182
s. XVI, 35, 78, 79, 128
s. XVII, 29, 34, 78

YUGOSLAVIA:
s. XV–XVI, 55

Index II

Dated Manuscripts

1229,	MS 214
1357,	MS 227
1391 [?],	MS 62
1396,	MS 94
1415,	MS 222
1422,	MS 225
1430,	MS 61
1440 [ca.],	MS 205
1442 [?],	MS 155
1452,	MS 20
1454,	MS 161
1454,	MS 3 (no. 45)
1458 [ca.],	MS 2
1461,	MS 58
1465 [ca.],	MS 228
1468,	MS 67
1469,	MS 67
1474,	MS 3 (no. 11)
1475,	MS 70
1476,	MS 226
1487,	MS 34
1502,	MS 162
1513,	MS 28
1515,	MS 104
1534 [?],	MS 59
1541,	MS 213
1550,	MS 35
1562,	MS 89
1564 [ca.],	MS 97
1576–1579/80,	MS 195
1578,	MS 18
1598,	MS 98
1606,	MS 139
1686,	MS 34
1704,	MS 11
1740,	MS 34A

Index III

General Index

"Alas, alas, alas is my chief song," 91
"A qui vens tu tes coquilles," 91
"A une damme," 91
"A vous sans aultre," 91
Abril, Pedro Simon. *See* Pedro Simon Abril
Acciaiuolus, Nicolaus, 197
Account Book, 94, 195
Accounts, 55, 222, 228
"Accueilly m'a la belle," 91
Adolph of Cleves, 230
Aelian: *De instruendis aciebus* (in Greek), 242
Aelred of Rievaulx: *De amicitia*, 157
Aemilius Paullus, 133
Aeneas Sylvius Piccolomini. *See* Pius II, Pope
Aeschines: excerpts, 63
Ages of man, seven, 243
Ages of man, ten, 163
Agogo Mago (Agosto Mago), 76
Agriculture, 233
Alagonia, Artaluccio. *See* Arthelouche de Alagona
Alain de Lille. *See* Alanus de Insulis
Alanus de Insulis: *Moralium dogma*, 102
Albertano da Brescia: *De amore et dilectione Dei*, 102; *Liber consolationis et consilii*, 102; *Liber de doctrina dicendi et tacendi*, 102
Albertanus Brixiensis. *See* Albertano da Brescia
Albertus Magnus: *Commentarii in librum IV Petri Lombardi*, 20; *De animalibus*, 77
Aldine Press, 59
Alexander of Hales: commentary on, 146
Alexander the Great, 194
Alexander VI, Pope, 9, 153
Alfonso I, of Naples, 167
Aloisius, Johannes Tuscanus. *See* Johannes Tuscanus Aloisius
Alphabet, tabular of Greek and Latin equivalents, 166
Ambrose: *De mysteriis* (extracts), 181; *De sacramentis* (extracts), 181; extracts, 80
Ambrose, pseudo-: *Epistola*, 146
Ambrosius Autpertus, attributed author: *Sermo*, 224

Ambrosius de Vignate: *Oratio*, 188
Amé Cassian, 90
Amphilochius: *Vita Basilii*, 177
Anastasius of Sinai: extracts (in Greek), 238; *Fidei notitia* (in Greek), 238; *Quaestiones* (in Greek), 235, 238
Anastasius, tr., 177
Andrea Bragadin: *Magister aucupatoris*, 232
Anglo-Norman, 60, 86
Anselm: extracts, 80
Anselm, pseudo-: *Epistola*, 111
Anthony of Burgundy, 129
Antiphonal, 78, 178
Antiphonal (fragments), 19, 55, 56, 178
Antoninus, St.: *Confessionale*, 4
Antonio Beccari. *See* Antonio da Ferrara
Antonio da Ferrara: *Canzoni*, 222
Antonio Grimani. *See* Grimani, Antonio
Antonio Loschi, 133
Antonio, Nicolas, 138
Archbishops, lists of, 163
Aristotle: *Analytica posteriora* (in Greek), 234; *Analytica priora* (in Greek), 234; *Categoriae* (in Greek), 234; commentary on (in Greek), 234, 245; commentary on (in Latin), 3 (no. 7), 21, 225; *De caelo* (in Greek), 234; *De incessu animalium* (in Greek), 234; *De interpretatione* (in Greek), 234; *De iuventute* (in Greek), 234; *De longitudine vitae* (in Greek), 234; *Ethica Nicomachea* (in Greek), 240; *Ethica*, Italian tr., 151; *Ethica*, Spanish tr., 29; extracts (in Latin), 63, 225; *Mechanica* (in Greek), 245; *Physica* (fragment), 21; Scholia on (in Greek), 234
ARMS
Alfonso II, Duke of Calabria, King of Naples, 143
Aston, Sir Walter, 97
Austria, Duchy of, 127
Babthorpe, Sir William, 97
Bacon, Sir Nycholas, 97
Barkeley, Sir John, 97
Bergen, 229
Bouchorst, 229

Bowes, Sir George, 97
Braye, Sir Edward, 97
Capell, Sir Edward, 97
Cary, Sir Henry, 97
Cattelen, Sir Robert, 97
Cheyney, Sir Henry, 97
Conwey, Sir John, 97
Coquille family, 217
Corvinus, type A, 145
Court [?], 229
Crechy, 229
Darcy of Chiche, Lord, 97
Darcy of Darcy, Lord, 97
Dethicke, Sir Gilbert, 97
Drury, Henry, 244, 247
Elizabeth I, Queen, 97
Eugène of Savoy, 226
Fairefax, Sir William, 97
Fauzonus, Francischus, 162
Fiennes, 229
Fitzpaterike, Sir Barnaby, 97
Florence, Santa Maria Novella, 42
Fulmerston, Sir Rychard, 97
Garnier family, 217
Gonçalez de Valdes, 35
Gresham, Sir Thomas, 97
Grey, Sir Arthur, 97
Gruythuse of Bruges, 229
Gui de Dampierre, 229
Guillaume de Termonde, 229
Harper, Sir William, 97
Hopton, Sir Owen, 97
Huet, Sir William, 97
Laud, William, 113
Leigh, Sir Thomas, 97
Lodge, Sir Thomas, 97
Lyttelton, Sir Edward, 97
Mallorye, Sir William, 97
Mortaigne, 229
Newporte, Sir Rychard, 97
Northe, Sir Roger, 97
Northwyck, 229
Parrey, Sir Thomas, 97
Piccolomini, 2
Poynes, Sir Nycholas, 97
Poynynge, Sir Adryan, 97
Prato, convent at, 42
Ryche, Sir Roberte, 97
Sheffelde, Lord, 97
Souche, Sir John, 97
Speke, Sir George, 97

Tinagero Rodríguez de la Escalera, 34
Trivulzio of Milan, 1
Umpton, Sir Edward, 97
Unidentified, 1, 9, 36, 76, 158, 229, 231
Weston, Sir Henry, 97
White, Sir John, 97
Williams, Sir Henry, 97
Arms, paintings of, 97, 230
Arthelouche de Alagona, 162
Arthurian Romances, 227, 229
Asceticism, passages on (in Greek), 238
Aston, Sir Walter, 97
Astrology, 67, 163, 166, 220
Astronomy, 163, 234
Athanasius: creed of (in Greek), 236; extracts (in Greek), 238; *Vita Beati Antonii*, 177
Attainder of Lord Cromwell, 40
"Au povre par nécessité," 91
Aubert le Mire, 214
Augustine, 28; *De ciuitate Dei*, French tr., 215; *Enarrationes in Psalmos* (extracts), 181; *Epigrammata* of Prosper Aquitanus, 15; extracts, 80; references to, 209; *Sermo* (extract), 181
Augustine, pseudo-: *De nativitate et passione Christi*, 80; *Disciplina monasterii*, 5; *Sermo* (extract), 181; *Sermo de annuntiatione*, 224; *Sermo de humilitate et obediencia*, 157; *Soliloquia* (in Greek), 236
Augustinian use, 134, 196
Autpertus, Ambrosius. *See* Ambrosius Autpertus
Avignon, 83, 206
Ayala, Pedro López de. *See* López de Ayala, Pedro

Babthorpe, Sir William, 97
Bacon, Francis: extracts, 75
Bacon, Nathaniel, 195
Bacon, Sir Nycholas, 97
Barbarus, Petrus, 104
Barbingant: *Chanson*, 91
Barkeley, Sir John, 97
Bartolomeo da Sulmona, 188
Basil the Great: *Ascetica* (in Greek), 235; *De libris gentilium legendis*, Latin tr., 179; extracts (in Latin), 63; (in Greek), 238, 241; letter to, 177; *Vita* 177
Basilici tyranni umbra, 45
Basilicus, Byzantine emperor, 45

Basin, A.: *Chanson*, 91
Beccadelli, Antonio, 69
Bede, astrological notes attributed to, 220; *Expositio super Lucam*, 80; extracts, 80; *Homilia* (extract), 181; prayers, 110; *Super Canticum Canticorum* (extracts), 80
Bedingham: *Chansons*, 91
"Bel Acueil," 91
Beltran de la Cueva, Duke of Alburquerque, 138
Benedict XII, Pope, 28
Benedictine use, 28
Berardinus Aquilius, 67
Berardinus Petrus, 67
Bergamo, 42
Bernard of Clairvaux: extracts, 5, 63; *Hymnus de Sancto Maluchia*, 177; *Vita Malachie episcopi*, 177; prayers, 16, 110, 134, 218; references to, 209
Bernard, pseudo-: *De nativitate et de passione Christi*, 80
Bernardine, St., of Siena: *Tractatus de restitutionibus*, 6
Bessarion, Cardinal, 113
Bible, 81-83, 126, 193 (fragment), 206; commentary on, 80, 154; commentary on (in Greek), 241, 249; extracts, 75, 80, 146; *Glossa ordinaria*, 126, 210; Matthew (fragment), 210; New Testament (in English), 125; New Testament (in Greek), 150, 246, 248; New Testament, commentary on (in Greek), 235; Numbers (fragment), 126; Old Testament, commentary on (in Greek), 241
Bible concordance, 19
Bible historiale, 129
Billinge, Jo, tr., 74
Binchois (Binchoys), Gilles. *See* Gilles Binchois
BINDERS
 Birdsall and Son, 105
 Bretherton, 59
 Chambolle-Duru, 99
 Cockerell, 150, 207
 Conti-Borbone, 103
 Gruel, 143
 Lewis, 168, 171, 217, 244, 247
 Lortic, 214
 Marius-Michel, 91
 Matthews, 41
 Miyar, 29

P. S. [?], 135
Ramage, 231
Rivière, 33
Thebaron, 158
Yale Library Conservation Studio, 17, 73, 129, 149
Zaehnsdorf, 65, 189
BINDINGS
 Armorial, 36, 113
 Armorial, Drury, Henry, 244, 247
 Armorial, Eugène of Savoy, 226
 Bruges [?], 246
 Cretan, 236
 Date?, 32, 55, 61, 80, 179, 206, 238, 248, 250
 Dated-1850, 59
 Dated-1899, 207
 Dated-1961, 150
 Dutch [?], 27, 84
 German [?], 27, 84
 Girdle-book, 84
 Greek, 243
 Levantine [?], 213
 Tuscan, 239
 with monogram, IHS, 104
 with monogram, Riant, comte Paul, 24, 31
 with monogram, Vitta, Baron Joseph, 91
 14th century, 102
 15th century, 4, 5, 12, 20, 27, 84, 87, 136, 145, 225, 239
 15th-16th century, 7, 60, 77, 212, 220, 221, 224, 237
 16th century, 9, 35, 89, 106, 127, 139, 153, 169, 187, 188, 190, 191, 196, 205, 208, 213, 243, 246
 16th [?] century, 67, 68, 177, 227
 16th-17th century, 25, 43, 78, 100, 134, 162, 163, 211, 219, 232, 235, 236
 16th-17th [?] century, 39, 57
 17th century, 36, 79, 104, 107, 113, 135, 172, 185, 216, 218, 228
 17th-18th century, 38, 42, 138, 155, 161
 18th century, 1, 2, 10, 11, 16, 26, 45-54, 63, 93, 101, 114, 125, 133, 151, 178, 199, 204, 226, 229
 18th [?] century, 34
 18th-19th century, 37, 64, 70, 82, 86, 94, 108, 124, 147, 156, 173, 175, 234
 18th-19th [?] century, 242
 19th century, 14, 15, 19, 24, 29, 31, 33, 41, 58, 59, 65, 66, 69, 74, 76, 81, 85, 90,

General Index

97–99, 103, 105, 109–12, 121, 122, 144, 149, 154, 159, 160, 164–68, 171, 174, 181, 182, 184, 186, 195, 198, 203, 207, 215, 217, 222, 223, 230, 231, 233, 240, 244, 245, 247, 249
19th/20th century, 143
19th–20th century, 6, 28, 30, 71, 72, 83, 88, 91, 92, 128, 137, 152, 158, 170, 180, 214
20th century, 17, 18, 73, 126, 129, 150, 157, 183, 189, 194, 197, 209, 210, 241
Birds, 13, 124, 162, 189
Birgitta, St.: *Orationes*, 24; prayers (in German), 24, 28; *Regula Sancti Salvatoris*, 5; *Revelationes*, 5, 24; *Vita*, 24
Bisticci, Vespasiano da. *See* Vespasiano da Bisticci
Bloodletting, 166
Boccaccio, Giovanni: *Filostrato*, 222; *Filocolo* (fragment), 3 (no. 38)
Boethius: commentary on, 85, 198; *De consolatione philosophiae*, 61, 84, 85, 175; *De consolatione philosophiae* (extracts), 63, 80; *De consolatione philosophiae*, French tr., 38; extracts, 225; references to, 209
Bonaventure: *Breviloquium*, Bk. 4, 146; Latin devotional text attributed to, 223; prayers (in Dutch), 153
Bonaventure, pseudo-: *Meditationes de passione Christi*, 27
Bonet, Honoré. *See* Honoré Bonet
Book curse, 214
Borromeo family, 37
Bourges, 217
Bovet, Honoré. *See* Honoré Bonet
Bowes, Sir George, 97
Bragadin, Andrea. *See* Andrea Bragadin
Braye, Sir Edward, 97
Bretigny, treaty of, 86
Breviary (diurnal), 7
Breviary (fragments), 3 (nos. 2, 3, 8)
Breviary, use of Carmelites, 41
Brigges, George, 195
Brittany, 18
Bruges, 110, 129, 190, 218, 226, 230
Brullinus, Aloysius, 98
Bruni, Leonardo, 14, 133, 179: *De primo bello punico* (in Italian), 194
Bruni, Leonardo, tr., 14, 63, 133, 151, 179
Brut Chronicle, 86

Buda, palace of, 145
Burial, anniversary of, 9
Burial, commemoration of, 9
Business accounts, 55, 94, 195, 222, 228
Busnois (Busnoys, Antoine de Busnes): *Chansons*, 91
Byzantium, 249

Caesar: *Commentarii de bello gallico*, French tr., 226; *Opera omnia*, 87
Caestre, Richard de. *See* Richard de Caestre
Calderini, Domizio: commentary on Martial, 64
Calendar, 7, 16, 17, 41, 88, 106–8, 110, 190, 196, 211, 217, 220, 248
Calixtus III, Pope, 110
Camaieu-gris, 108
Camargue, 162
Cambridge University, 75; Laws and Statutes, 11
Camillus Venetus, 242
Canonical obligations (in Greek), 243
Canzoni, 222
Capell, Sir Edward, 97
Carmelites, use of, 41
Caron (Firminus? Jehan or Jean? Philippe?): *Chansons*, 91
Carpianus, 248
Carta de foresta, 88, 89
Carta ejecutoria (in Spanish), 34, 35
Cary, Sir Henry, 97
Cassian, Aymé. *See* Amé Cassian
Castor *tribunus militum*, 45
Catalogus librorum, 59
Catena, 249
Catena on Isaiah (in Greek), 241
Cato, 133
Cattelen, Sir Robert, 97
Catullus: *Carmina*, 186
"Ce qu'on fait a quatimini," 91
Cecil, William, Lord Burghley, 105
Cenon [?], 217
"Chansonnier, Mellon," 91
Charles of Anjou, 233
Charles the Bold, Duke of Burgundy, 226
Charles V, Emperor of the Holy Roman Empire, 35
Charles V, King of France, 215
Charles VI, King of France, 94
Charm against thieves, 163
Charms, 163

Charter, Julianna, 86
Cheyney, Sir Henry, 97
Chivalry, 230
Choirbook (fragment), 209
Christian III, King of Denmark and Norway, 31
Chrysoloras, Manuel: *Erotemata* (in Greek), 239
Ciano del Borgo San Sepolcro: *Canzoni*, 222
Cicero: *De amicitia*, 157, 170, 179; *De officiis*, 158, 159, 170; *De senectute*, 179; *Epistolae ad familiares*, 92, 185; extracts, 75; glosses, 92, 185; *Orationes*, 93; references to, 209; *Tusculanae disputationes*, 152, 160, 169; *Vita*, 133
Cicero, pseudo-: *Invectiva in Crispum Sallustium*, 93; *Oratio antequam in exilium iret*, 93; *Synonyma*, 179
Civil law, 31, 39, 75, 88, 89, 104, 163, 212, 213
Civil Law (fragments), 3 (nos. 10, 30)
Civilization, prose sketch in Latin, 64
Claudian: *De raptu Proserpinae*, 180
Clement VIII, Pope, 36
Clement, Pope, 109
Codex Budensis Rhenani, 145
Cologne, 9, 24, 196
Columbus, Christopher, 128
Colyk, Medicyn for, 84
Comedy: extracts on, 73
Comestor, Petrus. *See* Petrus Comestor
Commandments, Ten, precepts on, 146
"Comme femme desconfortee," 91
Commendationes animarum, 9, 109
Comment on fait de nouuel vn empereur par election, 230
Commentary on unidentified Latin legal text, in French (fragment), 3 (no. 33)
Commonplace Book, Lawyer's, 75
Compte de la vennerie de Charles VI, 94
Confession, 163; precepts on, 146
Confession Manual (in Greek), 243
Conwey, Sir John, 97
Cookery, 163
Coquille family, 217
Coram Rege Roll (fragment), 62
Cornelius Nepos: *De illustribus ducibus*, 164
Corpus Iuris Civilis (fragment), 3 (no. 30)
"Corvinus Tacitus," 145
Corye, Henry, 195

Cosmas Indicopleustes: *Prologus in Psalmos* (in Greek), 249
Courgnilleroy, Philippe de, 94
Cousin, Jehan, 3 (no. 16)
Cracow, 225
Cramer, Daniel, funeral orations (in German), 99
Cremona, 210
Crescentiis, Petrus de. *See* Pietro de' Crescenzi
Crescenzi, Pietro de'. *See* Pietro de' Crescenzi
Crete, 104
Cristoforus Pyerius, 67
Crivelli, Leodrisio, 188
Cromwell, Thomas, Earl of Essex, 40
Cyril: *Epistola Synodica* (extract, in Latin), 181; extracts (in Greek), 241

Dalmatia, 55
Dancus rex, 127
Daniel, prophet, 163
Darcy of Chiche, Lord, 97
Darcy of Darcy, Lord, 97
Das Leiden Iesu Christi, 219
De modo tenendi Parliamentum, 86, 163
De spiritu Guidonis, 163
"De tous biens plaine," 91
Decembrio, Piercandido, 188
Demetrius Cydonius, tr., 236
Demosthenes, 133; excerpts, 63
Denmark, 31; laws, 39
Des droits d'armes, 230
Des Moulins, Guyard. *See* Guyart des Moulins
Dethick(e), Sir Gilbert: *Book of Arms*, 97
Diagrams, geometrical figures, 245; military tactics, 242; musical, 208; Syllogisms, 234; Tabernacle, 129. *See also* Drawings, Illuminations
Dialogus inter S. Basilium et S. Gregorium Nazianzenum (in Greek), 235
Diego de Valera: *Espejo de verdadera nobleza*, 230
Diego Guillén de Ávila, tr., 182
Diploma (in Latin), 98
Dives and Pauper, 228
Divine Office (in Greek), 139
Documents, collections of, 46–54, 55, 213
Dogs, 100, 121, 127, 232
Dominican Laurent. *See* Frère Laurent
Dominican use, 205

"Dona gentile," 91
Donatus: *De barbarismo et soloecismo*, 66
"Donnés l'assault," 91
Drawings, angel, 238; bird, 238; falconer with bird, 222; ghost [?], 222; heavenly ladder, 237; incubator for eggs, 233; knight in armor, 166; ladder of Divine Ascent, 237; lion, 121; schematic, 181; Soullart, 121; tabernacle, 129. *See also* Diagrams, Illuminations
Dreams, interpretation of, 163
Ducale, 104
Duchesne, Jean. *See* Jean Duchesne
Dufay, Guillaume. *See* Guillaume Dufay

Easter, finding the date of, 88
Eastern Orthodox Church, 187, 236, 238, 241, 243, 249
Ecclesiastical document, in Latin (fragment), 3 (no. 46)
Educational precepts, 209
Edward of Norwich, 2nd Duke of York: *Master of Game*, 101, 163
Eickstedt, Valentin von: *Pommersche Chronik*, 99
Elements of the world, four, 163
Elizabet Ebyn, 7
Elizabeth I, Queen, 11, 97
Emilius Probus. *See* Cornelius Nepos
Emperors, lists of, 163
"En soustenant vostre querelle," 91
"Enfermé suys je en la tour," 91
Epiphanius of Cyprus: *In Sabbato Magno* (in Greek), 248
Epistolary forms, 146
Erfurt, 225
"Est-il merchy," 91
Ethelred, St. *See* Aelred of Rievaulx
Eucharistic proof texts, 181
Eugenius IV, Pope, 37
Euphemianus, 45
Euphemius, tr., 177
Eusebian Canons (in Greek), 248
Eusebius: extracts (in Greek), 241; letter to, 177; letter to Carpianus (in Greek), 248
Eusebius Gallicanus: *De corpore Christi*, 181
Evagrius, tr., 177
Excerpta e gerontico (in Greek), 238
Excerptum de patientia (in Greek), 238
Exchequer, verses on, 163

Fairefax, Sir William, 97
Falconry, 76, 79, 90, 100, 103, 124, 127, 138, 162, 163, 232, 233
Fathers of the Church, extracts, 146
Fawkners' Glasse, The, 100
Fazio degli Uberti: *Canzoni*, 222
Federico Borromeo: *Vita S. Caroli Borromei*, 37
Ferdinand II, of Aragon, 213
Ferdinand V, King of Spain, 34
Ferdinand, King of Naples, 124
Ferrante I, of Naples, 91
Ferrara, 172, 222
Fether, William, 195
Filelfo, Francesco, tr., 63
Fishing, 101, 171, 233
Fitzpaterike, Sir Barnaby, 97
Five wounds of Christ, prayer to, 9
Florence, 3 (no. 41), 93, 114, 133, 151, 156, 158, 165, 168, 178, 221
Florence [?], 76, 87, 160
Forestry, law and legislation, 88, 89
"Fortune, par ta cruaulté," 91
Fragments. *See* Manuscript fragments bound in
Franciscan use, 78, 146
Franco abbas luginensis, 196
Frederick II, King of Denmark and Norway, 31
Frederick III, Holy Roman Emperor, 230
Frère Laurent: *Somme le Roi*, 204
Friedrich II, Emperor of Germany, 136
Frye, Walter. *See* Walter Frye
Fulmerston, Sir Rychard, 97
Funeral orations, in German, 99

Gadrip. *See* Ghatrif
Galen: scholia on (in Greek), 234
Gandino, Bernardo, tr., 30
Garnier family, 217
Gautier de Châtillon: *Moralium dogma*, 102
Gazeus *Rhetor*, 45
Genealogical table, 86
"Gentil madona," 91
Geoffrey of Bath, 157
Geometry, 225
Gerbertus. *See* Sylvester II, Pope
Gerson, Johannes. *See* Johannes Gerson
Ghatrif, 103
Ghent-Bruges, 9
Ghent-Bruges school models, 9

Giannozzo Sacchetti: *Canzone*, 222
Gigli, Giovanni. *See* Giovanni Gigli
Gilles Binchois: *Chanson*, 91
"Gimbel Hours," 190
Giordano Ruffo: *Marescalcia equorum*, 136, 161, 163
Giovanni Gigli: *Quaestiones de observantia quadragesimali*, 25
Girdle-book, 84
Glossa ordinaria, 126, 210
Glosses, 3 (nos. 1, 37), 57, 67, 72, 92, 185, 214
Gloucestershire, 75
Golden Number, 7, 88
Gonçalez de Valdes, Lope, 35
Gonçalez de Valdes, Pedro, 35
Gonzaga, Federico, duke of Mantua, 213
Gonzaga, Francesco, marquis of Mantua, 213
Gospels (in Greek), 150
Gracchus, Gaius, 133
Gracchus, Tiberius, 133
Gradual, 42
Gradual (fragment), 3 (no. 31)
Grammar, 66
Grammar notebook, 3 (no. 34)
Granada, 35
Great Britain: exchequer, 163; kings, 86; laws, statutes, etc., 88, 89, 163; Parliament, 86, 163; succession, 86
Greek grammar, 239
Greek language, 239
Gregorius Magnus. *See* Gregory the Great
Gregory IX, Pope: *Decretales* (fragment), 3 (no. 1)
Gregory of Sebenico, 55
Gregory of Tours: *Vita Sancti Brictii*, 177; *Vita Sancti Martini*, 177
Gregory the Great: *Dialogorum liber* (extract), 181; *Moralia in Iob* (extracts), 80; Prayers, 28, 110, 218
Gregory, Church of St., 55
Gresham, Sir Thomas, 97
Grey, Sir Arthur, 97
Griffolini, Francesco, tr., 167
Grimani, Antonio, 104
Gualterus Anglicus: *Fabulae*, 80
Guarino da Verona: abridged grammar (in Greek), 239; *Argumenta*, 67, 112; extracts, 63; verses on Catullus, 186
Guarino Veronese. *See* Guarino da Verona

Gubbio, 152
Guelloti, Brother Robertus, 3 (no. 46)
Guiart des Moulins. *See* Guyart des Moulins
Guicennas, 127
Guido de Corvo, Ghost story of, 163
Guillén de Ávila, Diego. *See* Diego Guillén de Ávila
Guillaume de Conches: *Moralium dogma*, 102
Guillaume de Lorris, 33
Guillaume de Saint-Amour, 199
Guillaume Dufay: *Chansons*, 91
Guillelmus falconarius, 127
Gulielmus de Sancto Amore. *See* Guillaume de Saint-Amour
Gulielmus Senonensis, stationer, 207
Guyart des Moulins, tr., 129
Guzmán, Nuño de, 151

Hainaut, 111
Hampshire, 88
Harper, Sir William, 97
Hawking. *See* Falconry
Hayne van Ghizeghem: *Chanson*, 91
Henry IV, King of England, 86
Heraldry, 97, 230
Herbs, 163
Hernán Pérez de Oliva. *See* Pérez de Oliva, Hernán
Herodian: *Historiae*, Spanish translation of Diego Guillén de Ávila, 182
Heron, Robert: *Argus*, 105
Hesines, Claude, 3 (no. 16)
Hewitt, Sir Thomas, tr., 74
Hierocles: *In aureum Pythagoreorum carmen commentarius*, 247
Hilary: extracts, 80; *Liber de Trinitate* (extracts), 181
Hilton, Walter, tr., 223
Hirtius, Aulus, 87
Historia Alexandri Magni, 194
Historia septem sapientum Romae, 163
Holy Grail, 229
Honoré Bonet, 230
Honoré Bovet. *See* Honoré Bonet
Hopton, Sir Owen, 97
"Hora cridar 'Oymè'," 91
Horace: extracts, 75, 112, 174
Horatian meters, 45
Horn, hunting codes for, 163, 200
Horoscopes, 166

Horses, 127, 136, 137, 161, 163, 244
Hours of the Blessed Virgin Mary: Premonstratensian use, 9; use of Paris, 17, 106; use of Rome, 16, 108, 110 (partly in Flemish), 190; use of Rouen, 107; use of Sarum [?], 109; use of Utrecht, (32) in Netherlandish); fragments of, 3 (nos. 28, 44), 19 [?]; use unidentified, 10, 191, 217
Hours of the Compassion, 9
Hours of the Cross, Short, 9, 17, 106–10, 190, 217
Hours of the Holy Spirit, Short, 17, 106–8, 190, 217
Hours of the Passion (in Low German), 218
Hubert, Nicolas, 3 (no. 16)
Huet, Sir Thomas. *See* Hewitt, Sir Thomas
Huet, Sir William, 97
Hugh of St. Victor, 13, 189, 196
Hughes of Fouilloy. *See* Hugo de Folieto
Hugo de Folieto: *De medicina animae*, 189; *Moralitates de avibus*, 13, 189; *Moralitates de lapidibus*, 13; *Moralitates de piscibus*, 13
Hugo de Salucces. *See* Hugues de Salve
Hugo de Sancto Caro: *Sermo*, 80
Hugo Folietinus. *See* Hugo de Folieto
Hugues de Salve, tr., 230
Hunting, 88–90, 94, 101, 103, 121, 124, 127, 149, 163, 232, 233
Hunting Calls, 163, 200
Hymns, in English, 163; in German, 122; in Italian, 12, 146; in Latin, 7, 8, 12, 43, 177; in Ripuarian, 196

I. M., 45
Iacopo Cecchi: *Canzone*, 222
"Il sera pour vous conbatu," 91
ILLUMINATIONS (*detailed list of subjects not given for MSS 27 and 229; consult the catalogue entry*)
  Abel and Cain, 215
  Abraham and wife going to Egypt [?], 215
  Adoration of Host, 16
  Adoration of Magi, 16, 108, 190, 217
  Agony in Garden, 110
  Ahasuerus and Esther, 83
  Ahasuerus, Esther, and Haman, 82, 206
  Ahaziah on deathbed, 206
  Alesia, surrender of, 226
  Amos as shepherd, 206
  Amos with sheep, God, 83
  Andrew and Peter, 42
  Angel and monk, 227
  Angel kneeling with harp, 196
  Angel with scroll, man in bed, 206
  Angel with scroll, Paul in tower, 83
  Angels, 17
  Angels carrying souls to heaven, 16
  Animal heads biting, 206
  Animals, 19, 129
  Anna, 190
  Annunciation, 108, 110, 190, 214, 217, 218
  Annunciation to shepherds, 16, 108, 190, 217
  Annunciation to Zechariah, 206
  Antony, 190
  Apuleius and Varro, 215
  Aquitanians, surrender of, 226
  Aristippus in a boat, 215
  Arma Christi, 42
  Arms, 171, 230
  Arms, book of, 97
  Army, 129
  Arrest of Christ, 227
  Arthur, King. *See* entries for MSS 227 and 229
  Arthurian Romances, 227, 229
  Ascension, 17, 108, 214
  Assassination of Caesar, 226
  Atuatuca, 226
  Babel, tower of, 215
  Barbara, 190, 218
  Baruch as scribe, 83, 206
  Battle *à l'outrance*, 230
  Battle near the Saône, 226
  Battle scene, 129
  Battles, tree of, 230
  Beans, 129
  Beheading, 83
  Berecynthia, 215
  Betrayal of Christ, 108
  Birds, 17, 83, 143, 165, 168, 189
  Birds, heraldic, 229
  Birgitta, 5
  Birth of Caesar, 226
  Birth of John the Baptist, 129
  Blackbird, 189
  Boethius, 61, 84
  Bonet presents book to Maximilian I of Austria, 230
  Bonet presents treatise to nobles and heralds, 230
  Britain, Roman fleet arrives in, 226
  Bust in profile, 143

ILLUMINATIONS (*continued*)
  Caesar, assassination of, 226
  Caesar crossing the Rhine, 226
  Caesar crossing the Rubicon, 226
  Caesar, birth of, 226
  Caesar's embarkation for Thessaly, 226
  Cain and Abel, 215
  Caladrius, 189
  Calling of Peter and Andrew, 42
  Candelabra, 42
  Cantors, 206
  Cantors at lectern, 82, 83, 220
  Catharine, 190
  Charles the Bold, Duke of Burgundy, 226
  Charles V, King of France, 215
  Children of Israel and Moses, 129
  Christ appearing to Mary Magdalen, 17
  Christ appearing to Virgin, 218
  Christ displaying stigmata, 37
  Christ in Majesty, 206
  Christ on the road to Emmaus, 17
  Christ seated, with two angels, 215
  Christ with Andrew and Peter, 42
  Christ with Mary, 215
  Christ, arrest of, 227
  Christ, betrayal of, 108
  Christ, nimbed figure [?], 82
  Coronation of Emperor, 230
  Coronation of Virgin, 35, 108, 190, 217
  Crane, 189
  Creation, six days of, 206
  Creation, seven days of, 83, 129, 214
  Cross with Arma Christi, 42
  Crowning of king of arms of France, 230
  Crucifixion, 16, 108, 190, 217, 218
  Cyrus building tower, 206
  Cyrus builds temple, 83
  Cyrus, King, 82
  Daniel in den of lions, 206, 214
  Daniel interprets Nebuchadnezzar's dream, 129
  David, 43, 108
  David and Goliath, 217
  David at carillon, 82, 83, 206, 220
  David harping, 82, 83, 220
  David in deep waters, 82, 220
  David in deep waters, God, 83, 206
  David kneeling, 190
  David pointing to eyes, 82, 83, 220
  David points to lips, 83, 220
  David, unction of [?], 82
  Death of Tobit, 129
  Delivery of letter, 83, 206
  Deposition, 218, 227
  Devil between two philosophers, 215
  Devil tempting the psalmist, 206
  Devil, with God the Father, 129
  Devils, 129
  Dionysius, with Rusticus and Eleutherius, 17
  Dogs, 83, 165
  Dove, 17
  Dragons and dragon-head terminals, 81–83, 191, 214, 226, 227, 229
  Eagle, 189
  Eagle, John with, 206
  Ego sum, 27
  Eleutherius, 17
  Elijah in the fiery chariot, 129
  Elimelech, Naomi and child, 83
  Elimelech, Naomi and two children, 206
  Elkanah and Hannah before altar, 83
  English frets, 143
  Entombment, 218, 227
  Esther, 82
  Esther and Ahasuerus, 83
  Esther, Ahasuerus, and Haman, 82, 206
  Esther receives scepter, 214
  Execution, 206
  Execution of a soldier, 129
  Execution of idolatrous Jew, 206
  Ezekiel eats the scroll, 214
  Ezekiel in bed, vision of 4 beasts, 83
  Falconer, 100, 162
  Fall of rebel angels, 215
  Finding of Moses, 214
  Fisherman, 171
  Flight into Egypt, 16, 108, 190, 217
  Flight of the Mandubii, 226
  Fool, 82, 83
  Four philosophers, 215
  Four rivers of paradise, 214
  Four soldiers on horseback, 129
  Frederick III, Holy Roman Emperor, 230
  Fruit and floral border, 42
  Fruit, bowl of, 143
  Funeral, 217
  Funeral mass, 106
  Funeral procession, 230
  Gaius Trebonius leads attack, 226
  Gaul, three parts of, 226

General Index

Gauls seizing Rome, 215
George and dragon, 161
Gnadenstuhl Trinity, 217
God appears to Obadiah in bed, 83
God the Father with Devil, 129
God, Amos with sheep, 83
God, David in deep waters, 83, 206
Gold cup, 83
Golden Fleece, Maximilian I awarding, 230
Goliath and David, 217
Gomer and Hosea, 206
Grapes, 129
Gregory, Mass of. *See* Mass of Gregory
Grotesques, 16, 121, 183, 217, 229
Habakkuk as scribe, 83
Haggai standing with King, 206
Haggai with banderole, 83
Haman, Esther, and Ahasuerus, 82, 206
Haman hanging, 82
Hares, 2
Harpies, 165
Harrowing of hell, 227
Heads, dragon or human, 229
Hell, harrowing of, 227
Heron, 189
Holofernes, decapitation of, 82, 83, 129, 214
Hoopoe, 189
Hosea and Gomer, 206
Insects, 9, 143, 168
Institution of herald, 230
James, 190
James with book, 83
Jeremiah and the people, 214
Jeremiah seated at writing desk, 129
Jericho, Joshua at, 214
Jerome at desk, 83
Jerusalem, 129
Jesse, tree of, 206
Jew, Mathathias slays apostate, 214
Jew asperging altar, 83
Jews before altar, 206
Jews disputing with King, two, 83
Jews kneeling in prayer, two, 83
Jews, Paul with two, 206
Job on dunghill, 82
Joel and two Jews, 206
John, 150
John as monk, seated, 83
John at desk, 83

John on Patmos, 217
John the Baptist, 190
John the Baptist, birth of, 129
John the Evangelist with poisoned chalice, 129
John, vision of St., 108
John with book, 83
John with eagle, 206
John with sword, 83
Joseph, 17
Joseph, selling of, 129
Joshua at Jericho, 214
Joshua made leader, the army departs, 214
Joshua's dream, 129
Josias with soldier, 82
Jude with book, 83
Judgment of Solomon, 82
Judgment, Last. *See* Last Judgment
Judith and decapitation of Holofernes, 82, 83, 129, 214
Justice, 35
King, seated, 35
King with two soldiers, 206
Kite, 189
Knight with three men, 227
Knights, 129
Labors of the months. *See* Occupations
Lancelot. *See* entry for MS 229
Lapidation, 83
Last Judgment, 110, 215, 218
Lion of St. Mark, 104
Love-knot, 203
Luke, 150
Luke as monk at altar, 83
Luke censing altar, winged man, 206
Madonna and Child, with Rodríguez family, 34
Magi, Adoration of. *See* Adoration of Magi
Malachi standing with scroll, 83
Malachi with two Jews, 206
Man and woman at altar, 83
Man in bed, angel with scroll, 206
Man standing, 206
Man standing, Paul in tower, 206
Man standing, Paul with sword, 206
Man, bust of, 143, 165
Mandubii, flight of, 226
Marie of Burgundy gives gold collar, 230
Mark, 150
Mark as monk, standing, 83
Mark as scribe, 82

ILLUMINATIONS (*continued*)
  Mark with lion, 206
  Mark, lion of St., 104
  Marne, Roman ships on, 226
  Marshall of France, 230
  Mary, Virgin, 17, 34, 35, 108, 178, 190, 217, 218
  Mary as child before altar, 196
  Mary Magdalen, 190
  Mary Magdalen, Christ appearing to, 17
  Mary with Christ, 215
  Mass of St. Gregory, 218
  Massacre of Innocents, 16
  Mathathias slays apostate Jew, 214
  Matthew, 150
  Maurice, 218
  Maximilian I awarding golden fleece, 230
  Maximilian I receives book from Bonet, 230
  Messalla and Cassius, 215
  Micah before city, 206
  Micah with banderole, 83
  Monk and angel, 227
  Monotheism, 215
  Moses and children of Israel, 129
  Moses expounding the tablets, 214
  Moses leading Jews, 83
  Moses on Mt. Sinai, 83
  Moses, finding of, 214
  Mourners around a coffin, 109, 190
  Musicians, 215
  Nahum and collapsing tower [Nineveh], 83
  Naomi, Elimelech and child, 83
  Naomi, Elimelech and two children, 206
  Nativity, 16, 108, 178, 190, 217
  Nebuchadnezzar's dream, Daniel interprets, 129
  Nervii, Romans battle, 226
  Nicolas, 190
  Nigidius and wheel of fortune, 215
  Nineveh, 83
  Noah, shame of, 230
  Noli me tangere, 17
  Obadiah in bed, God appears to, 83
  Occupations of the months, 217
  Old Law, 215
  Original sin, 215
  Ostrich, 189
  Owl, horned, 189
  Paradise, four rivers of, 214
  Paul and Peter, 190
  Paul disputes with three Jews, 82
  Paul in tower, angel with scroll, 83
  Paul in tower, man standing, 206
  Paul preaching, 82
  Paul with banderole, 82
  Paul with book, 82, 83
  Paul with scroll, 83
  Paul with sword, 83
  Paul with sword and book, 82, 83
  Paul with sword, man standing, 206
  Paul with two Jews, 206
  Peacock, 143, 189
  Pentecost, 16, 17, 108, 178, 190, 217
  Peter and Andrew, 42
  Peter and Paul, 190
  Peter with book, 83
  Peter with key, 83
  Peter, St., 104
  Petrus Comestor and William of Champagne, 214
  Philosophers discussing, 215
  Phoenix, 189
  Pietà, 7, 16, 110
  Pompey and Ptolemy, 215
  Portrait of owner, 217
  Portrait of scribe, 214
  Presentation in temple, 16, 108, 217
  Presentation of Samuel, 129, 214
  Presentation to Charles, Duke of Burgundy, 226
  Presentation to Charles V, 215
  Priest performing mass, 227
  Priest serving communion, 18
  Ptolemy and Pompey, 215
  Putti, 143, 145, 158, 165, 168, 231
  Quail, 189
  Rabbit, 83
  Rey Don Iohan [?], 35
  Rhine, Caesar crossing, 226
  Rodríguez family with Madonna and Child, 34
  Roman fleet arrives in Britain, 226
  Roman ships on Marne, 226
  Romans battle Nervii, 226
  Rome, 1
  Rome, Gauls seizing, 215
  Rooster, 189
  Rubicon, Caesar crossing, 226
  Ruse of Titurius Sabinus, 226
  Rusticus, 17
  Ruth removes kinsman's shoe, 214
  Sacrifice of burnt offerings, 129

Sacrifice of sheep, 83
Sacrifice of sheep, bull, doves, 214
Saints, 16
Samuel, annointing of, 206
Samuel, presentation of, 129, 214
Saône, battle near, 226
Saul on the road to Damascus, 9
Scribe, 152
Scribe, Baruch as, 83, 206
Scribe, Habakkuk as, 83
Scribe, Mark as, 82
Scribe portrait, 214
Scribes, three, 129, 206
Sebastian, 190
Seizure of Rome by Gauls, 215
Selling of Joseph, 129
Seraphim, 42
Seven churches of Asia, 83
Seven days of creation, 83, 129, 214
Shame of Noah, 230
Six days of creation, 206
Skeleton with scythe, 42
Skull and cross-bones, 42
Snails, 229
Soldiers on horseback, 129
Soldiers, King with, 206
Solomon knighting soldier, 83
Solomon on throne, 82
Solomon praying, 206
Solomon sacrificing sheep, 83
Solomon teaching, 83
Solomon, judgment of, 82
Stag, 83
Stork, 2, 189
Strawberries, 129, 217
Surrender of Alesia, 226
Surrender of the Aquitanians, 226
Swallow, 82, 189, 206
Swan, 189
Tent, 227
Three living and three dead, 108
Three Marys at tomb, 178
Three parts of Gaul, 226
Tobit, death of, 129
Tobit and swallow, 82, 206
Tobit, Raphael, Tobias, 214
Tournament, 230
Tower of Babel, 215
Tree of battles, 230
Tree of Jesse, 206
Trinity, 82. *See also* Gnadenstuhl Trinity

Two cities, 215
Valerius Maximus, portrait, 147, 221
Varro and Apuleius, 215
Vase, 2
Veronica holding cloth, 218
Venelli, ruse of Titurius Sabinus against, 226
Virgin and Child, 190
Virgin and Child enthroned, 17, 218
Virgin and Child on a crescent, 218
Virgin and St. John at foot of Cross, 218
Virgin, Coronation of, 35, 108, 217
Vision of St. John, 108
Vision of tetramorph, 206
Vision of 4 beasts, Ezekiel in bed, 83
Visitation, 16, 108, 190, 217
Vulture, 189
Wheel of fortune and Nigidius, 215
William of Champagne and Petrus Comestor, 214
Woman, bust of, 165
Zechariah, annunciation to, 206; receives prophecy, 214
Zechariah seated with book, 83
Zephaniah seated, 206
Zephaniah with banderole, 83
Zodiac, signs of, 217
Illustrations, Eusebian Canons, 248. *See also* Diagrams, Drawings, Illuminations
Indenture, article of, 60
Indicopleustes, Cosmas. *See* Cosmas Indicopleustes
Indulgences, 9, 28, 109, 110, 153, 218, 220
Innocent IV, Pope, 153
Iohannes Baptista Pegasus, 67
Iohannes de Burgh, 62
Isabel I, Queen of Spain, 34
Isidore: extracts (in Greek), 238
Isle-de-France, 106
Iuliano ciurczo, 124
Iulianus Pytius, 67

"Ja que li ne s'i attende," 91
Jacobus de Jüterbogk, 225
Jacobus de Paradiso. *See* Jacobus de Jüterbogk
Jacobus de Voragine: *Legenda aurea* 111, 224
Jacobus Mediolanensis: commentary on, 223; *Stimulus amoris* (in English), 223
Jacobus Utinensis: *Supplicatio oratoria*, 192
"Je ne puis vivre ainsy," 91

Jean de Limoges, 109
Jean de Meun, 33
Jean Duchesne, tr., 226
Jean Franchières: *La fauconnerie*, 90
Jenninges, William, 60
Jerome: extract on Seneca, 155; references to, 209
Jesuits, Latin poems on, 45
Joannes Climacus: *Scala paradisi* (in Greek), 237
Joannes Raithunus, 237
Johannes Fabri de Werdea: *Carmina*, 174
Johannes Gerson, 196
Johannes Okeghem: *Chansons*, 91
Johannes Regis: *Chanson*, 91
Johannes Shepey: *Sermones*, 15
Johannes Tinctoris: *Chansons*, 91
Johannes Tuscanus Aloisius: *Oratio*, 188
John Chrysostom: extracts (in Greek), 238; *Interpretatio Orationis Dominicae* (in Greek), 235; *Sermones* (in Greek), 235
John Damascene: *De dormientibus in fide* (in Greek), 248; prayers, etc. (in Greek), 236
John IV, Pope, 9
John of Damascus. *See* John Damascene
John the Evangelist, 185
John XII, Pope, 9
"Joye me fuit," 91
Joye, G.: *Chansons*, 91
Joys of the Virgin, Fifteen, 217
Joys of the Virgin, Fifteen (in French), 17, 106, 107
Joys of the Virgin, Five, 16
Joys of the Virgin, Seven, 110
Joys of the Virgin, Seven (in German), 28
Joys of the Virgin, Seven Spiritual, 12
Joys of the Virgin, Seven Temporal, 12
Joys, Seven, 12, 163
Juan de Sant-Fahagun, 138
Juan Páez de Castro, 245
Judgment, 15 days before, 163, 224
Judgment of Paris, 163
Juliana Berners, Dame, 163, 171
Julius II, Pope, 28
Justinus: *Epitome in libros Pompeii Trogi*, 168
Juvenal: commentary on, 73; extracts, 75; glosses, 67, 72; *Satirae*, 67–73, 112, 113; *Satirae* (fragment), 176; *Satirae* (in English), 74; *Scholia uetustiora* (in English), 74; *Vita*, 73

Kantzow, Thomas, 99
Kings, lists of, 163

"L'aultre d'antan," 91
"L'omme banny," 91
La manière de faire champ a oultrance, 230
La maniere de faire tournoiz et behours, 230
La mort au roy Artus, 229
"La pena sin ser sabida," 91
La premiere institution des roys darmes et heraulx, 230
La queste del Saint Graal, 229
La table des xij chapittres du blason darmes, 230
Lactantius: *Divinae institutiones*, 156; *Opera*, 114
Lancelot, 227, 229
Latin language, 66
Laude, 12
Laurentius Guillelmus Savoniensis. *See* Lorenzo Guglielmo Traversagni de Savone
Law, international, 230
Laws, of Denmark, 31
"Le corps s'en va," 91
Le livre de Lancelot du lac, 229
Lectionary (fragment), 3 (no. 8)
Lectionary (in Greek), 187
LeFèvre, Raoul. *See* Raoul LeFèvre
Legal documents, in English, 60; in French, 3 (nos. 16, 53), 46–54, 82; in Latin, 3 (nos. 11, 40, 41, 46), 46–54, 55, 213; in Spanish, 34, 34A, 35
Legal manuscript (fragment), 138
Legal precedents, 75
Legal text, unidentified (in Danish), 39
Leigh, Sir Thomas, 97
Lentulus, 185
Leo, archpresbyter: *Historia Alexandri Magni* (in Italian), 194
Leo, Pope: *Sermo* (excerpts), 80, 181
Leonardo da Vinci, 1
Leonicenus Omnibonus: *De arte metrica*, 66
Leonicenus Omnibonus, tr., 149
Leontius: *Vita Sancti Joannis Eleemosynarii*, 177
Les ordonnances aux gaiges de bataille en champ ferme, 230
Lheureux, Charles-Felix, 46–54
Lille, 226
Lima, 34A
Limoges, 108
Lisbon, 228

General Index 381

Lists of emperors, kings, archbishops, 163
Litany, 7, 9, 10, 16, 17, 28, 32, 106-10, 134, 153, 190, 191, 196, 205, 211, 217, 218, 220
Literary notes, 75
Liturgical manuscript (fragments of), 3 (nos. 2, 3, 4, 8, 28, 29, 31, 42, 44), 4, 55, 153, 187, 206, 209, 225, 235, 238
Livre du roy Modus, 121
Livy: *Ab urbe condita libri I-X,* 1
Lodge, Sir Thomas, 97
Lodovico il Moro, Duke, 1
"Loing de vo tresdoulce presence," 91
Lombardus, Petrus. *See* Peter Lombard
London, 89
Longinus, 45
López de Ayala, Pedro: *Aves de caça,* 79, 138
Lorenzo Guglielmo Traversagni de Savone, 66
Lorenzo Rusio: *Marescalcia equorum* (Italian tr.), 137
Loschi, Antonio. *See* Antonio Loschi
Louis of Bruges, Seigneur de la Gruthuyse, 230
Louis XI, King of France, 188
Luca Pacioli, 1
Lucan: extracts, 75
Lutheran Church: *Collectae,* 122; *Sacramentarium,* 122
Luxeuil [?], 193
Lyons, 3 (no. 44)
Lyttelton, Sir Edward, 97

"Ma bouce rit," 91
"Ma dame de nom," 91
Macarius: prayers, etc. (in Greek), 236
Maffeus, Timotheus. *See* Timoteo Maffei
Magdeburg, 7
Mago, Agogo. *See* Agogo Mago
Mago, Agosto. *See* Agogo Mago
Mainz, 41
Malatesta Novella, 167
Mallorye, Sir William, 97
Malopin, 90
Mandeville, Sir John, 86
Manettino da Firenze [?]: *Canzone,* 222
Manors, France, 46-54
Manuscript fragments, collection of, 3
Manuscript fragments bound in, 4, 5, 19, 25, 43, 55, 82, 88, 138, 153, 178, 187, 195, 196, 206, 209, 211, 225, 235, 238, 247
Manuzio family, 59
Manwood, John, 89
Map, Walter. *See* Walter Map
Marc Antony, 133
Marcus Eremita: *Consultatio intellectus* (in Greek), 238; *Quaestiones de baptismo* (in Greek), 238
Marie of Burgundy, 230
Martial: commentary on, 64; *Epigrammaton libri,* 64, 65; extracts, 75
Martin of Braga: *Formula vitae honestae,* 155, 184
Martin V, Pope, 151
Mary, Virgin, 7, 9, 12, 16-18, 28, 32, 41, 45, 106-10, 134, 146, 153, 190, 191, 196, 205, 217, 218, 224
Mass of the Dead, 18
Mass of the Virgin Mary, 16, 18, 190
Mathias Mercader: *Practica de citreria,* 124
Matthias Corvinus, King of Hungary, 91, 145
Maximilian I, of Austria, 230
Maximus the Confessor: extracts (in Greek), 238
Medical advice, 163, 220
Medical problems, unidentified table, 184
Medical recipes, in English, 84, 100, 163; in French, 90; in Italian, 124, 136, 146, 162, 232; in Latin, 84, 136, 146, 163; in Spanish, 138
Medici, Cosimo de', 93
Medici, Piero de', 93
Meditations (in Greek), 235
Melanchthon, Philip [?], 174
"Mellon Chansonnier," 91
Mercader, Mathias. *See* Mathias Mercader
"Mercy, mon dueil," 91
Merkyn, Robert, 195
Metrics, 66
Michael Glyzunios, 250
Michael of Ephesus: notes on Aristotle (in Greek), 234
Michael Psellus: *De psalmorum titulis* (in Greek), 249
Michelin, 90
Milan, 1, 169
Milbourne, manor of, 86
Military ordinances, 230
Miroir du monde. See Somme le Roi

Missal, 18
Missal (fragments of), 3 (no. 4), 25, 206
Moamin, 103, 127
"Mon trestout et mon assotee," 91
Monograms, Vitta, Baron Joseph, 91
Montbault, Catherine Amable de la Haye, 46–54
"Mort ou mercy," 91
Morton, Robert. *See* Robert Morton
Mottoes: *Endure fort*, 174; *Expecto*, 194; *Forte fide pugnat uigilat*, 199; *Vrai lui serai ami*, 162
Music, 208
Music, unidentified text, 225
Musical notation, 3 (nos. 3, 4, 31), 18, 19, 42, 55, 56, 78, 91, 122, 178, 181, 191, 193, 200, 205, 206, 209
Musical notation (Greek), 238
"Myn hertis lust," 91

"N'aray je jamais mieulx que j'ay," 91
Naples, 91, 143, 144
Nepos, Cornelius. *See* Cornelius Nepos
Neumes, 3 (no. 4), 55, 181, 191, 193, 206
Nevers, 217
Newporte, Sir Rychard, 97
Niccolò Azzone, 222
Niccolò Niccoli, 14, 133
Nicephorus: *Onirocriticon* (in Greek), 235
Nicholas de Burgh, 62
Nicolas Trevet, 38; *Commentarius in Boethium*, 198; *Commentarius in Boethium* (extracts), 85
Nicolaus Acciaiuolus. *See* Acciaiuolus, Nicolaus
Nicolaus de Azaiolis. *See* Acciaiuolus, Nicolaus
Nicolaus de Lyra: *Postilla super Psalterium* (fragment), 22
Nicolaus of Methone: *De processione Spiritus Sancti* (in Greek), 235
Nicolaus V, Pope, 37, 188
Nilus: extracts (in Greek), 238
Nominalium (fragment), 3 (no. 34)
"Non pas que je veuille penser," 91
Normandy, 18, 106
Northe, Sir Roger, 97
"Nos amys, vous vous abusés," 91
Nouveau dictionnaire historique, 26
Novae narrationes, 60
Novella, Malatesta. *See* Malatesta Novella
Novem Odae ecclesiae graecae, 249

"O fortune, trop tu es dure," 91
"O Virgo, miserere mei," 91
Obicinus, Thomas: *Motivo celeste*, 37
Obituary notices, 7, 161, 247
Odes, commentary on (in Greek), 249
Odes (in Greek), 249
Office of the Dead, 7, 10, 42, 107, 109, 191, 217, 220; Premonstratensian use, 9; use of Paris, 17, 106; use of Rome, 16, 108, 110, 190; use of Utrecht, 32
Ognibene dei Bonisoli, Leoniceno. *See* Leonicenus Omnibonus
Okeghem, Johannes. *See* Johannes Okeghem
Omnibonus, Leonicenus. *See* Leonicenus Omnibonus
"Or me veult bien Esperance mentir," 91
Osorio, Jeronymo: *Della nobiltà civile*, Italian tr., 30
"Ou doy je secours querir," 91
"Ou lit de pleurs," 91
Ovid: *Ars amatoria*, 183; commentary on, 174; epitaph, 174; extracts, 75; *Remedia amoris*, 174; *Vita*, 174
Ovid, pseudo-: *Opuscula*, 174; verses, 172
Oxaminus, 127
Oxford University, 75

Pacioli, Luca. *See* Luca Pacioli
Padua, 72, 166
Padua, University of, 98
Palimpsest, 184, 187, 191 [?]
Panormita. *See* Beccadelli, Antonio
"Par le regart," 91
Parabolae Salomonis, 102
"Paracheve ton entreprise," 91
Paraclitus Cornetanus, Frater, 188
Paris, 207, 242
Parrey, Sir Thomas, 97
Paschasius Radbertus: *De corpore et sanguine Domini* (extracts), 181
Passion of Christ, devotions on, 110; extracts on, 80; in German, 219
Paul II, Pope, 188
Paul, Apostle, 185
Paul, St., letters to Seneca, 155
Paulus de Worczin, Magister, 225
Pecia notation, 207
Pedro Simon Abril, tr., 29
Penitential Psalms, 3 (no. 28), 7, 9, 10, 16, 17, 19, 28, 32, 106, 107, 108, 109, 110, 190, 217, 218

General Index

Pérez de Oliva, Hernán: *Historia de la invención de las Yndias*, 128
Persius: commentary on, 58; epitaph, 112; extracts, 75; glosses, 67; *Satirae*, 67, 68, 69, 71, 112
Peter Lombard, 20, 207
Peter of Alcantara, 78
Peter of Poitier. *See* Petrus Pictaviensis
Petit Jan: *Chanson*, 91
"Petite Camusette," 91
Petrarch, 69; *Boccacii Griseldis historia*, 197; *Canzoni*, 222; *De remediis utriusque fortunae*, 203; *Epistola*, 197
Petrus Barbarus. *See* Barbarus, Petrus
Petrus blesensis, 196
Petrus Comestor: *Historia scholastica*, 3 (no. 37; fragment), 26, 214; *Historia scholastica*, French tr., 129
Petrus Damascenus: *Excerpta ascetica* (in Greek), 238
Petrus de Crescentiis. *See* Pietro de' Crescenzi
Petrus de Datia, Magister, 220
Petrus Hispanus: *Tractatus mirabilis aquarum*, 163
Petrus Pictaviensis, 26, 214
Phalaris, pseudo-: *Epistolae*, 167; extracts, 63
Philip II, King of Spain, 29
Philip IV, King of France, 230
Philip the Good, Duke of Burgundy, 216
Philoponus: notes on Aristotle (in Greek), 234
Philosophical definitions (in Greek), 235
Philosophical text (in Latin; fragment), 3 (no. 27)
Philotheus: *Sermo* (in Greek), 238
Phlebotomy, 166
Pierre le Mangeur. *See* Petrus Comestor
Pietà, 7
Pietro de' Crescenzi: *Liber ruralium commodorum*, 233
Pietro de' Faitinelli: *Canzone*, 222
Pilgrims' badges, 107
Pinelli, Frater Elia, 42
Pirano, 161
Pisa, 222
Pius II, Pope, 2, 9; *Bulla retractationum*, 197; *Epistolae*, 197; *Epistolae*, etc., 188; *Oratio*, 37
Platina, Bartolomeo: *Oratio*, 188
Plato, references to, 209
Plautus: extracts, 63
Plutarch: extracts, 63; *Vita Ciceronis* (in Latin), 14; *Vita Demosthenis* (in Latin), 14; *Vitae* (in Latin), 133
Poggio Bracciolini, 114
Poitiers, battle of, 86
Poliziano, Angelo, 182
Polyaenus: *Strategemata* (in Greek), 250
Polybius, 194
Pomerania, history of, 99
Pompeius Trogus, 168
Porphyry: extracts, 225; *Isagoge* (in Greek), 234
Possidonius: *Vita Augustini*, 177
"Pour entretenir mes amours," 91
Poynes, Sir Nycholas, 97
Poynynge, Sir Adryan, 97
Prague, 36
Prayers, in Armenian, 3 (no.45); in Dutch, 153; in Flemish, 110; in French, 107, 108; in German, 28, 122, 134, 218, 219; in Greek, 236, 243, 248; in Italian, 12, 222; in Latin, 7, 9, 10, 12, 106, 107, 108, 109, 110, 134, 211, 217, 220; in Latin (fragment), 88; in Middle English, 163; in Netherlandish, 32; in Ripuarian, 196
Precepts for students, 209
Premonstratensian use, 9
Printed texts bound in, 28, 188
Priscian, pseudo-: *De accentibus*, 66
Probo, Jacobo, conte di Pianelle, 213
Probus, Emilius. *See* Cornelius Nepos
Processional, 205
Procopius de Rabensteyn, 197
Prognostications, 163
Prosper Aquitanus: *Epigrammata ex sententiis S. Augustini*, 15
Prudentius: extracts, 174
Prudentius, Iosephus, 98
Psalmi de passione, 109
Psalms, commentary on (in Greek), 249
Psalms (in Greek), 249
Psalms (in Ripuarian), 196
Psalms, Penitential. *See* Penitential Psalms
Psalter, 8, 43, 191, 211, 220
Psalter (fragment), 3 (no. 29)
Psalter (in Dutch), 153
Psalter (in Ripuarian), 196
Psalterium sancti ieronimi, 109; in Ripuarian, 196

Psellus, Michael. *See* Michael Psellus
Ptolemy: *Harmonicorum libri III* (in Greek), 208
"Puis que je vis le regart," 91
"Puis que ma damme ne puis voir," 91
Punic war, 194
Purvey, John, 125
Pyrrhus, 133
Pythagoras, pseudo-: *Carmina aurea* (in Greek), 247; commentary on, 247
"Quant ce viendra," 91
Quentin, Mont-Saint-, 214
Quintilian, references to, 209

R. P. G., 45
Rabensteyn, Procopius de. *See* Procopius de Rabensteyn
Radbertus, Paschasius. *See* Paschasius Radbertus
Raithunus, Joannes. *See* Joannes Raithunus
Ramirez Tinagero, Don Bernardo Anttonio, 34A
Raoul de Praelles. *See* Raoul de Presles
Raoul de Presles, tr., 215
Raoul LeFèvre: *Le Recueil des histoires de Troies*, 216
Raynaldus, 3 (no. 11)
Recipes. *See* Medical recipes
Reform Congregation of the Spanish Discalceates, 78
Regis, Johannes. *See* Johannes Regis
Registrum brevium, 60
Religious text, unidentified, 225
Remigius of Auxerre: *Expositio super Matthaeum*, 80
Renaut de Louans. *See* Renaut de Louhans
Renaut de Louhans, tr., 38
Requests, Seven. *See* Seven Requests
Rex Federicus, 185
Rhetoric, 3 (no. 34), 66, 135
Rhine, Lower, 196
Rhineland, 191
Richard de Caestre: hymn, 163
Richard II, King of England, 230
Ríobamba, 34A
Ritual (in Dutch), 153
Robert de Borron: *Joseph d'Arimathie*, 227; *Lestoire de Merlin*, 227; *Lestoire de Saint Graal*, 227
Robert Morton: *Chansons*, 91
Robert of Bridlington: *Catena* on Romans, 154; *Catena* on 1 Corinthians, 154; *Catena* on 2 Corinthians, 154
Rockingham, 88
Rodríguez family, 34A
Rodríguez, Alfonso, 34
Roman de la Rose, 33
Rome, 113
Rome [?], 160
Rouen, 107
Rouen [?], 17
Rouge, G. le: *Chanson*, 91
Ruffo, Giordano. *See* Giordano Ruffo
Ruffus (Rufus), Jordanus. *See* Giordano Ruffo
Rusio, Lorenzo. *See* Lorenzo Rusio
Rusius, Laurentius. *See* Lorenzo Rusio
Ryche, Sir Roberte, 97

"S'il est ainsi," 91
Sages, Seven, 163
SAINTS (*The names have been standardized, for the most part, following F. G. Holweck, A Biographical Dictionary of the Saints* [*St. Louis, Mo., and London, 1924*]).
Achatius, 28
Aegidius, 10, 16, 28
Afra, 109
Agatha, 42
Agricola, 217
Alban, 10, 220
Albert of Trapani, 41
Albinus, 16
Aldegundis, 9, 110
Aldhelm, 220
Alexius, 190, 218
Aloysius Gonzaga, 45
Amalberga, 110
Amandus, 110
Ambrose, 28
Andochius, 217
Andrew, 28, 42, 109, 218
Angelus, 41
Anianus, 108
Anna, 7, 9, 28, 41, 88, 190, 205, 218, 220
Ansanus, 42
Anselm, 196
Anskar, 9
Antony, 177, 190
Antony abbot, 16, 190
Antony of Padua, 78
Apollonia, 16

General Index

Aredius, 217
Arigius, 217
Audomar, 16, 110
Augustine, 8, 9, 10, 28, 134, 177, 190, 196, 218
Augustine of England, 220
Austreberta, 107
Austremonius, 10, 220
Avia, 17
Barbara, 16, 28, 110, 111, 134, 190, 205, 211, 218
Bartholomew, 9, 28
Basil the Great, 41, 110, 177, 235
Basilius, 110, 190, 196
Bathildis, 220
Bavo, 109, 110, 190
Bede, 110
Benedict, 7, 28, 190, 191
Bernard, 9, 16, 28, 110, 134, 190, 196, 205, 218
Bernardinus, 218
Bernardinus of Siena, 190
Beroald, 205
Bertilia, 211
Bertin, 190
Birgitta, 5, 24, 28, 134
Blasius, 28
Boniface, 7, 218
Botulph, 220
Brictius, 177
Burchard, 7
Caprasius, 108
Cassius, 134
Castulus, 7
Catharine of Alexandria, 9, 16, 17, 28, 109, 134, 190, 205
Catharine of Siena, 37
Chad, 88
Christopher, 28
Chrysogonus, 28
Chuniald, 7
Cirycus, 217
Clara, 111
Columba, 10
Columban, 10, 191, 220
Consortia, 10, 220
Corbinian, 28
Cordula, 191, 196
Crescentiana, 41
Cunibert, 191, 196
Cunigundis, 7

Cuthbert, 10, 220
Cuthburga, 220
Cybard, 108
Cyril, 41, 177
Cyrilla, 10, 220
Daria, 10, 220
David, 88
Dionysius, 17, 106, 134
Dominic, 7, 190, 205
Dominicus, 28
Donatianus, 110, 190
Donatianus of Algiers, 16
Dunstan, 10, 220
Edmund, 10
Edmund Archbishop, 220
Edmund Campion, 45
Edmund King, 220
Edmund Rich, 220
Edward "the Martyr", 220
Edward the Confessor, 220
Egidius. *See* Aegidius
Eligius, 10, 16, 108, 190
Elisabeth, 28, 205
Elphege, 220
Ephrem, 177
Erasmus, 28, 218
Erentrude, 7
Ethelbert, 220
Ethelreda, 10, 88, 220
Eucharius, 191
Eucherius, 10
Eustachius, 17, 106
Ewald, 191
Faustinus, 41, 111
Felicitas, 42
Felix, 191
Fiacre, 108, 217
Florencia, 10, 220
Florentius, 134
Florus, 10
Fortunatus, 10
Francis, 28, 190
Francis of Assisi, 78, 80
Francis Xavier, 45
Fulgentius, 177
Gabriel, 108
Gallus, 191
Geneviève, 16, 17, 108, 109, 217
George, 28, 161
Gerald, 220
Geraldus, 10

385

SAINTS (*continued*)
 Gereon, 9, 41, 110, 191
 Germanus, 10
 Germanus of Alexandria, 16
 Germanus of Auxerre, 16
 Germanus of Paris, 16
 Germar, 220
 Gertrude, 16, 110, 218
 Ghislain, 109
 Gildard, 109
 Gislar, 7
 Godehard, 9
 Gregory, 9, 10, 28, 55, 110, 134, 177, 218
 Gregory Nazianzen, 177, 235
 Gudula, 190
 Henry, 205
 Henry Emperor, 7
 Heribert, 191, 196
 Hilary, 10, 108, 177
 Hippolytus, 108
 Honobert, 217
 Honoratus, 41
 Honorina, 16, 107
 Hubert, 109, 110, 190
 Hugo, 10, 28, 220
 Ignatius of Antioch "Theophorus", 177
 Ignatius of Loyola, 45
 Irenaeus, 10
 Ivo, 106
 James, 16, 28, 190
 Jerome, 9, 28, 83
 Joannes Eleemosynarius. *See* John the Almsgiver
 John, 218
 John and Paul Martyrs, 25
 John Chrysostom, 177
 John IV "the Faster", 177
 John the Almsgiver, 177
 John the Baptist, 8, 9, 16, 17, 25, 42, 109, 129, 190, 246
 John the Evangelist, 16, 28, 32, 41, 109, 129, 185, 205, 218
 Joseph, 41, 134
 Jovita, 41, 111
 Judas, 28
 Juliana, 16, 41
 Julianus, 10
 Julitta, 217
 Justina of Padua, 111
 Kenelm, 220
 Kilian, 7
 Lambert, 16, 110, 191
 Lawrence, 8, 16, 28, 42, 109, 134
 Lebwin, 110, 218
 Leodegar, 16, 217, 220
 Leonard, 10, 28
 Liphard, 217
 Longinus, 111
 Louis, 205
 Lucia, 3 (no. 11)
 Ludger, 191
 Ludovicus, 108
 Luigi Gonzaga. *See* Aloysius Gonzaga
 Luke, 150
 Lupus, 217
 Maclovius, 16, 18, 110
 Magloire, 16
 Majolus, 10, 217, 220
 Malachy, 177
 Marcellus, 10
 Margaret, 16, 17, 28, 109
 Mark, 104, 150
 Martialis, 108
 Martin, 7, 41, 177
 Mary Magdalen, 7-9, 17, 28, 109, 134, 190
 Mary, Virgin, 7, 9, 12, 16-18, 28, 32, 41, 45, 106-10, 134, 146, 153, 190, 191, 196, 205, 217, 218, 224
 Maternus, 191
 Matthew, 28, 150
 Maurice, 7, 218
 Maurus, 191, 217
 Medard, 16, 108-10
 Mellonus, 107
 Michael, 17, 108, 109, 122, 190, 246
 Michael archangel, 8, 9, 196
 Milburga, 10
 Monica, 134, 190, 196
 Nabor, 191
 Nicasius, 110
 Nicolas, 7, 16, 19, 109, 190
 Nicolas of Tolentino, 196
 Odilia, 7, 218
 Odilo, 10, 220
 Odo, 10, 220
 Olanus, 10
 Oswald, 7, 191
 Othmar, 211
 Otto, 7
 Pantaleon, 111, 191, 211
 Paschalis Baylon, 78

Paul, 8, 16, 25, 28, 78, 155, 185, 190
Peter, 8, 16, 25, 42, 78, 104, 134, 190, 205
Peter of Alcantara, 78
Peter, bishop and martyr, 211
Petronilla, 110
Petronius, 37
Philibert, 10, 220
Philip, 28
Protasius, 190
Quentin, 10
Quiriacus, 16
Quirinus of Tegernsee, 28
Radegundis, 10, 217
Raguel, 108
Raphael, 108
Reginswindis, 7
Rembert, 9
Remigius, 17, 190, 218
Richard King, 7
Richard of Chichester, 88
Rochus [?], 191
Romanus, 16, 107
Rudolph Acquaviva, 45
Rupert, 7
Saul, 9
Scholastica, 28
Sebald, 7
Sebastian, 16, 28, 190
Servatius, 9, 190, 218
Severinus, 9
Sigismund, 205
Silvester, 3 (no. 2), 10
Simeon, 3 (no. 3), 191
Simon, 28
Simon Stock, 41
Sixtus, 28
Stephen, 3 (no. 2), 109
Stephen protomartyr, 7
Suitbert, 191, 196
Susanna, 107
Swithin, 220
Taurinus, 10, 17
Thecla, 28
Theresa, 134
Thomas, 10, 28, 109, 205
Thomas of Canterbury, 10, 28, 109, 220
Thomas the apostle, 28, 111
Trudpert, 7
Ulric, 7, 218
Urban, 7

Ursula, 9, 16, 28, 134, 191, 205
Valeric, 190
Valerius, 191
Vedast, 110
Veronica, 28, 218, 220
Vincent, 205
Virgilius, 7
Virgin Mary. *See* Mary, Virgin
Vitus, 28
Walburga, 7, 190, 218, 220
Walburgis, 9, 10, 191
Wilgefortis, 110
Willehad, 9
William, 111
Willibald, 7
Willibrord, 7, 191, 211
Wolfgang, 28
Wulstan, 220
Zenobius, 42
Zuwarda, 109
10,000 Martyrs, 110, 190, 205
11,000 Virgins, 191, 196
Saints — Lives and legends, 37, 111, 177, 224
Salernian verses, 163
Salic Law, 212
Sallust: *Bellum Iugurthinum*, 231; *Coniuratio Catilinae*, 231; extracts, 75
Sallust, pseudo-: *Invectiva in M. Tullium Ciceronem*, 93
Salutati, Coluccio, 114, 133, 179, 221
Sant-Fahagun, Juan de. *See* Juan de Sant-Fahagun
Satire: extracts on, 73
Scholar's Notebook, 225
Scholastic text (in Latin; fragment), 3 (no. 47)
Scientific text, unidentified (fragment), 196
Scipio, 185
"Se je fayz dueil," 91
"Se mon service vous plaisoit," 91
Sebenico, 55
Secundo folio
  a ceste parlong, 215
  a tant, 229
  ab initio, 14
  Ad conseruandam, 5
  Adiscite, 179
  adnotat. Eius, 167
  aliqui habentes, 232
  anno ante, 169

Secundo folio (continued)
  aprez. Ceste figure, 230
  At uos exiguo, 186
  [expi]atos sordibus, 43
  auait esprigie [?], 227
  Aut diomedeas, 112
  Bel accueil, 91
  Benedecta, 12
  canetur, 25
  Capitulum de reclamacione, 103
  [falla]cem mutauit, 85
  Cest a dire, 129
  chosi fisamente, 194
  Circa uerbum, 146
  cognitum, 164
  Coment cesar se prepara, 226
  Comment Iupiter, 216
  Coniurant, 180
  corporis animalis, 77
  credere de, 102
  cum bonis, 1
  Cum leno, 72
  cum populum, 70
  Cum uero incipit, 127
  damnatum penam, 87
  de aere, 233
  de inflatura crurium, 161
  de medicamine, 232
  De prima, 214
  De sancto paulo, 111
  Dei nature, 181
  del uaissel, 227
  Denique supplicium, 65
  dicendi studium, 152
  dicens ite, 205
  die sundt, 219
  dirigens, 198
  disputatio. Nam, 156
  ea quae de officijs, 170
  [V]enatio et canes, 149
  erat Itaque, 197
  Et hec oblacio, 27
  et insuper, 20
  et prudentiam, 83
  et si boscum, 88
  eubulum Erat, 177
  Exul ab, 68
  exul ob, 69
  fieri uel, 66
  figulus, 147
  Flaminieam, 73

Gregorius in, 80
Gurgite, 71
Haec ego non, 67
How a man, 223
iam totam, 178
ihren vngebutzten, 134
ille durus, 203
in andriam ex, 185
in que libri, 151
inde suscipiunt, 157
inter coniugalem, 143
ire parum, 224
ita nox, 26
iusta et clemens, 165
KL Marcius, 41
Laprentis, 121
leua ung, 216
liber j., 221
ludere uellent, 133
lune que, 215
mansuete tractetur, 161
[ne]mine me uspiam, 2
Multa filij, 179
multa uero, 158
Nam cuncta, 145
[py]ne his flesshe, 223
Nec fonte, 58
Neque habitabit, 220
Nolueram, 64
nos futuros, 160
obripit, 179
oc værieløse, 39
Octauianus cesar, 27
[rati]onem. C. xij, 114
Pacem dum, 63
pagar, 34
Par enuie qui, 38
Parum est, 173
per se potest, 225
piena, 222
populum, 18
praemium, 13
Publij Ouidij, 174
Quanquam, 92
[la]queari debet, 136
Qui cecidit, 84
qui clauem, 212
qui tribulant, 211
Quid referam, 113
quis inuenta, 6
quod si eam, 163

reducere. Si, 207
rerum magna, 93
Rex et, 60
Rimari, 61
[ple]rique delicta, 231
rregla, 138
Semblot bien, 33
semiramide, 168
Seruantem, 166
sic inpij, 8
sint in philosophia, 159
soluas tu, 4
[woen]sten noch, 153
suer que, 227
[perscrip]ta sunt breuiter, 206
[dispu]tantem Quia, 179
[por]tato fioli tute, 76
[sen]tentiam et scipio, 144
Ti. Ante, 172
[in exi]tu hij, 41
vane glorie, 24
Uera eternitas, 15
uidentur, 221
un poco, 137
[nesci]unt subvenire, 199
[inpi]us incenditur, 191
Vostra Maiesta, 124
w^t thornes, 171
Seneca: *Epistolae*, 155; epitaph, 155; extracts, 63, 69, 102, 225; references to, 209; *Tragoediae*, 173
Seneca the Elder: *Controversiae*, 155
Seneca, pseudo-: *De quatuor virtutibus*, 184; *De remediis fortuitorum*, 155, 184; *De verborum copia*, 155; *Epistolae*, 155
Sententiae, 69
Sententiae (in Greek), 235
Sequences of the Gospels, 17, 106-8, 190, 217
Sermons, in Latin, 3 (nos. 5, 12, 13, 39, 42, 50, 52), 15, 80, 146, 224; in Greek, 235, 248
Serres, Macedonia, 150
Sertorius, 133
Servius: extracts, 57
Seven ages of man, 243
Seven Requests, 17, 106, 107, 217
Seven Sages, 163
Severus, Sulpicius. *See* Sulpicius Severus
"Seymour Gospels," 150
Sforza, Massimiliano, 1

Sheffelde, Lord, 97
Shepey, Johannes: *Sermones*, 15
Shorten, Thomas, 195
Sibilla de Burgh, 62
Silius Italicus: *In Ciceronis laudem*, 159
Silvester, Pope, 28
Simone da Cremona [?]: sermons (fragment), 3 (no. 12)
Sins, list of mortal (in Greek), 243
Sixtus IV, Pope, 9, 28
Sixtus XI, Pope, 28
Sjaelland, Denmark, 39
"So ys emprentid," 91
Somerset, 62
Souche, Sir John, 97
Soullart, Chien, 121
Sozomenus Pistoriensis: commentary on Persius, 58
Speciano, Cesare: *Propositioni christiane et civili subalternate a Dio*, 36
Speculum humanae salvationis, 27
Speke, Sir George, 97
Spiritual guidance, Middle English prose text, 223
Staggered thumb holes, 78
Statius: extracts, 174; *Thebaid*, 166; *Thebaid*, glosses on, 166
Statuta collegii reginalis, 11
Stiffkey mill, 195
Students, precepts for, 209
Subjects illustrated. *See* Illuminations
Sulpicius Severus: *Epistolae*, 177; *Vita Sancti Martini*, 177
Sylvester II, Pope: *De corpore et sanguine Domini* (extracts), 181
Symeon Euchaita: *Epistola ad monachum quendam* (in Greek), 238
Symmachus: extracts, 174

Tacitus: *Annales XI-XVI*, 143-45; *Historiae I-V*, 143-45
Tanno [?], 12
Talon, Omer, 135
Tariph. *See* Ghatrif
Tegernsee, 28
Ten ages of man, 163
Ten commandments. *See* Commandments, Ten
Terence: *Comoediae*, 165, 185; excerpts, 63; glosses, 185; *Vita*, 165, 185
Tertullian: extracts, 75

Themistius: notes on Aristotle (in Greek), 234
Theodoretus: extracts (in Greek), 238
Theological notes or texts, 3 (nos. 5, 17), 75, 105, 146, 195, 248
Theophylactus of Bulgaria: *Enarratio in Matthaeum* (in Greek), 235
Therouanne, 229
Thieves, charm against, 163
Thomas Aquinas: *In libros Ethicorum Aristotelis* (fragment), 3 (no. 7); *In tertium librum Sententiarum Petri Lombardi*, 207
Thomas of Woodstock, Duke of Gloucester, 230
Tibullus: Carmina, 186; epitaph, 186; *Vita*, 186
Timoteo Maffei: *Epistola*, 188
Tinagero family, 34A
Tinagero Rodríguez de la Escalera family, 34
Tinctoris, Johannes. *See* Johannes Tinctoris
Tiptoft, John, 149
Tomaso da Novara. *See* Obicinus, Thomas
Tommaso Nacci Caffarini: *Tractatus de stigmatibus*, 37
Toms, W. H., 107
"Tout a par moy," 91
Tractatus de reparatione hominis lapsi, 224
Tragedy: extracts on, 73
Tragedy, in Latin, 45
Treatise of Fishing with an Angle, 171
Trevet, Nicolas. *See* Nicolas Trevet
Trier, 191, 211
Trinity, prayer to (in Greek), 236
"Triste qui sperò morendo," 91
Trivulzio, Marshal Gian Giacomo, 1
Troy — Romances, legends, etc., 216
Tuscany, 3 (no. 38), 222
Tuscany [?], 87

Ubertinus, 196
Umpton, Sir Edward, 97
"Ung plus que tous," 91
Urban V, Pope, 28
Ursay, Barony of, 46–54
Utrecht [?], 32

Valdes, Lope de Gonçalez. *See* Gonçalez de Valdes, Lope
Valdes, Pedro de Gonçalez. *See* Gonçalez de Valdes, Pedro

Valera, Diego de. *See* Diego de Valera
Valerius Bergidensis, pseudo-: *De novae vitae institutione*, 146
Valerius Maximus: excerpts, 63; *Facta et dicta memorabilia*, 147, 221
Venetian document, 104
Venice, 104
Venice [?], 250
Vergil: adaptations, 105; *Aeneis*, 57, 172; *Bucolica*, 172; commentary on *Aeneis*, 57; *Georgica*, 172; glosses, 57; notes on, 174
Vergil, pseudo-: *Carmina*, 174; commentary on, 174; *Moretum*, 174
Vespasiano da Bisticci, 151
Villar del Aguila, 35
Vincenet: *Chansons*, 91
Vincent of Beauvais: excerpt, 177
Virgin Mary. *See* Mary, Virgin
"Virgo Dei throno digna," 91
Virtues and vices, 204
Vita di S. Petronio, 37
Vitae sanctorum, 177
Vocabulary lists, 3 (no. 34), 92
"Vostre bruit et vostre grant fame," 91
Votive masses, 18

Wagstaff Miscellany, 163
Walter Frye: *Chansons*, 91
Walter Hilton, tr., 223
Walter Map, 229
Walter, of England. *See* Gualterus Anglicus
WATERMARKS
  Briquet Ancre 381, 20
  Briquet Ancre 531, 243
  Briquet Ange 660, 250
  Briquet Ange 662, 30
  Briquet Armoiries 1656, 196
  Briquet Armoiries 1741, 226
  Briquet Armoiries 1876, 204
  Briquet Balance 2401, 137
  Briquet Balance 2411, 174
  Briquet Balance 2427, 20
  Briquet Balance 2489, 66
  Briquet Cercle 3134, 166
  Briquet Chapeau 3369, 194
  Briquet Chapeau 3370, 194
  Briquet Ciseaux 3668, 188
  Briquet Ciseaux 3737, 222
  Briquet Couronne 4639, 69
  Briquet Couronne 4640, 69
  Briquet Croix latine 5678, 128

Briquet Echelle 5904, 71
Briquet Echelle 5908, 71
Briquet Enclume 5961, 112
Briquet Étoile 6045, 173
Briquet Flèche 6285, 179
Briquet Fleur 6654-56, 228
Briquet Fleur 6690, 186
Briquet Fleur de Lis 7107, 37
Briquet Fruit 7397, 175
Briquet Huchet 7682, 152
Briquet Lettre A 7918, 70
Briquet Lettre P 8526, 233
Briquet Lettre P 8527, 204
Briquet Lettre P 8598, 8
Briquet Lettre P 8606, 77
Briquet Lettre P 8608, 188
Briquet Lettre P 8619, 24
Briquet Lettre P 8625, 24, 77
Briquet Lettre P 8636, 39
Briquet Lettre R 8941, 67
Briquet Lettres et Monogrammes 9747, 216
Briquet Licorne 10001, 188
Briquet Main 10793, 182
Briquet Main 11154, 138
Briquet Main 11417, 39
Briquet Monts 11678, 222
Briquet Monts 11706, 173
Briquet Monts 11719, 152
Briquet Oiseau 12127, 149
Briquet Oiseau 12203, 185
Briquet Oiseau 12220, 185
Briquet Sirène 13880, 103
Briquet Tête de boeuf 14247, 121
Briquet Tête de boeuf 14552, 174
Briquet Tête de boeuf 14579-80, 167
Briquet Tête de boeuf 14803, 179
Briquet Tête de boeuf 14873, 68
Briquet Tête de boeuf 14874, 73
Briquet Tête de boeuf 15102, 20
Briquet Tête de cerf 15548, 121
Briquet Tour 15865, 186
Briquet Tour 15937, 135
Harlfinger Ancre 67, 139
Harlfinger Chapeau 74, 236
Harlfinger Ciseaux 43, 166

Harlfinger Couronne 25, 242
Harlfinger Fer à cheval 5, 186
Harlfinger Flèche 12, 67, 71
Harlfinger Fleur 108, 186
Harlfinger Huchet 18, 72
Harlfinger Huchet 21, 72
Harlfinger Huchet 22, 72
Harlfinger Monts 78, 186
Heawood 259-262, 34
Heawood 294-295, 34A
Heawood 348, 40
Heawood 740, 34A
Heawood 743, 34
Heawood 2473, 25
Heawood 2475, 25
Heawood 3637, 200
Heawood 3638, 200
Piccard Fabeltiere III. 1342-48, 3 (no. 34)
Piccard Horn VII. 106, 188
Piccard Ochsenkopf I. 113, 3 (no. 10)
Piccard Ochsenkopf VII. 127, 188
Piccard Ochsenkopf XII. 732-35, 174
West Bagborough, Somerset, 62
Weston, Sir Henry, 97
White, Sir John, 97
Whitechurch, manor of, 86
Whittokesmede, 163
William of Champagne, 214
Williams, Sir Henry, 97
Wilson, John, 195
Wiltshire, England, 86
Wine recipes, 163
Wiseman, Sir Robert, 74
Wycliffite New Testament, 125

Xenophon: *De re equestri* (in Greek), 244; *De venatione* (in Latin), 149; excerpts (in Latin), 63; *Hiero* (in Latin), 14

Yatrib. *See* Ghatrif

Zealand, Denmark. *See* Sjaelland, Denmark
Zeno, Carlo, 2
Zeno *Imperator*, 45
Zeno, Jacopo: *Vita Caroli Zeni*, 2
Zodiac, signs of, 7, 67, 166, 220

Index IV

Illuminators and Scribes

ILLUMINATORS

Boethius Master, associate of, 215

Cristoforo Cortese, 147

Edward IV, shop of, 230

Francesco di Lorenzo Roselli, style of, 42

Ghent Associates, style of, 16
Gioacchino de' Gigantibus, 151
Grusch atelier, style of, 82
Guinifortus de Vicomercato, style of, 42

Jean Bourdichon, style of, 108
Jean Colombe, style of, 217

Loyset Liédet, similar to, 226

Master of Bruges of 1482, 230
Master of Louis de Bruges, similar to, 226
Mathurin atelier, style of, 82
Matteo Felice, shop of, 91

Nicola Rapicano, 143

Vincent Philippon d'Avignon, 162
Virgil Master, dependent on, 215

Willem Vrelant, similar to, 226
Willem Vrelant, style of, 190

SCRIBES

Angelus Vergecius, 242

Bartholomaeus Baldinotti, 58
Benedictus, 70
Billinge, Jo, 74
Bouberch [?], 199

Callistus, 238
Camillus Venetus, 208
Caspar Misnensis, 3 (no. 12)
Castantius Iottus, 213

Franciscus de Oddis, 98
Franciscus de Tianis, 2
Franciscus Seroddi Centinomius Phylaretus, 67

Gandino, Bernardo, 30
Gerhardus de Castris, 41
Greifenclav, Freiherr von, 24
Guillermus de fonte, clericus, 3 (no. 40)

Hansen, Pawel [?], 31
Hellin de Burchgrave, 226
Heron, Robert [?], 105

Ieronimo Sandei, 161
Ion., 220

Jacobus de Jüterbogk, 225
Jehan de Loles, 227
Juan Páez de Castro, 245

Langwith, Benjamin [?], 11
Larrillo, Antonio, 35
Laurence of Mechlin, 20

Manuel, 245
Manuel Chrysoloras, pupil of [?], 240
Melkiseth, 3 (no. 45)

Niccolò di Giovanni Cinuzi da Siena, 222

Paulus, Brother. *See* Wigg, Melchior
Petrus Iatrus Florentinus [?], 239
Petrus Visnadellus Cremonensis, 152
Petrus [?], 214

Sinibaldus C., 151
Sophronius, 139

Thatcher, John, 89

Victor Blanchus, 104
Vincent Philippon d'Avignon, 162

Whittokesmede [?], 163
Wigg, Melchior, 28

Zanetti, Camillus. *See* Camillus Venetus

Index V

Provenance

A. N., 239
Abdingkhoff, Benedictine monastery, 9
Adams, J. T., 68, 69, 164–68, 170, 173
Admont, Benedictine abbey of, 193
Agen, Jesuit College, 155
Agnes of Burgundy, Duchess of Bourbon, 204
Alfonso II, Duke of Calabria, King of Naples, 143
Allen, Henry, 112, 152, 168, 170, 175
Allen, Samuel, 112, 152, 168, 170, 175
Altschul, Frank, 26, 128
Ambrosini, Raimondo, 70
Ambrosius, dominus, 102
Amery, John S., 86
Amherst of Hackney, William Amhurst Tyssen-Amherst, 1st Baron, 100
Andrea Bragadin [?], 232
Andreini, Joseph M., 34
Andrews, William Loring, 1, 2
Angel, Elizabeth Day Seymour, 187
Archinto, Count Carlo, 151
Arquà [?], 146
Askew, Dr. Anthony, 1
Athanasius, 241
Athos, Mt. [?], 187
Austria, Duchy of, 127
Azzone family, 222

Baber, Rev. H. H., 125
Bacon, E. Champion, 97
Bacon, Leonard, 14–16, 19
Bacon, Mrs. Leonard, 195
Bacon, Nathaniel, 195
Bacon, Nathaniel Terry, 14–16, 19
Baggett Collection, 16
Baldanto Balducci, 87
Balken, Edward Duff, 126
Barbara Pfintzing, 205
Barbour, Humfrey, 228
Barry, Robert J., 198
Bartrop, Frederick Fox, 181
Beatrice of Aragon, 91
Beck, C. H., 24
Bedelaer [?], 32
Benjamin, 181

Bentley, John, 27
Berardinus Petrus, 67
Bergin, Thomas G., 221
Bernardus Kniperus of Lubeck, 9
Berners, John, 101
Bersohn, Robt., 203
Bindley, James, 11
Blickling Library, 217, 218
Bogardus, Anna, 32
Borghese, Prince Marco Antonio, 147
Borthwick, John, 223
Bou, Marquis de [?], 152
Brölemann, Henri-Auguste, 196
Bradish, James P., 60
Bradish, Theo. H., 60
Brancas, Duc de, 215
Brand, Rev. John, 171
Branford College, Yale University, 144, 193
Bretland, Benjamin, 181
Bretland, John, 181
Bretland, Martin, 181
Bretland, Samuel, 181
Bretland, Tho., 181
Browen [?], Robert, 109
Browne, John, 109
Brydges, William, 228
Buck, Albert H., 7
Buda, palace of, 145
Bula [?], Juan Antonio, 34
Burr, Harold S., 3 (no. 45)
Burrell, Sir William, 1
Bushnell, Charles E., 81
Butler, Charles, 165
Buxheim, Carthusian monastery, 3 (no. 12)

Campbell, Alexander, 154
Canonici, Abate Matteo Luigi, 37, 124, 167
Carter, Dr. Franklin, 28
Carter, Johannes, 3 (no. 34)
Castrumarquatum, S. Maria apud, 146
Celotti, Abate Luigi, 14, 114, 234, 239
Cenninis, Petrus Franciscus de. *See* Petrus Franciscus de Cenninis
Chardin Library, Paris, 207
Childs, Albert H., 38

Childs, Stanley W., 38
Clarke, Dr. Adam, 243
Clement, Franciscus, 217
Clements, William L., 153
Cockerell, Sir Sydney, 93
Colford, John, 45
Colman, Dudley M., 215, 226, 227, 229, 230
Cologne, Charterhouse of St. Barbara, 20
Compton, R. D. P., 45
Con. S. A. Neapoli, 173
Cone, William, 10
Cooke, Joseph J., 33, 36
Copinger, Walter A., 157
Coquille, Anthoine, 217
Coquille, Gilbert, 217
Corvinus, Matthias. *See* Matthias Corvinus
Cowper, Thomas, 60
Curtis, H. Holbrook, 28

Danet, Leonard, 89
Davenporte, Ambrose, 60
De Lahave, 106
Dell, William, 113
Demery [?], Mary, 10
Denison, Alfred, 171
Didot, Ambroise Firmin, 93, 214
Dietrichstein, Prince Alexander, 232
Dingley, Roger, 25
Disdotti, R. P. Jo. Ant., 42
Dominick, Marinus Willet, 106
Dommerich, Louis W., 217, 218
Donche, Jacques, 226
Dorsner, J.-P., 145
Drury, Henry, 168, 244, 247
Dunbar, K., 220
Dunn, George, 87, 212, 220

E. N., 203
Ecken, von der, family [?], 191
Ellis, William, 45
Ely, Cathedral library, 200
Emily [?], Philip, 228
Erfurt, Carthusians of Salvatorberg, 225
Ess, Leander van, 20, 41, 211
Eugène, Prince of Savoy, 226

F. C., 169
Fabriano, Franciscan convent [?], 80
Fairfax, Thomas, 15
Farnam, Mrs. Henry, 5, 24, 31, 39, 99
Faulkner, Stephan, 45
Faxon, Thomas, 200

Felippa da thano [?], 12
Fenton, Mrs., 106
Fenwick, M. T. Fitzroy, 215
Fieschi, Giovanni Battista, 169
Fletcher, Andrew, 242
Fletcher, Henry, 83, 86, 92, 125, 126, 154, 196, 199, 205, 207, 210, 212, 220, 231
Fletcher, Mrs. Henry, 196, 199, 205, 210, 212, 220, 231
Flirtmann [?], Henrietta, 16
Florence, Santa Maria Novella, 42
Florence, convent of San Marco, 93
Fordham, Edward Wilfrid, 106
Francischanus, Frater, 67
Francischus Fauzonus, 162
Franciscus, 67
Franck, A., 225
Frederick, Sir Charles, 107
Freeburg, Victor O., 42
Frezeau de la Frezelière, Carolus, 85
Frost, Dr. Lowell C., 80

G. W. B. I., 191
Galbraith, John B., 32
Galletti, Gustavo Cammillo, 186
Garnier, Dame Charlotte, 217
Gelsenthal, A., 9
Ghislain, abbey of St., 69
Gian Maria Ferduno [?], 57
Gimbel, Alva B. (Mrs. Bernard F.), 190, 206
Gio. Batt. Fliscus [Fieschi], 169
Godechon, Octave, 214
Godefroid, 19
Godfrey, Jonathan, 107
Goels, Jehan, 90
Gordon-Duff, Edward, 153
Gough, Richard, 125
Greenfield, Mrs. Arthur, 3 (no. 44)
Greenway family, Devonshire, 243
Gribbell, John, 93
Gruel, Léon, 214
Guilford Collection. *See* North, Frederick, 5th Earl of Guilford
Gunther, Charles F., 3 (no. 12)

Hachette, André, 214
Haerlem, 32
Hago, Martin, 108, 146
Hainaut, Cistercian abbey of Cambron, 111
Hamburg, Bischöfliche Seminar-Bibliothek, 24
Hanelle, 110

Provenance

Hapthauser, Werner, 134
Harkness, Mrs. Edward S., 145
Harriman, William, 109
Harrison-Broadley, Capt. John, 129
Haslewood, John, 171
Haslewood, Joseph, 200
Hastings, Reginald Rawdon, 89
Hawtrey, Rev. Edward Craven, 160
Hayes, John, 11
Heard, Sir Isaac [?], 229
Heber, Richard, 11, 222, 236
Hellman, G. S., 128
Henri, comte de Clermont-Tonnerre, 227
Herbert, William, 125, 171
Hibbert, George, 230
Hillhouse, James, 56
Hinnit [?], 10
Hodgkin, J. E., 59
Hodgkin, Thomas, 65
Hodson, Lawrence W., 93
Hormier [?], Jacoby d', 82
Hornung, Sebastianus, 135
Horton, John, 45
House, John Henry, 150, 187
Huntington, Enoch, 10
Huth, Henry, 231

Ioannes, 232
Isted, George, 171

J. B., 158
Jacobus de Jüterbogk, 225
Jacomo di Sterpeto [?], 72
James, Mrs. Doctor, 60
Jeaffreson, Christopher, 101
Jesse, Edward, 171
Joannes Pricaeus. *See* Price, John
Johannes Carter. *See* Carter, Johannes
John S., 181
Johnson, Samuel, 3 (no. 13)
Juan Páez de Castro, 245

Kalckreuth, Count Axel von, 190
Kalinowski, Maybelle M. von, 122
Karolus de Fortro [?], 166
Katzeskyriakos, Basil, 249
Keith, Susan Bacon, 14–16, 19
Keller, Friedrich Ludwig von, 93
Kendall, J., 109
Kennedy, George G., 60
Kennedy, Malcolm, 60
Kerr, Philip Henry, 11th Marquess of Lothian, 217, 218

Kingsley Trust Association, 224
Kingsley, Charles, 113
Kingsley, James L., 30
Knighte, John, 60
Kniperus, Bernardus, of Lübeck, 9

L'Ecuy, Jean-Baptiste, 26
Laing, Robert, 109
Lambarde, William, 121
Lammens, P.-P.-C., 246
Landau, Baron Horace de, 183, 186
Langomarsini, Girolamo, 93
Lantenach [?], Gaspar Vant', 218
Laud, William, Archbishop of Canterbury, 113
Laudegum [?], M. De, 153
Lebanon, monastery of Mt., 238
Leclerc, Henri, 158
Leconfield, Lord, 163
Leighton, W. J., 204
Leipziger, Mrs. J. L., 20
Leonardus Rubenus, 9
Lewisohn, Adolph, 155
Libri, Guglielmo, 157, 181
Lisbon, monastery of St. Catharine, 228
Lorenzzo Hilippilipo Strozzi, 194
Louis de Bruges, Seigneur de la Gruthuyse [?], 230
Lovell, J., 101
Lowe, Edward C., 200
Lucia, Church of Sta., 42
Luxeuil [?], 193
Lyell, James P. R., 86, 200

Mabbott, Thomas O., 105
MacCarthy-Reagh, Count Justin, 215
Madrid, Biblioteca Real, 138
Mainz, Carmelite convent, 41
Mallett, Etienne, 196
Malmesbury church, 86
Manasses, Archbishop, 139
Manolli [?] Notaras de sancta andrea, 235
Manson, Mr., 151
Manusso Chrisi, 250
Maria Forst, monastery of, 24
Marien Van Der [ie?], 191
Mariotti, Augusto, 245
Marosvásárhely, library of, 145
Marsden, David D., 135
Marston, Thomas E., 58, 59, 63–75, 112–14, 176–86, 191, 194, 223
Martin, Tho., 88
Martin, Thomas, 101

Martini, Giuseppe (Joseph), 144
Massey, William, 125
Matthias Corvinus, King of Hungary, 145
Maximilian I of Austria [?], 230
Meerman, Gerard, 235, 240, 244 [?]
Meerman, Johann, 235, 240, 244 [?]
Mellon, Paul, 91
Mendell, Clarence, 193
Merton, Wilfred, 87
Metzdorf, Robert F., 219
Milan, Trivulzio Library, 2
Milbank, Mrs. Samuel, 137
Mont-Saint-Quentin, abbey of, 214
Montagu, Jean II de [?], 215
Montbault, Catherine Amable de la Haye, 46–54
Monte, Diego del, 29
Montgomerie, Hugh, 223
Morot, Joanna, 217
Morris, William, 93

Name, Addison van, 9, 42
Naples, Con. S. A. Neapoli, 173
Naulot, Claude, 240
Newman, W. H. H., 108, 146
Newton, A. Edward, 84
Newton, Hubert A., 82
Niccolò Azzone, 222
Nicolutius Vingnutius de Fabriano, 80
Nonantola, abbey of, 87
North, Frederick, 5th Earl of Guilford, 241, 245, 248, 249
Nourry, E., 162
Nowell, Laurence, 121
Noyes, Laurence Gilman, 3 (no. 28)

Oberlin, Jeremias, 145
Odescalchi, B. G., 203
Odescalchi, Prince, 203
Offenburg, Capuchin monastery, 233
Ottolinus de busco, 210

Padoua 1678, 72
Paris, Jesuit College of Clermont, 235, 240
Paris, Chardin Library, 207
Paris, Musée Napoléan, 36
Parke, Edmaunt [?], 220
Parker, Thomas, 200
Payne, Thomas, 101
Pellicier, Guillaume, 240
Penniman, James Hosmer, 4, 11

Pennypacker, Samuel W., 195
Percy, Henry, 9th Earl of Northumberland, 163
Petrus, 214
Petrus Franciscus de Cenninis, 194
Petrus Iatrus Florentinus, 239
Pfintzing, Barbara. See Barbara Pfintzing
Phillipps, Sir Thomas, 130, MS 229; 292, MS 69; 345, MS 111; 485, MS 211; 573, MS 20; 772, MS 207; 890, MS 234; 947, MS 114; 963, MS 14; 1045, MS 227; 1227, MS 87; 2234, MS 77; 2738, MS 14; 3337, MS 244; 3397, MS 247; 3691, MS 189; 3873, MS 230; 3899, MS 212; 4202, MS 239; 4289, MS 237; 4359, MS 215; 4365, MS 94; 4468, MS 75; 4527, MS 246; 4739, MS 226; 4930, MS 241; 6758, MS 235; 6764, MS 240; 7220, MS 125; 7488, MS 245; 7682, MS 248; 7713, MS 249; 8385, MS 216; 8826, MS 222; 9072, MS 155; 9089, MS 166; 9178, MS 74; 9302, MS 125; 9314, MS 11; 9511, MS 66; 9516, MS 243; 9520, MS 15; 9551, MS 236; 10452, MS 250; 15644, MS 59; 15867, MS 238; 16244, MS 157; 25368, MS 160
Pickering, B. M., 33
Pierpont Morgan Library, 101
Pietro Paulo Santino, 57
Pius II, Pope, 2
Porte, Monsieur de la, 90
Porter, Mrs. John, 82
Potocki, Albertus Comes, 36
Prato [?], 2
Prato, Convent at [?], 42
Prentis, E. A., Mr. and Mrs., 109, 110
Price, John, 250
Priuli, 172
Pruden, Russell G., 109, 110

Quentin, Mont-Saint-, 214

Rabinowitz, Louis M., 129, 192, 214
Ramon, Alexander, 17
Rhenanus, Beatus, 145
Riant, comte Paul, 5, 24, 31, 39, 99
Ricketts, Coella L., 151, 152
Riddagshausen, monastery of, 122
Riggs, Rev. T. Lawrason, 104
Robbins, Rev. Howard Chandler, 106
Roche, James, 212
Rohn [?], Matteus, 91

Provenance 397

Rosenmeyer, Ant. Jos., 9
Rowden, Edward, 228
Rubenus, Leonardus, 9

Salamanca, 34
Santen, Gaspar Van, 218
Saragossa, Library of the Santa Iglesia del Pilar, 208
Sattig, Gustave R., 55
Saunders, Thomas, gent., 220
Scabinus, Andreas Schottus, 99
Schennis, Friedrich von, 180
Schwerdt, C. F. G. R., 76, 77, 94, 100, 103, 121, 124, 127, 149, 232, 233
Sebenico, Church of St. Gregory, 55
Sebright, Sir John Saunders, 79, 90
Senlis, Cistercian monastery of Royaumont, 207
Serra S. Quirico, convent of St. Francis, 80
Seville, 34
Seymour, Thomas Day, 150, 187
Shelf-marks, unidentified, 2, 3 (no. 38), 35, 41, 43, 75, 88, 92, 127, 152, 155, 156, 164-66, 169, 170, 172, 175, 179, 184, 185, 188, 191, 194, 204, 206, 208, 211, 216, 219, 221, 224, 225, 233, 238, 242, 243
Simkhovitch, V. G., 14, 155, 211
Sitwell, Francis, 181
Sitwell, Samuel, 181
Smily [?], Philip, 228
Sneyd, Rev. Walter, 37, 124, 167
Sotheby, C. W. H., 105
Sotheby, Col. H. G., 105
Sotheby, James, 105
Sparke, 86
Spiegel, Jacob, 145
Spitzer, Carl B., 57, 78, 102, 213
St. John, Mrs. George C., 150
Stacye, Tho., 181
Staycye, Iohannis, 181
Sterling, John W., 41
Stiles, Ezra, 27
Stokes, Rev. Anson Phelps, 209, 225
Stork, G., 36
Street, Augustus Russell, 17, 18
Street, Caroline M., 17, 18
Strong, Thomas B., 181
Strozzi family [?], 194
Strozzi, Lorenzzo Hilippilipo. *See* Lorenzzo Hilippilipo Strozzi
Suchier, Hermann, 103

Tanis, James, 3 (no. 52)
Teleki, Sámuel, 145
Tegernsee, Benedictine monastery, 28
Thatcher, John, 89
Thiele, Heinrich August Ludwig, 122
Thomas, 3 (no. 33)
Tobias, 181
Todd, Albert May, 207, 231
Tomkinson, M. F., 26
Towneley, John, 216
Trier, St. Maximinus, 211
Trigbor, Johan Georg, 91
Trivulzio Library, Milan, 2
Trowbridge, Francis B., 97
Trowbridge, Thomas R., 97

Vallardi, Giusseppe, 36
Vallardi, Pietro, 36
Vallière, duc de la, 26
Villar de Aquila, 35
Vitta, Baron Joseph, 91
Voynich, Wilfred M., 172

Wagstaff, David, 77, 79, 87-90, 93, 94, 101, 103, 121, 124, 127, 133, 136, 138, 147, 149, 151, 152, 155-75, 200, 232, 233
Wagstaff, Mrs. David, 77, 79, 87, 89, 90, 93, 94, 101, 103, 121, 124, 127, 133, 136, 138, 147, 149, 151, 152, 155-60, 163-75, 200, 232, 233
Waldbott-Bassenheim, Graf Hugo von, 3 (no. 12)
Warren, E. P., 169
Watters, Adam, 154
Watters, Frank S., 154
Weickhmann, Joachim Guilielmus, 99
Wells, Gabriel, 61, 145
Whittokesmede [?], 163
Wildgoose, John, 25
Wodhull, Michael, 1

Yale, Elihu, 27
Yarnold, Charles, 227

Ziskind Charitable Trust, 1, MS 242; 5, MS 245; 6, MS 234; 7, MS 240; 14, MS 241; 15, MS 249; 16, MS 248; 17, MS 246; 21, MS 239; 24, MS 235; 26, MS 236; 27, MS 238; 43, MS 243; 52, MS 250; 56, MS 247; 59, MS 237; 61, MS 244

Index VI
Other Manuscripts Cited

Arles: Bibliothèque municipale 133, 162

Beaver Falls, Pa.: Geneva College Library no. 1, 3 (no. 12)
Berlin: Kupferstichkabinett MS. 78.B.12, 16; — MS. 78.B.13, 16
Bloomington, Ind.: Lilly Library MS Ricketts 240, 42
Boston: Public Library MS q. Med. 137, 190
Bruges: Seminary 45/144, 229
Brussels: Bibliothèque Royale MS II 7057, 230; — MS 9475, 215; — MSS 9178-87, 214; — MS IV 669, 226; — MS 10607, 229; — MS 18295, 229

Camarillo, California: Doheny Library *Bible Historiale*, 215
Cambridge: Trinity College B. 14. 19, 223
Claremont, California: Denison Library MS Kirby 1, 226
Copenhagen: Royal Library Thott 399, 230

Florence: Biblioteca Laurenziana Ash. 125, 229; — Conv. Supp. 47 (= AF 2755), 240; — Laur. 35,27: 93; — Laur. 47,34: 114; — Laur. 48,25: 114; — Laur. 50,4, 2nd part: 114

Geneva: Bibliothèque Publique et Universitaire fr. 170, 230; MS lang. étr. 210, 1
Grenoble: Bibiothèque Publique MS 870, 215

Hague, The: Koninklijke Bibliotheek 133 A 5, 230

Katrineholm: Ericsburg Slottsbibliothek, 24
Klosterneuberg MS 205, 224

London: British Library Add. 10292, 227; — Egerton 1065, 230; — Harley 336, 25; — Harley 3989, 58; — Lansdowne 1178, 215; — Royal 15 E III, 230; — Royal 16 G VIII, 226; — Royal 17 A. XXXII, 163; — Sloane 7, 163; — Sloane 442, 163; — Vespasian B. VII, 86
Dulwich College MS 25, 109

Madrid: Biblioteca Nacional Vit. 25-5, 16
Malmesbury Church MS 2, 86
Marseilles: Bibliothèque Municipale MS 111, 229
Milan: Biblioteca Trivulziana 2163, 1; — 2167, 1
Munich: Universitätsbibliothek 2° Cod. 128, 224

New Haven: Yale Medical Historical Library MS 27, 163; — MS 40, 163
New York: Pierpont Morgan Library MS 766, 27; — MS 804, 215

Osimo: Collegio Campana MS XLIX. 17, 173
Oxford: Bodleian Library Auct. T. 4. 16, 169; — Buchanan e. 5, 218; — Canon. Class. Lat. 229, 172; — Canon. Liturg. 131, 172; — Canon. Liturg. 383, 172; — Canon. Misc. 251, 147; — Canon. Pat. Lat. 162, 169; — Canon. Pat. Lat. 177, 42; — D'Orville 161, 158 and 165; — D'Orville 209, 87; — Don. d. 85, 27; — Douce 202, 215; — Douce 208, 230; — Laud Lat. 48, 159; — MS Bodley 483, 163; — MS Bodley 596, 3 (no. 4); — MS Bodley 758, 27
Keble College MS 22, 181

Padua: Episcopal Seminary. 46, 2
Pamplona: Catedral MS 51, 207
Paris: Bibliothèque de l'Arsenal MS 562, 107
Bibliothèque Ste. Geneviève MS 8, 214
Bibliothèque Nationale fr. 20-21, 215; — fr. 95, 229; — fr. 1280, 230; — fr. 2005, 162; — fr. 5229, 230; — lat. 375, 83; — lat. 1076, 229; — lat. 4192, 2; — lat. 8823, 214; — lat. 8910, 2; — lat. 8911, 2; — lat. 11535, 214; — lat. 12692, 214;

— lat. 12947, 143; — lat. 16776, 214; — n. a. l. 540, 36; — n. a. l. 3104, 206
Philadelphia: Philadelphia Free Library Lewis European MS T 188, 203; — MS T 189, 203
Phillipps, Sir Thomas (formerly), 10396, 230

Saint-Omer: Bibliothèque municipale MS 252, 193
Salisbury: Cathedral Library MS 61, 181
San Marino: Huntington Library HM 64, 163; — HM 195, 28; — HM 1176, 28; — HM 28174, 163
Stratton on the Foss: Downside Abbey 26542, 223

Tampa, Florida: Public Library no. 1, 3 (no. 12)
Thompson, Henry Yates (formerly) MS LXXV, 227
Turin: Archivio di Stato MS *b*. III. 12 J, 129; Biblioteca Nazionale MS L.I.6, 129

Valencia: Biblioteca Universitaria 887, 91
Vatican City: Biblioteca Apostolica Vaticana, Ottob. gr. 452, 241; — Ottob. lat. 183, 42; — Ottob. lat. 1463/1, 114; — Pal. gr. 258, 245; — Pal. lat. 1557, 114; — Urb. lat. 393, 55; — Urb. lat. 404, 188; — Vat. lat. 648, 80; — Vat. lat. 738, 83; — Vat. lat. 1946, 188; — Vat. lat. 2829, 173; — Vat. lat. 11441, 66
Venice: Biblioteca Marciana Lat. XIV. 14 (4235), 113
Vienna: Österreichische Nationalbibliothek Cod. 2616, 230; — Cod. 13, 1

Würzburg: Universitätsbibliothek MS M, ch. f. 169, 80
Waddesdon Manor: Rothschild Coll. MS 10, 106; — MS 14, 107; — MS 9, 129 and 190
Warsaw: Bibioteka Narodawa 8003, 36

Zurich: Stiftsbibliothek MS Car. C 110, 163

Index VII

Incipits

A donna grande possente et magnanima, 222
A la S. C. R. M. de el Rey Dn. Phelipe, 29
A la veille de pentecouste quant tout li compaignon, 229
A solis ortus cardine adusque terre limitem christum canamus, 43
A tu amato dio superiore ogni cosa, 146
A vous tres exellent prince charles, 215
Ach du Lieber Herre Gott, der du uns bey diesen, 122
Ach mein hertzlieber herr, 134
Actiones nostras quesumus domine aspirando, 110
Ad dolorem pedum equorum qui euenit occasione, 127
Ad locum vnde exeunt flumina reuertuntur, 207
Ad patriam uenio longis a finibus exul, 186
Ad Sublime Pontificatus maximi culmen, 2
Adeste muse maximi proles iouis, 174
Adesto celsis Aemoniae iugis Vates loquaci, 45
Adoramus te christe et benedicimus tibi, 110
Adorate scabellum pedum eius quem sanctum est, 181
Adoremus dominum, 43
Adueniente et minime te tempore misericionum et misericordiarum, 27
Aduentus domini per quatuor septimanas agitur, 111, 224
Ah! quanta aethereos pertentant gaudia ciues, 45
Ai pisa uitopero delle gente, 222
Albius tibullus eques regalis insignis forma cultuque, 186
Alle forwondred of oure selfe auȝte vs for to be, 223
Aller augen warten auff dich Herr, 122
Aller suessister herr ihesu criste. Durch die wirdigkait, 28
Allmächtiger, Barmhertziger Herre Gott Vater wir bitten dich, 122
Allmächtiger Ewiger Gott der du dürch deinen Sohn Vergebung, 122
Allmächtiger Ewiger Gott der du durch deinen heiligen Geist, 122
Allmächtiger Ewiger Gott der du für uns hast deinen Sohn, 122
Allmächtiger Ewiger Gott, der du uns gelehret hast, 122
Allmächtiger Ewiger Gott ein beschützer aller die auf dich, 122
Allmächtiger Ewiger Gott, himlischer Vater, wir bitten dich, 122
Allmächtiger Ewiger Gott Vater, der du aus Väterlicher, 122
Allmächtiger Ewiger Gott Vater der du sehen lessest das, 122
Allmächtiger Ewiger Gott, von dem alle gute Gaben herkommen, 122
Allmächtiger Ewiger Herre Gott, der du den Irrenden das, 122
Allmächtiger Herr Gott, der du bist ein trost der traurigen, 122
Allmächtiger Herr Gott Vater der du bist ein beschützer, 122
Allmächtiger Herr Gott Vater verleihe uns einen bestendigen, 122
Allmächtiger Herr Gott, Vater wir bitten dich du wollest, 122
Allmächtiger herr Gott, verleihe uns, die wir gleüben, 122
Allmächtiger Herr Gott wir bitten dich hertzlich, du wollest, 122
Allmächtiger Herre Gott gib uns den rechten Warhaftigen, 122
Allmächtiger und Barmhertziger Gott himlischer Vater wir, 122
Allmächtiger Vater, Ewiger Gott, der du für uns hast deinen, 122
Allmechtiger ewiger parmherziger got Ain anfangk vnd endt, 28
Alma redemptoris mater, 9
Almächtiger Ewiger Gott, himlischer Vater, der du durch den, 122
Almächtiger Gott der du durch den Todt deines Sohnes, 122
Almächtiger Gott, Himlischer Vater, sintemal dieser Krancke, 122

Incipits

Almechtiger ewiger Got ich wie wol deines, 134
Almechtiger ewiger Gott Vatter Sohn, 134
Almechtiger schein des ewigen liechts durch das zaichen des, 28
Almectiger Ewiger Gutiger vnd Barmhertziger gott, 134
Almyghty god in trenite fadir and sone, 163
Als wy onsen heren sullen ontfaen so sellen wi gaen, 32
Am morgens froe Gottoitmoedelich, 134
Amoenus ipse amoenos fert flosculos Hymettus, 45
Amor se uuoi chio torni al giogo anticho, 222
An herte if he chased woll desyre, 163
Andechtigen Lieben Freunde in Christo dem Herrn Gegenwertige, 122
Anglorum Regi scripsit tota scola salerni, 163
Anima christi sanctifica me. copus [sic] christi, 110
Animaduerti sepe donate plurimos, 114
Anministrante [sic] rem publicam theodosio gloriosissimo, 177
Anno a virginis partu 492 Zeno genere Isauritus, 45
Anno nonodecimo imperij tyberij, 214
Ansellmus cantuariensis archiepiscopus et pastor, 111
Ante omnia fratres karissimi diligatur, 5
Antiqui philosophi quorum intellectus adeo, 232
Apres ce que Maistre Gautier Mappe ot tretie des auentures, 229
Apud Romam fuit quidam imperator qui dioclicianus vocabat, 163
Aqua mirabilis ad visum conseruandum, 163
Aquellos que las cosas antiguas declararon, 182
Ardua qua surgit Nabathaeo vertice rupes, 45
Argus, erat pastor prudens, doctusque minister, 105
Arma belluosa pubes Bellici propago Martis, 45
Arma uirumque cano troiae, 172
Associat profugum tidea primus polinicem, 166
Au temps que le Roy modus donnoit doctrine de tous, 121

Audiuimus ueracem magistrum diuinum redemptorem hunc manum, 181
Aue beatissima ciuitas diuinitatis, 9
Aue maria ancilla sancte trinitatis, 9
Aue maria immaculata e sancta, 146
Aue martir gloriosa barbaraque generosa, 110
Aue principium nostre creationis. Aue precium, 110
Aue regina celorum, aue domina angelorum, 107
Aue salus mundi uerbum patris hostia sacra, 110
Aue sanctissima caro summa vita, 18
Aue sanctissima maria mater dei regina, 9
Aue sanguis qui fluxisti de preclara carne, 110
Auegna amicho che la nostra barcha, 222
Auete omnes christifideles anime, 9
Augustinus in libro de fide ad petrum dixit miraculum est, 163
Augustinus sermone .4. ad suos fratres heremitas sic inquit, 3 (no. 12)
Aurora lucis rutilat celum laudibus intonat mundus exultans, 43
Austour et tersol naist an region chaude, 162
Auxilia humilia firma consensus facit, 102
Auxiliatrix esto michi sancta trinitas gloriosa, 110
Ave domina sancta maria mater dei regina celi, 107
Avete omnes anime fideles quarum corpora, 107

Barbara pyramidum sileat miracula memphis, 65
Barbarismus Est Vna Pars Orationis, 66
Barmhertziger Ewiger Gott der du deines Eigenen Sohns nicht, 122
Barmhertziger Ewiger Gott der du deines Einigen Sohns nicht, 122
Beata iustina filia regis uitaliani et regine, 111
Beata nobis gaudia anni reduxit orbita cum, 43
Bello Alexandrino conflato Cesar rhodo, 87
Benedecta verzenella madre de dio, 12
Benedicat me deus pater, 110
Benedico te Pater celestis Pater, 134
Benignissime domine ihesu christe respice super me, 110

Bereitet den Weg dem Herren, 122
Botrus cypri dilectus meus, 9

Caius autem gracchus siue, 133
Canti go [sic] zoiosi e dolce melodie, 12
Cantus sit modestus grauis, 5
Carmina qui quondam studio florente peregi, 61, 84, 85
Castissimum marie virginis vterum clausum ventris sponse, 224
Catonis genus principium dignitatis, 133
Ceci parentis regimen ac fexi, 173
Cento fiate nel pensier mi rutola, 222
Cernis vt frontem pugilis decoram, 45
Cesar itineribus iustis confectis nullo die, 87
Chi en droit dist li contes que quant Agrauains se fu partis, 229
Chi hà luoco principale appresso un Prencipe sauio, 36
Christe redemptor omnium conserua tuos famulos beate semper, 43
Christe redemptor omnium ex patre patris unice, 43
Christus factus est pro nobis, 27
Christus ist auffgefahren in die Höhe, 122
Christus ist umb unser missethat willen verwundet, 122
Christus ist umb unser Sünde will dahingegeben, 122
Christus von den Todten erstanden, stirbt hinfürt nimmer, 122
Ci qui la haute ce et la seignorie, 227
Cimba tenella tremit pelagus conscendere vastum, 188
Circa primum notandum quod preceptum est iussio uel, 146
Clarus inoffenso procedat lumine titan, 174
Coactus assiduis tuis uocibus balbe, 87
Cogis me frater karissime ut ea, 189
Cogitante ac diu tacite sollicitaque, 177
Collegi ea que pluribus modis dicerentur, 179
Comme il soit vray selon les anciennes escriptures, 230
Comt scepper gheest visentere dine dienaers inwendicheit, 153
Considerans beatus apostolus immensitatem benignitatis christi, 80
Consolationes tue letificauerunt animam, 198
Contra paganos uel achademicos, 177

Corinthij sunt archaici. Et hij similiter ab apostolo, 154
Cosi mi parto doloroso e lasso, 222
Credo nonnunquam tibi euenisse, 133
Credo tibi paule nunciatum esse, 155
Cremetis frater aberat peregre, 165
Criste mortalium spes vna, qui, 9
Cristoual Colon, Genoues, natural de Saona, fue ombre, 128
Cum ad hieronem tirannum simonides, 14
Cum defensionum laboribus senatoriisque muneribus, 169
Cum defentionum laboribus senatorijsque muneribus, 160
Cum deffensionum laboribus senatorijs muneribus, 152
Cum Deus egelido natus vagiret in antro, 45
Cum equs habet calorem pendet caput in terra, 127
Cum essem adhuc puer in scolis, 157
Cum ex virtute prudencie que inter bonum, 233
Cum fugeret dauid persecutorem saul inquiens ita, 181
Cum inter cetera animalia summo rerum, 136
Cum inter cetera animalia uiui hominis deputata, 161
Cum inter cetera animalia vsui hominis deputata, 163
Cum luna fuerit in Ariete bonum, 67
Cum multi ex romanis etiam consularis, 168
Cum paduanorum nobilissima ciuitas, 111
Cum scribere illiterato debeam non miretur, 13
Cupere te Princeps serenissime que nostra in legatione sunt, 37
Cura labor meritum, 155
Cy commence le prologue de ce present, 230

Da pacem domine in diebus, 78
Da zw dem ersten driualtigklichen per institutionem, 219
Danc segghen wi di almachtighe vader want du mi arme sondersche, 32
Dancus rex stabat in suo palacio et ante eum stabant, 127
Das der gross lerer Scotus vnd auch ander lerer mit jm sprechen, 28
Das heilige Euangelium sagt von funff weÿsen, 134

Incipits

Das verlangen der Elenden Hörestu herr, 122
Das Wort ward fleisch, 122
Das Wort ward fleish, 122
Dat erste pater noster hebbe ik gesproken to loue leue here, 218
De agide et cleomene que, 133
De cada dia ujeron los ommes, 138
De colligenda ut sistenda fuga temporis et non esse, 155
De comò deueys conosçer, 138
De effimera et eius cura, 184
De his libris dici potest, 114
De I. v pater noster vnd aue maria, 134
De liberalibus studiis quid sentiam scire desideras. Nullum, 155
De liuore seu invidio liuor tabificum malis fenenum, 174
De qual sera che si rallegri omai, 222
De septem donis spiritus sancti de quibus prius scire debes, 224
Defecerunt scrutantes scrutinio ait, 4
Dem gleübigen wird sein glaube gereihnet zur gereihtigheit, 122
Demostenis Pater demostenes ut Theopompus, 14
Demosthenis pater Demosthenes ut, 133
Deprecor te pijssime domine ihesu christe propter illam, 110
Der frid vnsers herren ihesu cristi, Das zaichen des heiligen, 28
Der Herr hat seinen Engeln befohlen über dir, 122
Describere hoc donum spiritus sancti ut gratum, 80
Deum inmortalem sepe numero precatus sum, 188
Deus cui proprium est misereris, 220
Deus cui soli competit medicinam, 9
Deus cuius misericordie non est, 9, 220
Deus cuius vnigenitis assumpte humanitatis probabile, 107
Deus in cuius manu corda, 220
Deus origo pietatis pater misericordie, 9
Deus qui beatam uirginem mariam, 109
Deus qui corda fidelium sancti spiritus illustratione, 110
Deus qui de beate marie uirginis utero, 109
Deus qui manus tuas et pedes tuos et totum corpus tuum, 110
Deus qui nobis sub sacramento mirabili passionis, 110
Deus tuorum militum sors et corona premium laudes canentes, 43
Dezimos asi que si el gaujlan, 138
Di pensier in pensier di monte in monte, 222
Di uento pasci chi techo si gloria, 222
Dic Epicure mihi cuium pecus, Herculis est ne, 105
Dicit Beda quod tres sunt dies, 220
Dicit ille populus nationum ille in prima electione, 181
Die ewigen rue gib herr allenn glaubigen selen, vnd das ewig, 28
Die straffe lieget auf ihn, auf daß wir friede hetten, 122
Dies nabugodonosor Regis omnis enim populus tradebat, 163
Dieselbige befihlet sich nun dem frommen, 122
Dilecte fili dilige lacrimas noli differre eas, 146
Dilecti filij salutem et apostolicam benedictionem. Saluator humani, 188
Dilectissimi non erit indecorum fideles, 177
Diri uulneris novitate percussi, 9
Dit is de dagh den de here gemaket hefft hute, 218
Diuitias alius fuluo sibi congerat auro, 186
Dixit Gatriph persicus Multi persiarum, 103
Doctor egregie paule mores instrue et mente polum nos, 43
Domine iesu christe qui in hunc mundum, 9
Domine Iesu christe salus et liberacio, 107
Domine Iesu christe, cui sanctus Petrus adeo fideliter, 78
Domine ihesu christe adoro te in cruce pendentem, 110
Domine ihesu christe fili dei uiui, 9, 107
Domine Ihesu christe filii dei redemptor mundi deffende, 107
Domine ihesu christe per amaritudinem mortis tue, 110
Domine ihesu christe qui hanc sacratissimam carnem, 107, 220
Domine ihesu christe qui portando crucem, 9
Domine ihesu christe qui septem uerba, 110
Domine ihesu christe Rogo te amore illius gaudij, 107

Domine non sum dignus vt intres sub tectum meum, 107
Domine sancte pater omnipotens eterne deus qui coequalem, 107
Domine sancte pater omnipotens eterne deus qui nos, 110
Domine sancte spiritus qui coequalis, 9
Domine spiritus sancte deus qui coequalis, 107
Dominum qui fecit nos, 43
Doulce dame de misericorde, 17
Dulcissime domine ihesu christe qui beatissimam dei genitricem, 110
Dum mea me genetrix grauido, 69
Duos cum haberet Demea adolescentulos, 165
Dye almcchtigkait gottes vaters die weißhait gottes Suns, 28

Ecclesiam tuam quesumus, 107
Eerstelich sollestu zuvor viertag, 134
Egli e manifesto beatissimo padre, 151
Ego omni efficio argumentum huius epistola, 185
Ego quidem frater vnanimis libellum, 177
Ego tibi hunc librum Colucij ex media, 179
Ehe sie ruffen, wilich antworten, 122
Ein kind ist uns gebohren, 122
El cauallo e di calda natura, 137
Emiliorum familiam in urbe roma, 133
En el nonbre del padre et del fijo, 138
En este libro de iohan de sant fagun, 138
En pallais de Roy ou dempereur appartient, 129
Eneas primo libiae depellitur oris, 172
Eo regum et potentum maiestates illustrissime princeps in, 188
Era di stelle il cielo ancor dipinto, 222
Ereyest du dich das du stirbst in dem heiligen cristenlichenn, 28
Erfrew dich du heilige magdalena, ein hailsame hoffnung, 28
Erstlich nach einer wahren vnd reinen, 134
Es ist aygentlichen zu wissen das man got mit dar, 28
Es ist mir schmertzlich leÿdt, 134
Es saintes couronnes de iherusalem, 230
Est belua in mare que dicitur grece aspis, 13
Est et non cuncti montasaba non frequentant, 174

Est vbi sidereas stant regia tecta sub auras, 45
Estando yo agora en Romà agora ha tres años, 182
Et autem corpus christi spiritualis alimonia pertinens, 181
Et si michi priusquam hunc locum conscenderem amplissimus, 188
Etas florida est multum superest vite, 203
Eterna christi munera apostolorum gloriam laudes canentes, 43
Eterne rex altissime redemptor et fidelium quo mors soluta, 43
Euch ist heute der heiland gebohren, 122
Euermore prime schal chaunge the furste day of new yere, 88
Ewiger got herr ihesu criste, schöpfer himels vnd der erden, 28
Ewiger vnd almechtiger got Erparm dich vber all edlendt glaubig, 28
Ex more docti mistico seruemus hoc ieiunium deno dierum circulo, 43
Ex re profecto discipulorum videbitur esse si ad capescendas, 209
Excedit quidem dilectissimj multumque supereminet, 80
Excellentissimo principi domino Karolo secundo, 233
Execrabilis et priscis temporibus manditis tempestate nostra, 188
Exigitis rem magis iocundam mihi quam facilem, 155
Expedit in cunctis mores seruare decentes. Nam solet, 209
Experior nunc nunc cerno ipsis oculis, 188
Explanationem librorum boetij de consolatione, 198
Exultet celum laudibus resultet terra gaudijs apostolorum, 43
Exurge apricis Calliope rosis, 45
Eya du ewigs wort geflossen auß dem herzen deines hymlischen, 28
Eya du parmherziger got ihesu criste dein grosse vnschuld, 28
Eÿa du tzarte moder aller gnaden, 134
Eya sote Ihesu ewige cruczigede wyszheit myn herte, 218

Fac mecum signum in bono, 220
Facturusne sim Opere precium si, 1

Incipits

Falso queritur de natura sua Genus humanum quod imbeccilla, 231
Farriti allaczare la uena della, 124
Festi laudes hodierni ritu ductas annuo ciues gaudio, 43
Filij Redemptor mundi deus miserere nobis, 107
Formosa virgo Zodiaci decus Amor leonis seu Marathonia, 45
Fortuna potens tantum iuris atrox que vendicas, 174
Fortune mere de tristesce, 38
Fraternas acies alternaque regna profanis, 166
Fremuit spiritu Iesus et turbauit se ipsum et dixit Iudeis, 107
Frew dich junckfraw maria ein muter vnsers herren ihesu cristi, 28
Frew dich o kunigin der himel widerpringer aller creatur, 28
Frew dich vnd frolock du außerwelts vas der heiligen kirchen, 28
Frondosis si nosse iuuat quam dulcia Campis, 45

Gallia est omnis diuisa in partes tres, 87
Gaude ergo de cetero et exulta mecum, 12
Gaude flore uirginali, 109
Gaude uirgo mater christi, 109
Gegroit sijstu schone hemelsche konynckynne Edel, 196
Gegruesset seist du aller lobsamiste muter gots rayne Iunckfraw, 28
Gegruesset seist du himlische kindel petterin, Du du vns, 28
Gegruest seist du allerheiligiste v̄berwinderin deiner, 28
Gegruest seyst aller heiligiste maria, muter gots, kunigen der, 28
Gegruet sijstu sterne des mers hoge godes moder, 196
Gegruetzet sijstu Iuncfrouwe eyn holtz des leuens werdich, 196
Gegrust seist du suesser herre ihesu criste Ain wort des vaters, 28
Gegrust seÿstu h. haupt vnsers Seligmechers, 134
Gegrutet sistu konigynne gegrutet sistu maria du czarte, 218
Gegrutet sistu maria ful gnaden de herre is mit dy, 218
Gegrutet sy dat erwerdige benedyde hovet vnses leuen, 218
Gegrutz sÿstu aller wÿeste Junffer, 134
Gegrutz sÿstu maria du bis ein einige, 134
Gegrutzet systu maria vol gnaden sich erlichen wael, 196
Gelaubige vnd cristenliche seel far hyn far hyn von diser welt, 28
Genera uolatilium uiuencium de rapina quibus utuntur, 232
Genera volatium viuencium de rapina quibus vtitur, 103
Generum uolatilium uiuencium de rapina quibus utitur, 127
Ggegruset sistu werde heilge muder, 24
Glorieuse vierge marie/ A toy me, 108
Glorieuse vierge marie mere de Iesucrist, 108
Gloriosa passio domini nostri ihesu christi nos liberet a penis, 107
Godt groisse dich maria eyn maget dei, 196
Gorgones nuper iacui cum fessus in antro, 45
Got gruys dich mynnentliche maget o moder, 196
Got heiliger geist, der du wo du wilt dein götliche genad, 28
Got vater von himel. Ich pit dich in dem namenn ihesu, 28
Gott gib friede in deinem lande, 122
Gott vatter von himmel ich bitten dich, 134
Gratias ago tibi domine ihesu christe pro sexaginta, 9
Gratias tibi ago omnipotens pater qui me, 110
Gruest seist maria genadenvol der herr mir dir, 28

Hanc uisionem reuelauit dominus zachiarie, 80
Hec diligenter adtende prudenter intellige sollicite, 181
Hechyra est huic nomen fabule hec cum hec data est, 165
Heer godstadighe in ons dattu heuest gewrocht in mi, 32
Heere doet vp minen mont te louene dinen alder, 153
Heere ghÿ sult open doen mine leppen Enn minen mont sal, 153

Heiliger martrer sand cristoff Ich pit dich durch, 28

Heiliger sand Thoman du apostel vnd sand pott des herren, 28

Heiliger vnd erwirdiger pischoff sant erasm edler gottes, 28

Helige junckfraw maria, die du deinen aingepornen Sun, 28

Helyas orauit ut non plueret super terram, 224

Here begynnyth the Boke of astronomye conciued and ymade, 163

Here bygynnyth the chapters of divers makyng and dyȝtyng, 163

Here ihesu christe die mit wille des vaters ende des heilighen, 32

Here ihesu christi ik bede dy an, an deme cruce hangende, 218

Here is describ'd the perfect ground, 74

Here may men se þe vertues of herbes which ben hoot, 163

Herr Allmächtiger Ewiger Gott, der du das gottlose wesen, 122

Herr Allmächtiger Gott, der du alles was da ist regierest, 122

Herr Allmächtiger Gott, der du der Elenden, 122

Herr Allmächtiger Gott, von dem alle gute und vollkommene, 122

Herr Allmechtiger Gott, himlischer vater, der du alles was da, 122

Herr Barmhertziger Gott, der du uns deinen Lieben Sohn Iesum, 122

Herr ewiger got wir pitten dein parmherzigkait mit andacht, 28

Herr got heiliger himlischer vater der du deinen aingepornen, 28

Herr Gott himlischer Vater der du aus Väterlicher Liebe uns, 122

Herr Gott himlischer Vater der du deinen Eingebohrnen Sohn, 122

Herr Gott himlischer Vater, der du deinen Sohn umb unser, 122

Herr Gott himlischer Vater der du deinen Sohn uns zum Heylande, 122

Herr Gott himlischer Vater der du deinen Sohn unsern Herrn, 122

Herr Gott himlischer Vater, der du die heiligen, 122

Herr Gott himlischer Vater, der du nicht Lust hast an der armen, 122

Herr Gott himlischer Vater der du uns deinen Sohn geschencket, 122

Herr Gott himlischer Vater du weissest daß wir in so mancher, 122

Herr Gott himlischer Vater von dem wir ohn unterlaß, 122

Herr Gott himlischer Vater wir bitten dich du wollest deinen, 122

Herr Gott himlischer Vater, wir bitten dich, du wollest durch, 122

Herr Gott himlischer Vater wir bitten dich du wollest uns den, 122

Herr Gott himlischer Vater wir dancken dir daß du mit deiner, 122

Herr Gott himlischer Vater, Wir dancken dir deiner grossen gnade, 122

Herr Gott himlischer Vater wir dancken dir von ganzen hertzen, 122

Herr Gott himlischer Vater wir dancken dir vor deine, 122

Herr Gott himlischer Vater, wir dancken, loben und preisen dich, 122

Herr Gott himmlischer Vater, der du deine Engel zum Schutz, 122

Herr Gott himmlischer Vater Wir bitten dich du wollest deinen, 122

Herr Gott, lieber Vater, der du (an diesem Tage) deiner, 122

Herr handel nicht mit uns nach unsern Sünden, 122

Herr Iesu Christe, du Sohn des allerhöchsten Gottes, 122

Herr Iesu Christe, du Sohn des Allmächtigen Gottes, wir, 122

Herr ihesu criste almechtiger ewiger got tail mir mit dein, 28

Herr ihesu criste der du vmb vnsers hails willen deinen lieb, 28

Herr ihesu criste hailer der welt, wir beuelhen dir, 28

Herr Ihesu criste Ich gedenck als du geopffert pist, 28

Herr ihesu criste Ich glaub das ich dich waren got vnd menschen, 28

Herr ihesu criste mein got nach deinem heyligen, 28

Herr ihesu criste vmb den grossen schmerzen den du an dem creuz, 28

Herre Gott himlischer Vater der du in der Tauff, 122

Herre handel nicht mit uns nach unsern Sunden, 122
Hersame frouwen aller frouwen de werdigiste, 218
Herzenliche danckparkeit ewigs lob, ere vnd alle säligkait, 28
Hesterna die cum ad me plerique, 177
Heu! heu rapaci gloria labitur, 45
Hic describitur modus quomodo parliamentum Regis Anglie, 163
Hic discribitur modus quomodo parliamentum Regis Anglie, 86
Hic iaceo putrida et stigia de fece deorum, 188
Hic inuicta patris capiunt veneranda quietem, 188
Hic nouus Alcides felix Sulmonis alumnus, 188
Hic queritum inter doctores theologicos Quid sit maioris meriti, 146
Hic vir despiciens mundus et terrena, 78
Hier beghint onser lieuer vrawen sauter der saligher maghet, 153
Hilff lieber Herre Gott daß wir der Newen lieblichen Gebürt, 122
His abluta plebs diues insignibus ad christi, 181
Historia de la inuención de las Yndias y de la conquista, 128
Historiam esse ueritatis testem, nuntiam uetustatis, 37
Hoc est uerbum patris altissimi quo caro factum est, 80
Hodie si uocem domini audierietis nolite, 80
Homo microcosmus id est minor mundus appellari, 189
Honorabili viro Willielmo Cicilio Domino ac Baroni Burleio, 105
Hostis herodes impie christum uenire quid times, 43
How a man or womman oweth gladly to have the passion of crist, 223
How a man shal knowe, whiche is the speche of the flesshe, 223
Huc ad regem pastorum Pastores currite, 45
Huc adsit omnis Pyramidum situs, 45
Huius autem operis professores sufficienter non tractauerunt, 127
Humilitas vera est timere deum, 5
Hunc Epicurum Argus, heu quo perduxit amice, 105

Hunc librum composuit Seneca nobilissimus orator, 155
Hwilken man annen slar i hiell. Oc vorter han gerpen, 39

I guardo i crespi e i biondi capelli, 222
I knowlich me to my lorde ihesu cryst and to his blessid, 163
Iam bone pastor petre clemens accipe uota, 43
Iam christe sol iustitie mentis deiscant tenebre uirtutum, 43
Iam christus astra ascenderat regressus unde uenerat, 43
Iam lux emoriens tacitam caligine noctem, 45
Iam nox hibernas bis quinque peregerat, 174
Iam tandem vir clarissime perfidiam fides auariciam, 197
Ic groet di inder afgronde diinre ewigher godliker minnen, 32
Ic sal dÿ belyden ower de vrawe. Want duer, 153
Ich armer sunder hochwirdig dich mit den stercksten, 28
Ich befelhe heut meinen Glauben, 134
Ich bidden dich heilige Ionffrouwen suysse, 196
Ich danck dir milter vater genädiger herr vnd parmherziger got, 28
Ich fahre auf zu meinen Vater und zu euren Vater, 122
Ich gebenedey vnd wolsprich dir o aller guettigister ihesu Wann, 28
Ich grossmach dich o aller suessister ihesu Wann, 28
Ich lob dich o allerdurchleuchtigister ihesu Wann, 28
Ich lob vnd ere dich o aller höchste weisshait Wann, 28
Ich pit dich du heiligs creuz dar an vnser hail, 28
Ich pit dich heiliger hochwirdiger martrer vnd kunig, 28
Ich pit dich herr ewiger got, du wollest mich heut genedigklich, 28
Ich sag dir großmechtig danck o aller suessister vnd, 28
Ich sprechen zoe dynen reynen hertzen O werdige, 196
Ich weiß daß mein Erlöser lebet, 122

Idcirco credo quia hoc tam aperte cum uiuentibus, 181
Ieronimus. Corinthij sunt achaici, 154
Ieronimus. post actam penitentiam scribit, 154
Igitur post excessum beati martini, 177
Ihesu corona celsior et ueritas sublimior qui confitenti, 43
Ihesu criste du genadenreicher schaz meiner seel gemahel, 28
Ihesu nostra redemptio amor et desiderium deus creator, 43
Ihesu redemptor omnium perpes corona presulum in hac die, 43
Ihesu saluator seculi redemptis ope subueni et pia dei genetrix, 43
Ihesus Christus den du hast empfangen von dem heiligen geist, 28
Ihesus nazarenus Rex iudeorum fili dei miserere, 163
Ihesus soisse gedencknisse du geues waer, 196
Ihesus soit en ma teste et mon entendement, 107
Ille super gangem super exauditus et indos, 170
Illumina domine oculos meos, 110
Imperatorie maiestatis est in palatio, 26, 214
In christi surgo nomine, 9
In deme Sondage sculle wij vnse herte dorch, 218
In der bicht nichts verschweigen, 134
In dien tiden Seide ihesus zinen iongheren Ghi, 153
In isto verbo praepostero ordine narrantur, 20
In manu tua domine, 43
In marche after the furste C, 88
In mein herz senck dein lieb du vrsprung aller genaden, 28
In milicias proficisci gnatum, 185
In militiam profisci gniatum, 165
In minoribus agentes nondum sacris ordinibus, 197
In noua terra credibile est fuisse omnia semina, 64
In presentia ueri corporis et sanguinis tui, 110
In quo patet casus hominis, 27
In quo uerbo .5. per ordinem ostendit et predixit, 80

In sua resurrectione dominus et saluator noster, 80
In uerbis istis de appocalypse sumptis ad laudem, 80
Incipit liber ruralium commodorum a petro, 233
Incipit prohemium cuiusdam noue copulacionis cuius nomen, 27
Incomenza vno interrogatorio confessionale in uulgare, 146
Initio et medio ac fini mei tractatus, 102
Initium est inchoatio uel alicuius rei principium, 80
Initium mei operis sergius galba, 143
Initium michi operis seruius galba, 145
Initium michi tractatus sit in nomine domini, 102
Initium mihi operis seruius galba, 144
Innocencia dei vera est que nec sibi nec alteri nocet, 15
Inter omnia digna memoria que annuatim recolit, 80
Interueniat pro nobis, 107
Inuenitur per scripturam quod animalia quedam audientes, 80
Inuenta secuit primus qui naue, 180
Inuiolata integra et casta, 107
Io ho nuouamente ordinato, 151
Io sono a te mandata padre santo, 222
Iste confessor domini sacratus festa plebs cuius celebrat per, 43
Iste magister non fuit mendax sed uerax, 127
Iste Prosper fuit equitaneus vir eruditissimus omniumque arcium, 15
Isti sunt due oliue et duo candelabra, 78
Ita fac mi lucilli vendica te tibi, 155
Ite procul laetae laeto cum carmine Musae, 45
Ite umbros eingnite [sic] siluas, 173
Item der heilig vater vnd pabst Siluester verleicht allen den, 28
Iunius Iuuenalis libertini locupletis incertum alumnus an, 73

Je souloye jadis penser, 38
Je suis soullart le blond et le beau chien courant, 121
Johannes du himlischer adler, Du besunder freundt gottes, 28

Incipits

Kircke om vigd vorter maa æy annen sinnæ vighes vtæn, 39
Kyrieleyson, Kyrieleyson, Kyrieleyson, Herr almechtiger got, 28
La gran fama signor di uertu carca, 222
La uerita malletta et dice pensa, 222
Labrum hoc erat lauatorium in quo sacerdotes lauabant, 80
Laist ons syngen dat goede ind dat suesse woert, 196
Las propiedades de la medçanas, 138
Laspro tormento che consuma et sface, 222
Lasso che quando immaginando uegno, 222
Le stelle uniuersali e i cieli rotanti, 222
Legerat huius amor titulum nomenque libelli, 174
Lehre mich, herr, daß ich bewahre dein gesetze, 122
Li premiers commandement que dieux commanda si est teulz, 204
Librum tuum quem nostro materno eloquio vt opinor, 197
Licet cunctorum poetarum carmina gremium tuum, 155, 184
Lieben Freünde! Demnach wir befinden, daß unser lieber Bruder, 122
Lieben Freunde es ist eine Kindelbetterin, die nachgehaltenem, 122
Lieber Herre Gott wecke uns auff, 122
Liquerat astrorum fulgentia culmina sedes, 45
Littera pitagore discrimine secta bicorni, 174
Litteris a fabio. C. cesaris consulibus, 87
Lo degno et dolce amor del natio loco, 222
Lo libro medesynal delli spariueri, 76
Lobent den herren all heiden, lobent in alle volcker, 28
Lors que ie me trouuay a par moy, 230
Lucius Annaeus Seneca cordubensis, 155
Lustris sex qui iam peractis tempus implens corporis, 43

Machet die thore weit, und die thür in der Welt hoch, 122
Magnitudo celestium beneficiorum angustias humane mentis, 181
Magno et excellenti ingenio uiri, 114, 156
Maintenant puis que vous veez comment, 230
Maintes gens dient que en songes, 33

Maior in exiguo regnabit corpore virtus, 174
Maiores statas solennesque cerimonias, 221
Maiores statis solennesque cerimonias, 147
Mantua me genuit calabri rapuere tenet nunc, 172
Marci Antonii uitam multiplici, 133
Marco Antonio auus fuit antonius, 133
Maria du gewaltige kunigin der himel. Du heilige kaiserin, 28
Maria Ik vormane dik der ouerflodigen stoude, 218
Maria Ioncfer Ontfanck die groisse die der van dem heren, 196
Maria muter rayen mayd, Zu mötten zeit ward dir herzlichs laid, 28
Marie klag die was so gross, da sy yr liebs, 28
Me tibi teque mihi genus etas, 69
Mein allerliebsten. Uns wird stets durch die Predigt, 122
Mein seel lobt auch got den heiligen geist durch des wurckung, 28
Mellifluum quisquis romanum nescit homerum, 174
Mentre che uisse il mio dilecto spoço, 222
Meretrix adolescentem cuius, 165, 185
Meth logh scal land bygges Æn vilde hwer man orues at sit, 39
Meum est propositum in taberna mori, 163
Min siel hait dich begert in der nacht Ind, 196
Miserere mi domine animabus que singulares, 9
Miserere mihi misero peccatori misericors, 134
Misericordiam tuam domine sancte pater, 9, 109
Mit frouden latet vns hilligen vnnd werdigen de gedechtnisse, 218
Molte fiate gia nobilisima donna auenne che io il quale, 222
Moralium dogma philosophorum per multa, 102
Morte poi chio non trouo a chui mi doglia, 222
Mortuus erat et reuixit legimus in quadam historia, 15
Mouet fortassis aliquos qui tamen modo, 80
Mout fu iries li anemis quant nostre Sires out este, 227
Multa filij sunt que me hortantur, 179

Mundi creator et redemptor ihesu christi qui, 110
Mundus modo ponitur totus in errore, 163

Nam eum qui pro omni ciuitate quid autem, 181
Nam ualerium asiaticum bis, 143, 144
Nam Valerium asiaticum bis, 145
Natus in ectelsis tectis carthaginis, 185
Natus in excelsis tectis cartaginis, 165
Ne cui sit uestrum mirum cur partes seni poeta dederit, 165
Ne cuj uestrum sit mirum. Cur partes seni poeta dederit, 185
Ne lintellecto nuouo pensier formasi, 222
Nec fonte labra prolui cabalino, 71
Nec fonte labra prolui caballino, 67, 68, 69, 112
Nec veneris nec tu bachi capiaris amore, 174
Necessarie igitur et hoc adicimus annuntiantes, 181
Nel primo punto quando amor percosse, 222
Nemo qui sanctorum uitas et exempla legerit ignorare poterit, 181
Nichil deo sic placet quomodo, 157
Nicolaus Episcopus seruus seruorum dej. Ad futuram rei memoriam. Vt pacis, 188
Nigra sum sed formosa, 9
Nobilis signis, moribus suauis, 177
Nocte surgentes, 8, 43
Noctu preterita priusquam me quieti committerem, 197
Non dubito fore plerosque Attice qui hoc genus, 164
Non è alcun dubbio (signor illustrissimo), 30
Non est fortasse mirandum, 133
Non semper viridem Cirrha superbiam, 45
Nonne plura sunt Rhetorices praecepta, 135
Nosse primum decet quantum sit femina turpis, 174
Nostre sires auoit mult danemis et auersaires contre, 227
Nuestro señor dios quando crio, 138
Nunc Theodidacte, hic dies est quia gratus ouilli, 105
Nuper legebam princeps Illustrissime Xenephontis, 149

O alder helischste maria moeder gods moeder ons liefs heeren, 153
O aller erwirdigiste kunigin der parmherzigkait, Ich grues dem Iunckfreulichs, 28
O aller erwirdigiste kunigin der parmherzigkait, Ich grueß den erwigen temel, 28
O aller höchste gothait, vngemeßne guet, aller guttigiste, 28
O aller liebster herr ihesu criste Ich betracht dein großpitters, 28
O aller liebster herr ihesu criste. Ich betracht vnd gedenck, 28
O aller raynigiste wirdigiste junckfraw maria, O du sälige, 28
O aller verwundtister herre ihcsu criste Ich sag dir, 28
O allerheiligister engel gottes herr dem diser mensch von got, 28
O Allerheiligste Jungfraw maria ich bitte, 134
O Allmächtiger Herre Gott, himlischer Vater, wir bitten dich, 122
O allmechtiger got herr ihesu criste Der du vns mit deinem, 28
O almechtiger ewiger got. Ich vnwirdiger sunder, 28
O almechtiger ewiger got vnd herre mein beschaffer erlöser, 28
O alre heilichste Ioncfer maria om dat swaer, 196
O alre mijlste moder godes neige zo min onseliger, 196
O amantissima christi sponsa summo, 24
O aula e masone della uniuerssale propiciatione, 12
O Barmhertziger Gott der du gelehret hast die hirten, 122
O bewaltiger schöpfer himels vnd der erdenn Herr, 28
O bone ihesu christe per tuam misericordiam esto michi ihesus, 107
O bone ihesu. O dulcissime ihesu. O pijssime ihesu, 110
O clementissime domine ihesu christe pro tua infinita, 109
O coninghinne der hemelen en vrawe der inghelen, 153
O coninghinne des hemels ontfanghe den lof zanck, 153
O crux aue spes unica, 107

Incipits

O domina glorie regina leticie. O fons pietatis, 110
O Domine iesu christe adoro te in cruce pendentem, 107
O du aller liebster here ihesu christe ich arme Sunderin, 219
O du aller liebster here ihesu christe mein erlosser, 219
O du aller liebster herr ihesu christe Schöpfer, 28
O du aller liebster herr ihesu criste Ich pit dich durch, 28
O du aller rainieste vnd wirdigiste muter meines herren ihesu, 28
O du aller soteste Iuncfrowe maria ik arme sunder, 218
O Du allerlieffte Jungfrawe maria ich ergeue mich dir, 134
O Du allersuessest Junfraw, 134
O du edle fraw sand Elizabeth erlang mir von got, 28
O du erwirdige kaiserin du heligen gepererin gots, 28
O du genadenreicher vnd heiliger herr sand .N. ein junger ihesu, 28
O Du gnadenriche vnd werdige Junffer, 134
O Du h. Geist der du de lieb, 134
O du heilige Iunckfraw vnd martrerin sand margaretha, 28
O du heiliger Sand Andre, zwelffpot vnsers herren ihesu cristi, 28
O du heiliger vnd wirdiger sand .N. ain warer ewangelist, 28
O du heiliger vnd wirdiger sand .N. ein junger ihesu, 28
O du heylige trinitet. O du ware aynikait du helige götliche, 28
O du hochgelobter vnnd hochwirdiger himelfurst vnd heiliger, 28
O du hochwirdiger vater sand .N. ain schein vnd zier, 28
O du hochwirdiger vnd strenger ritter gots heiliger sandt .N., 28
O du hochwirdiger zwelfpot vnsers herren ihesu cristi heiliger, 28
O du höchster got. O liebhaber menschlichs geschlechts, 28
O du hogeste prester vnde ware bisschopp Ihesu criste, 218
O du lobsamiste vnd raynnigste junckfraw vnd muter gotts maria, 28
O du mein aller höchster schaz vnd trost meiner armenn, 28
O du mein aller liebster here Ihesu christe ich sag dir meinem, 219
O du mein aller liebster herr ihesu christe du zier der engel, 28
O du parmherziger tröstlicher trost aller betruebten menschen, 28
O du rainiste vnd heiligiste junckfraw sand .N. du gesegnete, 28
O du reicher prunn der parmherzigkait, tail mit dein väterlich, 28
O du säliger apostel vnd ewangelist Sand matheus, 28
O du säliger vnd lieber peichtiger ihesu cristi heiliger, 28
O du säliger vnd wirdiger pischoff ihesu cristi heiliger sand, 28
O du schein des ewigen liechts. Wie pistu nun, 28
O du suess himelprot herr ihesu criste ain Sun gottes himlischen, 28
O du suesse muter gottes vnd vnuermailigte junckfraw maria, 28
O du trösterin aller betruebten Herzen. O du spiegel, 28
O du uth fletende borne der ewigheit wu bistu, 218
O du vnvermäligte Iunckfraw vnd wirdigiste muter vnsers herren, 28
O du ware speis der engel, O du wares himelprot der ellenden, 28
O du werdighe ewige Iungkfrowe maria du sote beschermerynne, 218
O du wirdige aller genaden heilige sandt .N. red ain guts wortt, 28
O du wirdige hochgelobte vnd rainigiste gepererin gottes, 28
O du wirdige muter der hymlischen kaiserin vnd aller raynisten, 28
O du wirdiger vnd strenger ritter gottes heiliger sand, 28
O du wirdigiste aller creatur zartte Iunckfraw maria, 28
O du ynnigkliche Iunckfraw ob allen Iunckfrawen, O du, 28
O dulcissime atque amantissime domine, 18
O Ehrentreiche Fraw O h. Maria gelich, 134
O Enedige vnnd barmhertige here ihesu christe Ik bidde dy, 218

O ewerdighe mich Dych tzo louen Beheiliche maget maria myt, 196
O ewige götliche parmherzigkait. O ernstliche gerechtigkait, 28
O ewige weishait herr ihesu criste meiner dursstigen, 28
O ewige weißhait. O gruntlose väterliche, 28
O Ewiger Gott und Vater, der du nicht bist ein Gott der Todten, 122
O Ewiger hymmelscher Vatter durch das leben, 134
O ewiger parmherziger got herr ihesu criste dein heiligs, 28
O eya du allerwirdigiste muter des aingepornen Sun gots, 28
O Genedige moder der barmhertzicheit, 134
O Gewarre ewiger Gott beslous, 134
O Ghebendide maghet maria moeder gods almachtich Ic biddu, 153
O Gloriose Jonffer maria ich grutzen dyn, 134
O Gloriose Jonffer maria moder aller genaden, 134
O Gloriose Junffer maria ontfanck zu ehren, 134
O Gloriose vrouwe Ind alre suesste maget, 196
O Gloriose vrouwe inde mylde maget O heilige, 196
O Got herr ihesu criste der du vmb erlösung willen, 28
O Gott almechtich vatter der barmhertzicheit, 134
O Gott der du fur der welt heÿl hast, 134
O Gott der du vns in deinen h. Leintwat, 134
O Gott meiner Seelen der du nit, 134
O Gott Vatter Sohn vnd heiliger Geist erbarm, 134
O Gude Ihesu. O Sote ihesu. O ihesu der iuncfrouwen, 218
O guede Jesu du bist dat wort, 134
O Guettiger herr ihesu criste Ich gedenck das du an dem palmtag, 28
O Gutiger pellican herr Jesu Christi, 134
O heer ihesu christe die alle tut voer ons gheoffert, 32
O Heere Jesu Christe sone vanden leuen, 134
O Heilige dach Ind eirlichen West gegruest ewelichen, 196
O heilige trinältigkait du ainiger got, Bross erschrockenlich, 28
O heilige trinitet warer ewiger got du hochstes güt ob allem, 28
O heilige vnuermäligte vnd gesegnete in ewigzeit Iunckfraw, 28
O heiliger engel gots dem ich auß götlicher fursichtigkait, 28
O heiliger geist vnd ewiger got vaterliche ewige, 28
O heiliger got, O starcker got, O vntödlicher got, 28
O heiliger herr sandt Cristoff der eren du bist ain wirdiger, 28
O heiliger vnd lieber herr sant cristoffel Ich pit dich, 28
O heiliger zwelffpot sant Iacob den wir glauben nach, 28
O heliger sandt Bartolmee, Du apostel vnsers herren ihesu, 28
O hemelsche coninghinne maria ontfanct goedertierlic, 153
O hemmelsche konigynne maria werdige godis muder, 218
O here dyr si lof ind eere du die vur ons, 196
O here mein got ich erman dich vnnd danck dir, 219
O herr almechtiger ewiger got Wir pitten dich durch deinen, 28
O herr almechtiger got ihesu criste, piß genedig nur, 28
O herr almechtiger got parmherziger himlischer vater, 28
O Herr erleuchte mir meine Augen, 134
O herr Gott himlischer Vater, der du aus Vaterlicher gnaden, 122
O Herr Gott himlischer Vater wir dancken dir für dein Väterliche Gnaden, 122
O Herr Gott hymmelscher vader ontfanck, 134
O herr Iesu Christe, der du zukünftig bist, 122
O Herr Iesu Christe Ich grutzen, 134
O herr ihesu criste des lebendigen waren gottes Sun, 28
O herr ihesu criste du ewiger parmherziger got, 28
O herr ihesu criste ewige suessikait, 28
O herr Ihesu criste ewiger parmherziger got Schöpfer aller, 28

Incipits

O herr ihesu criste Ich pet dich an am creuz, 28
O herr ihesu criste warer got vnd mensch du pist, 28
O Herr Jesu christe des lebendiger Gottes Sohn, 134
O Herr Jesu christe ich erman dich vnd danck dir, 134
O Herr Jesu christe, ich grose sunder, 134
O herr mein got künig ob allen künigen vnd, 28
O Herr vnd barmhertziger vader Schencke mich, 134
O herr vnd got Ich kom für dich als ain armer, 28
O herre got dir bekenn ich vnd gib mich schuldig, 28
O herre ihesu criste des waren lebendigen gottes, 28
O herre vorluchte myne ogen vp dat ik nimmier enslape, 218
O herzen lieber N mein dem almechtigen got, 28
O heylige drinältigkait du aynigs wesen, ewiger got, 28
O heyliger got. O starcker got. O vntötlicher got erparm, 28
O heyliger got, O starcker got, O vntodlicher got herr, 28
O himlischer künig mein got vnd herr ihesu criste. Durch, 28
O himlischer vater ewiger got, wer pin ich, oder wer hat mir, 28
O himlischer vater in der ewigkait du parmherziger got, 28
O intemerata, 16, 17, 106, 107, 109, 110, 190, 217
O Ioncfer marja salich is die mynsch die lieff, 196
O Jesu du Sohn des lebendigen Gottes der du vmb der Sunde, 122
O junkfraw gepererin gots maria lieb, freudt, kurzweil, 28
O kunigin der himel junckfraw maria trosterin aller betruebten, 28
O leue here ihesu criste des leuendigen goddis, 218
O liebe Herr Jesu Christe ierstete dat, 134
O liebe vnd aller liebste maria edle suesse kunigin Ich, 28

O lieber here ihesu christe gottes Sun vnnd, 219
O lieber herr ich opffer dir dis pater noster, 134
O Lieber herr Iesu Christe ein sohn, 134
O lieber herr Jesu christe diss Pater, 134
O Lieber herr Jesu Christe ich ermahne, 134
O Lieue herr du hast mit deiner, 134
O Lieue herr Jesu christe ich begere, 134
O Lieue herre ich bitten dich durch den floss, 134
O lieue selige inde heilige gebenedide Ionffrouwe, 196
O lux beata trinitas tres unum trium, 43
O maria ain laitter der himel, Ain saul, 28
O Maria du allergehorsamste dochter, 134
O Maria du edle junckfraw, Du liechter morgen, 28
O Maria du op brechende rode morgen van wilchen, 196
O maria du pist das wolgeriert vaßlem des heiligen geists, 28
O maria du suesse Iunckfraw, du heiliger tempel der heiligen, 28
O Maria ein hulperin in allen, 134
O maria ein Iunckfraw ob allen Iunckfrawen ein muter ihesu, 28
O maria ein kayserin des himels vnd der erden, 28
O Maria ein middelerm tuschen, 134
O Maria ein verluchterin die dar geboren, 134
O Maria ein weder brengerin, 134
O Maria eyn vursprecherin aller ellendiger, 134
O maria ghegroet si di in der helegher drie voudicheit, 110
O Maria hoege loefde gebenedide hemelsche, 196
O Maria moder der barmhertzigheit, 134
O Maria suesse maget ich vermanen dich der groisser, 196
O Maria vol genaden bewijse mir, 196
O Mein allergutigster Jesu du hast, 134
O Mein allerliebster Jesu O du geliebter, 134
O Mein geliebter vater allen gebenedeÿt, 134
O Mein geliebter verleÿhe mir gnad, 134

O Mein h. engel Ich dancke dir, 134
O Mein h. patronen meinen h. schutzengels, 134
O mein here ihesu christe pis ermant mit herczlicher, 219
O Mein Iesu ich komme zu dir deiner zugeniessen, 134
O Mein Jesu durch die verdeinsten, 134
O Mein Jesu O Jesu meines hertzens, 134
O Mein verwundter Jesu durch deine aller, 134
O mensch wiltu leben in sicherhait, So hab vmb dein sund, 28
O muter gots du engel zier, mit ganzer krafft schrey, 28
O Mylde Ionffrouwe maria alre heilichste moder, 196
O parmherziger got, O guettiger got, der du mit deiner grossen, 28
O pouerta cosi ti strugga idio, 222
O Sacrum Conuiuium in quo, 78
O säliger vnd großmechtiger martrer sand laurenz, 28
O scacci camera locus est mirabilis ille, 163
O strenger ritter vnd heiliger notthelffer sand Jorg, 28
O Suester her Jesu Christe, 134
O tite si quid ego adiuto curam, 179
O Unendliche Gute dir sag ich danck vmb, 134
O vlietende borne der eeuwicheit Hoe bestu dus versleghen, 153
O vlietende borne in der eewicheit, 110
O Vmbefleckede gnedige sunderlike iuncfrowe vnd moder, 218
O Vrauwe maria almechtich In der verbolgent heit gotz en, 196
O vrauwe maria moeder gods uwe helighe gratie, 110
O wee eenighe gheboren zone troost dijn, 153
O werde Iunckfraw maria O du himelische kunigin du zier der, 28
O werde moder gotz des almechtigen konynchs gewerdige, 196
O yr all lieb heiligen Die der almechtig got von ewigkait, 28
O yr aller säligisten vnd aller raynisten junckfrawenn in, 28
O yr allheiligen der nam vnd gedachtnuss ist geschriben, 28
O yr durchleuchtigistenn peichtiger ihesu cristi von got, 28
O yr heiligen engelischenn geist die der almechtig got, 28
O yr heiligen Iunckfrawenn die yr nun in keuschait vmbfangen, 28
O yr heiligen martrer die da vmb die lieb vnsers herren ihesu, 28
O yr heiligen patriarchen vnd propheten die den tag, 28
O yr heiligen peichtiger, die der almechtig got vmb bekennung, 28
O yr heiligen zwelffpotenn vnd ewangelisten Die der almechtig, 28
O yr hochwirdigen vnd heiligen himelfursten heiligen engelen, 28
O yr lieben heiligen apostelen cristi sand philip vnd iacob, 28
O yr lieben himelfurstenn Symon vnd Iudas apostelen vnsers, 28
O yr vnvberwindtlichenn lobsamen vnd heiligen martrer sandt, 28
O yr vnv̄berwintlichen ritter gottes vnd löblichen, 28
Obsecro te, 16, 17, 106, 107, 109, 110, 190, 217
Ocioso mihi nuper ac lectitare, 14, 133
Ogni arte et ogni doctrina, 151
Omni tempore diligit qui amicus est, 102
Omnibus consideratis ... [verse prayer in 10 parts], 109
Omnipotens et misericors deus quoniam non mortem sed, 107
Omnipotens sempiterne deus qui ezechie, 110
Omnipotens sempiterne deus qui gloriose, 109
Omnipotens sempiterne deus qui humano, 9
Omnipotens sempiterne deus qui unigenitum filium tuum, 109
Omnipotens splendor eterne lucis, 16
Omnis homines qui student sese praestare coeteris animalibus, 231
Omnis ostendacio non tacet suspicionem mendacij, 174
Omnis speculatio sapientialis inquisitiam altissimarum, 80
Onder wijst bidden wy heere hu volc en dwelke, 153

Incipits

Opere pretium est eciam illud inserere, 177
Optimum fratres inistis certamen aut equare, 177

Pallas Iuno Venus nemorosem vallibus Ide, 163
Pange lingua gloriosi prelium certaminis et, 43
Pantaleon filius senatoris pagani matris, 111
Paschalis admirabilis insignis et prodigiis, 78
Pater de celis deus miserere nobis, 9, 107
Paucitas dierum meorum timetur breui dimitte, 10
Paulus episcopus seruus seruorum dei ad perpetuam rei memoriam excommunicamus et anathematizamus, 188
Paulus Episcopus seruus seruorum dej. Ad perpetuam rei memoriam. Ineffabilis prouidentia summi patris, 188
Per che saccenda nel cor uolontade, 222
Per verum omnium sanctorum angelorum, 220
Pernassus gemino quam lambit vertice nubes, 45
Persius Flaccus Satiricus poeta uulterris nascitur omni mundi, 58
Pes in metro dicitur quod pedis, 66
Petrus apostolus et paulus doctor gentium, 78
Pharnace superato affrica recepta qui ex his preliis, 87
Pigliarite la herba chiamata, 124
Pis gegruesset sälige Iunckfraw vnd martrerin sand katherina, 28
Pis gegruest allerheiligiste maria, muter gots kunigin, 28
Pius episcopus seruus seruorum dei, 188
Pius .ij. pontifex maximus natione Tuscus fuit patria, 188
Pius et misericors deus qui te regem constituit, 188
Pja dei genetrix quamuis tua potestas nullis, 188
Poeta cum primum animum ad scribendum appulit, 165, 185
Poi che da uoi fortuna e rampognata, 222
Poiche, o Ludouico Principe illustrissimo, 30
Pollicitus fui praeclara gesta, 192
Polycletus Messenius quem proditionis apud ciues, 167

Posquam [sic] poeta sensit scripturam suam ab iniquis, 165
Post actam penitentiam scribit eis epistolam consolatoriam, 154
Post regis nostri conuiuantis conuiuia post patientis, 80
Posteaquam a me mane digressus es, 177
Postquam aliqua dicta sunt de trinitate dei de creatura, 146
Postquam poeta vetus poetam non potest retrahere a studio et, 165
Preoccupemus faciem, 43
Presbiter euagrius innocentio karissimo filio, 177
Presens autor prenomine publius nomine Ouidius, 174
Prima anime impressio in corpus est uita ita, 80
Prima die eriget se mare xl cubitus super, 224
Primero de la aves que son llamadas de Rapinya, 79
Primo dierum omnium, 43
Primo est considerare necesse est, 6
Primus habet libyam ueniunt ut troes in urbem, 172
Principium itaque huius religionis, 5
Prologo de el interprete al letor, 29
Protector in te sperancium, 107
Pys gruesset maria ein dierren der heiligen drinältigkait, 28

Quae est naturae humanae peruersitas ut quae imitari nos posse, 37
Quae tale Mauri prodigium Iubos, 45
Qual fie si duro cuor domo o di donna, 222
Qualis buccolicis quantus tellure domandi, 172
Qualquier ante, y qualquier doctrina, 29
Quam minime sim quietus etiam, 114
Quam pulcra es et quam decora carissima in deliciis, 181
Quamquam te marce fili annum iam audientem, 158, 159
Quamquam te Marce filij annum iam audientem, 170
Quando Crio el mundo e fizo, 79
Quant Je Regarde et congnois les opinions des hommes, 216
Quanti sit et fuerit semper, 114
Quas uobis pecunias dedimus Teucro, 167

Quattuor phalaridis epistolas quas nuper, 167
Quatuor Virtutum species multorum sapientum, 184
Quatuor virtutum species multorum sapientium, 155
Quedam dicta Boetij excepta de libro de consolatione, 80
Querebaris mecum nocte preterita quod amori operam dares, 197
Questa aulente rosa colorita et frescha, 222
Questa sie la legenda del nostro padre mesiere sam petronio, 37
Questio facta fuerat sponse a suis sodalibus, 80
Qui autem anima christiana quae ascensura es ex sacratissimo, 181
Qui dono lepidum nouum libellum, 186
Qui du corps dieu, 17, 106
Qui inchomincia la prima parte de libro chiamato Filostrato, 222
Qui natus fuerit in signo aquarij est honoratus in vno, 163
Qui uenetae urbis originem, 2
Qui uult esse bonus frater bibat semel, 163
Quid dicit omnis homo terra quando accipit sanguinem, 181
Quid est Rhetorica? Est ars benè dicendi, 135
Quid faciat letas segetes quo sidere terram, 172
Quid miri Aesonidem Phryxei uelleris igne, 45
Quid Nymphe resonae filia verulae, 45
Quintus mucius augur multa narrare, 157
Quintus Mucius Augur Sceuola, 170
Quintus mucius Augur sceuola multa narrare, 179
Quis me furor nunc sede ab infausta, 173
Quis me profundit dirus habitator stygis, 45
Quisquis fugacis lubricum mundi decus, 45
Quisquis lege versus oculo properante viator, 174
Quisquis prudentiam sequi desideras tunc per rationem, 155
Quo magis ingratus nemo fuit alter et idem, 188
Quod iam diu promiseram vt scilicet, 25
Quod predicant non missi uel non canonice, 199

Quodcumque uinclis super terram strinxerit erit in astris, 43
Quomodo peccata mundi tollat inquit quo ordine, 181
Quoniam deus magnus, 43
Quoniam in secunda parte legende uirginis beate katerine de senis, 37
Quoniam multi sunt qui in aduersitatibus, 102

Recte ergo sub ara martyres collocantur, 181
Regina celi letare, 107
Regina del cor mio, 12
Respice quesumus omnipotens deus, 9
Restitues hereditatem meam mihi, 6
Retribue seruo tuo uiuifica me, 134
Rex eterne domine rerum creator omnium qui eras ante secula, 43
Rex gloriose matyrum [sic] corona confitentium qui respuentes, 43
Ryght as poverte causeth sobrenesse, 163

Sacerdotii autem de quo loquimur aspice dignitatem, 181
Sacris sollemnijs iuncta sint gaudia et, 43
Saincte uraye croix aouree, 17, 106
Salich es die ghene die dinen name lief hebben, 153
Saloman in hys paraboles seith þat, 171
Salua me domine rex eterne glorie, 110
Salua nos christe saluator per virtutem sancte crucis, 107
Saluator mundi salua me qui per crucem tuam, 163
Salue mater Saluatoris fons salutis, 78
Salue sancte pater patrie lux forma, 78
Saluete vos omnes fideles anime quarum corpora, 9
Saluete vos omnes fideles anime que iacetis, 9
Salutem et Apostolicam benedictionem infructuosos palmates, 188
Salve Regina, 9, 107, 109, 134, 218
Sancta Birgitta ist geboren, 24
Sancta Maria succurrere miseris iuua, 78
Sancte gabriel sancte michael omnes, 220
Sapienciam antiquorum omnium exquiret, 199
Schaffe in mir Gott eine reines hertze, 122
Scienciam de animalibus secundum eam quam in principio, 77

Scilicet vt rosa quam ros educat, irriget imber, 45
Scripturus uitam serui tui prout tu dederis, 111
Se da gli antichi la uirtù cotanto, 30
Se mia uertute exprimer potesse, 222
Seit gruest all ellend glaubig seelen, 28
Selig sind die Todten die in dem herrn sterben, 122
Selon que dyent les trois maistres de faulconnerye, 90
Semper ego auditor tantum numquam, 68, 69, 70, 72, 112
Semper ego auditor tantum nunquam, 67, 73, 113
Semper quidem opere pretium fuit illustres, 177
Sensuit ung petit liuret fait et compouse par messire, 162
Sepe Philephe tue numos petiere tabelle, 188
Serenissimo et Inuictissimo Signore, 124
Seuerus desiderio fratri karissimo salutem, 177
Shall I alone for ever lend mine eare, 74
Si come il cigno quando a morte uene, 222
Si dormiatis inter medios cleros, 13
Si parentes vocari in ius liceret, 177
Si quem forte iuuat subidi sapienter amori, 174
Si queris miracula, mors, error, 78
Si quis ad malum legibus dominicis mannitus fuerit, 212
Si quis scire desiderat de arte bersandi, 127
Si quisquam est qui se placere studeant bonis, 185
Si quisquam est qui se studeat placere bonis, 165
Si vero .l. porcos furatus fuit, 212
Sic aestuanti glissit anhelitu, 45
Sic uolumus reliquis nequeas implere quod optes, 188
Sicut ante nos dixit quidam sapiens cuius sententiam, 181
Sicut ex multis scripture locis colligitur, 80
Sicut narrat sanctus ylarius magnus doctor ecclesie, 80
Sicut uerus est dei filius dominus noster ihesus, 181
Sio potesse ridir come comprese, 222

Siste focum te causa manet nunc altera iudex, 45
Sit dies ista tibi foelix Epicure peropto, 105
Sitte [?] hathe wonder that reason nat, 163
So oft ihr von diesen Brodt esset, und von diesen Kelch, 122
Solent plerique homines sublimis vir optimeque pater, 188
Solet aliquotiens in scriptoris ordo, 66
Soror tonantis hoc enim michi, 173
Sororem falso, 165, 185
Souente nel mio cor nasce un pensero, 222
Spente la cortesia spente larghessa, 222
Sperne lucrum vexat mentes vesana libido, 174
Spiritus sancte deus miserere nobis, 107
Stabat mater, 16, 107
Status royaulx touchant le fait de la guerre prins, 230
Stupor et mirabilia audita sunt, 24
Sub tuum presidium confugimus sancta, 78
Subbitamente amor con la sua fiaccola, 222
Subuenite sancti dei, 9
Succurre michi virgo virginum, 220
Sulpicius seuerus basule parenti venerabili, 177
Sunt lapides igniferi in quodam monte, 13
Sunt tria que vere faciunt me sepe dolere, 163
Suscipe domine animam serui tui, 9
Suscipe domine creaturam tuam, 9
Suscipere dignare domine deus omnipotens, 109

Tabula magistri petri de datia, 220
Take a lyne and leye hit to the louest here above the hoof, 163
Take caules and stryp hem from the stalkes and betes borage, 163
Tanto son uolti i cieli di parte in parte, 222
Te igitur, 18
Te precor sanctissima maria mater dei, 109
Te quoque uirgilio comitem non equa tibulle, 186
Tempore quo faedo regia Britannia bello, 45
Temporibus calixti pape secundi patriarcha, 111
Temporibus maximiani erat uir quidam, 111

Ten eersten male riepsi. O Wee een gheboren sone troost dijn eneghe moeder, 110
The Wyse man his sone forbede, 163
Theare be certayne tokens wherby a man maye chose them, 100
Theodericus rex francorum cum esset cathalones elegit viros, 212
Thesprotis et Mollossis post diluuium, 133
Thet hauer oc koning jæt riget at ængen man scal, 39
Thise ben þe wordis off, Salamon þus mych to sey, 228
Threicius quondam vates et fide creditur canora, 174
Thu that art a gentilman, 163
Tibi domine commendamus animam famule tue, 9
Titire tu patule recubans sub tegmine fagi, 172
To the honoure and reuerence of ȝou my worshupfulle, 163
To the Right Worshipfull Sr Robert Wiseman Knight all increase, 74
Tot vides gentes que sunt auersa loquentes, 163
Tous les filz de noe espartz par les climatz, 216
Tres hault tres puissant tres excellent victorieux, 226
Tria sunt utilia immo necessaria in enuntiatione, 80
Tristes erant apostoli de nece sui domini quem pena mortis, 43
Tristis hyems tumidis acuens Stridoribus iras, 45
Tulliorum familia que et Ciceronis, 14, 133
Tullius gratas raptabat in agmine turmas, 159
Tunc enim et sacrifici munda est oblatio, 181
Tzo loue ind zo eren der glorioser Iuncfferen ind moder godes, 196

Vedendo il negotio tanto graue per il quale mi sono, 37
Vellem malatesta novelle princeps illustris, 167
Venatio et canes deorum inuentio fuit, 149
Uenerabili in christo patri et domino spirituali, 233
Uenerabilis christi sponse deoque dicate uirginis, 111
Ueni creator spiritus mentes, 110
Venite adoremus, 43
Venite exultemus, 43, 178
Vera perceptio corporis et sanguinis tui, 107
Verba ista scripta sunt in euuangelio hodierno in quibus verbis, 15
Verba ista scripta sunt in psalmo et sunt verba spiritus sancti, 15
Verblijt dich heilige tempel godes serr, 196
Verbum hoc sumptum de euangelio beati Matthei est uerbum, 80
Verbum hoc sumptum est de euangelio beati luce quod, 80
Verbum istud sumptum est de euangelio beati luce. Et est, 80
Verbum istud sumptum est de euangelio beati luce et est uerbum saluatoris, 80
Uerbum supernum prodiens a patre, 43
Verbum supernum prodiens nec patris linquens, 43
Verschone Herr, verschone unser Sünde, 122
Uertice parnasi phebus phitona sagittis, 188
Vertu celeste in titol triumfante, 222
Victima tu christi virgo susanna fuisti, 107
Uidens pijssimus et misericordissimus deus hominem, 224
Vienne la maiestate imperatoria, 222
Vieron los hombres de como, 79
Vir bonus et sapiens qualem vix reperit ullum, 174
Uirgo templum trinitatis, 109
Vis consilij expers mole ruit sua vim temperatam mi sublime, 188
Vita in ligno moritur, 9
Vnde Lesbois animata neruis, 45
Uniuersum tempus presentis inde in quatuor, 111
Vocauit [nos] pius et misericors dominus ad sacram beati petri, 188
Volens igitur Boetius agere de consolatione, 198
Volentes aliqua de uirgine gloriosa predicare, 146
Uoluitur in primo fratrum concordia libro, 166
Voma superstitio egipti seruasque, 112
Uos nunc qui inter patrem et filium uoluntatem, 181

Incipits

Vos o Taenario quondam Ludibria regi, 45
Vos sancti dei incliti qui estis, 78
Uox clara ecce intonat obscura queque increpat, 43
Uox turturis audita est, 9
Urbanus Episcopus seruus seruorum, 5
Urbis Rome exterarumque gentium facta, 147, 221
Vt dies aduenit, Epicuro prospera cuncta, 105
Vt iuuet et prosit conatur pagina presens, 80
Vt pacis qua nichil desiderabilius in vniuersali, 188
Vtrum deum incarnari fuerit possibile, 207
Uxorem duxit Pamphilus phylomenam, 165

Washe the dogg throughly in Cowes pysse, 100
Washe your handes alwayes before you feede her, 100
Weest ghegroedt O alder wijste enn daerste moeder, 153
Welcher unwürdig von diesen Brodt isset, oder von dem Kelch, 122
Wen das kindlein in der noth daheime getauft ist, 122
Wer da gleübet und getauffet wird, der wird selig werden, 122
Wesche mich O herr ab von meinen, 134
West gegruet in verblijt O Conynckynne des hemels, 196
When her mewtes shew her to be surfyted, 100
Wiewohl er ihr in Kindesnöten, 122
Wir dancken dir herr Gott himlischer Vater von grund unsers, 122
Wir hören alle Tage aus Gottes wort erfahrens auch beyde, 122
Wir loben Gott den Vater, Sohn, und den heiligen Geist, 122

Xauerius. Fastidiosas terrere vlterius moras, 45
Xenophontis philosophi quendam libellum, 14

Yhesu lorde þt maydyst me and wt thy precyus, 163

Zu dem ersten kneende in de gedechteniss, 134

Ἀθανάτους μὲν πρῶτα θεοὺς νομῷ ὡς διάκεινται, 247
Ἄκουε ψυχὴ λογικὴ, κοινωνὲ τῶν ἐμῶν βουλευμάτων, 238
ἀλλὰ τοῦ μὲν ἀληθὲς εἰπεῖν ἐστι λευκὸν εἴτε μή, 234
Ἀπεδεξάμην ὡς πρέπουσαν τῷ σεμνῷ σου, 237
Ἀποκάλυψις Ἰησοῦ χριστοῦ ἣν ἔδωκεν αὐτῷ ὁ, 246
Ἄριστον καὶ πρῶτον μάθημα ἐστὶν ἐν ἀνθρώποις, 235
Ἁρμονική ἐστὶ δύναμις καταληπτικὴ τῶν ἐν, 208
Ἄρχε πρὸ πάντων, καὶ παθῶν, 235
Ἀρχὴ τοῦ εὐαγγελίου Ἰησοῦ Χριστοῦ υἱοῦ τοῦ, 150
Ἄσωμεν τῷ κυρίῳ ἐνδόξως γὰρ δεδόξασται, 249

βασίλειος: τί ἐστιν ἀρχή, 235
Βασιλεῦ οὐράνιε· παράκλητε ἀγαθέ· προσκυνητὲ θεέ, 235

Δόξα τῇ ἀπειροτάτῃ καὶ παναιτίῳ καὶ ζωαρχικῇ, 139

Ἐάν τις ἄπιστος ἢ ἰουδαῖος ἢ σαμαρείτης, 238
Εἰ διὰ τὸ λέγεσθαι φησὶ παρὰ ταῖς θείαις, 248
Εἰς πόσα διαιροῦνται τὰ εἰκοσιτέσσαρα γράμματα, 239
Ἐλάβομεν ἐντολὰς παρὰ αὐτοῦ τοῦ Χριστοῦ, 238
Ἐν ἀρχῇ ἦν ὁ λόγος. καὶ ὁ λόγος ἦν, 150
Ἐπειδὴ διὰ τὸ συμβῆναι ἡμῖν πολὺν χρόνον, 244
Ἐπειδὴ οἱ μὲν τέλειον εἶναι λέγουσι τὸ ἅγιον, 238
Ἐπειδήπερ πολλοὶ επεχείρησαν ἀνατάξασθαι διήγησιν, 150
ἐρώτησις .α΄. τὸ ὅλως ἔχειν τὸν ἄνθρωπον, 235
Ἔστι μὲν οὖν τὸ κυρίως καὶ πρῶτος μακαριστὸν, 249
Εὐλογεῖτε ἀπόστολοι προφῆται καὶ μάρτυρες κυρίου, 249
Εὐλογοῦμεν πατέρα καὶ υἱὸν καὶ ἅγιον, 249
εὐσέβιος χαρπιανῷ ἀγαπητῷ ἀδελφῷ ἐν κυρίῳ χαίρειν, 248

Ἡ ἀγάπη τοῦ Θεοῦ θέρμη ἐστι τῇ φύσει, 238
Ἡ περὶ φύσεως ἐπιστήμη σχεδὸν ἡ πλείστη φαίνεται, 234
Ἡ χάρις σου δέδωκέ μοι τὸ λαλεῖν πρὸς σὲ, 139

Θαυμάζεται τῶν μὲν κατὰ φύσιν συμβαινόντων, 245

Θεὲ ὑπεράγαθε πάτερ καὶ λόγε καὶ πνεῦμα τὸ ἅγιον, 139

Ἰωάννου δὲ τοῦ κολοβοῦ καθημένου, 238

Καθ' ἕτερον δὲ τὸ προκείμενον ἄπορον, 235
Καλὰ μὲν τοῦ βασιλέως πρὸς τοὺς ὑπήκοους, 235

Μακάριος ἀνὴρ ὃς οὐκ ἐπορεύθη ἐν βουλῇ ἀσεβῶν, 249
Μετὰ τὸν μωυσέα καὶ τὸν τούτου διάδοχον ἰησοῦν, 249

Ὁ ἀββὰς μακάριος πειραζόμενος ὑπὸ τοῦ διάβολου, 238
Ὁ βουλόμενος παντῶν τῶν παθῶν, 238
Ὁ κύριος ἡμῶν Ἰησοῦς Χριστὸς ἡ τοῦ πατρὸς, 238
Οἱ μὲν πρὸ τοῦ νόμου ἐκεῖνοι θεῖοι ἄνδρες, 235
ὁμώνυμα λέγεται ὧν ὄνομα μόνον κοινόν, 234
Ὄντος ἀναγκαίου χρυσαόριε καὶ εἰς τὴν τῶν, 234
Ὅρασις ἣν εἶδεν ἠσαΐας υἱὸς ἀμώς, 241
Ὅστις ἂν βούληται σωθῆναι πρὸ πάντων χρὴ, 236
Οὐκ ἔστι τὸ φαλτήριον δέσποτά μου βιβλίον, 249
Ὀφείλομεν πιστεύειν ὡς ἐβαπτίσθημεν, 238

πᾶσα τέχνη καὶ πᾶσα μέθοδος. ὁμοίως, 240
Πᾶσα διδασκαλία καὶ πᾶσα μάθησις διανοητική, 234
Πατέρα λέγεις ἄνθρωπε τὸν θεὸν, 235
Περὶ δὲ νεότητος καὶ γήρως καὶ περὶ ζωῆς, 234
Περὶ δὲ τοῦ τὰ μὲν εἶναι μακρόβια τῶν ζώων, 234
Περὶ δὲ τῶν χρησίμων μορίων τοῖς ζώοις, 234
Περὶ τοῦ πῶς δεῖ ἐξομολογεῖσθαι τὸν πᾶσα ἄνθρωπον, 243
πρῶτον δεῖ θέσθαι ὁρίσασθαι τί ὄνομα, 234

Τὰ τῶν βρωμάτων ἡδέα καὶ τίμια προτιθέμενα, 248
τὴν μὲν κατὰ τῶν περσῶν καὶ παρθυέων, 250
Τὴν παρὰ τοῖς ἕλλησι τακτικὴν θεωρίαν ἀπὸ τῶν, 242
Τί τοῦτο σήμερον σιγῇ πολλῇ ἐν τῇ γῇ, 248
Τὸν μὲν πρῶτον λόγον ἐπονησάμην περὶ πάντων, 246
Τοῦ ἀγαθοῦ καὶ ὑπεραγάθου καὶ παναγάθου, 237
Τρία μέρη λέγουσιν οἱ πατέρες ἔχειν τὴν λογικὴν, 238
Τῶν παρ' ἡμῖν αἰσθητηρίων τῶν ἐναργεστάτην τὴν, 241

φιλοσοφία ἐστὶ ζωῆς ἀνθρωπίνης κάθαρσις καὶ, 247

ᾠδή ἐστιν ὅσα θεωρίας ἔχεται φιλῆς, 249

Plates

Frontispiece	MS 229, f. 272v (*slightly enlarged*)
Plate 1	Binding Terms
Plate 2	MS 214, f. 30r (a. 1229)
Plate 3	MS 227, f. 12r (a. 1357)
Plate 4	*Above*: MS 225, f. 263r (a. 1422); *Left*: MS 222, f. 78v (a. 1415)
Plate 5	MS 61, f. 1r (a. 1430); MS 20, f. 317r (a. 1452)
Plate 6	MS 58, f. 77r (1461); MS 67, f. 36r (a. 1468)
Plate 7	MS 70, f. 10v (a. 1475); MS 28, f. 118r (a. 1513) (*slightly enlarged*)
Plate 8	MS 226, f. 197r (a. 1476) (*5/8 natural size*)
Plate 9	MS 89, f. 52v (a. 1562) (*slightly reduced*); MS 18, f. 78r (a. 1578)
Plate 10	MS 82, f. 150r; MS 26, f. 108v
Plate 11	MS 206, f. 209v; MS 83, f. 514r; MS 38, f. 13r
Plate 12	MS 215, f. 108v (vol. 3); MS 217, f. 48r (*4/5 natural size*)
Plate 13	MS 203, f. 87r; MS 108, f. 26v
Plate 14	MS 218, f. 159r; MS 190, f. 13v
Plate 15	MS 211, f. 68r; MS 205, f. 1r
Plate 16	MS 196, f. 15r; MS 9, f. 161r (*6/7 natural size*)
Plate 17	MS 154, f. 72r (*1/2 natural size*); MS 189, f. 9r
Plate 18	MS 81, f. 220r (*slightly enlarged*); MS 86, f. 11r
Plate 19	MS 27, f. 87v (*slightly reduced*)
Plate 20	MS 10, f. 81v (*3/5 natural size*); MS 163, f. 131v
Plate 21	*Above*: MS 178, f. 32r; *Left*: MS 138, f. 1r
Plate 22	MS 111, f. 48v; MS 152, f. 1r
Plate 23	MS 147, f. 1r (*7/10 natural size*)
Plate 24	*Above*: MS 114, f. 9r; *Left*: MS 221, f. 3r
Plate 25	MS 93, f. 49r; MS 133, f. 103v
Plate 26	MS 151, f. 1r; MS 64, f. 19v
Plate 27	MS 165, f. 1r
Plate 28	MS 1, f. 1r (*1/2 natural size*)
Plate 29	MS 247, f. 12r; MS 240, f. 20r
Plate 30	MS 239, f. 2r; MS 245, f. 22v
Plate 31	MS 246, f. 65r; MS 208, f. 1v
Plate 32	MS 27, Inside upper cover (*1/3 natural size*); MS 36, Upper cover (*1/3 natural size*)

PLATE I

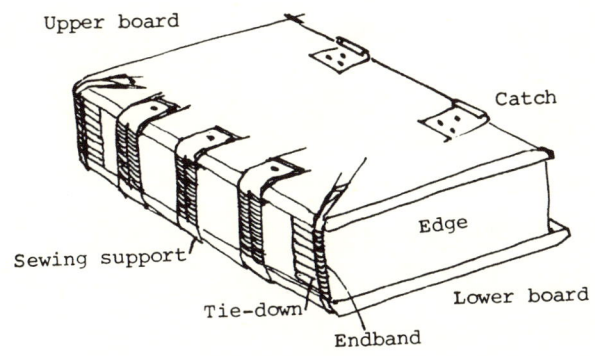

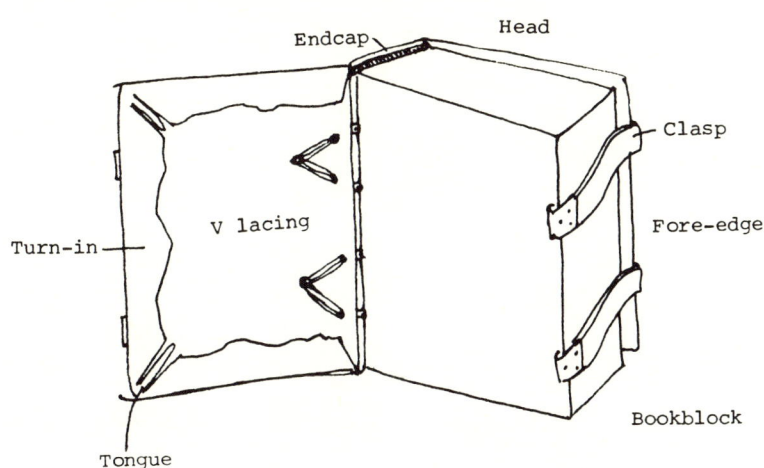

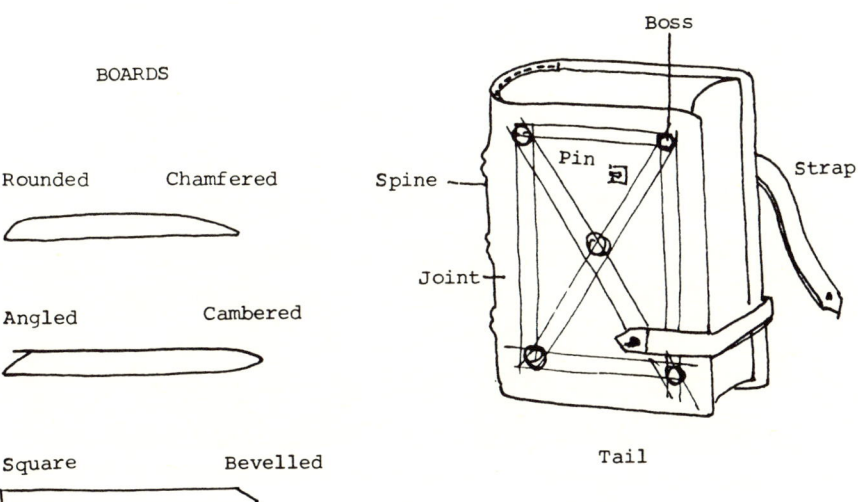

Binding Terms

Etiam he. v. distincte sunt ab hebreis. per. l. iiij. thomos. quorum tredecim precesserunt in genesi. Hec autem secunda partitio grece dicitř exodus. latine exitus. odos enim iter. uel uia dicitur. Agit enim de exitu isřł de egypto. Hebraice dicitur elesmoth a principio libri et sonat hec sunt nomina sicut nos a principiis suis psalmos nominamus.

Surrexit igitur rex nouus in egypto. longo tempore post mortem ioseph. Ab illo enim sub quo fuit ioseph qui egyptio nomine dictus est nemphres. octauus regnauit amonophis. sub quo natus est moyses. Regno aut̃ translato ad aliam domum. rex ille ob hoc q̃ nouus ignorauit beneficia ioseph. que contulerat egypto. et odiebat isřł. maxime ubi ait iosephus. quia inuiderunt eis egyptiis pr̃ uirtutem ingenii. et laboris industriam et affluentiam opum. et sobolis nobilitatem. Et ait rex ad ipm̃ suum. populus isřł fere

MS 214, f. 30r (a. 1229)

PLATE 3

MS 227, f. 12r (a. 1357)

PLATE 4

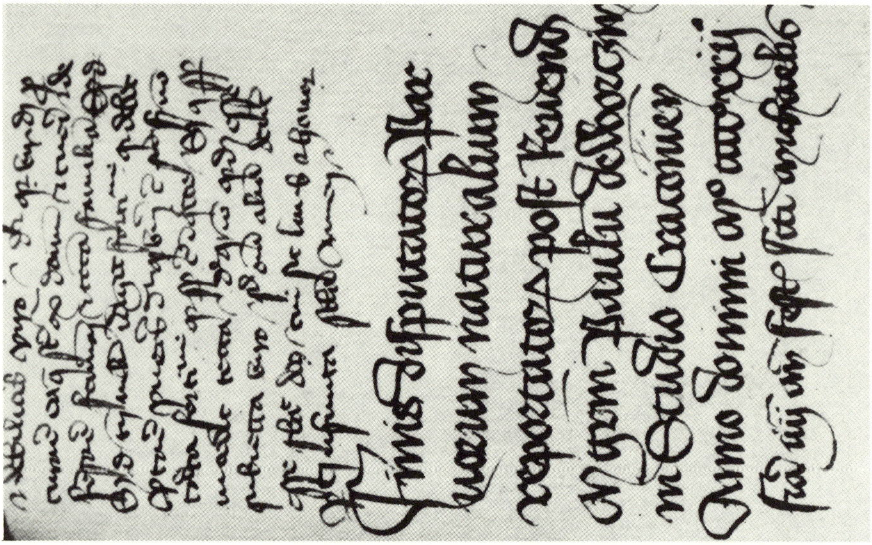

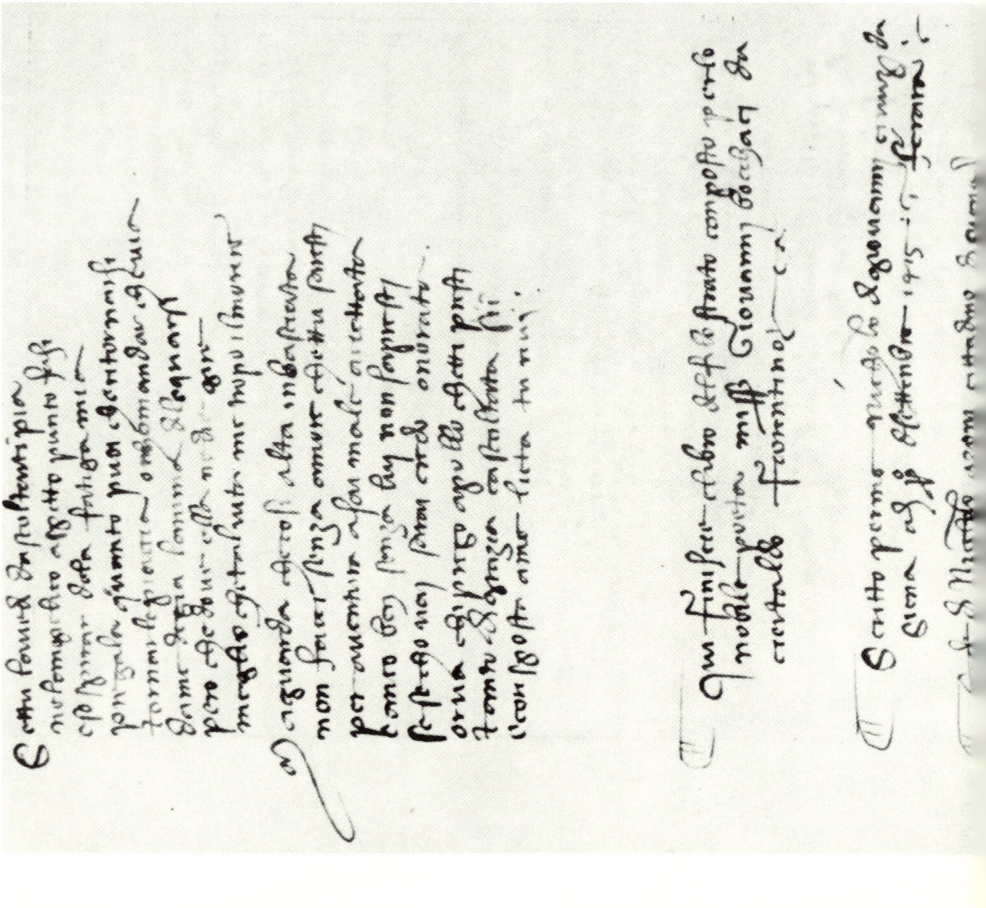

Above: MS 225, f. 263r (a. 1422)
Left: MS 222, f. 78v (a. 1415)

PLATE 5

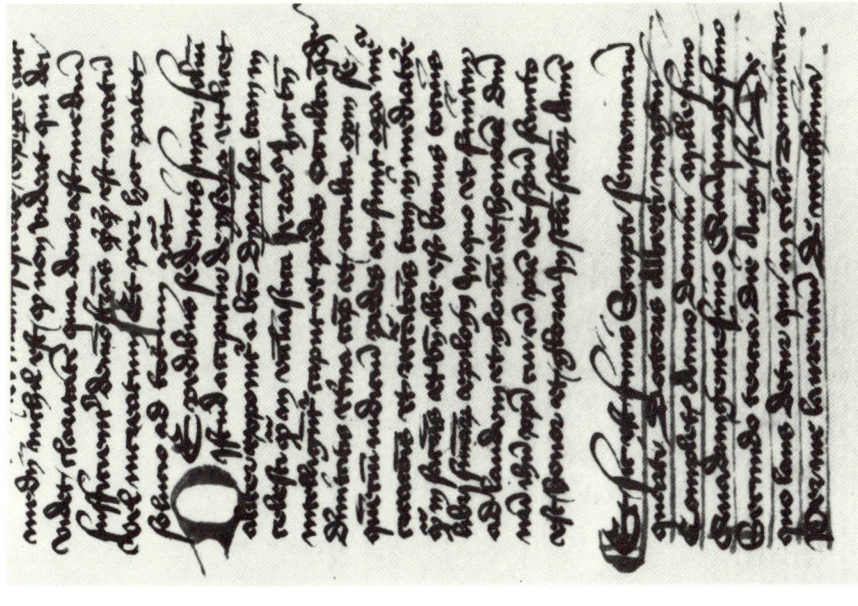

MS 20, f. 317r (a. 1452)

MS 61, f. 1r (a. 1430)

MS 58, f. 77r (1461)

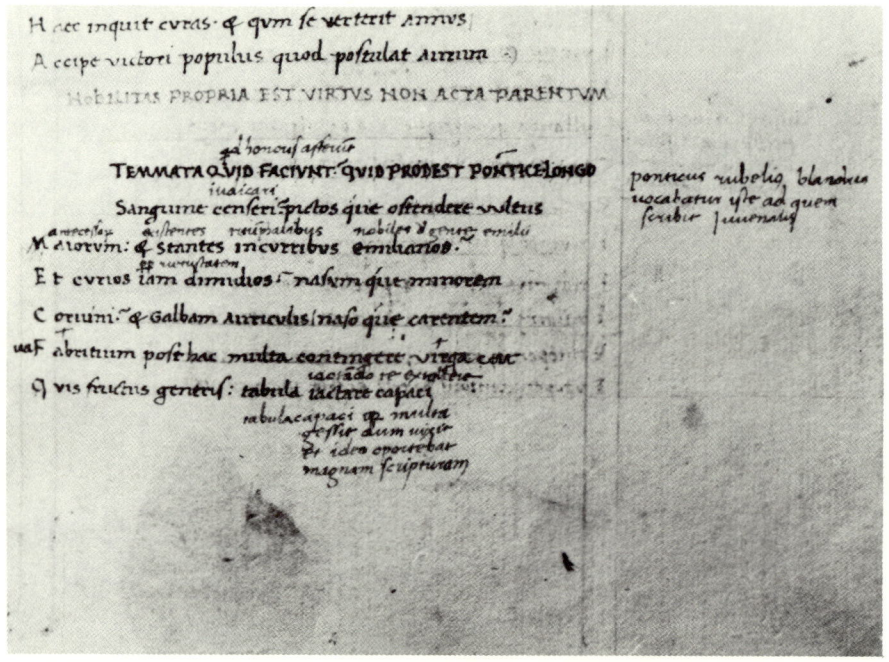

MS 67, f. 36r (a. 1468)

PLATE 7

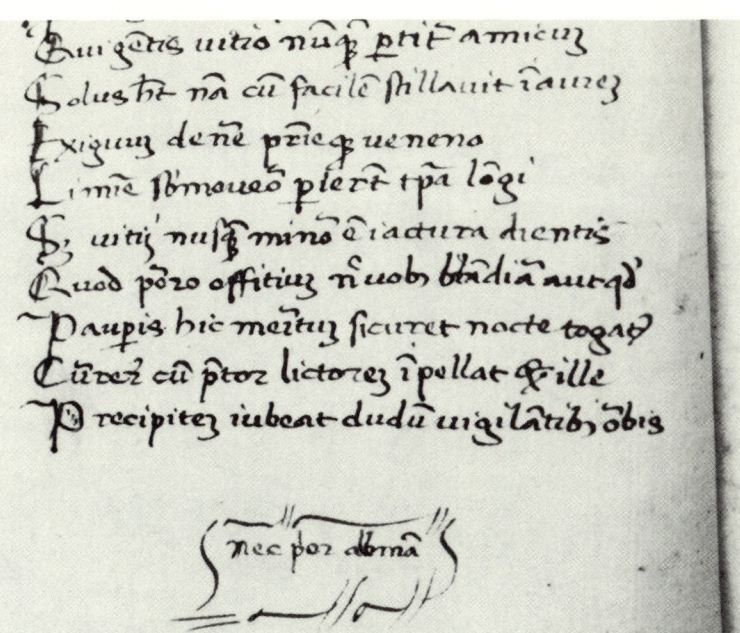

MS 70, f. 10v (a. 1475)

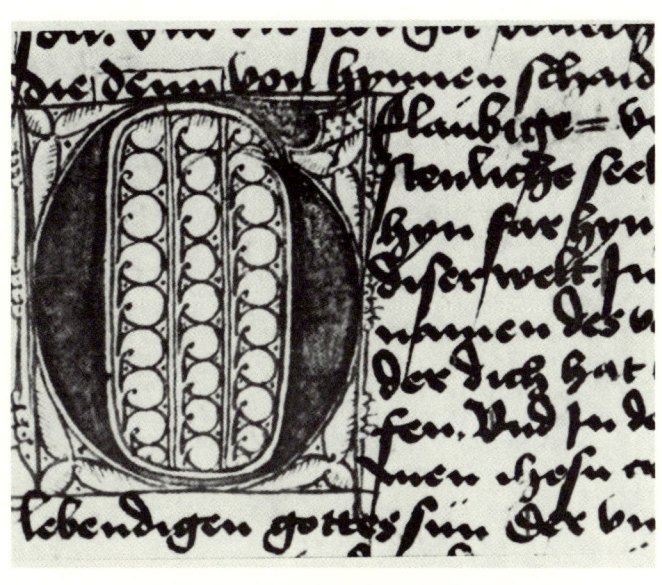

MS 28, f. 118r (a. 1513) (*slightly enlarged*)

PLATE 8

MS 226, f. 197r (a. 1476) (*5/8 natural size*)

PLATE 9

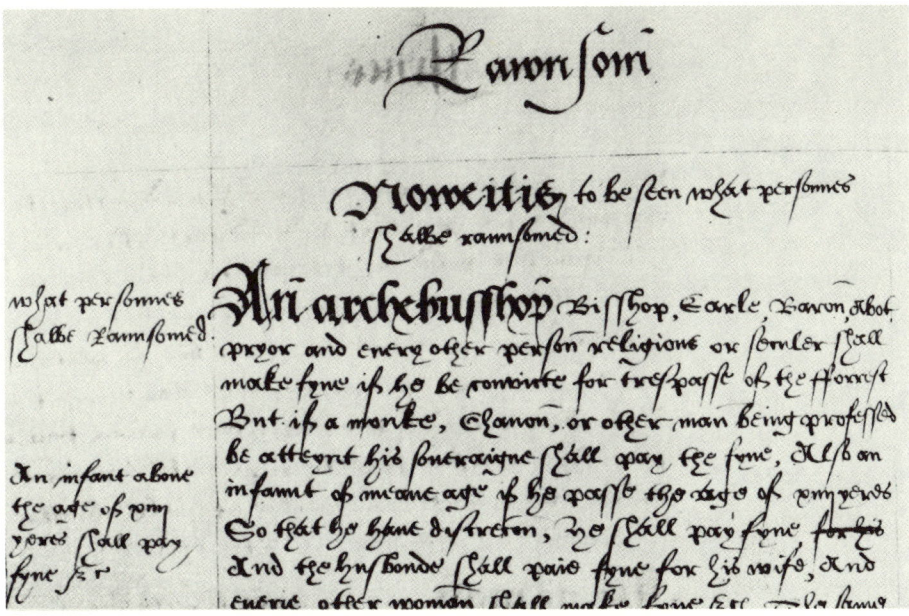

MS 89, f. 52v (a. 1562) *(slightly reduced)*

miserere populum tuum et domum patris tui.
Alleluya .v. Natiuitas gloriose virginis
marie ex semine abrahe orta de tribu iu-
da clara ex stirpe dauid. Initiu sci euang.
Liber gen̄ratio scdm matheum.
nis iesu christi fily dauid:
fily abraham. Abraham genuit
isaac. Isaac autē genuit iacob. Ia-

MS 18, f. 78r (a. 1578)

MS 82, f. 150r

MS 26, f. 108v

PLATE II

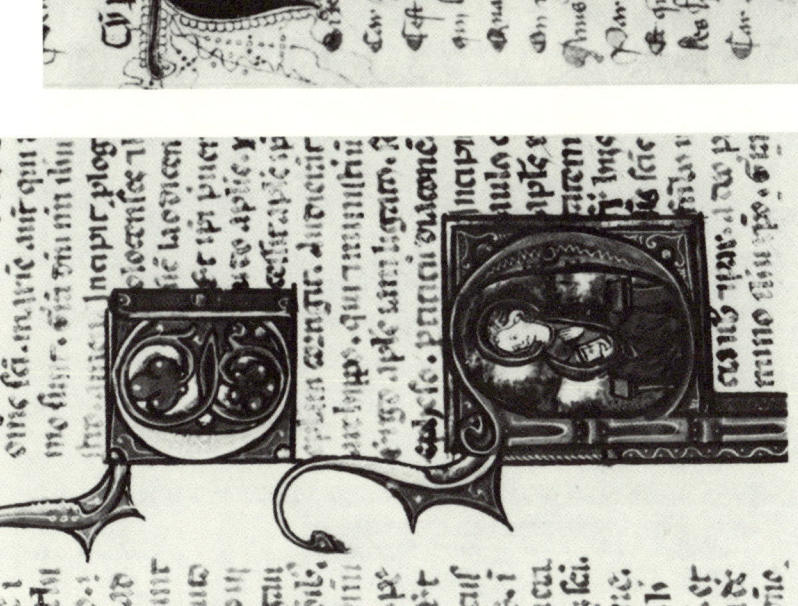

MS 38, f. 13r

MS 83, f. 514r

MS 206, f. 209v

PLATE 12

MS 217, f. 48r (4/5 natural size)

MS 215, f. 108v (vol. 3)

PLATE 13

MS 203, f. 87r

MS 108, f. 26v

PLATE 14

MS 190, f. 13v

MS 218, f. 159r

MS 211, f. 68r

MS 205, f. 1r

PLATE 16

MS 9, f. 161r (6/7 natural size)

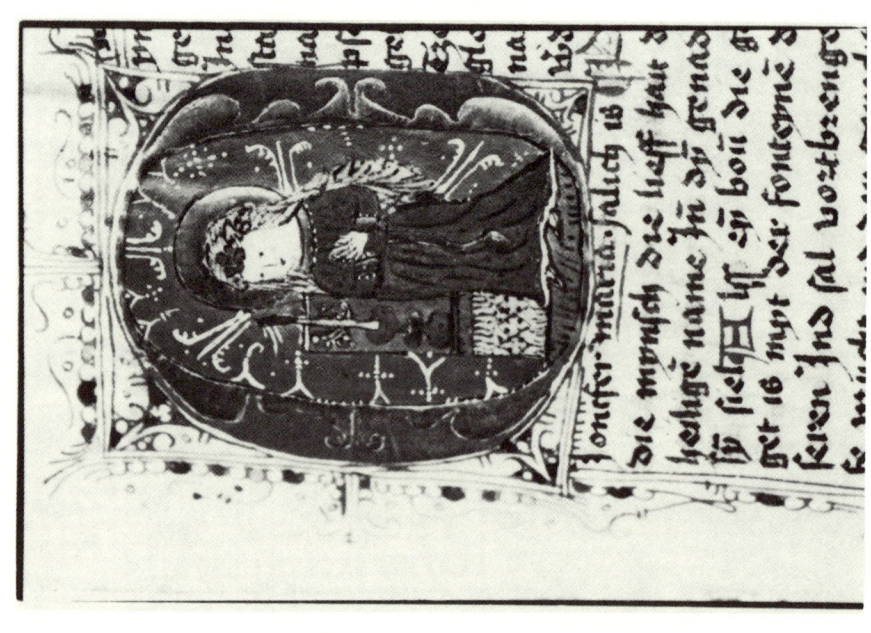

MS 196, f. 15r

PLATE 17

MS 154, f. 72r (*1/2 natural size*)

MS 189, f. 9r

PLATE 18

MS 86, f. 11r

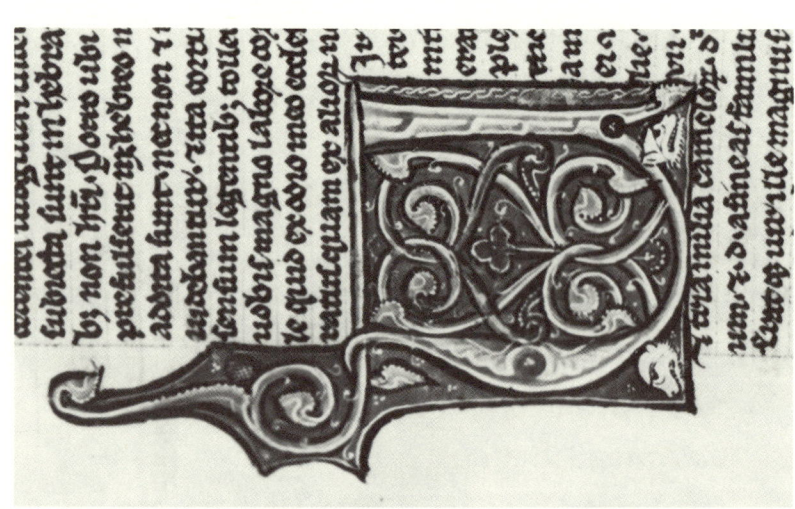

MS 81, f. 220r (*slightly enlarged*)

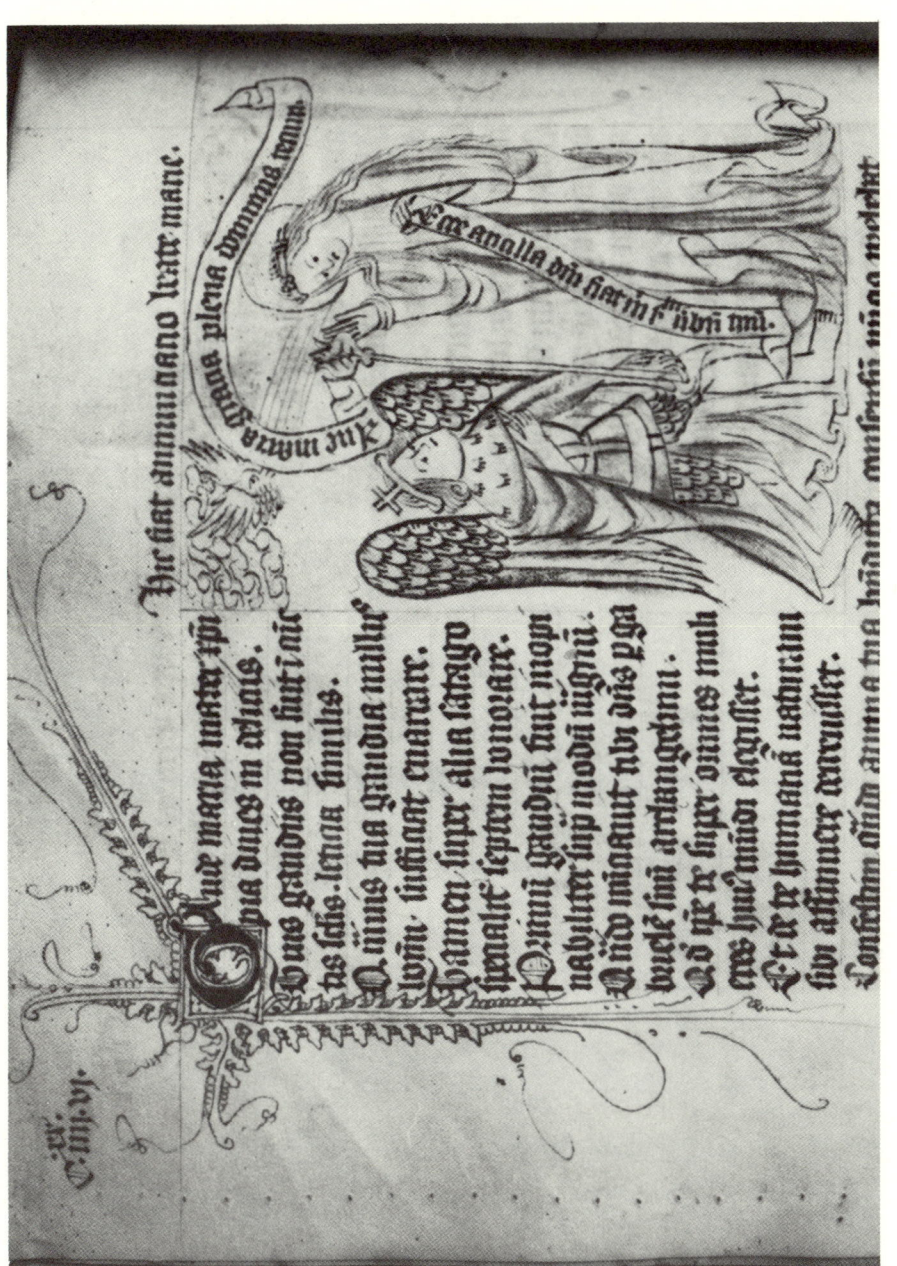

MS 27, f. 87v (slightly reduced)

PLATE 20

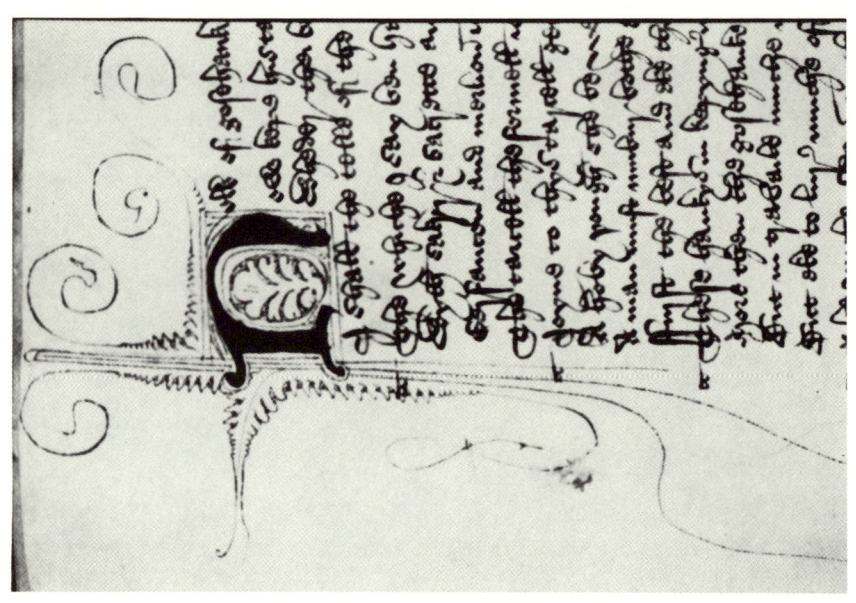

MS 163, f. 131v

MS 10, f. 81v (3/5 natural size)

PLATE 21

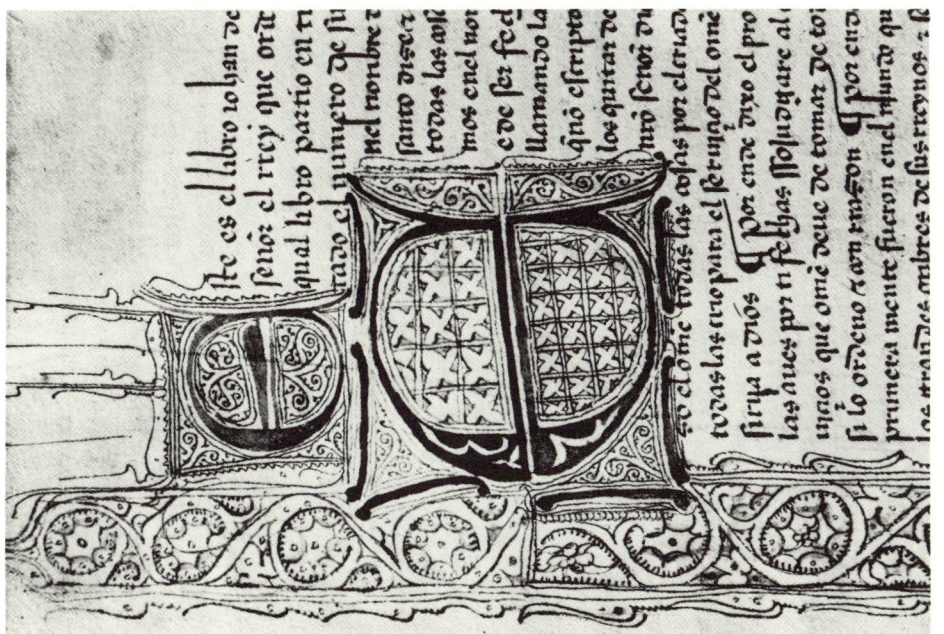

Above: MS 178, f. 32r
Left: MS 138, f. 1r

MS 111, f. 48v

MS 152, f. 1r

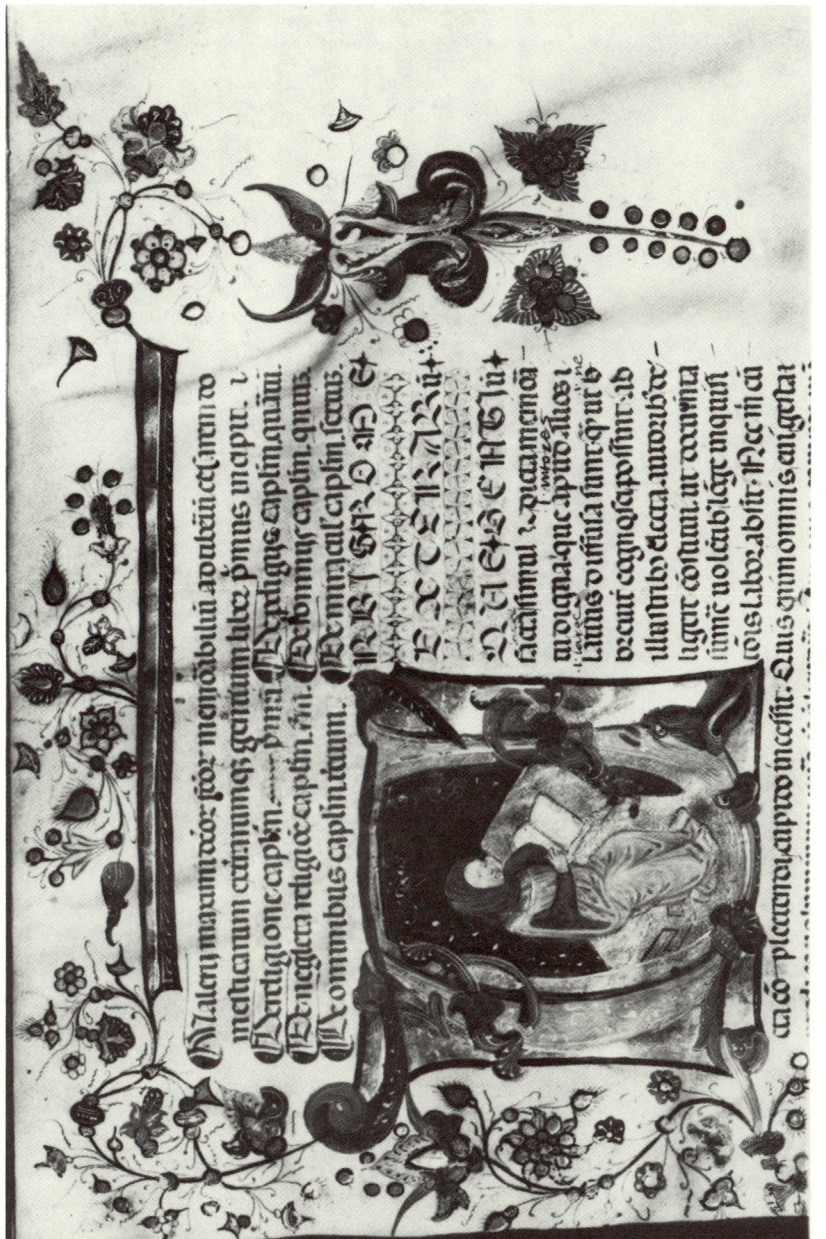

MS 147, f. 1r (7/10 natural size)

PLATE 24

Above: MS 114, f. 9r

Left: MS 221, f. 3r

PLATE 25

HESTERNO DIE .P.C. CVM .ME E
GITAS. a frequentia equitum. r. quibus sena
pere commosset. putaui mihi reprimendam es
dicam impudicitiam. cum is publicanorum ca
interrogationibus impedire. P. intullium siro nauare ope
cui totus uenerat. etiam uobis inspectantibus uenditare.
furentem exultantemq; continui. simul ac periculum iud
bus inceptis uerbis omnem impetum gladiatoris ferociam
tamen ignarus ille qui consules esset. tranquis atq; estua

MS 93, f. 49r

PREFATIO LEOHARDI AR
AHTOHII
MARCI AHTOHII V
uaria historiarum serie
tudine rerum uel mur
dam ad te salutate ī hoc libro m

MS 133, f. 103v

PLATE 26

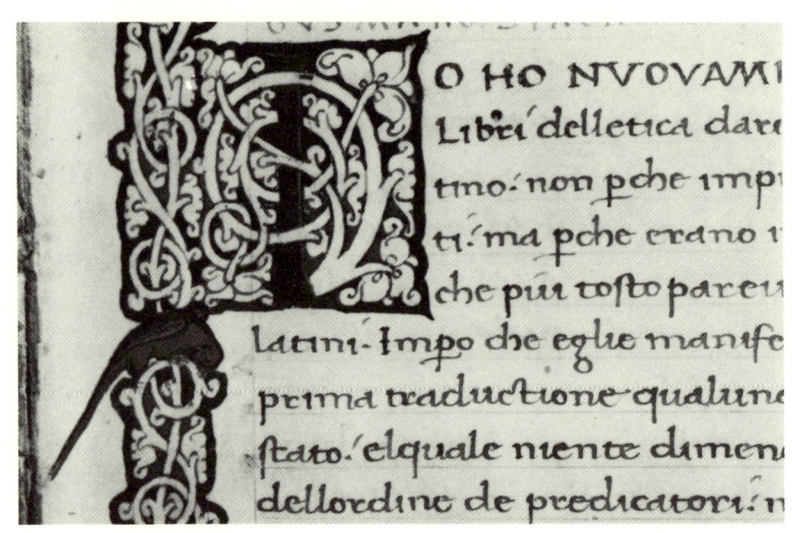

MS 151, f. 1r

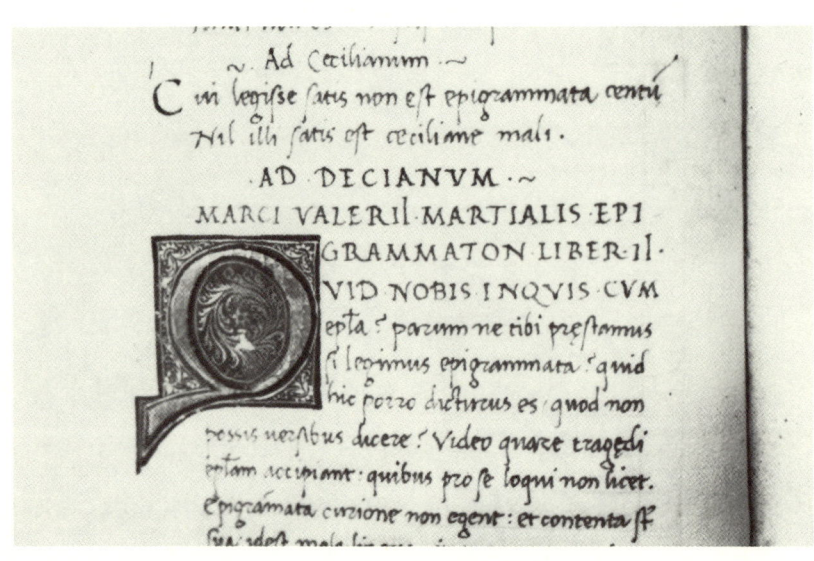

MS 64, f. 19v

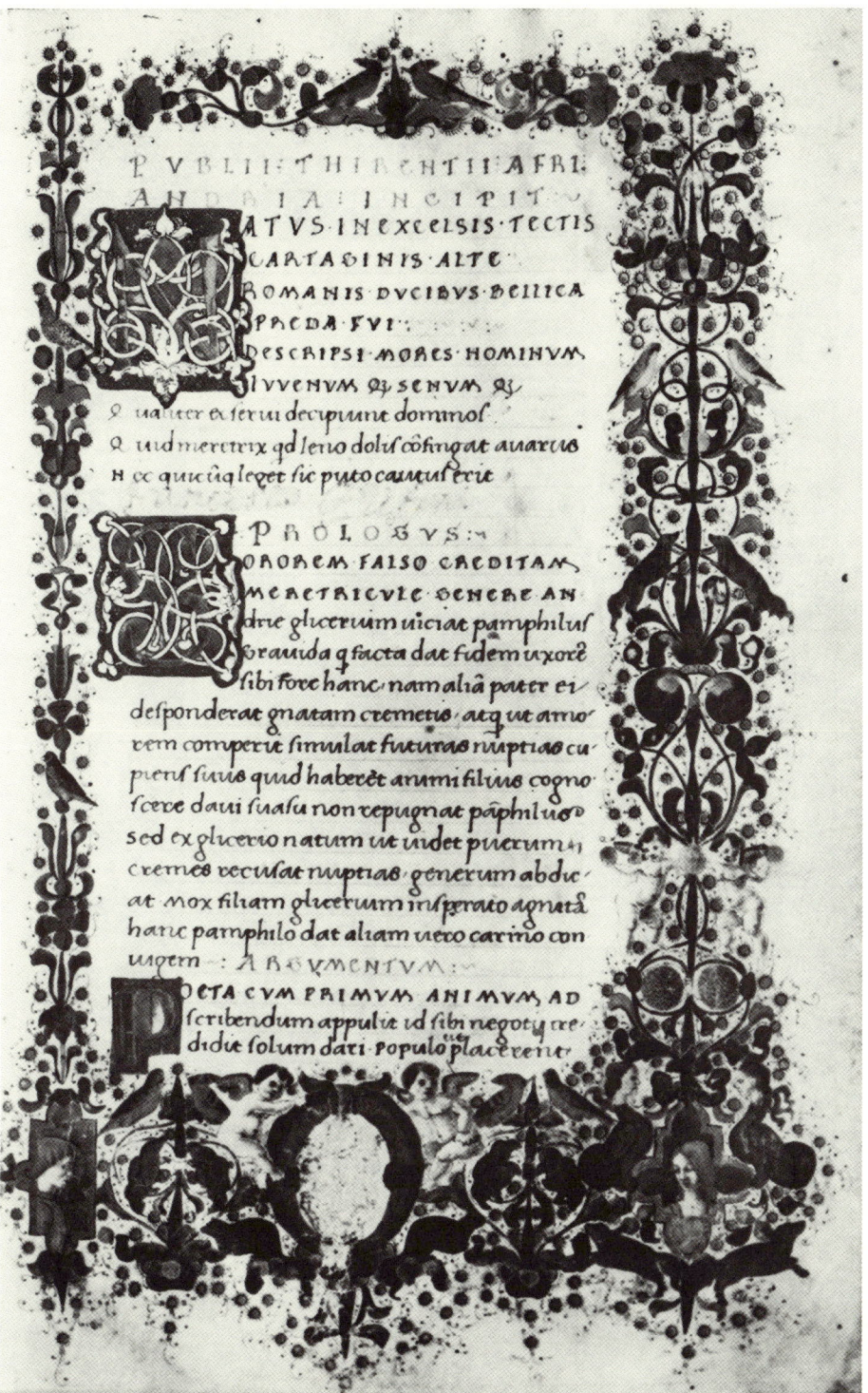

MS 165, f. 1r

MS 1, f. 1r (*1/2 natural size*)

MS 247, f. 12r

MS 240, f. 20r

PLATE 30

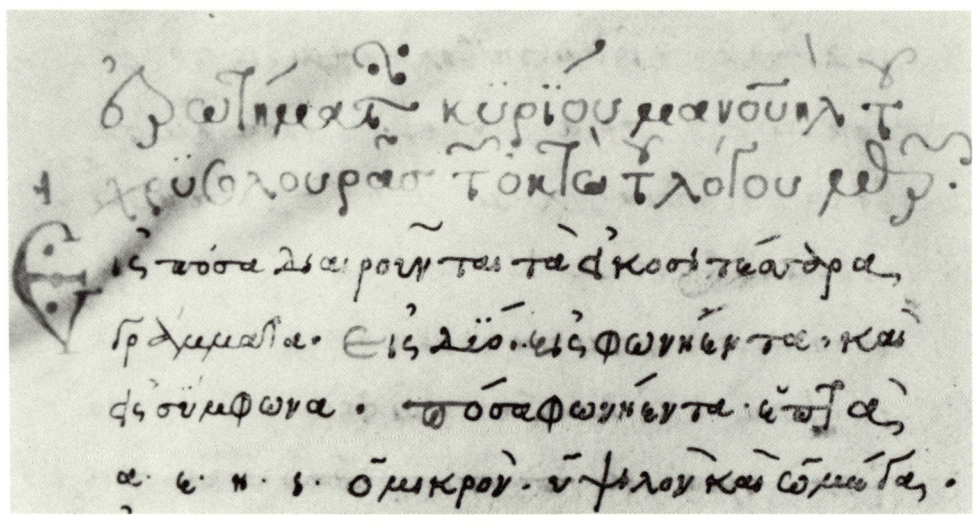

MS 239, f. 2r

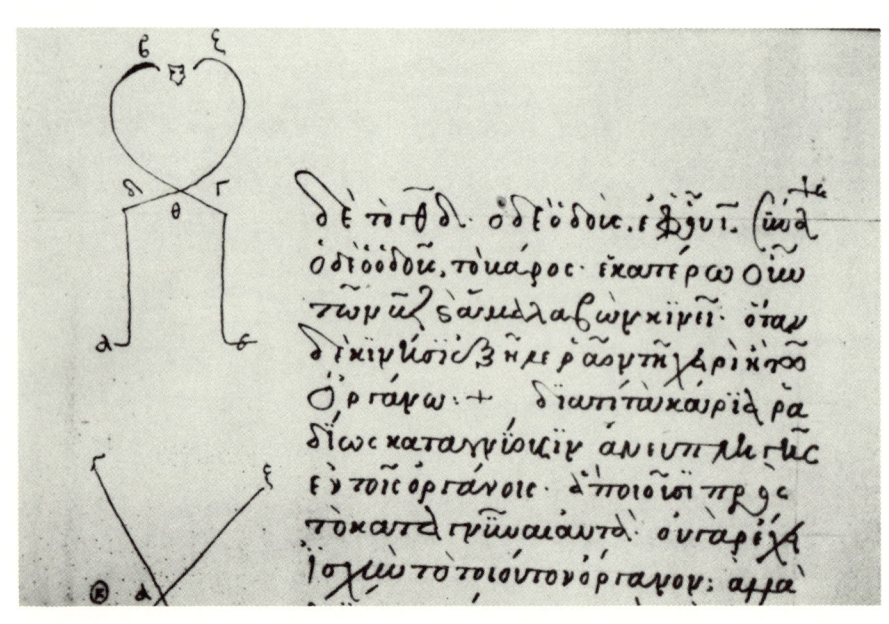

MS 245, f. 22v

PLATE 31

MS 246, f. 65r

Κλαυδίου Πτολεμαίου ἁρμονικῶν πρῶτον:–
περὶ τῶν ἐν ἁρμονικῇ κριτηρίων:–

Ἁρμονική ἐστι, δύναμις καταληπτικὴ τῶν ἐν τοῖς ψόφοις
περὶ τὸ ὀξὺ καὶ τὸ βαρὺ διαφορῶν. Ψόφος δέ, πάθος ἀέ-
ρος πληττομένου. Τὸ πρῶτον καὶ γενικώτατον τῶν ἀκουσ-
τῶν καὶ κριτήρια μὲν ἁρμονίας, ἀκοὴ καὶ λόγος. οὐ κατὰ
τὸν αὐτὸν δὲ τρόπον. ἀλλ' ἡ μὲν ἀκοή, π̅ς̅ τὴν ὕλην καὶ
τὸ πάθος. ὁ δὲ λόγος, π̅ς̅ τὸ εἶδος καὶ τὸ αἴτιον. ὅτι καὶ
καθόλου τῶν μὲν αἰσθήσεων ἴδιον ἐστί, τὸ τοῦ μὲν ἐγγὺς
γε ἀρετικόν, τοῦ δ' ἀκριβοῦς π̅ς̅δεκτικόν. τοῦ δὲ λόγου,

MS 208, f. 1v

PLATE 32

MS 36, Upper cover
(1/3 natural size)

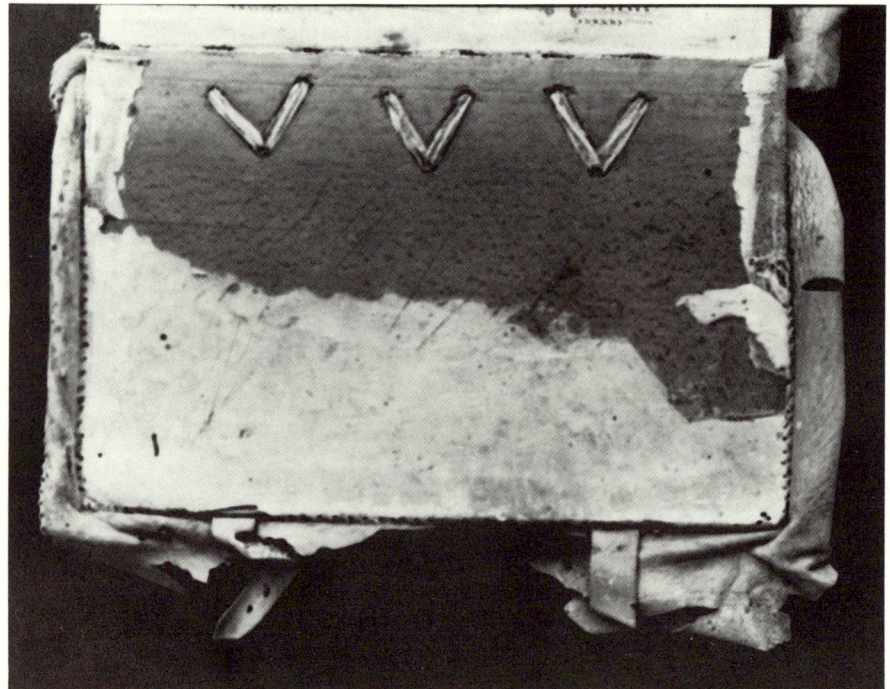

MS 27, Inside upper cover
(1/3 natural size)

Medieval and Renaissance Manuscripts in the Beinecke Rare Book and Manuscript Library, Yale University will be a three-volume catalogue describing in detail 500 manuscripts in the general collection and (Volume III) the 234 manuscripts in the Marston collection.

The Beinecke collection is one of the major holdings in the United States, a fascinating mixture of manuscripts of various dates and from far-ranging places. The **Catalogue** entries are rich and full, addressing manuscripts from the fourth to the eighteenth centuries, written in Latin, Greek, French, German, Italian, English, and even Icelandic and Nahuatl. Building on the work done by Cora Lutz, Professor Shailor provides detailed information on contents and physical makeup, relates the material to manuscripts preserved elsewhere, gives bibliographical data, and achieves a sound point of departure for further investigation by scholars and collectors.

Each entry describes the textual contents (including incipits and explicits), parchment or watermarks, foliation, flyleaves, dimensions, collation, scribes and scripts, decoration, binding, and provenance. Volume I is illustrated with fifty-eight reproductions. Seven indices, ranging from places and dates to incipits, and including persons, bindings, illuminations, watermarks, and scribes, complete this invaluable research work.

Barbara A. Shailor is Associate Professor of Classics at Bucknell University and Cataloguer, Medieval and Renaissance Manuscripts, at the Beinecke. She has published articles dealing with medieval and Renaissance manuscripts. She received a grant from the National Endowment for the Humanities (1981-84) to support her work on this volume and allow her to begin work on the second volume, scheduled for publication in 1985-86.

mRts

medieval & Renaissance texts & studies
is the publishing program of the
Center for Medieval & Early Renaissance Studies
at the State University of New York at Binghamton.

mRts emphasizes books that are needed —
texts, translations, and major research tools.

mRts aims to publish the highest quality scholarship
in attractive and durable format at modest cost.